Advance Praise for *Blurred Boundaries*

The distinction in writing about martial arts luminaries is often—as the title here perhaps unconsciously indicates—"blurred" indeed. Is it biography or a hagiographic adulation? Further, such writing often posits the subject in an equally blurry history, one without much cultural or social context.

This book addresses both weaknesses in a marvelous presentation of a man who was both legend and very human, who lived in one of the richest eras of Chinese history, and who was profoundly influenced by the society and politics of that age.

Blurred Boundaries is not only an enormous pleasure to read, it also affords insights into a unique character, and as important, his time. This is an essential volume for understanding the nature of a martial art and the personalities it can produce. [*Blurred Boundaries*] is an absolute must for the serious student.

—Dave Lowry, writer, author of *Autumn Lightning, Persimmon Wind, The Connoisseur's Guide to Sushi,* and *Chinese Cooking for Diamond Thieves*

This fascinating blend of storytelling and documentary; of martial spirit, principles, and strategy; of folk art and history, will captivate you for weeks, while you delve into facets of postwar Taiwan's radical social and cultural change—only partly known to Westerners. Hong Ze-han opens our eyes first to the draining of martial knowledge from China to Taiwan during the tumultuous time of China's civil war, and then to martial arts' two-folded usage (as a weapon for criminals and as a weapon to ward off criminals). Out of this milieu, Hong Ze-han draws a vibrant picture of the genesis, development, and dissemination of his father's art of Tangshoudao, which—rooted in traditions preserved by Chinese masters who fled from the mainland—grew out of the struggle of Chinese fugitives trying to gain a foothold in Taiwan, all while facing resentment, corruption, and social turmoil. Retracing and detailing his father's deep understanding of martial virtues and combat efficiency, this book gives us profound insights nearly lost in our modern martial culture of watering down the old ways. *Blurred Boundaries* will expand your mind in unexpected ways, whatever your martial background.

—Hermann Bayer, PhD, professor and academic dean (emeritus). Black belt ranks in Doshinkan Karatedo, Shorin Ryu Shorinkan, and Okinawan Kobudo Kokusairengokai (Shodan). Author of *Analysis of Genuine Karate: Misconceptions, Origins, Developments, and True Purpose* and *Analysis of Genuine Karate 2: Sociocultural Development, Commercialization, and Loss of Essential Knowledge*

Never has a work been so aptly named. [This book] reads as if sitting in a tea house in twilight, with an old storyteller weaving an epic out of lives both ordinary and remarkable, all at once. It meanders from one tale to another, interspersed with recipes and small illuminations, like fireflies in fog, explaining in succinct detail, the essence of this or that martial art. Hong Ze-han has done justice to a monumental father, writing of him as he was, truly larger than life, yet he has also retained the humanity and generosity of the man, something I remember from the one time I met him.

—Ellis Amdur, master instructor Araki-ryu Torite-kogusoku, Tenshin Buko-ryu Heiho, author of *Little Bird & The Tiger*

Blurred Boundaries: A Martial Arts Legacy and the Shaping of Taiwan is a martial arts masterpiece that is destined to become a classic.

Divided into one-hundred and fourteen often brief chapters, the book is instantly engaging. From page one the author, Hong Ze-han, paints a vivid world from personal memory and anecdotes gleaned throughout his childhood and later years. Supported by many rare photographs, the translation remains sympathetic to the original Chinese text, delivering a banquet of interesting information, tales of great sadness, as well as stories of derring-do. Being the son of a famous father, particularly in the world of martial arts, can prove too burdensome for some. This author, however, has continued to maintain the legacy left to him with great dignity.

Blurred Boundaries is at times an intimate look at how world events are experienced at ground level by people far removed from the politicians who start wars and the generals who prosecute them on their behalf. The book covers a lot of ground, but the landscape is always worth the view, always worth the pause to ponder the information. Translated from the original Chinese into English by Christopher Bates, the enormous value of this book is not limited to readers interested in the Chinese martial arts alone. Indeed, historians of Japanese karate will discover many previously undisclosed episodes in that country's historical links with the Okinawan fighting art.

Without hesitation, I recommend *Blurred Boundaries: A Martial Arts Legacy and the Shaping of Taiwan* and congratulate Hong Ze-han and Christopher Bates for delivering to the English-speaking world a book so well written and executed as to set the bar extremely high for all who would follow.

—Michael Clarke, kyoshi 8th dan Okinawan Goju-ryu, author of *The Art of Hojo-Undo: Power Training for Traditional Karate, Shin Gi Tai: Karate Training for Body, Mind, and Spirit,* and *Redemption: A Street Fighter's Path to Peace*

Not only a glorious deep dive into the world of Chinese kung fu, this biography is also a rich and revealing look at the post-WWII decades in Taiwan. We see traditional family life and folk culture, the colorful temple parades, and run-ins with gangsters. We experience the sometimes-violent tensions between the local Taiwanese and the newly arrived mainlanders, a crucible of modern Taiwan from which rose the truly impressive Hong Yi-xiang.

I believe *Blurred Boundaries* is one of the very best books written about Taiwan this century. It's a three-generation martial arts saga with a fascinating protagonist, interesting secondary characters, and momentous background historical events. To all of this, we get a front-row seat, courtesy of author Hong Ze-han's viewpoint as Master Hong's son. The book has been expertly translated by Christopher Bates, the perfect translator for the project thanks to his four-decade-long association with the Hong family, his knowledge of martial arts and Taiwan, and his writing/translating skills. His *Blurred Boundaries* translation shows admirable precision and fidelity to the original text, giving the prose an intimate Chinese flavor.

—John Grant Ross, author of *Taiwan in 100 Books* and
co-host of the *Formosa Files*, a history podcast

Blurred Boundaries is simultaneously a deeply philosophical and yet practical book. This work should take its place among the martial arts classics in the centuries to come. I wish there were already works like this one among the classics. The text is very quotable, and the translation is even poetic at times.

Hong Yi-xiang stands now in my mind among the greats who have changed the martial arts world. The stories and anecdotes in this book contain wisdom to be applied to any martial arts system or style.

Both Hong Yi-xiang and his son, the author, Hong Ze-han have a timeless vision and wisdom that is sure to enrich your practice and deepen your understanding of how the challenges of the past can inform our practices today.

—Matthew Krueger, host of the *Walking with the Tengu*
podcast. He practices BJJ, Shuai Jiao, and Iaido.

Blurred Boundaries: A Martial Arts Legacy and the Shaping of Taiwan by Hong Ze-han and translated by Christopher Bates hit all the right buttons for me as a reader. First, anything relating to martial arts history is immensely interesting, not only to me but to many people in the martial arts. The fact that the author is relating the story of his family's involvement with martial arts as it relates to the history of China and Taiwan makes for a story that is both personal and historical, resulting in a fascinating book. While my primary interest is judo, with its rich history of development in Japan, the author drew me into his family's story of how the Chinese boxing arts molded who they were, and who they are now.

Blurred Boundaries is a worthy addition to the library of every martial arts enthusiast.

> —Steve Scott, 8th dan Hachidan Judo, 7th dan Shingitai Jujitsu, author of *The Judo Advantage: Controlling Movement with Modern Kinesiology* and over twenty other books on judo, coaching, and martial arts

We often romanticize how martial arts might have been in days of old, but here is a gripping account of how brutal and unforgiving it really was. *Blurred Boundaries* is the first English translation of Master Hong, Tse-han's story of his father, Hong Yi-xiang, as he struggled to found Yizong Tangshoudao against the background of the civil war between the Tawain's Kuomingtang and the mainland communists. It vividly captures the turmoil of the times, as well as the inspirational real-life story of a historic martial arts master overcoming tremendous obstacles to further the art.

> —Gene Ching, 32nd generation disciple of the Shaolin Temple, publisher of *Kung Fu Magazine*

Blurred Boundaries

界疆榭揆

Blurred Boundaries
A Martial Arts Legacy and the Shaping of Taiwan

by

Hong Ze-han

Translated by Christopher Bates

YMAA Publication Center
Wolfeboro, NH USA

YMAA Publication Center, Inc.
PO Box 480
Wolfeboro, NH 03894
800-669-8892 • www.ymaa.com • info@ymaa.com

ISBN 9781594399800 (print)
ISBN 9781594399817 (ebook)
ISBN 9781594399824 (hardcover)

Copyright © 2023 by Hong Ze-han
Translated by Christopher Bates

All rights reserved including the right of reproduction in whole or in part in any form.

Cover design by Axie Breen
Photos provided by the authors unless otherwise indicated.
Edited by Leslie Takao
Copy edit by Doran Hunter
This book typeset in Garamond and Della Respira

20230926

Publisher's Cataloging in Publication

Names: Hong, Ze-han, 1955- author. | Bates, Christopher, translator.
Title: Blurred boundaries : a martial arts legacy and the shaping of Taiwan / by Hong Ze-han ; translated by Christopher Bates.
Description: Wolfeboro, NH USA : YMAA Publication Center, [2023] | Includes bibliographical references.
Identifiers: ISBN: 9781594399800 (softcover) | 9781594399824 (hardcover) | 9781594399817 (ebook) | LCCN: 2023947218
Subjects: LCSH: Hong Yi-xiang. | Martial artists--Taiwan--Biography. | Martial arts--Taiwan--History. | Taiwan--History--1945- | Taiwan--Social life and customs--1945- | BISAC: BIOGRAPHY & AUTOBIOGRAPHY / Sports. | BIOGRAPHY & AUTOBIOGRAPHY / Cultural, Ethnic & Regional / Asian & Asian American HISTORY / Asia / China. | SPORTS & RECREATION / Martial Arts / General.
Classification: LCC GV1113.H6 H66 2023 | DDC: 796.8092--dc23

This work is autobiographical. Everything here is true, but it may not be entirely factual. In some cases, the events have been compressed and certain identifying details have been changed to protect the privacy of the people involved. The events are portrayed to the best of the authors' memory.
  The author and publisher of the material are NOT RESPONSIBLE in any manner whatsoever for any injury which may occur through following the instructions in this manual.
  The activities physical or otherwise, described in this manual may be too strenuous or dangerous for some people, and the reader(s) should consult a physician before engaging in them.
  Nothing in this document constitutes a legal opinion nor should any of its contents be treated as such.

Printed in USA.

This book is dedicated to my father, Hong Yi-xiang, the founder of Yizong Tangshoudao school of martial art and to every renowned and unnamed teacher who taught at the Hong family's academy after being exiled from mainland China to Taiwan in the 1950s due to the civil war between the Kuomintang and the Communist Party.

Portrait of Master Hong Yi-xiang circa 1960.
Used with permission of Chris Bates

Acknowledgements

I first started writing this book in 2014, and when Chris and I were translating it into English in 2019, there were many details he asked about that I had to hypnotize myself through the words to reenter those lost places and memories, years of time and space, to reconstruct the mood and scene at that time. Special thanks to Christopher Bates for his hard work, patience, and tolerance during this lengthy, arduous, deciphering marathon translation process.

Thanks, too, to Thomas Argiro for copy editing and Marcus Brinkman for their generosity in making this book available in another language for everyone's enjoyment.

In the process of discussing the translation of the manuscript, I discovered many wonderful stories from the depths of my own memory that were not recorded in this biography. I hope that in the future I can find an objective way to present these past events.

Foreword

Using Love and Understanding to Soothe History's Wounds

In the 1940s, besides the 228 Massacre and The Great Retreat, there were other compelling cultural events and stories of the people on this island of Taiwan that flourished and then fell into obscurity.

Blurred Boundaries is the story, long past and covered in dust, of a Dihua Street merchant family's rise and fall. The author uses the life of his legendary martial artist father, Master Hong Yi-xiang, as the story's time axis, writing in a style like a movie screenplay, searching for the traces erased by time of his father's footsteps, while recreating the magnificent grandeur of the Dadaocheng area of Taipei in that era. This retrospective calls to mind one by one the youthful and passionate personages of outstanding ability sprinkled throughout that great age, conjuring them to reappear before our eyes and providing a fresh perspective on that extraordinary period.

This volume is a blend of reportage and non-classical Wuxia Romance. It features the author employing modern enterprise management and crisis management wisdom, replacing traditional martial arts fist and foot gongfu with clever and heartfelt sketches, anecdotal vignettes taking us back in time to the breakthrough moments of life's predicaments. Concealed within the background of each chapter's conflicts are expounded intricacies of understanding, change, and problem solving—worth savoring slowly, like sipping a fine old tea.

Tom Tsai

Tsai Cheng-wei, Chairman,
Republic of China
Olympic Committee
July 22, 2015

Preface to the Original Chinese Edition

THIS IS A BOOK THAT HAS BEEN DELAYED FOR TWENTY-ONE YEARS, after the passing of my father in 1993.

"Why not write down your dad's story?" In 1995 two years after my father passed away, the chairman of San Min Publishing, Mr. Liu Zhen-qiang, invited my family's seven brothers and sisters to dine at the Hankou St. Jiangsu restaurant, Fuxing Garden. It was here he spoke these heartfelt words.

At the time, when he uttered them, I dared not meet his eyes. There was the modesty of a son incapable of recording the biography of an extraordinary father; moreover, I had no way to face my father's friends and respected elders. Although Mr. Liu indicated he could send manpower to assist in the writing, after conferring with my brothers and sisters, it was decided for a myriad of reasons to decline his kind offer.

In the blink of an eye, twenty winters and summers had passed, during which time no one dared deliberately broach this subject. It was not until 2014, when I retired from Jihsun Bank, and could earnestly face retired life and myself, that I had time to reconsider. One day, when cleaning out my liquor closet, I spotted a special bottle of twenty-one-year-old Chivas Regal Royal Salute Scotch whiskey, and it reanimated deeply buried regrets. Chris Bates had presented that bottle of whiskey for the twenty-year memorial banquet of my father's passing. He had scoured the market and could only find a twenty-one-year-old vintage, so everyone agreed to gather again on the twenty-first anniversary to drink it. However, on that evening, I alone uncorked that bottle and drank it. Afterward, slightly drunk, I took my Samsung Note 2 in hand and began the work of writing this recollection.

Maybe it is just a personal prejudice, but I feel that were it not for this period of 1946 to 1993, an age of turmoil and tremendous change, Hong Wu-fan, Zhang Zhun-feng, Hong Yi-xiang, and the parade of personalities and circumstances in this book would not have emerged. These personalities, whether it was a hoodlum who failed to become a gang boss, the special operations assassin living deep in the mountains with his deranged wife, American soldiers far from home who came to fight in Vietnam, the CIA officer Robert W. Smith, who came to train Taiwanese intelligence operatives, Mr. C, who tried to get students to betray their teacher for personal gain, or the bellicose Westerner, the fighting fanatic Mr. K, nicknamed Sweet Potato, or… they were all, in many respects, the same. Each in their own way enriched that tragic and impoverished age, enlivening this story's various chapters and enhancing the glory experienced by the Hong family.

Except for a portion of events I had the good fortune to witness with my own eyes, the majority of the people, incidents, situations, were recounted to me from the mists of past memories by my grandfather, Hong Wu-fan, second uncle Hong Yi-wen, third uncle Hong Yi-mian, and my father, Hong Yi-xiang. I have relied on these memories, put them into words, and done some historical processing. To convey the richness of my father's remarkable life experience, and of those other remarkable people and events transpiring during this age of upheaval required that I occasionally take similar circumstances and condense them into the characters of representative personages, allowing these people and incidents of a similar age and environment to stand in as archetypes. To avoid the errors and distortions of memory—or, if in compressing incidents and people I have offended anyone through negligence, or disrespected or impacted the reputations of the characters or their descendants—I prefer to assert that this is a novel about the life and times of Hong Yi-xiang, and not a hagiography of a famous person. This is my original intent in naming the book *Blurred Boundaries,* and not *The Biography of Hong Yi-xiang.*

Through diplomatic eyes, I see the affairs of the world, including what is and what is not, truth and falsehood, good and evil, hard, and soft—all are relative to the circumstances of the moment, their relative relationship and subjective opinion; no position is absolutely right or wrong. A good person in the right age will do only good; in another age and from another value perspective, the same actions might be evaluated and appraised differently. And aren't many of the major and minor choices in life made in an environment of limited options and constant change, using fuzzy, blurred logic to make a decision? These types of decisions are neither made purely based on reason, nor are they made just with emotion. Therefore, the author considers that in all matters, a little more forgiveness and latitude for fault tolerance are called for. People should not skittle about assigning who is right and who is wrong, who won and who lost, so as not to rush to judgement.

I believe the most appropriate answers and solutions to even intractable, unsolvable problems can be found amid this blurry expanse. Fuzziness is by its nature not finalized. Doesn't the absence of finality express that there remains unlimited potential?

My father, Hong Yi-xiang, was born in 1925 and died abruptly in 1993, at the age of sixty-eight. I was born in 1955, hence my life overlapped with my father's for only thirty-eight years. Deducting the time when I was an unaware infant, my times of schooling and work, and my several years at university, I was with my father morning, noon, and night, practicing gongfu and teaching boxing, seeking out fine foods, paying calls on friends, and chatting with martial artists. But the time I spent truly close to him was not actually all that long, and this limited my understanding of my father's excellent life. I felt I could not really do justice to the precious source of material he embodied and the result merely skims over surface of an amazing life. I hope as I loosen my grip on this work, I can, as the saying goes, "release this coarse brick and get back a piece of fine jade in return."

Not long after my father was put in his coffin, the chairman of the Republic of China Guo Shu Federation, Mr. Chen Shou-shan, and the chairman of the Taipei Guo Shu Federation, Mr. Huang Shan-de, led a delegation from the martial arts community to visit our family's mourning hall at Dihua Street to pay their respects. They entreated, "Please allow us to do something to express our respect and appreciation for Brother Hong Yi-xiang!" However, a funeral committee formed of his disciples and those who had received benefits or kindnesses from him in life had already made the arrangements. Amongst my brothers and sisters, we could not think of some special way they could honor my father's life. The funeral committee decided, "Let his coffin be draped with the national flag." On the day of his burial, the blue sky, white sun, and red earth, symbolized in the flag of the Republic of China, was displayed on his coffin.

A "Black Arm Band Team" of one hundred-twenty local and foreign disciples, walked on foot, pulling on a white sash, dragging the bier, making a circuit around the entire Dadaocheng area, as they all accompanied him on his final stroll through this place best known by him. Along the way, merchants and stall owners who had no other way to say goodbye, set up their own prayer offerings on tables along the route. I, steely eyed up to this moment, now let loose a torrent of tears and emotions.

Finally, I wish to again express my deepest appreciation to Chairman Liu Zhen-qiang. If not for his ardent hope and encouragement in 1993, I would not have had the courage to dig up deliberately neglected and evaded memories of the past, to face once again those images and circumstances of bygone days. If not for his righteous and impassioned support, the day of this volume being sent to press would not have come. In addition, I want to thank my wife, Huang Bi-xia, for these many months during which she sometimes assisted, as she read the proofs and seized on errors, allowing obscure terms intertwined in the volume to be explained to the average reader.

Story Background

IN 1949, AT THE TIME OF THE GREAT RETREAT OF THE NATIONALIST Chinese government to Taiwan, Mr. Hong Wu-fan, the orphaned son of an impoverished Taiwanese farmer had built north Taiwan's largest manufacturer of candles and charitably took in a large number of martial arts masters who had made the ocean crossing to Taiwan. He invited them to live in his compound and teach Chinese Boxing, sparking the interest in and talent for martial art of the family's five children, thus establishing one of North Taiwan's illustrious martial art clans.

Hong Yi-xiang was the fourth in line of his sons. In the 1970s, Hong Yi-xiang was invited to the Nippon Budokan in Tokyo to demonstrate China's internal school of martial arts and received challenges from many exponents of various systems of karate, his victories in these matches shaking up Japan.

He was the first to receive the All-Japan Budo Alliance award of "International 9th Dan Black Belt Teacher," the highest honor awarded to a foreigner.

He was the Taiwanese instructor of unarmed combat fighting skills to American GIs transiting in Taiwan during the Vietnam War.

He was the private martial arts instructor to the American CIA agent stationed in Taiwan, Robert W. Smith.

He was the featured master in the 1980 BBC *The Way of the Warrior* series episode focusing on the Chinese internal school of martial arts (this series was broadcast around the world to a global audience and received great acclaim).

Finally, it is the story of three generations of martial arts transmission, Zhang Jun-feng, Hong Yi-xiang and Hong Ze-han.

This is not an orthodox biography of a famous person, nor is it a cut-and-dried martial arts romance. It is one son's attempt to leave the faintest of traces for disciples and successors, so they might come to follow the path and pay homage to his father. Of course, it is also my expression of infinite longing for and memory of a bygone era of elegance and intellectual brilliance. Because this spans forty to fifty years, a huge number of characters and events are dragged in. For this reason, although all the characters are real, and the events are real, for the purpose of presenting so many people and events, the author had no choice but to select some characters and some events and combine them into a limited field of representative characters and events, portrayed as occurring together.

I am not a professional author; I rely solely on the perspective of one son's unquestionable filial piety to his father and foolish bravery, thinking to leave behind some evidence of his father and his era. I only hope that these necessary compressions and changes do not distort the facts. Perhaps someday, on another plane, I will meet these characters again; from the bottom of my heart, I hope that I can carry them news from this modern age, and that they will find, from this account, comfort and affirmation of their existence and past struggles.

Notes on the Translation

IT HAS BEEN MY GREAT HONOR AND GOOD FORTUNE TO HAVE HAD the opportunity, in 1982, to become one of Master Hong Yi-xiang's students. On his passing, I continued training in the lineage, and encouraged his son, Master Hong Ze-han, to continue teaching when I moved back to Taiwan in 2006.

Here, acting as translator, I would like to comment on this work and some technical details about translation.

In *Blurred Boundaries* Master Hong Ze-han has written a fine book, not a vapid hagiography. It is a folk history of a dramatic period in Taiwan during the second half of the twentieth century, full of heart, passion, courage, desperation, and dedication. With Hong Ze-han's pen, it is also filled with great compassion for the human condition and touching humor. Knowing Hong-Ze-han's love of the book *The Da Vinci Code*, it is also filled with hidden secrets of the martial arts for the industrious and clever reader to decipher.

It was my goal to retain the flavor of the author's distinct voice and that of the language in which the book is written, Mandarin Chinese. This can lead to some awkwardness for the reader, but I wished for the reader to come away from this experience having read Chinese, in English. For this reason, in some dense or long, flowery, or self-deprecating passages, I have retained the original flavor.

Some readers may take exception to my choice of methods for Romanizing Mandarin. With very few exceptions, I have used Pinyin for romanization purposes. Where I have not, such as in the city names of Taipei (pinyin Taibei) or Keelung (pinyin Jilong), I have done so because the alternative is more widely known or employed. I have broken with convention in Romanizing names by putting a dash between the two characters of the given name, Yi-xiang for example, rather than adopt the current convention of dropping the dash.

Throughout the book, Hong Ze-han addresses his father as 老四懿祥, literally Old Number-Four Yi-xiang. In every instance, whether it is in a conversation with his father or brothers, or among his friends, I have retained this usage throughout the book even though it means "fourth *brother* Yi-xiang" (not fourth son).

For some martial art technical terms, I have used translations closer to the flavor of the original, rather than simpler terms frequently seen in martial art teaching materials. An example would be 連根拔起, liangenbaqi, simply translated in Taijiquan texts as "uprooting" but I have gone with the more prosaic, "Pulling Up by the Roots."

Finally, in the English translation, any deficiencies are my fault alone. I hope they will not hobble your enjoyment too much.

Christopher Bates—Taipei, Taiwan

Reflections on Editing and Proofreading *Blurred Boundaries*

It has been my sincere pleasure and privilege to be the editor and proofreader for this outstanding work by Master Hong Ze-han. I have trained in Yizong Tangshou Tao Xingyi and other martial arts with Master Hong for several years, and his martial arts skills, knowledge, and instructional talents are indeed first rate. So is his talent as a writer, and it becomes very apparent in reading this engaging and exciting work that Master Hong's integrating of his family's generational history, Taiwan's history, and his own martial arts journey, practice, development, experiences, and wisdom, provides a unique and valuable insight into Taiwan's deeper martial arts culture.

Again, it has been my great honor and privilege to have been a part of this fine project, in working closely with both Master Hong Ze-han and Christopher Bates, and I expect that this work will achieve the status of an instant classic in the realm of martial arts literature.

></br>Thomas Robert Argiro, associate professor of English (retired)
></br>Department of Foreign Languages and Literature
></br>Tunghai University, Taichung, Taiwan, ROC

Contents

Acknowledgements vii
Foreword viii
Preface to the Original Chinese Edition ix
Story Background xii
Notes on the Translation xiii
Reflections on Editing and Proofreading Blurred Boundaries xiv

1– Genesis 1
2– A Moment of Chaos and Escape 4
3– The Silent Flute 7
4– Taipei Main Station 11
5– Black Snake 13
6– Black Turtle 16
7– Street Race 19
8– Ragged Clothes 22
9– Dihua Street Hong Wan Mei 24
10– You Will Understand When You Grow Up 29
11– Minced Pork Stewed with "Ragged Clothes" 30
12– Blasting Away Pestilence for Lantern Festival 32
13– A Secret Plot 37
14– Artillery Barrage on the God of Pestilence 40
15– Crying Uncle 44
16– Toughening Up 45
17– Blockheaded 47
18– No. 11 Floodgate 49
19– Another Heaven 51
20– Jiangshan Winehouse 54
21– Sanyi Market 61
22– Hangzhou Tearoom 66
23– Daojiang Meeting Hall 70
24– Bid Rigging 101 75
25– Speed Determines Everything 77
26– The Dark Hidden Stream 81
27– Outreach 84
28– Eldest Brother's Demise 89

xv

29– The Human Chopping Board 91
30– The Hall of Encouraging the Good and Commie Spies 96
31– Eating Noodles, Drinking Tea, and Talking Gongfu 99
32– A Contest 104
33– One-Ton Head and Ten-Ton Stomach 108
34– Taiji Push Hands on the Riverbank 111
35– Goading into Action 116
36– Celebrating the Dragon Boat Festival 119
37– Assisting in Training 124
38– Challenging the Master 128
39– A Renowned Teacher's Bearing and Conduct 132
40– The 228 Conflict 137
41– Our Own People 140
42– Lunchbox Sushi 141
43– Panel Beaters Street 143
44– 1949 146
45– Connecting to Another's Mind 148
46– Calling on the Master 151
47– A Decision 154
48– A Master Down on His Luck 157
49– Talking about Xingyi 160
50– Discourse on Bagua 166
51– Speaking of Taiji 172
52– Taiwanese Essence of Change 176
53– Making Obeisance to the Master 180
54– Planting the Seed 185
55– Marking Territory 190
56– The Roar of the Wanli Turtle 193
57– The One Punch Kill 197
58– Brewing Tea, Chatting, and Withholding a Technique 204
59– At the Speed of Thought 208
60– A True Gentleman Quietly Observes Chess 217
61– Reverse Grip Sword 221
62– Guanyin Confrontation 225
63– First Seek the Conventional, Then Seek the Unconventional 230
64– A Renowned Teacher and Lofty Disciples 236
65– Harsh Training and Metamorphosis 239

66– Guandu	244
67– The Battle of Guandu	247
68– The Fired Brick	255
69– After the Fired Brick	262
70– So Just Call It "Yizong Tangshou"	268
71– Outwitting the Ebony Stupa	274
72– The Secret Training Base in the Central Mountain Range	283
73– Agent Smith of the CIA Part 1—Undiluting Diluted Secrets	289
74– The Hermit Deep in the Mountains	294
75– Agent Smith of the CIA Part 2—All Warfare is Based on Deception	300
76– The Long March to Japan Part 1	304
77– The Long March to Japan Part 2	310
78– The Long March to Japan Part 3	315
79– The Long March to Japan Part 4	321
80– Dark Arts and Dirty Tricks	327
81– The American Military Training Base	330
82– The Master Prepares a Banquet Part 1	336
83– The Master Prepares a Banquet Part 2	342
84– Taiji Master Chen Pan-ling	349
85– Movies, Gongfu, and Tea Part 1	355
86– Movies, Gongfu, and Tea Part 2	364
87– Old Bai	369
88– The Western Fanatic of Martial Arts Part 1	373
89– The Western Fanatic of Martial Arts Part 2	382
90– The Western Fanatic of Martial Arts Part 3	391
91– Matsumoto and Okuyama	401
92– Luodong Shaolin Hong Boxing	410
93– BBC Way of the Warrior Part 1	418
94– BBC Way of the Warrior Part 2	425
95– BBC Way of the Warrior Part 3	430
96– BBC Way of the Warrior Part 4	436
97– BBC Way of the Warrior Part 5	446
98– BBC Way of the Warrior Part 6	449
99– Across the Equator to Transmit the Art in Australia Part 1	454
100– Across the Equator to Transmit the Art in Australia Part 2	460
101– Across the Equator to Transmit the Art in Australia Part 3	464
102– Across the Equator to Transmit the Art in Australia Part 4	470

103– Across the Equator to Transmit the Art in Australia Part 5	476
104– Miaoli Vagrant Boxing	481
105– A Pot of Tea Shared in the Demimonde	487
106– Natural Boxing's Master Wan Lai-sheng	492
107– Conversations with My Old Man on the Balcony Part 1— The Stratagem of with the Grain versus against the Grain	497
108– Conversations with My Old Man on the Balcony Part 2— Focus on Strength and Get Powerful, Focus on Mind, and Get the Total Solution	500
109– Conversations with My Old Man on the Balcony Part 3— Involuntary Muscles	504
110– Conversations with My Old Man on the Balcony Part 4— Tilt Your Head, Don't Tilt the Taco	507
111– Downfall of the Strong	511
112– That Damned "Swallow Skims the Water"	519
113– The Paradox of Increase Is Decrease	523
114– My Plan B: Jerry-Rigged Saw on a Pole	527
About the Author	*531*
About the Tranlator	*532*

1– GENESIS

Most early drafts of our history are written with the pen dipped in fresh blood. In those pages interweaving histories of blood and tears, the records of foreign invaders are few. Many more record the evil and vicious behavior inflicted by our own on our own.

Scene: Dihua Street, Dadaocheng District, Taipei, Taiwan

IT WAS AN AGE OF UNINTERRUPTED CONFLAGRATION. Having endured the torment of the Second World War with great difficulty, the Chinese civil war between the Nationalists and Communists ramped up without pause. Unlike World War II, this was a military disaster between our own, exactly as the stories told in China's histories of dynastic rise and fall. The two sides in this war, no matter how despicable and base their hidden motivations, could at the same time both spout moving grievances and resentments, point fingers, pursue "justice" with no regard for the consequences, hurl invectives at their opponent for "damaging the country and causing suffering to the people." And on the battlefield, they exchanged abuse, showering spit and pent-up hatred, but both without hesitation turning on the innocent commonfolk to pay the bill.

Whereupon the largest refugee exodus across the sea in the modern history of China or the world was created. Whereupon martial arts exponents of each style and from all over China, each with their similar miserable excuses, but driven out most efficiently, were herded and aggregated together on this strange southern island—Taiwan. Whereupon these martial arts masters or wanderers of the martial forest, insinuated between the forces of dark and light, accompanied the Nationalist government gangsters to this foreign land for the same humble reasons, forced to exchange in this alien place their acquired martial skills and wisdom for the requisite chips used in the dangerous casino of survival. Whereupon, with the backdrop of this cruel history and motivated by petty survival, all manner of the impossible became possible, and anything might happen.

❈ ❈ ❈

Hong Yi-xiang's father, the elder Mr. Hong Wu-fan hailed from Taipei municipality, Danshui, Ting He Xiang Zhou (present day New Taipei City, Luzhou District). He was an orphaned peasant, raised with the help of his father's younger brother. With his special qualities of honesty and dogged perseverance, during the Japanese colonial period, he earned the favor of a Japanese engineer who passed on to him without reservation the latest candle manufacturing technology. With the full support of his eldest son Hong Yi-qin, step by step he became Northern Taiwan's largest supplier of candles and fireworks. Due to his personal interests, and due to the requirements of doing business in that rough and tumble era, the elder Mr. Hong Wu-fan embraced a high degree of passion for traditional martial arts.

Before and after 1949, following the Great Retreat of the Nationalist Government to Taiwan, came famous martial artists, swimming like shoals of fish across a river. Among these were martial artists who, through direct and indirect relationships, received relief and help from the Hong family of Dihua Street, and in repayment for the helping hand extended to them by Mr. Hong in the darkest moments of their lives, they permitted themselves to teach the Hong family without reservation, like emptying their pockets of secret treasures. In that time of turmoil and mutual mistrust, to protect the wealth they had acquired in their business and not be pressured by the extortions of dark elements, the Hong family thought of helping these martial arts experts to come and protect their business and family members. Mr. Hong never imagined that the ardor and sense of debt of these "Security Guards" would inspire the natural martial talents of the five children in the Hong family. The sons' enthusiasm further spurred the elder Mr. Hong to throw money into their training, enlisting the services of those martial arts exponents who had crossed the sea to Taiwan. They came to reside in the Hong compound and transmit their arts. Thus, because of a string of fateful circumstances for the Hong family, and if not for the confluence of the above social elements at the time, there should not have been a Master Hong Yi-xiang and the creation of this school of martial art—"Yizong Tangshou."

※ ※ ※

During the crossing of a dark stream of turbulent sea, a middle-aged man accompanying the retreating Nationalist government sat powerless and paralyzed on the deck, staring blankly at the many devastated and war weary old martial artists. They were thoroughly exhausted in body and mind, and unable to bear the torment of wave on wave of destitution and difficulty.

One after another, they dropped.

One after another, although not guilty of anything, they were compelled to forfeit their precious lives.

To a man, they were formerly famous in Chinese martial art circles, and here on this great unfamiliar sea, one by one their bodies were abandoned to the sea. Their martial skills and cultivation refined over a lifetime vanished, sealed within their lifeless forms, slowly sinking into the deep, inky black, becoming eternal corruption beneath the waves.

He looked at the hand-written boxing manuals in a bag entrusted to him by an oldster now expired, and muttered a whisper, "Pa, you have not even any life left. What's the sense in leaving this behind?"

Like a soulless puppet he hoisted that bag and lurched toward the aft of the ship, removed the handwritten tomes one by one, tore the pages out, and handed them to the sea breeze like they were devalued dollar notes.

2– A MOMENT OF CHAOS AND ESCAPE

It is known that keys open locks, but who has considered a key carried to a foreign land in a time of crisis and exodus, what meaning can it claim in a new place? Even more so, what is the significance of a key left behind with no lock to open?

Scene: Port of Qingdao, Mainland China, 1949

Every speck of earth along the shore of Qingdao harbor was packed with all manner of military and private vessels rushing to load refugees fleeing this ancient place. A bird's eye view revealed that even out into the open sea, the water was jammed with passenger and cargo ships slowly navigating out of the crowded harbor. Beyond them, more ships and boats of all sizes lined up, preparing to enter the port, ready to take on passengers, take on wealth.

On the shore were lined brokers of the nation's treasure, directly facing refugees begging for passage who were being charged exorbitant prices. In this setting, paper currency was worthless; apart from gold bars, boat ticket sellers would not even lift an eye to consider jewelry, paintings, and antiques that had no recognized value. Refugees desperate to sell off precious family heirlooms to obtain gold of sufficient weight were observed by antique merchants off to one side waiting to appraise and negotiate.

※ ※ ※

"We're old. We can't take the tossing about on the high seas, you go and don't worry," his mother said.

"I'll take care of your mom; we'll await your return," his father said.

"Pa!" The son, tears and snot streaming down his face, kneeled on the ground. In his hands only two tickets for passage, not enough to transport the destiny of a family of three.

Who could say how this final farewell would end? Would the son, unable to cast aside the fetters of family ties, surrender the tickets just obtained to some other refugee, and stay with his aged parents to face an unknown fate? Or would he comply with his father's will to continue the family line and burn incense at the alter to his ancestors, which meant turning and boarding the ship to face yet another unknown fate on his journey? In that moment, there was no one who cared about this tragic scene or touching story. And no one with enough heart or position to decide—who should stay behind? Who should leave?

In an era when war must be employed to decide cardinal questions of right and wrong, or have and have not, it is from the barrel of a gun or bore of a cannon that such human-destroying instruments of war issue their awful judgments. They cannot distinguish who is the evil person that should die, who is the kindhearted filial son on whom mercy should be shown. In the key moment when firepower decides everything, the wisest men of old have never stepped forward to protect the weak and preserve life.

※ ※ ※

Leaving the shoreline on a sampan, a wealthy family of six mouths plus their servants squeezed onto the deck, their brows knit, their two arms clutching the one precious bag each allowed by the captain, staring at the anxious and chaotic scene. In the bottom of their hearts they were clear, no matter how influential and illustrious their family had been, no matter how well socially connected, once they left the coast, any asset they could not carry was sealed up for safe keeping. For those things that could not be carried, sold, or shipped to someone to manage, they relied on an old lock, like a trusted servant who would refuse to yield, to seal up all their things until that day—that day when things were better, that clear and sunny day after the storm—when they could return from overseas, reclaim their land, wield their key, open their gardens, and resume the family business.

Only no one knew whether this old lock would be like Wang Bin-chuan, the virtuous wife of Peking Opera fame, able to resolutely protect the memories enshrined in the courtyard during the long absence of her husband. Who could say as soon as the boat left the coast, as the nation's masters changed, what claims this key making the ocean crossing could make? What did it prove? For a refugee fleeing turmoil, I am afraid that only the few precious items they pressed to their chests could be relied on to face an unknown future in a new land, relied on to protect them.

※ ※ ※

"Ai! Didn't I just change the lock this morning? How could the government fall so completely the same day, what's the rush?" On a small craft laboring against the current in the busy harbor stood a middle-aged man, his face lined with his thoughts, his back to the wind on the bobbing sampan. Gazing at the far shore and the hazy images of constant life-or-death encounters as people scrambled to escape or say farewell, he thought he saw his own silhouette. He could not tell if it was his spirit torn from his body by the war or his physical body. Only the icy spray of the ocean water clashing with the hot tears flowing on his face woke him to his existence. On the overcrowded deck, he strained to create a small space and dropped to his knees, his two hands clutching the gunwale, his head pointing in the direction of that ancient land where he had grown into a successful man. He bowed his head against the gunwale over and over, again and again, vowing, "When the war is concluded, I will return."

In that moment of his great pledge, on that enormous sea, besides the sound of a steam whistle's cry, neither heaven nor earth offered any reply.

3– THE SILENT FLUTE

The reason for life's perplexity is just because the reality and the ideal are blurred, the false and the real are hard to distinguish! And mankind indeed has some subliminal instinct, always thinking that out of chaotic disorder can emerge order or regularity, but in the end to no avail. Because chaos, fuzziness, is an innate quality of life. Always amidst our blunders, we mistake our own feelings and expectations. However, man's greatness is precisely because, having erred, we make our amends, our hair grows white, we say our goodbyes, and inevitably pass away...

Scene: A ship carrying refugees escaping Mainland China through the Straits of Taiwan, 1949

A mid-sized merchant ship is navigating toward Taiwan in the Taiwan Straits. The passengers move with the ship, the vessel moves with the waves. Jolting, bumping, splashing, no one is spared. The passengers talk or interact little partly due to the wave of seasickness, but mainly because of bewilderment and fear of an unknown future.

From their parochial, Middle Kingdom heartland perspective, Taiwan is just a remote island near the southern frontier. According to the mainstream historical view, the significance of Taiwan to China's historical rulers was that during periods of internal unrest, the island served as a foothold for the evil remnants of the previous dynasty in its last throes. Then, during times of foreign aggression, the island transformed into a bargaining chip tossed away to protect the motherland from the Great Powers negotiating "unequal treaties."

Which rebel parties and evil elements had occupied and seized the island in the past?

Which foreign nations and races have governed it?

How many times has the motherland declared its full-throated love for this piece of land, then sold it out, ceding it away, over and again?

It is not just the refugees and compatriots on this ship who are trying to escape from war and unrest who lack a full understanding of this disgrace. Even eminent scholars with a profound knowledge of Chinese history do not comprehend this island, which has tarnished the national glory and is often deliberately omitted in history annals or recorded only in unpopular chapters.

However, at this moment the shipboard compass is pointing toward this unfamiliar island and the future and fate of these passengers.

During the development of the Chinese civilization, this isolated isle has never been given even the slightest consideration in the official history books, resembling an illegitimate child never cared for by its natural parents.

By a strange serendipity, these parents and children, who once lacked mutual trust, suddenly find their destinies entwined at this critical moment. Is there enough generosity to accommodate shipload after shipload of brothers and sisters born of a different mother, coming to rely on their distant siblings?

Is the shoulder strong enough to bear the weight, to carry this group, representing the national assembly members elected in perpetuity, legislators, and government dignitaries of the legitimate regime?

Is there enough depth to bear the thousand-year-old treasures stored in the National Palace Museum and the thousands of tons of gold in the national treasury?

No one knows.

No one knows what will greet them when the ship reaches the shore, and the gangway drops—cold steel and guns? Or a warm shoulder?

At this key moment of universal desperation, will these islanders, forsaken by their great motherland on numerous occasions, their bastard genes never lovingly recognized, turn heartless their emotions, fall out with their counterparts, seize the opportunity to unburden accumulated rage in the face of a thousand years of indifference?

No one knows.

The departure from the mainland represents a departure from the mainstream Chinese civilization and the heartland of China. A legitimate political regime turns into rebel scum overnight. When the reins of political power in the motherland change hands, the power to write and interpret history is passed on to this bunch you regard as illegal usurpers. No matter whether you are fighting to "Oppose the Qing and Restore the Ming Dynasty," or fighting to topple the "Thoroughly Vicious Commie Bandits," or rally under the flag of "Liberate the Motherland's Comrades," history only provides one answer:

> *No one has ever been able to successfully restore the Chinese nation and recover political power from this island.*

※ ※ ※

"Stay with me, my dear," the old lady whispered her plea as she supported her feeble husband.

"It's the end of the road. I can't go with you," the old man said.

The old lady silently yielded to a stream of tears.

"Give this to Jun-feng." The old man took a hand-transcribed copy of *Swimming Dragon Bagua Consecutive Palms—A Clarification* from the duffel bag he held in his arms, handing it over to his wife.

"Look for him here," he said while pointing at a couple of characters written on the book with a fountain pen. It was an address: Hongwanmei, Dihua Street, Taipei, Taiwan.

The old man summoned what little energy was left in his body to inhale a mouthful of moist and salty ocean air. He forced open his eyes to look around at this stretch of unfamiliar sea. "Such a beautiful flute song." After the words were finished, a stale exhalation quietly leaked from his mouth; he closed his eyes and serenely passed on to the next world.

At the stern, on top of a messy pile of freight, a lone middle-aged man fingered a copper flute while looking out over the vast ocean, no sound. No melody.

On the deck, there was no unnecessary mourning or ritual. Only a piece of worn-out wooden board carried the old gentleman's body after his soul left. His once magnificent physique, now frail and thin, was carried with the help of several refugees to the railing of the ship, the board inclined, and he slid into the embrace of the great ocean. His wife stood at the rail for a long time, her arms folded across her chest as her husband's had been when he slid into the ocean, her eyes helplessly staring at the place where this old man, a mutually supportive companion of nearly a century, slowly, slowly submerged into the sea, silent and without tears! Only the noise of that *Swimming Body Bagua Consecutive Palms—A Clarification* book in her arms, pages flapping in the cold, ocean wind.

※ ※ ※

After sending away her true love, she closed her eyes slightly, trying to marshal her own flagging will to survive. She embraced the rare martial arts tome that her husband had written by hand with a lifetime of painstaking effort. With the other hand, she gently combed the gray hair that was disordered by the ocean wind, her expression solemn and respectful and with a dignified bearing, she slowly walked to the stern of the ship.

She blankly gazed at the long strip of the vessel's wake, linking her back to her home port. Already she couldn't distinguish the exact location where her husband had just slipped into the sea, nor was she sure in which direction her hometown was behind the ship. She turned around to observe one more time the disappointment on the faces of the unfamiliar refugees. She no longer cared for the world in which she lived. She cared even less about any significance or possibility in the words "Hongwanmei, Dihua Street, Taipei, Taiwan."

With both hands she embraced the precious relic entrusted to her by her old husband and fell back peacefully in the direction she thought most probable was that of her hometown. Her mind returned to the days of her youth when she and her beau met and fell in love, when she was fresh and pretty, so beautiful, so beautiful.

She, a martial arts woman who had won dozens of national championships with the Taiji Long Sword, thus died for love in the most poignant way, accompanying a master of the Northeast Internal School of Boxing into the boundless unknown. And together all their glory, legends, and experiences created over a lifetime in the field of traditional Chinese martial arts disappeared. No vestige. It was as if she and he had never existed.

4– TAIPEI MAIN STATION

Objects and energy always gravitate in the direction of least resistance. Courage is not the absence of fear, it is clearly knowing the fear and bravely standing firm, to do all one can without giving up.

Scene: Taipei Main Train Station

IT IS 1947, IN THE TIME JUST AFTER THE JAPANESE DEFEAT AND unconditional surrender in WWII, not long after they had departed from Taiwan. On the streets, each day, there were more and more mainlanders hailing from Tangshan Guangdong Province and places further inland from China, wearing their long male gowns, speaking with the accents of each region. Deep in the alleys, however, wearing their Japanese-style pajamas or undergarments, scores of Taiwanese continued to shuttle back and forth greeting each other in Japanese. In that time, the language barrier was a common, daily phenomenon. Although both parties tried hard to understand the other, and tried hard to help the other understand, it was like twins separated at birth to grow up in a different country, a different family. Even when they are joyfully reunited and embraced by their own parents, who would be able to overcome pernicious cultural barriers in the short term? In the markets, in shops, one often heard a brilliant cacophony, like chickens trying to talk to ducks. At the train station, on the street, one frequently saw conflicts, maybe big maybe small, continuing to erupt.

※ ※ ※

In the past, Taipei Main Rail Station was always the convergence point of a stream of people and goods moving north and south, a key transport hub. Near Zhengzhou Street was the rear of the station. Although it afforded access to passengers, it primarily served as a dock for large goods and raw materials to be off-loaded. Parked on the plaza in front of the Rear Station, facing the right side of the ancient main city gate of Taipei, was a long line of trishaw pedicabs awaiting passengers. Some of the drivers lie alone on the passenger seats, their bare feet propped up, conical bamboo hats shading their faces, taking naps. Others squatted in whatever shade could be found next to their machines and played checkers on the ground with chips of red brick and white mosaic as pieces, gambling for small change to while away the boredom. Along the left side of the plaza stood a line of what were popularly called "Push-Pull Depots," large hand-pulled freight carts. Coolies,[1] wadded burlap bags padding their shoulders and a ceaseless flow of sweat beading their bodies, moved a cargo of candle wax arrived from Keelong harbor on the loading platform to the carts.

Zhang Jun-feng, attired in a long traditional men's gown, a cloth sack hanging on his right shoulder, an ivory-handled large black umbrella in his left hand, entered the Rear Station from the train platform and stopped at the wooden gate to inquire of the ticket taker, "Please, how do I walk to Dihua Street?"

In Taiwanese, "Don't understand. Go ask the trishaw drivers," replied the old wizened ticket taker who did not comprehend his heavily accented Shandong Mandarin.

There was nothing Zhang Jun-feng could do but feign understanding of the old station employee pointing in a direction. Just as he was strolling across the Rear Station main hall, a street urchin of about three years old suddenly scurried around him. At that moment, a coolie bearing two large heavy sacks of paraffin blocks on his back was rushing in the opposite direction and just about to collide. The child was so small that the collision banged him away like a bullet from a gun, and he staggered back and fell on the floor. The coolie made every effort to arrest his forward momentum, but the one hundred pounds of paraffin followed the laws of physics and hurtled forward toward a crushing impact on the child.

"Ai, this is bad!" the coolie thought of the unfolding peril and could not help but shout out.

It happened in an instant, but Zhang Jun-feng was as quick as a spark. His left foot circled inward with a Bagua button step and his body followed to the right rear turning 180 degrees, placing him in a flash between the coolie and the child. His body released the centrifugal force of his turn into his right shoulder, colliding with one of the bags of paraffin and knocking it away. He shifted into a right bow-and-arrow stance and released Bagua's Upholding Palm, shoving away the second burlap bag. Without a hair's breadth to spare, he had agilely eliminated a thorny crisis. When he determined that both parties were safe and sound, he collected himself and calmly stood up. He reached out and helped the child up first, turned and picked up his umbrella and the sack dropped in haste, then sauntered out the main door like nothing had happened, leaving behind the coolie who had yet to collect his wits and a station full of gawking passengers.

---

1 Coolie is not a Western derogatory term but originates in Chinese as *kuli* 苦力, 'bitter strength,' denoting someone working at hard physical labor.

5– BLACK SNAKE

Train platforms and seaside docks are not merely places where we see off departing guests and meet new arrivals, nor are they only a stage on which we fondly say farewell to our departing fathers. Generally, in places at the intersection of large flows of goods and people, there are always resources and opportunities, and they are focal points coveted by both black and white, by forces of darkness and light.

Scene: The Plaza Behind the Taipei Main Train Station at Zhengzhou Street

ZHANG JUN-FENG HAD NO SOONER STEPPED DOWN FROM THE platform at the rear of Taipei Main Station, his foot taking its first step on Taipei soil, when Black Snake, with excellent snake weaving technique, swerved into the head of the line of trishaws. "This one's mine! You take the next one." Although Black Snake's face sported the professionally insincere smile of a cabby touting for passengers, the tone of his voice carried a "take it or leave it" frostiness. Black Turtle intervened, "Stealing business. This is bad." Zhang Jun-feng would never accept this outrageous, brazen public hustle and glared at the cabby taking his measure. At a glance he could see this fellow worked all year outdoors, his skin nut brown from over exposure to the sun, lean sturdy build, dressed in shorts and a tank top, a conical plaited bamboo hat on his head, an old, faded scarf around his neck, on his feet he pedaled in "ninja shoes" popular among workers at the time (a mid-rise cloth boot with a space for the big toe and four little toes). From his active, shifty eyes, he subtly revealed the arrogant bearing of a ruffian, with an "I'm the boss, put up or shut up" attitude. "Yeah, don't ride his cab!" Black Turtle shouted, full of invective.

Although at the time Zhang Jun-feng did not understand the words being spoken, relying on many years' experience traipsing through all manner of markets, ports, and depots, he understood the nests of vipers that harbors and stations were, entangling all manner of interests and disputes. From the contemptuous tone of voice, he was already roughly informed of the subtle relationships between the two parties here at the station. So as not to step on any mines in a new place, nor having any desire to provoke people, he did not turn his head to see who shouted, instead feigning ignorance. But he firmly rejected riding on the trishaw of this boldly rapacious cabby. He insisted on getting onto the first pedicab that had been waiting in line.

"It doesn't matter. He's one of us. It's fine, just ride his," the good natured, old cabby said, removing his hat and waving his hand to signal he was willing to give up this ride. Faced with the cabby's non-confrontational acquiescence, Zhang Jun-feng first felt a bit of doubt. He looked back at that line-cutting guy with his implacable "I told you so" bully's expression and thought he should not take his cab. In the end he strongly resisted his heart's annoyance and resentfully boarded.

"We're all friends here, Master," in Taiwanese. "What's your pleasure, sir? Do you want to go to 'Hong Wan Mei'?" Black Snake asked.

"I'm going to Dihua Street, Section 1, No. 177," Zhang Jun-feng said.

"Okay, take a seat," Black Snake responded.

Zhang Jun-feng had barely boarded and had not even turned around to seat himself, when Black Snake eagerly put some juice into his pedals, and the pedicab shot out of the station like an arrow. To his utter embarrassment, Zhang Jun-feng was caught unawares by the sudden acceleration and was thrown awkwardly into the two-seater bench.

"Your leg strength's not bad!" Zhang Jun-feng exclaimed as he hastily arranged himself in the seat.

"I have the fastest legs in Dadaocheng. From the city gate at the back of the station to Dalongdong Pig Slaughterhouse, nobody is faster than I am." After watching Zhang Jun-feng take a spill into the back seat, Black Snake felt quite full of himself. "That was called a Speedy Getaway. Pretty cool," the Black Snake said with pride on his face, having taken pains to dash away quickly.

"What did you say?" Zhang Jun-feng had an inborn fear of speed, but it did not show on his face and he feigned calm. His two hands, however, clutched the wooden armrests without letup.

"Don't understand, no matter. It's all cool," Black Snake said to himself.

"Master, I'm in no hurry. You don't need to burn so much energy," Zhang Jun-feng said.

"This is only 30 percent. I can go even faster!" Black Snake replied.

Perhaps he did not understand, or he wanted to intentionally make his fare suffer, but Black Snake continued in an ever-accelerating serpentine path through the traffic.

This was a small microcosm of what it was like back then, when so-called foreign provincials from the mainland and Taiwan provincials interacted. Hindered by language barriers and life's necessities, there was unavoidable contact and unavoidable collisions and friction. Provided an odd spark did not fall onto a pile of dry grass, provided the two sides employed a little good-will and forgiveness to show consideration to the other party, if bystanders ardently assisted or came forward to try to dissolve disputes, then any sparks resulting from social collisions and friction would help everybody to see clearly the beauty of their differences and understand their mutual boundaries and limits. Thus, not only would events not evolve into intractable problems, but they would also contribute to mutual respect, forgiveness, and fusion between different cultures and social groups.

This is entirely rationalized, wishful thinking and good intentions alone, since the origins of conflict and slaughter were often hibernating beneath the veneer of peaceful coexistence, well camouflaged to look like, "This is for the good of all." Yet pressures constantly would build up until one day when they had reached their limits, they would give vent with earth-shattering force. And that boundary kept in place to maintain harmony, to avoid overstepping into conflict, has always been blurred, since humans have no way to understand or control it. Without a fixed demarcation, it nevertheless exists.

When the majority have the homecourt advantage, they will demarcate the boundaries: "We aren't letting you interlopers suppress us." Later, the minority, controlling the military resources of the nation, commands, "You are not allowed to defy the powerful." Watchful people, standing between these two opposing forces, observe closely the aftermath of such chaos, to see the opportunities and possibilities for redistribution of resources and power, for at these times the watchful can grab golden prospects, netting twice the result with half the effort.

6– BLACK TURTLE

Labor is mankind's most primeval, and cheapest commodity. Within the Labor Market beneath the Taipei Bridge, to provide for their families, aging laborers still had to struggle to hold out. Those for whom strength had given out relied on skills; those without sufficient skills just marked time.

Scene: The Plaza Behind the Taipei Main Train Station at Zhengzhou Street

ON THE PLAZA BEHIND THE TRAIN STATION, COOLIES LIKE WORKER ants resigned to their fate endlessly trudged back and forth with a fixed rhythm, struggling to transfer a pile of paraffin blocks bag by bag onto a large lorry. The coolies on the bed of the truck busied themselves receiving the paraffin and piled it up layer after layer. From start to finish, laborers would busy themselves with this for at least an hour and only fill one lorry.

In that age entirely dependent on manual labor, many people arrived in Taipei from south and central Taiwan seeking to make a living. If they did not have enough capital of their own to invest in a small business, or if they temporarily could not find full time employment suitable to their skills, so long as their body was healthy and they had two arms and two legs, in such a commercially vibrant city most could find some temporary manual labor employment. The snag was that whether it was hot or cold, rain or shine, those seeking to make a living this way had to sacrifice their sleep, rise from bed in the dead of night and hurry to make it to the Labor Market underneath the Taipei Bridge before dawn at 5:00 a.m. Here they awaited the decision of the foreman to pick them for one day's wages of temporary work, selling their one day of labor in exchange for a pittance of income to raise a family. Here, over half of the laborers awaiting work orders were middle-aged, in their hometowns some had been farmers, some fishermen, others had repaired roofs, were plasterers, or carpenters, or metalsmiths. They came from each corner of Taipei, other villages all over Greater Taipei and from the north and west coasts; their backs hunched up at the black, star-filled sky, they rode their "iron horse" bicycles for the journey to assemble at Yanping North Road Section 2, the Labor Market under the Taipei Bridge.

In that dark cavern under the bridge assembled group upon group of older men, all sporting different accents. Seeing the longing in their eyes that the god of fortune might shine on them, it was hard not to feel the weight and pressure on these breadwinners. For these elders any work order received from the foreman would do. It didn't matter if it was carrying loads or street cleaning, or if it did not require special skills, provided they could get any job order. This waiting continued until 7:00 a.m., by which time all jobs had been assigned. Of those who had not succeeded in getting a work order, some trudged away despondently to the train, sad to return home, some preferred to remain under the bridge with other leftovers who had been rejected and play Chinese Chess, whiling away the entire day, unwilling to return home to face their families and their wives' scorn.

The group of coolies working behind the train station had Black Turtle as their leader and were a gang relying on strength in organization. Assembled into a gang, they seized control of this lucrative spot that was the main traffic hub of Taipei. Every day at dawn, he would appoint a foreman to the Labor Market, sent to select for work as porters those waiting lambs; obedient, hard-working, and willing to surrender a cut of their wages. Most of the rest of the gang members were reprobates or thugs mixed up with local gangs, responsible for protecting the turf, or "additional laborers," used to pad the payroll, but these gang members were not expected to, and definitely would not, lift a finger to carry any burdens.

"Move out," his eyes noting that the truck was already finished loading, Black Turtle shouted from a shaded spot where he smoked a cigarette, the pack of New Paradise smokes rolled into his T-shirt sleeve. After issuing the order, he cast a glance to several footmen and immediately three chaps who were doing nothing jumped on the back of the truck. The three coolies who had been shouldering the heavy lifting were given not a moment to catch their breath. They removed the cloth pads from their shoulders to vigorously shake off the paraffin chips and dust, then scrambled for their lives to grab hold of the pile of burlap bags as the truck pulled out.

"Hit the road." Black Turtle flicked his butt away like a bullet and slapped the truck door hard, urging the driver to be on his way.

"You, you, you, you three are escorts. Collect the fee," Black Turtle ordered. The loafers immediately sprang into action, nimbly jumping one by one on board the back of the truck.

"What the fuck are you gawking at? Get on board." Several coolies who had just finished moving goods to the truck and with nary a moment to drink a mouthful of water nor catch a breath were pressed to climb on board. They had no choice but to drag their knackered frames onto the truck and await with weary resignation the next round of heavy labor, off-loading into the go-down.

Zhang Jun-feng, filled with martial vigor, arrived in Taiwan as a fruit wholesaler, 1947.

7– STREET RACE

My hand inserts the green rice shoots into the paddy,
My lowered head sees the reflection of the sky in the water,
My mind is a tranquil square in the Way,
To retreat in the end is to advance.

—Liang the Burlap Monk, "Rice Planting Hymn"

Scene: Zhengzhou Road and Dihua Street

ZHENGZHOU ROAD—ALL ALONG IT ARE THE KINDS OF SHOPS frequently seen along bus routes, inns, guest houses, hardware stores, variety shops, and farm implement stores. The master craftsman of the old shop selling wooden buckets and tubs, dressed head to foot in semitransparent underwear made of fine white bamboo fiber, a wool obi sash, popular among Japanese, around his waist, leads by the hand, his grandson, dressed in Japanese-style pajamas, to urinate in the open gutter in front of his own shop house. The master craftsman lifts the grandson up, opening the large convenient crack in the pants exposing the grandson's behind and wiener. Aiming his wiener in the direction of the gutter, the master craftsman whistles to stimulate the grandson's urge to pee. The naughty boy, on the one hand peeing, on the other hand playing with himself and directing the flow like from a fountain, now far, now close, now high, then low, now left, then right, provoking his grandpa and giggling away.

In those days, Taipei's gutters were all uncovered, open sewers. Moreover, they had been built primarily with the stone that had been recovered when Taipei's old city wall had been torn down. Because of the enormous number of abandoned flagstones, to dispose of them would have taken considerable human and monetary resources, and yet the stones, although old, were strong and durable. So, after research and commercial discussion, these flagstones were turned into building materials. It is said that, apart from the stones used to build the Taipei Prison and the perimeter walls of some official residences, the remainder were employed to make the two sides of the gutter and to prevent soft asphalt road from washing away. Who would have thought, in the early days, something used to divide the political boundary of the inner city and the outer city over time would separate us from criminals and provide the channel for the flow of sewage? Looking back on those days, I was studying at the Yongle Elementary School, and my baseball teammates and I would form a single line, our feet straddling the two sides of the "Century Old Taipei City Wall," fish out our not-yet-matured peckers, and gloriously take a leak into the open sewer of Yanping North Road. Unfortunately, during this heroically bold and unconstrained action, I ran into a coed who I had long pined after, and with the suddenness of the encounter at a key moment of liberating pleasure, I had no time to halt the flow nor recover the liberated tool. Accordingly, years spent pursuing a pure unrequited love were entirely flushed down the drain with this great flow of juvenile piss missing the mosaic of the gutter, never to return.

※ ※ ※

"Why are they still wearing Japanese-style clothes?" Zhang Jun-feng could not help asking with a smile.

"Ah, this. Eh, easier to take a leak," Black Snake replied casually without thinking.

"Oh, spoken truly. Heh-heh," Zhang Jun-feng could not think of a better reply.

After seeing the tike take a leak, the trishaw turned from Zhengzhou Road into commercially prosperous Dihua Street. Before one's eyes the street scene transformed into one of flourishing activity. Lining the street were fabric stores, tea wholesalers, Chinese herbal medicine pharmacies, goods from north and south, seed stores, agricultural implement shops, paint stores, all manner of shophouses stuffed to the brim with glittering surprises. Some of the larger wholesalers put their inventory on the pedestrian archway or on the road in front of the shop, to make deliveries and pickups easier. Others who had just completed a transaction buying inventory, busied themselves supervising pedi-trucks[2] delivering the mess of goods and removing them from the street.

"This is Dihua Street. The richest street in Taipei. It's lively," Black Snake remarked.

"Really bustling," Zhang Jun-feng said.

"Sir, where did you say you wanted to go?" Black Snake asked.

"Section 1, Number 177. Selling candles," Zhang Jun-feng responded, knitting his brows.

"That's gotta be Hong Wan Mei," Black Snake said.

"BAHHHHH!"—a loud sound suddenly split heaven, interrupting the two

---

2 These trucks, totally different from the pedicab trishaws and called Li A Ka—plough carts—were man-powered carts. Later, when loads became bigger, besides strengthening the truck beds, they added engines, making them into motorized carts that were called Iron Buffaloes, that can still be seen occasionally in southern Taiwan.

men's conversation. The truck filled with paraffin that had left the train station after them had caught up with the trishaw, pulled right up to his rear, and laid on the horn, demanding that the trishaw make way.

"Fuck your mother! You're dealing with Big Daddy here," Black Snake blurted out.

"Ba-BA-BAHHHH!" the truck replied even more urgently to his greeting.

"I'll fuck your ancestors. The road is only so wide. Big Daddy's not giving way—see what you can do about it!" Black Snake ratcheted up the invective to include ancestors, determined not to yield.

The two vehicles remained deadlocked on the narrow single-lane way and Zhang Jun-feng, his ears no longer able to stand the blaring horn, waved his hands, imploring the trishaw driver to yield. "Little Brother, just let them go first," Zhang Jun-feng said. Only then did Black Snake resentfully pull his trishaw over to the right and the big truck immediately passed on the left, the two vehicles shoulder to shoulder. "Fuck your mother! You're dickless, pedaling so slow, can't get out of the way when you're honked at!" The ruffian sitting in the truck's passenger seat hurled this invective, then the truck stepped on the gas and passed by.

Black Snake could not swallow being taunted as a loser, and his two legs shot the trishaw forward like a rocket, so that it pulled into the arcade at the same time as the truck. Actually, this awkward situation was just a symptom of the dangerously narrow and crowded roadside scene at Dihua Street. Never in his dreams had Zhang Jun-feng on the trishaw imagined he would be drawn into such a conflict; besides praying with all his might to the gods for protection, he could only clutch at the arms of his seat to avoid being spilled out of the cab.

"I fuck, fuck… FUCK your mother!" Black Snake panted the invective. He had chased the truck as if his life depended on it to deliver this four-letter greeting to the truck driver's mother, to have the last word with his last strained breath conveyed with sufficient intimidation and hurtful force. Before he could even finish his invective, the wastrel derisively mimicked Black Snake's swearing by panting and contorting his face. "No more chasing, just let them be. I know they are afraid of you," Zhang Jun-feng implored to smooth the cabby's ruffled feathers. "Fuck… His mother… Big Daddy's gonna let you be reincarnated first!" Black Snake slowly regained his composure, converting to a third-person invective to conclude this battle without a victor. In the end Dadaocheng's Fastest Legs was no match for the new technology, but on the road, Black Snake remained unrepentant in cursing the opponent to a bad death, to regain his lost breath, to regain that lost bit of dignity in the demimonde.

8– RAGGED CLOTHES

"Ragged Clothes" is a type of bitter astringent fruit of the Sebastian Plum shrub. After slow cooking, pickling and fermentation, it develops a beautifully sweet flavor. In days past, it was an accompaniment to a breakfast of light porridge intended to stimulate the appetite, but now its principal use is as a sublime flavoring for steamed fish.

Scene: Hong Wan Mei Trading Company, Dihua Street

AT NO. 177 DIHUA STREET, SECTION 1, IN THE OPEN-AIR COURTYARD between the three Hong family residences, there stood neat rows of sun-withered dry radishes, grapes, and cucumbers on a Fujian Minnan-style double swept red tile roof. A petite maid carefully stepped on the depressed rain channels between the red tiles turning over one by one the drying cucumbers to be pickled. The courtyard was filled with jars of all shapes and sizes, tall, short, slender, fat, for putting up foodstuffs. Auntie Wu-fan[3] sat on a wicker stool, pulling up her wide sleeves, exposing on her wrist a fine imperial jade bangle streaked with ochre and a delicately crafted gold bracelet. That blood-colored jade bangle had been broken into three pieces one time when she slid and fell at the well. According to ancient legends, a good jade bangle will protect and bear the calamity for its owner. Therefore, Auntie Wu-fan always believed that this was her favorite jade bangle, for at the critical moment it took for her the brunt of one of life's unavoidable spills. To express her heartfelt gratitude, she sought the oldest gold jewelry shop on Yanping North Road, the goldsmiths of Gold Luck Mountain, to help. The cost was more than buying a new pair of jade bracelets. Tastefully reticulated carvings of flowers created a gold sleeve joining the broken jade pieces, elegantly renewing it into a three-section bangle.

Without any hesitation worrying about the fine jewelry, she directly plunged her hand into the thick sauces, one by one plucking out pickled cucumbers, fermented bean curd, "ragged clothes," pickled cabbage hearts, and other preserved foods, afterward using her other hand to squeegee the excess sauce, piling it into the extraordinarily large, coarsely thrown pottery bowl brought by Crabby Auntie.

---

3 Although this person is the author's paternal grandmother, she was referred to as Auntie Wu-fan by friends and neighbors, and so the author has used this designation. Similarly, the author's grandfather is referred to as Uncle Wu-fan, and an unrelated wife of an employee is Crabby Auntie.

"Is this enough?" Auntie Wu-fan asked.

"Auntie Wu-fan, your preserves are the best. Roast pork with these 'ragged clothes' is the absolute favorite of my old man and Black Turtle!" Crabby Auntie exclaimed.

"They like the 'ragged clothes,' huh? Okay, then take some more." Auntie Wu-fan said cheerfully.

Auntie Wu-fan again extended her arm and fished into the jar, pulling out a chunk as big as your face of "ragged clothes," then gingerly stacking it in the already over filled giant bowl, like a seven-story pagoda. Crabby Auntie busied herself with her free hand, stabilizing this critical tower of pickled vegetables so as to avoid making this architectural wonder collapsing.

"I'm such a glutton. Every time I take so much." Crabby Auntie bowed at the waist to express her heartfelt gratitude.

"Ai! Don't speak this way; if you don't help me consume some of this, Uncle Wu-fan will certainly ridicule me as a stingy wretch, and he'll say the vegetables are too salty, so no one wants them," Auntie Wu-fan said.

"Apologies and many thanks," Crabby Auntie said.

Crabby Auntie continued to bow her thanks as she backed up to the entrance and walked out.

9– DIHUA STREET HONG WAN MEI

The lanterns of myriad families light the night, beautiful turns and marvelous abundance please the heavens.

Scene: Dihua Street Hong Wan Mei Trading Company, Jiang Cheng Long Funeral Supplies

OUTSIDE, UNDER THE PEDESTRIAN OVERHANG, LEANING AGAINST the columns at Jiang Cheng Long Funeral Supplies, were two unfinished wood coffins serving as samples for customer comparison and displaying the selection of the quality of materials used. Here were sold only two styles of coffins; Shanghai and Fuzhou, and their differences in price depended entirely on the choice of material selected by the customer. Because their target customers were all high-level officials and the well-off at the top of the food chain, the shop always kept in stock a large supply of the finest woods. Usually seen was Formosan Conifer, Chinese Juniper, Red Juniper, Camphor, False Cypress, and others. Only after the customer confirmed the wood selection would carving and lacquering proceed, according to the customer's specifications and color choice.

The shop's hunchbacked master carver was wielding a sharp hatchet, splitting a section of Grade-A Phoebe Laurel. The distinctive fragrance of the essential oils in Formosan Conifer wafted about the entire workshop. Employing neither blueprints nor carpenter's lines to demarcate, relying entirely on his direct senses and touch, he could accurately split the wood and get two identical pieces of auspicious size when measured by the mystic ruler. No one knew that this talented and robust middle-aged man was the grandson of the wealthy owner of a six-branch chain of protection services[4] in Northeast China. He had been his grandfather's favorite and was expected to succeed him in the business, but due to an intolerable dispute within the family over assets and the trauma of World War II, the depraved breakdown of family feelings, and a sense of powerlessness and desperation, he chose to cross the seas alone to Taiwan, preferring to disappear into the cities of this southern island and lead a life of self-exile.

To make a living, he had no choice but to turn to the martial skills he had

---

4 Protection Services, BiaoJyu, were convoy guard services in China. They also came to act as a means to move funds quickly in China, providing promissory notes. In this sense they were like an early version of Wells Fargo in the American Old West.

trained so hard in his youth, TanTui and Cha Quan boxing, wielding his hatchet to split coffin panels. When required he would also help the bereaved children and grandchildren take care of the ancestor's corpse to supplement his meager wages in this strange land. His neighbors did not know much about this hunchbacked master shuttling between the two worlds of shadow and light. They only knew that he could frequently be found muttering aloud in conversation with ghosts and demons, but no one ever had the temerity to ask about the content of these conversations. Maybe the reason was that everyone felt the darkness surrounding him was too heavy, so they dared not get to know him well. Thus, no one even knew the real name of this gloomy, joyless Northeastern Chinaman, nor any details about his background. They knew only that every day at dawn when he was at the banks of the Dan Shui River, he practiced his martial art with uncompromising attention to detail, suggesting that in the deepest, darkest recesses of his heart, there remained a thread of passion and lofty intent that could not be destroyed by his present circumstances.

Next door to the coffin shop was the northern district's largest licensed salt wholesaler, Gao Jin Salt. In front of the salt seller were parked several heavy-duty ox-drawn carts, on top of which were piled salt baskets made of woven bamboo, waiting to be off-loaded. The first ox to arrive had already had its yoke removed, and having passed under the archway, lowered its head and was chewing on some fresh hay. Another large yellow cow stood both chewing hay and gushing forth a great stream of yellow cow piss. A little puppy, reared in the city, stood on the side and curiously took a lick with its tongue at the splashing puddle of urine. An old cat squatted on top of a cement trash receptacle surveying this scene with total indifference. As for the puppy's opinion, perhaps cow urine is an acquired taste.

The trash receptacle under the old cat's feet was that year's city government masterpiece of urban design standardization. The regulations of the time stated that each shop had to have one of these cement trash receptacles that looked oddly like a shrine to the Earth God installed in a standardized fashion at the left side of each archway. The top of the receptacle was a wooden cover nailed together. Every night at dusk, a municipal cart would come by to recycle this garbage. This public garbage collection cart was a giant box pulled by a man pushing a wooden armature, assisted by a sturdy shoulder strap fashioned from thick canvas sailcloth. The box had to be pushed and pulled this way just to get it to budge. On New Year's or other large holidays, when the volume of garbage was huge, extra people had to be enlisted to push on the cart from behind. Besides moving the cart, they still had to collect the garbage from every residence, which was extremely onerous work. At least there was one good concession made by the regulations of the time: food waste that could rot, and kitchen scraps, were separated and retrieved by a "Swine Rearing Association" to be fed to the pigs as slop, so usually this was not put in the trash receptacles.

In that era, before the appearance of flush toilets, there was yet another type of manual labor not highly sought by the average worker— the so-called "Liquid Manure Brigades." According to memory, nearly all the street sweepers and manure bearers of the Nation's Glory Brigades seen at Dihua Street were of the same stripe: hard-luck, demobilized soldiers from mainland China. These old laborers toiled every day for meagre wages, but without their sacrifice and enduring humiliation in carrying out their work, even cultured, high class, rich families would have found life unbearable.

When New Year's rolled around, shops and families would all prepare a HongBao red-envelope gift of money to express thanks for their year of wretched toil. Some families would take some unused daily-use items or clothing still in good condition, clean it properly, and give it to them. In that age when nothing was plentiful, it did not matter if one was giving or receiving; everyone felt a sense of preciousness and gratitude. Although people ordinarily lived simple, impoverished lives, it is what one looks back on fondly from this era.

Each household and shop appointed someone to carry the human waste out to the Brigades. Mr. Hong Wu-fan gave strict instructions to the Hong family children never to turn their nose up to this job. He said that stuff was the product of our own bodies, and these old uncles from mainland China were helping take on the task of handling it, so we should have heartfelt appreciation and never belittle their work with any loathsome expressions. When I was small, I always thought this was torture; only now that I am old do I understand this expression of consideration.

To the right of the salt shop was the Qing Brocade Spirit Table Shop, a century-old establishment specialized in selling shrines and alter tables. The master lacquerer was holding a large bowl full of lacquer in his left hand and applying a second primer coat to an Eight Immortals Table. The Hong Wan Mei Trading Company was thus placed directly facing the Gao Jin Salt Wholesaler, so it was no surprise that the prettiest daughter of the salt merchant's boss later became the wife of the Hong family's second-generation son, Hong Yi-kun, and thus the two large Dihua Street clans, Hong and Gao, became relatives.

The truck transporting paraffin came to a stop at the gate of Hong Wan Mei and three laborers shouldered the paraffin raw materials into the storehouse next to the rundown furnace, as number four among the sons, Hong Yi-xiang, moved around the truck taking inventory of the number of bags, and frequently calling out to the coolies to put a bag down on the ground, randomly selected to check for weight and purity. "Okay. The rest you take over to the Anxi Street warehouse; my brother is waiting there for you," Yi-xiang ordered, and the coolies organized the truck as instructed, reattached the chain at the back and climbed aboard the bed waiting for the truck to pull out. At this moment, Zhang Jun-feng, riding on his pedicab, pulled up to Hong Wan Mei's gate, paid his fare, and got off the trishaw. Then he saw Black Snake walk over to fourth son Yi-xiang after taking his fare and ask for a tip.

"I've brought you a really awesome boxing idol, give me a bigger tip," Black Snake said.

"How do you know he's awesome?" fourth son Yi-xiang asked.

Black Snake forked his two fingers, pointed at his own eyes, and said mysteriously, "I rely on this, one glance and I knew it all."

Fourth son Yi-xiang knew it was BS, but according to their practice, he handed over a $5 note to Black Snake, and hinted to Black Snake to return the fare he had just taken from Zhang Jun-feng.

"He gave me more than you did, so I am returning yours. That's right, in Taiwan pedicab rides are free." So saying, Black Snake disappeared, slithering through the traffic, leaving Zhang Jun-feng looking astonished and unbelieving.

"It's okay. It's my Pa's rule. A respect to old masters," fourth son Yi-xiang said with a laugh, beckoning Zhang Jun-feng to come into the shop.

"Please, how shall I address you, Master?" Yi-xiang asked.

"Surname Zhang. I came to buy candles," Zhang Jun-feng replied.

Realizing Black Snake had bilked him out of five bucks, Fourth son Yi-xiang muttered, "That deadbeat," from the corner of his mouth. "In that case, come on in and take a look." He turned and courteously showed Zhang Jun-feng into the shop.

※ ※ ※

On the wheels of the truck's departure, Black Turtle rode up on a bicycle, appearing at Hong Wan Mei's shop gate. "Freight's all delivered. Pay up," Black Turtle said.

"According to the rules, we pay after the freight is off-loaded," fourth son Yi-xiang said.

"Rules. Peh! You made 'em up. If you don't pay, I'm getting your old man." Black Turtle strode into the shop on his own. "Uncle Wu-fan. Pay up!" Black Turtle yelled.

"Oh? Altogether, how many laborers?" Uncle Wu-fan asked.

Black Turtle counted the three on the truck who had done the work and the other three loafers who stood smoking. "Including myself, that makes seven. Let's make it six and a half!" Black Turtle said.

"There were only three who actually moved anything, why have you doubled up?" fourth son Yi-xiang said, reaching the back room.

"Ai, that's weird, you didn't see the three guys I had guarding the truck?" Black Turtle asked.

"There was no theft, no pilferage, guarding what?" Yi-xiang scoffed.

"These are the trucker's rules, got it?" Black Turtle said facetiously.

"Okay, six and a half it is." Uncle Wu-fan pulled open the drawer from the counter and took out the money to give Black Turtle.

Just as Black Turtle was extending his hand to take the money, Crabby Auntie emerged from the courtyard with a large bowl heaped with pickled vegetables, supported by her two hands, on her wrist hanging a bag of pork belly cooked with pickled yam leaves. Two people, four eyes, met; Black Turtle hurriedly averted his glance and stuffed the money just put in his hands into his pocket. "Ai! One bad turn after another," Crabby Auntie said. She shook her head and disgustedly headed out of the shop.

A mother seeking a hand-out of free pickles from her employer's family, a son trying to extort excess wages from a shop; one embracing gratitude, one bringing threats, mother and son unexpectedly running into each other—this scene, both contradictory and conflicting, was all witnessed by Zhang Jun-feng's eyes, who had only come by chance to buy candles. When the eyes of the proprietor of the shop and his guest unexpectedly met, all was understood without anything having been said.

10– YOU WILL UNDERSTAND WHEN YOU GROW UP

Things we don't understand when we are young, we don't necessarily understand when we've grown up.

Things we think we understand after we grow up usually are not the reality. This is because people always only believe what they are willing to believe, so in the end, that is what constitutes their understanding, but that is not necessarily a true understanding.

Scene: At the Hong family dinner table at Dihua Street

"PA! WHY DO YOU PUT UP WITH THESE SCOUNDRELS?" FOURTH brother Yi-xiang asked resentfully.

"It's only pocket change. Don't bicker over it. It's the same as when your ma hands out pickled vegetables to people," the elder Wu-fan replied.

"Making pickles to give to people, that's to help our children and grandchildren acquire good karma. How is it the same?" Wu-fan's wife said.

"Yeah, how is it the same?" fourth brother Yi-xiang said.

The elder Wu-fan forced a smile but did not reply.

"Pa said it's the same, so it's the same. Cut the nonsense and eat dinner," the eldest brother, Yi-kun, stood up and shouted.

The third brother, Yi-mian, who had just been vigorously shoveling food in, was so startled by the outburst that he not only dropped the chunk of stewed fatty pork but also his chopsticks onto the table. "What are you thundering about!? Scared me to death," Yi-mian said loudly in reaction.

Amused by his preoccupied gluttony and cluelessness, the whole family laughed so hard they choked. The elder Wu-fan just gently nodded his head, acknowledging the eldest brother Yi-kun's timely intervention, but he also reached out and patted fourth brother Yi-xiang's hand on the table. "When conducting business, there is a trick to talking, and some things are better left unsaid. It's not necessarily logical. Later you will understand."

11– MINCED PORK STEWED WITH "RAGGED CLOTHES"

Life is short and hard, you must do something, something that well proves to you this life was not wasted.

Scene: A rear alley off Dihua Street, an illegal construction site facing Anxi Street

UNDER THE YELLOW GLOW OF TUNGSTEN LAMPS, THERE WAS A table set for dinner; a dish of fried peanuts, a soup of sweet potato greens, and a clay pot of minced pork stewed with "ragged clothes." As Crabby Auntie busied herself feeding her tubercular, invalid husband, Black Turtle came in from outside, stole a sideways glace at her back, and without a word slipped behind toward his dark room. Crabby Auntie heard the sound and knew it was Black Turtle returning; although the anger in her heart was still not extinguished, she could not but ask, "Have you eaten?"

Black Turtle arrested his steps at the doorway, but neither answered nor turned around.

"Come, let's eat together," Crabby Auntie entreated.

Black Turtle turned around and saw on the table a bowl of glutinous rice his mother had already filled for him, and not daring to disobey, he walked over and sat down without a word. Crabby Auntie watched him take several swallows of rice but never move his chopsticks near the food on the table. In the end, she could bear it no longer and took a piece of meat with her chopsticks and lifted it toward Black Turtle's bowl. At first Black Turtle resisted, but then reached out the bowl to receive it. From the corner of his eye he espied on the kitchen cabinet a half chunk of raw pork and that large bowl of pickled vegetables. He forced himself not to let the tears that welled up in his eyes flow down his cheeks, but in his mind's eye he replayed the earlier, intense argument between him and his mother.

"Take your money," Crabby Auntie had said.

"Ma, you wanna be poor? Why are you so heartless forbidding yourself and Pa to enjoy life?" Black Turtle pleaded.

"Your money is filthy. I wouldn't feel right using it," Crabby Auntie replied.

"Ma, I beg you, okay? Look at the world, is there any money that is not tainted?" Black Turtle entreated.

"I can't understand your nonsense," Crabby Auntie said.

"If you want our money to grow, there are only two ways: by conning or taking it by force, all other ways are just bullshit," Black Turtle said.

"Heavens! You know what you're saying?" Crabby Auntie pounded her ears against that which she did not want to hear.

"Ma! It's a dog-eat-dog world. If not this, how can poor people get a toe hold?"

"If this is getting a leg up, then I don't want it."

"Are you really content to rely on the charity of others to get by? Don't you want a little dignity, a decent life?" Black Turtle implored.

"Of course I do. But absolutely not by you relying on your tricks to bilk some cash. And another thing, you listen up. The Hong family gives us respect, love, it's not charity," Crabby Auntie said with finality.

And so it was: one table, three diners, each with their own thoughts, over a long, silent dinner.

12- BLASTING AWAY PESTILENCE FOR LANTERN FESTIVAL

All religions solicit donations to spread the word, but over half of it goes to serve man's greed.

Scene: The Xiahai Town Guardian Spirit Temple and Hong Wan Mei Trading Company

ON THE 15ᵀᴴ DAY OF THE FIRST MONTH OF THE LUNAR CALENDAR falls Yuanxiao, The Evening of the First Full Moon Festival, when, according to customs, the entire family will gather to eat glutinous rice ball broth and prepare decorated lanterns. At that time, if the rice balls, also named Yuanxiao in association with the festival, were not stuffed with a center, they would not be considered to be First Full Moon rice balls. The lady of the house, regardless of whether she was the mother-in-law or the wife, would normally start preparing these delicacies two days prior to the festival by pre-soaking the glutinous rice grains for an entire night in an aluminum pot filled with water so as to allow the grain to soak up the water and soften. The next day they would carry the pot to a place specializing in grinding services, which used machines to crush and grind the grain into a paste. Typically, these grinding service providers were small food processing factories making traditional steamed cakes, bean curd, or dried bean curd.

Most of the large merchant families on Dihua Street kept their own stone grinding mill for their family use. During New Year's festivities, the whole family, big and small, seven hands and eight feet, would push together on that grinding millstone to make rice paste. When grinding rice paste, the main job of the women was to match the rhythm of the turning millstone precisely, adding scuppers of water and soaked glutinous rice one by one into the receptacle of the mill while it was turning. The role of strenuous laborers assigned to pushing the millstone fell to the men and boys of the family. The paste that came out of the millstone's lip was gathered in a moistened cloth bag that would be three-quarters filled and then removed. The bag would be tied closed and laid down on top of a long board, with another bamboo carrying pole or wooden staff, placed atop it, then rope would be bound around the two and twisted tight. On the morning of the festival, after checking to make sure the excess water had been squeezed out, they would proceed to steam a chunk, knead it together with more raw dough, and fold and knead it repeatedly, carefully creating a dough of perfect chewiness. To increase the holiday spirit, some white dough balls would be colored a festive red by using an edible dye known as Rouge paste. Seeing an entire pot of red and white mixed together, plump and roiling, steaming hot glutinous rice balls on a cold winter's night, just added to their tasty deliciousness.

For youngsters, The Evening of the First Full Moon Festival is The Lantern Festival. Generally speaking, most boys who were a little older did not like the traditional lanterns sold by the corner shops; no matter if they were the hand-held halberd-shaped lanterns or the wheeled battleship lanterns one rolled on the ground, battle tank lanterns or annual zodiac animal lanterns, in their eyes, these were toys for "babies." In that era, nearly all middle- and high-school-age boys knew how to make their own lanterns and afterward would band together with friends to seek out those dark alleys, dead-end lanes, or abandoned buildings they dared not ordinarily go, to explore in the dark of night. Among the homemade lanterns, the most frequently seen were modified and constructed from empty KLIM milk powder cans. They were simple to make. First, one used a large nail to punch ten or so air holes into the bottom of the can, afterward driving a small nail through the bottom so as to anchor the candle and loop a wire through to act as a handle. Thus, one made that year's "bestest, brightest, most unblowoutable" lantern. Although such lanterns were in no way refined and had no shape to speak of, this did not decrease, one bit, their fascination for children. If one happened to live near a spinning or weaving mill, often one could pick up some discarded yarn spools. These round, conical wooden spools, tapered big at the head, small at the tail, were shaped like the Olympic Torch. One only had to wad up a rag, drip kerosene on it, stuff it into the end of the spool, and light it and you had the trendiest victory torch. Kids who carried this kind of victory torch, without calling for a show of hands, could take the lead as Captains of Team Explorers.

Besides this, Dihua Street had yet another rousing folk art activity called NongHanDan. Nong meant to "blast away." According to folk custom experts' explanations, HanDan means pestilence or represents the God of the Plague. To pray for favorable weather, a prosperous nation and a people at peace, everyone on the evening of the festival would NongHanDan, Expel the Pestilent Spirits. During traditional folk parades—besides viewing the local spirit statues being carried on palanquins, traditional drums and horns, strolling effigies of the Spirits of Rewarding the Good and Punishing the Bad, the Guardian Spirit Who Sees All and the Guardian Spirit Who Hears All, among others, the main event of the Lantern Festival was when the temple spirit mediums would take on the role of the God of Pestilence and allow the pious believers to use firecrackers to blast him, in the hopes that the God of Pestilence, so symbolized, would be driven away, never to harm the world. From memory, the *spiritista* who plays the role of the God of Pestilence would paint his face into a ferocious mask. According to Taoist religious rituals, after a spirit brush is used to write on the body of the *spiritista*, the "God of Pestilence" stands atop a flexible sedan chair made of bamboo, his chest and back bare, a cattail leaf fan waving in his hand, and anybody can throw all manner of firecrackers at him. Because of the spirit writing on his body, the protection of his spiritual gongfu, and the protection of the cattail fan, these talismans were the equivalent of Golden Bell Armor + Iron Shirt = Knives and Spears Cannot Penetrate.[5] Of course, the most important matter was to have access to some secret burn and blast treatments. According to what has been traditionally said, only newly picked banana leaves possess this miraculous curative effect on inflammation and blisters. (This is only a rumor heard by the author, and not tested, whatever you do, don't try it lightly.)

※ ※ ※

Before the Lantern Festival, pretty much the day after the shops had reopened following a New Year's celebration, everywhere along Dihua Street one could see groups from shrines, temples, and Lion Dance troupes, raising donations. Forming bands of three to five people on a mission, beating drums and gongs, they would circulate in and out of all the shops one by one soliciting donations for the parade expenses. The person demanding sponsorship would wear a yellow bandana on his head, inscribed with magical Taoist figures, while another led the way swinging an incense censor, and the one in the back followed closely, holding the statue of the spirit in his arms, all the way down the road proclaiming themselves the exclusive and legally appointed representatives of all manner of spirits, conjuring a road filled with extortioners, "You don't pay up, we're not leaving; what's that do for your business?" All day long, among this mix of people from shrines, temples, and Lion Dance troupes, their mouths like blood-red basins of betel nut juice, their bodies covered with tattoos of dragons, phoenixes, and demons, not a one of these gang members hadn't been in and out of reform school, like making casual repeated trips to a restaurant bathroom. In that time, temples and lion dance troupes were nearly equivalent to breeding grounds and havens for undesirable elements recruited by secret societies. About their using temple activities to unfairly extort money from shop owners, while everyone dared to be angry, no one dared speak out. One could only console oneself: "So, let's just pay respects to the Gods. Otherwise, who knows what? The police and officials will be of

---

5 Golden Bell and Iron Shirt are gongfu practices purported to imbue the master with invulnerability, the Knives and Spears Cannot Penetrate being a false exhortation believed by the Boxers of the Boxer Rebellion. It did not work for them.

no help." Because of this tolerant attitude of appeasement among the Ah-Q,[6] the hoods' appetites for making unlimited demands grew ever larger. From the intersection of Anxi Street and Liangzhou Street, extending all the way through the administrative district, down to Taipei Bridge, this was one of Taipei's two largest lion dens of gangsterism.

※ ※ ※

"Uncle Wu-fan. You're the headman of Dadaocheng, you should set an example and contribute a bit more," the fundraising rascal said.

"Yeah, yeah, yeah, I already gave more than usual," Uncle Wu-fan said.

Uncle Wu-fan handed over a red envelope he had prepared for the man facing him. The leader hefted the red envelope in his palm, appraising its thickness and weight and said dissatisfiedly, "Selling incense, prayer candles, and fireworks, all Hong Wan Mei profits flow from the wealth of the Gods. Uncle Wu-fan, when you take a sip of water, think of where it flowed from," the leader said on behalf of all spirits and Buddhas expressing their dissatisfaction and admonishment.

"Okay. So how about this, enough?" Uncle Wu-fan concealed his annoyance, reached into the drawer, and grasped a pile of cash and respectfully conveyed it to the other party.

"I'm too greedy. Remember to prepare extra firecrackers. On Lantern Festival Eve everyone can blast away to their heart's content." The leader and his party took up the so-called funds intended to pay respect to the Gods, beat on the drum, clanged the gong, and continued on with their procession to "Raise Charitable Contributions" to "Bring Glory to the Gods."

---

6 *The True Story of Ah-Q* is a famous novella by the Chinese author Lu Xun about a pitiful Walter Mitty-esque man who in his deluded imagination overcomes his enemies and shortcomings, while continuing to live a life of poverty and rejection.

Commemorative photo of Master Zhang Jun-feng, the Hong family and students in front of Hong Wan Mei Trading during the Lantern Festival, circa 1952.

13– A SECRET PLOT

You must first set your target and then choose your strategy to reach it; this avoids in the end having to clean up after your poor decisions.

Scene: Hong Wan Mei Trading Company

IN THE SECOND SECTION OF THE FACTORY AT HONG WAN MEI Trading Company, on a work bench arranged neatly according to firepower, were all manner of fireworks. Second brother Hong Yi-wen was earnestly explaining the function and specialty of each, so that the Hong brothers could make their battle plans.

Flung Firework—About the size of a peanut, they explode when thrown against the ground, when discharged from a slingshot, they are quite effective, well adapted to sniping, a weapon hard to defend against.

Pulled Fireworks—Diameter one-third centimeter, length four to five centimeters, at each end there is a red cord, take each cord and pull hard in opposite directions to produce an explosion, the explosive force is minimal, belongs to the category of "practical jokes for mischievous tikes." Normally deployed when plotting against an annoying guy by tying to his door, this kind of firework has been adapted for modern weddings and is called Party Poppers.

Dancing Fireworks—Scrubbed against a rough surface or concrete, or thrown against the ground, these fireworks will erratically jump about with loud reports, a plaything to amuse little children.

Rat Fireworks—Slightly larger than Pulled Fireworks, deployed by touching a lit incense stick to the fuse, they explode. Size is small, report is small, destructive force not great, for general people learning to use fireworks, classified as a gateway product, once they get the knack, they graduate to bigger products.

Great Dragon Fireworks—So-called because the body of the firework has a green dragon printed on it. Diameter of about two centimeter, height five centimeter, loud report, explosive force great, considered to be a grade-ten upgrade from Rat Fireworks. If one first places an empty can over the body of the firework and uses a lit incense stick to light the fuse sticking out under the can, the explosion is sufficient to blast the can up to a height of three to five stories. New Year's best seller.

Arc Flash Fireworks—The older brother of Great Dragon Fireworks, loud report, flash is bright, suitable for deployment at night.

Aquatic Ducks Fireworks—The shape and size of a pencil, short version is six centimeters, long version is ten centimeters, the end containing black powder can be directly struck on a match pad to ignite, upon striking will first emit a cloud of white smoke but not explode immediately; waterproof, it is suitable for land and sea battles. Because of its special delayed explosion, it can be deployed when rain or mud puddles are available.

Flower Tubes—Diameter of six to seven centimeters, height fifteen centimeters, when deployed they are stood on end and the fuse lit with a lit incense stick, will spray a magnificent display of sparks of all colors after which the body of the firework will explode. Very resounding report. It functions like a flare, similar to today's fireworks display boxes, and with its excellent sound and light, it was the firework of choice for Blasting Away Pestilence shows.

Heaven and Earth Fireworks—Diameter of six to eight centimeters, height of twenty centimeters, the fuse is located in the middle of the body, after lighting, the lower half will explode, shooting the upper half of the firework to a height of five to ten stories after which it explodes, modern firework display boxes are the equivalent of a mix of Flower Tubes and Heaven and Earth Fireworks.

Soaring Skyward Fireworks—The same as modern bottle rockets, except without the safety feature of the plastic cap, suitable for surface-to-air, surface-to-surface, air-to-surface, and air-to-air battles.

Chain Explosion Fireworks—Shaped like the magazine of a rifle, medium-sized firecrackers arranged horizontally, wrapped in a fixed cardboard shape. Two rows of firecrackers have their fuse mouths facing each other slightly offset, with ten to twenty firecrackers per row. The main fuse contacts the firecracker fuse down the center, once lit it will ignite the firecrackers in order, these are firecrackers commonly used today to welcome wedding couples, pay respects to the Gods, or in prayer ceremonies.

※ ※ ※

"If we want to fix these swindling rascals, then we have to grab this rare chance," second brother Yi-wen said.

"Right! Then let's use Soaring Skywards to blast them into oblivion," third brother Yi-mian interjected.

"Nix on that. Soaring Skywards scatter, it won't be good in the off chance the audience coming to see the excitement gets hurt," second brother Yi-wen judged.

"So just use the Great Dragons to blow them to smithereens," third brother Yi-mian said eagerly.

"Again, not gonna' work. The Great Dragon's head is too big, too easy to bat down with the cattail leaf fan. Bigger is not better if it doesn't make those cult con artists hurt," offered fifth brother Yi-kun.

"So, the problem isn't the choice of firecracker. It's making it so they can't bat them away," fourth brother Yi-xiang thought aloud.

"Right," Yi-wen, Yi-mian, and Yi-kun all said at the same time.

"In that case, let's use Rats," fourth brother Yi-xiang said.

"Idiot, Rats are so small, only for the dickless," third brother Yi-mian chided.

"Exactly, small is fearsome. We get some really sticky rice paste and smear it on the ends of the Rats, we chuck them so they stick on the spirit mediums' bodies, it doesn't matter how they try to swat them, they won't be able to swat them off," fourth brother Yi-xiang said.

"Won't it be even more ferocious if we use Great Dragons with the paste?" third brother Yi-mian said.

"No way. Great Dragons are too heavy, too obvious, and too destructive. In the end, we won't get the desired outcome," fourth brother Yi-xiang said.

"But the blast of Rats is too small, basically it will just massage them, like scratching an itch," fifth brother Yi-kun said.

"All you need to do is wrap the Rats in heavy kraft paper, bind 'em up tight, and the explosive force will be multiplied a couple of times," hidden off in the corner, the silent oldest brother Yi-qin could not restrain himself any longer and pointed out, though he remained alone and did not join the group. With eldest brother's quiet support of Yi-xiang's idea, the morale of the troops was rallied.

"Yeah! We disperse and lay in ambush in the audience and chuck them in from all directions."

"Stick 'em all over their bodies."

"Blast until they shit and piss themselves!"

"Blast until they cry 'Uncle'!"

The brothers seeking to teach the leader of these hoods a lesson, united in their efforts, scheming and strategizing, everyone more enthusiastic the more they talked it over, all way into the wee hours as midnight came and went, and they still did not feel tired.

14– ARTILLERY BARRAGE ON THE GOD OF PESTILENCE

No matter what the outcome of a war is, it inevitably conceals the seeds of the next war.

Scene: Dihua Street neighborhood

ON THE 15ᵀᴴ DAY OF THE FIRST MONTH OF THE LUNAR CALENDAR, the evening of the Lantern Festival, on Dihua Street in the Dadaocheng area, with Hong Wan Mei Trading Company at its center and extending for ten shophouses to the left and right, each shophouse had already hung between its columns facing the street a string of firecrackers to be used that evening to drive away the God of Pestilence. These strings of firecrackers were hung from the long bamboo poles used as scaffolding at construction sites and were double braided into long kebabs of firecrackers. The firecracker skewers all exceeded six meters in length, and to avoid getting dampened from contact with the ground the fuses were all arranged to point up. Hemp rope was used to tie them to the columns, awaiting the start of the spectacle when the fuse tail would be draped on the ground and lit.

In the days before television, besides opportunities to watch traditional opera and puppet shows during festivals, nothing could surpass as entertainment for the masses "watching the hot and raucous" New Year's local parades. Idlers who enjoyed getting in on the action would all scout out the scope of the "military preparation" two or three days in advance. Judging from the number of firecrackers on display, they could accurately discern that for this year's Blasting Away Pestilence, the Hong family would be the center of operations and the pinnacle of liveliness for the festivity. For these reasons, as soon as New Year's was over, people young and old living around Dadaocheng looked forward to watching Blasting Away Pestilence at Hong Wan Mei. Some wags, who enjoyed peddling news about others, would undertake intelligence runs to inquire about the state of "military readiness" at the Hong family site, more fodder for the trivia they shared around the tables at teahouses. And loose-lipped third son Yi-mian was always the "Deep Throat" they relied on to dig out the news!

That year there were two favored vantage points to view Blasting the Pestilence on Dihua Street. One spot, of course, was from the plaza in front of the Xiahai

Town God's Temple, but by religious customs, courtesy, and ceremonial form, that place was reserved for honored guests welcoming the spirits to the temple. Moreover, the Xiahai Town God's Temple on Dihua Street had the prior year started to take donations from Buddhist devotees, which went into the budget to procure "munitions."

The other main viewpoint then was, of course, Hong Wan Mei. Because the company's main business was incense, candles, and fireworks, a trade directly related to religious beliefs, they would always take the opportunity to invest money and effort on processions to welcome the spirits, thus returning to the spirits of the temple and their neighbors the consideration Hong Wan Mei had been shown during the year. So it was here one could see Taipei's largest scale, most frenetic, most intense, most satisfying, and most able to make-one-for-get-one's-troubles fireworks.

On the ensuing night, people rushing to see the spectacle would take their dinner early, or eat their fill of steamed rice cakes, flocking from all directions, as entire families, young and old, would carry their own bamboo stools or wooden benches and crowd into the site, relying on the previous year's experience, to scout out the best viewing location, after which they would take their leisure waiting for the show to begin. These spectators came from all over; there was no lack of them, all the way from SanChong, Yonghe, Guandu, Huwei, and other places, rushing over on the train. Before the arrival of the procession, old friends one infrequently ran into, old classmates, or distant relatives, everyone would use this rare opportunity to chitchat and chew the fat. One looks back fondly at that memory of a time when society was transitioning from an agricultural to an industrial base, and the simple, honest, and deeply connected manner of people then!

From when the BaoMaZi[7] Scout emerged, until the sound of the approaching processions, gongs and drums became audible, the mood of the audience was elevated in rhythm with the drums and gongs, surging and reaching a boil. The main event of the parade was always arranged to be toward the end, when the palanquin bearing the spirit was in front of the shop of the biggest contributor, so the space on the street in front of Hong Wan Mei was kept clear. The spirit mediums, under the spell of the Taoist priests directing them, first let loose some loud belches, after which their bodies began to tremble uncontrollably. The Taoist priests used branches of green leaves they carried to douse the bare chests of the spirit mediums with water they had blessed and traced magic signs on their bodies. The spirit mediums entered a religious trance; one by one

---

7 A BaoMaZi is a character in the Blasting the God of Pestilence procession. His accoutrements are very particular, sandal on one foot, the other barefoot, a traditional umbrella on the shaft of which hangs a pig's foot and a wine gourd, a farmers hat, a bruise plaster on the left shin, and thick rimmed glasses. He is a combination of rodeo clown and grand marshal.

they got onto the flexible bamboo pole sedan chair and the performance was ready to begin. Moving to a quicker tempo of the gongs and drums, the sedan chair bearers began to shake, tremble, and vibrate the chair to the rhythm, and the fireworks were to commence with a salvo of three small strands of firecrackers being ignited by the oldest son of the shop owner, Hong Yi-qin. Immediately after, several dozen "Flower Tubes" were ignited simultaneously, spraying golden flashes of sparks to a height of three stories; their fiery displays illuminated the open space like a light show at a concert.

In clouds of gunpowder smoke, the four Hong brothers and some laborers from the shop lay in ambush according to plan, spread out within the masses of spectators. On orders from fourth brother Yi-xiang, they started a continuous attack from all directions, constantly hurling the Rat Fireworks specially prepared with the sticky glutinous rice paste. The spirit mediums on the sedan chairs rocked and swayed to the rhythm of the chair and had already completely entered into a world with no self. Although they were able to swat away the "bullets" flying in from all directions with their cattail leaf fans, these specially fabricated Rats could not be dislodged once they stuck, until one by one the spirit mediums all looked like porcupines with fireworks hanging on them. According to the length of the fuse, these would explode, sometimes one detonating another. The spirit mediums, for whom the magic signs had not been written deeply enough, were the first to be awakened from their trances; those for whom the guardian spirit had already departed their bodies now writhed to the tempo of the explosions on their skin, energetically concealing the scalding and pain from the explosion of the fireworks plastered to their body. No one in the audience watching this spectacle could fathom why the spirit mediums this year were so intensely energetic in their performance, only that this year's Blasting Away Pestilence was exhilarating, truly a marvel to watch. And they all believed to the bottom of their hearts: "To have given the God of Pestilence such a drubbing, this year is certainly going to be prosperous and fine."

And so it was, the entire performance area was filled with resounding applause, the spirit mediums climbed or were carried down one by one. Ear rattling drums, gongs, and firecrackers continued incessantly, and from the boundless clouds of smoke emerged Zhang Jun-feng mingling with the spectators, happily participating in this event and the strange local flavor of this southern island's temple culture. But unlike the perspective of the average audience member, he clearly saw the ambush and crisis faced by the spirit mediums on the sedan chairs and even more clearly saw the several Hong brothers scurrying in and out among the audience like devils' shadows. He saw fourth brother Yi-xiang amidst the chaos, calmly directing the battle dispositions and shifting the application of force. Third brother Yi-mian, amid the crowd, made his opening moves with precision, courage, and vigor.

Driven by his curiosity, Zhang Jun-feng intentionally moved across the street, seeking to ascertain the ruse hidden in these fireworks. After inadvertently meeting the eyes several times of an old spectator sitting casually on a rattan chair, he was pretty sure the oldster knew the cheap trick the youngsters had played. What he did not know was that this gentle looking old man, besides having worn a grin during the entire procession and witnessed his own children secretly carrying out their revenge plot, was simultaneously plotting in his own mind his next steps, when he would need to face the counterattack of that group of temple rascals. "Ai! This Yi-qin didn't stop. Forget about it. Let them have their fun. As for the rest . . . cross that bridge when we get to it." Elder Wu-fan's mind was thus preoccupied, and he repeatedly muttered to himself.

The elder Hong Wu-fan in his favorite rattan chair enjoying tea with his son Hong Yi-xiang, 1982.

15– CRYING UNCLE

When an arrow precisely strikes the hunted, in the hunter's eyes there is only the prey, there is no self. Whereupon the hunter himself becomes the prey in the eyes of another.

Scene: Hong Wan Mei Trading Company

THE DAY AFTER THE LANTERN FESTIVAL, ELDER WU-FAN SAT AT the head of the dining table with a rare expression of severe earnestness.

"We won't do it again," four brothers cried at the same time.

"Ai, the money was trifling, but blasting people that way," elder Wu-fan said.

The four brothers in trouble for the calamity they had wrought all stood before their father and eldest brother with heads slung low, wringing their hands.

"Didn't they say the gods would protect them?" third son Yi-mian asked.

"Still have something to say!" eldest brother Yi-qin shouted at him to stop further talk.

"After dinner, you all go to the alter room and kneel on the hard floor while one incense stick burns down. Yi-qin, you're in charge of supervising," Wu-fan's wife enjoined to bring this farce to a close.

"Ma, eldest brother he also . . .," the straightforward Yi-mian blurted out, seeking to plead their case.

"Alright already! We eat and then kneel," Yi-xiang interjected, to block his further talk.

"Eat," the eldest Yi-qin said while staring daggers at Yi-mian and muttering out of the side of his mouth, "Pig headed."

The five brothers sat down respectfully to eat. Artless Yi-mian's appetite did not seem to have been affected at all; he took big gulps of meat and soup, like nothing had happened. His mother, father, and elder brother all looked over at him and barely managed to contain their mirth.

16– TOUGHENING UP

The bounty of delicacies on the dining table are not benevolently bestowed by nature. In the law of the wilds and jungles the weak are the prey of the strong; there is not a species that can presume to act mercifully and naively. To give the impression of weakness is only a pretense to preserve one's life when things have taken a turn for the worse; to retreat is to anesthetize the enemy's protective instincts. Without bearing these humiliations to add control, add pressure, there would be no way to lay low and renew enough energy to counterattack. Because you must first squat down before you can spring up!

Scene: Hong Wan Mei Trading Company

OUTSIDE THE SHOP, REVELERS STILL MINGLED IN GROUPS. IN FRONT of the countertop a mess of bent, broken, and faded candles covering the table had been dumped by A-Bula and several fierce looking hoods who charged at other customers and pounded the table. Fourth brother Yi-xiang diligently inspected and compared the size and specification of these defective products.

"These are not Hong Wan Mei candles," he said.

"You still want to blame someone else. Everybody knows that north of Taizhong, the Hong family supplies everyone," A-Bula said.

"This pile of crap, really, they are not from our stock," fourth son Yi-xiang said.

"The proof is laying in front of your eyes. If you don't want us to tear up your shop, you better 'fess up," A-Bula said.

"You dare!" fourth son Yi-xiang responded.

Elder Wu-fan interceded, "No problem. Sir, in your view, what is the best way to handle this?"

"Pa! Don't fall for this, our machines don't even produce this specification of candle," fourth brother Yi-xiang implored.

"It's okay, I'll handle it alright," Elder Wu-fan said. "Sir, you tell me how to handle this."

"Candles made so shamelessly, I don't want replacements. Give me a cash refund," A-Bula said.

"Okay. Settle in cash," Hong Wu-fan opened the strongbox and took out some cash, counted some out, and handed it to A-Bula.

"Are you fucking joking? So little. How are you compensating for the damage to my business reputation?" A-Bula pushed.

"Business reputation? Where is your shop? What business reputation loss are we going to pay you for?" fourth brother Yi-xiang said.

"Okay, okay, okay. Is this enough?" Hong Wu-fan added two stacks of paper cash, handing it over to A-Bula.

"This is about right. Little friend, if you want to do business, you need to take some more lessons from your old man. Let's go." Elder Wu-fan silently watched this group of greedy rascals swagger out with the money.

"Pa! We gotta think of something. If it keeps going on like this, the business you sweat to build will be destroyed," fourth brother Yi-xiang pleaded.

Elder Wu-fan did not answer, but in his heart an idea had already taken firm root.

"I think I really made a mistake. I should never have expected mercy from these lowlifes. If I keep putting up with it, matters will only get worse the further on it goes. Ai! Having lived to this age, only now do I understand that having money but no power is just like a beautiful paper spirit house to be burned as an offering—you can't live in it. To continue, I am going to have to toughen up my family."

17– BLOCKHEADED

Intelligence and analysis in the end transform into the capacity to change and improve; people today who are good at employing this capacity have skills that in the eyes of our forefathers would be seen as magic or clairvoyance.

Scene: The factory of Hong Wan Mei Trading Company

WITHIN THE FACTORY, SEVERAL DOZEN TOYO CANDLE MOLD machines arranged in rows on the left and the right lay idle. In the aisle between them were stacked some wooden crates on top of which was paraffin raw material; one pile was powdered hard paraffin and another pile was blocks of soft paraffin. The Hong family brothers were all intently listening to big brother Yi-qin's detailed explanation.

"Tell me the truth. Did you make it according to the proportions I set or not?" big brother Yi-qin asked.

"Sure. I definitely put the two types in," third brother Yi-mian said.

"What I asked you is, did you put it in according to the proportions?" eldest brother Yi-qin said.

"Yeah. But with the weather colder, the candles are cracking when we pull them from the mold," third brother Yi-mian said.

"Haven't I told you before, when it is under 15 degrees Celsius outside, it needs more soft paraffin?" big brother Yi-qin said.

"But when we add more soft paraffin, and the weather warms up, don't the candles deform and droop easily?" third brother Yi-mian asked defensively.

"That's why I want you to take the weather into account when we produce," big brother Yi-qin said.

"So troublesome. Isn't there an easier way? Why do we have to make it so complicated?" third brother Yi-mian asked.

"That's right. Elder brother, couldn't we find a formula that is suitable for winter and summer?" second brother Yi-wen asked.

"It's a conundrum. For the time being it is difficult to overcome this limitation of the technology. Maybe there are some additives, but which ones? It is a production secret. We will have to rely on our own continuous groping in the dark to discover some improvements," big brother Yi-qin said.

"So, I beg you, do us a solid favor. Come up quick with that new formula!" third brother Yi-mian said.

"Fuss and bother! I don't want to manage it. You find another person to take responsibility, okay?" third brother Yi-mian said.

"Such a simple task you consider a nuisance. Making candles is the same as becoming a man; when you need to be soft, be soft, when you need to be hard, be hard. The only way is to continually accommodate to circumstances in order to improve, I am begging here," big brother Yi-qin said.

"I beg you back! I beg you not to beg me, okay?" third brother Yi-mian remonstrated.

"Brother Four, from now on you are responsible for factory production," big brother Yi-qin said.

"Elder brother, I'll take responsibility for mixing the ratio and controlling the temperature. Third brother is better at production," fourth brother Yi-xiang said.

"You work it out between yourselves. Ai! How can you be so blockheaded?" big brother Yi-qin said. Yi-qin let out a long, long sigh, and strode out like a defeated rooster. This elder brother who carried the weight of heaven for his old man appeared, from behind, more stooped and ashen than his father. No one imagined that he would depart this family, this world, earlier than his papa.

18- NO. 11 FLOODGATE

A perfect defense does not simply avoid the attack but sets up one for victory.

Scene: Outside the Danshui River No. 11 Floodgate, the open-air pensioners tea stand by the river

WALKING THROUGH THIS GIANT SLUICE ARCHWAY THAT IS THE No. 11 Floodgate takes one to the spot that was the source of old Taipei's prosperity for centuries, the mother river, Danshui. It is said that in those days the Danshui River water was clear, not troubled by silting and mud. Small- and medium-sized boats and motorized junks could directly carry on trade all the way between the mouth of the river and Monga. Old folk familiar with Taipei history said that the entire city grew up layer after layer from the bank of the Danshui River; from Huanhe North and South Road to Dihua Street to Yanping North and South Road to Chongqing North and South Road to Chengde Road to Zhongshan North and South Road to Jilin Road to Songjiang Road . . . in parallel fashion pushing into the mainland and developing.

At a temple outside the dike, in an empty space facing a grove of banyan trees, Elder Wu-fan had not missed a day in decades to rise early, train boxing, and exercise by the riverbank. The Taizu Boxing and Shaking Crane Boxing he trained were the most common boxing forms in that era among Taiwanese. They were necessary defense skills studied by the ancestors who had crossed the sea to Taiwan in search of virgin lands. After Taiwan's retrocession from Japanese colonialism, most lion dance troupes, militias, and formal martial art training halls taught this type of traditional boxing.

"Uncle Wu-fan, this is Master Tu," Uncle Green Brocade said. "Master Tu is a distant relative of mine. He's from Fuzhou, but what he trains is Northern Boxing."

"Oh? Northern Boxing?" Elder Wu-fan asked.

"That's right. From when I lived and trained in Tianjin and Beijing with several Taijiquan masters," Master Tu said. "Taiji Boxing is a type of internal boxing style. It especially emphasizes softness to overcome hardness, cultivating health inside and repulsing enemies outside, not the same as the external boxing style Mr. Hong was just now training. Roughly, external styles of boxing train an obvious, overt strength, while internal styles train hidden and adaptive strength. External styles inculcate that the shortest distance between two points is a straight line, relying on speed and power to extract victory, and internal styles seek the arc of least resistance and maximum flow, taking advantage of angles and clever use of strength to decide the victor. One hard, one soft, you can say these are the two main columns in the construction of Chinese martial art," Master Tu said.

"Master Tu. Gracious, how rude of me, I really don't quite understand, but . . ." Elder Wu-fan looked back at Uncle Green Brocade and made a small nod of agreement.

"Master Tu, Uncle Wu-fan is seeking a private tutor of martial art. Of course this is for his family of five sons' self-defense, but there is still an ulterior motive," Uncle Green Brocade said.

"This I understand. Those trifling complications that crop up when one does business, just let me take care of them," Master Tu said.

"Truly, many thanks. But I really hope the kids can learn something with which to protect themselves. As for those problems in the field of business, if you only have the effect of frightening them, that's worth it," Elder Wu-fan said.

"I understand. Within those proper limits, I will make things difficult for them. Please rest assured," Master Tu said.

"Well, this is settled then. Let's go have some tea," Uncle Green Brocade said, inviting the two to imbibe.

And so it was that as the three sat at an open-air tea vendor, eating their sweetened millet porridge and baked buns, on a sandy space even closer to the river was faintly visible the agile silhouette of the hunchbacked craftsman from the Jiang Cheng Long casket shop, training alone in his Tan Tui and Cha Boxing. If one were to inspect closer the sandy spot on which he launched his fists and planted his feet, to one's surprise there would be not one footprint, showing the consummate martial attainment of this lonely, taciturn Northeasterner.

19- ANOTHER HEAVEN

Every instance of conflict is a proclamation, a resolute warning to the opponent that they have clearly crossed a line.

Scene: Another Heaven Fuzhou-Style Restaurant

THE LOFT OF THE FUZHOU STYLE RESTAURANT, ANOTHER HEAVEN, on Minle Street, was permeated with the fragrance wafting up from the kitchen, an aroma of tasty dishes and cooking smoke. In order of their age, the male members of the Hong family sat at the large round table occupying the private room. The dining ambience at this Fuzhou restaurant, situated within a group of unauthorized buildings at the Sanyi Wet Market, was really lacking, but in that era when people were not fussy about decorations or ostentation, if the chef was able to put together some locally flavorful dishes, then the business would catch fire. Interestingly, if one wanted to eat in this crude loft, nevertheless there were certain "rules." It didn't matter if you were a tycoon or an important government official, you had to bow down to enter, because this loft was squeezed out of a small space stuck up near the roof; the ceiling was low and slanted, so if you did not bow, you could not get in. Due to this special dining environment, some Mandarin scholars had penned a commemorative sign with the nickname "Pavilion of Bowed Heads." With this clever endorsement from the "literati" and word of mouth from their diners, their Fuzhou dishes became known far and wide, so if one wanted to book this private loft room, one had to make reservations two to three weeks in advance.

Besides Elder Wu-fan, there were two empty seats of honor set aside at the big round table next to the low window. As was customary on the table, an assortment of salt fried melon seeds and red earth peanuts was displayed, but no one dared make a move to serve themselves. Elder Wu-fan struck an uncharacteristically firm tone: "If you quarrel in anger, it is a momentary conflict; if you fight over ideals, it is a conflict for a lifetime. I am not only thinking of making minor changes. I am thinking about an entire turnaround. But it all depends on luck and opportunity. Just like when you are fishing, you cast your lure out, then you can only wait patiently. On the surface, it appears as if the fisherman is doing nothing, and this is the hardest part, the hardest part is patiently holding your tongue.

"From our foothold on Dihua Street, every day we must be accountable for fluctuations in market competition and our cost of raw materials. To remain unchanged is actually harder. Really, if we change or not it is the same; both have attendant risks and costs to be calculated. Compared to the treachery of the marketplace, those guys aren't too bad. If we can use money to smooth things out, it is no big deal.

"I just caught a whiff of a scent that something big is going to happen," he said, tapping the side of his nose with his finger. "An intuition that we have to act first. I have always believed in this kind of premonition. Therefore, we need to strengthen our capacity to meet an emergency. Thus we can increase our chance of survival during great change. But before we make a move to transform, we first must think clearly about what basically needs to be changed. Do we have the ability? Is it cost effective? Because as soon as we start to move, it's like a sword being drawn from its sheath, an arrow being released. Very difficult to return to the starting point.

"It is reckless to disregard the consequences of change, it only invites disaster. Moreover, we have to be like a lobster shedding its shell—before the transformation is complete, it absolutely has to stay hidden. My great uncle said, 'Make your opponent believe you have no plan or capacity to strike back. Only then do you have a chance of success.' If all of this cannot be accomplished, well, then to stay put is better than to move." Elder Wu-fan calmly described how he had survived in isolated and adverse circumstances after being orphaned, his first-hand experience of how in a dog-eat-dog competitive workplace he had grown from a small to a big player. Because he did not have much book learning, almost all his words were tinged with his daily blood and sweat and evening tears, one drop at a time.

"Did you get all that?" eldest brother Yi-qin asked.

"Huh." The other four brothers were not certain why their old man had suddenly raised this topic, but still nodded their heads in unison.

"Pa, so what are we gonna do?" second brother Yi-wen asked.

"Going into hiding like the lobster?" third brother Yi-mian wondered.

"Transformation, of course it starts with you. If you don't change, how can you hope the world will change?" eldest brother Yi-qin asked.

"Brother, only relying on ourselves, how can we transform? Besides doing trading, we basically don't know anything. We are powerless to even deal with those rascals, aren't we?" fourth brother Yi-xiang said.

"That's right. So, we need to strengthen our capacity to win. Without a capacity to win, we have no power to demand peace."

As if on cue at the key moment, Master Tu and Uncle Green Brocade pushed open the door and appeared. "This is Master Tu. Uncle Wu-fan has spent a tidy sum to especially secure instruction for you lads in martial arts from the master!" Uncle Green Brocade announced.

The five brothers were all thoroughly roused by *this* decision to transform. What sort of transformation would this extraordinary act bring? No one knew.

But the Elder Hong's heart held tight to his belief: the challenges one faces in life are all the same, and no matter how thoroughly one plans or completes one's preparations, risk will not be completely eliminated. The only wise way when hazards arise is to bravely approach them head on, honestly face them, and quickly make amends. After all, to the Hong Family, maintaining their position at Dihua Street was the key battle they faced at the moment.

"Pa! Can they bring on the food now?" third brother Yi-mian asked.

"Good. Serve the dishes. Let's eat and chat," elder Wu-fan said.

Thereupon, Another Heaven Fuzhou Restaurant's most expertly prepared specialties were brought to table: Crispy Fried Marinated Eel, Seasonal Fish Head in Claypot, Curled Slices of Steamed Sea Bass, a Soup of Fish Dumplings and Shark Meat Balls, Fried Saltwater Snails, Fried Razor Clams, Crispy Sweet and Sour Pork Kidneys with Jellyfish, one after another were served to the table.

20- JIANGSHAN WINEHOUSE

You don't know who you are, so you require a false identity to blend into the scenery. And everything you now own props up your false identity...

> *A sheep, even if it is hiding under a tiger's pelt, will be delighted when it sees a lush, beautiful grassland and will quake when it sees a vicious wolf because the tiger's pelt only changes the outside appearance but cannot change the sheep's own innate character.*
>
> *— Cao Zhi, a noted poet and calligrapher of the Three States Period*

Scene: 181 Guisui Street Jiangshan Winehouse

SITUATED AT 181 GUISUI STREET, DURING THE JAPANESE occupation, the Jiangshan Winehouse was Taipei's most famous venue of sensual pleasure. "To ascend the Jiangshan Tower, indulge in Taiwan delicacies, listen to artistes sing" were the era's most fashionable, most luxurious socializing activities. Nearby were The Mayflower, The Black Dahlia, The Penglai Pavilion, The First Dance Hall, The Celestial Music Dance Hall, The Singapore Dance Hall ... all of which were most beloved by businessmen entertaining government officials, so of course these venues benefited from being hives of scheming snakes and dragons.

In that era, Guisui Street, between Ningxia Road and Yanping North Road, was like today's Huaxi Street next to Wanhua's Longshan Temple, a closely packed assortment of night market vendors. Hawkers and their merchandise commonly seen in the night markets included fresh venomous snake soup, martial arts bruise liniment, mynah bird oracles, tortoise shell fortune readers, ring-toss games, head-lice removers, roundworm expulsion medicine vendors, second-hand and stolen items, fake watches, fake antiques, counterfeit works of art, forbidden books and magazines, pornographic novels, pachinko, pinball games to win sausages, meat rolls, Chinese herbal sishen soup, fried rice vermicelli, shrimp potage, duck potage, mochi, agar jelly, oily cake with meatballs, leaf wrapped steamed glutinous rice dumplings, fried intestines, and pig blood cake, all packed into this section of street not five hundred meters long, like a daily temple festival where anything your heart desired could be found. Hidden in darkened alleys perpendicular to this Guisui Street night market, mingled among some squat residences, were several dozen unlicensed brothels. To avoid guests seeking pleasure from entering the ordinary residences by mistake and causing a ruckus, the brothels all used red or green cellophane to cover their windows, allowing colored light to glow outside, on the one hand to differentiate them, on the other hand to arouse the visitors with their hazy light and the suggestion of pleasures awaiting.

In the main hall on the second floor of the Jiangshan Winehouse, one table of seven young drifters from behind the railway station sat around Black Turtle, drinking and shooting the shit.

In a drunken soliloquy, Black Turtle said, "Shit. Where is the fairness in this world?"

"The rich use money and roll the money over. The more they roll it over, the more it snowballs."

"The poor work to death and can't even grab pennies."

"My old man played by the rules his whole life as a lackey at Hong Wan Mei, laboring away, dozens of years, what did he get? Worked until he had tuberculosis and couldn't even turn himself over in bed."

"The Ruler of Heaven doesn't love the naive, He dotes on the wealthy."

"The wealthy pray to Him, they kill their pigs and sacrifice their lambs; the poor pray to Heaven with two empty hands save three sticks of incense. If you were God, who would you choose to bless?"

"Why bother praying? Where do you think so many poor people came from?"

"I detest the wealthy, but I look down on the poor even more."

"Because if you're poor, you're stupid. Wishfully relying on Heaven, the more they depend on prayer, the poorer they get."

"Poverty. It's basically a disease passed on from generation to generation. The poorer you get, the stupider you become, the stupider you become, the poorer you get, passed on down and down, there is no end."

"To turn this around, one must completely overturn the social order and how benefits are distributed."

"If we complacently go along with the current situation and rules of the game, poor people need not even think about ever getting turned around."

"Create chaos, then redistribute. That's the day poor people can raise their heads up."

"This is an 'everyman for himself' world. The rich just see you as a piece of meat on their chopping board, meant to be an accompaniment to their dishes."

"You want to know the truth? All their righteousness and morality is just a load of fucking bullshit."

"All the myths exhorting goodness, the sutras read in the temples, they are all just spells to hypnotize you, just made-up crap! You believe you can lie in the ice water and catch a carp?[8] Do you believe in samsara and karma?"

"You know who you were in a former life? Would you recognize him?"

"Shit, of course you wouldn't recognize that bastard; much less, how come you are taking on the inexplicable burden of his sins?"

"It's all just a fabrication, a con. Only fools believe it."

"Only the *Romance of the Three Kingdoms* is real. The generals, Cao Cao, Liu Bei, taking advantage of turmoil to overturn heaven, they didn't rely on words of goodwill and morality, they relied on *not* talking about their thick skin and black hearts."

"I want to be just like Cao Cao, whiter than white and blacker than black. You know?"

"It doesn't matter if I am a hero or a scoundrel. To me, having enough money to live comfortably, that's what matters."

"You don't have to listen to me, go ahead keep believing what you believe. But don't expect to drink good wine and eat good meat."

"To sum it up, if you got no money, no power, no learning, then you'll always be poor."

"Businesspeople buy low and sell high, what a con. They are making profits from deceit. Not a one of them is a good person."

"We rot away an entire life. Wanna turn yourself around? There is no such path. Wanna beg, become a hobo? Don't wanna be a hobo, become a gangster. Anyone in between is just an idiot waiting for death to come around."

"If you are not willing to gamble with your life, don't expect to live on easy street."

"What we are getting out of those merchants on Dihua Street is just chump change."

"With more people come opportunities; I want to play big time."

"The real big money is all hidden away in the dance halls and winehouses."

"If you want to live high on the hog, you gotta rely on your smarts, not your fists."

"Courage in numbers."

"With enough people, even the devil will fear you. You know what I mean?"

"With more people, then we talk about organization, we talk about a brotherhood."

"If you don't talk about brotherhood, only how awesome you are, then you are not going to win for long. Sooner or later, you will be sold out and betrayed. You know what I mean?"

"Boss. You've had a lot to drink. We're with you, not to eat and drink. We've bought into your speech about brotherhood, right guys?" one of the more

---

8 From *The 24 Tales of Filial Piety*, in which a son lies in the ice water to catch a carp to feed his mother in winter.

senior gang members said to Black Turtle, after he had vehemently presented his views, rousing their righteous indignation. "Damn Right!" the load of eating, drinking, brown-nosers responded, hoisting their glasses and toasting themselves.

"Fuck your mother, doesn't matter if you're telling the truth, lying, or if it is just flatulence, I hear this and I just feel swell. Bottoms up. Down the hatch!"

After an orgy of toasting with millet wine, Black Turtle vigorously vented his discontent with society and expounded his philosophy of the underworld. Once upon a time he had been a good all-around student, highly regarded by his teachers, but because of his family's impoverished circumstance he was forced to drop out and enter into the dark orbit of gangsters. Although relegated by society to a dim and gloomy corner, still remaining and surviving in his heart was a flicker of lofty aspiration that had been stomped on but had risen time and again. Sadly, surrounding him were helpers whose civility and class were much lower than his, to a man a bunch of mooching, incapable wine sacks and rice bags. Neither able to communicate their misery and bitterness nor escape from it, they choked it down their throats by drinking strong Zhuyeqing and Wujiapi spirits. Black Turtle straightened his neck up to let the liquor flow straight to his gut. Only when the alcohol was enough, then his mind became hazy, dead, forgetful. If only to forget, then all would be well. If only for a moment, that was enough.

In the middle of the avenue fronting the winehouse, five or six trishaws in a procession arrived from which alighted a continuous flow of a dozen crewcut local mobsters, all dressed in floral shirts. The discerning bystander would immediately know that they were all big dragon bosses. A bunch from Niubuzi, under the orders of the Bandit Leader, had been waiting across the street and were led over to join the group.

"You see that sausage seller? Don't let him squeal on us." As soon as he crossed the street the Bandit Leader ordered his people to control the lookout posted outside the winehouse.

"They are all inside. Should have drunk enough by now." An ugly, shifty-looking snitch immediately ran over and whispered to the Bandit Leader his intelligence report.

"In a moment, what do you want us to do? We'll take your lead," the leader of the Sikanzi gang said.

"Okay. There's not many people inside. We won't have to use the furniture, just pile it up outside first, grab it when we need it," the Bandit Leader said.

"Before we make a move, let me make this clear. After we grab this turf, future profits won't be carved up unevenly, three parties get equal shares."

"Alright. We have your word," the leader of the Sikanzi gang said.

"Let's not add to our troubles. Today we just rough up people, not trash the place. Just avoid the area where the government people sit, we don't want their hassle," the Bandit Leader said.

"Understood." Everyone as directed was prepared to beat people up and carried watermelon knives, katana, hunting knives, iron rings, baseball bats, and sickles . . . all manner of weapons employed in gang fights of that era were fished out and displayed next to the reception counter at the entrance, as according to length they were arranged, leaning against the wall.

"You bunch take care of the main entrance," the Bandit Leader said. "You lot circle back in the alley to the back door, don't let that son of a bitch slip out."

"Check," several responded with a shout and ran off.

"The rest of you, come with me. Let's go!" the Bandit Leader said.

On entering, there was a scout already sent in preparation for the ambush who signaled with his eyes to the Bandit Leader the location of Black Turtle. As soon as the Bandit Leader confirmed the direction, he waved his hand, ordering the gang to surround and outflank. "Which one of you is Black Turtle?" the Bandit Leader asked.

"Me for sure. What the fuck?" Black Turtle said.

"Yeah, it's you. I'm the Niubu Bandit Leader, today it's just between me and him. The rest of you beat it if you want to live," the Bandit Leader said.

Hadn't they just finished talking about the underworld and the code of brotherhood? Except, the only message at that moment lodged in the brothers' noggins was "Courage in numbers," those scant words. As soon as they saw so many opponents, these "dining companions" lost all heart. They took one glance at each other, and all scurried off like the frightened son of a bitch rats they were, leaving behind only two plastered loyalists, one on the left and one on the right, unsteadily standing their ground beside Black Turtle. No one was sure whether these two wise guys with their blurry eyes and mental confusion were true stalwarts or not. Or were they just too drunk and their legs too wobbly to run?

Black Turtle said, "Fuck, you got balls, so you and me go at it, but you brought so many people, what kind of hero is that!" Before he could finish speaking, the Bandit Leader signaled with his hand, and the men surrounded them. Although Black Turtle was nimble, swift, and fierce, even a ferocious tiger cannot take on a horde of monkeys. Before long he was overpowered, brought to the ground, and beaten black and blue.

"Fuck your mother! What age are you living in? Who would take you on mano a mano? Pig-headed fool monopolizing the whole rear of the train station."

"You, you, and you, and all of you in the winehouse, listen up. Starting from today, the rear of the train station, around the traffic circus, Dihua Street, Yanping North Road, base of the big bridge, from Sikanzi to Niupu—all shops, winehouses, tea houses, brothels, night markets, and wet market kickbacks go to me. And you soft-shelled turtles, never let me lay eyes on you again. If I run into you, I'll kneecap you then and there. Beat it!" The Bandit Leader proclaimed his leadership and sovereignty at the top of his lungs to the winehouse staff and all the dining patrons.

※ ※ ※

From start to finish, the door of the winehouse's most secluded, largest private room was open. From there, Jin Yuan Long Shop's Boss Jin sat fussing with his pipe, one cold eye on the curtain being lowered on this dramatic production he had personally directed.

"Done the way you wanted. Right Boss Jin?" the Bandit Leader asked.

"As long as the turf was grabbed, I don't particularly care what tricks were used. These guys are like a flock of birds, pick off the leaders and they disperse. What I really care about is not this," Boss Jin responded vaguely.

"These pig heads occupied the fattest loading platforms for the longest time and were only able to use them to generate chump change. To not snatch these treasures from them would be a true waste of this gold mine," the Bandit Leader said.

"Besides taking a cut on deliveries, I want to profit from everything moving in or out of the Dihua Street wholesalers. I want to create an opening between the manufacturers and wholesalers, a valve, pinching-off between the two ends of supply and demand, then I can employ this water valve to control the flow and the price. Like soybeans, flour, and cooking oil, these staple goods with a huge daily flow into the market, just add a decimal place to the price and it's like printing money. *This* is what I am really after," Boss Jin said.

"So, what do you want me to do with the rest of his crew?" the Bandit Leader asked.

"Clever people aren't reliable. Except Black Turtle, the other hoods if you need 'em, keep 'em, anyway, they don't have anybody they can run to," Boss Jin said.

"Okay, these trifles I'll manage," the Bandit Leader said.

"I am connected into the train station management and local police station. I'll spread a little grease to take care of them. Tonight, everyone's worked hard. Let's drink. Bring on the food!" Boss Jin shouted the order, and the most popular dishes of the time were delivered: squid and snail fried with garlic, sliced abalone, sautéed mullet gizzards, mullet roe soaked in spirits and baked in salt . . . course by course delivered to the table.

The quick-witted maître d' saw that the mood in the room had warmed up and immediately flourished his hand, striking up a band with an accordion, guitar, and drums, and the sounds of music and rejoicing filled the hall. In single file a gaggle of young women purported to be the most beautiful and high class in Taipei, wearing tight tailored silk qipao, gracefully swayed and beguilingly sashayed in to crowd this private room where gold was shoveled like dirt.

The hoods who had participated in this turf battle, regardless of whether they had raised a fist or exerted themselves, all had contributed to the asymmetrical victory and great days to come, and so, unruffled by sentiment, they went on a drinking binge. With his arms wrapped around women to his left and right, Boss Jin downed a whiskey proffered by one of the beauties, and with the liquor doing 30 percent of the talking and his lofty ambitions the remaining 70 percent, he said, "Next step, go after Hong Wan Mei!"

21– SANYI MARKET

To prove the existence of God is difficult, but to prove the nonexistence of God is even more difficult. Therefore, it doesn't matter what the situation is, they're all the same. In the end, it's between you and God; the rest are just innocent implicated third parties.

Scene: Sanyi Market

SANYI MARKET WAS FRAMED BETWEEN ANXI STREET, MINLE Street, and Guisui Street on a plot of land set aside for a park. Before it was turned into the Dadaocheng Park and underground parking facility, this approximately 1,300 tsubo piece of land had been the site, since early in the Japanese colonial era, of hundreds of irregular, illegal buildings closely packed like the scales of a fish. These ramshackle dwellings were all roofed with those black, undulating, Japanese-style tiles. On this small plot of land crowded several hundred families from all over China, each of the provinces, and from varying cultural backgrounds, among which people from Fuzhou were the most represented. Over half the dwellings fronting the street were rented out as shophouses, none deviating from offering the daily essentials of life, such as barbers, tailors, comestibles, food stalls, hardware, housewares, stationers, and bike and clock repairs. If you needed it, they had it, a microcosm of all the vendors between Dihua Street, Yangping North Road, and down to the train station.

On Minle Street, there was a family-owned factory, the largest manufacturer of combs made of buffalo horns in Taipei. The owner was from Fuzhou and was a famed craftsman of fine, exquisite combs. Usually heaped outside of the factory was a large quantity of imported water-buffalo horns. When walking past, one would frequently see the Fuzhou craftsman at work making combs from the horns. Top-grade combs were then inlaid with mother of pearl decorations by hand, stylized lucky decorative symbols like flowers and birds.

It did not matter if the comb were made of the more expensive white or cheaper black horn, they had the same properties of durability, they did not cause static electricity when combing hair, and they helped preserve one's hair and scalp. A good, horn-made comb would last for several decades, compared to a common wooden or plastic comb, since they would resist wear and tear many times over. However, this traditional craftsmanship died with the demolition of the Sanyi Vegetable Market and decline of the old ways of hand crafting, and I fear it is a skill now lost. In those days, with no high-capacity automated production, most daily use products and tools relied on hand craftsmanship to produce. For this reason, hand crafting skills and secret techniques passed down within the family were all on view in the places where the common people gathered. The common man only needed one special skill to ensure a livelihood for taking care of his family, keeping them clothed, and growing their future. This is unlike today, when these opportunities to make a livelihood have nearly all been seized by large corporations and financial holding companies, leaving an ever-shrinking space for a commoner to scrape by barely making a living. People can nowadays only squeeze into the narrow crevice between what automation and computers can't do, and what they don't want to do, pursuing an ignoble existence gathering the crumbs and dregs.

Besides being a place where one cherishes the memory of past customs and the environs of myriad crafts, hidden within Sanyi Market's illegal construction there was yet Dadaocheng's largest Four-Color Card[9] gambling den and the Speed drug supply center. Speed is a variety of cheap narcotic belonging to the amphetamine family, highly addictive and greatly injurious to health. Here the junkies selling drugs were themselves amputees because they had abused the injection of these poisons. Whether ingested, inhaled, or injected, when they had exhausted their family's assets to satisfy their habits, in the end they would all become drug pushers, becoming the ghosts of victims devoured by a tiger who then helped the tiger find new victims.

To the uninitiated visitor, how could they not see that this unprepossessing dilapidated acre was such a snake pit of lawless, rapacious exploitation, such that people zipped their lips about this forbidden zone? During weekday sunlit hours, the people entering and leaving this district were nothing but those customers coming to make purchases or assistants of distributors delivering goods and coolies contracted for transport. After night fall, on this same stage, the curtain would rise on a completely different show, with the actors all made up and ready to enter the drama, each bearing the weight of their own addictions, as they would be playing one of the five traditional roles of Chinese opera,[10] and in the dark world of the gambling or drug dens would liberate the lusts of their own hearts.

Huddled within a low-roofed dwelling down a gloomy and dank alley, across its door a dark green army blanket providing cover preventing the yellow glow of a bare tungsten light bulb inside from seeping out, enveloped within the haze

---

9 Four Color Cards belongs to the rummy family of card games, with a relatively long history in China. The cards, 112 in number, are based on the pieces in Chinese Chess and with four color families.

10 The five key roles in Chinese opera are Sheng—male lead; Dan—female lead; Jing—male character with a brightly painted face; Mo—an elderly man; Chou—a clown or jester like character.

of smoke from all brands of cigarettes, each breath of the human occupants emitted all manner of smells and noises. Under the glow of the light around the gambling table clustered the pig butcher, the master of dried sea cucumber and fish skin, the mid-wife, the boss of the cloth store, the tea shopkeeper, the wife of the local surgeon, the Chinese herbalist, the patrolman from the police station, the matron from the temple who exorcises fears, the school inspector from the municipal government Ministry of Education, and the dancing girls who had just left the Celestial Dance Hall. One by one, under the cover and beckoning of nightfall, they stripped off their daytime disguises and exposed their naked original natures.

The gamblers here were neither differentiated by profession nor identity, rich, poor, high, low, if one had chips in hand to stake, everyone was of equal class and equal rights. In this murky world, few people cared about anything but winning or losing. Here at the Four-Color Card table, everyone used a different kind of ethical yardstick to satisfy their most primordial longing: to answer the question, "How deep is God's love for me?"

For thousands of years, "gambling" has suffered the reproach and censure of the upright; however, it is the same as a virus embedded in our genes, coexisting with humans, never eradicated. It originated when humans faced unclear prospects, a lack of information, moments when it was hard to differentiate between disaster or fortune, a skill used to decide special requirements when experience or the facts at hand were limited. In the laboratory, this type of integrated decision-making skill can impel the elevation of civilization, but in the gambling den it is a huge force dragging down human nature. Every day, in mundane and work-related fields, this strategic need to discern the unknown appears in all manner of distinct manifestations, compelling us to make a clear choice between zero and one. It does not matter how much—"there is no option but," or "as a matter of course"—the appraisal process considers. In reality, it always comes down to winning or losing determining whether the decision was right or wrong.

Here, the rule around which the world turns is not the karmic doctrine of "you are right, so you can win" but a results-only doctrine: "you won, so you are right."

This completely subverts the values perspective by which the common man abides and is familiar. Of course, some people care about one's original intent, some people care about process, others care about results. There are even people who use the principle of proportion to measure truth and error, right and wrong. This is like the saying, "Where a benevolent person sees benevolence, a wise person sees wisdom"—different people have different views. Looking narrowly at this skill of prediction or discerning the unknown, it is hard to employ standards of common sense, morality, law, or religion to clarify its position and value. However, if this innate human power of discernment is turned at the gambling table into a tool for victory and defeat, or a profession, and from that arises all manner of greed, wicked dealings, and vicious behaviors, then this transformation and abuse becomes an unpardonable evil not to be tolerated.

Crabby Auntie's home was deep up this viper's nest of an alley. She was using pressure point therapy to apply herbal liniment to the bruises and contusions all over Black Turtle's body.

"Ai! Serves you right. Be like a normal person, go out and get a normal job to do," Crabby Auntie said.

A speechless Black Turtle suffered in silence.

"Just the other day, I brought it up with Auntie Wu-fan. Asked her to help you secure a job in the candle factory."

"Ma, you and Pa have worked like oxen there for over ten years, hasn't enough time been wasted? I don't think like a regular guy, one who's willing to slave away in someone else's house," Black Turtle said.

"You don't want to be someone else's slave. Great. You grew a backbone. But like this? Who doesn't want to be top dog? You're an adult now, you have to accept your fate, your station," Crabby Auntie said.

"All you and Pa do is accept your station. For our whole lives we've been enduring these bitter days. You're used to poverty. Paralyzed. I dread poverty. I am still young, I can no longer endure these days of not even being able to look up to myself," Black Turtle said.

"Who doesn't want to turn their lives around and enjoy their days? But for what, if it is not relying on an honest job?" Crabby Auntie asked.

"Ma. Didn't you work just like that your whole life? But what did it get you? What's changed? You talk about conscientiousness. In my schooling, was I not conscientious enough, not outstanding enough? But what use was being conscientious? In the end, in the end . . ." Black Turtle did not have the heart to finish the sentence.

"Don't say another word. It's like we owe you—owe you our lives, right?" Crabby Auntie said.

"Ma, I am not blaming you and Pa, this is between me and God. I just want to let you understand that, in so many matters, just recognizing your station and working hard is useless," Black Turtle said.

"Well, you also can't squabble with God—walked your own evil road, you did. What if something bad happened to you, how would we two oldsters manage?" Crabby Auntie said.

"Ma, didn't the puppet show we saw at the Little West Garden say, 'The horse without guts won't get fat off the grass. The person not harsh and unreasonable, won't get wealthy'? Believe me. Awaiting the final result according to one's station and a resignation to fate is only a road to death. Down to their marrow, those wealthy big bosses will chew you up and swallow you whole. Which one is not a monster? The bright path and the dark path are the same.

It's all about the money," Black Turtle said.

"Don't talk nonsense about black and white," Crabby Auntie said.

"No. I am absolutely not talking nonsense. This is the way the world is—daytime is for people, nighttime is for demons. Since there are no seats at the white table for poor people, they are at the black table. If it were not that the stupid eyes of God were not shining on us, who would willingly become a gangster? Since He gives me nary a glance, I go that direction. You just have to have a big enough following, and naturally good days will come," Black Turtle said.

"Ai, being a gangster, you will be a laughingstock," Crabby Auntie said.

"Ma. Having no money makes me a laughingstock. If you are a gangster with a big enough following, they fear you like they fear the devil himself. Who would dare look down on me?" Black Turtle said.

"Ai! You're talking the twisted reasoning of someone who has lost their will. From a tike, Uncle Wu-fan had no mother or father, his situation was even worse than ours. But he did nothing but walk a straight path, relying on his effort and exertion, and only that way built today's business," Crabby Auntie said.

"I don't believe the bullshit those rich folk say *after* they are successful. We are living in a squatter's shack in Sanyi Market. We hide amidst dark demons; to stick our necks out, I must become a gangster. A gangster with a big following," Black Turtle said.

"Ai! You are only afraid you haven't stuck your neck out yet, but that's when your head gets whacked off," Crabby Auntie said.

"Ow!"

Crabby Auntie used extra force on the pressure point therapy of a head bruise, making him cry out a yelp of pain.

22– HANGZHOU TEAROOM

Teahouses aren't wonderful, refined, airy-fairy places to sip renowned brews; teahouses are beehives of converging rumors and the site for trading of intelligence. Any people who look like they are having a casual conversation have all come with an object in mind, and just like bees gathering honey, they also distribute pollen.

Scene: The Hangzhou Tearoom on the banks of the Danshui River

ON AN EMPTY SPOT ADJACENT TO THE DANSHUI RIVER, A WOODEN ship, its enormous bulk sitting on the banks of the river at an angle, lay abandoned in a pile of gravel and weeds. The equipment, fittings, and rigging, including the masts, wheelhouse, and wheel, had long disappeared. The parasites, like barnacles and mussels, that normally would adhere to the bottom of the hull, had been scraped off by naughty children. All that remained was an empty bloated hull that refused to disintegrate, propping itself up on dry land. On the bow of the vessel, in paint that had long ago peeled and faded, could be made out the vessel's name, *Success*. Although it had barely survived riding the wind and cleaving the waves of the black seas with some remaining dignity, it did not want to allow the trials it had endured to be forgotten and swamped by the mighty torrent of time. However, why was there never any person who cared to inquire where this mighty vessel had come from? Why? When? Discarded by whom in this most unseemly location? Nor did anyone know when, nor who had had the creative inspiration to surprise and delight by opening a place of unique charm on this slanted, beached vessel a pensioner's tea house called the Hangzhou Tearoom.

Before dusk, this was purely a tea consumption spot, with genuine goods and realistic pricing. It didn't matter if one was drinking aged Tieguanyin, Dongding Oolong, or had brought one's own tea leaves, there was a uniform price of about NT$5 per pot with unlimited refills of hot water. If one's tea became bland and tasteless, the proprietress would proactively refresh the tea leaves at no charge. On the wooden bar was arrayed a line of earthen jars and cans marked with their contents: salt roasted watermelon seeds, red earth peanuts, tortoise shell fried pastries, plum pastries, salty moist cakes, phoenix eye cakes, winter melon candy, and all manner of sweets preserved in sugar or honey. The tea accompaniments were all priced at NT$1.50 per plate. The large pots used to boil water for tea were the same kind used to make millet congee in those days. When the water boiled, steam from the roiling water would rush out of a small orifice and make a crisp and clear *Wooo* whistling sound. The fuel used to heat the water was the most commonly seen fuel of the time, "lotus briquets." It was bits and pieces of coal compressed into a round briquet; one piece would burn for about twelve hours, very durable. Their major deficiency was they did not protect the environment, friendly neither to the planet nor to human lungs.

Every Monday, Wednesday, Friday, and Sunday, the proprietress would arrange for a Chinese storyteller to come to the teahouse on the ship to tell legends of the past, the cost of which was covered by the basic tea charge. The stories never deviated from the classics: Mulian Saves his Mother, Hairui of the Qing Palace, Investiture of the Gods, The Seven Knights of Five Justices, The Righteous Thief Liao Tian-ding, Huang Chao Tries the Precious Sword, and others; books of anecdotes teaching lessons in righteousness and piety through entertainment and folksy tall tales. Occasionally, one would run into a more politically aware storyteller, and the story would drift intentionally or unintentionally into current political affairs. When such a performance was finished, although it might result in a war of words between the storyteller and the audience, it was a duel of wagging tongues only, not damaging the refinement of the place.

The tearoom's proprietress was a veteran beauty who had seen many storms; reportedly, she was the lover of Shi Xing Da, a high-level police official. Toward such programs inappropriate to the times, she would usually open one eye and close the other, rarely intervening. But if she got a report from a mole, in order that the guests and tearoom operation not be impacted, she would come out and give a shout. All she had to do was take a stand, no one dared mess with her.

With nightfall, this pensioner's teahouse outside the dike would automatically change its colors into what was vulgarly called a Lecher's Inn of Tea Groping, where walking about were underage children used for erotic entertainment. Although this belonged to activities that were both against public morals and the law, yet its gaudy flag had been hoisted for many years. Neither local hoods nor stupid cops came looking to collect protection money; indeed, hidden deep in its dark recesses were actually high-placed officials who propped it up.

Around five o'clock in the afternoon, the sun dipped below the mountains in Sanchong across the Danshui River. The yellow dusk illuminated the small ripples on the river as the tide went out, like golden fish scales bedazzling the eyes. Seated in the Hangzhou Tearoom staring at the backlit silhouettes at sundown, one could see the five Hong family brothers training together on the riverbank with Master Tu, learning Yang-style Taiji. Master Tu's performance embodied relaxation, softness, slowness, evenness, like clouds passing and water flowing, a complement to the soft beauty of the golden twilight of the heavens and river. Simply an *al fresco* edition of Lin Huai-min's "Moon Water" modern dance, except that the bunch of chumps in back had no way to divorce themselves from their stiff and hard pattern of Southern Shaolin boxing. From start to finish, they were a stark contrast to the form of Master Tu who stood out front. But in that authoritarian era, regarding the lessons transmitted by a teacher, the foundation of discipleship was that there was no room to talk back to the master; one trained what the teacher taught. However, concealed within the doubts of the five brothers, like soap bubbles getting bigger as they joined with each other, their worldly reveries outdid one another . . .

"Hey, uncle, are you a sloth or snail? Pick up the pace. People back here want to pass!" third brother Yi-mian muttered.

"Pa must really be getting old. How could he want us to train this sluggish dance?" oldest brother Yi-qin remarked to no one.

"Fuck. This shit's so squishy soft, can it really be used to fight people?" second son Yi-wen asked.

"Wow, spare me. This speed is driving me nuts!" Yi-mian commented.

"Gracious, in which year of the republic will we finish doing this form?" brother five Yi-kun complained.

"Why do we train it slow to use it fast? Shouldn't we train it the way we intend to use it?" queried fourth brother Yi-xiang.

"When the Bodhisattva Avalokitesvara was coursing in the deep prajna paramita, He perceived that all five skandhas are empty. Thus He overcame all ills and suffering. Oh, Sariputra, form does not differ from the void, and the void does not differ from form. Form is void and void is form; the same is true for feelings, perceptions, volitions, and consciousness," eldest brother Yi-qin recited the Heart Sutra to himself. *Do I care about you? Or not. Pray you bring this class to a close!* he thought.

"Waiter, I'll have a plate of stewed meat on rice and a bowl of stewed day lily with meat, extra day lilies, and make it extra meat, too," third brother Yi-mian daydreamed.

"I'm taking a test tomorrow on the *Compendium of Materia Medica* and the *Book of Prescriptions in Rhyme*, and I am here . . .," second brother Yi-wen said, worriedly.

"I've gotta find a way to skip class, I'd rather be in my room studying electrical schematics," fifth brother Yi-kun thought.

"Eh, gotta think of a way to invite her out to the movies tomorrow . . .," fourth brother Yi-xiang said, considering.

Thus, the five brothers were of one mind, vigorously employing reverie to endure that which they could not avoid, while not a-one was able to internalize the skill of this miraculous soft art.

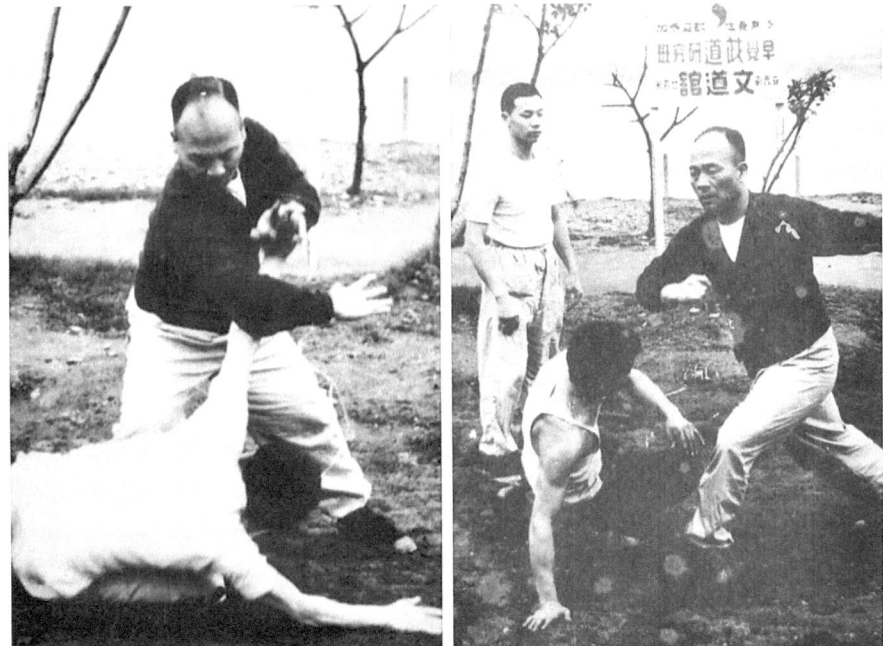

Hong Yi-wen focused his training on Xingyiquan, joint locking and foot stomping. Strength training included whipping a six-meter pole.

23- DAOJIANG MEETING HALL

A place that in the daytime serves as a hall for a funeral wake, in the evening could also see gorgeous strippers grinding their stuff on the stage at a wedding banquet. In that time of shortages, people were the universal measure. And all rules and taboos were set by people.

Scene: The Daojiang Meeting Hall on BaoAn Street

SITUATED RIGHT ACROSS THE STREET FROM THE MAIN POLICE AND railway workers' dormitory, the Daojiang Meeting Hall was solely used for rental to local residents holding wedding banquets or for large local funeral ceremonies. Any colorful or sad events in the YanPing district would all be held here without worry. The scale of the average restaurant was insufficient to cope with the popular customs of the age. Some public schools had large auditoriums used for parent teacher association meetings and would rent them out cheaply, accepting token rental or cleaning fees to alumni and local residents to use as wedding party or banquet halls. For this reason, one would often see elementary school students during PE class carelessly knocking their ball against the outside of the auditorium, where a temporary banquet kitchen was set up. In the past, people paid attention to a show of extravagance. Weddings and birthday parties could easily have a hundred or more tables, a very magnificent sight. Especially among the local elites where a wedding was concerned, the host's family and the guests feared being rude to each other, all apprehensive about a loss of face, so some invitations could not but be sent. Although the people who received the invites might complain about the damage to their pocketbooks, those who did not receive invitations felt they had certainly lost face to the extent they would complain that the groom's family was looking down on them.

As for enormous three- to five-hundred table occasions, these were also not unheard of. When one came across this sort of extravagance, besides filling the school auditorium, there was only enough room if the tables spilled outside onto the athletic field. Sometimes, to improve the quality of the food, when the number of tables exceeded a certain amount, a banquet might employ two caterers. This was commonly known in Taiwanese as "Dueling Tables." Besides considering the scale of the food, beverages, and service the venue was equipped to support, the host had to take into consideration business relations and how to spread the grease around so as to avoid giving favor that offended the party that did not get sufficient business.

These outside caterers were running around the countryside all year round, and their style of business operations was not any different from the demimonde of the Rivers and Lakes. Say if one had no background or connections in the demimonde, the fee for the banquet might not be so easy to collect. Especially at such enormous guest banquet venues, if banqueters had no background in or were not backed up by gang bosses, they were wise to refrain. Employing such occasions to test the strength of their connections, warm or cold, deep or shallow, generally speaking even large business owners would not dare to display such ostentation.

When there were local or national elections and it came time to buy off influential people and collect votes, the characteristics of this very special ecosystem were leveraged. The money men and fixers behind the candidates, and the influential who could swing votes, all would go through these uncouth outsiders to manage this conniving on their behalf, thus avoiding much undesirable awkwardness. This hucksterism should be considered an unintended special business opportunity derived from the election culture of the time.

If it was confirmed there would be two caterers, a red velvet rope would be erected in the auditorium or plaza of the temple, creating a passage through which the dishes could be delivered to the tables and to set the boundaries in the venue. Besides using different colored tablecloths to distinguish the two sides of the banquet, all the courses delivered would be different. To build reputation, face, and relationships, the teams of the two sides would both exert themselves to the limit. Each would demonstrate epic waitering techniques, thus seeking the banquet guests' approbation and judgement, over which each side's food and presentation were more "flamboyant."

In that era, for a caterer, the diners' public praise was the best way to disseminate and guarantee new business solicitation. If one was offered this kind of occasion to make direct comparisons right at the dining table, the great chefs had hardly any choice or right to bow out or not accept the invitation. Once the food was on the table, not only could they not let the host lose face, worse, they could not let their own image take a hit under the glaring stare of the crowd.

Facing this life-or-death struggle, the two combatants would temporarily put aside all thoughts of cost control on the ingredients, labor, and profit, and from the moment they confirmed the order, would activate their "military preparations." Foremost were the ingredients to be used; they strictly demanded the highest quality, freshest, most masterful Grade-AAA ingredients. Seafood is the tentpole dish at a Taiwanese banquet, so if one's ingredients were not fresh, one lost the battle. It did not matter how gifted the chef or marvelous the table-waiting skills, defeat was assured.

Besides the freshness of the ingredients, the artisanal skills of the chef, the management of the venue, and the ability to smooth emergent situations were points of comparison. Generally speaking, it was the sous chefs who did the cooking when catering. The master chef managed the discussion with the host about dish selection and pricing, establishing the menu to control the overall appearance and cost. On the day of the banquet the master chef would focus solely on standing guard between the dining hall and the kitchen as dishes emerged. Observing the situation in the banquet hall, he would control the speed at which courses were delivered, the temperature and the pace. All prior preparations and efforts came down to these two hours of the banquet repast, having the optimal presentation when the courses were delivered.

The expectation of Taiwanese is "Eat While It's Hot" because, optimally, fresh seafood flavors should be consumed within fifteen minutes of being steamed or fried. Even the best of ingredients and most skilled preparation are ravaged by time. For this reason, how one mastered the pace would be the deciding factor of this most important key to divine flavor. At wedding banquets, the program mixed in the arrival of the newlyweds, the ceremonial witnessing of the vows, and toasting, so it was imperative to exert control to avoid delivering courses at the wrong time and thus spoiling the whole enterprise with one misstep. In every respect, this was essentially a battlefield. Chef versus chef, chefs versus guests, chefs versus the ingredients, and a battle of chefs versus time.

Besides this, outside catering had one enormous difference related to inviting guests to a restaurant, and that was caterers had to bring to the table sufficient portions; excessive to the point they could not possibly be consumed at the banquet. Once they had their fill of the fine cuisine, guests attending banquets would always think of the unspoken wish in large families of the time and take doggy bags home to share with family members who could not attend. So, sitting at a table with twelve strangers, on the arrival of each course of the meal, twelve plastic bags would also accompany the meal to allow the guests to carry home portions they hated to part with, or were too full to consume. Leftovers not consumed and not taken home by guests became "banquet tailings" distributed by the host to the people who helped manage the banquet and to neighbors.

In that era, it was not discourteous to extend an invitation to friends or neighbors to come over to eat "banquet tailings." This kind of considerate sharing of good fortune is seen too little in today's society. Maybe it is because we have too much stuff. People have nearly forgotten the joy and camaraderie of sharing.

On this occasion, the Daojiang Meeting Hall was being prepared for a competitive bidding meeting, organized by a large Japanese trading house. At the entrance to the main hall was hung a large poster on which was written with an ink brush, *Japan Tokyo Municipal Electricity Power Cut Meeting to Bid on Lighting Candles.*

Because the purchase quantity was huge and the value large, nearly all of Northern Taiwan's mechanized-scale candle factories were enthusiastic to participate in this rare opportunity to bid. Since the Bandit Leader had merged many small gang leaders to form an underworld coalition after snatching the fertile territory behind the rail station, he continued according to plan, progressively expanding the range of pies into which he could stick his fingers. Now, they guarded a narrow corner near the entrance to the bidding hall that had to be passed to enter the hall, using street muscle to obstruct the arriving merchants' representatives coming to place their bids. One by one they took the cowed merchants to face the Big Boss.

"You have your bid?" the Bandit Leader asked.

"It's here!" the merchants meekly handed over the bid.

"You want to bid, not die, right? Bidding such a low price, your cost of materials might only rise 5 percent, 10 percent, and it would be a miracle if you didn't die," the Bandit Leader said, shredding the document.

"No way. Unless there was a natural disaster, why would the cost of materials suddenly rise in price?" the merchant asked.

"Because you're my bitch! The supply of goods is completely in my hands, wouldn't you say whether the price goes up or not is totally up to me?" The Bandit Leader flicked his head back, signaling for his minion to hand over a bid document prepared in advance. "In a moment, just use this bid. If you play a trick on us, we'll take out your whole family."

"How is this price even possible?" the merchant asked.

"What of it? Haven't you ever carried the palanquin? You haven't fixed the prices? You earn the same," the Bandit Leader declared.

Those merchants' representatives, who were powerless to resist, under the threat of these bid-rigging robbers, took the bloated bids and dispiritedly walked into the bidding hall. Several bidders who did not want to sully themselves, or whose factory was small and could not justify such a bloated bid, simply gave up on the idea of bidding, turned, and went for the exit. Industry acquaintances waiting outside the bidding hall, thinking to chat or say hello, saw the hoods step in and froze their tongues, silently stepping aside.

※ ※ ※

"Director, you are still playing around with the bids. That's not good. You take the advantage of every opportunity this way, it's not fair to other good and honest merchants," the Bandit Leader said.

"No rule it can't be done this way, everyone makes money," Director Wang of a coalition of manufacturers said.

"Everybody makes money, that's okay. But only if I get to fix the profit distribution," the Bandit Leader said.

"You make the distribution? On what basis?" another Director Lin asked.

"Fuck. When Big Daddy speaks, does he need a basis?" the Bandit Leader said.

"Then… how to distribute?" Director Xu asked.

"Subtract the cost. I take 70 percent of the net profit, and the remainder is split among everyone else," the Bandit Leader said.

"In one breath you strip away so much, and then what's left for distributing?" Director Xiao said.

"Fuckin' bitch. You all don't need to do anything, I spend money to buy you off to take a hike and you still complain," the Bandit Leader said.

"You keep the money to get us to walk, we don't need it," Director Xu said.

The Bandit Leader could see the directors relying on their numbers could not be budged; he pointed to his muscle standing near the door, who at the same time intentionally let hidden watermelon knives slide down their sleeves to their hands, where they were exposed.

"You dare!" Director Xu said.

"If you have guts, take a chance, see if I dare or not!" the Bandit Leader said.

"Forget about it. Such a big bid, I don't believe they will swallow it anyway. Let's go."

Several of the more cowardly partners hurriedly pulled back Director Xu, seeking to avoid a verbal spat intensifying into a blood-spattered conflict. And so it was that a determined veteran of bidding wars, with a solid bid, had no choice but to lower his head in surrender to the threatening gleam of a gangster's knife.

"Off so soon? Won't you wait for the opening of the bids?" Always hidden and controlling in the background, Boss Jin intentionally chose this moment when the bids were soon to close to make his appearance, coming face to face with the defeated group of veteran bidders.

"When I win the bidding, I will yet trouble you all to do contract work for me. By all means, please help," he said with sufficient courtesy, but no one was willing to look back and regard his despicable features. These old hands of the demimonde knew too well that when the time came for him to hand out the work, it would be unappetizing and unprofitable, but nonetheless they would be unwilling to turn it down. Jin Yuan-long had relied on his deep financial resources and cultivated influence with the mob to rise quickly. He chose to create a monopoly at the source of the raw materials supply and thereby control the price. After getting a taste for it, he would progress to employing all manner of parasites to digest this whale, stealthily finessing the seizure of the bids won by the smaller players and letting these larger, more automated producers make profits for him with shrinking margins. Until one day they could not prop up their businesses anymore, and he would swoop in and acquire their secondhand equipment at extremely low prices and take their existing customers, thus completing the construction of a fully vertically integrated conspiracy and hegemony.

24– BID RIGGING 101

You can get much farther with a kind word and a gun than you can with a kind word alone.

—*Chicago Crime Boss Al Capone*

Scene: The Daojiang Meeting Hall on BaoAn Street

AFTER THE COERCION BY THE LOCAL BANDITS OUTSIDE THE HALL, the numbers of merchants' representatives attending were clearly reduced by more than half in the competitive bidding assembly set up at the Daojiang Meeting Hall, to the extent that the hall looked a bit deserted. Only some people who had been tricked despondently placed their bids into the sealed wooden box. Jin Yuan-long sat in the front row in the center of the bidders, frequently looking back to scrutinize each corner of the bidding hall, to confirm whether the only remaining competitor he had on his mind, the Hong family, would, according to his scheme, fail to come forward to place a bid. As the time to close the bids drew near, his face was already lit up with the joy that this was in his grasp. Ringing in his ears was the intel the Bandit had reported to him the night before: "According to our mole's report, the equipment at Hong Wan-mei that can produce this specification of candle is not more than fifty production lines. With the scale and delivery time requirements taken into consideration, they definitely cannot swallow this whole order." He had not completed this reverie when he saw the fourth son, Hong Yi-xiang, enter the bidding hall at the last moment, carrying a coffee-colored brief case and hurriedly complete the inspection of the bidder's qualifications. At the last moment, before the bidding was closed, he slipped the last bid of the day into the box.

"Times up. I welcome all the bosses who have participated in the bidding. Thank you for your enthusiastic participation. According to the regulations, I hereby repeat the relevant stipulations for this invitation to tender. Our commercial organization has on this occasion opened a tender for bidding on the following items: white candles twenty centimeters in length, with a diameter of two centimeters, weight for each is not to be under fifty grams. The tender is for a total quantity of ten thousand cases, altogether ten million pieces, ten candles per paper box, each case packed with one hundred boxes shall be made of wood to prevent the breakage of candles during shipment. Any product that is bent, deformed, faded, cracked, or under-weight, will be judged as rejects, and the reject rate cannot exceed 0.5 percent. Rejects will be handled according to the penalties established in the contract. Under circumstances where delivery is delayed or cannot be made, according to the penalties in the contract, 1 percent of the total contract value will be fined, how many days late will be fined how many days. If the contract is reneged on, besides forfeiting the deposit, the vendor will be liable to pay the buyer three times the contract value. These terms have already been clearly communicated in the two-party agreements, and here we want to highlight clearly: the necessity of this tender is to cope with an urgent need in the Tokyo metropolitan area experiencing an electric power shortage. For this reason, the priority factor in deciding the winner is a delivery time not exceeding ninety days, with price a secondary consideration. We expect that within ninety days of signing a contract, the goods must ship, distributed into three deliveries. Good. Now we will begin the opening of the bids. Huitong Merchants has given up. SanXie has entered a bid of 120 days with each case NT$500; the delivery time is unacceptable."

Seated behind Jin Yuan-long, the Bandit leaned in, his mouth close to Jin's ear, and said, "When we get the deal, I'll take care of the production."

"The penalties are severe. Can't have any mistakes," Jin Yuan-long said.

"Rest 120 percent assured. What you want to worry about now is that guy," the Bandit said.

"We have carefully reckoned Hong Wan Mei's capacity, if that old man still insists not to tear up his bid, it will take him at least five or six months to deliver. Time is the key factor in the tender, so unless his price is really attractive, it is no use."

25– SPEED DETERMINES EVERYTHING

Only if you raise the right question can you find the right answer. Einstein said, "If I had an hour to solve a problem and my life depended on it, I would use the first fifty-five minutes determining the proper question to ask, for once I know the proper question, I could solve the problem in less than five minutes." Only by employing a new angle can one see the old problem.

Scene: Inside Hong Wan Mei #2 Candle Factory

WU FAN-BO PERSONALLY CHAIRED THE EMERGENCY MEETING IN the Hong Wan Mei factory. "Our machines that meet specification can produce fifty candles per shot, fifty machines operating at the same time can manufacture two thousand five hundred candles per shot. The problem is that after we have put the liquid paraffin in the molds it takes thirty minutes to cool the molds down to the point at which we can remove them. Not accounting for our scrap rate, we can only make five thousand per hour. If we maintain twelve-hour workdays, the most we can produce per day is sixty thousand sticks. Estimating at this rate, ten million sticks will take at least 167 days to get it out. That is to say, even if we don't experience any issues, we need at least five and a half months to finish. This is to say nothing of running the machines overtime, in which case the molds can fracture any time, and assessing that impact is difficult," said Wu Fan-bo.

"If we can't resolve these issues, the problems caused will be enormous," oldest brother Yi-qin said.

"So, tell them right away, we don't accept the order," third brother Yi-mian said.

"No way. Our entire deposit would be forfeited," second brother Yi-wen said.

"You idiots were just looking to win the order and not taking care of how to produce it. Couldn't you do the math? You want to kill us?" third brother Yi-mian declared.

"Brother, I was not being greedy. The domestic market is saturated, so if we don't pry open a new market or transform our business right away, our traditional business will certainly wither away. If we can slog through this opportunity and break into the Japanese market, it is a whole new road for us. But to break into the Japanese market we have to let them see our quality and efficiency. This is a rare opportunity, passing on it would be a true shame," fourth brother Yi-xiang said.

"Truly spoken. When doing business, if you only strike at the safe balls, you only end up striking out."

"I have to believe there is some smarter way. This problem can be solved. If we only talk about scale, our capacity ranks No. 1 in Taiwan. If we can't swallow this order, I trust no one can," fourth brother Yi-xiang said.

"You are just paying attention to whether people can take on the order. But we don't have five to six months so we can't cough it out. You have to be clear about this," third brother Yi-mian said.

"Unless we split the order up, find some small factories outside to help outsource the work," fifth brother Yi-kun said.

"The risk and cost are too high. One, small factories all too easily skimp work and are stingy with material, so it's hard for us to control quality. Two, if we give them our process and formulas, isn't that the same as leaking our production secrets to them?" second brother Yi-wen posited.

"Let them figure it out for themselves. If they take on the order, serves them right," third brother Yi-mian said.

"Let's not just talk about the downside. Everybody get your brains in gear, see if there isn't a way we can expand production," Wu Fan-bo said, encouragingly.

"The fastest way to expand production is to add production lines," fifth brother Yi-kun said.

"New machines would have to be ordered from Japan; with placing the order, shipping time, clearing customs, installation, and testing to reach scale production, it is a minimum of three months. In addition, we need twenty to thirty new lines to fill the gap; if it is only for digesting this one order, is a rash factory expansion worth it?" second brother Yi-wen asked.

"True enough. And to cope with this order, the deposit we have placed on the paraffin materials is huge, so I think we don't have spare capital to put into adding production lines. This route isn't feasible," eldest brother Yi-qin said.

"Since increasing production lines is a no-go, is there some way we can squeeze extra speed out of the production process?" fourth brother Yi-xiang asked.

"Have you suffered a brain injury? We just finished saying that cooling down the tools takes thirty minutes; that's in the winter, it's summer now, and it will take forty minutes or more, otherwise there is no way to release the candles from the molds. You are all really wasting time; the way I see it, there is absolutely no solution," third brother Yi-mian declared.

"Yi-mian!" Wu Fan-bo checked his son's disparagements.

"Eh, so the key is the rate of cooling. Brother, is there some way to tweak it?" fourth brother Yi-xiang asked.

"Hmm, you put your finger on it. Putting aside other problems, we just have to increase the cooling rate; it works out to be the same as increasing capacity," eldest brother Yi-qin said. All eyes now focused on Yi-qin, who got out a pen and some thick craft paper on the table, speaking as he drew. "These are the machines in the factory. After liquid paraffin is put in the molds, we presently use manual labor to put the molds into a vat of water to cool down. But when the molds have given up their heat to the water, the water gets hot, reducing its cooling effectiveness."

"So, we need to use running water," fourth brother Yi-xiang said.

"Hmm," eldest brother Yi-qin gave an approving glance to Yi-xiang.

"If we are continuously replacing the water, not only are we wasting labor, we will increase our water consumption a lot. It's too wasteful," second brother Yi-wen said.

"True, we can't waste water and we shouldn't waste manpower," fifth brother Yi-kun said.

"So, we need to elevate some of the machines and install a water pipe around the factory. We can pump water up from the underground well to the water tower on the roof, then connect the piping to the water tower and install a flow valve on each machine to control the water entering the cooling vat. This way we can use Yi-xiang's idea of running water." With head lowered as he drew, eldest brother Yi-qin continued to illustrate for the others the blueprint in his mind.

"Flowing water transforms the original closed-loop cooling vats into an open-loop system, letting the cold water from the well enter here for cooling. Afterwards, at the other end of the cooling vat, we have an exhaust port at the bottom, letting the warmed-up water discharge into our gutter, and from here it will flow back into the well to get cooled off. The water will not only have a continuous cycle, but we can increase the rate of cooling several multiples, right?" Fourth brother Yi-xiang picked up a pencil from the table, and on eldest brother Yi-qin's hand-drawn sketch, drew a filling port and an exhaust port and used his pencil to point out the direction of the water flow.

"Eh, correct," eldest brother Yi-qin said.

"The rate of cooling is sped up. Doubling the capacity shouldn't be a problem. Excellent!" fourth brother Yi-xiang said.

"Okay, we have a solution. Let's get to work," Wu Fan-bo said.

Thereupon, Taiwan's first open-loop water cooled system was born of necessity in the hands of the self-taught engineers.

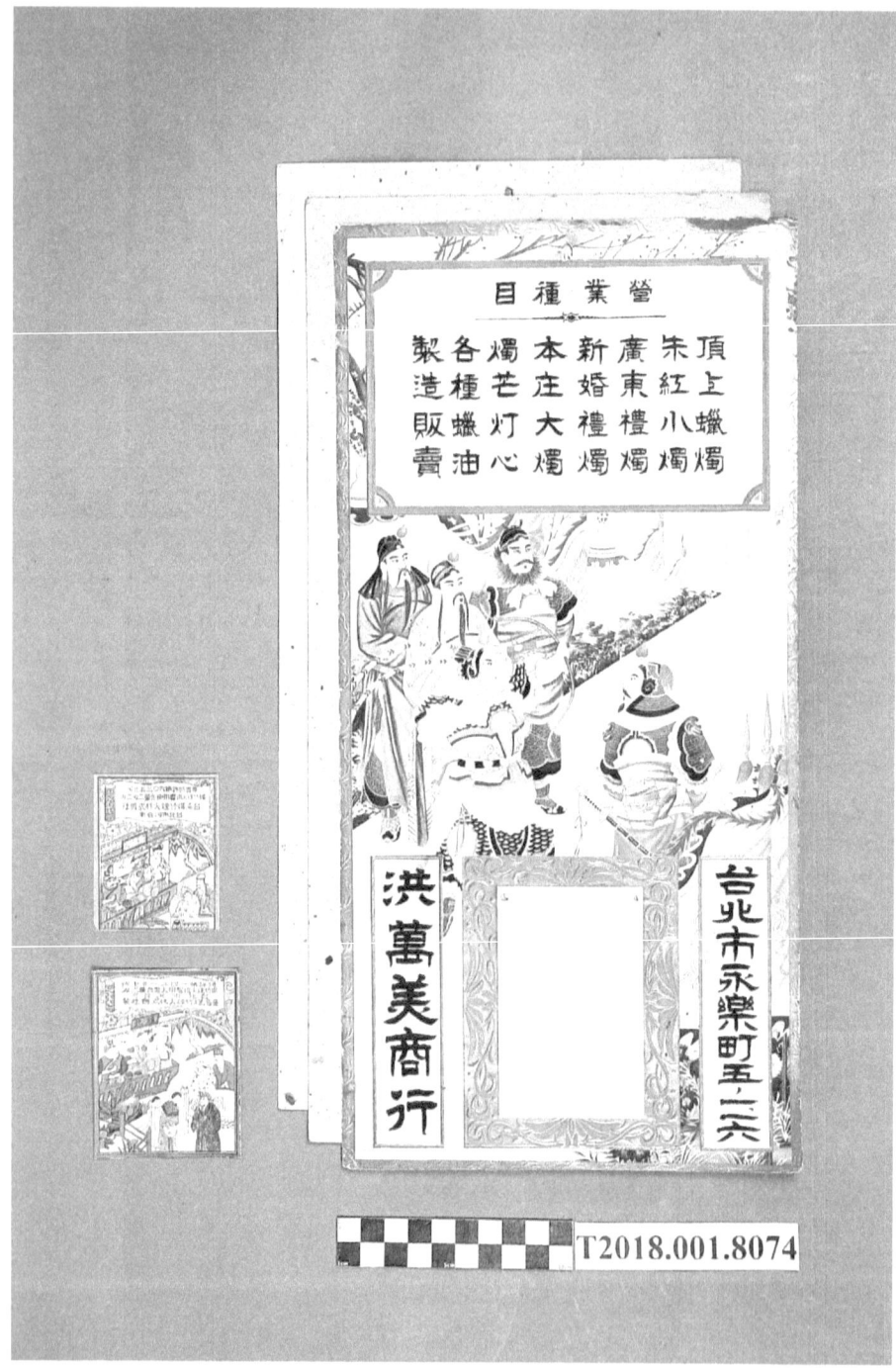

An advertisement for Hong Wan Mei candles from the period on display at the National History Museum in Taipei.
Used with permission of Taiwan's National History Museum

26– THE DARK HIDDEN STREAM

In the cracks where law and morality fail to shine, religion is mankind's final salvation and comfort to the spirit.

Scene: Hong Family Candle Factory

According to plan, the Hong family candle factory completed reengineering on the "Recirculating Water-Cooling System." They also rearranged the production lines so all those machines capable of producing the tender-specified product were closer to the furnace. They then did a thorough cleaning of the large furnace used for red candles, converting it into a furnace for white wax. Under the din of the motorized bellows, scorching hot flames hastened the melt of paraffin, bringing it to a constant boil.

Black Turtle, bare from the waist up, was standing on a highchair next to the furnace, scrupulously measuring and adjusting the temperature and proportion of soft to hard wax in the melt. The highchair on which he stood was precisely the station at which his father had toiled in a former life. In the last stage of his career, Black Turtle's father had rejoiced at the opportunity to pass on his decades-long accumulated experience at the side of the high temperature furnace to his only son, who was determined to change his evil ways and return to the fold. This gave him a foundation on which he could rely to secure his future and raise a family.

"Black Turtle, well done. You have your dad's knack," cheered on some old factory hands, watching Black Turtle handle the furnace with thorough competence. Observing much of his father's grace and refined movement, they could not but directly express their admiration and acclaim. In the heat of the furnace flames Black Turtle's body glowed red, the lines of a half-finished tattoo on his back were swollen and took on an especially surreal three-dimensional effect. It was a tattoo motif rarely seen, of the mythological Emperor of the Mysterious Heaven, his one foot stepping on a turtle, the other foot on a snake. The turtle and the snake in the myth were taken from the Emperor of the Mysterious Heaven's guts when he was cleansing his intestines in the river to show his determination to Buddha and were left behind to become the organs of humankind. Having been exposed to the essence of the Sun and the Moon, these organs became evil and intent on harming people. Afterwards, when the Emperor of the Mysterious Heaven received the Jade Emperor's edict to descend to the mortal world and subdue demons, he took the spirits of the turtle and snake as his mounts and spirit animals, the two helping him to bring bounty to the villagers.

This fairy tale, handed down by temple con artists to temple devotees, was a preposterous myth that could not stand up to reason, yet it had become a solace to Black Turtle on encountering the dual blows of bad luck with the loss of his turf, and his father's death, thus he had no choice but to hang his head low and trust in this myth. It was on the seventh night of mourning, half in dreams, half awake, that he saw his old man return, his stooped body scrawny and tormented by disease, and taking his hand and with great difficulty, guided him to the side of the large furnace at the Hong family factory, there to take direction from his old man, to train and practice the requisite skills over and over again. Maybe this was just a kind of hallucination, a figment of his imagination injected by his sub-conscious. But in the end, he could not stand to let his old man, dead of disease, still carry such a burden after his death.

After the dream, he disregarded the folk edicts not to enter the temple to worship during the mourning period and knelt piously in penitence before the many gods at the main Ma Zu Temple on Yanping North Road. He took faith in a charm delivered to his mother, Crabby Auntie, after her prayers: "There is no easy return from a life of wandering and dissipation, obstinately refusing to repent future darkness, the turtle and the snake chanced to meet the Lord of Rectitude, then abandoning darkness and entering light, now none can deceive them." He came to believe such talk, which he had previously turned his nose up at. He believed that in those gaps where law and morality could not shine, religious conviction was mankind's sole final source of redemption and spiritual retreat.

Basket upon basket of coal, borne on carry-poles by a herd of bearers, their skin black from the coating of coal dust, were continuously dumped into the fuel bin ready for use. The cardboard cartons specified in the order were being urgently completed by the paper and printing factories on Anxi Street. There was the so-called Materials Hut of Jinzhou Street, where at several shops specializing in materials for wooden crates there was the pervasive din of saws cutting wood and hammers hitting nails. In the kitchen, Auntie Wu-fan commanded the "Kitchen Brigade": vegetable washers washing vegetables, vegetable cutters cutting vegetables, fish scalers scaling fish, soup cookers cooking soup. No one was idle. The air was filled with the anticipation of reward and happiness. One large order, and its attendant flow-through business, besides its significance to the expansion of one family's enterprise, brought direct business opportunities and participation to peripheral enterprises, thereby improving other families' incomes and futures.

A successful businessperson can be very devious, or can be very merciful, or he can be both devious and merciful. And the key that determines what he is, sometimes is just his natural instincts, sometimes just his destiny, sometimes both, sometimes neither. Speaking of that businessperson, does it matter if, in the eyes of bystanders, he is great? Or if he is despicable? It does not matter. Because all torment and resentment come back to the most basic starting point. Perhaps he is simply an ordinary person, uttering a humble prayer for adequate food and shelter. Isn't it true? Accordingly, if you can benefit others and yourself, you benefit others and yourself. Sometimes, the fish and the bear's palm have no way to both be satisfied, in which case Nature listens to Heaven to decide fate. As a result, some people profit and some people take a loss.

Of profit and loss in business, some adopt a philosophical approach, some are just sore losers. Since they cannot afford to lose, and cannot let it go, such people in the end seek a means of settling scores through the demimonde. Consequently, success and failure in the field of business directly translates into grudges and animosity in the demimonde.

That one risky move on the chess board of the Hong family won for them the opportunity to open new markets but upset the beads arranged nicely on Jin Yuan-long and the Bandit Leader's wishful abacus. Hidden beneath an atmosphere of happy celebration, a black strand of retaliation and petty destructive plotting flowed underground, gathered speed, pooled, surreptitiously grew, ominously expanded.

27– OUTREACH

In the concrete jungle or the forested jungle, it's all the same; neither is a place to cultivate mercy or virtuous ideas. True peace springs from a balance of power between two parties; not dictated by heaven or human nature.

Scene: The plaza behind the Taipei Main Station

AFTER THE LOCAL GANG BOSS, BANDIT LEADER, AND THE MONEY laundering Jin Yuan-long had linked up, step by step, according to plan, they integrated the business horizontally and vertically. If there was any profit to be made, they squeezed their brains to think of ways to employ their relations and influence, black and white, to bring it under their sphere of control. After they had captured control of the strip of territory between the rear of the Taipei Main Station to DaDaoCheng, such things as smuggled cigarettes and liquor, prostitution, gambling, narcotics and other obscenely profitable illicit enterprises, without exception became part of their money-making machine, operating without a hitch.

After they secured this illicit income, they used this filthy lucre to buy influence with corrupt officials, and then used their influence with these corrupt officials to dig out more sources of money. Rolling people in money, and rolling money in people, the more they rolled, the bigger the pile of cash became. Anyone with a say over purchases or procurement in military, public, education, and other sectors, who gave the slightest hint to them, naturally found a "middleman" inserted in the loop, converting his decision-making authority into personal gain.

And these corrupt officials in key posts were happy to keep their hands clean, let others convert their connections into cash and enrich themselves. Legend has it that one time Jin Yuan-long went, through the introductions of a retired official of the Bureau of Investigation, to pay a visit directly at the house of a general responsible for the procurement of military supplies. During the visit, whether intentionally or not, the general expressed admiration for the solid gold pocket watch Jin Yuan-long always had with him. Without another word, Jin Yuan-long took off the watch and presented it to the general. From then on, Jin Yuan-long became the largest supplier of food provisions to the military in that area. In that age, when strongmen over-ruled the law, the fastest path to growth for a big company was to collude with officials. And the middlemen who operated between the black and the white more often than not were retired directors or operatives from the Bureau of Investigation. Once they had built up well-oiled relations with police, military, government, and investigators, these businessmen naturally had a way to convert relations into cash transactions. As they employed their talent to the fullest, goods flowed freely, and the benefits were spread around like mist, so they were successful in every endeavor and there was nothing they could not accomplish.

"We relied on our skills to win the tender, what's this about the big taking advantage of the small!" second brother Yi-wen said.

"Don't you love to put it that way. Stealing the tender is your family's skill. In that case, refusing to make deliveries is our skill, everyone relies on their native abilities, everybody tries hard, what's the harm in that!" the Bandit Leader said.

"Above board, fair competition is our native skill. You refusing to transport goods, this sneaky move is just pulling our legs out from under us, what kind of skill is that?" second brother Yi-wen said.

"A sneaky move is just a move. If it works, it's a good move, that is a native skill," the Bandit Leader said.

"You won't transport, okay, just let other trucks haul. Shit or get off the pot, don't stop outside trucks from coming in," third brother Yi-mian said.

"Outside trucks entering the station are only allowed to discharge, they can't load cargo, these are the rules of the loading dock, I didn't make 'em! You ask me, who do I ask? The drivers at the station wait in line to toil under the noon sun, in one day they can only make two or three deliveries, if it is opened up so outside trucks can come in and steal business, won't they starve to death?"

"You want to talk about rules, okay. Please, what is the rule that says you can refuse business? Is it because we did not pay? Or we did not pay enough? If you really want to guarantee the drivers at the station have enough to eat, then you shouldn't forbid them from moving our goods. If it weren't for you hiding at the station fucking around, why would we need to look for outside trucks to haul freight. Everything you said is a pack of contradictory lies," second son Yi-wen expressed with his thoughtful and clear eloquence, tongue tying the local mobster with his refutation, so that he had no answer.

"Even if you say 'die,' it won't change anything. Your family's freight is forbidden to be hauled, period. Doesn't matter who you send. This is the back of the train station, not your house. I have no obligation to listen to your orders. If we don't want to earn your money, is it breaking any laws?" the Bandit Leader said.

"You scumbag, see how you like it when I stuff your balls down your throat," third brother Yi-mian said.

"Three!" Yi-wen said grabbing Yi-mian.

"Oooo. I'm shaking in my boots. If you got the guts, make a move," a tall and sturdy tough standing beside the local hood said, intentionally provoking third brother Yi-mian, who could barely restrain himself.

"I'll ask you one more time, what do you want, what's it gonna' take to get you to be willing to send trucks out?" second brother Yi-wen asked.

"Alright. I'll tell you clearly one more time, let you bury this idea, what you can do now is…head home and just wait to die," the local hood said.

The conversation having reached this point, there was already neither goodwill nor common ground, since there was no hope to peacefully settle this impasse.

※ ※ ※

"Brother Four, besides the Taiji, are you still keeping up with your judo?" eldest brother Yi-qun asked.

"Ah. Taiji is too abstract for my taste, too hard to make sense of. I rely more on the speed and destructive power of judo," fourth brother Yi-xiang said.

"What's your level of conditioning?" eldest brother Yi-kun asked.

"Still good. I am on the same level as Huang Cang-lang and Chen Mei-shou, no problem," fourth brother Yi-xiang said.

"In a street fight?" eldest brother Yi-kun asked.

"Depends on the opponent and the situation. If we are talking about ordinary guys, handling two or three should be okay," fourth brother Yi-xiang said.

"No. Just one is enough."

"You're thinking of making a move?"

"Mmm. The cargo is all stuck at the depot and we can't get it out, so I am afraid we will have to risk a skirmish," eldest brother Yi-kun said.

"Understood."

"Of course, we talk first, if talk really doesn't work, then we take action," eldest brother Yi-kun said.

"Brother, this is not just about a grudge from the bidding hall, that's just an excuse is all," fourth brother Yi-xiang said.

"I know. Hidden in the back, pulling the strings, is Jin Yuan-long, they want to use this as a pretext to dip their fingers into all the trade at Dihua Street."

"So, isn't any talk just hot air?"

"No. It's reasonable, this step can't be skipped. I think tomorrow, just let Brother Two do the talking, you stay close by his side and do as you see fit. If we can use money to buy peace, that's best, if it's really not possible, then make a move. You will have to decide quickly on the spot," eldest brother Yi-kun said.

"Okay. I know. But how far do you want me to take it?"

"Just far enough to get them to release the cargo."

"So, I want to capture their king, put them in checkmate."

"Right. You want to control the top guy."

"Check."

"One more thing," eldest brother Yi-kun said, "Make it a surprise attack. I know you and brother three are both capable fighters, but this time, no showing off, it has to be one move to take him out, let them be caught completely off-guard, that will intimidate them."

"I understand. What about Pa? Will he agree to this?" fourth brother Yi-xiang asked.

"This is a life-or-death juncture. If we can't fight our way through, then Hong Wan Mei credibility in the marketplace is finished. I think he will make allowance for that," eldest brother Yi-kun said.

"Oh."

"Another thing, don't let brothers two and three know ahead of time, avoid influencing the results of the talks."

"I know, brother three likes to mouth off…"

Brother four Yi-xiang could hear his eldest brother Yi-kun's warnings ringing in his ears from the private conversation the night before. Looking at the impasse before him, he knew eldest brother's conclusion was correct. He set his mind, then with no warning, surged forward from behind brother two, as fast as a peal of thunder that gives no time to cover the ears, he struck. One hand seized the Bandit Leader's right arm, and shifted his body deep under his armpit, so that when he was in position, he immediately sprung up from the waist and executed his favorite seoinage shoulder throw, in a flash dropping the Bandit Leader's large body heavily onto the asphalt. As soon as this was accomplished, he immediately gave a firm kick to the opponent's jaw knocking out this cruel bastard. Because the accumulated rage was deep, and this surprise attack was both fierce and swift, both parties were entirely dumbfounded in the moment, not knowing how to respond. Only after a pause to recover did the Bandit Leader's brethren at his side grasp that the war had already begun, and a group of men immediately swarmed over to surround them.

Third brother Yi-mian narrowed his eyes on the tall and sturdy tough taking the initiative rushing forward, he instinctively surged ahead to guard fourth brother Yi-xiang's front, feinting with a right fist to attack the opponent's face, whereupon the opponent raised his hand to block it, the right hand instantly reversed, folding down taking a firm grasp of the sturdy tough's testicles. His hand secure, he squeezed tight and lifted, that sturdy tough could not overcome the acute pain searing from his privates, and unable to maintain a brave face, he howled loudly in front of everyone.

To witness one's own leaders brought down in a flash by others, one lying on the ground in a dazed heap and oblivious, one crying for his mother as a man crushed his balls, this was an embarrassing situation. Immediately this mob lost its fighting spirit and motivation, with entirely no idea of how, or whether, to keep fighting, as one by one they froze in their tracks, not daring to take further rash action, for a deep-seated fear that if they did not respond properly, their boss's ability to have children was at risk.

"Tell 'em to back off!" third brother Yi-mian said, continuing to put the squeeze on his opponent's testicles.

"Back off! Listen to him. Quickly! Aiii! Hurry. Mother!" the sturdy tough spouted in a cold sweat and tears.

"Black Snake, bring the trucks in," fourth brother Yi-xiang, standing outside, confidently bellowed.

In an instant, dozens of pedicab trucks that had been hiding just beyond the station in wait for the all-clear sign, immediately sped like a flight of arrows into the station, within seconds filling the plaza behind the station depot. On the cargo bed of each pedicab truck stood two porters who did not wait for the vehicle to stop but sprang off the trucks and into action.

"Black Turtle, over to you!" Black Snake said.

"Go, into the depot, let's move that cargo!" Black Turtle commanded, and immediately led ten men into his familiar territory.

"Fuck, what was with that move!" third brother Yi-mian said.

"Eldest brother made it clear last night, the cargo had to be moved to the factory today!" fourth brother Yi-xiang said.

"Understood. Trying to talk sense with this bunch is basically a waste of breath," second brother Yi-wen said.

"If you were going to make a move, it wouldn't have hurt to tell me earlier," third brother Yi-mian's grip on the balls had not released in the slightest, parading their boss' agonized face in front of the little hoodlums, whose own faces became pained at the sight.

In and out of the station, coolies shuttled back and forth, exerting themselves to move the materials that had been hoarded for several days on the platform to the trucks, their faces hard to suppress the joy of the success of this surprise attack. The bags of paraffin were moved one by one from the station depot out to the plaza, and then the tricycle pedicab trucks one by one sped out from the plaza.

28- ELDEST BROTHER'S DEMISE

The mystery and impenetrability of life's meaning rests in its utter unpredictability. Goodness is rewarded, evil has its retribution, but it is the vagaries of life faced by the common folk that leave them speechless and disillusioned.

Scene: Hong Wan Mei Trading

TEN MILLION CANDLE STICKS—WITH THE UNITED EFFORTS OF THE Hong family father and sons, they broke through technical barriers and human obstructions one by one, passed the rigorous inspection and shipped without a hitch before the deadline. At the same time, because the quality of the goods delivered was approved, a long-term supply contract was obtained from a Japanese trading company. Black Turtle and Black Snake, the two fellow sufferers who had both lost their turf battles, under the sincere guidance of fourth brother Yi-xiang, shed their past intemperate lives, thoroughly reformed themselves and entered into the Hong family enterprise, starting life afresh. The latecomer, Black Snake, owing to his innate talent and ingenuity, was put in charge of material supply and delivery work. Black Turtle owing to the precious experience his father had handed down to him, was responsible for quality control and production supervision. After entering the Hong family enterprise, communications between the two became more amicable, they frequently exchanged knowledge and traded responsibilities, becoming the two most important cadres in the Hong family enterprise, the left and right hands of management.

Who would have thought that at this moment when business was on its most harmonious and glorious development path, that this family's brightest, most capable son, expected to continue the family business, the eldest son Yi-qin, would succumb to illness and depart this world alone.

In his capacity as the eldest son, he had always been the greatest helper at his mother and father's side. It did not matter if it was family or business matters, he toiled without complaint or regret, devoting all his mental and physical efforts to the family. During the early days of setting up the family business, any details or important matters that his father and mother had been unable to take care of, he shouldered as an honor without second thoughts. Compared to his father, who grew up as an orphan from when he was small, this eldest brother seemed more like a father in the eyes of his younger siblings than their old man.

Compared to second brother Yi-wen's natural gifts of painting and Chinese medicine, third brother Yi-mian's courage and never say die nature, fourth brother Yi-xiang's ability to discern the key element at a glance, the gift of directly pointing to the core of a problem, and fifth brother Yi-kun's special knowledge of electronics technology, what this eldest brother Yi-qin possessed was a holistic wisdom about leadership and an ability to resolve disputes. But he was called to Heaven at this moment. Leaving behind that work of genius created purely from self-taught resources, the "Recirculating Water-Cooling System," he departed. This tremendous and remarkable invention caught the notice of Japanese candle manufacturers and trading companies who visited Taiwan and came to call. They paid visits because no one in Japan could believe that, solely relying on fifty old machines and the brief ninety-day period, anyone could produce such a large quantity as ten million candles.

For the longest time, this large family could not exit the haze of their grief. With every recollection of this exemplary eldest brother, family members invariably wept. When faced with the enormous sorrow of a grey-haired father burying a black-haired son, the normally introverted and taciturn Wu Fan-bo, whose countenance belied neither joy nor anger endured this with spine, holding himself up, not allowing himself to crumble. In the middle of the night, however, as he lay on his back staring at the awning of his rosewood bed, tears gathered at the corners of his wrinkled eyelids and one by one streamed down his face, all the way until morning.

29– THE HUMAN CHOPPING BOARD

The biggest difference between a human chopping board and a vegetable chopping board is a that a vegetable chopping board can do nothing but bear repeated hacking, whereas an able and intelligent human chopping board can endure all those cuts and strikes and turn them into precious experience and personal assets.

Scene: Danshui Riverbank

ACROSS AN EMPTY SPACE NEXT TO THE HANGZHOU TEAHOUSE, THE dusk of the setting sun painted the surroundings and the wall of the dike a golden hue, so that even the decrepit wreck of the old beached wooden ship was resplendent. Facing the river, in the gleaming reflections off the water, the dark silhouettes of several figures shuttling back and forth were vaguely recognizable, as Master Tu was directing the four Hong brothers in combat applications. Time, effort, and instruction had honed their skills from a muddling awareness of form to a focused application of intent. Third brother, Yi-mian, was flailing his two fists, going after fourth brother, Yi-xiang, with all his might, in a kamikaze-like "all attack-no defense" fierce assault. Fourth brother Yi-xiang skillfully made clever side-steps, always just avoiding the focus of the fist and feet, as he cleverly employed advances and retreats, bobbing and weaving, accurately keeping himself just out of range of his opponent. Third brother, Yi-mian, although his blows fell into empty spaces, the more he was frustrated the bolder he became, ceaselessly employing all variations of hand methods and angles, fast hands and quick feet constantly attacking, no reduction in the firepower of his attack.

"Third brother, cut out the brute force craziness!" fifth brother Yi-kun said.

"Capture his foothold, bite into his maneuvering room!" second brother Yi-wen said.

"Don't butt in! I'll fight him my way. I can't believe I can't hit this louse," third brother Yi-mian said.

"It is not a question of speed. Fourth brother is already wise to your habits, if you don't mix it up, attacking faster isn't going to help," Master Tu said.

"I am wearing him down, let's see how he can escape!" third brother Yi-mian responded.

"Idiot. He's not getting tired but you are!" second brother Yi-wen said.

"You're the idiot," third brother Yi-mian cursed.

The more third brother Yi-mian attacked, the more his ire was raised, the hotter his temper, the less disciplined his assault. All along he believed the universal martial dictum that nothing trumps speed, so even if his life depended on it, he was unwilling to listen to the guidance offered from his brothers on the sidelines. Blindly accelerating the speed of his attacks, he was determined to wear down Yi-xiang. However, it appeared that fourth brother Yi-xiang not only did not collapse in fatigue, on the contrary, he grabbed the opportunity of a gap between Yi-mian's shift from left to right, to switch from defense to attack, his right foot first taking a half step back, his body pivoting back to the right 45 degrees, cleverly absorbing an incoming right fist. At the same moment, Yi-xiang's right hand spiraled up from the inside, wrapping around third brother's right wrist, connecting with his hand while at once hooking and lifting it, as he immediately sank his body and entered into Yi-mian's stance with his left foot, his left hand piercing and rising up against third brother's right ribs, mixing Taiji's Left Diagonal Flying technique with a sudden explosive reverse rotation of his body, shocking third brother to fly five of six steps backward before he regained control over his feet.

"If this isn't losing!" Fifth brother Yi-kun could not help but mock his stubborn third brother.

"Fourth brother cheated, just dodging is not attacking, it's not fair!" third brother Yi-mian protested.

"If your boxing is brainless, it's really hard to win," second brother Yi-wen observed.

"Actually, third brother's constant rapid attacks are not necessarily bad. Taiji employs the slow to generate the fast, if one can't calmly cope with the opponent's fast attacks, then the training is wasted. And fourth brother was constantly passive, defending without countering, although he won in the end, but that is not necessarily the essence of Taiji. You must remember, once attack and defense both become second nature, they are both very dangerous!" Master Tu said.

"I was waiting for my chance to counter," fourth brother Yi-xiang said.

"One can't just wait and not take action. When there is a bridge, take the bridge, when there is no bridge, proactively build the bridge. Even though this is Taiji, its basis is not entirely passive. With a bit more proactive and aggressive spirit, you can see another facet and might of Taiji Boxing," Master Tu said.

"'Taking the initiative and being aggressive'?" fourth brother Yi-xiang asked.

"Right. You must try it yourself," Master Tu encouraged.

"Okay," fourth brother Yi-xiang said.

"Third brother, your fists are fast enough, but your techniques never land because you are in a hurry to switch to another shot, the shortcoming is your follow through and speed, no wonder you are easily evaded!" Master Tu instructed. "Remember, the power of your launch just gets the fist on the way to its target, only the power of your follow through has killing force. If you can increase your mix of long and short techniques, the loser will not necessarily be you. Understand?" Master Tu asked.

"I intentionally let him. He's my younger brother, how could I try to hit him," third brother Yi-mian spuriously defended his face.

"Bullshit. I am also your younger brother, when your blows land on me, aren't you the first to say so!" fifth brother Yi-kun interjected.

"That's because you suck. You're talking nonsense. Next time I'll punch you in the mouth," third brother Yi-mian said.

"Somebody's a sore loser, such a quick about face. Everybody look," fifth brother Yi-kun said.

"Okay, okay, okay. You made your point. I'll settle this with you later!" third brother threatened.

"Furthermore, while it's true speed is good, there are limits to how fast your fists can be. Angles are the key to internal boxing's finesse. All of the changes in angle born out of your younger brother employing the shuttling 'swallowing and spitting' of his body serve to neutralize your speed. So, real exponents need to understand how to use changes in speed to control the tempo, to use breaks in the timing and unseen angles to wipe out the opponent. All that is necessary is to grasp the secret of rotational speed and angle changes, slow becomes fast, fast can be slow," Master Tu instructed.

"Teacher, it's too complicated. Isn't there a little easier way?" third brother Yi-mian complained.

"Heh-heh. The opponent throws a thousand variations at us, we need to have ten thousand adaptations, how do you simplify it? Something that can't be avoided in the process of training martial art is you start out complicating the simple, later you arrive at simplifying the complex. The road is long, but toto reach the end of it, it takes a little more persistence!" Master Tu said.

"I knew it, this world never gives me what I want," third brother Yi-mian said.

"Teacher's right. Third brother's just a stupid cow. He only pays attention to hitting what he wants, he doesn't care what the opponent's up to," fifth brother Yi-kun said.

"Bullshit. It's nothing like you're thinking. You think I have no strategy? I display this punishing firepower at the get go, if it doesn't work, I immediately switch it up, constantly forcing the opponent to busy himself blocking me, leaving him no time to counterattack," third brother Yi-mian said.

"Not bad. But you must increase the penetration of your attacks. You must step in a bit more, only in this way will your surge have force, you know? Here is an even more intelligent way, if you can attract the enemy in, let him deliver himself into a collision with your fist, wouldn't the effectiveness increase?" Master Tu asked.

"I knew that already. Actually, to tell you the truth, I was just going easy on him," third brother Yi-mian said.

"I don't buy this. In practice sparring to prepare for combat, you can yield with the amount of force, you can't yield in the attacks. If you go easy on the attacks, he will leave with a misconception, falsely thinking he is safe, on the contrary, this is hurting your training partner, you understand?" Master Tu said. "Okay. Number four, since you won, you get to continue. Come on. Use two handed pushing, give it a try, see if you can use your judo to throw me," Master Tu said.

Whereupon teacher and student, two people, four hands, faced off and began executing the training method "Active Stepping Two Hand Pushing." It could be seen that Fourth brother Yi-xiang's original nature was to put more weight on defense than attack, only this time he was more obviously proactive and taking the fight to the opponent. Following Master Tu's lead, he repeatedly tried to use the Taiji methods of Roll Back to absorb and Press, so as to connect closely, testing if he could break his opponent's center and create an opportunity to attack. Occasionally he would throw in some feint or facial expression, hoping he could increase the strength of his deception's effectiveness. It is just that Master Tu frequently closed his eyes, relying entirely on the tactile sense of his two hands to respond to all the information transmitted by the opponent. Several times fourth brother tested dropping his body down and in, hoping to penetrate into Master Tu's torso, but from start to finish he was unable to prevail.

"To employ your hands to Listen to Energy requires focus and relaxation of the mind and spirit, only in this way can you accurately detect the meaning of the faint messages transmitted by the body," Master Tu said.

"Gotcha,'" fourth brother Yi-xiang said.

But to listen to energy, one must understand energy, requiring much more practice and contact, so Master Tu latched onto a gap at the end of one of Yi-xiang's feints, his two hands dragging Yi-xiang's center of gravity to Tu's right rear, so that Yi-xiang could not help himself falling forward, but Master Tu then with a reverse binding technique, put Yi-xiang into a neck lock, giving him no chance of escape, at the same time arresting the technique but also not letting him fall. The third and fourth brothers, in the process of training with their brothers, thus played the role of Master Tu's "Human Chopping Board," allowing Master Tu to demonstrate on them, the application and detail of every skill, as much as he wanted.

On the surface, becoming the teacher's chopping board is certainly a poor way to curry favor with the teacher. Besides getting frequent thrashings, one also runs into teachers who don't show an understanding of their student's face, who readily wound their disciples self-esteem. However, it is not every resilient person who can take on the role of the human chopping board. To be the teacher's punching bag one must be especially clever, and it is a rare kind of smarts.

Amid the process of analyzing the teacher's method, one must be able to grasp the teacher's progression of the attack in the flash of the moment, and yet estimate correctly the teacher's power and tempo. Only in this way can one not betray any sign of defending one's own body or dignity in the moment when the teacher manifests his true skill. A human cutting board who is up to the task can usually receive most of the teacher's authentic transmission. In the process of being rolled into a ball and flattened out by the teacher, through the actual hand to hand contact and the collision of fist on body, one can accurately grasp the subtle movements and changes embodied when each technique's deception becomes the real attack. These subtle hand methods and minute variations, if not experienced directly on one's body, would be like only allowing someone to watch closely, yet they would not be able to discern the wonder of the technique. So, if one seeks to train for real skill, one must not try to preserve one's hide or fear pain, otherwise, one can train a lifetime and only skim the surface, never to immerse deeply into the mysteries of the fist arts.

30– THE HALL OF ENCOURAGING THE GOOD AND COMMIE SPIES

The horror of war is not limited to the carnage of the fighting, rather it is the suspicion and fear that creates White Terrors and unlimited evil.

Scene: The Hall of Encouraging the Good on Liangzhou Street

THE HALL OF ENCOURAGING THE GOOD IS A PRIVATELY OWNED temple situated on Liangzhou Street, the site being near the convergence of the Dihua Street Commercial area and the Liangzhou Street culture and education district. From the temple's statues darkened with the smoke of incense, and the wooden columns, one can see its history. But because it is a privately owned temple, to increase their income the temple committee attached a pensioners' tearoom on the terrace.

The tearoom was positioned cattycorner from the south gate of the Yongle Elementary School, adjacent to the street corner where the Dihua Area Police Station maintained public order and was itself under the watchful supervision of the mysterious spirits and deities. So, this was an honest to goodness tearoom with real goods and fair prices, but it was not like other tearooms, for selling tea was just a front, while selling sexual pleasures was its main source of income.

That age was not like today, where specialty coffee shops have sprouted up everywhere. Pensioners' tearooms were places where everyone chatted, listened to old stories, discussed business, cut their deals. For this reason, besides the presence of people discussing business, frequently at the tables one could see gang bosses dividing their spoils, assemblymen arbitrating profit disputes, the government procurement officers grabbing their kickbacks from businessmen, tax assessment officers hitting up shop owners for money, and Education Ministry school inspectors helping publishers to sell textbooks…from this one microcosm, one could observe the appearance of the accepted social conventions of the time, and various underground commercial machinations. People entering the pensioners' tearoom were not necessarily old nor idle, nor was their purpose necessarily to sip and enjoy tea. A pensioners' tearoom was a hive for the rapid circulation of all manner of information regarding market conditions.

In an age when the relations between the Kuomintang (KMT) and the Chinese Communists were at a nadir, so-called Commie Spies would frequently mix in such places, the main consideration being the ease of receiving and delivering messages. One hears tell of an Investigation Ministry cadre in the company of a local cop and the neighborhood boss, publicly arresting a commie spy right in front of all the tea patrons and the statues of the gods. What is ridiculous, that so-called commie spy was only a poor kid living in a hovel within the Sanyi Market, a kid that besides doing odd jobs would normally take refuge in this tearoom, helping give backrubs and foot massages for spare change. That day, for a meagre sum, he was helping a stranger who had paid him to hand out leaflets. Totally illiterate and feeble minded, how could he know that the cost of making a living could be so ruthlessly high.

Several years later, when a neighbor caught sight of him, he was lame, hunchbacked, almost toothless, and his entire body had a gait like he had suddenly aged twenty years, having become a homeless street person. Even more heart rending, during the period of his incarceration, the investigator seeking a quick win, searched for the boy's family to harass them and extort money. His two aged and dependent parents, no longer able to endure this blood sucking bureaucrat's poison and the torture of an indifferent world, chose a freezing cold night on which to hang themselves, escaping to the bitter relief of death.

This was the era of the White Terror, when these little stories would unfold right next to you on the street. The media of the time was completely in the vice-grip of the authoritarian government, so that when some untoward incident occurred, no one dared stand up to make probes into these hell-bound offenders, or inquire, did the sentence fit the crime? Or, had the hapless accused been smeared? After the incidents had gone down, it was even less likely that anyone would need to take even a speck of responsibility for the vicious behavior that had led to the unjust persecution and unwarranted executions.

Within the temple, the various Buddhas and Gods enjoying incense, offerings and tributes of the believers maintained a persistent silence on topics of a political nature, never once revealing a Spirit or demonstration of Celestial might about the intolerable, the unfair, the unjust, so as to reveal to the masses the truth about these oppressive government curs, to truly deliver the wrath of Heaven and retribution in this world for their conniving, arbitrary imprisonments and draconian executions. They could only affirm that in that age of authoritarian government, to be an official was to be greater than the Gods, and if they said you were wrong, you were wrong. What are you going to do about it?

This lack of rectitude at the top only encouraged the unrighteous to seek government posts through fair means or foul, increasing the number of hands raised to heaven and yet concealing their earthly evil and increasingly unrestrained rapaciousness. Such types knew clearly, this is a coldly indifferent, gutless and forgetful society. One just needed to lay low and be resilient, just needed to have good enough connections, and insist on not preserving one's face, not indulging in regrets, not admitting that the unfairness was not principled, that even the Gods can't pull you up. Wasn't that the wretched reality?

And the pensioners' tearoom was only one stage on which the drama of this age was writ, with all manner of shows playing every day at the tea tables. Each guest who came here cracking watermelon seeds between their teeth and sipping tea, actually, they all wore makeup to play their roles. They listened to the opera, they watched the opera, even sold tickets to the opera, all believing they were themselves not a part of it. Few recognized that what happened on the stage and off the stage was all part of the show, the audience was truly the show, and they influenced the arc of the opera outcomes.

Some of the old customers not only would arrive at the same time each day, but it was their habit to sit at a fixed table, even going so far as to use the same tea utensils and tea leaves brought from home and left for their use at the tearoom. Of course, these old customers would not think of stiffing the proprietor of the tearoom because they had brought their own tea, that is a deficiency of today's society's growing lack of human feelings and mutual consideration for the buyer and seller. Person to person, it usually just takes a miniscule amount of consideration to bring out a wealth of warmth and responsiveness. So, customers, as soon as they had no other pressing matters, would run there, and once a pot was steeping would remain a whole morning or entire afternoon, even during Chinese New Year celebrations, without exception. I have forgotten which famous writer it was, perhaps Balzac, who had a sign over his door with a classic saying for his visitors who paid him a call: "I am at the coffee shop, otherwise I am on my way to the coffee shop!" Coffee and tea are different in strength but applying this saying to that age and those people is the same. Sometimes, even though one might not run into friends, and sat alone steeping in the tearoom, to just prick up one's ears and listen to the boisterous harangue at the next table was excellent amusement.

31– EATING NOODLES, DRINKING TEA, AND TALKING GONGFU

Traditional street side eateries, with a depth of flavor built on decades of life experience forging the recipes, are best able to represent the essence of a locale's food culture.

Scene: Yan-zi's Noodles at the Hall of Encouraging the Good

BEFORE THE DRAGON BOAT FESTIVAL, ON A RAINY, MISTY SUNDAY afternoon, the factories and shops were all closed for the day. The specialty dried goods shops on Dihua Street were doing a brisk business in seasonal ingredients like dried bamboo leaf steaming wrappers, dried mussels, dried krill, dried scallops, shiitake, potato, dried chestnuts, chopped preserved vegetables, salted duck egg yolks, and fried onion, etc., used to make the festival's notable snack, steamed glutinous rice dumplings—*Zongzi*. Dried bamboo leaves take up considerable space and were sold in huge volume, so they were always tied in bundles and stacked in the rafters, even overflowing out into the street. Paying no heed to the weather, masses of shoppers filled the street with an atmosphere of festive joy.

From Dihua Street, if one walked north to Liangzhou Street was Noodle Vendor Yan-zi's stall, renowned near and far for their cut noodles, the most authentic pasta products in Taiwan. Their dumpling soup and dried noodles were "must order" flagship dishes for visitors. Other dishes were braised meat, steamed chicken, fatty pork, smoked shark, shredded liver, intestines, and pig heart, etc. A bowl of especially tender and tasty pig head scraps was set aside by the boss for special customers as his "private reserve." At Noodle Vendor Yan-zi's stall, before 11:00 in the morning, that special bowl of pig head scraps would never be given to casual customers, because the two generations of bosses reserved them for fourth brother Yi-xiang. Only if he did not come by 11:00 would they sell the "private reserve" to other customers.

This is the way it was in that age; a proprietor and his customers formed this kind of relationship beyond the commercial transaction. Perhaps, when viewed from an economic perspective, it was small change, but it created such a strong human connection. In today's marketplaces chasing profits and efficiencies, I am afraid we will never see this kind of gracious offering again.

That day, after eating a sumptuous breakfast at Noodle Vendor Yan-zi's stall,

Master Tu and fourth brother Yi-xiang, as was their habit, sauntered over to the pensioners' tearoom attached to the Hall of Encouraging the Good, to drink tea and chit chat. As usual, they took a table under an archway and savored an aged high mountain Tie Guanyin tea that Yi-xiang had especially brought back from a business trip the day before, to honor his teacher. Because these are highly fermented and aged tea leaves, as one would expect the beverage is a burnt ochre color, with a dark, deep, fragrant flavor, not the kind the average tea customer can appreciate, but Master Tu was an old hand at tea and enjoyed the bitter as if it were sweet.

Fourth brother Yi-xiang was well practiced in tea preparation and took the first rinsing steep of the leaves and dumped it in the bowl of cups to clean and heat them, then Master Tu took his own cup and poured himself some brew. Fourth brother Yi-xiang quietly waited for the water to cool, and only then poured the hot water from the kettle to the teapot from an elevation because when poured at the right temperature from the right height, although the color of the brew was slightly lighter, the flavor was still full-bodied, and as soon as it entered the throat it would dissolve and wash away any lingering oil from their breakfast.

After two or three cups of strong tea, the range of topics discussed would expand. At that time, few practitioners of martial art did not drink pensioner's tea, and tea drinking practitioners of martial arts would rarely sit and drink tea without talking about gong-fu. The topics discussed between master and disciple, rarely diverged from Master Tu's experience during his youth in mainland China, when calling on masters seeking instruction, and anecdotes of time spent in the martial forest. When the old stories were exhausted, the topics slowly moved on to an exploration between the master and disciple of each style of martial art and their strengths and weaknesses.

"Master, what method can be used to quickly disable an enemy, make the enemy lose all fighting capacity in an instant?" fourth brother Yi-xiang asked.

"First you have to ask what the outcome you want is?" Master Tu returned the question.

"Like judo shoulder throws or great reaping throws, these are big moves, injurious or deadly, all you need is to execute this technique and the opponent is done for, and at the same time other opponent's will think twice in their fright," fourth brother Yi-xiang said.

"Such techniques *should* exist in each style of martial art. But the key is not in the technique itself, but the timing of using the technique and the degree one has ingrained in the training. If you can't take him by surprise, as soon as you expose the move, any deadliness is gone," Master Tu said.

"Does Taijiquan have this kind of deadly technique?" fourth brother Yi-xiang asked.

"Although Taijiquan appears soft, warm, and friendly, don't forget, even a bull with short horns is equipped with the power to kill and maim. Like when using some tendon tearing and bone breaking hand techniques, for safety's sake, I usually only employ 30 percent of my force. If I used full force, with one push or one roll-back, I could immediately tear up the opponent's joints, so don't underestimate the power," Master Tu said.

"But those hand techniques, don't they require controlling the opponent to apply them? They should be not so easy to use by those who are scrawny," fourth son Yi-xiang asked.

"Not necessarily. It is not only a death grip that constitutes 'control.' For instance, Taiji's Shoulder Butting—Kao, you can, on the one hand, intercept your opponent's wrist from the inside, at the same time employ Turning Body Force using your own body to shoulder butt the opponent's elbow from the outside. The applied forces of two opposing trajectories thus are released simultaneously, creating a formidable shearing force, so that fundamentally it does not require a strong death grip." Master Tu took fourth brother Yi-xiang's hand, demonstrating and dissecting the technique as he spoke.

"You only need to control at the instant of releasing the force?" fourth brother Yi-xiang asked.

"That's right," Master Tu said.

"So how do you intensify the release of force at the right moment?" fourth brother Yi-xiang asked again.

"Taiji's release of force—*Fajin*—is a technique of instantly unifying and liberating the power of the entire body. The key is in grasping the moment of explosion, grabbing the instant when the opponent is off-balance and his force is dissipated, releasing the force of your body without delay. Thus, the destructive power is maximized. For this reason, sometimes you must seize the moment and the circumstance to directly employ your body's "swallowing and spitting" and inner strength on the spot, to release force," Master Tu said.

"Is power released this way enough?" fourth brother Yi-xiang asked.

"You must look at the situation. The clever use of force to control the enemy in Internal Boxing, so called Clever Energy—Qiao Jin—is using just the right timing, the right technique, and the appropriate amount of strength, to arrive at the destination of controlling the enemy and producing victory. But some teachers make a big deal out of this so as to exaggerate the power of Fajin and avoid talking about Clever Energy. I think it's a con. Actually, what Fajin delves in is relative, not absolute power. You must know that victory or defeat in a fight is not decided by how much force is employed," Master Tu said.

"Where is the difference between relative and absolute power?" fourth brother Yi-xiang asked.

"When weightlifting champions compete, a pound more is the winner, a pound less the loser, this is absolute power to determine victory. In martial arts victory or defeat, strategy, experience, and technique count, with power adding bonus points. It is enough to be just slightly stronger than the opponent. Besides, if you become more powerful, will you be able to hit harder than a Western boxer with a couple hundred pounds of force? So, whatever you do, don't buy this Fajin myth!" Master Tu said.

"Understood," fourth brother Yi-xiang agreed.

"To secure victory through cleverness, one must immerse into strict training. If you can diligently hone an ordinary technique through tens of thousands of repetitions, the power will quite naturally become extraordinary. When you have sunk into your horse stance, maintained it for long enough, naturally, like flowing water digging a ditch, the results will appear," Master Tu said.

"It's like Master always says, 'the guy who practices a fist set a hundred times, and the guy who repeats it ten thousand times, are no longer training the same thing,' right?" fourth brother Yi-xiang said.

"Right. This is the principle of quantitative change and qualitative change. Correct. Not bad, my words have stuck in your mind!" Master Tu said.

"So finally, is there a special way to train this kind of 'instantly disabling the opponent' martial art?" fourth brother Yi-xiang asked.

"In the hinterlands of Southwest China, I heard tell of one kind of secret skill called 'The Art of Controlling the Bull,' specializing in seeking this kind of ability to instantly disable the enemy. But because this martial art technique is too sinister, too easily employed by bad people, after being passed down several generations, it abruptly went quiet and into hiding. Some say the school was destroyed by a rival enemy, so the transmission was not passed down and it was lost. Some say it went underground and is no longer openly taught. Theories about its transmission are many, but no one knows the truth."

"Ai. Yet another fighting skill withering in the light of day. Seems like the world's peerless martial skills suffer the same curse, all of them disappearing just when I have heard of them. Never letting the living witness their veracity," fourth brother Yi-xiang said.

"On this I have a different opinion, I think a lot of fake stuff is actually a reflection of subliminal aspiration and need. Those who truly set their minds to it, who can disregard the cost of following this path of study, will find one day they have accumulated enough knowledge and experience; the fake can then become real!" Master Tu said.

"Put this way, the things I can't see with my own eyes now, doesn't mean they don't exist?" fourth brother Yi-xiang asked.

"Eh. The separation of real and fake is not so absolute. The boundary between them is fuzzy, blurred, obscure, very unstable, and can change at any time. In different times and places, the false can become true, the same way that the real can become fake. Sometimes, the quality can change the quantity, sometimes the quantity can change the quality. This is like the relation between the body and the spirit. Some things the body can do that the spirit cannot. Some things the spirit can do, like crossing a burning expanse, the body cannot do. When they are both present and aligned, they both pull each other, a mutual check and balance, both influencing the opponent and influencing the self," Master Tu said.

"I'm gonna have to spend some time whittling on this to understand it," fourth brother Yi-xiang said.

"You're too serious. Busting your chops over tea, no need to take it seriously, just listen. Actually, I am just being glib, I don't necessarily understand it all. Maybe it's just my character. I feel that regarding profound mysteries passed down, maintaining a little blur, a little romantic longing, is actually a good thing. Doesn't it make the whole world more interesting? Heh, heh, heh!" Master Tu laughed.

32- A CONTEST

When you draw your pistol, you must be mentally prepared to be killed by the other gunslinger. A fight between schools is like a game of chess, once you make your first move, then there will be a winner and a loser. And the victory and loss on the field, often causes grudges off the field, add to that the exhortation and catalyst of by-standers, and it is too easy for situations to devolve into intractable problems.

Scene: Outside of the dike, near The Palace of Heavenly Water

IN THE AFTERNOON, OUTSIDE THE DIKE ON THE RIVERBANK, LEFT of the Palace of Heavenly Water, in the tangle of a banyan tree, it was tranquil with nary a soul stirring, only the two figures of Master Tu and Zhang Jun-feng facing each other, the two dressed in white T-shirts exposing their shoulders, loose fitting white pants and a black leather belt around their waists. In those days, this was the usual classic attire of martial art practitioners in Taiwan.

"Brother Jun-feng, I have received the Hong family elder's request to find a famous teacher of Northern Boxing, I am so thankful for you taking a break from your busy schedule to condescend to teach!" Master Tu said.

"Brother Tu, I am just a businessman trading in fresh fruits, not a dedicated martial arts expert. Since my youth, I yearned for the easy and elegant life of chivalry in the martial forest, so I frequently took the opportunity on my business travels to call on famous masters and exponents who had withdrawn from society, hoping that from my friendships with them, I could widen my horizons, but today I have not come to be recruited to teach," Zhang Jun-feng said.

"Oh, in that case, we won't bring up teaching. Only that you and I both share the love of martial arts, and the elusive Bagua Palm trained by Brother Jun-feng is rarely seen in Taiwan, so I don't know if this could be my lucky chance, to use my Taijiquan and your Bagua Palm to learn from each other, widen our horizons a bit?" Master Tu said.

"So long as Brother Tu doesn't disdain my being an amateur dilettante and is willing to waste his precious time to accompany me in my dabbling, then that is truly all I could wish for," Zhang Jun-feng said.

"Great. So, we don't treat it as a teaching post, winning or losing is not the purpose. Purely a mutual exchange!" Master Tu said.

"That works. Since you are deigning to grant instruction in Taijiquan, so I will use Bagua Palm to face the attacks, besides which I have this suggestion;

for today's comparison we only use techniques from our original styles for the interaction, not mixing in other techniques, and at the same time there is no need to intentionally pull techniques. Okay?" Zhang Jun-feng asked.

"Interesting. The differences and subtle profundity of the different martial art systems should become even more apparent. Still, although this is an interschool match, you and I are just exchanging views, so it doesn't involve a loss of face between the schools," Master Tu said.

"That works for me. Beyond the walls of the dike, this exchange simply never happened," Zhang Jun-feng said.

"Tu Kang-mu, Yang style Taiji, a disciple of Hebei Yang Cheng-fu. Please," Master Tu formally introduced himself.

"Zhang Jun-feng, Cheng School of Bagua, a disciple of Hebei Gao Yi-sheng. Please," Zhang Jun-feng returned.

"Wait a moment," Master Tu suddenly called out.

"Huh?" Zhang Jun-feng asked.

"There is still another rule!" Master Tu said.

"Please speak up," Zhang Jun-feng said.

During our match, we cannot harm these little brothers crawling on the ground!" Master Tu said.

"What is this?" Only then did Zhang Jun-feng discover that around the two men's feet, he did not know when or how, but a riot of small crabs covered the ground.

"Fiddler crabs. This place is their territory where they make a living, today we two are just interlopers borrowing their turf for our trial, so for the sake of the God of the Earth, we cannot but respect them," Master Tu said.

"As you say. Whoever steps on them, buys the tea," Zhang Jun-feng said.

"Okay. Proceed!" Master Tu said.

A match between Northern boxing schools, such as the southern island of Taiwan had not seen thus, quietly unfolded in this secluded grove outside the dike. One was a Taiwan local professional martial arts teacher, one was a martial arts amateur from Shandong province, each expert at their respective fist arts, here at this quiet location along the Danshui River, separated from the hubbub outside, a pact was reached to have a friendly exchange. The two parties agreed this was not to pursue victory or defeat, not to seek fame, and as there were no witnesses, there were no referees, only several local stray dogs sluggishly dozing in the shade of the tree, and on the slick, muddy surface where the tide water had retreated, several mallards that had migrated from the north and refused to return to colder climes, and some nameless northern wild fowl, scrabbling in the mud in search of food.

The competition of fists and feet commenced according to the stipulations in the gentlemen's agreement. Master Tu employed Yang style Taiji, Zhang Jun-feng used the Swimming Body Consecutive Bagua Palms seldom seen in the south. The two styles of martial arts had big followings in Northern China. In Hebei, Shanxi, Tianjin, Beijing, Nanjing, each had a large number of disciples, but in Taiwan in the 1940s, these two fist arts were rarely seen. At the time, the most frequently seen martial arts in Taiwan, besides the Japanese arts of judo and kendo handed down during the colonial period, were primarily the Chinese Southern Shaolin external fist arts. And the source of instruction in these martial arts were mostly lion dance troupes attached to temples, independent lion dance troupes, or bone setters who taught boxing part-time. Only the few businessmen who had travelled to the North, or people who had read about them, would have the opportunity to be exposed to this kind of profoundly deep and concealed combat skills, totally different from external boxing.

The prelude to this encounter between Master Tu and Zhang Jun-feng was actually more complex than their conversation initially revealed. The death of his oldest son from tuberculosis had produced in old Mr. Hong Wu-fan an emotional and nameless resentment toward the external boxing originally practiced in his family. When Master Tu had announced he was moving his family south to Central Taiwan and had resigned as teacher, Hong Wu-fan hastily called especially requesting Master Tu to seek a substitute exponent of Internal Boxing. Due to this unexpected turn of events, Zhang Jun-feng was invited to participate in this selection.

The two renowned martial art exponents of their age, on that sandy riverbank alive with fiddler crabs, thus commenced a battle shuttling their way back and forth, finding footholds between the crustaceans. One unhurried, soft, and graceful, the other undulating as a dragon and snake coiling about each other; one taking advantage of opportunities, the other changing to create opportunities. The aura of one was grand and expanding, the other swirling in eddies. The two persisted in their contest for a dozen or more rounds, no less than 20 minutes. Although a friendly exchange of learnings was agreed beforehand, as experts engaged in a contest, minus any ill will or violent temper nothing else was lacking. The fists flying and the kicks snapping were the real thing, bones hitting muscles. Fortunately, the two were both experts in the accumulation of inner force to protect themselves, and after fighting this long road, besides dripping with sweat, they were left with minor scrapes and light injuries, no major wounds.

"I've met my match, truly a pleasure!" Zhang Jun-feng declared.

"It's still Brother Jun-feng who is the luminary, moving back and forth among the crabs, your stepping and posture remained casual, elegant, like a skilled butcher guiding his knife through the joints!" Master Tu said.

"That is a gift from my masters, they designed this sticking to the ground, foot sliding motion called Mud Wading Stepping, only this allowed me to protect myself with some difficulty on this sandy surface. If not for Brother

Tu's kind heartedness, at several key junctures pulling me back, I fear my two clumsy feet would have committed sins. So, I must insist on hosting our tea today!" Zhang jun-feng said.

"You are too modest, if you had not secretly pulled some of your shots, I would be black and blue. I truly admire you," Master Tu said.

With the unpredictable maneuverings of General Crab, this ground-breaking contest had become more fraught with risk, cleverness, excitement, and challenges.

33– ONE-TON HEAD AND TEN-TON STOMACH

Defense is not passive, reactive non-action. A successful defense more often than not is born of an effective counterattack.

Scene: Left of the Palace of Heavenly Water in the banyan tree grove

"I heard tell in the past about how crafty and cunning Bagua Palm is. Today I can see that sure enough it lives up to its reputation. Brother Jun-feng is such a hidden gem of an expert, if the Hong family misses this chance, it would be a real pity," Master Tu said.

"You are too kind. Brother Tu's Taiji, like needles hidden in cotton, is unfathomable, I never imagined Taiwan harbored such an expert," Zhang Jun-feng said.

"I am saying this without fear you will deride me, if it weren't that I took a good stance and played with some of my tricks and these crabs distracting your attention, I fear that early on I would have fallen to you," Master Tu said.

"Ah, the troops, strange in their ways. Part of Master Tu's calculus for victory, you winning was inevitable and right. I was, after all, bold but clueless. Ha-ha-ha," Zhang Jun-feng laughed.

"Brother Jun-feng, if you do not think it too forward, please allow me to state again my sincere view, can you reconsider this teaching position?" Seeing that Zhang Jun-feng did not object to this subject, Master Tu continued to speak. "Although the elder of the Hong family built his fortune in the world of business, he conducts himself sincerely and righteously, not like the average businessperson bent solely on profit, and he has been especially loyal and financially supportive of we lovers of the martial arts, never letting us down. More importantly, the several young bucks in the Hong family are each good material for training martial arts, if they can receive a transformation under the guidance of a famed master like Brother Jun-feng, then northern fist arts will take root on this southern island, and I believe that the spirit of Bagua Palm's progenitor will be happy in heaven with this outcome."

"Transmitting northern boxing in the south, planting shoots of Xingyi and Bagua in Taiwan? Eh, I never thought about it before. Let me give this matter some careful thought," Zhang Jun-feng said.

"Good. Anything less than a rejection can be managed. Taiwan's local boxing development has been impacted by excessive street performance and religious processions; many originally effective techniques have already been buried under operatic movements on the stage. Even the Taiji I train has become tame, it originally had combat effectiveness in a fistfight, but by degrees it is losing its original character and wild nature. Looks like it is just a matter of time before it will unavoidably lean toward the fate of being 'calisthenics,'" Master Tu said.

"I have the same feeling as you, Master Tu. Actually, I don't know where the situation is heading in China either. Traditional martial arts already can't keep up with the trends of the age, the road gets narrower the longer we go. Besides being reluctantly preserved as a body building exercise, I am afraid there is not much of a rosy future we can expect," Zhang Jun-feng said.

"These skills passed down hundreds of generations, we shouldn't let them go dark in our generation, we must think of a way to pass them on," Master Tu said.

"Although I am passionate about martial arts, after all I am just a businessman, most of my mind is on buying and selling. Considering Master Tu's words, to tell you the truth, I have never looked that far ahead. Never thought deeply about it," Zhang Jun-feng said.

"So, you must plant some shoots, just pass it down, then it will survive. You only need one or two talents sufficient to pick up the craze, then you don't have to worry about it not continuing," Master Tu said.

"Brother Tu, I understand your intention. Please rest assured. I will think about this matter, give me a little time," Zhang Jun-feng said.

"Fine. Besides this, Little Brother has a request," Master Tu said.

"Too polite, please just tell me," Zhang Jun-feng said.

"In Taiwan martial arts circles, word has it there is a lost martial art skill called One Ton Head and Ten Ton Stomach. I have heard tell that Brother Jun-feng's inner qi of your dantian is famed in Northeast China, I don't know if I could be so fortunate to see it?" Master Tu asked.

"That is a method of energy training exclusive to our school. After I underwent an alchemic transformation under my senior, Wu Meng-xia's direction, despite great concentration and austerity, in the end I was unable to achieve the result. However, since Brother Tu has not turned his back on me, Jun-feng will give Brother Tu a clumsy demonstration of my lack of skill." Whereupon the two men stepped back from each other, each concentrating on their breath.

"Ready. Brother Tu, it's time to release your force, but you must be mindful of your wrist." Zhang Jun-feng took a Bow and Arrow Stance and stuck out his stomach, his two hands supporting his waist, fully prepared to perform the Ten-Ton Stomach.

"Ready. Brother Jun-feng, you also take care!" Having spoken, Master Tu placed his full attention and energy into his two feet, the soft sand under foot immediately giving way, sinking an inch, awaiting the release of force when it reached its apex, the rear foot springing forward launching the fist toward Zhang Jun-feng's dantian the center of his energy below his navel.

Facing this full power attack from Master Tu, Zhang Jun-feng, who had accepted the challenge, did not put his entire focus onto his own body, contrarily, he ploughed his attention into the speed and distance of his opponent's oncoming attack, at the same time employing the precise rhythm matching the opponent's attack. Before, his body was bowed, sunken back like a prawn with his energy concentrated on the point that would receive the strike, his Cinnabar Field. Waiting until the approaching fist was a distance of two handwidths away, he suddenly locked his breath and flexed his abdomen surging forward a half step, and with the method of "The Best Defense Is an Attack," collided with Master Tu's right fist as it was striking in.

This unyielding, nay surging forward, counter force counterattack of Zhang Jun-feng's was completely counter intuitive to principles of attack and defense, such that all of the preparation Master Tu made to release his punch, all the planning of an effective distance to land the attack, suddenly became shortened. This forced his fist before it had reached an optimal point of impact to hit its target early. This seemingly insignificant change, conversely at the key moment, created an extremely destructive action. The collision of a fist on a stomach suddenly switched their attack and defense roles, the attacking weapon became the target of a counterattack, all the momentum and mass was entirely returned to the weakest point, and the contact point of these two bodies in motion was precisely where Zhang Jun-feng had specially reminded caution, the wrist joint. With the sudden occurrence, there was essentially no time to put on the brakes or modify the technique, hence the ligaments in Master Tu's wrist let out an audible "snap", and because of the severe pressure put on the joint, it was severely twisted, such that intense pain immediately filled Master Tu's body and his frame drained of spirit in defeat.

Master Tu bore the pain to his marrow and said, "So that's how it is. Worth it. It's worth it."

34– TAIJI PUSH HANDS ON THE RIVERBANK

It is not that "Four Ounces can Overcome a Thousand Pounds," and also not ""Using the Few to Attack the Many." It is avoiding direct confrontation, creating a relative circumstance, forcing the absolute majority to be dispersed by the unknown minority, and allow the absolute minority to concentrate into a relative majority. Afterwards, again the relative majority defeats the relative minority. Therefore, in the end it is the many victorious over the few. During the Shogun's Bakufu rule in Japan, when samurai faced "One against Many" disadvantages, the only strategy that could turn the tables on victory was just one word "Flee." However, this flee was not a "running for one's life" flee. It was intentionally fleeing so as to have the enemy give chase. Each person's capacity to chase and give fight is not the same. This variation will naturally take the advantage of the large group and break it up into several smaller units. The samurai took opportunities to flee on the one hand and watch for a chance to turn and face an opponent one on one on the other hand, thus finishing off his enemies individually.

Scene: On the riverbank

"CAN FOUR OUNCES TRULY PARRY A THOUSAND POUNDS?" FOURTH brother Yi-xiang asked.

"This is the same as the principle of The Few Attacking the Many," Master Tu said.

"To hear Master tell it, intuition can't be that simple," fourth brother Yi-xiang said.

"And it's not that complicated either. However, these techniques or strategies don't exist on their own, they require other prerequisites and conditions to accompany them to work," Master Tu said.

"What conditions?" fourth brother Yi-xiang asked.

"Force is directional. A fist striking out, besides its force in the direction of the target, is very weak in other axis," Master Tu said.

"Like a bicycle barreling in at me, it's dangerous if I try to face it head on and stop it, but if I move to the side, just a little push and the bike will topple," fourth brother Yi-xiang said.

"Eh, this example is spot on. The key to 'Four Ounces Parrying a Thousand Pounds' is 'Avoiding the Substantial and Attacking the Insubstantial,'" Master

Tu said.

"So, it is not four ounces taking on a thousand pounds head-to-head. It is taking action at the flank or the weak point of the thousand pounds?" fourth brother Yi-xiang asked.

"That's right. The reason why Taijiquan can "use the soft to overcome the hard", the alprincipal skill is to lead the opponent, and when the opponent's force is over extended, divert it off its original track, letting it 'fall into emptiness,' causing the opponent to lose balance. Take advantage of this momentary gap to strike from the flank," Master Tu said.

"Is this method of absorbing what is called 'Transforming Energy'?" fourth brother Yi-xiang asked.

"Hmm, but you are not transforming all of the opponent's incoming force," Master Tu replied.

"So how do you do it?" fourth brother Yi-xiang asked.

"If you have no capacity to seize an opportunity and counterattack, then one attacks while one defends, until it is a stalemate, so doesn't the result end up with the same old confrontation? You should put the opponent's force to good use, let him eat the fruit of his own effort!" Master Tu said.

"How to do that?" fourth brother Yi-xiang asked.

"Use a feint to draw out an energetic response from the opponent, then use a yielding technique to break his balance, remove his ability to defend, afterward seize the opportunity to shove him or hook his feet, completely borrowing his own projection of force to injure him," Master Tu said.

"So, I must seize the instant of the opponent falling into emptiness to strike?" fourth brother Yi-xiang asked.

"Right. This is the moment when the efficacy of your strike will be best, this is the secret of Four Ounces defeating a Thousand Pounds. With this method I have faced opponents using Iron Shirt and Hard Qigong, it is just as effective," Master Tu said.

"It can even bust through Hard Qigong?" fourth brother Yi-xiang asked.

"Yeah. Because when a person loses their balance, their mind goes blank, they can only think about regaining their center. In that instant, any innate tendency to defend themselves or the ability to react is temporarily lost. It doesn't matter what you have been training, it is all the same," Master Tu said.

"I will remember this," fourth brother Yi-xiang said.

"Another point. Between attack and defense, you can't misinterpret the intention of the quiet producing the active, only defending and not attacking, always passive is not right either. The ultimate aim of defense is to counterattack, only this is correct. Only a timely and effective counterattack, is the best way of ending a fight," Master Tu said.

"Good. I will be diligent in amending this weak point," fourth brother Yi-xiang said.

"Usually, we infer many different countermeasures for responding to an opponent's attack. However, the key is that you must understand how to use the intended result to create your push back, thinking about how you want to counterattack, then you have to make your opening move," Master Tu said.

"At the same time, I am dissolving the opponent's attack, I set up the counterattack?" fourth brother Yi-xiang asked.

"Right. The design of the forms is following this logic, simulating all manner of possible situations. After going through repetitive and incessant training, take these hypothetical possibilities and implant them in your reflexes, allowing them to become a type of instinctual response," Master Tu said.

"Undergoing persistent repetitive training, it makes attack and defense become an innate response?" fourth brother Yi-xiang asked.

"Not only that, you have to link attack and defense together, until the merger of attack and defense is effectively overlapped. In a real fight, you can't follow the sequence of the training form, using it in fixed order. You mustn't stubbornly stick to a couple of techniques you think are handy," Master Tu said.

"Master, is what you are pointing out termed 'crossing the bridge and building the bridge?'" fourth brother Yi-xiang asked.

"That's right. If you have a bridge to the opponent, then cross it, if you don't have a bridge to the opponent, then build it. You can't just embrace one subjective view of the fight from start to finish, you want to allow your intuition in the moment to rule, thus you will not be influenced by fixed patterns," Master Tu said.

"I feel that Pushing Hands is a method of training to break up fixed patterns and return to reality. Seen only on the surface, Pushing Hands nearly operates to a fixed pattern, but actually the person pushing is sensing tactile information from which myriad rapid changes can be launched, and moreover, in the moment, you must immediately respond to the opponent's probing and attacks, so basically there is no time to think," fourth brother Yi-xiang said.

"Right. They say there is yet another kind of secret transmission called 'Strolling' or 'Dispersing Hands.' This form of facing training is freer—you can stick and adhere or lose contact with their arms, you can employ fixed stances or be mobile, presenting a myriad of changes, all treacherously unpredictable!" Master Tu said.

"Will we be able to train this kind of gongfu?" fourth brother Yi-xiang asked.

"I have only heard tell of it. Sadly, until this day, I have never had a chance to see it with my own eyes," Master Tu said.

"I hope I have the chance to experience it!" fourth brother Yi-xiang said.

"That reminds me. A couple of days ago, I received your father's instructions, directing me to help you seek out an even more illustrious master. After interviewing a bunch of them, I was fortunate enough to run into a businessman and exponent from China and sparred with him. When we had a go at it, although the opponent did not use full force, I am very clear that this chap's gongfu is better than mine in all respects. He trains two types of internal boxing from northern China, called Xingyiquan and Baguazhang," Master Tu said.

"How are they different from Taijiquan?" fourth brother Yi-xiang asked.

"Xingyi, Bagua, Taiji are the three main axis of Chinese internal martial art. Internal boxing trains three kinds of force, overt, hidden, and changing. Bagua Palm methods are cunning and varied, it trains covert, hidden energy. Xingyi fist principle is to use the simple to overcome the complex, it trains the one punch kill overt energy. Overt, covert, changeable energies, although each stands alone, they complement one another and cover each other's deficiencies. If one is thinking to receive the entirety of Chinese internal boxing method's essence, I feel one should enter from Xingyi boxing's overt energy, proceed with Bagua Palm's covert energy and finally study Taiji's changeable energy. If one can follow this process immersing oneself in hard training, it shouldn't be too difficult to reach the highest levels of internal martial arts," Master Tu said.

Master Tu and fourth brother Yi-xiang, were standing atop the nine-nine-meter high, 0.6-meter wide dike, training fixed stance pushing hands attack and defense. With this kind of elevated activity, any slip up could result in serious consequences. Moreover, this specialized training method was a way Master Tu thought up for fourth brother Yi-xiang to overcome his fear of heights. They, master and student, always used this extreme method to force themselves to face their own weaknesses. To force themselves under pressure that could not be evaded or retreated from, to strengthen their bodies most intuitive, most instinctual capacities. They would push and then chat, trying attacks and defense, until the surrounding light became the color of deep water, like a pendulum swinging back and forth they attacked and defended, from a clear blue cloudless sky changing to the resplendent riot of sunset pinks, until the quiet of evening filled the entire firmament, until a vast sky of stars framed the moon, they, master and disciple, the two of them shuttled back and forth, not stopping, not resting, their figures could be seen clearly atop the wall.

Hong Yi-xiang demonstrates the control method of sticking to a visiting karate expert, 1987.

At the Hong Kong Goju Ryu Karate headquarters, Master Hong teaches close quarter combat, 1976.

35– GOADING INTO ACTION

Under certain circumstances, the many must be subordinated to the minority. A barrel's capacity to hold water is not determined by how many of its wooden slats are long, but by the length of its shortest slat.

Scene: Dadaocheng's Guide Street

ALTHOUGH DADAOCHENG'S GUIDE STREET WAS ONLY A NARROW, four-meter-wide street, but here was hidden a colonnade of Dutch style architecture. The people who lived nearby all knew, if the subject was the refinement of the architectural adornments and grandeur of the interior decoration, the luxury residences here beat out the homes of the Dihua Street merchants many times over. If the subject was financial power, the owners hidden within these grand residences held in their hands the market and lifeblood of the underground lending for the Greater Taipei area, and on the surface these wealthy tycoons' business was cloth, tea, or imported items.

The front hall of the Cai Family Tea Shop was a place used for discussing business, the rear was a courtyard filled with all manner of flowers and herbs. To be able to stand among the Western styled buildings at Guide Street was to have made it to the big times. The owner's son, Cai Wan-cheng, together with two brother students from the Taiji class, Luo Ying-jian, and Hong Wan Mei Trading House's fourth son Hong Yi-xiang, were all three relaxing outdoors on the second-floor balcony, drinking tea and chatting. Only Luo Ying-jian, contrary to his usual happy go lucky, self-confidant style, put on a face like he had just swallowed bitter melon, drinking cup after cup of tea in low spirits.

"Hey, this tea's quite costly, you're gulping it down like a cow at a trough, you're drinking through a mountain of gold's worth of tea," Yi-xiang said.

"Yeah, what is it, your wife run away?" Wan-cheng joined in mocking him.

"It's no use training this. What we're training is fundamentally not genuine Taiji. Basically, it is not up to facing off with anyone," Ying-jian declared.

"What are you blathering about?" Yi-xiang asked.

"What? That fellow showing off outside kicking the steel plates? Where'd he come from?" Wan-cheng asked.

"Came from Shanxi, family name's Wang, what he plays is the real Taiji, ours is anything but," Ying-jian said.

"Genuine or fake is not determined by you alone winning or losing. You're not that great," Yi-xiang said.

"Yeah, I agree with what Yi-xiang said!" Wan-cheng said.

"But isn't the result the same, our training can't overcome the other guy!" Ying-jian said.

"That's just your skill not being up to the other guy's. It is not enough to represent whether a school is good or bad. You are just representing yourself—you know?" Yi-xiang asked.

"That's right. What you said doesn't square with reason. And it's not fair to Master Tu either!" Wan-cheng said.

"But the spectators at the scene watching the commotion just see the result, if you lose on the basis of your fists, you can't win afterwards on the basis of your mouth," Ying-jian said.

"You bastard. One guy showing off stirring up trouble, and the teacher and whole school have to take responsibility," Yi-xiang said.

"So, what can I do about it?" Ying-jian asked.

"Apply yourself. You lost face, you should train harder, win back your face based on your fists," Yi-xiang said.

"If it's just training the same old thing, then for sure there is no regaining face," Ying-jian said.

"You…at the time you started this, how come you didn't think of this outcome?" Yi-xiang asked.

"Yi-xiang, I got your meaning. But if he can't win his face back, it's really letting down Master Tu!" Wan-cheng said.

"Thanks for nothing. Such confidence in me," Ying-jian laughed bitterly.

"And you can still laugh about it," Yi-xiang said.

"Seems I am now loathed by others whether I cry or laugh," Ying-jian said.

"You! Serves you right," Wan-cheng said.

"Since this is the way it is, so as not to drag down everyone, I'll just quit," Ying-jian said.

"You lose so you quit, leave a mess for others to clean up, where is the victory there? You quit or not it's your choice. You must face your own conscience, though," Yi-xiang said.

"Yi-xiang, if he goes and loses master's face in front of a big audience, it can't be gotten back, our school won't be able to face the public," Wan-cheng said.

"If not for his boasting, who could force him to make a fool of himself? If one dares to deliver the challenge, one has to take responsibility for winning or losing. The loser is blaming heaven and others, even complaining that Master's teachings are not genuine, this is really a loss of face," Yi-xiang said.

"Winning and losing is a common event, the thing is to get over it and make in-roads," Wan-cheng said.

"I understand this in principle, but there is really no way I can persuade myself, to waste more time training this stuff that clearly can't beat other people," Ying-jian said.

"Okay, so you tell me, how did you lose face that day, I will use the same 'stuff' to prove it to you, that it is your fault, it is not a problem with Master's teachings." Yi-xiang's competitive spirit was already aroused.

"That guy's stance was so stable, I heard that he won many push hands championships in China, he is best at 'dropping roots into the earth' and uprooting. With these two skills in combination, no one who has crossed hands with him has been able to evade this move," Ying-jian stood up and imitated the moves the opponent had used that day.

"Okay. Let's find a day to meet up with him, not for a match, I just don't believe there is a move that can't be broken down," Yi-xiang said.

As soon as Luo and Cai heard his determination to take up the challenge, the two of them could hardly hide their joy, knowing that their ruse had worked. They exchanged knowing glances, but their faces were yet resolute with righteous indignation. "That's too good. Finally, someone is willing to stick their head out to demand justice. Tomorrow we will go over together," Ying-jian said.

"Tomorrow? You go yourself tomorrow," Yi-xiang said.

"What the hell? Backing out?" Ying-jian asked.

"No. Sun Zi's Art of War says, 'First seek victory, then seek battle,' Round One was lost already, besides the opponent is a mainland China push hands champion. Since this is a matter of honor or disgrace for our teacher and school, I don't want to cross hands without careful consideration, I have to make sufficient preparation, must seek out a route to crack his strength, then cross hands with him," Yi-xiang said.

"Right. Tomorrow is just to start your preparations. Then we'll make the courtyard downstairs our secret training base, I'll be responsible to sort out all the equipment, food, and drink." So as to encourage Hong Yi-xiang to step up and do battle for the sake of the school, Cai Wan-cheng shared his excitement like he himself was taking up the challenge.

"In that case I'll take responsibility to recruit some good sparring partners to be fist fodder," Ying-jian said.

"Most importantly, don't let Master Tu know," Yi-xiang said.

Thereupon, a Taiji Push Hands challenge match, under the scheming of the two diehard sidekicks, Cai and Luo, goaded fourth brother Yi-xiang toward an unknown battlefield.

36– CELEBRATING THE DRAGON BOAT FESTIVAL

The street is the best training hall. No rules, no referee, no rest between rounds, no "fair and just," no problems with cheaters breaking rules. Street fights have only one simple rule: the first to go down is the loser. Any martial art that cannot thoroughly protect the artist against an unexpected conflict, overcome the enemy and create victory, even if it always wins in the ring, is not worth a dime.

Scene: Guide Street—The Cai family courtyard

"Fifth Month, Fifth Day, Dragon Boat Festival, Shout Hooray!" According to the customs passed down by the ancestors, on the day of the Dragon Boat Festival, children will all don a "fragrant pouch" hand stitched by the clever hands in the family. The elder women suspend bouquets of Sweet Flag and Lemongrass above the lintel to ward off insect pests and evil spirits, only to take these fragrant herbs down after nightfall, place them in a large wok in the kitchen, and infuse them in a special bath water. It is said that bathing in this kind of lemongrass-infused water prevents mosquitoes from biting.

At the balcony of the second floor of the Cai home, womenfolk and servants divided themselves into two groups, each busily stuffing salty and sweet glutinous rice dumplings. In the kitchen, the old grandmother still wielded authority over all Cai family matters besides business. In line with her experience over decades as a daughter-in-law dominated by her mother-in-law, she commanded the womenfolk to put the cooked short-grain glutinous rice into the large iron pot. The broth in the pot was first made by sizzling yellow onion and ginger slices in sesame oil until their fragrance exploded, then in succession adding golden hook shrimp, shiitake mushrooms, and fatty pork belly cut into chunks, where they were stir-fried together, finally adding homemade soybean oil and braising until done. When the lightly colored and plump glutinous rice kernels were dumped into the rich and fragrant decoction, it immediately was colored a beautifully delicious golden yellow color. The women of the kitchen stir fried the oily rice with large wooden handled spatulas, straining to toss the glutinous kernels in the wok, entirely distributing the sauce among the grains, allowing each and every one to be coated with juice. A round steamer made of Chinese Juniper could hold five or six strings per round of the prepared dumplings, wrapped in bamboo leaves and tied up. For a large family like the Cai family or the Hong family, one Dragon Boat celebration would require at least five steamers, only thirty strings of dumplings or more would be sufficient for the family members, and to deliver to people.

In that era, between neighbors, relatives, and good friends swapping homemade *Zongzi* rice dumplings, exchanging tastes and cooking styles was a frequent and cordial custom. Especially the week before and after the Dragon Boat Festival, amidst the lunchboxes carried by middle and high school students attending all day classes, there was a single, solid color of dark green *zongzi* wrappers. When lunch time arrived, classmates always exchanged stuff to eat, the better to try out all manner of different flavors. Local students then had a chance to taste Southern Taiwan *zongzi* brought by classmates, and first timers were usually not used to the entirely different texture. Northern *zongzi* use flavored and cooked glutinous rice packed with the stuffing ingredients. Inside there might be found: braised pork belly chunks, salted duck egg yolks, chestnuts, dried mussels, pickled radish bits, yam chunks, ginkgo, etc. After wrapping in the bamboo leaf, the *zongzi* is put in the steamer until it is cooked. Southern *zongzi*, on the other hand, takes uncooked washed glutinous rice, mixed with the sauce, and with raw peanuts for flavor and texture. To this is added all manner of stuffings, which are then wrapped in the bamboo leaf and placed directly in boiling water to cook, until the rice is done thoroughly. The special quality of this method of cooking is that it allows the raw glutinous rice in the *zongzi* to expand, so that the space between the kernels is squeezed tight, turning it into more of a cake, unlike Northern *zongzi*, in which each kernel is defined. So, when Northerners eat Southern *zongzi*, they always feel the rice is a little mushy. And when classmates from the south ate Northern *zongzi*, they also couldn't quite accept them, feeling that the Northern *zongzi* was just oily rice stuffed in a wrapper, the rice, wrapper and stuffings had not integrated into one whole. One can't say one is the "correct" *zongzi*.

Objectively speaking, Northern *zongzi* are best eaten hot, while if you can let Southern *zongzi* cool first and then eat them, it brings out the delightful chewiness of the cakey rice and special flavors. I don't know if habits influence subjectivity, or subjectivity influences habits. Civilizations always clash over differences, creating new preferences and values. Happily, the differences in food culture are not measured in 'right or wrong,'

The clever ways of making Taiwan *zongzi*, "Northern Steamed/Southern Boiled" are not the same, but generally speaking, it does not matter if short or long grained glutinous rice is selected for use, in the kitchen-art mastered in these homes, most all of them would use "old rice" to pack the dumplings. So-called "old rice" refers to rice that has been in the bin for over a year, because the moisture content of newly harvested rice is too high, so that when it is steamed, it will become mushy, not like "old rice" thoroughly dried, the rice texture and mouth feeling will be chewier. Furthermore, according to what gourmands say, to judge whether a rice dumpling is delicious our not, the key is not whether the stuffing materials are extravagant and expensive, but the mouth feeling of the rice and the balance of flavor between the rice and the stuffing. For example, at the popular and long standing Liu Family Meat *Zongzi* shop next to the 18 Kings Temple on the north coast, the best of the many kinds of *zongzi* sold there is not the one with the most plentiful stuffing, or the most precious and expensive ingredients. Conversely, the best is often the most ordinary, cheapest *zongzi*. The reason is not because it is the cheapest, but that it sticks to the original intention, the deliciousness of a *zongzi* is in the balance of the bamboo leaf wrapper, the rice, and the fillings, as one entire flavor experience. Excessive additions of precious ingredients from mountain and sea, besides being a crass grab for the consumers' purse, don't really add anything to this traditional rice specialty.

In the open space of the Cai family courtyard, a group of youth were participating in this instance of "secret planning," and they were all the more animated because the meeting was "secret." According to the techniques described by Luo Ying-jian, they were industriously trying to fathom the action and usage of two skills: "Sinking Roots into the Ground" and "Tearing up by the Roots," or Rooting and Uprooting. They strove to research all possible variations that would arise on a changing battlefield and what countermeasures to take. They took their turns partnering with fourth brother Yi-xiang in pushing hands contests, without exception seeking some way to allow this warrior, carrying the hopes of the group, to defeat the peerless master in one fell swoop and win back the face that had been lost. From the start, not a one of them had put his mind into considering deeply the repercussions might be of taking on this challenge to win back face? They trained straight through to noon, when the old grandmother herself brought a bamboo tray of this year's freshly steamed meat *zongzi*, and everybody took a lunch break. The richly stuffed meat *zongzi* of a wealthy family's kitchen accompanied by the heavy fragrance of a high-quality *Biluochun* tea brightened the spirits of all the guys. For this group of carefree wealthy lads, to have a shared purpose and ideal, everyone pulling hard to advance a shared objective, and for the time being not discussing the final outcome of the battle, brought color, beauty, and a touch of romance to their youth, truly a wondrous inspiration.

"Brother Yi-xiang. When you finish the meat *zongzi*, take a rest. Later this evening I have arranged for several enthusiasts, who have crossed hands with Shanxi Wang, to come and help feed you some techniques!" Wan-cheng said.

"Fine," Yi-xiang said.

"Having invested so much blood, sweat, and tears, you gotta win this fight!" Ying-jian said.

"Strange. Everyone pitching in so enthusiastically to help, its only right I should be feeling grateful, so why do I feel like I have been set up by you, and am being used?" Yi-xiang pointed out.

"Haha! Indeed, nothing escapes you. If it wasn't this way, would you do it?" Wan-cheng exposed his crafty plot with an awkward smile.

"That's right. If you don't step out of your comfort zone, how will you know how great you can be?" Ying-jian said.

"To each his own training. What good is making comparisons? Besides, didn't you already test him?" Yi-xiang said.

"I volunteered to be the pawn ahead of you, our knight, helping you to clear the path, test the water," Ying-jian said.

"Who is gonna believe your BS," Yi-xiang said.

"Yi-xiang, if you can win this back, it constitutes glory for our teacher and school, someone has to stand up and face him. Our school will establish a position in the demimonde of the Rivers and Lakes," Wan-cheng said.

"You've read too many military chivalric novels. This is today's real society, where is the realm of the Rivers and Lakes?" Yi-xiang said.

"No, no. This *you* don't understand. The will of the people, that's the Rivers and Lakes. The Rivers and Lakes is omnipresent, and there are hazards everywhere. You are immersed in it, you just don't realize it," Wan-cheng said.

"Alright. So, we'll just continue with your Rivers and Lakes dream," Yi-xiang conceded.

"This is just one battle, but there is yet another layer of substantial significance of which everyone has lost sight. Think about it, if you take on and defeat a real famous master, afterwards, would any incautious bastards dare come to Dihua Street, to run amuck or try to extort from us," Ying-jian said.

"Humph. I suppose not," Yi-xiang said.

"Isn't this the reason we are training together with the Hong family?" Wan-cheng asked.

"Okay, okay. Let's get back to training and cross those other bridges when we get to them. My heart just feels it is not right to make a move on someone else's turf," Yi-xiang said.

"You think too much. The guy who dares to publicly claim he is king of the mountain, to set up a training hall and accept students, the one who is a veteran of a hundred battles, is the one to worry. Not you worrying for the other guy," Ying-jian said.

"It's a question of attitude. There is no evil intention, just a benign request to receive instruction. Then you don't have to think so much," Wan-cheng said.

"It's all I think about," Yi-xiang said. "You're right. The past few days of training, I've cracked Master Wang's strategy. It is, first break the opponent's center of gravity, then from below pushing upward on the opponent to overturn them. So the key should be the ability to shift the center of gravity in any direction. I am afraid you will have to find several sparring partners with more stable stances or who are heavier, use tonnage to make up for any deficiency of rooting skills."

"Rest assured. The ones I found to come train are all judo or sumo exponents, they won't let you down," Wan-cheng said.

"That's good," Yi-xiang said.

"Ai! You both care too much about technique and theory. Isn't the common expression 'First courage, second strength, third ability'? All along Dadaocheng, who doesn't know you and third Brother are naturally gifted with prodigious strength, what's with this putting aside your gifts and not using them. I think the simplest way should be to use your strength to overcome him, that's best," Ying-jian said.

"Shut up and eat your *zongzi*. You're the one who didn't think enough and got your ass kicked, now telling others to think less," Wan-cheng said.

"I don't think relying on brute force beats people. This is to be a test of skill, not a street fight. Besides, if you overly rely on strength, what do you do in the off chance you come across someone stronger," Yi-xiang said.

"Little Lord Hong, although this is not a street fight, it is also not a formal contest in the ring. This kind of test of skill has no rules, no referee, so whoever goes down, loses. No one will care whether you used skill or brute force. Put another way, isn't the skillful use of force a skill?" Ying-jian asked.

"Yi-xiang, what you said isn't without reason. These streetside tests of skill are very shady. You can't be too naïve. You can't not protect yourself from the opponent using hidden techniques. Furthermore, using strength to knock down the opponent, is also a strategy, to the extent that breaking the rules and cheating are all a part of competitions. So, what is worth having these arguments over scruples? If the opponent can't neutralize the force, it just means that he hasn't perfected his art, one can't blame others," Wan-cheng said.

"I know, at the time, I will act accordingly, looking at the opponent's situation and responding. I just don't want to go into this for winning and losing by hook or crook," Yi-xiang said.

"No, winning and losing is key. Don't forget our original purpose. Isn't it to win back our face?" Wan-cheng said.

"And I just don't like this way," Yi-xiang said.

"Okay, drink your tea. On the field of battle, I doubt you will remain so Confucian, moral, and high minded," Ying-jian said.

37– ASSISTING IN TRAINING

The victorious warrior first prepares for victory, only afterwards seeking battle.
The defeated warrior first engages in battle, then seeks victory.

— *Sunzi's* Art of War

Scene: On the banks of the Danshui River

AT DUSK ON THE DANSHUI RIVER, WITHIN COMPETITIVE LANES separated by floating balls, dragon boat teams were about to enter the final heat of the championship. After heat upon heat of advancement and elimination, the teams that could survive were the elite among the skilled. Only by undergoing an entire day of trials had these select rowers arrived at this juncture, their physical capacities pushed to the limits. Facing this final heat, what would truly determine the margin between victory and defeat was how strong the entire team's will power was to strive for victory. And the source of this striving for victory was frequently how many years of resentment had accumulated on the water. By looking at previous winners, these teams that had pushed their way into the finals were old enemies, well familiar with each other. Over the course of many years, their victories and losses on the water had already become something of a folklore tradition in their villages, and this tradition supported them, spurring on the primordial energy of their bitter training, year after year. Because the winning side always treated the closely guarded hard won victory as tradition, they would never countenance lightly handing this glory and honor over to share with another party. And the losing side, harboring brooding regret over a victory being wrested from their hands at the last moment, pledged to snatch the trophy out of the hands of their enemy, bringing honor to their ancestors and glory to their village. Objectively speaking, their mutual contest often was only about winning and losing, not about improving their technique and certainly was not about so-called sportsmanship. Afterwards, it is only when they bared teeth in the midst of the fight, that technique emerges or improvements were made to the equipment, thus even strategy emerged as a competitive development. Maybe, the origin of civilization itself is just such a fortuitous by-product of this kind of accidental adaptation.

In that era, it did not matter who you asked about the Dragon Boat Festival. You could ask the competitors on the water straining at the rudder and the oars to contest for victory, or the musicians on the shore beating their drums and gongs to rouse the audience, or the spectators enjoying their *zongzi* to tell you the origins of this custom and tradition of the Dragon Boat Festival. They could tell you what but not tell you why.

Besides the elderly familiar with Chinese historical tales or those literate in written Chinese, the average *hoi poloi* would ask, "Who is Qu Yuan? Also, who is Physician San Lyu? Why did he want to jump in the river to kill himself? What did he use his death to make a stand on? What changed after he died? Why do we wrap glutinous rice dumplings on this day anyway? Also, why do we hold the Dragon Boat Races contest on this Danshui River, ten thousand kilometers away from the Miluo River? As for how many years these threads connecting classic stories from history had been hanging out there in a vague mist of space, few people cared to ask.

Besides the master storytellers in the teahouses and temples, or the puppet theaters set up in the open-air gardens, few could recount these old historical events gathering dust. Perhaps this kind of sad tale was insufficiently grand and exciting to rouse the spirit of the people. Perhaps because, in the long flow of China's river of history, there were too many such tragic heroes giving their life for their country. Even more, perhaps during the long periods of foreign domination or colonization of Taiwan, the umbilical cord carrying culture had dried up and withered, with no one to attend to it.

In the age of the Yamato and Japanese Imperial military rule, it was impossible that Japanese language textbooks in the schools would preserve chapters or sections elaborating on Chinese history. The customs handed down among the people from before the incursion of the colonizer's culture were passed on by rote with only superficial understanding, preserving only with difficulty the vestiges and appearance of the age-old customs and traditions. This might be the main reason why, in the common man's awareness, the characters of the Tale of the White Snake—the two juxtaposed roles of the gorgeous, infatuated demoness, and the stubborn old monk with no knowledge of mundane feelings, triangulating with the naïve and handsome youth—are all better known than Mr. Qu's loyalty to his sovereign.[11]

---

11 Qu Yuan was a patriot, poet and advisor to the King of Chu during the Warring States period in which seven feudal states contested. His advice to his king was to ally with one of the states to prevent the Qin state from taking over. Other officials slandered him and he was exiled. When he later learned that Qin had taken over, he drown himself in the Miluo River. The customs of the dragon boat race and zongzi are symbolic of the rescue attempts and offerings to his or the river spirits. There is another origin story for the races also involving a slandered loyal official executed by his sovereign, hence the authors ensuing description of how good men are turned corrupt.

Some people have said, "Under heaven the two most pained and most unredeemed figures are: A hero at the end of the road and a beautiful woman past her prime." Once a proud and loyal official loses the trust and respect of the sovereign, the wisest and most elegant choice is to resign and depart, to write love poems, roam the mountains and eat, drink, and be merry. It is wiser to never again take an interest in the rise and fall of the realm, who is gaining and who is declining in the mundane world of dust. It's only that if we survey China's many millennia history of officialdom, or the world of privilege, those upright, loyal officials who could truly see through privilege, truly make an elegant departure, truly not leave under a cloud, how many were there? History clearly reflects blood and tears, every intellectual, the more books they read, the more determined they were to enter the capital to seek their fame, enter the court and display their talents, to render service to the high and mighty, or to the muddled or tyrannical sovereign and system of authority.

People! Once they become stubborn, they do foolish things. An official who has made it into office and squeezed into the circle of power and influence, once they discover they have lost the power or influence they relied on, it does not matter whatever the reason for being beaten down, they feel stripped naked and without any security. Whereupon, to remedy this abandonment, this sense of loss at being side-lined, they will exhaust any means necessary to return to the core of power.

When people are determined to do something no matter the cost or consequences, when the motivation to reach an objective exceeds everything else, they lose their reasoning and are completely unscrupulous. Hence, writing poisonous rumors to frame someone, using precious jewels and baubles to bribe officials, employing beautiful call girls to entice bigwigs…as one would expect these lowlifes playing scumbag tricks rationalize their actions as pragmatic expedience. Consequently, as past history and even the unwritten future will show, all treacherous officials and villains were once heroes at the end of the road, or pure hearted loyal officials who lost influence, because they had served a licentious, immoral ruler with all their hearts, and were perfectly happy to sink from "honest to heaven and earth" to "have no choice but to" to "by hook or by crook" to "might makes right" to "committing all manner of crimes" regressing into crafty, fawning, vicious scumbags. Isn't it so?

Maybe it is because they didn't know better, maybe it is because they could no longer bear their own circumstances, even more so because they no longer cared. Some tragic epics thus became diluted in the flood of time, by faded memory, by change, simplified into the customs of wrapping steamed dumplings and competing in the Dragon Boat races. Anyhow, this moment of racing on the river, the oarsmen on the boats and the cheering villagers on the banks, one's heart only vested in one thing, keeping the opponent's boat far behind, so as to be able to carry the gleaming glory of the trophy cup back home and bask in the approval and admiration of neighbors, parents, relations, young and old, for the coming year. So, the supporters on the shore, cheering, beating their drums and cymbals, rooting their team on, invested as much energy as the competitors, and cared even more about victory.

On the banks of the Danshui River, to the left of the Heavenly Water Palace temple, in an empty space filled with a thicket of banyan trees, secret training was underway for another showdown. Under the cover of the trees were six tiger-backed, bear-shouldered stalwarts, each relaxing in the shade to cool down. Several were active members of the provincial judo team, several had been sent to Japan to receive formal instruction in sumo wrestling, all were experienced sparring veterans, all were given generous gifts by Cai Wan-cheng, to serve as sparring partners.

"Elder brothers, this is the fourth son in the Hong family, brother Yi-xiang. Seven days from now, he will challenge the Taiji Push hands Master Shanxi Wang on Yuan Shan. So his challenge can succeed, please exert all effort. Under no circumstances do you want to hold anything back. After seven days we hope to destroy Shanxi Wang's undefeated legend," Ying-jian said.

"Ying-jian is just exaggerating. Nobody takestakes it seriously. It's just out of curiosity, I want to go up against Yuan Shan to seek instruction from my elder. Master Tu often says, 'If there is a way, there is a way to break it.' I hope we can all compare notes, see if we can find a better way to break down his unique skill," Yi-xiang said.

"Brother Yi-xiang, rest easy. Winning or losing is not so important to us, whether we can find a technique to beat him is also not important. Anyway, we all have the same interest, just being able to compare notes is a happy thing."

"Great. So, everyone exert yourselves to 'compare notes,'" Wan-cheng said.

In the middle of the river channel, the result of the final heat of the Dragon Boat Race was announced with the reports of a barrage of firecrackers. The audience favorite, the Guandu Dragon Boat Team, had once again defended the championship. Under the banyan tree, the push-hands training, loss by loss unfolded. From time to time, one could see a burly recruit fallen to earth… from time to time, one saw a man flying out…from time to time, one suddenly saw a loss of balance and a body tumbling head over heels…but from start to finish, no one turned tail and gave up. Martial spirit is hard for outsiders to understand. If it is not for prize money, not for the glory of a trophy, not for a place in history, why would anyone happily endure aches, bruises, bleeding, even the pain and injury of broken bones, to pursue skills without complaint or regret, that one might never use one's whole life? Who knows?!

38– CHALLENGING THE MASTER

To come prepared is not as good as adapting to circumstance. All preparations made before the event are for the purpose of increasing adaptability on the field of battle. In the showdown on Ganryu Island, Miyamoto Musashi of the Two Sword School employed a single wooden oar to beat the divine swordsman Sasaki Kojiro, and not the dual swords he was famed for. If a swordsman is excessively stuck on details of victory, and does not know how to adapt, he will miss all key opportunities.

Scene: Yuan Shan

From the moment the two men contacted hands, fourth brother Yi-xiang immediately felt an inner force that could not be pinned down, a ceaseless pressure emanating from the opponent's two palms. This strength sometimes seemed like an underground stream of water, concealing hidden turbulence, attacking straight to one's soul; sometimes it was like a grand wave collapsing swift and heavy in a chaotic roil, swallowing up without a trace any capacity to resist. On making contact, the pushing hands master Shanxi Wang, famed throughout Taiwan, sure enough suffocated the opponent with his immense aura and physical presence. At first, the two men used soft, gentle pushing, like they were warming up, testing from all manner of possible and impossible angles, tossing out "interrogating hands," both feinting and real, to probe the opponent's response and habits, hoping that from these weak and chaotic signals, they could quickly converge on the detailed outline and main threads of the opponent's skill and weakness, all the better to avoid errors and traps. And from the limbs and trunk of his opponent's "answering hands," Shanxi Wang, faintly detected something deeply reserved and elusive. He perceived that this youth in front of him was clearly not like others who had come to challenge him in the past. This fellow was not eager to attack, at the same time seeming to have no intention to bring the fight to him. Conversely, he was more like a partner with whom a tacit agreement had been made ages ago, allowing Wang to just take his time, grudging the use of any ruthless technique to bring this encounter quickly to a close and break the concord. Although both reason and experience reminded him, "This is a siren's song, to be lured is a fatal error," but this well-matched opponent, this feeling of a kindred spirit, let Shanxi Wang decide to continue to accompany playing with this youth. Of course, he was confident his own strengths were sufficient to back himself up at the key moment, to launch a mortal attack. Whereupon he just let his hands direct the opening and closing, rising and falling of the rhythm between them. For that very brief instant, the two competing opponents forgot about winning and losing, forgot antagonistic intents and purposes, as letting go of themselves they entered into a harmony between man and heaven, allowing that kind of joy when one chances upon a new friend who keenly appreciates one's talents to pervade the entire mountain.

And so, this atmosphere was maintained for a period, the two in a rhythm of coming and going, then they seemed to enter a new phase of surging forward with great momentum, at times like giant waves crashing on the shore, billowing and excited, at times like scattered flashes of lightning and thunder from all directions. Shanxi Wang incessantly used all manner of varying speeds and techniques, from all manner of varying angles to launch a series of feints, the purpose being to quickly reach a conclusion about what lay behind the false and the real. Suddenly Shanxi Wang became like a giant inflatable bop bag, now pushing forward then drawing back, now entering left and dragging right, now shouldering up then yanking down, incessantly initiating all manner of attacks, enticing the opponent to extend his hand and counterattack. As soon as the bystanders to this battle saw these wind-up moves, they knew the push hands master would soon launch his *coup de grâce*, "Pulling Up by the Roots." Sure enough, the figure of Shanxi Wang, though ever changing, teasing spectators with fascinating skills, inexorably began to settle deeply. Already as stable as Mt. Tai, in this moment it seemed as if thousands of tendrils of roots spread out from his feet, each tendril insinuating itself into any crack or void in the rock, firmly seizing the bedrock underground, a foundation that could not be shaken on the surface.

However, in a flash of insight, fourth brother Yi-xiang had a distinct epiphany, at the last moment deciding to rewrite the playbook, unexpectedly dropping his original plan and drafting new countermeasures. Because he preferred to trust his own intuition based on comprehension of new intelligence obtained through hand-to-hand contact with the push hands master as a substitute for preconceived battle plans, he preferred the risky impulsive choice. To check Shanxi Wang's "Sinking Roots into the Earth," he thoroughly gave up thoughts of competing with the push hands master at sinking and stability. In this moment, his mind was clearer than anyone's, that against that kind of practical fighting skill accumulated over decades, he absolutely could not vainly rely on a couple of days of secret training to attempt a coup. He could only let himself be like a boat crossing the ocean, persisting amidst the ever-changing swells awaiting a moment of balance to act, only in this moment to launch a victorious attack "Pulling Up by the Roots" until there were no roots left to pull.

One was an invincible Taiji master whose "Pulling Up by the Roots" shocked everyone in Taiwan by routing famous teachers of Taiji, one was a martial genius relying on a flash of wisdom in the immediate moment to rise to prominence. Two experts from different generations, an elevated encounter by lucky chance, each trying to use all their skills and tricks to "persuade" the opponent. "Lift!" Shanxi Wang as expected used the same technique previously tried on Luo Ying-jian, employing the moment of his body sinking down and "Sinking roots into the Earth" to unify his whole internal strength. What was seen, was his originally silky soft and gentle twin palms suddenly issue hidden force, from above pushing down, catching fourth brother Yi-xiang's two wrists, with the intention of forcing the challenger to lose balance and topple forward, then waiting for the instant Yi-xiang exerts counterforce upward, to suddenly slacken his hands, immediately eliminating the resistance and yielding to the challenger's upward inertia, firmly grasping this brief moment of weakness, both palms reversing course to conform with the challenger's momentum releasing the force of a mighty river welling up from below, thus turning the opponent's body into a great tree, ripped up by the roots and cast flying away.

This category of miraculous skill "yielding to force to borrow energy and exert force" on the one hand is borrowing the opponent's own rising strength from below to above, on the other hand it is utilizing one's own forward momentum to seize an opportunity to lift (like handing off a heavy platter), and thus create twice the effect with half the effort in one stroke, thereby lifting the opponent off the earth and making the receiver of the technique fly out in response. This, then, was the master stroke that had laid low innumerable martial art exponents—"Pulling Up by the Roots."

In the martial arts there is a taboo: "expose your move, the strike will fail." And so it is, even the most brilliant techniques one should avoid using over and over, abstaining from "over-cooking" the maneuver. Once a maneuver is exposed to the light, it is very easy for the opponent to break it down and counter. Fourth brother Yi-xiang had adopted a strategy of dynamic equilibrium, to which was added the mystery and clever skill he had grasped of the opponent's Pulling Up by the Roots killer stroke, and for this reason, when he became aware of Shanxi Wang sinking lower, he already accurately foresaw the movements that followed precisely. His two hands feinted upward resistance, enticing the opponent to falsely believe he had fallen for the trap, while secretly holding in store 70 percent of his strength, awaiting Shanxi Wang to exert full force in his master stroke, his epiphany allowed him to abandon his originally designed counterattack, and to decide amidst the skirmish to beat him at his own game.

He imitated Shanxi Wang's method of borrowing force to exert force, and in a flash as Wang's arms started to try to lift him like a platter, he circled his arms around and down, applying the same Pulling Up by the Roots, to deal with

Shanxi Wang's original Pulling Up by the Roots. This deft sudden emergence of change, completely contrary to Shanxi Wang's expectations, coupled with his extremely over-confident application of fully committed force, resulted in a moment during which Wang had no foothold. On top of this, the young challenger yielded to his own direction of force, anteing up the stakes as he lifted up, instantly disintegrating the tight hold of Wang's root on the bedrock, so that his entire body was like it was hit with the great force of a ground swell, nearly uprooting him.

But human instincts in such an instance of impending victory and defeat produce pivotal actions. And so it was, with the outcome of this battle at this critical juncture, fourth brother Yi-xiang's heart took a turn, suddenly terminating the force he had prepared to launch, not allowing the advantage he had accumulated to make good on realizing his victory. On the contrary he withdrew his force and pulled back, stabilizing the opponent's body, so preventing the old master from being humiliated in front of all his students. Already on a dangerous precipice, this sudden unexpected change allowed Shanxi Wang the opportunity to restore balance and catch his breath; moreover, in this instant of give and take, he felt two contradicting hidden forces rush through his body. Although he was not clear what motive was hidden within, making the opponent give up a victory within his grasp, experience told him that when situated within this kind of vague disadvantage, to never rashly seize the opportunity to counterattack. Whereupon he yielded to the opponent's guidance, allowing the interaction, attack, and defense to slowly and gently decrease, in such a way that outsiders could fathom nothing, hence peacefully concluding this challenge between the two champions of their age.

39– A RENOWNED TEACHER'S BEARING AND CONDUCT

"Fighting for victory" and "holding on to victory"; neither is simple. But at the end of "fighting for victory," bitterness is exhausted and sweetness follows, whereas in "holding onto victory," when bitterness is exhausted, more bitterness follows.

Scene: Taipei North Gate Parapet

HIGH AND WIDE WALLS ONCE GUARDING THE CITY HAD LONG AGO been torn down deserting the Gate of Receiving Favor (aka North Gate) leaving a lone sentry. Although its body had stood tall and proud through time's mighty torrent, its intention was now on its last gasp. It insisted to proclaim to future generations its past glory and resplendence, except now its body, faded by the march of time, could no longer command the people of the world to give it even a charitable passing glance. Like an old soldier stripped of his armor with no capacity left to fight, set against the onslaught of traffic from the south traversing the avenues and circus, it continued to steadfastly guard over the historical meaning it symbolized, becoming a nostalgic model that even itself was at a loss to comprehend.

Perhaps. All meaning and value of existence in this world, all of it, is self-opinionated perspective and impractical one-sided reverie. If one does not have the support of those in power or is intentionally repurposed, even this ancient ruin cannot prevent being forgotten in the end, torn down by karma. Unless it can enlist the help of heaven to create a new universal value, one endorsed by mainstream culture, otherwise no matter what protection it provided the people in the past, the torso of this already fragmentary wall must humbly retire from the stage under the grand rotation of time. Thus, its bits and pieces are replaced, turned to dust, and disassembled into the building elements needed for a healthy and strong new world.

Ever since the push-hands challenge at Yuan Shan, Shanxi Wang and fourth brother Yi-xiang surprisingly became the best of friends. The two frequently arranged to take tea or a meal together, and over their post repast tea would chat about all manner of rumors, anecdotes, and incredible phenomena of peerless fighting skills from the martial forest.

Most of these topics were like Pegasus soaring across the sky, unverifiable crazy talk and fantasy, but if not for the romance and omnipotence woven into the imagination of these fallacious ravings, how could so many talented dreamers be drawn into researching and renewing the arts? How could Chinese martial arts have developed with the flourishing vitality we see today? Who can verify if the ""genuine goods at fair prices" was the true gongfu seen today, and was not in its creative inception blended by accident with much make believe turned into reality? However, even if it developed out of accident or delusion, after myriad forgings of real combat and incremental revision, it might yet evolve step by step, morphing into a skill of attack and defense worthy to be passed down to a hundred generations, with the leaves and fruit of its branches scattered the world over.

Embracing this zeal these two martial arts fanatics and friends would regularly seek out the places no one went. Deep into the mountains and green gorges they ventured together to train, exchanging martial skills. There they endeavored to explore all manner of the miraculous and the possible within the inner universe of the human body according to the health cultivation methods of Daoist alchemy. Among their chosen secret training retreats, this old city Northgate tower, nearly forgotten by humanity, was their favorite. Perhaps training within the ruins of this ancient battlement heightened their awareness of a grand air of ancient, awe-inspiring, unyielding integrity. Perhaps the ancient tower was already old to the point where no one bothered to even look at it.

"I circulated the news myself!" Shanxi Wang said.

"Why do this?" Yi-xiang asked.

"Of course, it is to protect myself," Shanxi Wang said.

"How can that be?" Yi-xiang asked.

"People's talk can be dreadful. Rather than allow other people to spread embroidered stories and malicious gossip, better to push the truth out myself," Shanxi Wang said.

"Elder. You care about these rumors and gossip?" Yi-xiang asked.

"Who doesn't fear it? In brief, once I clearly explain myself, there is no reason for others to talk," Shanxi Wang said.

"I never imagined there could be this kind of blowback," Yi-xiang said.

"Don't blame yourself. Losing, winning, it's normal. If one fights, one must shoulder the loss or the victory. To speak of it, I have been occupying that perch too long. Enough. To speak the truth, in that moment I worried I would suffer an even more embarrassing loss. I want to thank you for extending a hand of mercy, so I can use this way to leave the ring without losing my old face!" Shanxi Wang said.

"Besides apologizing, I truly don't know what to say," Yi-xiang said.

"No apologies need be said. Over the long term, letting you face even more challengers in your youth is right, then you will be compelled by distinct challenges to develop quickly," Shanxi Wang said.

"I have a long way to go. Tell you the truth, ours fundamentally cannot be considered a fair competition," Yi-xiang said.

"No. Martial art is originally about those with intent beating those without intent, the fast overcoming the slow. Doesn't matter if the intent was spur of the moment or premeditated, once fist and feet are employed to determine winning and losing, so the win and loss in that match is *the* verdict," Shanxi Wang said.

Yi-xiang waited for the old fighter to continue.

"It is also better for me this way. Using this opportunity to climb out of the ring, my face is preserved, my high rank is also preserved. Also, I had an ulterior motive in promoting the young generation. Ai! Me. I have played Taiji Push Hands all my life, and this was the pushing I am most proud of. Ha, ha, ha!" Shanxi Wang laughed.

"Elder, it was pure luck I got away with it. I can't shoulder this burden," Yi-xiang said.

"I am not being polite, when we push again, let's see if I can't win back my confidence in the same way," Shanxi Wang said.

"Really, I have the same feeling," Yi-xiang agreed.

"For your part, you need this pressure on you to continue your rapid development. For my part, now the thing I want most is to find again this kind of simple pleasure," Shanxi Wang said.

Yi-xiang was silent in his thoughts.

"To be unable to lose, this is a heavy burden. It made it so for a long time I have not been able to enjoy this kind of light-hearted Push Hands," Shanxi Wang observed.

"If that was the case, why did you continue to accept challenges?" Yi-xiang asked.

"Some things we cannot control. Once standing on that perch, it becomes a duty. A duty to be another's moving target, can't be avoided. Just like playing chess, if there is no conclusion, can you call it a game?" Shanxi Wang said.

"Hmm," Yi-xiang muttered.

"From when the non-polarity of the primal chaos divided into yin and yang, the chaos of a battle becomes clear with a winner and a loser. Although we know there is a winner and a loser, one day when you are, in the words of others, a 'great master,' your students, your family, their respect for you and their expectations of you will make it so you simply cannot lower yourself," Shanxi Wang.

"As far as I am concerned, this is all too remote, too abstract," Yi-xiang said.

"No, believe me, you are not far from that step. When I reflect on the past, before I became a great master, every time I challenged an exponent and won, I admit I felt very happy. But I could even more appreciate after losing a fight, that feeling of immersing myself in hard training, so as to find a way out, the carefree satisfaction of going after a clear goal with all my might," Shanxi Wang said.

"When we were doing the training in secret, that's the way I felt," Yi-xiang said.

"Even at this age, I still really love that kind of hard focused training, the thrill of going for it. My experience tells me, every setback is a message from life compelling you to transform and advance. If a person remains too long in one place, it is easy to become complacent. Over the past decades, I have relied on opponents being unable to deal a shock to my rooting, after I discovered that strategy of Pulling Out by the Roots. Because I was never defeated, it made me more rigid in this strategy, mistakenly believing that only sticking with this proven technique was enough to deal with all comers. Who knew that dynamic equilibrium of yours would make it so for a moment, I had entirely no idea what was best," Shanxi Wang said.

"I took advantage by trickery, pirated your own technique," Yi-xiang said.

"No. You used strategy, outsmarted me. Outsmarting is the final goal of the martial art. When two powerful contenders are matched in strength and rank, the more agile thinker between them will certainly emerge victorious. Martial arts training in the end comes down to your wisdom in the ring. Not your skill with fist and foot," Shanxi Wang said.

"Thank you for being willing to tell me so much," Yi-xiang said.

"I also want to thank you for presenting me with this precious bottle of wild mountain ginseng wine, come. Let's toast a glass together!" Shanxi Wang said.

"Bottoms up," Yi-xiang said.

"Finally, I want to share with you an insight I have traded a lifetime of experience to obtain. That is, under no circumstances do you let people start calling you 'Grand Master' too early. I tell you, it's no fun!" Shanxi Wang said.

"I know. It's the only way to preserve my right to make mistakes and enjoy the happiness and unlimited possibilities martial arts brings me," Yi-xiang said.

"Hmm. Unlimited possibilities. I like this way of expressing it, full of hope. Come. Bottoms up!" Shanxi Wang said.

Because it was still early, the automobile and pedestrian traffic on the avenue remained sparse. Without the separation created by the old city wall, the central part of the city mainly Boai Road and Chongqing South Roads, and the Dadaocheng area, mainly Dihua Street and Yanping North Road, were fused together early on into a functionally complementary, mutually symbiotic section. Moreover, at this intersection where Yanping South Road and Boai Road split, to allow old steam engines coming from the south to smoothly access the nearby Taipei Main Station, the safety gantries at the intersection would drop for half an hour or more, in complete disregard for the winding dragon of pedestrian and automotive traffic backed up several hundred feet. Though this set people to cursing and gnashing their teeth at the gantry, it assured that each train could smoothly arrive according to schedule. It also played the role in this modernizing world creating a new kind of border between the inner city and the outer city. Today after electrification and tunneling, besides relieving the traffic nightmares of that period, even this vestige of a dividing line has been wiped away, forming in the jigsaw puzzle memories of the post-war baby boom generation a hard to replace piece of another blurred boundary.

40- THE 228 CONFLICT

No single event exists in isolation. Each "randomness" has its own element of inevitability. Even something seen with one's own eyes is only a unique perspective of a moment in space and time, not necessarily the truth of the whole picture.

Scene: Dadaocheng

ON FEBRUARY 27, 1947, TWO SPECIAL AGENTS FOR ANTI-SMUGGLING in the Monopoly Bureau, Ye De-gen and Fu Xue-tong, led six policemen near the Pegasus Teahouse to crack down on private cigarette sales by Lin Jiang-mai, a woman selling imported cigarettes illegally, and a dispute broke out when they moved to confiscate the smokes and cash. In the fray, the special agents opened fire, injuring the old lady Lin, and accidentally killed an onlooker, Chen Wen-xi, fueling the crowd's fury. The mass of local onlookers arose, chased, and beat the Monopoly Bureau's agents, and gathered at Police Headquarters and the Military Police Central Command, demanding the relevant authorities of the government give a fair response to these events. On the day of February 28, because of this demonstration by the crowd, the citizens of Taipei suffered completely unjustified executions at the hands of government officials, creating a disastrous bloodbath, henceforth igniting within the populace long pent-up dissatisfactions and violent conflict.[12]

On the street, when one side was larger, they would chase and beat the smaller side. In the beginning, maybe only because the dispute had not been handled equitably, some people filled with righteous indignation and rage stood up, out on the streets unburdening themselves of accumulated rancor and discontent. In alleyways, when the outnumbered got backup manpower, they would return to beat back the original larger side.

In the beginning, maybe it was only a response to an innocent emotional backlash. By the end, after people had been injured in the rioting the entire incident slowly devolved into a deeply personal animosity in which no one could fathom who was right and who was wrong. Even worse, those with the power and authority to arbitrate matters of right and wrong, truth and error, to maintain fairness and justice, demonstrated no capacity at this key moment in history to manage this thorny issue, to employ a humble sincere attitude and a way to let the masses have faith and feel consoled. Conversely, they wielded the

---
12 For more about the 228 Incident, see Graham Kerr's *Formosa Betrayed*.

power and gunfire against the citizenry, thereby initiating a cruel suppression and a succession of bloody massacres. Whereupon this entire isolated island sank into perpetual terror and factional polarization.

In the dark of a new moon night, an urgent pounding on a gate, immediately followed by two youths shackled together, dragged out of a squat building by armed escorts, closely tailed by their two elderly parents. A soldier originally acting as an armed guard at the door, hesitated on the orders of his commander, then unskillfully placed a burlap sack over the bodies of the two youths. A guy wearing a Zhongshan jacket[13] snatched a rifle away, out of the hands of a soldier, and used the butt to smash the two men in the burlap sacks down to the ground.

"Tie 'em up. Load 'em on the truck."

That's the way it was…an entire night, employing the same unyielding, uncaring tactics, carrying out the bloody orders of their superiors one after the other, breaking apart warm circles within homes, one by one. From start to finish, using loads of large coarse burlap grain sacks, bag after bag trussed up, one after another, the elites of Taiwan were roughly piled onto bed after bed of large military trucks. Leaving behind family after family of relations wailing helplessly, and a countless number of neighbors peering furtively through the cracks in their doors, fearfully spying on the entire tragic occurrence.

That's the way it was…in the dark of night, their eyes witnessing this tragedy. In the light of day, employing whatever muscle or implements they could muster. In streets, lanes, and alleys, they sought possible targets on which to vent their anger, they released the rage and terror accumulated over the long, dark night, without any real consideration for how much "these people" and "those people" actually were related. Whereupon the men sent on their mission the night before, slowly began to feel justified and motivated to carry out the mission they had formerly resisted. Whereupon the daylight counterattacks and the evening massacres interacted as cause and effect in a ceaseless, vicious cycle of Samsara.

Under the dim yellow light of one bare bulb, one official document handwritten in small characters, one chop of the government seal deciding life and death, in the crimson color of fresh blood, was heavily pressed down…On the Taipei Bridge straddling the Danshui River, in the steel span's mid-point dividing line between Taipei city and Sanchong, coincidentally also the coldest and deepest part of the river water, were parked many military trucks laden with heaps of burlap bags. Bag by bag, they were roughly heaved down, bag by bag they were chucked into the river, into the ink black below, with only the cries

---

13 A Zhongshan jacket is a tailored jacket with no lapels, and with a collar or not, worn by government people. It is named after the style of Western apparel adopted by Sun Yat-sen (Sun Zhong-shan) the father of the Chinese revolution, but in the West it is referred to as a Mao jacket, because of its association with Mao Ze-dong.

of the victims and the sighs of history to be heard.

"Why kill these youngsters?" several grunts responsible for tossing the bags in the river knelt down paralyzed and exhausted by the censure of their better nature. But what history gave them was not the consolation of mercy. Instead, from their commander's rifle magazine spat forth bullets, the rusty smell of blood covering everything; the burlap bags one by one heaved in the river; the magazines of bullets one by one firing. The government's crimson seal, the burlap bags, all became instruments of death. It is just that those hidden in their government offices sealing the fate of people, were more loyal and dependable, more resolute, more efficient, and more willing to pursue justice, no matter the cost, than the grunts in the field carrying out the executions.

Among the masses who personally experienced this tragic history, none could fathom why the spirits and supernatural beings overseeing right wrong, good evil, and karmic retribution in this world, would tolerate such a regime, employing these inhuman means to inflict such great suffering on kind-hearted citizens. In that moment, even among the most devout disciples of religion, I am afraid none would yet dare wildly hope that those men giving the orders would in the end receive God's punishment, that they would truly get what they deserved.

41– OUR OWN PEOPLE

The things people make an effort to emphasize in their speech tends to be that which in the bottom of their hearts they lack, or of which they don't approve.

Scene: Taipei, Taiwan, Dihua Street

AT SECTION 1 NO. 177 DIHUA STREET IN TAIPEI, HONG WAN MEI Trading Company, second brother Yi-wen, third brother Yi-mian, fourth brother Yi-xiang and fifth brother Yi-kun huddled together, their bodies shivering behind the steel shutter. Through a slit in the shutter they espied ten large military trucks hurtling past. Each truck deployed several soldiers, rifles at the ready, their faces solemn, their eyes ceaselessly scanning the locked shutters of each residence on each side of the street. Heaped two or three deep on the bed of each truck was a mass of writhing burlap bags, some of them moaning.

"There's really people in the bags!" Yi-kun spoke.

"Where are they taking them?" Yi-mian asked.

"Shush! Keep it down. If you are not careful you will wind up arrested like them, and end up at the bottom of the Danshui River," Yi-wen said.

From the pitch darkness behind the four brothers there was a sigh, "Didn't they say they embraced us as their own?" Oldest brother Yi-qin sighed deeply.

42– LUNCHBOX SUSHI

If you were rain, it would be better to fall on a place lacking water.

Scene: Shuanglian Train Station

ONE RAINY AFTERNOON, THE GROUND STILL WET AND GLISTENING, on Wanquan Street near Shuanglian Station, the proprietor of a factory making grass jelly was using a thick rubber hose, pouring the liquid of the grass jelly cooked several hours into square metal tubs covering the ground. On the other side, several crones, hired as laborers, busied themselves dumping already cooled and congealed grass jelly from the metal tubs and carved it up into cubes of standard size.

As soon as summer hit, the street vendors of these cooling summer treats, like grass jelly, bean jelly, and cold rice noodles, would arrive with their roving carts, on a daily basis, at a fixed time, to replenish their inventory. They would typically put the precut grass jelly into a bucket of clean water, letting the grass jelly soak in the ice water, so as on the one hand to maintain its cooling flavor, and on the other hand, to dilute the bitterness of the herb so as to increase its tasty and refreshing delectability.

Facing the grass jelly factory were several small diners selling an assortment of cooked dishes. After the peak time of the midday meal rush, and the dishes on the display had been thoroughly picked over, and the number of customers had dwindled, the remaining customers were all stall keepers and street peddlers. To do even a little bit of last business, , all of these street vendors would wait until the average customers had already eaten lunch, before folding up their stands and settling down for their own meals.

"Boss, I want two bowls of yam porridge and this, and this dish." A mother wearing a navy blue short sleeved *qipao,* a small boy holding one of her hands, an infant swaddled and strapped to her back, was standing in front of the shop ordering shyly in Beijing accented Mandarin.

"Okay," the boss turned, picked up a bowl and began to ladle out the porridge.

"This shop doesn't sell to you foreigners!"[14] A thin middle-aged man appeared before the shop, preventing the proprietor from conducting his business, and

---
14 People of Foreign Provinces, *waishengren,* 外省人, was how Taiwanese used to refer to people who arrived from Mainland China in the 1940s with the Great Retreat. They were seen as interlopers.

although by outside appearance this man did not look the part of a local thug, his eyes and tone were cold and sharp, like he had the capacity to kill.

"Don't be this way…," the boss said, expressing his embarrassment.

"Taiwanese have to grow a backbone, not just do anything to make a buck," the middle-aged man said.

"Then…I don't want it, Boss, sorry." That mother made pains to avoid the fierce stare of the man, timidly bowed her head to the proprietor and apologized.

"Ma! I'm hungry…," the little boy said.

"Precious, we will go back to eat…" The mother hastily pulled her son out of that diner. Quickly walking the length of the road, she kept her head lowered, daring not to meet the eyes of others, hoping to exit that scene as quickly as possible, never expecting that as she turned into Liangzhou Street, the road ahead would be impeded by a large foot blocking her way.

"Come, this is for you, don't let the little guy go hungry!" Fourth brother Yi-xiang had just returned on the train to Taipei from collecting payment for a delivery in Taizhong, and when he alighted at Shuanglian Station, he espied this interaction unfold, yet hindered by the tense atmosphere that prevailed in society, he found it inconvenient to interject himself at that moment, rather waiting for the woman to leave the scene, when he then walked double time to catch up to the woman and give her a "Wooden Sushi Lunchbox" bought on the train.

"Thank you!" the woman said.

"He's not a bad man. He's…also hurting."

In that time, under those circumstances, facing that kind of persecution, no one knew what kind of bitter and deep-seated hatred was hidden behind some evil conduct. What great terror had been suffered to lead them astray, allowing these demons to conceal themselves behind "rights" and gun barrels pointed at other people, using other people's two hands to execute their bloody missions. It is simply that with the exception of a minority willing to stand up and use their own bodies to face the bullets and burlap bags, to face this immense State apparatus, anyone would be the same. Those who could do it were few, those who lived to talk about it even fewer.

43– PANEL BEATERS STREET

Life is an endless forging in the red furnace and the martial training hall.

Scene: Panel Beaters Street

"Just here, pull over to the side." Fourth brother Yi-xiang had the trishaw driver stop on the side of Qinxi Street, and walked himself across the road, strolling into what locals called "Shuanglian Panel Beaters Street" of Chifeng Street's alleys and lanes. From Chifeng Street up to Wanquan Street, this part of town was devoted to the manufacture of machinery, repair, and metal working. Within the narrow alleys and lanes, no matter where the eye looked, everything was covered in a red rust color. On the side of the road were piled all manner of rusted ironware and heavy machinery. Walking through here, the ear was filled only with the great clanging sound of the forging presses and the piercing high pitched whine of the metal working lathes. It was within this cacophony of metal attacking metal, each ferocious clangor louder than the next, that faintly sandwiched within the din was the barely discernible sound of a Daoist priest chanting sutras, the noise seeping out from little gaps in the sound waves. When fourth brother Yi-xiang had walked the length of the street to its end, outside a building he saw a temporary simple mourning hall constructed of bamboo poles, metal brackets, plastic tarpaulins, with white bereavement scrolls offering the black and white images of the deceased, drawn in charcoal.

"Auntie Hao, I have come to offer incense for the twins," Yi-xiang said.

"You shouldn't have," on seeing that the son of her husband's employer had made a special trip to extend condolences, Auntie Hao, who had been folding spirit money and reciting the sutras with the Daoist priest, quickly got up and lit a candle and a stick of incense and holding them in two hands, offered them to fourth brother Yi-xiang.

"The *fengshui* and dates are all set?" Yi-xiang asked.

"Oh, Yi-xiang, our two eldest, their whole lives they were law abiding, keeping their heads down, they didn't have any enemies, no grudges against them, how could they come down on my two well-behaved children this way?" Auntie Hao asked.

"Alas. No one knows why it turned out this way," Yi-xiang said.

"These two boys listened to reason ever since they were young, and when they went out into the world, they never gave us a day of worry. Who knew it would just take one night, they are all given up to the clutches of the Danshui River! I hurt so, you know? One was studying to be a doctor, the other a lawyer, both so exemplary, then like this, in one night, vanished," Auntie Hao said, choking on her sobs.

"Auntie Hao, you must control your grief. You have to be strong in this time, you have to go on living. My father will take care of this." Yi-xiang solemnly placed a thick white envelope of money at the base of a candle holder burning a large white candle.

"Ai, they had not even left their youth. What more can I hope for?" Auntie Hao said.

"On the day, I will send Black Snake and Black Turtle over to help. Please set your mind at ease," Yi-xiang said.

According to the local customs, when visiting a grieving family to offer condolences, the guest must not bid farewell on leaving. Red eyed, fourth brother Yi-xiang quietly departed the mourning hall, wishing he could say something more to comfort the bereaved, but the words got stuck in his throat like fishbones. He knew these words would only release more tears, giving the grieving not one bit of succor, and in the current moment, what was more important, was how to allow his own family not to get caught up in this tumultuous spreading conflict. To preserve their own sufficient financial resources and influence, only in this way, when others needed their help, would they be able to extend a bit more effort.

Uncle Hao was an expert in welding metal, who all along helped the Hong family factory to do periodic maintenance and repair on machinery. Although there was no formal employment agreement between them, every week he would spend three or four days in the factory, taking care of problematic busted pipes leaking wax on the machines. During peak season, to help keep up with rush orders, he would be right there twenty-four hours a day, coping with emergencies as they happened. When they were short of hands, he would proactively fill in, helping to deliver on time, and usually he took three meals a day with the rest of the crew.

Privately, Uncle Hao and eldest Hong family son Yi-qin had especially hit it off well, because both were experts in tinkering to improve machinery and manufacturing processes. Most of all, Uncle Hao's spouse of many years had originally grown up in the Sanyi Market and had previously labored for the Hong family. Through the Hong family's eldest son's, Yi-qin, string pulling, they had gotten to know one another and were married, so for this reason, the two of them, were especially close to the Hong family .Afterwards, although eldest son Yi-qin died in the prime of life, the Hong family never regarded them as strangers.

When the Hao family ran into their fated misfortune, the Hong family wanted to help, but could not. Because at that moment, what they faced was a regime that did not speak their language, wielding the hammer of national authority, and to find oneself in that political moment unable to speak out, not to mention the average urban denizen, even financially secure wealthy tycoons, all were as silent as cicada's in winter. No one dared challenge this kind of opponent head on! To the extent that repressed emotions hidden deep in the dark corners of hearts constantly accumulated, increasing, increasing… heightening…

44–1949

When a strange town becomes your hometown, you can no longer be physically here, but emotionally there.

Scene: Dockside at Keelong Port

In 1949 CE, Keelung dock and harbor were filled with all manner of ships, following the Nationalist government's great retreat from mainland China and the surge of refugees, they spilled out of boat after ship after vessel, like a load of fish dumped from a trawler. This was not a sizeable port, so it was burdened to swallow the enormous weight of Chinese tradition and history suddenly entrusted to it. This included: the millennium old collection of treasures from the Imperial Palace of the Forbidden City, ten thousand tons of gold from the National treasury, and refugees from each strange corner of every province. This dynastic rotation and end of an era forced changes both vast and rapid. The matter at hand was too great, too fast. Besides merely facing and bearing it, no one knew, what the next step should be? What would they encounter?

   The local people, separated at a distance and quietly watching this historic flood of humanity unfold, felt apprehension in their hearts. "Haven't we just ushered off those defeated Japanese, how is it we are welcoming this bunch of refugee Chinese?" The interlopers, cautiously treading their way down the gangway, were going from one strange world into another unfamiliar place. Their minds had not yet caught up and considered what turmoil and changes they themselves and their family members might face on this southern outlying island. Although history and bloodlines told both sides that everyone was progeny of the Yellow Emperor, their mutual recognition and interaction could not compare with this island's colonization by the Japanese or Dutch.

   In the coming months and years, how would they mutually treat each other? At this moment it was too early to say, the people who had stepped off the ships were not even clear about what their very next step would be. Besides the infants and wives they held, the degrees they carried in their bosoms, their identities and whatever finery, valuables, and professions they carried from their former lives, everyone was the same, knowing nothing, having nothing, not even a return boat ticket. And those standing on the shore, gazing outward, kept ruminating: what impacts and turmoil will this tsunamic surge of human refuse bring upon our originally quiet lives?

On the pier, amidst the tide of humanity pushing and shoving, Zhang Jun-feng constantly shuttled back and forth in an arduous search, hoping that out of all of these strange faces he might find his own longed-for relations or an acquaintance from his hometownhometown. Although he had received word that his family members had no possibility of catching up to the Nationalist Party's great retreat, he preferred to maintain a single thread of hope, keeping watch on the dock every day, trusting that in this foreign port, some happy surprise, some miracle, might occur. But miracles are all the same, indifferent, merciless, granting neither comfort nor compassion to past human suffering. He watched as ship after ship off-loaded, wave after wave of people dispersed. When he finally gave up hope, his tears would not stop from red eyes that had not slept for days on end.

Starting with that moment, the link between his past and his future was broken.

Starting with that moment, he realized that he must resign himself to a new fate in this strange speck of land, and begin again, learning anew how to live.

Starting with that moment, he was no longer a passing traveler coming and going as he pleased, he must adapt as quickly as possible to all things new here, accept all things new here, and at the same time find a way for the local people to accept him…

45– CONNECTING TO ANOTHER'S MIND

Little matters employ the brain, big matters employ the mind.

In many matters, even though you have seen it with your own eyes, heard it with your own ears, how can you be sure that the lackadaisical person in front of you just a moment ago was not cultivating the Tao? That in the next moment they will not be striving to achieve Zen.

"Connecting to Another's Mind" employs something like the technique of a religious trance to enter humanity's crystal-clear, universal self, using the mind and the mind's dialogue, making the critical distinction between accurate and false, according to the life experience and degree of understanding of the person employing the art.

Scene: A small inn behind the Taipei Main Railway Station

ON A PITCH-BLACK NIGHT, ONE MATCH IS STRUCK ILLUMINATING A square table and igniting a single white candle placed at its center. Under its yellow glow one can see the narrow confines of the room in which Zhang Jun-feng and Mr. Hong Wu-fan sit face to face, separated by the small wooden table.

"Why do you want to help me? Don't you know I am from a foreign province?" Zhang Jun-feng asked.

"Here, we are all from foreign provinces. Some came first, some came later."

"Aren't you afraid of implicating your family and your business?" Zhang Jun-feng asked.

"It's not that I am not afraid, but if I don't act, my heart cannot rest."

Zhang Jun-feng's eyes fixed on this thin, small, mild-mannered old man. From outside appearances he would never be able to see through the façade of this person, who could not even speak Mandarin, that he was a renowned North Taiwan businessman who sheltered martial arts masters from China to act as guards. He really didn't know which mind reading technique he should use to penetrate into this Southern Chinese businessman's true thoughts and character. Accordingly, as he spoke he extended his two hands, larger than an ordinary person's, and thickened from intense internal arts training, toward Mr. Hong, and placed them palm up on the table.

"That incident hurt everyone. In that critical moment, no one could say how this incident came about, or what really happened."

Old Mr. Hong also extended his two hands, placing them on the palms of the person opposite. Zhang Jun-feng closed his eyes, clearing his spirit and focusing his attention. Using the esoteric art of Connecting to the Other's Mind, his entire spirit concentrated on sensing the internal landscape of the person sitting opposite. "Please continue to speak," Zhang Jun-feng said.

"Some matters, unless you are there and see the whole thing with your eyes…"

"Everything your eyes see, usually it's just a fragment…"

"It may not necessarily be the whole truth…"

"That it could evolve into such a big conflict, besides how the basic incident was handled, so many factors influenced the development afterwards, certainly beforehand there was an accumulation of too much friction and resentment…"

"So many sacrificed already…"

"Can't vent this way again…"

"If the two sides both harbor emotions…"

"Then we won't have the truth…"

"I'm just a businessman…"

"So much I don't understand. I don't know how this could have turned out this way…"

"They must quickly provide a clear account, otherwise the longer they delay the worse it will get…"

"I don't know why there is a refusal to admit to errors…"

"Maybe there is fear, after mistakes are admitted to, that the situation will run out of control…"

"It seems there is too great a divide between what the Big Man wants and what the populace wants…"

"No one is willing to admit to mistakes on their side…"

"I just think, facing this kind of conflict…"

"The great and powerful, they really need to understand how to bow their heads and take a step back, the situation would then ease up…"

"Otherwise, hostility is going to burn hotter and more rampant…"

"One instance of conflict, once it has turned into a feud, is passed on generation to generation, endlessly…"

"If it goes down this way, this island is finished…"

"What I mean is, both sides are the same…"

"I am an orphan; I have never held a grudge against my people. It's not because I don't have the capacity to strike back, it's what my uncle taught me, that no matter how strong you are, one needs to know when to bow one's head and yield. Those who persist in just trying to win, in the end they lose. The defeat comes in not yielding. Those who bow their head and admit defeat, win. They are winning without struggle."

"Once things settle down, I hope you can come and help teach my five boys." Old Mr. Hong had already stopped speaking a long while before Zhang

Zhun-feng slowly took his spirit back in, gradually opened his eyes and fixed his gaze on that bright, steady, unflickering candle flame between them. His forehead was beaded with pearls of sweat the size of soybeans. The two men sat as before, silent.

46– CALLING ON THE MASTER

Small matters are up to people, the big things are up to heaven. When the political situation is turbulent and chaotic, no one knows which will come first, tomorrow or a calamity.

Scene: Taipei Main Station at Zhengzhou Road

THE AREA ENCLOSED BY THE FOUR ROADS OF ZHENGZHOU ROAD, Chengde Road, Nanjing West Road, and Chongqing North Road is commonly known as the back station business district. Many wholesalers specializing in garments, farm tools, hardware materials, and chemical raw materials are gathered here. And Huayin Street, which runs through Chengde Road and Chongqing North Road, is also a mix of many shops of different sizes in the narrow alleys, engaging in sales of a variety of daily necessities. This place was regarded as the most complete market ecosystem in Taipei City. In this block, all the things needed for daily life could be purchased at one go.

Located near the intersection of Taiyuan Road and Huayin Street, the Jinlong Lodge, was an old, rundown, small hostel, barely large enough to pack in seven or eight rental rooms. In the narrow guest room passageway on the second floor, the owner of the hotel took the rent from the tenants and stepped down the tight and steep wooden staircase carefully. On the platform between the stairs, he happened to meet Master Tu and fourth brother Yi-xiang. The proprietor recognized the Fourth Young Master of the Hong family at a glance, and immediately greeted them with a friendly smile, but on seeing fourth brother Yi-xiang's two hands full, carrying a big bag of daily necessities, he tactfully yielded sideways and let the two visitors go upstairs first.

"Brother Jun-feng! Is it convenient to introduce a young disciple to you?" Master Tu asked.

"Welcome, welcome! Please come in and sit," Zhang Jun-feng said.

In the simple, crude, small and narrow guest room, there was only a tiny, scarred wooden table slapped together from scraps, a chair that had been disemboweled by an unruly guest with a knife, letting balls of stuffing bulge out, and a small wooden plank to sleep on with threadbare linens. There was nothing on the table except a glass lined thermos and an iron cup, whose enameled outer layer had started to peel. To prevent Zhang Jun-feng from being embarrassed, Master Tu dragged him to sit together with him on the edge of the bed.

"Yi-xiang, just sit there!" he said, signaling he wanted fourth brother Yi-xiang to sit on the sole small chair provided.

"Everything okay? Brother Jun-feng?" Master Tu asked.

"All good. Just need to spend some more time to sort out my head. I originally hadn't made plans to live here long, I didn't expect the state of the world to suddenly become like this!" Zhang Jun-feng said.

"How are the family members over there?" Master Tu asked.

"I heard that the situation is chaotic, but who knows the real status!" Zhang Jun-feng said.

"Wow! Small matters are up to people, the big things are up to heaven, there is no use being anxious. The most important thing now is that you have to settle down first. This is Yi-xiang, the fourth son of Hong Wan-mei on Dihua Street, the family's several sons practice a little Taiji with me. Today, I brought him specially to meet you," Master Tu said.

"Master Zhang, how are you. Pleased to seek your advice," said the fourth brother Yi-xiang.

"Mr. Hong, hello. Pleasure to meet you," Zhang Jun-feng said.

"Brother Jun-feng, you're busy and preoccupied these few days. If there is anything where he can be of help, just please call Yi-xiang," Master Tu said.

"Brother Tu, I appreciate the trouble you have gone to. Right now, I really can't think of anything to ask!" Zhang Jun-feng said.

"It's okay. No rush. I hope I can help!" said fourth brother Yi-xiang.

"Brother Jun-feng. I'm here to say goodbye to you today. Because my wife's parents in Lishan insisted that we move over to live together and help take care of farming in the orchards. I think you are alone and have no language skills, so in particular, I would like to introduce you two to meet each other, so in the future you will be well looked after," Master Tu said.

"Brother Tu. Thank you for your concern. But you too must take care of yourself!" Zhang Jun-feng said.

"Thanks be to old Mr. Hong for not giving up, he let his kids practice gongfu with me for a few years. If Brother Jun-feng settles down and can spare a little time, I would entreat you to give them some direction," Master Tu said.

"I wouldn't dare. Even though I have practiced with Master Gao Yi-sheng for several years, after all I'm just playing around. I've never pursued it seriously, not to mention teaching others. Brother Tu, I really don't dare to do this. I am truly sorry," Zhang Jun-feng remonstrated.

"No. No matter. This is just a parting suggestion, Brother Jun-feng, by all means ignore it," Master Tu said.

Amidst tumultuous change, no one knows how to face future tomorrows. When you only have a little pocket money left, and you are earning less than you spend, the days become harder and more severe. Under this kind of real-life pressure, it is very easy to sink into predicaments, it being hard to determine what is good, what is right. When faced with others who sincerely want to help, in the moment it is difficult to express what help one needs.

When faced with a crisis, Zhang Jun-feng the businessman became a full-time teacher of martial arts.

47– A DECISION

The misty rain of Mount Lu and surging tides of the Qiantang River,
To not behold them would be regretted a lifetime;
Having come to behold them there is bugger all to do,
Mount Lu is misty raining and the tides surge on the Qiantang River.

—Su Dong-po, Song Dynasty

Scene: Sanzhangli

IN THE 1950S, THE STRETCH OF LAND FROM THE EASTERN DISTRICT of Taipei to Sanzhangli was still a sparsely populated grassland overgrown with weeds. Standing there amidst the wasteland were only infrequent illegally constructed huts made of scrap building materials and corrugated asbestos board, barely held together. One was the temporary hovel of Zhang Jun-feng and several fellow compatriots from his old village in Shandong. All had fallen into hard times because of the war and landed in this strange place. In a narrow space less than eight square meters were crammed five or six big guys from Shandong scratching out a meager existence. Between simple and crude rooms with one bunk bed each, there was only a narrow passage. Everyone's belongings were all stacked on the sleeper, and when they went to bed at night, belongings had to be piled up to make a space where they could lie down. Cooking, bathing, and washing, all these activities were done outside the house under a rain tarpaulin.

The most painful thing about living in such a remote wilderness was not the inconvenience of daily life and transportation, but nightfall when all the blood-sucking insects and mosquitoes in the grasslands would fully mobilize forces and gather, assembling in these houses to hunt humans, suck blood and forage. The tall and sturdy Zhang Jun-feng slept on the lower bunk, and when night came, he was often bitten by bedbugs and fleas, which were secreted in the grooves and crevices of the bed plank, and thus he could not sleep the whole night. Sometimes, to avoid the harassment of these blood-sucking demons, the only thing to do was to walk out into the moonlight shining on an empty space in front of the hovel and practice his gongfu. Practice until he was bone tired, forcing himself to let these demons wreak their havoc and devastation while he slept.

That night, Zhang Jun-feng spread the meagre handful of banknotes and copper coins on the bed and carefully counted. On the back of a spent piece of calendar paper he wrote down his name, and then wrote down all the names of close and distant relatives and one by one the names of people and organizations with whom he could connect in Taiwan that might generate meaningful contacts and assistance. He then used a straight line to connect names from whom a network could be woven, a network that could sustain his life and lead to a future here. Several times he toyed with the idea of connecting the line to Hong Yi-xiang's name. Even he could not fathom the reason, but that line was always drawn halfway and never connected. All the way into the wee hours, he still couldn't finish drawing the line that would determine the rest of his life.

Finally, to avoid loafing and squandering the little resources he had, Zhang Jun-feng, with the assistance of friends from the same hometown, scoped out an unused gentle slope at the base of the mountain behind Yuan Shan. Everyone worked together to root out the stumps of trees on the slope and the roots exposed on the ground. This grudgingly yielded a small patch of yellow earth used as a training field. A small wooden sign posted to the side began to attract students and early bird oldsters to practice health cultivation, longevity skills, and easy-to-learn push hands. He was thereby hoping to slowly wean himself of support from the Hong family.

On Dihua Street, the Hong family had reached out to assist when Zhang Jun-feng was most helpless, but ever since Master Tu reached out to invite him to teach at the Hong family home and he had politely declined the offer to live there, no more requests were made by Master Tu. He avoided embarrassing Zhang Jun-feng by requesting that which he was unwilling to do.

The days slowly settled down. In addition to teaching the oldsters exercise and fitness, after class, when the students had all dispersed down the mountain, Zhang Jun-feng stayed on the slopes for self-training almost the entire day. He used the Cheng school Gao-style Baguazhang learned from Gao Yi-sheng, and the Xingyiquan learned from Wu Meng-xia, one by one, lesson by lesson, earnestly drilling, his personal performance strictly self-examined, technique by technique. Because, after making an inventory of his life that night, he had made one thing clear to himself: "If the resources of the family are cut off, the matter of the second half of my life is up to what *I* can do with my own two hands."

The son of a wealthy family finally recognized his current situation under the urgency of real survival, and pragmatically adjusted the attitude and role he would pursue to face up to life. At that moment, the only thing he could rely on seemed to be the Bagua Palm which he had learned purely for the sake of an idle pastime. Although he never dreamed that the second half of his life he would live off his martial art in a strange place, he changed his mind, thinking, "doing my favorite thing all day long might be the best arrangement God could make." Of course, if one is not in such a desperate situation, I believe that no matter how romantic one is, you wouldn't make such a decision. So, he told himself: "Let's do it. What's next…I'll cross that bridge when I get to it."

48- A MASTER DOWN ON HIS LUCK

One cannot use a northern brain filled with steamed buns and noodles to pursue a life in the south filled with rice and sweet potato!

Scene: Sanzhangli

A CONTINUOUS PERIOD OF TORRENTIAL RAIN FOR OVER A MONTH had completely disrupted the lives and livelihoods of everyone. For those who had to work outdoors all day to make a living, it was a disaster and torture.

On Yuan Shan, the yellow earth training field had only recently been cleared. The topsoil layer that could prevent the erosion of the earth and the stumps and roots had all been stripped out. It could not withstand the disorderly ravages of the great rain and was washed away all at once. With the open-air venue gone, there was no training and without training there was no income.

To make matters worse, this was closely followed by a strong typhoon, another bout with heavy wind and rain. The abundant rainwater and gale force winds turned northern Taiwan once again into a disastrous baptismal font. The previous one-month of torrential downpours had saturated the mountains surrounding the Taipei Basin already seriously exceeding the limits of soil moisture and runoff water. With the heavy rainfall brought by the typhoon wind, the yellow and turbid mountain rivulets and rivers converging from the various paths and waterways, grew from small to large to unstoppable, and the deluge surged down like a discharge from a reservoir. The rampant flooding filled the rivers and streams of the Taipei Basin, instantly raising the water level. The dikes and drainage canals were immediately overwhelmed, and the water reversed, invading the urban areas within the dikes from the gates of the dikes and the various drainage canals. Overnight, the entire Taipei Basin was immersed in fetid, filthy water. All kinds of unexpected things were scattered on the floodwaters floating by. The swollen corpses of drowned animals, pots, bowls, and basins could be seen everywhere, an appalling scene of devastation.

Zhang Jun-feng's residence in Sanzhangli was of course not immune to this natural disaster. The corrugated asbestos board on the roof used for shading and avoiding the rain was simply held in place with a few bricks pressed on it. The wall panels and doors of the facade were also barely pieced together with various construction waste materials and did not provide particularly good shelter from the elements in the best of times and presented no resistance to the uninterrupted strong wind. When the single door panel gave up the fight, surrendered its guard duties and was blown away, the entire roof was immediately torn off by the strong wind that rushed in from all sides.

The gale laden with sheets of rain expressed an irresistible power in the pitch-black night, demonstrating its primacy over the land. Employing asymmetrical force, it easily laid waste to the dwellings in this basin of land, now timid, trembling and bowing before it. Finally, even the plywood and iron sheets on the wall were confiscated by the heavens, leaving only a few simple wooden beds soaked in the yellow water like desolate islands.

In the completely hollowed out "atrium," five Shandong heroes versed in martial arts were all curled up like pangolins in the upper bunk of a double wooden bed, shivering in the wind and rain. With one hand, they clutched their valuables tightly to their chests, and with the other hand, they grabbed the last remaining piece of tarpaulin, hoping to survive the wind and rain's ruthless attack from above and below, and the physical and mental violation.

"What kind of demonic weather is this? I don't want to live in this horrible place anymore."

"Everything's ruined! Even the pots, bowls, and basins are gone. How will we get by?"

"Don't worry about the pots, bowls, and basins. I wanna go home! This place is not for us."

"Can you go back? Careful you're not executed as a spy."

"But staying here, isn't it a dead end, too?"

"I would rather die in my hometown than live here."

"Wow! To be faced with this, and speak this way, whatever for?!" Zhang Jun-feng said.

"But look at this place, look at yourself, there is nothing left, what can you do if you don't leave?" said one.

"Could it be you have all forgotten the people at home?" said another.

"I have not forgotten. So, let's not be discouraged!" Zhang Jun-feng said.

"But…"

"No more 'buts.' Believe me, our day will come, just wait," Zhang Jun-feng urged.

"Ugh, I can't even make it through this, yet you talk of hopes and dreams…"

"You can't be deflated by this. Only before that day comes, we have to make some changes," Zhang Jun-feng said

"Changes?

"Yes, change! Here is different from our place, Shandong. We can't obstinately employ brains used to eating steamed buns and noodles to eke out a living in a land of rice and sweet potatoes. It must be changed!" Zhang Jun-feng said.

"Change? Change what?"

"Attitudes!" Zhang Jun-feng said.

The men were silent.

"No matter how hard the storm is, it will pass. But if we don't change our attitudes and don't try to learn to live here, the days will only get worse and worse!" Zhang Jun-feng said.

His compatriots looked at him, glum and uncomprehending.

"When the rains stop and the water recedes, we will go out together, blend in, live with the locals here, and learn together. They can survive here, there is no reason we cannot. The most important thing is that we can't be physically here while our hearts are over there!" Zhang Junfeng said.

In that expanse of unsheltered land, no one knew how many houses and illegal squatter's sites were blown down by strong winds and destroyed by floods; how many refugees were living in this foreign land because of the war, huddled in the wind and rain, on a wooden bed, on the verge of despair, the yearning for hometown and family affection strengthening their will to survive. If not that they chose to believe these empty comforts could finally be realized in the end, it would only take a change of the mind, a release of two hands, and in a flash, they would become corpses carried away in the torrent.

In the eyes of the gods, mankind has not learned true humility, has not given up self-righteous judgements and ridicules, has not truly relinquished their own dignity. Until mankind humbly kneels down and kisses this muddy ground and happily submits to receive both the good and the bad this land offers, then these oaths are just words. Whether uttered on a night of howling wind and rain, or on a beautiful sunny day, it is all the same. No person or God will care about regrets and realizations bemoaned in the test of this storm. You want to live, you want to die, as you wish, you want to pull yourself out of the mess or sink into oblivion, as you wish, including whether you want to believe or not believe, as you wish. In any case He is just playing the role of this impartial, merciless, unfeeling, nonacting, and unnamed Spirit.

49– TALKING ABOUT XINGYI

Xingyiquan: Originated from ancient spear techniques. Put down the spear, the spear technique becomes fist technique. So, when training the fist, although there is no spear at hand, one still carries a long invisible spear in the mind, as with the spear, the two hands move in concert, the front hand builds the bridge, the rear hand crosses the bridge.

Scene: Zhang Jun-feng's new residence

AFTER THE STORM, PEOPLE REBUILT THEIR HOMES, DEMONSTRATING astonishing powers of recovery, and soon everything returned to its original order and life. Even many new business opportunities emerged because of this disaster. The true essence of the interplay of calamity and good fortune is evident in our real lives every day, manifesting varying versions and plots in a true and subdued manner. In the process, it is inevitable that some people will be unable to withstand the torture and trials and are toppled, but there will always be people who are renewed and stand up again, employing a resilient toughness difficult to destroy. They bring together all the broken resources and continue to face the way forward.

Just like in the ecology of the Amazon rain forest, when a great tree falls because of disease or the inevitable natural disaster it makes way for new growth. The space and sunlight it monopolized is soon occupied by other species coming forward, jockeying to fill the vacancy, including that lifeless trunk. It will soon be decomposed by a whole host of symbiotic lynchpins into nutrients for the survival and growth of yet other organisms.

If one knows how to look at the ups and downs of the world with this kind of rational and calm attitude, one can also perhaps understand the real reason why an omnipotent God always chooses not to meddle, not to interfere, and not to act. Because He knows all life that He has created must face crises of extinction and understand they must find their own way to survive down the ages. As for those tortured souls who fall, they are only an inflection point in the overall scheme of things. Only through this seemingly ruthless and cruel mechanism can resources be efficiently transferred to those who have the ability to integrate and use them. Isn't it inevitably so?

After enduring this baptism rending heaven and earth, Zhang Jun-feng chose to believe in the fact that in the near term he would not be able to return to his hometown. He tried to employ another mindset to treat Taiwan, originally just a stop along the road, as a home in which he must settle down. On this hot and humid southern island, he had to relearn ways of coexisting harmoniously with typhoons and earthquakes. After he had made the shift from his cherished longing, he finally allowed himself to surrender his pride, to calmly accept the beneficence of the Hong family providing a new residence.

On that day, relying on the memories of his hometown cuisine and the ingredients and condiments cobbled together with much difficulty from the neighborhood vegetable market, Zhang Jun-feng spent a whole morning setting a lunch table of authentic Shandong hometown dishes. To be faithful to the original taste, he insisted on cooking by himself. Although fourth brother Yi-xiang was in place to lend a hand as early as noon, at the insistence of the Shandong chef he could only stand idly by. He waited patiently until about 1:30 in the afternoon for a table of hometown masterpieces that seemed out of place. All this to express Zhang's heartfelt gratitude for the emergency relief from the Hong family, but also to share a bit of Shandong with his young disciple and somehow say goodbye to Shandong. So, in this new home, two people happily tucked into a seriously delayed lunch, one speaking heavily accented Shandong Mandarin to one speaking heavily accented Taiwan Mandarin. With copious amounts of ginseng deer antler wine to help catalyze and translate, as soon as they opened their chatterboxes, these two-men fond of martial arts, let their lofty sentiments filling their hearts spill out.

(The following is a monologue by Zhang Jun-feng.)

"Classified in the roughest way, Chinese martial arts can be divided into two types of boxing, External School and Internal School…

"Generally speaking, the External School is mainly based on North and South Shaolin. Of course, it can actually be subdivided into many different schools.

"Internal School boxing is based on the three linked main axes of Xingyiquan, Baguazhang, and Taijiquan.

"In the past, the concepts and boundaries separating sects were relatively deep, and martial arts practitioners rarely crossed over to study under other sects.

"At the time, it was seen as deceiving one's teacher and turning one's back on ancestors, a crime of betraying the teacher and school.

"But then things opened up, the taboos disappeared, and mixed learning became a natural thing.

"From my point of view, this is definitely a good thing.

"With such stimulation and comparison are newer and better things created.

"Take the example of your Hong family's candles. Traditional Chinese candles are made of rushes and dried straws that are rolled into a candle wick, and then manually soaked in hot wax layer by layer. Although candles made with this technique burn longer, they are time-consuming and labor-intensive to produce and cannot be quickly mass manufactured. In the past, because there was no comparison and competitive stimulus, this old craft was regarded as a sacred and unchangeable tradition that was passed down. No one had the courage and wisdom to challenge the things passed down by those ancestors.

"I once visited the production line of your family's factory. To my knowledge, your methods have adopted the water-cooling production technology improved by the Japanese. The production speed is dozens of times faster than the traditional method. The shortcoming of it is that it uses cotton string as the wick, because the wick is soft. When the weather is hot, the candle is easy to bend and deform. But I have heard from your esteemed father that, to overcome the shortcomings resulting from this new technology, your eldest brother used hard wax and soft wax to experiment and improve the product, and finally formulated several different ratios to overcome the problem that arises with candles at different ambient temperatures. Something newly created by breaking through traditional restrictions will definitely have some shortcomings in the beginning. If you can persist to seek solutions, frequently you end up the winner. I think this should be the reason why your Hong family dominates the Taiwan market.

"The principle in learning martial arts is the same. Cross-training will also run into contradictions and walls. If you can push through them and reason through the main threads, you can be outstanding.

"Practicing martial arts is a long-haul effort, it must fit in with the students' physical and mental maturity and be learned in a planned way. Young people should learn martial arts from Northern and Southern Shaolin. They should first develop strong muscles and bones, amplifying their innate strength as much as possible, imprint it and after three to five years, switch over to practice the internal school with Xingyiquan.

"Xingyiquan practices *Ming Jin*, which means overt, obvious, clearly expressed power, a technique that internalizes the original power of the External School.

"Xingyiquan uses the five main elements of metal, water, wood, fire, and earth, to evolve into five mother strikes. This is originally a life and death combat technique used on the battlefield. To facilitate the teaching and training, it has been changed. Myriad offensive and defensive actions, converged into the five most effective prototypical actions, simply said:

From high to low	"Pi—Splitting"	(metal)
From low to high	"Zuan——Drilling"	(water)
From inside out	"Beng—Pounding"	(wood)
Cutting diagonally up	"Pao—Cannon"	(fire)
Shifting left and right	"Heng—Crossing"	(earth)

In addition, straight and angle lines, curved lines, arc lines, and spirals:: these five ways of exerting force and changes contain the five corresponding paired elements of rising and falling, opening and closing, expanding and contracting, relaxing and tensing, and piercing and buttoning. Mutually generating, mutually overcoming, they emphasize the use of simplicity to overcome complexity, the fist does not leave the center, and the boldness and overt power of the one punch kill.

"According to what my senior Wu Meng-xia said, the original form of Xingyiquan evolved from ancient spear techniques. If you put down the spear, the spear technique is an unarmed boxing technique. So, when you practice boxing, you must have an invisible long spear in your hand. When you practice cultivating power, to grow skills rapidly you need to use a long spear to help.

"The spear method is light and agile, the emphasis is on attack, not defense, heavily weighted toward piercing, not bludgeoning. It specializes in finding small angles with hidden openings to directly pierce and thrust into, while trying to avoid large-angular contact with the enemy as much as possible. If you collide with an opponent's weapon during the piercing, the enemy's weapon will be deflected with the rolling strength of the spiral drill, as in the Drilling and Crushing technique of Xingyiquan, the most classic application. Even the power and angle used in Crossing are also less than 45 degrees when released.

"The five mother fists of Xingyiquan are not a beautiful performance routine, but a practical way of training alone, which is convenient for repetitive exercises between the left and the right, until the moves are practiced into instinctive reflex.

"The five element mother fists of Xingyiquan are all single exercises, but they are all related, mutually generating and overcoming each other. They can be arranged on the spot in any permutation to form a variety of instant impromptu countermeasures. This is just like the Chinese children's toy, *Tangram*. Seven small boards of different shapes and sizes are assembled to form an image of all things. It is an exceptional internal martial art."

"In addition to the five original mother fists, later exponents used the original concepts to derive the Five Element Consecutive Boxing, Eight Powers Boxing, the 12-forms of five birds and seven beasts, Mixed Hammers, and the 12 Great Hammers, Cannon Protecting the Body, etc., but the most critical and core techniques are all included in the five simple actions, and the others are all supplementary moves.

"Before I formally came into contact with Xingyiquan, I had practiced Baguazhang for seven years, but when I actually tried to use it, I couldn't beat a friend who practiced Praying Mantis boxing. Later, my senior asked me to go back and practice Xingyiquan. After synthesizing these two martial arts, the one who fought with Mantis Fist was no longer a match for me.

"Of course, this is just my opinion of Xingyiquan. Without the gorgeous ease and clever variety of Baguazhang, Xingyiquan is just simple and effective, a fighting skill to extinguish the opponent. An analysis of its customary technique is the forward hand builds the bridge as an opening gambit, then the rear hand directly attacks. Its tactics are: first, the front hand uses the techniques of button, pluck, parry, press, and slap to destroy the opponent's defense and balance and cause the opponent's body to fall forward. The rear hand uses the five methods of splitting, drilling, crushing, pounding, and crossing as the main attacking force. To achieve the goal of a one punch kill, when Xingyiquan releases power in the strike, the target point is set behind the enemy, so that the force of the strike penetrates the muscle tissue and goes through the protection of the muscles and sinews, and directly pierces the internal organs, destroying the enemy's capacity to retaliate. It is the most direct and most effective battle force. It is extremely practical.

"If you are interested in learning internal boxing, Xingyiquan is definitely the gate through which most people must enter training."

Hong Yi-xiang in the Three Bodies Posture of Xingyiquan Splitting Fist, circa 1960.
Used with permission of Chris Bates

Hong Ze-han performs elements of the
12 Animal Form of Xingyi: the Roc, Swallow, Snake,
Monkey, Hawk, Dragon, and Horse.

50– DISCOURSE ON BAGUA

Baguazhang: It is a halberd with a hook. A head stab is a feint, as soon as it makes contact it returns, hooking, carrying, pulling, first sucking the opponent in to destroy his balance, then exerting force to attack. For this reason, the opponent within this maelstrom has his sense of direction disordered, his breath and blood reverse flow.

Scene: Zhang Jun-feng's new residence

(THE FOLLOWING IS A MONOLOGUE BY ZHANG JUN-FENG.)

"Different from other internal martial arts, the path walked by Baguazhang is to create stillness from action, a kind of extremely proactive and predatory martial art.

"Among the three internal martial arts it also got its start latest. In Chinese fist arts, regardless of the size of the school or when it originated, it inevitably shrouds itself in a thick and mysterious light, it's just those farfetched legends are of no real benefit to the development of martial arts. It's alright to listen to, but…

"The disadvantage to a boxing art that got started late is often that the completeness can be lacking. But its advantage is that the nature of skills will be of a higher level, because after all, its framework is created on top of the existing technical levels. There are more models and theoretical foundations to be referred to.

"Baguazhang is an internal martial art based on palm methods and mobility.

"During practice, imagine the enemy is in the center of a circle, and use two stepping methods, button, and swing, to walk around the circle outside of our enemy, and change the palms concurrent with a button step to initiate the attack.

"The purpose is to use constant movement and change to disrupt the enemy, so the enemy has no way to focus smoothly and marshal an attack. It trains you, when moving and changing steps, to find openings into which you can reach. Because of the focus on attack, we especially emphasize an intention to strike unexpectedly and using fast hands to strike the slow.

"This kind of continuous and circular training method is said to be a cultivation method employed by Taoist priests circling the incense burner 'orbiting the Celestial Worthy' to seek enlightenment. Its biggest advantage is that one can do unlimited exercise in a limited space.

"Of course, the first obstacle you have to face when practicing Baguazhang is circle walking, because going around in a circle is not a habitual human action.

"Obviously, when you go around a circle, your eyes have to stay on a fixed point. It's easy to make people dizzy.

"To walk the circle, you have to correct the angle of the button and swing steps according to the size of the circle.

"So, the inner foot must be swung, and the outer foot must be buttoned. Of course, there is also a reverse training method that involves turning around and walking the other way around the circle.

"In the early stage of training, the diameter of the circle should not be less than three meters. After you have mastered that, you can adjust the size of the circle at will. The smaller the circle, the greater the angle of the button step. The twisting of the body must also correspond.

"After you are proficient in the button and swing steps, the next is to train mud stepping.

"The mud step is like treading carefully on a slippery mud surface. To avoid slipping and falling, you must place your body's center of gravity on the back foot, first use the front foot to probe the ground, then move the center of gravity to the front foot, and then repeat with the back-foot probing ahead.

"Mud stepping is a dynamic qigong for practicing essence, vitality, and spirit, it is not used in fighting moves.

"The mud step requires the weight of the whole body to ride on the back foot while the front foot empties and lifts up probing forward. The ultimate goal is to be able to unify the whole-body power; toes clutch the ground, the soles of the feet empty, and the intention rises from the Bubbling Spring point. Pull up the sphincter, let the innate true Qi pass up through the Ren and Du channels to achieve the effect of nourishing bones.

"Ordinary people are content with a superficial understanding. When walking in the circle, regardless of the inner foot or the outer foot, their entire foot's sole is imprinted on the arc of the circle. This kind of training, even if you go around the circle for a lifetime, it is equivalent to practicing for nothing.

"Because of that kind of practice, the angle of the button and swing steps are both diluted by the circle, the spiraling energies cannot emerge. The correct practice should be: When the inner foot is swinging to the outside, you should step so the heel of the front foot is inside of the circle and let the heel of the rear foot press on the outside of the circle. When the rear outer foot is button stepped inside, the heel of the foot is pressed on the circle, while the back heel stays outside the circle. This is the only way to practice the essence of the button and swing step.

"Besides button and swing steps and mud stepping, the biggest characteristic of Baguazhang is that palms are employed more than fists. Among them, the most important method is the piercing palm. When the piercing palm reaches out, the spiraling force is like a steel rasp drilling out, forcing the opponent to make contact. As soon as contact is made, you will immediately pull back your wrist with a reverse rotation, and your fingers should grasp the opponent's wrist like thorny steel hooks and yank down. The purpose is to disrupt the opponent's balance. He loses the ability to defend.

"The most foundational palms of the Baguazhang are single, double, following, back, embracing, turning, rubbing, and overturning. These eight moves are all performed left and right as single exercises, most of which are to pull the enemy onto the perimeter. They are not directly entering the center of the circle to attack.

"And this system I practice is based on the Baguazhang of grand master Cheng Ting-hua and my master Gao Yi-sheng, who spent a lifetime of effort refining the original palms into: snake following palm, dragon piercing palms, turning back to fight the tiger palms, swallow overturning palms, turning the body to the back palm, twisting body horse palm, shaking body piercing back palm, stopping body, moving capturing palm, eight Pre-heaven palms and named it 'Swimming Body Consecutive Baguazhang.'

"At the same time, the fighting applications taught by these sages were reclassified and reorganized according to usage and characteristics as 'Post Heaven Bagua Sixty-Four Palms.' The Post-Heaven Palms are designed to intensify combat effectiveness. There are hand techniques, elbow methods, and body methods. There are throwing methods, leg methods, and joint control skills. To facilitate learning and use, they are all left and right single exercises.

"In addition, to increase the force of one's release of energy, this school yet has a set of exercises to strengthen the tendons and fortify the bones called 'The Ten Celestial Stems.' They are extracted from the Pre-Heaven and Post-Heaven palms and called Move, Chop, Hang, Collide, Button, Crush, Grasp, Sway, Obstruct, and Relax. Ten commonly used movements to specially strengthen the central axis of the body, the dragon-pillar and the four-limbs, connecting the main muscles and traditional Chinese medicine channels of the body core. If you practice patiently according to the key principles, you can achieve the magical effect of shedding one's mortal body and exchanging one's bones, returning to your pre-birth state. This technique is to develop our innate energy, but the real key lies in the word "diligence," as in the saying "Heaven Rewards the Diligent." If a person cannot diligently practice it daily, it is like he has learned a peerless martial art but is unable to display its true greatness and value.

"Generally speaking, Xingyiquan practices straight and curved lines. When confronting the enemy, it uses the seven-star footwork to build bridges and opening moves. Once you decide to attack, you will adopt a direct approach seizing the target, using great power and force to a quick conclusion. Bagua Palm practices arcs and loops, but you definitely do not want to lock the enemy in the center of the circle, and then pointlessly circle him. This misunderstanding will only have two results: One is that your enemy will laugh to death, the other is that you will be struck dead by the enemy.

"Bagua Palm's combat strategy is to take the enemy's line of advance and retreat as a reference point, extending it forward and backward as a central axis, and then lock on this line, shuttle back and forth across it, and constantly use the penetrating palm to disturb and lure the enemy, waiting for the opportunity to ripen, then cutting in from the flanks, attacking with the superior offensive of your two hands taking his one hand. The 'Boxing Bible' says: "Abandon the direct, choose the outside angle, when you capture his flank switch to a straightaway surge, your front foot seizes his rear heel, your rear foot shuttles in, launching your hands will lead to success." This is the truth. In battle, Baguazhang adopts an indirect, flanking style of attack. Once you have buttoned down your opponent, use full force to yank them on a transverse plane, and then immediately switch to a direct surge to launch an attack toward his side. In the end, it is 'the center' that has been captured, a kind of dynamic center. It may sound abstract, but you will understand it slowly after practicing.

"Different from Xingyiquan's direct attack, Baguazhang chooses a more indirect and three-dimensional style of play. It will first use the methods of button, pick, enter, lead, yank, and obstruct to destroy the enemy's balance, first guiding the opponent in a false direction to make the opponent misjudge, when he forcefully tries to reverse direction, you then reverse direction in your attack. It instantly confuses the opponent and forces the flow of blood to reverse.

"Even people who have practiced hard iron cloth shirt *qigong*, if they are in a situation where the *qi* and blood reverse flow, they will immediately find themselves deflated and enervated, and then there is no qi barrier to protect the internal organs. So, fundamentally without relying on brute strength, you can cause great damage.

"These kinds of tactics to bewilder and misdirect the enemy are not simply a back-and-forth direction. It uses left-right-left, left-right-right, left-right-down, and left-right-forward…These seemingly random continuous assaults—people fundamentally don't know how to defend against them at all.

"Of course, this style of play requires close coordination of body shape, hand technique, and footwork. It is a more complex and superior style of play. If you lack the foundation and actual combat experience, employing such complex maneuvers to face the enemy is, conversely, very dangerous indeed.

"I have made this mistake in the past. That's why I never beat others.

"If you can mix and match Baguazhang and Xingyiquan, you can achieve a complementary effect. When the situation permits, use the overt energy of Xingyiquan to directly capture. When the situation is not obvious, use the circuitous outflanking strategy of Baguazhang to cut in from the side. The two fists complement each other to boundless miraculous effect."

When martial arts practitioners talk about martial arts, they seldom just talk with their mouths. The two talked with increasing excitement, lively fists and feet flew as student imitated master in the not-so-spacious living room. Fourth brother Yi-xiang under the enthusiastic guidance of Zhang Jun-feng, finally formally entered the realm of internal martial arts, a peek into the wisdom and mystery accumulated by Chinese martial arts over thousands of years.

Ji 戟, the Chinese character for a halberd, the weapon that describes the actions of Baguazhang.

Hong Ze-han performs Pre-heaven Bagua Piercing Palms, 1994.

51- SPEAKING OF TAIJI

Taiji Boxing: Taiji is not simply a set form, moreover, it is a model and catalyst. Any action can be put through this model and catalyst and be turned into Taiji.

If you try to grasp water with your hand, when your fingers start to close, the water will escape through the cracks between your fingers. This is not stemming from water's innate strength, but it is water using your strength to escape.

Scene: Zhang Jun-feng's new abode

(THE BELOW IS A MONOLOGUE FROM ZHANG JUN FENG.)
   "Taoism cultivates Yin and Yang, Taiji boxing trains in hard and soft.
   "Yin and Yang are good, hard and soft are all very good, actually both are only representations of extreme states. This is a binary concept. At one time this concept was considered very advanced.
   "But after several hundred years of sustained exploration and progress, we made a discovery—between dual extremes of Yin and Yang, birth and death, black and white, clear and obscure, true and false, there exists an overlap with an undefined gaping, chaotic, fuzzy space.
   "In the traditional concept, Yin and Yang already contain everything, including this undefined fuzzy space, and everything is within the operation of these two polarities; moreover, in the process of their operation, they created their interactive meaning and value.
   "Take life and death as an example. Birth is an instant, death is also an instant, in between these two poles there still exists a process of moving from weakness to strength and from strength to weakness. Even if we are talking about the brief life of an insect, it's the same process of transition.
   "Using the same logic to infer, between hard and soft there exists the same fuzzy yet enormous capacity and possibility.
   "Before we discuss Taiji boxing, if one is not aware of this, then it is easy to lose one's way in the myth of hard and soft and never find the path out.
   "The average person speaking of internal martial arts is always talking about the mutual benefit of hard and soft, but this kind of talk will never reveal the opposition and limitations to these two elements hard and soft.
   "Everybody loses sight of the admixture of these two elements, what kind

of new changes and new elements will be produced. I believe ultimately that internal boxing is exploring these particular inner energies. In the past I never knew how to describe this condition, but afterwards I discovered there was something that could very suitably describe this situation.

"So. It's like a high gluten dough, a very active or alive condition. If you press on it, it recedes in, and as soon as you release your hand, it rebounds back. As soon as you pull it, it stretches longer, as soon as you release your hand, it contracts back.

"This state more closely describes Taiji's strength than water.

"In Taiwan, how do you describe this kind of elastic tenacity?

"Q? Yes. It's QQ—like your delicious chewy noodles! This is Q power.

"Therefore, to train Taiji boxing one must first grasp the three principles of hard, soft and Q.

"Taiji boxing is not a fixed pattern. Moreover, it is a model of movement. This type of model can be a vehicle to convey all manner of attack and defense.

"Any style or form, doesn't matter if it's Shaolin boxing, Xingyiquan or Baguazhang, if it channels this medium, and complies with it as a model for its actions, it will be absorbed by Taiji boxing.

"The opposite is also true. We can perform a Taiji boxing movement using Shaolin boxing style and it will become Shaolin boxing, or maybe tough Taiji.

"In any event, the names we give boxing styles are created by people, boundaries are also written by people. As far as I'm concerned, if it can defeat an enemy, strengthen my body and improve my health, then it's all good.

"Do you know why I emphasized first defeating my enemy? Because things which strengthen my body and improve my health are not necessarily martial arts.

"The original purpose of martial arts is to overcome one's enemies. Strengthening the body and improving the health are its secondary attributes. But so many people do not comprehend the logic of this progression. Hence, Taiji boxing has become Taiji calisthenics.

"Boxing and calisthenics are all good things, but the motive of the training is not the same, and the results achieved in the end are not the same.

"If one is training boxing, then we must be particular about form, intent, method, overt, covert, and adaptable technique. During training, our mind must be focused on imitating the application of the technique, just like we are facing an opponent. After thousands, tens of thousands, of repetitions, when these applications take root in our mind, they become a reflexive response, this sets the standard for martial arts training.

"Taiji gymnastics focuses on breathing cultivation and life extension, the purpose is greatly different. Taiji boxing becoming Taiji gymnastics is not inherently bad. But it's Taiji gymnastics. Not Taiji boxing. You can't jumble them up together.

"Taiji boxing talks about adaptable strength, but in application it must be mixed with overt strength and covert strength, thus can a better victory be achieved.

"Adaptable strength is a technique to control and use the opponent's strength.

"It's like a car hurtling down the road at high speed. From the perspective of the car, with only a slight change in angle of the steering wheel it is sufficient to alter the direction of the car to fatally crash into a person.

"Of course, Taiji's premise is that you want to coax out the opponent's strength, and only then can you lead and guide it.

"If you understand how to cultivate opportunity, and you understand how to counterattack, then you have mixed Taiji and Bagua, this will give rise to unimagined power.

"In general people consider that Taiji boxing is a comparatively benign, passive martial art. This is a very superficial view. The Golden Envelope Poem states: "The martial does not produce the good, and from form who can know emotion." When in combat, it is all about the ultimate aim of overcoming the enemy and achieving victory. For this reason, do you want the process to be diabolical? Or benevolent? Do you want it to be taking the fight to him? Or passive? It all depends on what is necessary to win. It's absolutely not a matter only of flailing your arms.

"When I have decided that a matter cannot be resolved peacefully, then I have to grasp the opportunity to move first, to attack first and to control the opportunity, this is a key to producing victory.

"If I feel that there is no route to victory, then I also have no right to demand a peaceful resolution. Maybe the principle of what I've said is not necessarily correct, but this is my strategy. So, all along I have never considered Taiji boxing to be so passive or peaceful."

The two men continued to talk, continued to compare, continued until the embers had died out, and the entire pot of Northeast Chinese sour cabbage soup had become cold, yet the two men had still not stopped, they continued chatting, continued gesturing…and no one could know just how long it would be before they stopped.

Master Hong demonstrates the Single Whip of Taijiquan, 1982.

52– TAIWANESE ESSENCE OF CHANGE

Reality is like a giant, ideal-swallowing monster. As soon as it is expedient, often in the blink of an eye, one careless slip is enough to force life and world changing compromises. This principle applies equally to a street side portrait painter, as well as to a resident martial art teacher.

Scene: Dalongcheng's studio

IN AN AGE WHEN FILM CAMERAS WERE NOT VERY COMMON, AMONG ordinary people film processing, enlargement and reproduction were considered very advanced and fashionable professional skills. To alleviate the feelings of longing for hometown and relatives, people travelling far from home would never forget to put a small black and white photo of the family portrait in their wallet when they left. Over time, the photos in the wallet would slowly turn yellow, fade and blur. To retain all the sentiment embodied in these images, a professional painter who specialized in painting portraits on behalf of customers would be employed to take the figures in the small photos and copy them, via a fine meticulous brushstroke technique, onto graph paper. From this, artists with good skill could not only recreate the family member's face with charcoal pens on drawing paper, but also, according to the needs of the customer, make the person in the photo fatter, thinner, add wrinkles or change the costume. This kind of time-bending skill can be regarded as the pioneer of Photoshopping.

Artists usually fixed the photo on the easel, and then mounted a magnifying glass to view all the features and details to be highlighted, and then transferred the image to graph paper. From the photo to the small squares the angles and proportions, the size, the contour lines and shadows of the portrait in the photo were transferred to many small simple units within small squares. Because the delineated image will become simple elements and lines, provided the artist can accurately grasp the angle at which the lines appear in the grid, and use a pen to draw the lines on the drawing paper, these divided small squares will magically recombine into the original image. Even if it is magnified several times, it can still be replicated beautifully. In addition, people's memories of images and appearances always become blurred with the lapse of time, so as long as the charm and feeling of the portraits was not too far from reality, it was good enough for the clients seeking the portraits.

The tools required for painters to make a living on the street are very simple.

They only need: an easel, a magnifying glass, a clip lamp, a few sheets of drawing paper, a few pens, and a couple of completed portraits of famous people or their proudest work as a signboard. One could open a business in a small shop or an arcade of less than three to five square meters. This was a profession and skill of an earlier time in an agricultural society.

Later, the camera became common and this was the enemy of the portrait painting industry. The skill of portraiture could not beat out competition from new imaging technology. Today, the business of street painters in Ximending or Tamsui Old Street has transformed into quick sketches of tourists, capturing a snapshot of the tourist's vacation mood. The kind of cherished memory of hometown and relatives outlined in black ink in the past required a completely different emotional register. In that era, painters of portraits and movie posters were often graduates of Fine Arts schools who failed to become artists. Perhaps in the beginning, they thought it was a temporary expedient, simply to earn three squares a day, for which they must lower their heads and make a living. However, under the strict pressures of reality, the temporary expedient eventually became the unavoidable compromise of a lifetime and the only way forward.

On this day, Zhang Jun-feng looked through his suitcase and found two small, yellowed photos, one of his grandmaster, Cheng Ting-hua, and the other of his master, Gao Yi-sheng. These two precious photos had always been separately sandwiched within the title pages of two martial art manuscripts, "Golden Letters Verses" and "Art of the Cosmic Orbit." Since he had decided to officially pioneer the establishment of a school, by accepting disciples and teaching the art in Taiwan, he thought everything must be attended to according to traditional rules. On that day, he and fourth brother Yi-xiang made a special trip by trishaw to Dalonggang to call on a famous painter, now retired. The painter, impoverished, living alone up a cold back alley, still maintained the artist's toughness, insisting that he had retired and was unwilling to paint for money. After a long heart to heart talk, he nodded and agreed to paint the portraits of the two Cheng School Gao-style Baguazhang masters. He insisted Zhang Jun-feng describe the life stories and personality traits of the two masters in as much detail as possible, because in the words of this famous artist with severely degraded eyesight, without supporting background information on these personages, the final image drawn would only be a picture, a piece of paper not infused with life force. Such a portrait could be hung at the end of a hallway, but it was not suitable to go on a family altar for receiving people's prayers and veneration.

It was precisely because of this insistence and conviction that fourth brother Yi-xiang was willing to expend a price several times more than what was typical for the efforts of ordinary painting hacks and beseeched the retired artist to make quality portraits of the two Baguazhang masters. After the two parties agreed on the time for the interim inspection and the final collection of the paintings, the two men, master and disciple, departed to the "Lin Wu-hu Fortune Telling Studio," located near the Rosy Seas Temple of the City God, on Dihua Street, to request Master Fortune Teller Lin's help in selecting an auspicious day for the opening of Zhang Jun-feng's 'Taiwan Beginnings—Essence of Change School' and to ask him to perform the necessary preparatory work.

Zhang Jun-feng's seal used on certificates—
Taiwan Beginnings Essence of Change.

Martial arts luminaries attend Zhang Jun-feng's opening of the Taiwan Beginnings Essence of Change school, 1953.

Opening of the Taiwan Beginnings Essence of Change school, Zhang Jun-feng (center) Hong Yi-xiang to his left, 1953.

53– MAKING OBEISANCE TO THE MASTER

All boundaries within the world of Nature are blurred. For survival, when mankind lacks a teacher, we frequently imitate Nature. However, after the mechanisms for passing on traditions are developed, people no longer need to risk their own flesh and blood to recreate the learnings and experience already conceived by other people. They can simply stand on the shoulders of their forebears and view the whole world. Diligent people, even in the course of daily life, can extend their learnings; intelligent people can transform learnings into experience and wisdom; even more intelligent people understand how to put to good use the creations, experience, and wisdom of these other people.

Scene: Hong Wan Mei Trading Company

Hong Wan Mei Trading Company sprang into action for this special day, and specially posted an announcement three days in advance, to notify the day of suspension of business. To not break with the proper etiquette, Wu Fan-bo deliberately invited elders familiar with the customs and traditions of both Taiwan and North China to his shop, to advise on arranging a dignified and grand Obeisance to the Master gathering. Large celebration wreaths sent by friends in the business and martial arts world festooned the pillars on the road outside the shop. On the lintel of the door, there was a huge embroidered vertical silk banner of the Eight Immortals and along its top border was another embroidery of calligraphy announcing "Taiwan Beginnings–Essence of Change Groundbreaking and Obeisance to the Master Ceremony."[15] The calligraphy was both powerful and energetic, like dragons and phoenixes dancing. With a single look one knew this was calligraphy by the hand of the second brother of the Hong family, Yi-wen. The embroidery had been commissioned to the shop at the entrance to Dihua Street specializing in silk embroidery, and the chief of the famous shop took nearly a month to meticulously stitch the artwork to perfection.

In the shop, the original merchandise display cabinets and the large checkout

---

15 *BaiShi* 拜師 is a ceremony in which the pupil submits themselves to the Master, entreating to be accepted as a formal disciple in the lineage. It is sometimes translated as "apprenticeship ceremony," but in the Western term, apprentice, has a commercial connotation. A closer translation is Making Obeisance to the Master.

counter were all covered with red cloth. In the main hall, a set of high-legged altar tables and square Eight Immortal tables exquisitely carved out of the best Chinese cedar were arranged. A statue of the Zen patriarch Damo, Master Bodhidharma, was enshrined atop the cedar altar table. Fourth brother Yi-xiang had earnestly sought the work of the chief carver of the Lushan Pavilion, a famous Buddhist wood carvings shop on Yanping North Road and selected first rate ebony to be slowly and meticulously carved. As Master Bodhidharma had crossed the seas from India to propagate Buddhist teachings in China, and Indian's have a darker complexion, the use of dark ebony to carve out the master teacher's statue created the right effect without needing to stain the wood. People who train martial arts venerate Damo as the founder of martial learning, and most admire his "Punch my teeth out and make me swallow blood, I set my jaw and train harder" spirit of determined ascetic practice and fortitude.

In front of the high-legged altar table, on the shorter Eight Immortals table, there was a vertical mahogany picture frame that could be folded in two. Mounted in the two picture frames, were those two large charcoal portraits executed with utmost care by the retired painter at Dalongdong. The two black-and-white portraits expressed a graceful might, an imposing aura. It is hard to imagine that a nearly half-blind, decrepit painter could fathom how to paint such a realistic portrait of a person from those small, yellowed, faded and torn photos, and scattered oral recollections. A downtrodden, unknown painter who spent his entire life on the streets eking out a living still had within his paintings the ability to isolate that piece of his inner landscape, the artist's soul and vision, not yet overwhelmed by reality and not yet completely extinguished by time.

In the small incense burner at the front of the table, burned high quality "Laoshan Wuchen" saturating the air with a solemn religious dignity. To the left and right of the Eight Immortals table, sitting on one side was Zhang Jun-feng, painstakingly dressed and made up, his bearing noble and imposing. Sitting on the other side was a ninety-five-year-old local elder. Gathered together at the banquet on behalf of Zhang Jun-feng sat all the celebrities and masters in the martial arts world who had followed the government's messy retreat to Taiwan at that time. To accommodate the egos of these different sects, Zhang Jun-feng had bothered to adjust the seating arrangement dozens of times, but there was still some unavoidable unhappiness and "the teeth of the upper and lower jaw not aligning" on the day of the ceremony. People are vain regarding the ranking of seniority; even when in the awkward situation of being stranded in a strange land, still they would rather die than yield. Fortunately, these episodes were all dissolved by the smiling welcome of the host, Black Snake.

The honored guests sitting next to the local elder included almost all of

Dadaocheng's highly regarded big bosses. The layout of the spectacle, the invitations for the guests and the seating arrangements showed that for the Obeisance to the Master Ceremony, Wu Fan-bo's plans were prudent and attentive. In addition to sincerely expressing the respect of the Hong family to the martial arts world, the artful display also cleverly raised Zhang Jun-feng's position in the future development of Taiwan's martial arts world. This was an integration of the martial arts community with the business community. It was the first time on the home island of Taiwan that the financial strength of the business community had supported a Mainland Chinese martial art. This act was unprecedented. Of course, all of the publicity generated by this grand affair, building on Hong Wan Mei's positioning as a daring and influential business leader on Dihua Street, and indeed, in Northern Taiwan, was one of the motivations behind Wu Fan-bo's meticulous plan.

The ceremonies were kept in accordance with the ancient rituals for apprentices in the martial arts world. The young squires of the Hong family followed the command of the master of ceremonies, and one by one ceremoniously presented a cup of tea and kowtowed before the images of the patriarchs and Master Zhang Jun-feng. From that moment on, Zhang Jun-feng, a businessman who came to Taiwan to do business, officially became the martial arts master of the four young masters of the Hong family, and he was also the first-generation master of the "Taiwan Beginnings—Essence of Change" founding sect. As the ceremony of Making Obeisance to the Master was reaching a conclusion, several ruddy faced, burly chaps who had been watching from outside the shop shoved their way in, followed closely by the face of the man who had just that year failed to finesse the large tender to produce candles, Jin Yuan-long.

"Mr. Hong, you must really love Taiwan, not! There is not one single local boxer you don't look down on. Conversely you pick a 'mountain man'[16] who can't even speak a word of Taiwanese. You are deliberately humiliating Taiwanese!" Jin Yuan-long declared.

"You…" Third brother Yi-mian, seeing that Jin Yuan-long was intentionally looking to pick a fight on this occasion, immediately stiffened up and rose, itching to gratify these troublemaking ruffians' perverse intrusion by delivering a public lesson to them. He was grabbed by fourth brother Yi-xiang, who began urging him to calm down and observe.

"You put on this show, so big and so ostentatious, your backup must be impressive. Why not take this opportunity to show your hand and let everyone see how powerful the Northern Internal school is!" Jin Yuan-long said.

"Boss Jin, today is a teacher apprenticeship ceremony, it isn't convenient. If you are really interested, I will invite you to visit another day!" said second brother Yi-wen.

---

16 Here the guest is insulting Zhang Jun-feng calling him an uncouth mountain man. Zhang hailed from Shandong Province, East of the Mountain Province.

"Ai! Changing the date is not as good as the spur of the moment. Besides, there are so many people here looking for excitement, let's just do it today. What's everybody say?" Jin Yuan-long egged on the crowd to jeer.

The curiosity of the crowd, escalated with the deliberate heckling, combined to make the scene suddenly very awkward. Wu Fan-bo understood in the bottom of his heart the trick being played, but he did not want to be hustled into a tight corner. Just as he was about to speak up his objections, he saw Zhang Jun-feng had stood up and walked towards the interlopers. "Although I don't speak Taiwanese, I do understand everything you said. Since this friend is interested in the Internal School of boxing, let's have a go!" Zhang Jun-feng said.

"Fresh. I like it. In order not to let people say that we bully outsiders, I'll let you pick which among my brothers here," Jin Yuan-long said.

Fourth brother Yi-xiang stepped forward. "Great. But this is our place of business. It's not suitable for getting down to this kind of work. If you really want to test us, you send whomsoever. Master Zhang does not need to show up, I can take care of it. Since you want to see Internal Boxing, give me three months, then I will use the Internal School boxing to do battle." Fourth brother Yi-xiang understood what was on his father's mind, and destroyed the opponent's tricky intent with "no-intent."

"What a good disciple. You were only just admitted as your Master's student, and you can't wait to help the master by stepping in for him." Jin Yuan-long's original intent was just to disrupt the ceremony, to kill the highfalutin,' overweening atmosphere of the apprenticeship ceremony the Hong family had organized. He never thought that the Hong family's fourth son would deliver himself up for a drubbing, so he restrained the delight he felt in his heart, outwardly only clapping his hands, but his face deliberately bore an expression of reluctant acceptance. "Okay. We'll do it your way. Three months from now, we'll contest in front of the Chenggonghao Suzhou teahouse. Everyone's welcome to attend and give guidance. Ha-ha-ha…," Jin Yuan-long said with a frivolous smile, and swaggered off.

"Yi-xiang! What the…?" Zhang Jun-feng started.

"It's okay. Master, you're a foreigner, its inadvisable that you get mixed up in such a trivial trouble at this time. Don't worry!" fourth brother Yi-xiang said.

Fortunately, this unexpected episode did not impact the whole apprenticeship ceremony. Wu Fan-bo forcefully concealed his unhappiness and concerns, as usual, and treated a few children to the Red-Faced Turtle cake from the Shizixuan Pastry Shop to celebrate the apprenticeship, then presented the same to guests and the crowd of onlookers.

At the conclusion of the ceremony, a banquet was held in the back street area of Dihua Street, and a continuous stream of fine food was served at more than twenty tables as the honored guests were generously feted. During the banquet, Wu Fan-bo, liberated with a little wine and rare pride, officially welcomed all neighbors and martial arts friends to practice boxing and strengthen the body. Hong Wan Mei would fully absorb and bear all tuition expenses and equipment during the study period. Because of the meticulous pre-planning and unexpected incidents during the process, the ground-breaking of the "Taiwan Beginnings—Essence of Change" won immediate fame and influence. Especially, the match scheduled on the banks of the Danshui River three months hence became a highly anticipated spectacle for the crowd of gawkers.

The grievance in the market had not vanished with time or one side's forgiveness. It worked according to the machinations of conspirators, hiding in concealed places, choosing to employ all manner of different disguises and tricks, awaiting its opportunity to reemerge. Of course, using a test of martial strength to settle a commercial grudge is not the best alternative; however, in places where the light of law and morality do not shine, to protect oneself and survive, counterattacking at the right time is the only option.

54– PLANTING THE SEED

A solitary seed can grow into a giant tree, can sprout an entire forest, or can just remain a seed. But so long as it is a seed, it can remain dormant underground or in a deep freeze for a hundred generations, a thousand years, and preserve all its possibilities of existence.

Scene: Hong Wan Mei Trading Company

"Training internal martial art doesn't have quick-fix shortcuts. Three months is too brief. Yi-xiang, you are taking too many risks," Zhang Jun-feng said.

"They came prepared, if master had accepted the challenge then and there, the risk would have been even greater," fourth brother Yi-xiang said.

"This I know. However, you are entirely uncertain about what's up with this opponent. Accepting this challenge was really impulsive," Zhang Jun-feng said.

"I had to stabilize the situation, and then think about how to handle it, anyways we still have time to prepare, rest assured," fourth brother Yi-xiang said.

"Asking around the martial arts world, the word is that on that day, the group standing to the side should be considered wanted bandits and criminals who fled the Mainland. This gang, mixed in with the tide of people on the Great Retreat, conspire to link up with local hoods, to grow their own influence," Zhang Jun-feng said.

"So long as they don't come packing guns, there should be a way to handle 'em," third brother Yi-mian said.

"This gang is not an orthodox martial art group, their hearts are black, black. Who knows what dirty tricks they'll use," Zhang Jun-feng said.

"Teacher, you're underestimating fourth brother. Even without using internal boxing, those guys aren't necessarily a match for him. In Taiwan judo circles, besides the exponents Huang Cang-lang and Chen Mei-shou, few can surpass him. Not long ago after a crash program he successfully challenged the Taiji push hands master and fought him to a draw," third brother Yi-mian said.

"I heard about this. This can only be considered a victory of strategy. It can't be considered to be true gongfu. This opponent is mixed up with crime gang bad guys, not related to the genuine techniques used by martial art masters," Zhang Jun-feng said.

"Teacher, don't worry, let me try. Since I have already agreed to use internal boxing to do battle, I still need Teacher's help," fourth brother Yi-xiang said.

"Quick fix short cuts, eh, I'll have to borrow from Xingyiquan, simplify the complex and drill, drill, drill it into you. And since you are already good at judo, I'll pick out some Baguazhang throwing techniques to put to use," Zhang Jun-feng said.

"Baguazhang has throwing techniques? Fantastic!" third brother Yi-mian said.

"The Post-Heaven palms training of Bagua has many techniques derived from Mongolian wrestling, even more solid and easy to employ than Japanese judo," Zhang Jun-feng affirmed.

"Good. Let's use this strategy. Outside of the arena if those guys really dare to wield dirty tricks, second and third brothers are responsible to frisk them. Inside the arena, I'll be careful, I won't give them a chance to play tricks," fourth brother Yi-xiang said.

"No worries. Leave those wise guys to me!" third brother Yi-mian said.

"The way I look at it, I am thinking perhaps the conclusion to this fight…it might be to the death. Don't forget, you cross hands with one of these desperados, you can't have a stitch of mercy or goodwill. The one who goes down, I am afraid is not just the loser. In matters of life and death, you can't be careless," Zhang Jun-feng said.

"I know. This is a no time limit, no holds barred, fight to the death. Winner take all, no good or evil, no right or wrong. I don't protect myself, I'm done for," fourth brother Yi-xiang said.

With this kind of prelude in Taiwan, Zhang Jun-feng's newly established Taiwan Beginnings—Essence of Change School cleared the field, took root, and sprouted. Every morning the four brothers of the Hong family, Yi-wen, Yi-mian, Yi-xiang and Yi-kun and an assortment of the rich sons of Dihua Street merchants with the shared motivation of building their physique's, working out, and protecting their family enterprises, banded together and one by one entered the school, starting with training the rudimentary lessons of Xingyiquan from Zhang Jun-feng. Every day, starting at dawn, they would train straight through, only dismissing class at noon. After noon was when Zhang Jun-feng and fourth brother Yi-xiang trained, one on one, in fighting.

For this one match, Zhang Jun-feng trained fourth brother Yi-xiang with a state of mind like he himself was going into the ring. The sentiment between the two of them included his gratitude for the helping hand extended when he was at his most isolated and downtrodden. He remembered the cordial hospitality the Hong family extended by investing effort, money, and heart into the baishi ceremony; including for the thoughtful consideration shown when he had shown his face to stem the provincial conflicts of local riff-raff and including this fight to elevate his influence in the martial art circles of Taiwan in the future.

Of course, even more importantly, the passion for training hard in Chinese martial arts without complaint, and the innate courage and talent shown by this young man were the reasons for not holding back in passing on practical sparring skills to fourth brother Yi-xiang. Zhang Jun-feng sought out many martial arts fellow enthusiasts, skilled in bare knuckle fighting, to assist in training and sharing techniques. These martial art exponents, who had been baptized in the chaos of war and a bitter life of homeless exile, served as "Resident Martial Art Instructors" to the Hong family.

Besides assisting in the training, according to their skills they also entered the candle factory production workforce, even serving in transport, delivery, and debt collection. Besides receiving a fixed stipend for teaching, even if they only helped out in the factory, they all received an additional wage supplement. Besides taking into consideration the efficient use of manpower, Wu Fan-bo regarded this arrangement as an expression of thoughtful care and compassion extended to these exiles far from home. This financial aid normally continued until the person made an arrangement with a government unit, or their friends from their old hometown helped them, at which time it would stop.

Later on, this elder generation of martial artists arranged through a veteran's affairs unit to go to the central mountain range, to trailblaze and open up land for agriculture, plant orchards, or participate in the Central Cross Island Highway engineering effort. To survive in quiet remote mountain areas far from civilization they had to take care of each other and mutually console their feelings of homesickness. They gathered local materials and simple tools, and as callouses grew on their hands and feet they built together, one by one, their family settlements.

In the end, whether they were able to pass down the martial skills they had spent a lifetime refining, no one knows. From being respected boxers of the martial forest barking out commands to students, they were transformed into vegetable or fruit farmers living a secluded life in the mountains. This process of change was most certainly not like flipping an electrical switch. From "on" to "off" one must only lightly press down a button, and it is easily completed. Their interval between "on" and "off" was no doubt entangled with many heartbreaking tales of blood and tears. The elegies of that great age accompanied their departed spirits, heads lowered, forever buried in the remote, misty, lofty mountains of a strange land.

Hong Ze-han demonstrates the Colliding Palm of Baguazhang's Post Heaven 64 Palms, 1994.

Blurred Boundaries

Hong Ze-han demonstrates Double Embracing
Palms of Baguazhang, 1994.

55– MARKING TERRITORY

What is a territory? A territory is just a place animals mark with their pee. When lions and tigers see a tree, they can't help but raise their hind legs and let loose a spray, declaring their sovereign right to eat to their fill gratis in that territory.

But in the law of the wilderness, where the strong prey on the weak, if you can only take a leak everywhere with no ability to protect your turf, pissing even more is just a kind of pointless self-consolation.

Scene: Mayflower Restaurant

"THE HONG FAMILY'S FOURTH SON IS JUST A RICH YOUNG MASTER, not a real martial arts player!" Jin Yuan-long said.

"I think so, too. Taiwan, this little snot-nosed backwater, shouldn't be able to hatch any tough guys," Bandit A said.

"But those martial artists at the banquet are all well-known in the Mainland. I am worried that these people will lend a hand and make things worse," Jin Yuan-long said.

"On this you can rest assured. Chinese people! If they were capable of working together, history would not look like this. Those martial artists, they all have their own schemes. They are not capable of being so magnanimous, or happy, to see the one surnamed Zhang be the first to dominate in Taiwan!" Bandit A said.

"For sure?"

"Those men came to show their faces, the bottom line for them was nothing more than their status and influence in the Taiwanese martial arts world. Didn't you see how red-faced they already became that day just about the seating assignments? Don't worry about these people going to battle for Zhang!" Bandit B said.

"Right. If those stupid pigs really knew how to cooperate to fight an enemy, then we meat eating tigers would have to become vegetarians instead. Ha-ha-ha…" Bandit A said.

"Good, good. It's just this fourth son, he doesn't always play the cards dealt. I have suffered losses from him in the bidding, better to be a little careful!" Jin Yuan-long said.

"Boss Jin. We brothers crossed the sea to come to Taiwan to put down roots and prosper, not to be temporary guests. When we fight, we will help you win back in spades the loss of face you swallowed at the tender," Bandit B said.

"Yeah. For our brothers, this battle is not a question of face but a question of filling our bellies. Don't worry," Bandit A said.

"Okay. Since you are so worried about this guy, I want to make you feel reassured. Starting tomorrow, can I trouble you, Boss Jin, to help our brothers arrange some human fodder to act as sparring partners, practice our skills. At night according to your expansion plan, we can start with any bars and dance halls at Nanjing West and Zhongshan North Roads that you are targeting. We will get even more practice. Pick a few big ones and we'll begin trashing them; kill the chickens to scare the monkey."

"Good, good. Practice during the day and practice at night. I guarantee you will get enough pre-match training every day. Ha-ha-ha!" Jin Yuan-long said.

Enterprise does not distinguish between expensive or cheap, good or evil. If great profits are there for the taking, there will always be people hiding in the dark, currying favor and waiting for opportune moments. It doesn't matter if they take the high road, or the low road, there is always someone with unique insight. At a glance they can see the huge benefits hidden in the gray blurred zone between the dark and light worlds. In the eyes of ordinary people, this kind of gray business opportunity bordering between legal and illegal is too risky to dare enter without careful consideration, but they cannot imagine that in the torrential ebb and flow must be stored tremendous power and resources.

In these dangerous areas where ordinary people dare not tread and explore, there are also potential hidden business opportunities submerged below the surface. Therefore, organized crime and the wealthy are always under the protection of the government and the police, allowing unbridled, rapacious exploitation of these resources. Therefore, in the process of creating profits, there are always some incidents offensive to heaven and reason that are fabricated intentionally or unintentionally. At this time, White Knights, pretending judicial righteousness, can ride into the scene and right the course, becoming accomplices able to overcome all obstacles smoothly. Whereupon even greater evils can all be manifested, their bad luck turns good, for them it is smooth sailing and all systems go.

It is possible the original intention of these people was to simply provide warm food and clothing for their families, old and young. But later their appetites grew. The definition of "warm food and clothing" was magnified infinitely, whereupon they slowly moved further and further from their original intention. There is too much evidence making them believe that provided they can seize power and wealth without repercussions, all crimes can be smoothed over by using power, using money to bribe, and using stories to bleach the truth. Is this not the way it is?

They even have a psychological justification to shed guilt and have a twisted road to salvation, and the incentives for crime are magnified at the same time, so the whole of society's elites will naturally compete for these grey zone preferential treatments. This "not to be spoken of" and unspeakable secret has never even slightly altered due to the changing of the times or the advancement of technology. The profit-seeking world is like a wild jungle, as soon as someone stumbles, immediately others will circle around to distribute the spoils, distribute the meat of the fallen's resources. Afterwards, they continue to strive to advance, continue to repeat the same plot, reenacting and reincarnating again and again, passing from generation to generation, lifetime to lifetime.

56– THE ROAR OF THE WANLI TURTLE

Rules are made to be broken. Nothing under Heaven is absolute. Turtles Roar. In fact, originally this was just a place sea turtles came ashore to lay eggs, so Taiwanese called it Guikong (龜空)—Turtle Space or Guikong (龜孔)—Turtle's Recess. Later, what reason was Guikong (龜孔) changed to Guihou (龜吼) Turtle Roar"? This is a mystery of the ages, even the local elders can only say the what and not the why.

Scene: Wanli Turtle Roar Village

IN WANLI, THERE IS A SMALL HARBOR FOR LOCAL FISHING BOATS called Guihou Village. It has always been a place of small fish catches, low productivity, so small that it did not attract people's attention. However, because of its remoteness and unobtrusiveness, it fully met the needs of smuggling and blockade running. And so this humble small fishing port became a strategic location of underworld influence. The coastal defense forces that had just been stationed in the local area and the public security units on the ground carried out coastal patrols round the clock to prevent smuggling, blockade running, or infiltration of spies from the other China. At this moment when the confrontation between the two sides of the Taiwan straits was the tensest, there were often United Front pamphlets from across the strait dropped from planes or washed up on shore, aimed at advancing a "silent war," and attracting extremist elements who were dissatisfied with current affairs and "willing to leave the reactionary side and cross over to the side of progress," to become Chinese Communist sleeper cells.

To counteract this, the local government authorities, of course, also set up a huge defense budget, through various channels and methods of political warfare and propaganda, to encourage fighters from the opposing camp to surrender to Taiwan. Different rewards were offered according to the propaganda value to the United Front. At that time, the highest reward was to encourage the Chinese Air Force pilots to fly the MiG fighters over to surrender. If they could defy death to dash across to the halfway mark of the straits, those who treasonously abandoned their homeland would immediately get a reward of ten thousand taels of gold and become anti-Communist and anti-Russian National heroes. Today we look upon these inducements as absurd, but then it was the open and grandiose Anti-Communist government policy, and people will never be able to penetrate the absurdity and nonsense of this old world.

It could well be asked, what kind of standard can be used to clearly identify the anti-communist principled man, which one is really surrendering for the sake of ideals and beliefs? Which ones, bewitched by the allure of quick bucks, choose to flee their homes and betray their country by deserting and taking the big roll of the dice? Therefore, although coastal patrol operations were carried out every day, night and day, driven by huge profits, things that shouldn't happen were still happening, and heaven knew, the earth knew, you knew and I knew.

Originally, most of the local people who lived in the Guihou area fished offshore for a living, but for many months of the year they could not fish due to the influence of the seasonal winds. During fishing's off season, they planted crops on infertile sandy farmland to supplement their households. However, the salt content of the coastal farmland is too high, and the wind and sand are too overpowering, so the crops grown in the fields far from made up for the economic shortfall of being unable to fish. Therefore, in addition to the main business of farming and fishery, when the ocean currents are not right, the schools of fish are not coming, and the gods do not bestow rice, they had to rely on some sideline business to support the family's livelihood. Willing to take risks to support their families, these fishermen formed a symbiotic bond with the military and police on frontier defense who provided special industries outside the law with transportation, mooring, tools, and necessary protection. The particular circumstances of the time and place, plus practical considerations, provided sufficient nutrients and incentives for all illegal business deals, whereupon, with the integration of "interested parties," these scattered motivations and de-mobbed soldiers gradually converged to become a giant network of accomplices. This food chain included coastal defense, public security, coordinated communications between the two sides of the strait, ocean transport to China, the fencing of stolen goods, bribery management, profit distribution, and crisis management in emergencies.

This was a large and complex machine. If it weren't for powerful characters with remarkable reach manipulating the levers of authority behind the curtains, weaving this complex network and relationships, at every turn relying on "Articles for Temporary Mobilization During Periods of Unrest" to serve the interests of illegal deals, how could ordinary public officials and local grassroots security units afford to play such a high stakes game. Stuck in the same historical rut, the law enforcers themselves are often the players and masterminds establishing this criminal organization. In other words, to the high-level ringleaders hidden behind the curtains, the ones doing the arresting and the ones arrested are just the difference between the left hand and the right hand. No matter how big the risk, it is nothing more than rearranging and redistributing the vested interest. In the process of interest reorganization and distribution, the losers are the chumps who really took risks, who no longer are of use and not knowing when to get off the gravy train, of course, become scapegoats!

Of course, those who pursued these illegal activities were not completely without taboos. At the time, anything connected to "cross-strait politics" was a sensitive issue, even those aces specializing in wandering the boundaries of the law took pains to avoid this taboo, lest they come up short. This was the era of the two Chiang's dictatorship. No one wanted to disturb that murder hornets' nest. In the end this "taboo" evolved into something the wealthy and privileged used to eradicate political enemies, a weapon to sell each other out and frame each other. Human ingenuity was really on display in the hands of these scoundrels who truly employed talent to the fullest, made the complete use of the land, exploited everything to the full to the point they felt they were omnipotent. This proves the common saying in southern Fujian: "If there is a law, it must be broken." Nothing is absolute in the world. Isn't it?

※ ※ ※

On a night without stars or moon, flickering lights of "three long and two short" appeared on the dark sea's horizon, and from the shadows of the shore came the immediate response of "two short and three long" lights. After a brief while, a motorized sampan could be seen emerging from the pitch-black ocean, heading toward the beachhead. Several guys who had shown their faces at the apprenticeship ceremony rushed down the sandbar to meet the people getting off the sampan.

"Big Brother. You had a rough ride," Bandit A said.

"It ain't easy for you either. Everything's fine!" Ba San said

"Thank you, Big Brother. All the brothers here are fine. All is arranged according to your plan," Bandit B said.

"And this is?" Ba San asked.

"Big Brother Ba San, my name is Jin, I welcome you to Taiwan!" Jin Yuan-long said.

"Thank you. I feel I troubled you to come here in person," Ba San said.

"No, no. That's as it should be!" Jin Yuan-long said

"Okay. I hope that with your help, our brothers can make great achievements in Taiwan. Haha,," Ba San chuckled.

"'Ba San' was the nickname of 'Scarfaced Elder Brother #3,' a gang member roaming southern China. He was a rare and cruel character in the gang with real gongfu. His life was vicious and cunning, and although he carried the burden of the many men he had killed, he possessed remarkable abilities, every time evading the dragnets of the law authorities and luckily escaping like a rabbit from a trap, to continue actively pursuing all manner of illegal activities in the coastal areas of South China. He got the scar on his face while fighting to take control of the gang, given to him by the boss that had raised him up, now not so lucky.

This time around, he came across the sea from Xiamen because most of the bureaucrats he originally colluded with had retreated to Taiwan with the Nationalist Government. The original power structure that dominated the overall situation lost control in China, so the profit-making structure and mechanism collapsed. All vested interests vanished into thin air. If he continued to stay on the mainland, not only would he not continue to profit, but he would likely lose his life as everyone settled old scores. So, he sent his brothers to sneak across and scout to see if they could connect with Taiwan's local criminal forces and replicate the original profit model from China, setting up their kitchen on the tropical island.

It seems that the Hong Family and Jin Yuan-long's contest at the Chenggonghao Hangzhou Tea Room was no longer a commercial grudge. The complex variables mixed within were a situation no longer possible for ordinary businessmen to contemplate.

57– THE ONE PUNCH KILL

In many matters, if one does not establish the preconditions, then there is no answer. Once one has set the preconditions, there can never be objective reality.

Scene: Danshui River—on the open space outside the Hangzhou Tearoom

THE HANGZHOU TEAROOM, SET IN THE TRENCHES DUG INTO THE banks of the Danshui River, was originally equipped with operating equipment of an old ship, now included: a charcoal stove, a big teapot for boiling water, teacupteacup sets, various refreshments, including cakes, and tables, chairs, and benches…all moved to the open space outside the cabin for this martial arts contest. The business-minded lady boss deliberately rented extra tables and chairs, used to enclose the originally empty venue into a square contest arena. Mobile stalls from all over the province, that usually appeared only during festivals or for welcoming the gods, or who followed the "theatrical troupes," were lined up selling various popular dishes: stir fried rice noodles, squid stew, oil cake, Sishen soup, grilled sausage, roasted sweet potato, roasted fart beans, Taigu pie, sponge toffee, etc. Vendors were stretching fresh noodles, coating skewers of haw with sugar, creating sugar sculptures, running rattan ring hoop games…whether they came to sell food or sell amusements, it is not known from where they heard the news of the event, but all of them descended on the venue a day early to personally scope out the best locations, in the hopes of getting their fair share of the business opportunities accompanying the tide of spectators.

The entire riverside square was as lively as a holiday market or a religious procession. After enjoying lunch, joyous idlers came in groups of friends carrying benches to occupy the best spots in advance. They exchanged information they had acquired beforehand about the fight prospects, predicting the possible winner and loser. In the eyes of people watching the contest, winning or losing in the field was often more important than the dispute, right and wrong, black and white, righteousness and evil.

At five o'clock in the evening, the sky was still bright, but it was cooling down. Besides the crowds watching the match and the vendors doing business, the entourages from both sides were already in place, and they chose their locations based on who got there first. Normally the riverbank outside of the dike was rarely patrolled by policemen. Today they were there in force, fully armed with rifles and billy clubs, surveying the perimeter of the arena and patrolling the area. Of course, also mixed in with the crowd were many plain clothes policemen and Investigation Bureau officers. What is more special is that even the Intelligence Bureau sent a military jeep to bring a foreigner to the scene to watch the battle. This foreigner was a military intelligence officer sent by the USA to assist Taiwan in establishing a network behind enemy lines and training the personnel—Colonel Jim Dolenz.

In that era under martial law, a popular martial arts contest was not a trivial matter. Were it not for the motives of highly placed people, this kind of high profile event would not be allowed to take place. The two sides and the spectators watching the excitement would never know how many public security units' attentions had been secretly aroused, and how many unknown specializations and mobilizations were set in motion by this event.

"This competition was agreed on by both parties. There are no rules. There are only two restrictions, one, this is unarmed fighting, and the other is that when one side goes down or admits defeat, the fight must be terminated immediately. Agreed?" The referee said.

"Okay," Guo Shan-hu said.

"Good," said fourth brother Yi-xiang.

The referee for this fight was Zhang Ying-wu, a well-known giant in the north. He was more than two meters tall and was unusually well built. As soon as one stood before him, all the sunlight was blocked. Although his movements were not very agile, and he had never practiced a day of gongfu, he was gifted with immense strength. He was asked to serve as a referee mainly to prevent both sides from crying foul in case someone was unwilling to yield according to the rules, and so long as this towering god stood in the middle, it would be difficult for either side to continue fighting.

The fighter Jin Yuan-long sent out from his team to respond to the challenge was known as Guo Shan-hu—Traversing the Mountain Tiger. This fellow was about thirty years old and 1.8 meters tall. His whole body was very muscular without a thread of flab. This is what is commonly called "Iron Boned Body" in Taiwanese. When Mountain Tiger was young, he had trained several years in the External School of hard gongfu, but because of his cruel and wild nature, even if he was sparring with his fellow students, he would often beat them until skin ripped and blood flowed from top to bottom without relenting. No one wanted to fight with him anymore, and later he simply stopped practicing. From then on, he decided that boxing arts were useless. So, he turned to the streets to seek purpose and excitement, and from street fighting, he accumulated a wealth of practical experience. For more than ten years, the Mountain Tiger had gathered crowds and gangs in South China, looting casinos, taverns, and brothels in various provinces, cities, towns, and villages along the coast. Nary a day went by without his knives, guns, or cudgels lapping up some blood. After being thrown in prison, it is not known for what reason, he landed in the hands of Ba San and became his enforcer. Today he came out fighting on behalf of Jin Yuan-long, implying that the two underworld forces in China and Taiwan had already successfully opened a new milestone of sincere cooperation between the two factions.

The way humans make a living starts from the most basic supply and demand. Because of environmental conditions and species characteristics, a food chain with elements of both interdependence and competition among its inhabitants is derived. Some people work hard every day, tilling, weaving, fishing, and raising cattle, so as to exchange the same for a meagre income barely enough to maintain a family's food and clothing. Other people buy these labors and products at a low price, and then package them into sellable goods seeking to gain greater profit from them. Others scheme to create games or scams, enticing and bewitching to human nature, in a search for huger profits. And then there are those who do nothing, just concentrate on taking the resources of others as their own. And such gangs as Jin Yuan-long and Ba San's are just like ferocious beasts at the top of the food chain, relying on their great claws and strong jaws, willing to do anything to "feed on the enemy."

However, just as in the natural world, plants extract nutrients from the sunshine and embrace of the earth to grow their seedlings, herbivores fill their bellies with these plants to survive, carnivores follow closely to hunt these herbivores, and finally these animals die one after another. They are decomposed by insects and bacteria into nutrients and nitrogen, which forms a complete cycle of the interlocking food chain. And the species at the top of the food chain, to survive and multiply, inevitably seem to resort to deception, plunder, and slaughter. If we use the viewpoint of the survival of the fittest through natural selection to explain all of these behaviors, provided they are for these two purposes (survival and propagation), no matter what means are used, they can be justified and rationalized.

With the modern transformation of civilization, people continued to elaborate on various interpretations of the definition of "survival," until the simple line between right and wrong became blurred such that no one could any longer discern it. Whereupon, some people would say, "The world has not met my preconditions, so there is no answer I accept." The problem is that if preconditions must be met, there can never be objective reality and/or Truth. Isn't it so? Therefore, the distinction between bad people, good people, bad things, and good things, is always subjective. The relative relationship is not absolute. Just as good people occasionally commit stupid acts and do bad things, bad people also show compassion and do good deeds. Only by independent observation and taking into account the specific time and place can it come to be differentiated.

Fourth brother Yi-xiang and Mountain Tiger formally saluted each other, the right fist clasped in the left palm, then saluted to the left and right.

"Start!" the referee Zhang Ying-wu declared the start of the fight with his giant's unique voice.

Before the word was out of the ref's mouth, Mountain Tiger stole the initiative, rushing in, fists swinging, pouncing to the attack. Judging from the look of things, it really had the appearance of a fierce street fight. Fourth brother Yi-xiang seemed shocked by the opponent's ferocity and might. He retreated involuntarily, and barely avoided the iron fist of the Mountain Tiger aimed at his face, the energy of which blew the hair up on his forehead. And so it went, the Mountain Tiger employing sharp footwork while swinging punches from left and right, fists punching, elbows striking, knees thrusting, head butting, shoulders colliding, all the parts of his body that could be used to injure people were employed in his offensive and transformed into extremely lethal attacks. It was indeed a simple and efficient way of attacking. His fierce attack in this first volley, forced fourth brother Yi-xiang to only dodge to the left and bob to the right to hold him off, leaving no spare energy within the passive defense to deploy a counterattack.

In the interval, the Mountain Tiger had already thrown more than thirty punches in a row, and he couldn't get his opponent to hit the ground, but with this round of fierce attacks the uproar and cries from the crowd increased his determination to win. Facing such an incompetent opponent completely unable to hit back, he could savor the thrill of slowly torturing his opponent in front of the crowd. Because he was the odds-on favorite to win, in the spectator stands Boss Jin and Ba San happily toasted their teacups to each other, ready at any moment to accept the victory and cheers from the crowd. And from the jeep, the American Dolenz seemed underwhelmed by the entirely one-sided match and felt disappointed, constantly shaking his head and sighing.

Seeing that fourth brother Yi-xiang had fallen into a weak position from the start of the fight, and that there seemed no possibility of reversing his lot to victory, Zhang Jun-feng furrowed his brows, quietly regretting he allowed this young man to substitute for him and put his neck on the line to face such a hazard.

When he looked, with shame and regret written on his face, at Wu Fan-bo, he unexpectedly saw in the old man's countenance the same twinkle in his eye as during the fifteenth day of the first lunar month at the Blasting the God of Pestilence festival, a confident look—"everything is accounted for!" Seeing this strange twinkle, he then instinctively turned his head back to look at the battle in the arena, because instinct told him: "Something is going to happen." Sure enough, it did.

"Aahhhh!" There was a mournful wail from the arena, and the Mountain Tiger fell stiff as a board to the earth and did not get up. Because it happened so fast, it was only after he was fully crumpled on the ground that the visual image of the whole process could be replayed clearly on the inner screens of the spectators minds. They only saw fourth brother Yi-xiang withdraw his left foot a half step, just avoiding the straight left jab of the Mountain Tiger. At the same time, he intercepted the Mountain Tiger's punch, grabbing the wrist with his left hand, and following the twisting momentum, dragged the Mountain Tiger's body to the left, back, and down. With the suddenness of this parrying diagonal opening move, the Mountain Tiger immediately noticed that the situation was different and instinctively withdrew his body and pulled back. When he pulled back his left hand with all his strength, he unexpectedly found that the opponent applied no resistance at all, he was trying too fiercely, and in the wink of an eye his imbalance caused him to stumble backwards. Just as he was seeking to stabilize his center of gravity, he saw his opponent smashing toward his face with his right palm. After that he felt as if the earth itself had given him a violent impact, his vision blackened and spinning. He vaguely remembered instinctively stretching out his right hand to block this splitting palm, but this was immediately followed by a searing pain above his left elbow, and then…and then he passed out.

At a contest in which the players seemed grossly mismatched, no one expected that after less than three minutes into the event, such a huge reversal would occur. In an instant, all the audience, vendors, officials, Investigation Bureau, and Intelligence Bureau personnel present fell silent. "This is not an accident. This was an awesome strategy. He really has the one punch kill skill!" Dolenz blurted out.

With one resounding surprised gasp from the crowd, the entire contest concluded. It had lasted less than three minutes, but this brief three minutes fueled post-match discussions, boasting and exaggeration far exceeding the interval of the fight by many thousands of times.

With the end of the fight the crowds dispersed. Zhang Jun-feng remained alone on the riverbank, facing the sunset, watching as it gradually turned orange-red, boundless thoughts and feelings welling up in his heart. This fight gave play to his lofty ambitions. With such a disciple, he began to believe that "Tai Shi Yi Zong" would no longer be just for making a living, not just a temporary expedient. In this moment, long-lost self-confidence and pride emerged in his heart, and he really hoped to make good use of Chinese Northern Boxing to settle down in Taiwan and cultivate its branches.

"Commander, welcome back to the team!" the intelligence guy on the jeep suddenly jumped out of the jeep and greeted Ba San deferentially.

Ba San leaped into the back seat of the jeep. "Wow! Even in my dreams I didn't dare hope to still see you. Ha-ha-ha! Get in the car and talk while riding!" Ba San said.

"Yes, Commander!" The intelligence officer then got back into the jeep and turned it around toward the direction of Shilin Yangming Mountain and started driving.

"Well. It's great to be able to get out, but I really don't know whether I came back in vain!" Ba San said.

"Political warfare clearly is not a black and white job. If something is done on behalf of the country, no matter what is done, none of it can be considered evil," Dolenz said.

"Humph. Even if it's not considered evil, it's blood that can't be washed away with one hand. I wish I could start anew in Taiwan and live the normal life of an ordinary person," Ba San said.

"It's not a simple thing for people like us to live normal lives," Dolenz said.

"Yeah? What do you think of the young man named Hong just now?" Ba San asked.

"He's not a simple character. I heard that he has been practicing internal boxing for only three months," Dolenz said.

"This kind of no holds barred fight, the key to winning or losing is not in technique. This guy won by virtue of his courage and his brains," Ba San said.

"I heard that you have the supernatural power of 'The Eye of Heaven' fortune telling. Let me ask, do you think this guy could become a master of Chinese martial arts in the future?"

"Don't believe the bullshit in your files on me. This was simply a win or a loss, it determines nothing. Keep observing, digging. If Hong can make it, then I need not fear having no disciple to pass on this 'Art of Controlling the Bull,'" Ba San said.

"What is the Art of Controlling the Bull?" Dolenz asked.

"The Art of Controlling the Bull is…"

After the National Government moved from China to Taiwan, an agent of Military Intelligence who spent half his life undercover in a gang deeply feared remaining on the mainland with no one to bring him in from the cold. He had to resort to arrangements between the underworld and intelligence units to smuggle himself into Taiwan. Only the unit that greeted him was no longer the unit to which he originally belonged, but the Intelligence Bureau. Will this be the beginning of a new lifestyle and a new identity? No one knows. And his resurrection seemed to coincide with the emergence of a martial arts superstar born in that excellent match that had just taken place.

Hong Yi-xiang teaching Xingyiquan to Robert Smith, circa 1961.
Used with permission of the Estate of Robert W. Smith

58– BREWING TEA, CHATTING, AND WITHHOLDING A TECHNIQUE

Withholding a technique really isn't "withholding never to pass down," it is establishing a filtering threshold. The logic is present. If your heart is diligent and attentive to your pursuit, you will arrive at the same location your predecessors spoke of. It is like the discovery of gravity; it can be said the luck of Mr. Newton discovering the law of gravity under the apple tree was better than the poor chump hanging around under the durian tree!

Scene: The "Hall of Encouraging the Good" Pensioner's Tearoom

(THE FOLLOWING IS A MONOLOGUE OF HONG YI-XIANG.)

"Internal martial arts has been promulgated in China for so many years and there are more factions than hairs on an ox. Who told you Master Zhang's teaching is not orthodox?

"'The greater number of people who practice it, the more orthodox,' is not the most important thing.

"From the perspective of the Manchu Qing dynasty, the folks in the revolutionary party back then were a chaotic rabble that toppled the orthodox regime.

"Conversely, from the perspective of the Republic of China, the Manchu dynasty was a scourge that had allowed the great powers to force China to eat its fill of suffering.

"Which was the chaotic party? Who was the scourge? It doesn't matter. What the common folk care about is whether they live well or not.

"Besides, which orthodox sovereignty would be transformed if not by revolution or foreign invasion?

"If you succeed in seizing power, you become the mainstream and orthodox. You fail, and you can only remain the party of chaos.

"So orthodox or unorthodox? History is written by the winner, crowned if successful, beheaded if you fail.

"What I should care about in my martial arts training is whether I can make myself stronger, don't use those silly limitations that disturb the feeble minded.

"Many things develop to a limit, a ceiling. New thinking is like boiling water—the water vapor rises to the top and creates a head of steam. Similarly, martial arts have reached an apex, and the traditional boundaries will naturally be breached. Xingyi, Bagua, and Taijiquan did not exist at the start of the universe when Pangu opened the sky. If there is a core concept linking the past, the present, and the future, even a newly created technique can extend the value of an orthodox tradition.

"I don't reject orthodoxy and tradition at all. I just don't want to be trapped by that circle and miss out on many things that are clearly better.

"The 'Cheng School Gao-Style Bagua Palm' passed on by Master Zhang emerged with this logic, and it was originally different from the Bagua Palm of other schools. Entering the system to learn the art is like participating in a relay race. After the baton has been passed to you, you still must continue running hard to advance. You can't just grab the baton on the track field and stay still. Every generation, every passing of the baton, must inject some nutrients or add some new ideas into the system for it to remain healthy and strong.

"The two terms for Master are originally different in meaning. Shifu—Master—is the honorary name for people who have professional skills. Shifu—Master—or Teacher Father,[17] is someone to whom we have personally served tea and undergone the grand ceremony of kowtowing. A Master is someone who helps us become stronger. If what you want is someone who can beat you up, then what you need is a sparring partner, not a Master.

"A champion master of boxing may not necessarily cultivate a champion disciple. On the other hand, there are many champions whose teachers are just unknown boxing masters, but this does not detract from the fact and value of their having cultivated a boxing champion. Some people can become good fighters on their own, some people can help others become good fighters, and some people are both good fighters themselves and know how to help others become good fighters. Which one would you choose to learn from?

"Withholding a technique? It doesn't matter how many techniques the teacher keeps. The key is whether you have internalized what was taught. If you haven't trained it into your very marrow, it's like you dabbled in the eighteen kinds of weapons but mastered none. A student fundamentally need not be greedy about that one withheld technique.

"You say, 'How come I can never beat others?'

"Continue to make corrections and practice harder. Who promises that after training, you will definitely win. Sometimes a minor loss means winning.

"You lost. That means the opponent is stronger, doesn't it? There are too many factors that impact winning or losing, you can't use the final result to deny the value of the previous effort.

"No one likes to lose. But sometimes when you lose you end up winning

---

17 The two terms being elucidated are homonyms Shifu 師傅 Master Teacher of a skill (like carpentry) and Shifu 師父 Teacher Father. The two terms are frequently interchanged in modern Chinese, but the author here is differentiating between them. This is the term known by some in the West as Sifu (a Cantonese pronunciation).

more. Because when you win, you usually only get applause. But if you lose, it will make you see your own deficiencies and take needed improvements seriously. I think the mindset with which you face defeat can determine the meaning and value of winning or losing.

"Of course, you can give up and not practice, but is not that the same as losing? Otherwise, what is it?

"Are you thinking of seeking an even more ferocious old master to teach you?

"This wouldn't be bad. It's only that if you do this it will make people think that you are only putting your loss on the guy who taught you.

"Also, what do you mean by 'old master'? What is your logic? You don't know what an old master can prove, besides proving his age. Just like wine aged in an earthenware pot, if you put rice wine in it, even though you age it in the wine cellar for a long time, it won't become sorghum spirits. The value of time accumulated is determined by what's inside, isn't it?"

A conversation is the matching of wits and the interaction of consciousness and energy between people. Most people who practiced gongfu in that era liked to brew tea and chat. Although the information exchanged with each other never steered far from boxing and some trivial gossip, and these topics were often repeated again and again, masters rich in life experience were always able, within these casual chats lacking any fixed focus, to analyze the logic of one's thoughts and inner mind. From this subtle sense, the direction and depth of the student's gongfu training could be determined. There is no single wise method on earth that can cover all "holding back a hand" decisions, but every master always has a measuring stick in his heart, and that ruler measures naked humanity after disguises have been stripped away. Masters often rely on the results of long term, searching observations to choose who will carry their mantle. For martial arts masters, the inheritance of boxing is just a continuation of mind and tradition. When passing on an art, there are many more considerations, much more important than money.

As for those who are receiving the art, there has not been a single day for thousands of years not governed by the traditional concept of respecting the teacher and honoring the teachings, but between students of the same generation, privately, they will question and debate the boxing method taught by the master. What they care about is whether the boxing technique taught by the master is authentic or not? Ferocious or not? And did the master in the end retain some method for himself? If so, what method was held back? How ferocious was it? Based on highly subjective opinions, a persuasive conclusion on these topics cannot be reached through words alone. As the nature of human suspicion is inherently deep-rooted, a couple of succinct words alone cannot dispel it.

To be convinced, only martial art methods can handle doubts in the martial arts. And a frequent problem among seekers of the arts is that they are greedy to learn more and to learn fast. They hope the master can teach them that kind of "earth shattering martial skill unknown to anyone on earth," but are unwilling to acknowledge the fact that martial skill is acquired through training, not teaching. Few imagine that even with the most authoritative system of certification and the best master to teach you the strongest martial arts in the world, if you can't get rid of extraneous thoughts and concentrate on diligent, painful practice, it will be in vain.

Once a person selects a single skill as his lifelong goal, if he can invest at least ten thousand hours into focused hard training undistracted by other interests, it would be highly unlikely that he does not acquire true gongfu. If in one year, for 365 days, he trains three hours a day, it will take almost ten years to reach this number of hours. This may be the origin of the expression "ten years to polish one sword." In this lengthy process of diligent drilling, it is inevitable that one will encounter some technical bottleneck or physical and mental setbacks. Provided one can face the torment of these hurdles steadfastly and bravely, one can break through and enter a different realm.

Some unforgettable life experiences often accompany the process of breaking through to a new level. The experience is like dropping into a wormhole and travelling through time and space, connecting across time, and entering into dialogue with the founder of the boxing system. In that moment, only the person involved knows what is going on. And he will also know why even a small thought arising will have such a huge impact on the final result of one's cultivation. At the same time, he will deeply understand where the truth of "What Buddha said cannot be expressed in words" is coming from. In a conversation between people not at the same level, many principles can be vocalized but it's just hot air. So, in the end, what the master has withheld from teaching you is not the issue, but the question of whether you understand that which the master has already taught you. The question is, "Have you sunk ten thousand hours into hard training?" Isn't it?

59- AT THE SPEED OF THOUGHT

Thought is not under the control of gravity. The speed of muscle and bone can never catch up with the speed of the mind. A nameless swordsman once said: "To win by surprise, you must dispose of the normal state of habitual thought. When crossing blades with experts, I always cut their sword first, then the people." Aim at the blade of the katana two-third the distance from the tip, forcefully attacking it, utilizing the mass, length, and shocking power of your sword, you can shatter his weapon.

Scene: Home of Zhang Ying-yi in Daxi, Taoyuan

ZHANG YING-YI WAS ORIGINALLY A FAMOUS MASTER OF SWORD forging whose skill had been passed down in his family on the Mainland for generations. Every sword he forged suitably combined unpretentiousness and elegance, lightness and strength, feeling balanced and refined to the touch. However, this master swordsmith had a principle that no one could change, that is, he would not sell ready-made swords, because he insisted that every blade he forged recognize only one master. It must be tailor-made according to the height and arm length of the swordsman and his style of brandishing the weapon. If not according to his rules, no matter how much money was offered, he would never accept it. He was a principled and self-disciplined master.

When he retreated from the Mainland China to Taiwan, he stayed at the Hong family compound teaching for nearly a year. Later, with financial support from his hometown migrants, he moved to Daxi, Taoyuan, established residence and married a local Daxi beauty. Because his age was close to fourth brother Yi-xiang, although he taught several sets of ancestral swordsmanship during the Hong residence teaching period, they insisted on being sworn brothers. In addition to the family heirloom skills of forging and fighting with swords, Zhang Ying-yi was also expert in a boxing art rarely seen in Taiwan—"The Eight Drunken Immortals."

After Zhang Ying-yi moved to Daxi, fourth brother Yi-xiang often used "business" as an excuse to visit. When he was passing in the general vicinity of Taoyuan, Xinzhu, or Miaoli, he would bring special local produce from various places, just to pay a visit Martial arts practitioners attach importance to comradeship and hospitality. When the two would meet, Zhang Ying-yi always tried his best to get fourth brother Yi-xiang to stay overnight. With a few plates of stewed vegetables and a pot of old wine, the two could chat free of worry on all manner of subjects the whole night long. When roused to the occasion, Zhang Ying-yi, in his cups and uninhibited, would get up and demonstrate his "Eight Drunken Immortals."

Referring to the special characteristics of the eight Taoist immortals of myth and legend, eight different boxing arts were developed, of which the most distinctive is "Staggering Drunk Stepping." This style is to imitate the dim, out of control state of mind of a person who is plastered, transforming it into the offensive and defensive actions of boxing with what appears to be "unbalanced" steps, staggering and ready to fall. The body shape is like a staggering drunk, avoiding hard knocks, attacking weaknesses, as from this emerges: absorbing, dodging, toppling, falling, overturning, bumping, leaning, pressing, up-lifting, etc., all are concealing murderous tricks, like:

Han Zhong-li's Stagger Step Elbow to the Heart
Uncle Cao's Immortal Wine Toast Throat Grab
Zhang Guo-lao's Drunken Cup Toss with Consecutive Kicking
Li Tie-guai's Cripple Lunges with the Knee
Han Lan-zi's Seizing the Arm like a Flute and Elbowing the Chest
Lu Dong-bin's Drunken Lift of the Thousand-pound Wine Jar
Lan Cai-he's Single Toast to Grab the Waist and Throw
He Xian-gu's Swaying Elastic Waist with Drunken Steps

This special martial art is a technique of mind and body control. Even when not inebriated, it can also simulate drunkenness and exert force.

※※※

"Apart from the style of boxing technique, I think speed, angle, and knowing the opponent's habits are the three most important elements to control the enemy!" Zhang Ying-yi said.

"Yes. But I think there is another element that cannot be ignored!" Yi-xiang replied.

"What?" Zhang Yingyi-jian.

"Foresight!" Yi-xiang said.

"You mean clairvoyance. Oh, really! Only a few days since I last saw you, can it be you are already half Immortal? Ha-ha-ha!" Zhang Ying-yi said.

"Old Brother, said that way, it's ridiculous!" Yi-xiang said.

"Then why do you suggest martial arts is a magic gateway, can it be you're drunk?" Zhang Ying-yi said

"I have my reasons. But first I want to hear your opinion!" Yi-xiang said.

"Alright. It does not matter whether the martial art is from the internal or external schools, don't they all require to intentionally strike the unprepared target, a fast hand striking a slow hand? Can it be you have never heard the principle in all martial arts under Heaven, 'Only speed cannot be cracked?'"

Zhang Ying-yi said.

"Of course, I have heard it. But I think of speed as a dynamic with a relative relationship. It is enough to be a half beat faster than the opponent, you don't have to overdo it. After all, blindly seeking speed is not the most intelligent method. Moreover, the speed of the limbs cannot be divorced from gravity, faster still, and there are set limits. Beyond that limit, speed is very hard to increase," said Yi-xiang.

"There is nothing wrong in what you said. But in the end, it's speed that can take advantage," Zhang Ying-yi said.

"No. If you really want to put it that way, I think the quickness of the mind is more important than the quickness of the body," Yi-xiang said.

"Also true. No matter how strong gravity is, it can't control how fast your mind turns over after all," Zhang Yingyi said.

"It's not just that. With a baseball pitch 100 kilometers per hour is fast enough. But if you face a ball velocity of 150 kilometers every day, when you look back and face 100 kilometers, you will naturally feel it is not fast, right? So, speed is just a relative dynamic. Once your mind adapts, the relative advantage disappears," Yi-xiang said.

"I agree with this statement. The princess of my family, she got it from her mother, very fast mental arithmetic, even faster than using an abacus!" Zhang Ying-yi said.

"Wow! I didn't expect you to have such a smart and clever daughter. Come on, a toast to your daughter and your blessings," Yi-xiang said, raising his glass.

"Ai! Girls. They get married and belong to someone else in the end," Zhang Ying-yi said.

"The times are different. Now daughters are more caring, and sons go off and get married to someone else," Yi-xiang said.

"Ha-ha-ha! Anyway, in the end, only the old man and his old wife remain, depending on each other, right?" Zhang Ying-yi said.

"True, true," Yi-xiang said.

"Speaking of how fast one's mind turns over, chess players who play Go are even more powerful. Spectators only see two people sitting quietly facing each other, but in fact, their minds are busy," Zhang Ying-yi said.

"Yes. Mental arithmetic is only turning numbers over in the mind, with a single fixed answer. Chess is a two-way, interactive offense and defense, and each move does not exist in isolation. On the chessboard, every slight change drives a chain reaction through the entire board. Therefore, the placement of each piece in the hands of a chess player is determined only after an omnidirectional, multi-interrelated deliberation, before removing his hand. Each piece has multiple purposes of laying traps, correcting previous errors, sewing confusion and countermeasures. This is a method of high velocity, complex thought training," Yi-xiang said.

"In martial arts, the person who uses the *jian* also possesses this kind of rapid calculation. The body of the sword is frail and cannot bear a heavy attack, so when facing the enemy, out of multiple possibilities, I must find a path that avoids a direct clash with heavy weapons. When it's really unavoidable, you can only parry the opponent's attack from the side," Zhang Ying-yi said.

"Generally, I only know that the *jian* moves quick and agile, I never thought that hidden within were such profound theories. Really interesting," Yi-xiang said.

"Not only that, but only the two edges of the tip of the entire *jian* areare sharpened, giving it lethal power, so the main attack with it is a stab. The stab strikes at a single point, unlike a *dao*, which traces a full arc. On the arc traversed by the *dao*, all contact points along the arc have lethal potential. Because of this innate limitation, the person with the *jian* must make clever use of its lightness and agility to take quick and proactive offense. Also, one must stay a step ahead of the opponent to accurately predict their style and where their weapon will make contact, so that the *jian* will not be broken in two by the opponent. Therefore, the person wielding a *jian* must have a faster mind and eyesight than the person using a *dao*, to be able come out okay. Only in this way during the chaotic clash of *jian* and *dao* can he perceive the tiny gap into which his *jian* pierces the heart!" Zhang Ying-yi said.

"If one can practice boxing as sharp as swordsmanship, then you can enter a higher realm. Most people who practice martial arts only understand the hard work of the physical and technical levels. If they don't put time into the mental game, they will reach a certain point, but surely won't progress beyond that. No wonder the Internal School pays so much attention to the demands of the mind. Excellent. Brother Ying-yi, just listening to these words is worth the price of the train ticket!" Yi-xiang said.

"Ha-ha-ha! You. You drank too much plum wine. Your words come out so sweet!" Zhang Ying-yi said.

"That's just your good wife's craftsmanship, putting up such delicious wine," Yi-xiang said.

"If you like it, take a jug back with you and enjoy it slowly!" Zhang Ying-yi said.

"Well, it would be impolite for me to refuse," Yi-xiang said.

"I can accept your view of speed. Just don't forget that the limits to speed of the physical body can be surmounted with technique!" Zhang Ying-yi said.

"I understand this. Like the methods of rising, drilling, falling, and overturning in Xingyiquan, and Bagua palm clasping the wrist and pulling back are intended to draw the opponent in and let the opponent collide with the attack," Yi-xiang said.

"Yes. The shortening of the distance equals a doubling of the speed. At the same time, it can also disrupt the opponent's balance and make the injury worse!" Zhang Ying-yi said.

"Naturally this is a smart way, but under any scenarios, you can't ignore the opponent's countermeasures and changes!" Yi-xiang said

"So, if you can occupy a safe and effective angle, won't you have a greater chance of winning?" Zhang Ying-yi said.

"Yes. But when you encounter Taiji's Changeable Energy, a single 'swallowing and spitting' can eat up any advantage of the angle you took," Yi-xiang said.

"No. No, I don't agree. Even if they use Changeable Energy, they can't escape from the habituation I mentioned. As long as you grasp inertia of the opponent's limbs, swallowing and spitting, coupled with the speed and angle, you can definitely drive the opponent's surrender," Zhang Ying-yi said.

"Okay. What you said makes sense. But I still have a different view. Let's have a drink first and moisten our throats," Yi-xiang said.

"You drink up. I will treat that as your admission of defeat," Zhang Ying-yi said.

"Ha-ha-ha! The war is not over yet!" Yi-xiang said.

"I don't believe you can do anything," Zhang Ying-yi said.

"Okay. Let's talk about habituation, then I will use cats as an example, because cats are the best animals at fighting alone," Yi-xiang said.

"Yeah. I have the same impression," Zhang Ying-yi said.

"Although cats are not large, they can push their physical possibilities to the limit. In a common cat-dog skirmish, at the beginning, the cat will always huddle in the corner and arch its back to prepare for battle. This reduces its area that can be attacked and makes it able to launch an attack in an instant," Yi-xiang said.

"Yes. Cats usually use their front feet to make probing attacks first. Once, twice, three times, until they have ascertained the dog's habitual reactions, they will suddenly put all their strength into launching fast and continuous effective assaults. Although the cat may not win in the end, but its tactics and combat skills are completely in line with characteristics of martial arts. That's why I put habituation as one of the three essential factors of humans," Zhang Ying-yi said.

"Yes. The cat's style of fighting is completely in line with the principle of 'The enemy does not strike, I do not strike; if the enemy makes the slightest move, I strike first.' Before launching an attack, it will calmly observe and probe, and after determining the real and the fake, only then will it choose the most appropriate time and technique for taking action. Therefore, true masters can always observe clues from the enemy's inadvertent actions, predict the opponent's possible timing, angle, technique, and attack tactics, and then carry out the necessary countermeasures," Yi-xiang said.

"Isn't this the habituation I talked about?" Zhang Ying-yi said.

"No. Still a bit different. Habituation is nothing more than repetitive actions taken to protect oneself against novel situations or opponents. In the eyes of an experienced fighter, these repetitive actions are rapidly analyzed to enable control of the habitual pattern. But prediction is an ability to holistically judge, just like when we see a line of ants moving home, we know that we might be facing a heavy rain. This is accumulated knowledge and experience coupled with the ability to continuously verify and make corrections," Yi-xiang said.

"It's just a difference in terms. Essentially, I still think we are talking about the same thing," Zhang Ying-yi said.

"No. It ain't the same. Challenges taken on by a master are a type of mind game. Smart opponents must understand how to make clever use of the strategy of alternating between the strange and the expected. In turn they use habituation to mislead opponents. So, in addition to grabbing onto their habituation, you still need more data to make judgments, this is the predicting I am talking about," Yi-xiang said.

"What you're saying is still very abstract and difficult to understand," Zhang Ying-yi said.

"Okay. Then I ask you, do you watch baseball on TV?" Yi-xiang asked.

"Of course. It's a matter of national pride, I never miss a game," Zhang Ying-yi said

"Okay. On a baseball team, a good catcher has a more important task than squatting to catch the ball. It is to be familiar with the habits of every batter, including the speed of swing, which angles they are good at hitting, favorite flight path of the ball, etc., and then according to the current situation, provide the pitcher with suggestions on the pitch. But, if you think about it, don't the opponent's batters use the same method to analyze the pitcher?" Yi-xiang said.

"Are you saying that all this is not enough, still not enough, to determine who will win and who will lose?" Zhang Ying-yi asked.

"Yes. According to your theory, aren't speed, angle, and habits all that need be taken into consideration?" Yi-xiang asked rhetorically.

"Wait a minute. Let me think about it. Where's the problem?" Zhang Ying-yi asked.

"Okay. As you think about it, listen to me. I heard that an American professional baseball pitcher, when he throws a fast ball, it's not even a second and the ball goes into the catcher's mitt. In other words, the speed of the fast ball is much faster than our brain's reaction time. If you add the time required to twist the waist and swing the bat, it will be even worse," Yi-xiang said.

"Do you mean that the batter must swing at the same time as the pitcher moves to get the ball?" Zhang Ying-yi asked.

"Yes," Yi-xiang said.

"Really? Don't just cook up stories to cheat me out of a jug of wine, deceiving me as you please," Zhang Ying-yi said good-naturedly.

"The exact data I don't remember, but it is true," Yi-xiang said.

"So, as far as the batter is concerned, basically, it is *not after* seeing what ball has been pitched that he decides how to hit it!" Zhang Ying-yi said.

"Yes. But, of course, there are right and wrong predictions, so it is only right that we still keep correcting them," Yi-xiang said.

"It's really interesting. I didn't expect to use a scientific point of view to explore traditional martial arts, it truly opens up a new vista!" Zhang Ying-yi exclaimed.

"These are experiences accumulated after long-term observation. Only after analyzing and categorizing is a common context and trajectory derived, then, based on the deduced results, an ability to discriminate and predict is developed. The level of predictive accuracy is greatly correlated to personal experience, cultivation, and innate talents. If the person's temperament is insufficiently clear and settled, if they are subjective and over-bearing, it will affect the accuracy of judgment," Yi-xiang said.

"How come you know so much?" Zhang Ying-yi asked.

"My kid is a baseball player, so I know something from him," Yi-xiang said.

"Which one? The oldest or the second?" Zhang Ying-yi asked.

"The one who doesn't practice boxing!" Yi-xiang said.

"Ha-ha-ha! Are you talking about your second son?" Zhang Ying-yi said.

"Ai! This kid is a mixed-up thing, not an obedient guy, don't mention him!" Yi-xiang said.

"Ha-ha-ha! Keep talking about your clairvoyance," Zhang Ying-yi said.

"This kind of predictive ability must be cultivated slowly in actual partner training. And it also needs to be constantly fine-tuned according to people, time, and force. Master Zhang said that true transformation often requires the help of external catalysts and stress. Only then can it be transformed into an instinctive adaptability. This kind of opportunity can only be chanced upon, not sought," Yi-xiang said.

"Brother, I think you have this potential," Zhang Ying-yi said.

"I think you're drunk!" Yi-xiang laughed.

"No, no, no. The wine in our house, only inebriates the guests, not the owner…" Zhang Ying-yi chuckled.

Some people say: Only those who are not drunk can proclaim that they are drunk, and those who are really plastered will never admit that they are drunk. No one knows how deep into the night these two friends drank and chatted, did they really get drunk? Or were they not really drunk…?

The two men spoke agreeably, the wine flowed, and besides critiquing literary and martial arts, even arranging the marriage of their children was a topic influenced by plum wine. A verbal agreement was concluded between them. Only after waking up did both quietly shelve this commitment, and no one dared open their mouths to raise the topic again.

It was not until many years later that the second son of fourth brother Yi-xiang[18] became a director of a TV station. He was busy working day and night, and often had to go out and not return home to sleep, and for a long time there was no news about whether he had a girlfriend. As an aging father, Yi-xiang was worried about his child's work and health, and secretly he felt some glee in his heart; wishful thinking that words in jest under the sweet haze of plum wine might become the Will of Heaven. To reveal his secret arrangement, he took advantage of an opportunity to find his son and have a talk.

"Zhang Ying-yi of Taoyuan is getting on in years. He has never found a worthy disciple to whom he can pass down his Drunken Boxing form, and leaning on my friendship with him, he means to accept you as a disciple. He wants to pass on these unique skills to you. Can you take a long vacation, go to Taoyuan with me, visit the teacher, and learn that set of boxing?" entreated Hong Yi-xiang.

He kept on with his nagging in the same way for several years but did not get any response. In the end, unable to hold back, he put his cards straight on the table: "Let me come clean. Zhang Ying-yi's daughter is well-mannered, also tall, smart, and gorgeous. She is a famous beauty in Daxi. A few years ago, we arranged a match for you. Can you just listen to me once and come to Taoyuan with me, I promise, I guarantee, you'll like it."

As for the repeated requests from his elder to go to Taoyuan to apprentice the art, his son apologized that he was swamped with work, and because of his lack of skills, begged off. However, once the ruse behind this boxing training was exposed, it spoiled a good thing. In the end, this post-drinking marriage contract was a promise between the two martial arts masters, a promise that neither could fulfill in their lifetimes.

---

18 I.e., the author of this book, Hong Ze-han.

Hong Ze-han performs a sword cut with Eight Battles Sword at the Zhishanyan training ground, 2016.

60– A TRUE GENTLEMAN QUIETLY OBSERVES CHESS

In the game of chess, before you place a piece down, there are limitless possibilities. But soon as the chess piece leaves the hand, all possibilities merge into one.

Scene: Yanping North Road Mazu Temple

IN THE ERA OF THE TRANSFORMATION OF AN AGRICULTURAL SOCIETY into an industrial and commercial society, centers of local faith and religion were often the core of the local economy. Such was Taipei City Dihua Street Xiahai Temple of the City God, Yanping North Road's Mazu Temple, and Monga's Longshan Temple. Around these big temples, a cooked delicacies district unique to temple streets would surely blossom. On Yanping Road, in front of the Mazu Temple there was a wide plaza. The surrounding fence of the temple was planted with old banyan trees thick with branches and leaves. The wide and dense shade of the trees was a place favored by pensioners for enjoying the cool open air, chatting and playing chess in the summer.

Outside the temple wall, up against the outside of the back fence, there were dozens of open-air vendors of delicious snacks. In addition, there were also many vendors selling snacks on both sides of the alley leading to Yanping North Road. At the entrance was a grilled sausage stall.

The sausages sold in this shop were made of lamb intestine casings. The pork hind leg meat filling in the casing was mixed with five-spice powder, minced garlic, and sorghum spirits. Because the lamb intestine casings are smaller, this family's sausages were rolled into a whole circle and grilled over the fire. Customers could select how much they wanted and that much would be cut to order. The taste was salty, fragrant, and delicious. The meat was succulent and juicy. After eating, there would be a heavy sorghum spirits aftertaste. Especially the scorched crispy casing at the bursted part of the skin was a favorite of diners. Looking at sausage flavors sold in the entire market in Taiwan today, most of them have been standardized by the "Tainan Black Bridge." Many of the original flavors with strong family traditions and local characteristics have been erased because of lack of confidence in their craft.

Behind the grilled sausage stall was a stand selling duck stew. This duck stew vendor styled himself as the favorite of the silver shop proprietor and bridal shop proprietresses on Yanping North Road. He chose boneless breast meat. Before putting it in the pot, meat slices were rubbed with marinade. Freshly boiled and freshly eaten, soft and tender, not dry, or tough, blended with the crispy, sweet Napa cabbage, the thick broth balanced between sour and sweet, so delicious.

However, with the changing times, the shop went downhill. The craftsmanship was not passed on. Those traditional delicious flavors all followed the disappearance of that age and those people, they were lost to history. And now, few people know or remember these people, these things, this past…as if they never existed at all.

Today, you can go to any western restaurant and eat a large serving of pan-fried Yilan cherry-blossom duck breast meat, but the traditional delicacies had traditional sentiment and hooked the tastebuds. No matter how many years old you are now, just wait until one day, you'll be so old that only the tastes of your memory will satisfy your buds and definitely the traditional tastes on the tip of your tongue are what you will yearn for.

At that time, Yanping North Road was what we call today's "Marriage Boulevard." The betrothal gifts and dowry required before marriage, by both men and women could be purchased at one go on this street, for example: gold jewelry, suit fabric, wedding dress, wedding photography, etc., were all available. Even the most popular restaurants for eligible men and women on introductory blind dates, "Bolero"[19] and Kentucky Western Cuisine, were both near the intersection of Yanping North Road and Minsheng West Road. It is said that all the early Japanese-style Western cuisine chefs in Taipei City were "graduates" of "Bolero." Go further toward the North Gate, and the section between the crossroads of Nanjing West Road and the traffic circus of Chongqing North Road, there was the Jinling Hotel and Da Guangming Restaurant, the top choice of the day for engagement, wedding, and "first return of the bride to her parental home" banquets. Nanjing East Road, which is now called the "Wall Street" of Taipei City, then could only be described as "there are more weeds than people."

Under the shade of the old banyan tree at the temple, Zhang Jun-feng and fourth brother Yi-xiang, who had just had a lunch of duck stew, sat at a stone table arranging their pieces to play chess, while second brother Yi-wen and third brother Yi-mian sat to the side eating watermelon seeds, drinking aged Oolong tea and watched the battle while concurrently providing a running commentary. Second brother cool-headedly deduced the tactics and layouts of both sides, while third brother was up next to fourth brother incessantly urging lousy chess moves, impassioned meddling one bad idea after another. Pushed beyond tolerance fourth brother Yi-xiang pointed sternly at the chess board

---

19 When courting his Taiwanese fiancée, a dinner at Bolero was de rigueur for the translator even in 1978.

and quoted the adage, "A True Gentleman quietly observes chess, A Man of Character leaves his piece on the board without regret". Within a few minutes, third brother not only relapsed into the old problem, but also moved a chess piece.

Third brother heckled, "If you play like this, you're seeking your own road to death. Listen to me, I won't steer you wrong. Yeah, kill 'em!"

Second brother smacked him on the back of the head. "What nonsense are you talking about. Don't you know the opponent is our master. 'Kill 'em,' sheesh!"

"No matter. Playing chess, it is just me and the enemy, there's no great and small. Ha-ha-ha!" This time even Zhang Jun-feng smiled and let out a chuckle.

"If you speak again, may you have diarrhea on the spot," second brother laid out a venomous curse hoping to shock third brother into keeping his mouth shut with no more interruptions. Sure enough, third brother zipped his lips and watched the battle. But it was not three or four moves before he could not help himself, grabbed the shoulders of fourth brother and said, "Little brother. I beg you! On this move listen to me. I'll gladly rush back to the out-house now!" After that, the three big men in the field were all rolling in laughter.

Zhang Jun-feng left-center in a playful mood with students Hong Yi-mian front center and Hong Yi-xiang center, circa 1950.

61– REVERSE GRIP SWORD

If you desire to be first, you must aim for it. It is like two equally skilled masters facing off in chess, if one places each of his pieces just to face-off the pieces of the opponent, he will definitely lose. What makes a miraculous move miraculous is that it dares to be intimate with error and danger, while seeking newer perspectives and opportunities.

Scene: Guanyin Township

"This is the famous boxer Master Zhang Jun-feng. He is a family friend from my hometown in Shandong. Master Zhang is the current martial arts instructor to the Presidential Palace. These two are the third young master Yi-mian and the fourth young master Yi-xiang, squires of the Hong family on Dihua Street. They are all the direct disciples of Master Zhang entering into their instruction here in Taiwan. The three are all martial arts masters who can go one against ten opponents."

After listening to this flowery introduction, Zhang Jun-feng became vaguely aware that the situation was not "simple." He instinctively turned his head and looked back at fourth brother Yi-xiang thinking to give him a warning. When their eyes met it was obvious fourth brother Yi-xiang also had become aware something about the situation was off. Using this way to introduce business partners meeting for the first time, the Shandong family friend was clearly implying an unusual, cooperative relationship between the parties. However, due to the etiquette of being a guest, it was best to bear patiently the disquiet that had arisen in their hearts and just observe the changes. "Mr. Tact" third brother Yi-mian, obliviously chatted with the wait staff.

"This is Mr. Chen Da-li, my partner in business for many years. What a coincidence. I didn't expect that the first time you three came you would happen to bump into us during this awkward scene of us breaking the partnership, but this is also good. In this matter of splitting up, a fair and powerful third person must be the witness. That avoids people going back on their word or not acknowledging their debts after the fact." Huang Chang-mao remained relaxed.

"Didn't you say we came to Zhuwei fishing village to eat seafood?" asked the third brother Yi-mian.

"Yes, yes. When this is done, we'll go," Huang Chang-mao said.

"Such an important matter, I think it's better for the two of you as parties to this dispute to talk it out. It is inconvenient for us outsiders to get involved. We'll first accompany Master to go strolling in the fishing village." It was already clear to fourth brother Yi-xiang that today's scene was not a hometown friend wanting to reminisce about the past. It was clearly a set up by Zhang Jun-feng's fellow villager, intending to use their martial arts background to control a situation. He did not want Zhang Jun-feng and the Hong family to wade into this muddy water, so hoped to extract themselves.

"Brother Jun-feng, please let your two apprentices wait for me a moment. You came all the way from Taipei to see me, how can you not let me extend my hospitality," Huang Chang-mao pulled on Zhang Jun-feng entreating them to stay. Hindered by sentiments for an old family friend, in the end Zhang Jun-feng relaxed the annoyance he felt at the pit of his stomach.

"Okay. Let's make a long story short, Brother Da-li, I want to know if I quit and leave the entire factory to you to operate, then how much capital can I get back?" Huang Chang-mao asked.

"You well know that the equipment is old and dilapidated. Moreover, we've distributed profits several times in the process. The initial investment funds should already have been recouped by you several times over. The remaining equipment is probably not worth any money," Da-li said.

"Okay. No matter. Not worth much is still worth how much? Just name a number," Huang Chang-mao said.

"The residual value doesn't exceed 100,000 yuan," said Da-li.

"No way," Huang Chang-mao said.

"Brother Chang-mao. Don't forget, whoever takes it over has a group of old laborers to support," Da-li said

"I know this. But after so many years of hard work, I have accumulated many established customers and orders. Isn't that worth a little money?" Huang Chang-mao asked.

"If you are still so optimistic, then you should remain and continue to cooperate and work hard together. Why do you want to tear it down?" asked Da-li.

"Tearing it down is because I have another plan," Huang Chang-mao said

"Then 150,000 yuan," said Da-li.

"Can't it be more?" Huang Chang-mao asked.

"In recognition of so many years of cooperation, just give a bit more," third brother Yi-mian interrupted suddenly and thoughtlessly.

"Elder brother. We outsiders don't interrupt in this business matter," fourth brother Yi-xiang said.

"Okay. I'm just simply reminding everyone of the key-point. When you have talked it through, everybody's going to eat seafood." The rude interjection of third brother Yi-mian almost messed up Huang Chang-mao's position. Fortunately, fourth brother Yi-xiang came forward and stepped on the brakes in time, not letting things continue to develop that direction.

"It can't be more. For the factory to continue operating, some cash sufficient for turnover has to be retained." Chen Da-li estimated that if he chomped down hard on this number and didn't let go, he should be able to considerably reduce the cash spent, and so he didn't want to yield an inch.

"I think it should be worth at least 180,000 to 200,000 yuan," Huang Chang-mao said.

"Don't utter 180,000 or 200,000 such an outrageous price. If we reversed roles and you were to buy it, I would also get 150,000 from you." Chen Da-li quietly speculated that although his opponent deliberately sought out three 'helpers,' judging from the current situation, the opponent did not seem to have any special chips or trump card to play, so Chen boldly switched from defense to offense, forcing the opponent to yield and conclude this not so excellent negotiation.

"Well. Since you can't increase the price, I can only trust your professionalism and sincerity," Huang Chang-mao said.

"Then that's settled. Good friends. Let's all part without hard feelings. This way no one gets the worst of it," Da-li said.

"Right. Good friends! Part without hard feelings. No one at a loss. Here is 160,000 yuan in cash. I respect your suggestion and switch to buy it from you. I am adding another 10,000 yuan to the price you suggested to buy it. This way is really sincere and generous." Huang Chang-mao finally revealed the "dagger hidden in the scroll"[20] and thrust his backhand sword.

"You! You son of a…" Even in his nightmares Chen Da-li never expected that a partner with whom he had been cooperating for many years would go on the offensive at this critical moment and resort to such an insidious trick, but because of his own words in front of all of them, if he wanted to renege he feared he had neither circumstances nor logic as legs to stand on. Facing the bag of money that Huang Chang-mao had already prepared and placed in front of him, he was filled with bitter remorse. "Hmph! Aren't you ruthless? Employing such a poisonous crafty plot to undermine cooperation with your partner of so many years," Da-li said.

"Ai. But I gave you more than you were asking for. In the business, you place your bets and have to be willing to suffer the loss," Huang Chang-mao said.

"You…" Da-li was speechless in his rage.

"Mr. Chen, if you have no other proposals, then can you please make yourself scarce. I yet have three guests to entertain, so I won't be sending you off. In the future you're welcome to come here for tea anytime," and with one sentence, Huang Chang-mao turned his partner into a roadside stranger.

"Hmph! If you bite it off, you have to be able to swallow it. We'll see." For more than ten years, he had toiled, hands and feet calloused, with the

---

20 This refers to a historical incident in which a court assassin sought to kill Emperor Qin by hiding a dagger in a scroll he was presenting to the emperor.

employees to build his kingdom of telephone assembly. Because of a moment of greed, I am being swept out of the house by another. Chen Dali's heart was full of vexation and regret, but no matter how discontented he was, it was of no avail. He resentfully grabbed the bag of money on the table and stormed out the door.

"Okay. The matter was resolved consummately. So, let's go to Hongmaogang to eat crabs together," Huang Chang-mao said.

"No. Thanks. Brother Chang-mao, I am already very happy to see you. But a meal we will not share with you. Take care." Never dreaming that a hometown acquaintance might thus exploit an old friendship, Zhang Jun-feng took the two young masters of the Hong family on this special trip, only to come here and play this kind of role. And while it seemed that the other party was also not kindly, his fellow countryman showed that he had clearly dug a hidden trap waiting for his business partner of many years. Zhang couldn't persuade himself to waste another minute eating in the company of such a man.

"Okay. Since you don't want to eat, I won't be seeing you off," Huang Chang-mao said.

Hoodwinked by friendship the three martial arts exponents representing two generations had played a disgraceful role. This life lesson showed them clearly a reality: a martial artist not only has to lead a clean life cherishing one's good name, but also must understand how to choose friends carefully, otherwise the influence of the activities of a martial arts group can easily become a pawn used by ambitious people.

62- GUANYIN CONFRONTATION

Life's biggest lecture hall is not at school, but in the commercial district, among the multitudes.

Scene: Guanyin Township Hongmaogang Seafood Restaurant

LOCATED IN GUANYIN TOWNSHIP ON THE WEST COAST OF TAIWAN, before it was built into a modern industrial area, the wasteland of the coastal area was scattered with simple, crude factories built with corrugated asbestos boards. They specialized in all manner of light assembly and contract industries, including radios, hand-cranked phones, motors, etc. It was close to Zhuwei Fishing Port so there were several restaurants specializing in Taiwanese seafood in the densely populated streets of the industrial zone. Being not a wealthy town, most of the restaurants were very simple. The majority of tables and chairs were set up for business outside the shops under the shade of trees. Although its location was remote, the seafood sold here was all the catch of the day, and even with a simple preparation was extraordinarily delicious. Every holiday, it always attracted many diners, groups of friends roped in to come here for fresh food and drink.

In the open-air Hongmaocheng seafood shop dining area, Zhang Jun-feng and the two Hong family brothers, ordered a whole table of fresh, in season seafood delicacies: sand prawns steamed in lotus leaf, steamed large black hairy crabs, deep-sea fish belly fried with basil, grilled squid, roasted phoenix snails with hot peppers, stir fried tofu with shark, duck tongue cooked Three Cup style, steamed flower shell crab, Yaoshan mudfish soup, etc. No matter how advanced the times, how deep the generation gap, these traditional Taiwanese seafood delicacies are a path to bridge across the moat of time and space or generational differences. For thousands of years, the external material civilization has continuously evolved and changed, but the taste buds of people have always been the same, and almost no one can resist seasonal seafood.

Zhang Jun-feng and fourth brother Yi-xiang were both serious connoisseurs in picking out seafood but nothing compared to third brother Yi-mian.

He had been a conscripted Japanese soldier during World War II and stayed in a small fishing village in the Philippine Sea for nearly 2 years. Because of this fateful turn, he was not picky about food, but as a blessing in disguise, he also cultivated the unique skill of a refined palate for seafood. It is said that the Japanese warship he served on was sunk by a torpedo from an Allied submarine in the South China Sea. He clung to the wreckage of the ship and spent several days adrift. Relying on rainwater and two water-swollen roots of wild mountain Korean ginseng his mother had given him to sustain himself, he survived at sea until he was found by a local fishing boat, rescued, and taken to shore. He remained in the village until he was tracked down and returned to the Japanese army, then repatriated to Taiwan by returning ships.

According to his own recollection, if he had not already been betrothed to marry in Taiwan, he would have become the son-in-law of a South Seas Philippine island tribe. At the time, the family received notification of his death from the military that his ship sank and disappeared in the South Seas, and they all resigned him to an unmarked watery grave. No news was shared even as the transport was off-loaded at Keelung Port, he disembarked, took the train to the Taipei Main Station, and then took a pedicab home. When his gaunt, unkempt figure appeared in front of the Hong Wan Mei Shop on Dihua Street, everyone thought "A ghost has returned!"

For this reason, the three big guys who practiced martial arts faced a whole table of surging seafood flavor overload, and the rancor they felt being used by a friend was already dispelled far beyond the clouds. Like wolves and tigers they pounced on the shrimp soldiers and crab generals. Just when the master and disciples were tucking into their fill of seafood, none surrendering to the tense moment just passed…

"Master, something's up," fourth brother Yi-xiang said in a low voice. Having just personally witnessed the scene where Huang Chang-mao set a trap and forced his partner away, fourth brother Yi-xiang intuitively believed the curtain on this matter would not fall so easily. He wanted to leave this disputed place as soon as possible, but because third brother Yi-mian insisted on eating seafood before he would be willing to leave, the only solution was according to the original plan to take their meal at Hongmaocheng Seafood Shop. Therefore, from start to finish of the meal, he maintained his composure while quietly scanning the surroundings and street outside for activity. Sure enough, on the street behind Zhang Jun-feng, an armed mob surged hurriedly towards the factory Huang Chang-mao had taken over.

Chen Da-li, who took the lead, caught a glimpse of the three people dining under the shade of a tree ten steps away, and immediately raised his hand to signal that the team stopped. A tattooed man who seemed to take the lead by his side continued to walk forward slowly. On seeing this situation, third brother Yi-mian felt the adrenaline rush kick in, put down the big crab claw in his hands and prepared to stand up.

"Brother. Don't step on the snake, don't make a move. I'll go suss them out." Fourth brother Yi-xiang was afraid Yi-mian would rush in and make more trouble, so he pressed down on third brother Yi-mian's thigh, pinning him to the seat for an instant. He knew at this moment that the only thing sustaining the courage of the mob to fight was overexcited hormones. Under such a situation, people are blind and incapable of rational judgment. If they spun out of control and rashly struck out, the three of them could be sucked into the quarrel and become the object of rage.

"Keep eating, I'll go scope out the situation." Fourth brother Yi-xiang calmly picked up a big crab claw on the table and handed it to third brother Yi-mian, signaling he should continue to eat, and then he casually got up, never putting down his sharp bamboo chopsticks. He moved forward mirroring the tempo of the other, and the two stopped at the same time a distance of five paces from each other… In the hand of one was a samurai sword in its black lacquered sheath; in the hand of the other a pair of sharp bamboo chopsticks for eating seafood. The tattooed boss's face, fierce and proud, revealed no anger; fourth brother Yi-xiang displayed a quiet amiable smiling expression. During these few seconds that both parties did not budge, fourth brother Yi-xiang espied the three Chinese characters "Open Tai Mother" written above a dragon tattoo on his chest. In his heart he had the strange feeling of déjà vu.

"Which path are you on?" the tattooed boss asked.

"Businessman," fourth brother Yi-xiang said.

"Doing business? You sure did a big business. Popping up on my turf," said the tattooed boss.

"I just came looking for a friend and happened to run into it." Fourth brother Yi-xiang maintained a cordial voice. If you didn't see the scene of the two sides, if you only listened to the tone of their speech, you would think it was just a greeting between friends talking about the weather, not morale boosting prior to a brawl. Just when the tattooed boss was trying to think of invective to use to intimidate the other party, a skinny lackey ran up from the mob and whispered into the tattooed boss's ear.

"Oh! Really?" The tattooed boss sought confirmation from the younger brother, only to see the lackey express absolute certainty, facing his boss and nodding up and down.

"Are you the fourth son from Hong Wan Mei in Dihua Street?" The tattooed boss's tone was clearly much calmer.

"Yes, I am. You are…," fourth brother Yi-xiang inquired.

"I'm Wujiaozi, the head of the Opening to Taipei Mazu Temple in Bali[21]," said the tattooed boss.

"Then you are Black Turtle's Maternal Uncle," said fourth brother Yi-xiang.

"That's right. How come you're messing around with that profiteer Huang

---

21 Bali Kaitai Empress of Heaven Palace, commonly known as Kaitai Mazu Temple (hence the tatoo on the fellow's chest), is the center of worship in Bali District, New Taipei City. Together with the Guandu Temple and the Danshui Fuzuo Temple, these three are also known as the three great historical temples at the mouth of the Danshui River.

Chang-mao?" the tattooed boss asked.

"It's my master's hometown acquaintance, I thought they were just going to chew the fat, who knew…," said fourth brother Yi-xiang.

"He set you up?" the tattooed boss asked.

"Well, it looks like it. We originally came to eat seafood, but who knew it would become like this," said fourth brother Yi-xiang.

"The whole strip along the West Coast is the territory of the Opening to Taipei Mazu Temple gang. Today, this kind of collusion to bury my friend alive and swallow his business happened on my turf. It really riles both men and gods, and I can't ignore it. But my brother just brought it up that during the Eight Seven Floods, the victims of Guanyin and Zhuwei had eaten the rice distributed by the Hong family at the Mazu Temple. We seaport people know to whom we should show gratitude, and against whom we should feel resentment. Regarding the matter, we demand payback. Today's problem has nothing to do with you. But in the problems of that bastard, you best not meddle," said the tattooed boss.

"Thank you for your understanding, much thanks. Would you sit down with us and have a drink?" fourth brother Yi-xiang asked.

"Another day. That problem has yet to be dealt with," said the tattooed boss.

"Okay. Then when you come to Taipei, you're welcome anytime," said fourth brother Yi-xiang.

The tattooed boss turned around and took two steps, then suddenly stopped in his tracks and looked back. "That Shandong guy, is he really the martial arts coach of the Presidential Palace?" the tattooed boss asked.

"Yep. He is a good person. Good gongfu and good character," said fourth brother Yi-xiang.

"Hmm. Very well. When autumn cools down, we'll invite you, master and disciples, to make the trip out to Bali to help our troupe learn some punches and kicks," said the tattooed boss.

"Okay. I'll set it up," fourth brother Yi-xiang agreed.

"That does it. If you teach well, I'll invite you to eat big crabs," said the tattooed boss

"With a word, we seal the promise," said fourth brother Yi-xiang.

"With a word, we seal the promise," said the tattooed boss.

Benefiting from the accumulated hidden virtue created by old Mr. Hong's kindness, coupled with the low-key response of fourth brother Yi-xiang, a violent conflict that might have been "clean knives in and red knives out," dissipated without a trace just like the salty sea breeze of the West Coast. Though calm when facing the crisis, the three of them, master and disciples, knew in their hearts that every war, no matter what the outcome, surely plants the seeds of the next war. After this turmoil, they had a deeper appreciation for the darkness of society and sinister human nature. A martial artist or a martial arts gym must know how to be cautious in words and deeds and cherish their reputation. Otherwise, if not careful, they will easily become the target of designs and exploitation by conniving people.

63– FIRST SEEK THE CONVENTIONAL, THEN SEEK THE UNCONVENTIONAL

Respecting tradition and seeking through tradition new ways forward, are both the highest forms of praising tradition.

Scene: Open-air pensioners tearoom in Tianshui Temple, Danshui

"Master. Have you noticed that the fourth brother Yi-xiang seems to have regressed recently?" asked the third brother Yi-mian.

"Oh. How did you come about this feeling?" Zhang Jun-feng asked.

"When I saw him practicing boxing, many of his movements were off track," said third brother Yi-mian.

"Mm. Not bad. Your power of observation is quite sharp," Zhang Jun-feng said.

"Then why don't you set him straight?" third brother Yi-mian asked.

"Why set him straight?" Zhang Jun-feng countered.

"Because it's a deviation. If it's not standard, it's not right. Isn't it?" said third brother Yi-mian.

"This is an interesting question. I ask you. Will the appearance and personalities of brothers from the same father and mother grow up to be the same?"

"One needn't think about it to know. I am the only brother who has women friends. During the war in South Seas, a local maiden grabbed me and almost made me become the chieftain's son-in-law," said third brother Yi-mian.

"Really? Well, it's not a bad thing to have confidence in yourself. Then let me ask you again, will the results of two different people studying the same thing together be exactly the same?" Zhang Jun-feng queried again.

"Yeah. Master, is it that obvious? Actually, I don't want to hurt my brothers' feelings, but there is no way, they just can't keep up with me," said third brother Yi-mian.

"Okay. Yi-mian, let's not talk nonsense. I know you deliberately pretend to be stupid in front of others. I believe you must have experienced life-and-death events in the South Seas, but you don't have to be so negative. I know you care about fourth brother Yi-xiang's situation and hope to go through me to drop him a hint, right? Don't worry, I can see all. You need to understand, in practicing martial arts, what is trained is the inner idea and the marrow, the essence, not just studying the outer appearance of the forms," Zhang Jun-feng said.

"I know this," said third brother Yi-mian.

"Generally speaking, in the initial stage, you must go according to the rules. Like writing Chinese characters, the stroke structure of the characters must be drawn according to the prescribed frame, like painting by numbers, otherwise no one will understand what you are writing. But once mastered, everyone's characters will have their own distinct merits, right?" Zhang Jun-feng said.

"Right," said third brother Yi-mian.

"The beauty or ugliness of the characters is not the key. It is more important to make people understand. The purpose of writing characters is to record and communicate. The purpose of learning martial arts is to overcome the enemy and strengthen the body. So, the key should be knowledge and usage. As for the appearance, whether it's standard or not, it's not that important. There are many boxing techniques that are imitations of animals. The most common are tiger, eagle, snake, monkey, swallow, etc.. The real purpose of learning these animal forms is not for you to imitate the perplexed expression of a monkey scratching its head and ears, but rather pushing you to take as a model their skills of body control and fighting. Like the grabbing, probing, jumping, and body shifting monkeys are good at, they can be transformed into martial arts movements by adding the concept of offense and defense," Zhang Jun-feng said.

"So just take their spirit, not their appearance," said third brother Yi-mian.

"Yes! Do you know that in addition to Xingyiquan's mother fists, the Five elements of metal, water, wood, fire, and earth's simplify the complex? Why do we yet practice the twelve-animal boxing of five birds and seven beasts? Isn't that complicating the simple?" asked Zhang Jun-feng.

"I don't know," said third brother Yi-mian.

"The twelve boxing forms represent the characteristics and combat strategies of twelve different animals. The purpose is to awaken the long dormant fighting potential of humans by learning the fighting skills of these animals and help us return to the time before humans were domesticated by civilization; the kind of survival techniques that can meet the challenges of various beasts in the wilderness. This is a training method that can multiply your fighting ability. It is a pity that after this method has been passed on for several generations, the intention has slowly deviated from the original, leaving only five birds and seven animal routines and movements. Everyone only knows the paint by numbers approach," Zhang Jun-feng sighed.

"Master, so how do you rediscover these errors?" asked third brother Yi-mian.

"Actually, it was only after I came to Taiwan and spent many years of intensive training that I slowly learned from experience. People, it's only when facing desperate situations that they earnestly take measure of what they have in hand. Only when they take inventory do they realize that which they require, they always had within themselves. They never mulled it over and digested it properly, but that's how people are. Let's say I had stayed at Master Gao's side, perhaps my whole life I would never have uncovered this realization," Zhang Jun-feng said.

"So is what you are passing on to us now the same as what the Grand Master passed on to you back in the day?" third brother Yi-mian asked.

"The foundational skills at the start of training should be very similar; strict imitation in the beginning is a necessary process. But the high-level movements and usage are not exactly the same. Just like when a river is filled to its banks, water will naturally find new outlets. If there is a chance to go back to the mainland during my lifetime, I think my brothers may also say that my boxing has morphed and is unpalatable. It is the same principle as you said that fourth brother Yi-xiang's boxing is off track," Zhang Jun-feng said.

"So fourth brother is not wrong to practice this way?" third brother Yi-mian asked.

"Provided it can be used and can guide the body to surface hidden capabilities of the body, this really is the key. Standard or Conventional or not, not so important. Just like your personal characteristic is lean and agile, in the five elements you belong to wood (Beng Quan, Crushing Fist), and in the twelve forms, monkey. Yi-xiang belongs to the earth and water (Heng Quan Crossing and Zuan Quan Drilling) in the five elements, and the dragon and the bear combined in the twelve forms. You must understand your own inner characteristics and potential, and only then can you develop your own gongfu true to your nature," Zhang Jun-feng said.

"Why is fourth brother earth, also water, also dragon, and also bear? How can it be so complicated," said third brother Yi-mian.

"Fourth brother's natural gifts are not the same as yours. He is a generalist, an all-rounder, you see that no matter what boxing he trains, he can quickly grasp the key points, and immediately derive many different changes, and the systems he has learned, even if he hasn't reviewed the moves for a long time, he doesn't forget them. This kind of talent is rare," Zhang Junfeng said.

"Yeah. Fourth brother has been like this since he was young. Every time he learned a new routine, he was always the first to master it. Didn't matter if we forgot it later, we just asked him anyway because he would remember. So, you usually see him quietly keeping to himself, but in our house, almost all the brothers listen to him," said third brother.

"Actually, you are also very good, you fight very well," Zhang Jun-feng said.

"Master, when you put it this way, it makes me embarrassed. But I still don't understand why we can accommodate changes in the form of the movements?" asked third brother Yi-mian.

"Okay. Let's explain it in another way. A brilliant musician, no matter how complicated the music he plays, he can play every note accurately. Right?" Zhang Jun-feng said.

"Since he is a *brilliant* musician, it should be like this," said third brother Yi-mian.

"Very good. What if you are a master?" Zhang Jun-feng asked.

"He should be even more accurate. Isn't it?" asked third brother Yi-mian.

"Okay. What is the difference between accurate and more accurate?" Zhang Jun-feng repeated.

"This, I don't understand," said a perplexed third brother Yi-mian.

"Actually, the master may not be able to play more accurately," Zhang Jun-feng said.

"How can that be? Must be a fake master," third brother Yi-mian said.

"In fact, even a real master might not be more accurate. Because the master usually uses this song and these notes to express his emotions. In different situations, there will be different performance and emotion, and different emotions naturally have different ways of expression. They will never chase accuracy at the expense of sacrificing an expression of the emotion. Therefore, as long he is a master-level musician, he will never waste his spirit chasing the accuracy of every note. Sometimes they might even deliberately be inaccurate," Zhang Jun-feng said.

"Why do they want to do that?" asked third brother Yi-mian.

"'Accuracy' is to master the spirit and intent of the original work. 'Inaccuracy' is to interpret the original repertoire in your own way, to express your personal understanding and awe of the original piece. If you are stubbornly demanding accuracy, use a machine to play the notes most accurately, but that kind of sound is lifeless and unmoving. Understand?" Zhang Jun-feng said.

"This is really hard to understand," said third brother Yi-mian.

"It's okay. Slowly you will understand. Learning anything is the same. Some people make great efforts to maintain the original appearance of the tradition, and some people's strong suit is extracting nourishment from tradition to create new possibilities. These two efforts are not good or bad. So long as you use the right method, either way you can achieve fine results and progress," Zhang Jun-feng said.

"No way. I still can't accept this theory of deliberately performing inaccurately," third brother Yi-mian said

"It's okay. Don't force yourself to accept this concept. You and fourth brother are precisely two different archetypes. Just follow your own feelings and work hard, that is what is right for you. The most important thing is that in the end you must be able to use your own feelings to express the power and grace of your boxing," Zhang Jun-feng said.

These principles are just like the knowledge we derive from reading and listening. In the end, you must be able to use your own way to tell a complete story, which means that you have successfully internalized the power of the story and turned it into your own wisdom. Being able to earnestly listen to stories told by others and being able to clearly tell stories so that others can understand, are both very important self-trainings. Stories often contain many unspoken motives and purposes. Understanding and allowing others to understand your purpose is more important than the story itself, isn't it?

Hong Yi-mian practiced by the Danshui River every morning and often had full contact exchanges with other martial arts friends, circa 1982.

Hong Yi-mian training Xingyiquan's Snake Form, circa 1982.

64– A RENOWNED TEACHER AND LOFTY DISCIPLES

Every famous teacher understands that their depth and breadth is derived from their body of students.

Scene: The Family Worship Hall on the second floor of Hong Wan Mei's rear court

(THE FOLLOWING IS A MONOLOGUE BY ZHANG JUN-FENG.)
"It's time. I really love them, but now's the time to let go of them.

"Only by letting go of them and letting them be independent can I compel them to 'shed their bodies and exchange their bones' and move on to the next level.

"I have placed all the gongfu that I have learned in my life, without reservation, all in Hong family.

"For the same reason, I really need to take care of myself, I need to let go and fly solo.

"I will never forget the first typhoon night I spent in Taiwan. We were besieged by the flood water on the only remaining wooden bed, a desperate situation, isolated and without help, not a friend in the world. If you hadn't let the two brothers, Yi-mian and Yi-xiang, pedal the trishaw over facing wind and rain, wading through the flood to come to rescue me, then I would have become a corpse floating on the water of a foreign land.

"At the moment I was rescued, I sat on the pedicab and looked back at the vast water, it was like I saw my own soul still sitting alone on the wooden bed, it did not leave with the pedicab. In that moment of brief enlightenment, I knew from the bottom of my heart that the original me was already dead. Dead in that storm.

"But as I calmed down slowly, watching from behind as the two brothers Yi-mian and Yi-xiang strained to pedal the tricycle in the wind and rain before the stagnant water subsided, that true feeling of risking their lives to help another, the empty shell of my body seemed to be filled again with a new life.

"I should have died at least once. This life was reborn in Taiwan, and it was given to me by the Hong family. Without the Hong family's unsparing support, hard work and expenditure with no expectation of recompense over the years, there would be no Zhang Jun-feng and Taiwan Beginnings-Essence of Change toehold.

"Independence is the best choice for the second generation of the Hong family and for myself. The course is finished, and I have nothing new to hand down to them. What they need is to spend time on chewing, digesting, and establishing their own system instead of continuing at the food trough. And I also have to take advantage of my own strength and vitality at this age and build a career here where I can settle down and support a family.

"In the future, I will continue to teach boxing for a living and promote 'Taiwan Beginnings-Essence of Change' in Taiwan.

"To thank you for your help when I was most troubled and helpless in my life, the Xingyiquan and Baguazhang I teach in the future will not exceed 80% of what I have taught the Hong family.

"No. Please don't exhort me, this is the only thing I can give back to the Hong family. Whether you agree or not, I will do it.

"Precisely because this was not the Hong family's intent, it made me decide to do this.

"Technology is so advanced, in the future these things may not be worth a penny.

"But I still have to follow the rules established by the grand master.

"Handing down the profound learnings of an orthodox school is not a business transaction, one's character and moral fiber are more important than money.

"Getting by these many years, I believe in my intuition and judgment. What is rare is that these three kids have good temperaments and innate talent; Yi-wen has a rigorous and focused personality, and is proficient in medicine and art, he is devoted in the research of Xingyiquan and internal strength. He is thorough, clear, eloquent, and is peerless in the theory of boxing. Yi-mian's natural disposition is bold and unrestrained, gutsy, highly artistic, brave, and battle wise. If he specializes in the Post Heaven Bagua Palms, no one can be his match. Yi-xiang is ingenious and intelligent. Any abstract, incomprehensible internal and external boxing skills he can grasp at a touch, and once touched he will not forget it for a lifetime. If this kind of rare talent continues to immerse himself into his training, he will become world-class in the future, a master of martial arts. To have such disciples should be considered my blessing.

"Looking back at the time spent and transformations we have experienced together over the years, it really seems like an illusory dreamscape. If it wasn't God's will, I don't know how to reasonably explain these karmic relationships? Were it not for the civil war, who could have had such a big influence, to persuade so many talents and resources to move to the isolated island of Taiwan in an instant? Were it not for the civil war, I should still be a northern businessman shuttling between the two sides of the strait and engaging in trade. Were it not for the civil war, so many stories would not be what they appear today. For our generation, is such an encounter lucky? Or unfortunate? Until today, I have no answer. I only remember the process was too traumatic. Living through this age of mutual antagonism and mutual hatred, it doesn't matter if you were Chinese or Taiwanese, both suffered hardships. In the end I don't know what method can be used to resolve the problems caused by politics and the historically accumulated indignation. Maybe foolishly follow the trajectory of history, use another bigger and more devastating war to destroy the other side? Maybe some smarter people will come forward and use greater compassion and wisdom to smooth those irremediable scars, use greater understanding to stop the endless slaughter and reincarnation. Maybe in our lifetime we won't see it. We can't wait for it, that path to an intelligent solution. We can only wait while abstaining from doing further harm, wait until time slowly erases these scars and memories, until another larger or more shocking event completely buries them. Who knows?

"Maybe. In my lifetime, I'm afraid I won't have a chance to return to my Shandong home.

"Taiwan is my home, the Hong family are my closest relations.

"So, even if I go out to train independently in the future, I will never forget that I am still a member of the Hong family.

Time passed imperceptibly, Zhang Jun-feng had already been teaching at the Hong family compound for more than ten years. During the period with the Hong family, with the unflagging financial support of old Mr. Hong, he was able to regularly organize martial arts conferences with friends and provide timely support to down and out martial artists who were struggling in Taiwan. This financial support of martial arts activities and charitable acts also invisibly enhanced Zhang Jun-feng's influence in Taiwan's martial arts circles. The three Hong family brothers under his full training gradually displayed their lofty talent in the martial arts world of Taiwan, solemnly becoming the most renowned and able fighters among the younger generation of martial artists in Taiwan.

65– HARSH TRAINING AND METAMORPHOSIS

It's not just that a big number looks pretty, but the principle of quantitative change and qualitative change. After hammering out a routine more than ten thousand times, in its essence, it is no longer the original thing. 10,000 repetitions ÷ 3 per day = 3,333 days ÷ 365 = 9.13 years. So the adage "ten years to forge and hone a sword" is reasonable. If you still complain it is not fast enough, then you can increase the number of daily repetitions, but if you reduce the element of time, it is hard to avoid that the temper and flavor will differ to some extent.

Scene: Outside the Danshui River embankment

(BELOW IS ZHANG JUN-FENG'S MONOLOGUE)
"A training pattern has been passed down for hundreds of years, how many people have diligently polished and refined it during that interim. After so many years and so many people, it still survives after repeated forgings. It must have its own marvel and existential value.

"When learning boxing, until you have tested it, don't rush to judge whether it's good or bad, or you won't be successful in learning anything.

"No matter what kind of boxing technique, after learning the basic applications, you still must incessantly and repeatedly practice.

"If you want to be outstanding, you have to endure the time and loneliness consumed.

"To achieve results with a boxing form, you must perform at least 10,000 repetitions before you can squeeze out the full flavor of the juice.

"Disassemble a complete routine into component parts, and then carefully repeat the polishing one by one. Confirm the intent of the move and the possible response and countermeasures of the opponent, again and again. Only repeated forgings will do.

"Repeated training, not mindless repetition of the same thing.

"Instead, try to employ all manner of different thinking and points of view to mull over and decode it.

"What seems like pointless repetition, for the diligent creates a deep communication with the original ancestral teachers. In a place that is invisible to the naked eye, the borders between yin and yang overlap in space and possibility. When absorbed in hard training, when the mind becomes empty, those ideas and energy will naturally enter.

"Western boxing's basic moves are few, and there is no special mystery in it, but Western boxers always do sufficient homework on these foundational skills. Whether straight punches or uppercuts, before they step through the ropes and enter the ring, which action did not go through hundreds of thousands of repeated practice, until the intent, spirit, and power reaches a pinnacle of practiced ease.

"There is no other shortcut, only oneself striving through the blood and sweat of hard training. Anything less is insufficient to break out, not enough to become the top exponent.

"Take the half-step crushing fist of Xingyi we are practicing now. Its progenitor is called the step-through crushing fist. It used the front foot generating the power, and the back hand moves forward when the rear foot is stepping through, synchronously launching the crushing fist. It is suitable for longer distance attacking.

"It is rumored that Guo Yun-shen, our Xingyiquan ancestor, was imprisoned because of an incident. While he was still in prison calming his heart seeking repentance, he practiced boxing to dissipate the evil tendencies in his heart. The shackles on his feet and the heavy iron ball restricted his action, so he changed the original step-through crushing fist to half-step boxing to practice. The additional constraints on his feet and resistance of the iron ball, imperceptibly enhanced the internal strength and power of the crushing fist. When he was released from prison, the fetters of shackles and iron ball were removed. His half-step crushing fist was invincible, and his generation extolled the beauty of his "half-step crushing fist conquering the world." This is just one simple move practiced in prison by ancestor Guo Yun-shen. After tens of thousands of repetitions of forging and polishing, after insights revealed the detail, the spirit and marrow, of crushing fist, and after adding his own creativity, he turned his stint in prison into a successful transformation.

"There is also an even more supernatural legend, just listen to it as an anecdote. It is said that Guo Yun-shen once lodged in a friend's protection service headquarters. One day early in the morning, after completing a routine morning exercise, he passed by the horse stables of the protection services. When he saw eight horses side by side and their heads bowed down eating forage. On a whim, he secretly gathered the qi of his whole body, and with his famed half-step crushing fist instantly summoned the release of power into the rib cage of the first horse. Probably because the horses were focused on eating hay or maybe due to a limitation of space, in response to that one punch the eight horses actually collapsed like dominoes. This is the anecdotal legend of the so-called "Diagonal Crushing of 8 Horses.

"As for the veracity, you don't have to invest too much effort investigating it. The main purpose of these stories is to emphasize the power of the half-step crushing fist. Because of the additional resistance of the heel dragging on the ground, even though this is a 'one-inch punch,' the power is nearly the same as the step-through crushing fist.

"The more basic the thing is, the more quintessential it is. But those who learn boxing tend to forgo what is close at hand to seek what is far afield, pursuing the branch before the root, blindly chasing dazzling magnificent gongfu.

"Like Xingyiquan's Splitting-Drilling-Crushing-Cannon-Crossing fists, this kind of simple, practical and unflowery move is the most useful in actual combat. Unless there is a wide gap in the ability of the two sides, in a real life and death fight, there is rarely a chance for you to display overly complex and mysterious moves.

"When it is a life-or-death fight, rules provide no restrictions and protection. Losing means going down, means dying.

"The Bagua Pre-Heaven Palms provide a new angle of thought and possibilities. Later, to improve its practicality for facing attacks, the Bagua Post-Heaven 64 hand maneuvers practiced left and right were added to strengthen its combat effectiveness.

"In most skirmishes, the fighter selects the shortest straight line between two points as the fastest and best to exploit.

"But fighting is a dynamic, mutually corresponding relationship, so the opponent certainly also understands to use the same logic to counteract you. The target you originally set your sights on, the opponent only needs to slightly turn, weave, and sidestep, or change his body shape, and your move will be defeated.

"Therefore, Xingyiquan's straight-in and straight out and Baguazhang's twisting body turning circle must be mutually reinforcing and arranged without discernible pattern to have increased chances of winning.

"This is also the main reason why after many years of training Baguazhang I went back to learn Xingyiquan.

"Strive to fathom each sentence I have said, and you will achieve a different level of perspective."

Alone in the dark of night outside the embankment, following the path of the dyke Fourth brother Yi-xiang, performed:

Splitting-Drilling-Crushing-Cannon-Crossing (the Mother Fists of
  Xingyi Five Element boxing)

Eagle, Hawk, Swallow, Chicken, Roc (Five birds)

Dragon, Snake, Tiger, Bear, Horse, Monkey, Water Strider (Seven
  beasts)

Opening, Uplifting, Yanking, Probing, Rising, Shouldering, Covering,
  Coiling/Wrapping-Heaven Trigram-Snake-form Flowing Posture
  Palm

Intercepting, Flower Concealed under the Leaf, Hacking, Peeling, Two Sages Transmit the Way, Tiger Pouncing, Phoenix Seizes the Nest, Chain of Rings—Water Trigram—Dragon Form Piercing Palm

Piercing, Moving/Transporting, Plundering, Blocking, Stopping, Overturning, Strolling, Turning—Mountain Trigram—Turning Body Tiger Striking Palm

Pushing, Upholding, Tying/Carrying/Hooking, Guiding/Collaring, Touching, Connecting, Following, Sticking/Adhering—Thunder Trigram—Swallow Overturning Covering Hand Palm

Propping/Slamming, Coiling, Dropping, Goring, Twisting/Crossing, Obstructing, Piling/Stacking, Drilling—Wind Trigram—Spinning Body Back Covering Palm

Chasing/Converging, Stomping, Swinging, Hanging, Kicking, Checking/Intercepting, Trampling, Colliding—Fire Trigram—Twisting Body Forward Searching Palm

Tucking/Pressing, Squeezing, Tricking/Clamping, Capturing, Crushing/Collapsing, Crashing, Buckling, and Moving—Earth Trigram—Shaking/Undulating Body Backward-Inserting Palm

Pounding/Passing, Leopard Cat, Perching, Gathering, Rocking/Undulating, Dodging, Crossing, Leaping—Marsh Trigram—Stopping Body, Moving and Hooking Palm

To the left and the right repeatedly, he refined his skill through bitter training, Master Zhang Jun-feng's exhortations and final teachings imparted on that farewell banquet echoing in his ears.

Hong Yi-xiang training Xingyiquan's Splitting Fist and Three Bodies Posture, circa 1955.

66– GUANDU

An expert skilled in the purchase of tuna fish said: The place where the head and the body of the fish are connected is the most deliciously flavored part of a fish. In the same way, where rivers meet the sea, there is always a bounty of fresh seafood treasures.

Scene: Guandu

GUANDU, LOCATED ON A WIDE PLAIN BETWEEN TAIPEI CITY AND Huwei (Danshui), was a small waterside village where farmers, fishers, and livestock farmers make a living. Most of the residents rely on planting rice as their main business, and harvest twice a year. For a long time, farmers near the sea have used their spare time fishing offshore to help out with family expenses. With its location at the junction of rivers and seas, the freshwater blends with the salt water so there were bountiful fish catches. Overfishing and pollution from upstream industrial wastewater gradually decreased the offshore fishing resources.

During the fishing season, whenever a fishing boat returned to port, there were always many fishmongers or seafood restaurant bosses waiting on the shore to buy out the most popular highly prized seasonal fish in the market. At the bottom of the net there were always some small, irregular, or unclassified fish. These were commonly called "low grade, sundry fish." To the fish monger and fisherman, these fish were a "not good enough to eat, but too good to throw away" by-product.

As was customary at other villages and towns near rivers in Taiwan, on farmlands near the river and sea a whole strip of land would be built up with "Duck Coops" where ducks were raised. These "low grade, sundry fish," which originally lacked economic value, became a godsent feast of fresh seafood delicacies for flocks of duck every day. Raised on freshly caught seafood, every duck had a shiny and healthy coat. The eggs laid by these duck hens are rich in nutritious essences and astacin peptides of small fishes and shrimps, so the round and firm egg yolks appear fresh, gorgeous, and naturally red as cooked shrimps, commonly known as 'red kernels,' completely different from the eggs produced by captive ducks fed commercial fodder.

This kind of duck egg is used to make 'terra cotta salted duck eggs.' Provided the salt percentage and time are sufficient in the preserving process, the yolks of the salted eggs will appear like onions, with a layered structure wrapping the yolk. Cut it in half with a knife, the 'red kernel' egg yolk will ooze bright red and translucent like chili oil. Anyone who has personally tasted them will proclaim that the egg yolk of 'terra cotta salted egg' compared with the egg yolks used in mooncakes or steamed lotus leaf wrapped rice dumplings on the market today "are not the same thing at all". The eggs laid by ducks raised on commercial feed can at best be described as egg-flavored "sweet potato puree". Use this kind of 'terra cotta salted duck egg' in clear porridge or white rice.— that is really full of flavor and lip smacking good; once tasted a flavor not to be forgotten!

Just like other towns and villages, the Guandu Mazu Temple has always been the center of faith, culture, and commerce for local residents. The chairman and director-generalship of the temple is usually held by local chiefs or elders in turn. Seeking to rid the villagers of the evil habits of gambling, making wine, and quarreling during the seasonal slack periods, the local chief and committees of the temple jointly initiated the 'The Guandu Dragon Boat Team.' It was regarded as the most positive agricultural slack activity for the villagers in Guandu, Lion Head, Zhuwei, and Danshui. Already expert swimmers familiar with water and fishing boat operations, when organized, promoted, trained, and incentivized with a real prize, the Guandu Dragon Boat Team was an invincible squad in the Taipei City Dragon Boat Race for many years.

Guandu Mazu Temple, resplendent in candlelight and incense perfume, was a major patron of Hong Wan Mei incense, candles, spirit money, and firecrackers for many years. And, aside from donations, the commodities supplied by the Hong family were also the main source of income for the temple. The villagers of the Neighborhood Association proposed to increase martial arts exercise training during the slack period so the local chief and chieftain sought an introduction from the chairman of the Mazu Temple. He personally led the main members of the dragon boat team carrying two red-faced Muscovy ducks and a bamboo basket filled with terra cotta salted duck eggs—a gift of local specialties. This vast and mighty group of people took a train from Guandu to Shuanglian Station and walked ceremoniously from the station to Dihua Street to call on elder Mr. Hong hoping to invite fourth brother Hong Yi-xiang to Guandu as a martial arts instructor in the village. Whereupon the commission of this voluntary teaching appointment became a turning point influencing the fourth brother Yi-xiang's life.

Group photo of Hong Yi-xiang and early students, 1972.

Leitai Free-fighting Champions, 1973.

67– THE BATTLE OF GUANDU

In the eyes of a gambler, not placing a bet is a choice between wagering and not wagering, a bet in itself, so in the end, not betting is betting!

Scene: Guandu, in the open space in front of Mazu Temple

ON THIS DAY, IN THE SMALL HARBOR IN FRONT OF THE TEMPLE square of the Guandu Mazu Temple, the river was filled with bobbing electric powered bamboo rafts and sampans. Due to the influence of the seasonal monsoon, the offshore wind and waves were too strong, and all the boats fishing along the coast joined in the "closed fishing period" for safety. In addition to personal safety considerations, the prohibition of fishing also took into account the ecology of the ocean, because that period coincided with the breeding season for most fish, shrimp, eel, and shellfish in the sea. The respite allowed overfished endangered species to recuperate and reproduce.

Beside a duck pen, a flood-prevention earth embankment was already covered with idlers from nearby towns and villages making a special trip to see the ruckus. On a piece of fallow farmland next to the embankment could be observed almost all the adult men from the entire Guandu area who could lay down their work and gather here to watch an oft-awaited event. For several years, on this square mound made of packed earth, who knows how many well-known martial arts masters seeking glory came forth to "test their hands" and many had to be carried off.

And the key person who created this result was one guy, Chen Mi-lan, the captain and coach of the Guandu Dragon Boat Team. Chen Mi-lan was 175 centimeters tall and weighed 85 kilograms. He was the three-time heavyweight champion of Western boxing in the Taiwan Provincial Games. At each competition, from the preliminary to the championship rounds, all ended with knockouts, no exceptions. He said that he did not deliberately want to make these martial art contenders look bad, but he believed that the teachers of traditional Chinese martial arts always talked more ferociously than they fought. He didn't want to waste time learning useless things from such people who had no real practical knowledge. "Talking about gongfu is just flatulence! Who has the ability knock me out, that is who I will admire." "What is the goddam use of practicing so many ferocious paper tiger forms. If it is truly good and practical, a few tricks are enough." This was his unwavering conviction after practicing many years of boxing, and it is also the main reason why he had never given up on boxing since he was selected as a member of the Western Boxing Team in junior high school.

In this arena, Chen Mi-lan fought barefoot, treading with smooth graceful steps, his sturdy body moving light and lively like a butterfly, constantly employing jabs to launch exploratory attacks on Hong Yi-xiang around whom he circled. The referee Chen Qing-bo had repeatedly reminded both parties that this was a friendly match, only "light contact" and definitely not a full contact match. However, once a person is in the ring, once there is an audience, once there is a prospect of winning or losing, all the reminders become just wind around the ears. In such an atmosphere, exhortations that the contenders let go of the prospect of winning or losing is purely said for the sake of the audience. From the sound of his punches and breathing, it was clear that winning or losing was obviously more important than friendship.

Hong Yi-xiang had seen Western ring boxing, but this was indeed the first time in his life that he had formerly crossed hands with a Western boxer, and the first time he faced such a powerful opponent at the level of "Provincial Champion". Sure enough, from the start Chen Mi-lan relied on his rich experience in the ring to easily gain the home court advantage. Facing the fast and pragmatic style of Western boxing, besides struggling to adapt to the speed of the opponent's punching and movement, Hong Yi-xiang was locked in a circle of fire of incoming punches, only able to react to the opponent's jabs, and for a while it seemed there were no active countermeasures that could reverse the situation.

"Doesn't seem like much!" Chen Mi-lan taunted.

"Bagua? Isn't that for fortune telling?"

"Chinese martial arts—lots of famous schools, no real power, not up to the test!"

"Yeah. It's Taiji all over again, it's Bagua again, all wrapped in mystery, wrapped in bullshit!"

"This is fun. Isn't the Bagua Palm going around in circles? How come I'm the one doing the circling around you. Ha-ha-ha!"

The crowd, not impressed, expressed their views.

"I can fight like that."

"They just started, you worried already?"

"They're not making a move, just dodging. When you gonna' fight back!"

"This isn't even a street fight. Maybe he has some strategy!"

"I'll give it to you straight. A fist fight is not that complicated. Without real power, what is the use of strategy alone on the street. In the end, aren't you just beaten down to surrender."

"Fight back. Are you waiting for a sign from the gods before you make a move?"

The spectators who stood on the sidelines were always thirstier to see fire and blood than the boxers in the ring.

After several rounds of probing attacks, Chen Mi-lan believed that he had grasped his opponent's habitual responses, whereupon he began to encroach with bolder 'combination punches' to make continuous and destructive attacks. Although several fierce attacks were dodged by clever footwork, Yi-xiang was still forced to ward off blows with no room for counterattacks. However, neither did Chen Mi-lan's rapid punches land an effective blow. To force Hong Yi-xiang to take an active shot thus revealing an opening, Chen Mi-lan decided to change his tactics. He deliberately lengthened and deepened the jab and switched to an offensive of alternating left and right punches. He hoped to mess up the opponent's footwork and force him to fight back. The difference between this powerful cross punch and the probing jab lies in the speed and strength. Normally, the "jab punch" penetrates shallowly, focusing on speed. The 'cross punch' is based on strength and is relatively slow speed. But for a boxer of Chen Mi-lan's level, even cross punches are incredibly fast!

"Look at the momentum and you know who will win the round. Look. The young master of Dihua Street is not our Mi-lan's equal after all."

"No. I see Hong Yi-xiang's body shifting and footwork is neither hurried nor chaotic, it's too early to call the victor."

"Fuck off, you spineless dick! You root for outsiders but not your own. Place a bet if you dare."

"Fuck your mother! My spineless dick will fuck your corpse. Put your money down. Afraid of you, peh!"

"What's the bet?"

"Just bet on the winner and the loser,"

A sensitive nerve of the entire audience was immediately stimulated by this one word 'bet.' In an instant, the person who was invited to make a wager took on the identity and mission of the 'House.' He squatted down and picked up a pebble under his feet, and drew two circles, one large and one small, on the yellow earth. He wrote the word 'rice'[22] in the big circle and the word 'flood'[23] in the small circle. "This is for our own people, I drew the ring big since there must be a lot of people betting on Chen, it has to be big enough!"

"Fuck your mother! Are your heads all busted? All betting on Mi-lan, no one betting on that Dihua Street guy, how is that going to work. No, no, no one wagers that way, somehow divide the bets up to another bookie…"

A small, unexpected episode on the sidelines of a passionate crowd of villagers, instantly turned into a frenzy of betting on the winner. The crowd, originally scattered around the mound to watch the match, also flocked to the House where the casino was sketched on the ground, and one after another took out their banknotes and silver coins in their pockets According to their

---

22 Mi 米, rice grain, is part of Chen Mi-lan's given name.
23 Hong 洪, flood, is Hong Yi-xiang's surname.

subjective view of the action in the ring and from the mysterious and unseen influence of the "Mother of Heaven" in Guandu Temple, they placed their bets. The martial arts training program, which was originally arranged to eliminate the pernicious gambling habit of the villagers, turned on its head into Game Central. And the two martial arts masters continuing their duel in the ring were turned miraculously into slot machines. Even the upright spirits of compassion sitting in the Guandu Temple could not avoid becoming accomplices to the House as bettors turned to them and prayed for a windfall.

This is where the all-pervasive, all conquering magical power of the word 'gambling' emanates from; its existence pools everyone's interests in profit and harm together. The originally pointless tussle and victory or loss in the ring, was now instantaneously tied to personal opportunity to profit. The two sides facing off were representing the glory and honor of their respective schools. The principles they stood for and the legends behind the bitter training, all would be judged after the conclusion of the fight. Only then could it be determined which had won the right and value to be lauded.

When any technical competition is reduced by gambling to the outcome of winning and losing, whether you like it or not, success or failure becomes the universal value that dominates the world. In the eyes of gamblers, even 'not betting' is considered a 'wager.' In essence there is no difference from those who make their wager 'To Gamble.' For them, any prediction, choice, decision, or judgment carrying an element of uncertainty is all related to 'Gambling' with a direct blood-tie, like twins. The difference being some people have more chips to play, and some people have fewer.

In even more wishful thinking, they feel that 'gambling' is the opportunity God gives the poor to change their destiny. Only 'Gambling' can leapfrog over talent, education, and connections, the levels of constraints and hard-work necessary to crawl up, directly leading to the back door of plenty, wealth, and joy. It is an investment filled with hope and romance. Deliberately ignored behind this romantic fantasy is hidden a huge price. Although the moment from placing the bet to the instant the winner or loser is revealed is full of excitement and all manner of possibilities, once the addiction to gambling is on your back it is no longer "quitting while you are ahead" or "cutting your losses," that kind of "I can do what I say," that kind of easy, relaxed happiness…

Only after all the bets were placed did the enthusiasm of the crowd return to the competition in the ring. Ignored as insufficiently captivating and put on "pause" thanks to the help of the punters on the sidelines, the scene all of sudden became lively.

As planned, Chen's deep, extended jabs successfully broke through the opponent's closely guarded defense and smoothly penetrated past the elbow block's—the last line of defense. Chen Mi-lan's mind quietly plotted, "I just have to skip in a little deeper, get a little greater angular twist on my waist and rachet up the push off of my step at just the right instant, then I'll be within an effective attacking range." In this way he would have sufficient purchase to cleanly bring this bout to a conclusion. So, he deliberately pulled his body away creating a buffer, making the margin they had taken great pains to narrow between them suddenly pull open wider.

This is like the situation where the sea will suck back and retreat before the tsunami arrives, and then return with a thunderous force collapsing heaven and earth. It is easy for people to overlook the deadly threat hidden behind. From the sidelines, the audience with years of armchair observation, faintly smelled blood signaling the curtain was about to close on this great game. To a man their eyes opened wide and fixed their gaze on the changes taking place in the ring lest they miss the instant of the most crucial moment.

Sure enough, the action of Chen Mi-lan's deceptive feigned retreat allowed his opponent to relax his centerline defense, and the hands that had been guarding his chest hung down slack. Seeing this sign, Chen Mi-lan was delighted, and immediately dug in his right rear foot to surge toward the opponent, restricting Hong Yi-xiang's ability to adapt with two consecutive left jabs. This was followed instantly with a heavy right uppercut long lying-in ambush to the opponent's "off-limits" left chin.

Hong Yi-xiang, heretofore forced to continually retreat, suddenly changed at this critical moment. He was seen to take a sidestep forward to the right and hunch his back, just like a cat's action before launching an attack. As he shifted his position, his left forward hand used the leverage of "clever energy" to gently intercept the opponent's ferocious right uppercut, followed up in a hair's breadth of time with a right cannon fist "point striking" Chen Mi-lan's right biceps.

This "point striking" is a special method used by Internal Boxing to "strike acupuncture points," using the second knuckle of the index finger, focusing on striking dense clusters of nerves and lymph nodes. The deadliness of this hand technique might seem trivial, but the force is very concentrated, instantly rendering the struck point sore, numb, paralyzed, and/or feeble, in the blink of an eye depriving the ability to attack and defend. The moment Chen Mi-lan was struck, his arm muscles cramped, his entire right arm was seized with pain such that he could not straighten it.

However, Chen's strong will to win made him resistant to the severe body pain. He firmly believed if he could only withstand the pain, he could drive a final, fatal combination attack according to the original plan and the one who would first hit the canvas would certainly not be him.

With this conviction, he put all the energy of his feet shifting up into the left arm swinging out. Hong Yi-xiang was seen to use his left front hand to press down and hold Chen Mi-lan's left uppercut, and then he stepped deep behind his opponent's left leg, accompanied by a right backhand slapping grab of Chen's right arm and a lower outer side sweep of Chen Mi-lan's legs throwing him onto the soft ground. This combination attack of "Xingyi Cannon Hammer," "Bagua Pulling Palm," and "Sweeping Legs" is a simultaneous expression of the three energies of internal boxing, Overt, Covert, and Adaptive.

Chen Milan, lying on the ground, his head blank, unable to fight anymore, heartily accepted such a result. This result beyond everyone's expectations not only determined who would go home with that pile of bets in the big circle on the ground, but also determined that Hong Yi-xiang would start from Guandu to commence a new milestone in his career teaching boxing.

※ ※ ※

"Isn't Baguazhang good at shooting on the move?" Chen Mi-lan asked.

"It depends on whether you are standing in the circle or outside," Hong Yi-xiang said.

"Then why didn't you move just now?" Chen Mi-lan asked.

"Because you kept moving. Isn't it?" Hong Yi-xiang said.

"Why could I never hit you?" Chen Mi-lan asked.

"Because I am standing in the center of the circle, a slight angle shift is enough," Hong Yi-xiang said.

"But my speed was always faster than you," Chen Mi-lan said.

"I use angles to offset your speed, and my thinking is a bit faster than you."

"How is it faster?" Chen Mi-lan asked.

"Quick eyes, quick mind," said Hong Yi-xiang.

"Can you make it clearer?" Chen Mi-lan asked.

"I observed your physical and tactical habits," Hong Yi-xiang said.

"But I used a lot of feints, why didn't I deceive you?" Chen Mi-lan asked.

"I seized the moment at the end of your techniques," Hong Yi-xiang said.

"Is it the gap between the previous movement and the next movement?" Chen Mi-lan asked.

"Yes. But a little earlier," said Hong Yi-xiang.

"I was unable to change mid-move, and the subsequent moves naturally couldn't be launched," Chen Mi-lan said.

"Yes. This is a mixed style of Xingyiquan and Baguazhang," said Hong Yi-xiang.

"Sure enough, Neijiaquan is really terrific. In the end Western Boxing doesn't cut it," Chen Mi-lan said.

"No, Western boxing is a very pragmatic and efficient boxing skill. It eliminates many useless and inefficient techniques, leaving a few simple moves, focusing on speed, strength, and coordination. It is a combat art worthy of respect," Hong Yi-xiang said.

"But in the end it can't beat Chinese boxing," Chen Mi-lan said.

"A single win or loss cannot determine the quality of a boxing school. At best, it is just a win or loss between you and me," Hong Yi-xiang said.

"Master Hong, what do you think is the key to winning or losing?" at this point Chen Mi-lan was finally happy to formerly call Hong Yi-xiang "Master Hong".

"My personal view of Western Boxing is not necessarily correct, but I think there are too many restrictions."

"For example?" Chen Mi-lan asked.

"Western boxing attack stipulates that only punches with the front of the fist face can be used. It sacrifices the use of fingers, elbows, shoulders, waist, and head, not to mention backfist, hammerfist, and single knuckle strikes. Many clever functions can be employed, like the fingers can spot, wrap, pluck, grab, twist. And our feet, in addition to moving, we can kick, stomp, hook, sweep, trip… If it's a competition, it's only the difference between winning and losing. If it's a battlefield, then the price paid for these limitations is huge," said Hong Yi-xiang.

"Understood. In a real fight, there is only win or lose, life and death, You can't limit yourself, no one can blame the opponent for 'breaking the rules' if you go down," Chen Mi-lan said.

"If you can't fully protect yourself when the enemy breaks the rules, it is considered a loss," Hong Yi-xiang said.

"I will keep it in mind. The rules only exist in competitions. You must not use the same tactics outside the ring," Chen Mi-lan said.

"In fights without rules or restrictions, it is the purpose of martial arts to protect yourself and overcome the opponent. In addition, the key to winning or losing a fight may not be the boxing style itself. Your current status and the opponent's situation are both big variables," Hong Yi-xiang said.

"So today I lost on the strategy to do battle," Chen Mi-lan said.

"No. You should say, 'Today I won because I obtained many different ideas for free!' didn't you," said Hong Yi-xiang.

"Well said. You've convinced me. In the future, please share more 'ideas,' Master Hong," Chen Mi-lan said.

Evening calisthenics training, rolling forward on the knuckles, 1973.

68– THE FIRED BRICK

Two opposing sides must exist at the same time, the harder the thing, the more brittle. All that is needed is to find the universal physical properties, then one can find the easy way to crack it.

Scene: Yanzi's noodle stall, the US Army PX Center on Zhongshan North Road

IN THOSE DAYS, CHEN MEI-SHOU WAS THE TOP PLAYER IN TAIWAN'S judo circles. During the Japanese occupation, he and Hong Yi-xiang studied judo in the same gym. Later, due to his family, Hong Yi-xiang changed his training to Chinese martial arts while Chen Mei-shou chose to remain in the judo world to cultivate and develop, and he was as famous as the well-known judo master Huang Cang-lang. These notables were the soul of Taiwan's early promotion of judo.

This morning, he and Hong Yi-xiang met to have breakfast together at the Yanzi Noodle Stall. Both ordered dried noodles and dumpling soup, and asked Boss Ye to help them select an arrangement of crispy fried red-yeast meat, raw intestines, liver, and smoked shark and other signature dishes of the kitchen. Of course, this included the pork head scraps the stall set aside for Hong Yi-xiang every day. The two ate the dried noodles in one go, and then they talked while eating the dumpling soup.

(The following is the monologue of Chen Mei-shou)

"I have taken charge as judo instructor for the US military in Taiwan.

"Three days a week. Every lesson two hours.

"Westerners are pragmatic. You have to beat 'em to earn their respect.

"Yeah. They are all soldiers fighting the Vietnam War!

"Going to the battlefield to fight to the death, if it's not practical it's not suitable!

"Those soldiers are well-nourished and big, of course it's not easy to teach 'em. But the tuition fees are quite tasty!

"The Guandu battle, that was a pretty win!

"Many masters and well-known teachers were decked at the hand of that western boxing champion.

"There is an event coming up, you have to participate.

"It's specially assigned by the top-brass.

"On the night of Mid-Autumn Festival.

"Yeah. Foreigners don't think there is anything special and different about the moon that day.

"Definitely go. The top-brass of the Sino-US command have specifically named you.

"There is another special person who wants to meet you.

"It's not convenient to say, you'll know at the time.

"The PX opposite the Zoo on Zhongshan North Road seems to be a welfare center dedicated to the US military.

"There's gonna be many domestic and foreign reporters attending.

"The Big Guy is afraid of losing face. I have to find a few who can fight, able to hold their own. This kind of face can't afford to be lost.

"Several old timers are publicly promoting you.

"Unacceptable. You gotta go.

"Because…the event will have all you can eat delicious cheeses and American steaks, ha-ha-ha."

※ ※ ※

The day before the Mid-Autumn Festival, the "US Army Welfare Center" canteen occupying a large area on Zhongshan North Road was completely cleared and was arranged as a performance space to hold a medium-sized gala. In this instance the performances to be demonstrated one by one on the stage were not ordinary dance recitals, but martial arts routines with swords flashing, rapiers flickering, sticks flying . The martial art groups invited to demonstrate their skills were all elites selected by the National Martial Arts Association under the decree of higher authorities. Almost all well-known martial arts masters and up and coming stars from Taiwan were recruited.

The evening of the event, only the headmasters of the schools sat in the hall while the large number of participants were arranged to wait outside the venue. They entered the arena one by one according to the schedule. The content of the program was all-encompassing, including routines, partner training, weapons, grappling, seizing, empty-handed defense against knives, iron head skills, iron throat skills, iron bridges, driving nails with bare hands, and all variety of power breaking. Myriad schools competed for the admiration of the crowd.

Although they had been screened beforehand, however, the quality of the routines was mixed, with weeds stuck among the flowers, and the event was unbearably chaotic. The main reason was that the National Martial Arts Association responsible for screening and inviting could not beg off all the personal pressure exerted on them. No school would think of missing this opportunity to show their face in front of reporters from home and abroad. No one knew what practical benefits of being invited might be in the end, but they felt that if they were not invited, they would have been eliminated and ignored by others. Therefore, in deference to the influence of all parties, the so-called "screening out" in the end became "screening all in." Provided the martial gym had paid the "membership fee" according to the rules every year, almost all of them were successful in becoming candidates on the list. Consequently, a performance that was originally scheduled to conclude within two hours, had been in full swing for nearly three hours and still didn't end.

Subjected to those long, tedious, highly repetitive martial arts masters "giving it all they had," early-on the guests had started to shift restlessly in their seats with bewildered expressions on their faces. It was only due to the friendship between allies China and the United States that a mediation outreach took place on the quiet with the director general of the National Martial Arts Association secretly asked to eliminate as many programs as possible, to end this tedious martial arts performance before nine o'clock. Immediately after the top US military official attending gave a brief speech, the floor was open to media from various countries to ask questions of the heads of the martial gyms. At that time, although Hong Yi-xiang had already started teaching in Guandu, it was of a charitable nature and he had not formally registered to set up a martial arts gym. He had been especially directed by higher authorities to participate, but in deference to his elders he sat in an inconspicuous seat in the back row.

"In modern warfare, what is the practical value of traditional martial arts?" a reporter asked.

"During close hand-to-hand combat, you can kill the enemy. You can save your life," to the first question from a foreign reporter an old master sitting in the center of the front row, who seemed to exude the special quality of a leader, replied with an attitude that only he was up to representing the entire Chinese martial arts tradition of thousands of years.

"Thank you for the master's answer. So in the event of war, you will still carry these big swords, big war hammers, seven-section steel whips, and meteor hammers to fight with you?" the reporter asked. This barbed question immediately dispelled the originally dull and boring atmosphere, and provoked laughter from the VIPs and reporters.

"…" The venerable oldster was taken by the surprise ambush of this cold spear, and his mind went blank for a while, not knowing how to respond to this plot against him. Those who originally struggled to sit in the first row, rushing to face the media and cameras, only then realized that this front row of seats was basically the execution ground for the firing squad. Facing this kind of dilemma, some people chose to close their eyes and meditate. Others chose to pretend chit-chat, and no one was willing to stand up at this moment to face the tart and impolite questioning of this foreign journalist.

There was a far-off voice from the back corner, but a voice that was loud enough for everyone present to hear clearly, as Hong Yi-xiang responded to this question. "In the training of long weapons, some are intended to increase fundamental strength, and some are for the sake of tradition. It might not all be related to combat. Internal boxing uses the long spear and *zhang er* long pole to exercise strength of the core and foundation. The principle is the same as Westerners using barbells and dumbbells to increase muscle stamina. These traditional techniques cannot be interpreted through your perspective. What you see and what you call to mind may not be the key. On the other hand, I would like to ask you this, Mister, do you use dumbbells as hand grenades in Vietnam?" The clever, inspired analogy was like the "needle hidden in cotton" of Internal Boxing, easily dissolving this pejorative provocation, following the opponent's oncoming force and responding with a humorous cheekiness to lob it back to the opponent.

"Apologies. Your question touches on national security and secrets of the United States. I am afraid that only the Secretary of Defense can answer your question." The experienced reporter used more humor to easily defuse the awkwardness. But after such a response, other reporters were embarrassed to use disrespectful ways to ask questions so as not to humiliate themselves.

"Just now we watched a lot of power-breaking performances, which are wonderful. They look great, but there are many tricks in them. Like your Japanese-style roof tiles, they are piled very high, and they seem to require a lot of force to break. But everyone knows that this kind of tile is dried in a low temperature kiln, and the hardness is not great, plus the curved tiles collapse like a wave. What I see is a technique depending on physics, not real martial arts skill. If power breaking is supposed to show skills, why don't you choose to use more realistic materials and methods," A foreign reporter speaking very formal Mandarin exposed this commonly understood problem in the martial arts industry.

"Even if it is a technique depending on physics, it is part of gongfu. Anyway, everything has been smashed up. If you have doubts, we can't re-do. Anyway, believers will believe, if you don't believe, it doesn't matter what I say." The master who had just done the bare fist breaking spread his hands on the table and explained helplessly.

"That's not necessarily so. Masters one and all, are you interested in trying this?" It seemed that the interviewing reporters came prepared. No sooner had he spoken than an assistant took out two light yellow bricks and put them on the long table in front of the masters.

"It's fired bricks." People in the know could see at a glance the origin of the two large bricks on the table.

"Correct. These are high-density refractory bricks for kiln building. They're thicker, harder, and have no curvature. Can someone break two refractory bricks without spacers—with one punch? Then we'll really admire Chinese martial arts." The reporter looked around at all the masters on the scene with a wry smile, hoping that someone would stand up and give it a try.

"It's kilned at a high temperature—over a thousand degrees—it's harder than stone."

"Fuck! It's clearly a trap set up in advance. You deliberately pull these wonderful things out to suck us in."

"Restrain yourselves, whatever you do, don't touch it. You don't know the characteristics of things you haven't struck before. Don't fall into the trap."

"Yes. Restraint. Don't pay attention to them, in a moment the Chinese Martial Arts Association will come to our rescue."

"Fuck his grandma. What kind of demonic press conference is this. I'll never participate in this kind of damned meeting anymore." The masters at the table whispered to each other reminding and complaining, but no one emerged to stand up at this juncture to challenge these two bricks.

"I am very grateful to this reporter for his diligent preparations. Today's performance has exceeded the original schedule. The masters here have been preparing for today's performance for many days, and they should be tired. I suggest we don't try the matter of this brick today. If there is a chance in the future, our National Martial Arts Association will make another arrangement, okay?" The director-general of the Association came forward to circle up the wagons at the critical moment. "Yes. It's too late. We have to rush to get the night train back south. Let's talk about it next time," the masters on the table responded in unison, regardless of school. And the people in charge of taking interview notes and the people in charge of the photography displayed disdainful smirks when they heard the news from the Association.

"Slow down. I'm willing to try it." Hong Yi-xiang got up from the back row and walked to the front table. He hefted the two heavy fire bricks and carefully evaluated their weight and quality. The atmosphere at the event, which had become sullen like a concert breaking up, suddenly became lively again with this change. The staff at the venue immediately arranged the space and lighting according to the requirements of the on-site photographers. Although the scene was bustling and chaotic for a while, it was also very efficient. In less than ten minutes, dozens of still and movie cameras were in place, glaring like the eyes of covetous tigers viewing prey, and ready to pounce on the headline image of tomorrow morning's newspapers. Whether it was a shattering of rock surprising Heaven, or the making of a fool in front of everyone, the headline and the manner of the report would entirely be determined at the instant the camera shutters flickered open and closed.

Hong Yi-xiang seized the brief gap in the schedule as the venue was arranged, and after a simple warm-up and breathing on the sidelines, he entered the venue alone to face all the lenses and attention. At this time, Mr. Wang Cheng-zhang, the chairman of the National Martial Arts Association, took pains to step forward, express his concern and encouragement, and briefly introduce

Hong Yi-xiang's martial arts school and background to all the distinguished guests and the media. "Mr. Hong, in order for every photographer to take the best shots, would you please cooperate and wait until we count one, two, and three before hitting it."

"No countdown. When I raise my hand, you'll definitely have enough time to press the shutter."

"Hey. A guy who can't be pushed around." In the VIP seat, an American military officer whispered into the ear of Jim Dolenz beside him.

"You have to break them clean, only then do you get bragging rights. Otherwise…" The end of the derisive statement was too late to be uttered. The flashes and shutters of dozens of cameras at the scene were like hundreds of tracer rounds under a night sky, at the same time, a shattering burst, shocking every heart on the scene.

"Did you take the shot?"

"Took it. But I don't know if I got it. I have to go back and develop it to know," All the photographers were concerned about whether they caught the right moment when they pressed the shutter button. Only after that did someone wonder out loud, "Did it break?"

The next morning, at the newsstands by the city bus ticket booths on the front page of all the newspapers, the headlines were different, but the photos published were almost identical—Hong Yi-xiang's left hand grasping the sides of the two fired bricks, the right fist pressed on top of the brick, and under the fist the scar of an obvious fracture, running down the side of the bricks.

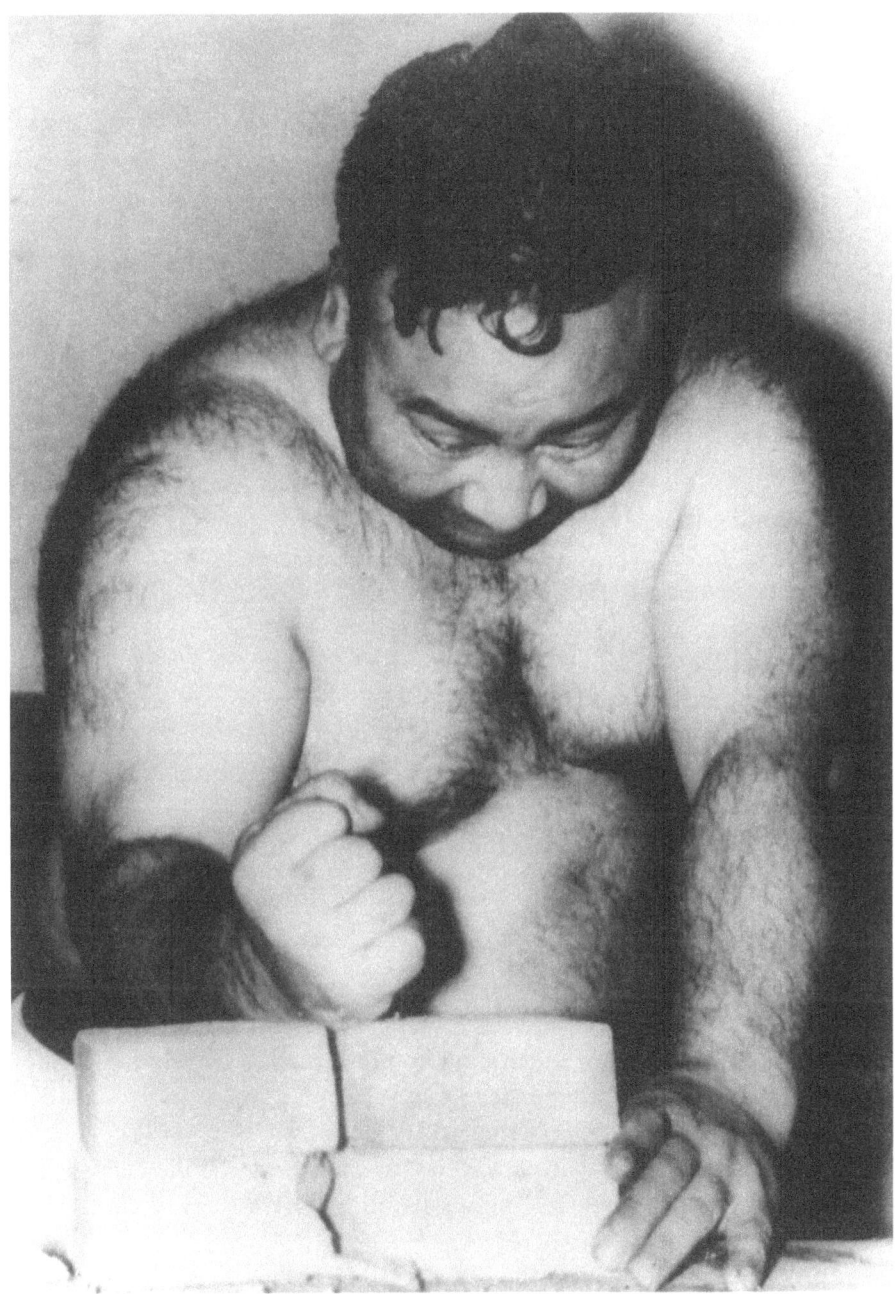

Hong Yi-xiang demolishes two fired kiln bricks with his bare hands, 1960.

69– AFTER THE FIRED BRICK

Reality tells us, you must first prove that you have the strength to win before you are qualified to sit down and talk about the right to peace. Therefore, everyone made a nuclear weapon to prove to the world that they have the right not to use nuclear weapons!

Scene: US Military Welfare Center, Zhongshan North Road

"Breaking bricks is breaking bricks. Not real gongfu," said Hong Yi-xiang

"Why?" The media reporter asked.

"Bricks are inanimate. People will dodge, will respond. They'll fight back," said Hong Yi-xiang.

"So what do you consider to be real gongfu?" the reporter asked.

"Martial arts are man to man, a skill of the internal and external mutually interacting," Hong Yi-xiang said.

"Since it's not real gongfu, why did you still attempt the break?" the reporter asked.

"Because it broke. It is convincing. Isn't it?" Hong Yi-xiang said.

"What if it didn't break?" the media reporter asked.

"This should be asked the other way around. If it didn't break, how would your report be written?" Hong Yi-xiang said.

"Definitely more provocative than if it broke," said the media reporter.

"I think so too. Sorry to disappoint," Hong Yi-xiang said.

"Excuse me, do you rely on technique to break bricks? Or power? A simple answer is enough, please," the reporter said.

"What do you say?" Hong Yi-xiang asked back.

"You broke the bricks, it's up to you to say," the reporter replied.

"Okay. But you all only ask questions and don't answer them?" Hong Yi-xiang said.

"We're journalists, it's our bound duty to ask questions," said the reporter.

"Makes sense. But if there is no premise, there is no answer. This time you have to answer my question first. Question, do you care about 'striking' or 'breaking'?" Hong Yi-xiang asked.

"It would be about 'striking.' Whether you break it or not, we still have a story. If it breaks or not, this is not something we can control. For the media, 'fist hits brick'—the goal is reached. Provided there is news and pictures, we are done. Our report is determined by what happened at the event. Although we always hope the unexpected happens. So under this premise, we must have someone step up to make news, right?" the reporter said.

"What if no one steps up?" Hong Yi-xiang asked.

"Don't worry about this. Trust me. Someone will always be pushed into the water," said the media reporter.

"No fear, I can swim. Actually, at that moment, what I wanted to do most was to smash the brick with a hammer, and then tell everyone that in Taiwan we all use this method to break bricks. Not by hand. Would that be okay?" said Hong Yi-xiang.

"Ha-ha-ha…This result would be even more awesome," The media reporter said.

"I was afraid you couldn't accept such a big discrepancy," Hong Yi-xiang said.

"So you stepped up and shouldered this risk? Have you ever thought about it, what if it didn't break?" the reporter asked.

"In that case, just write that I am not proficient at my art and lack vigor. But, I can't let you write that Chinese martial arts aren't up to the test," Hong Yi-xiang said.

"One guy taking on all the risk, that makes you remarkable," said the reporter.

"I am the son of a merchant from Dihua Street," said Hong Yi-xiang.

"Mr. Hong, you haven't answered my question yet," the media reporter reminded.

"Okay. Let's go back to your question. Breaking is a corresponding relationship between people and objects and can't be separated from one's grasp of the physical characteristics. Therefore, in addition to technique and power which you just mentioned, one must also have knowledge and judgment, two important elements. Of course, you also have to have some luck," Hong Yi-xiang said.

"May I ask, what physical characteristics did you see in that hard brick?" the media reporter asked.

"Two opposite sides must exist at the same time. The harder the object, the more brittle. Fired bricks used to build furnaces are heat-resistant, the texture is hard, but it is not resistant to impact," Hong Yi-xiang said.

"So?" the reporter asked.

"Providing you catch the resonant breakpoint, the effect will emerge. Strictly speaking, in that instant I struck down twice," Hong Yi-xiang said.

"But we only saw one strike clearly," the media reporter said.

"I used my left hand to secure the lower brick, and then used a two-stage splitting-energy to strike. I first hit the upper brick with crushing power. When it rebounded on impact, I opposed the rebound force with internally twisted pressure and used the brick that popped up to hit the brick below," said Hong Yi-xiang.

"So you were using the upper brick to hit the lower brick?" the media reporter asked.

"You could say that. But you still have to have enough energy in reserve. Because it is completed in an instant, it's not easy to detect. This is the two-stage power of Neijiaquan 'breaking the cover of the golden bell' of hard qigong. First strike relaxed, then strike with penetration," Hong Yi-xiang said.

"Is that really the way it works?" asked the media player.

"Before the camera was invented, no one believed that people's images could be captured on film?" Hong Yi-xiang said.

"Everyone, it's getting late. Let's ask the last question now. We have to prepare for the banquet," said the director general of the National Martial Art Association.

"Mr. Hong, what do you think is the most difficult to break?" the reporter asked.

"Balls. Under normal conditions, I can't bust balls," Hong Yi-xiang said.

"Oh. Why?" the media reporter asked.

"Because if they're busted, no one has any fun," Hong Yi-xiang chuckled.

"Ha-ha-ha…"All the guests laughed.

"That's really interesting. He's not wrong at all."

※ ※ ※

After the breaking of the two "fire bricks," everyone relaxed and took a breather. The organizer of the banquet announced the end to the day's performance and cleared the venue as planned, quickly arranging it into a Western-style buffet. On the main wall of the venue was projected an artificial moon allowing everyone to enjoy the moon while eating indoors. Several long tables with clean white tablecloths displayed a bounty of sandwiches, ham, steak, fried chicken, cake, fruit, cocktails… At the tableside, two extra-large ice chests cut from big oil drums were set up. On beds of crystal-clean ice were bottles of beer, and soda-pop. All of the guests forgot the toil of the just concluded performances and tucked-in to their heart's content into the sumptuous delicacies. This type of ground-breaking American style feast, in that era of shortage and hardship, was already regarded as a great treat.

During the banquet, the media was free to roam and interview. All the masters who participated in the meeting, having eaten and imbibed their fill, came forward boldly and recounted to reporters from various newspapers that Chinese martial arts were extensive, profound, all-encompassing, and indomitable, all manner of fantastical and unverifiable rumors and apocryphal stories…and in that moment when all were unabashedly enjoying the delicious cuisine, off in a VIP room several senior media representatives and senior officers from the Sino-American command hosted a meal with Hong Yi-xiang and Chen Mei-shou. At the dining table was served freshly squeezed juice, freshly baked bread, steak hot off the grill, lobster, and aged whiskey. With the help of an American translator, everyone had a chat while eating.

"I once saw a karate master in Japan, smashing a ball empty-handed," an American military officer said.

"Wow! That's incredible," said a veteran reporter.

"May I ask, was the ball fixed? Or was it loose?" Hong Yi-xiang asked.

"Yeah. Good question," the American officer said.

"What's the difference?" another reporter asked.

"There's a big difference. Mr. Hong, do you always see the key to the problem at a glance?" Dolenz asked.

"No. Just naturally curious. Actually, the power sought by martial arts is a relative superiority, not absolute power. Frankly speaking, to break a rib or destroy a joint, it doesn't require much power. Strength is not 'the stronger the better,'" Hong Yi-xiang said.

"I agree with this. Using just the right amount of strength is correct. Can you explain what 'borrowing energy' is?" Dolenz asked.

"Simply put, borrowing energy is to use the opponent's strength to counter-attack. The greater the strength you apply, the greater the harm to yourself. In the concept of Internal Boxing, we emphasize release. Release the appropriate amount of strength in the right place. Like a free fall, there is no resistance in the middle except for the air. But most people are not comfortable with this, thinking that the harder the better, so the innate things they were capable of, conversely are covered up. After learning a lot in accordance with the rules, only then do they discover how to release, let go. It's a pity. But it's also very interesting," said Hong Yi-xiang.

"Mr. Hong, is there a way to learn Internal Boxing in the shortest time?"

"It's not easy. But it should still be possible to think of a way," Hong Yi-xiang said.

"Brother. It seems you rarely say 'no,' do you?" Chen Mei-shou said.

"I just think if it is something I have not done before, I always have to try it first, then say what's what," Hong Yi-xiang said.

A seemingly relaxed and ordinary dinner chat was in fact, an interview specially arranged by the US military for the selection of unarmed combat coaches for the US military who was escalating the fight in Vietnam. The purpose was to improve their survival rate in the Vietnamese jungle. Also at the banquet was Jim Dolenz, a senior military intelligence officer who had come to Taiwan to assist the Taiwan military in training operatives to infiltrate behind enemy lines. Together, they conducted the most stringent examination of this Taiwanese middle-aged martial arts master. In fact, before this interview, secret surveillance had been going on for some time and even Chen Mei-shou, the judo master who was in charge of the invitation, didn't know the inside story. Both martial arts masters thought this was just a sumptuous and delicious meal.

Hong Yi-xiang and Chen Mei-shou participate in the opening ceremony of the extracurricular training of American military forces, 1960.

Hong Yi-xiang breaking a stack of ten boards with no spacers, 1965.

70– SO JUST CALL IT "YIZONG TANGSHOU"

Sixty percent traditional martial art, plus twenty percent foreign martial art, plus twenty percent newly created martial art equals Yizong Tangshou.

Sixty percent real applications paired training, plus twenty percent forms training, plus twenty percent exploration of boxing theory equals Yizong Tangshou.

Sixty percent fist and foot skills, plus twenty percent weapons skills, plus twenty percent health cultivation equals Yizong Tangshou.

Scene: Hangzhou Tearoom

WITH THE NECESSARY COOPERATION OF THE MILITARY AND THE media, an event planned to use "fired brick breaking" as a test of efficacy successfully completed its mission. The next day, the print media of various countries explained their views on Chinese martial arts in their own subjective terms. Of course, no one carefully probed whether the claims written in the newspaper were in line with the claims made by the parties on the scene. This was a mundane matter unimportant to the grand plans involving the people's livelihoods, so once over, it was over, and it left few traces in history.

However, outside the dike next to the Danshui River in the 'Hangzhou Tearoom' built in the cabin of an abandoned ship, on a bare table with exposed cracked wood grain, there was a pot of high mountain aged Tieguanyin tea, small plates of salt-flavored melon seeds, red earth peanuts, haw jelly cake, and a foreign-language newspaper with a headline, "Master of Internal Boxing Breaks Kiln Bricks with One Strike."

"Look at it for yourself, the hair all over your body is standing up, it's frightening," Chen Mei-shou said.

"Yeah. It's really scary. Even I was shocked when I saw it myself. Ha-ha-ha…," chuckled Hong Yi-xiang.

"How much did you pay the newspaper in private for advertising? So many people performed on stage that evening, but the papers picked you alone and printed a photo of this size. It's unfair," Chen Mei-shou said.

"I fed them the news and picture, I threw 'em a bone, they gave me a steak," Hong Yi-xiang said.

"You! You really have an affinity for the media, they wrote you so well," Chen

Mei-shou said.

"Yeah. Even I don't think I am as good as what they wrote," Hong Yi-xiang said.

"Seems you have some self-awareness. Some people forget their own weight as soon as they become famous," Chen Mei-shou said.

"Rest assured. I'll never suffer from that kind of big-headedness," Hong Yi-xiang said.

"Right. I guess that important person should be Jim Dolenz. Did you notice?" Chen Mei-shou asked.

"Is he the one who asked the questions when we were eating steak?" Hong Yi-xiang asked.

"Yeah," Chen Mei-shou said.

"What does he want?" Hong Yi-xiang asked.

"I thought he would put his cards on the table then," Chen Mei-shou said.

"No rush, some people have already surfaced, and sooner or later they'll have to take action. Just wait for them to show up," said Hong Yi-xiang.

"There is something I have to remind you first. It is something someone reminded me when the US asked me to teach judo. Just teach okay, don't ask about other things or touch on other stuff. Don't have personal relationships with foreigners, avoid stirring up trouble," Chen Mei-shou said.

"Understood. We're under martial law. I have to be careful about everything," Hong Yi-xiang said.

"I remember when I first started teaching, I was under surveillance for quite a while, but then somehow they disappeared," Chen Mei-shou said.

"So why don't you simply not teach it at all. You're not lacking for money, why bother looking for trouble?" Hong Yi-xiang asked.

"That's also a no-no. Can't afford to offend Uncle Sam," Chen Mei-shou said.

"Like holding a bird, squeeze and it breaks, loosen up and it flies off. It's a dilemma," Hong Yi-xiang said.

"Isn't this just politics," Chen Mei-shou said.

"Then just go with the flow. It's them seeking me, not me looking for them, they're the ones who should worry about it," said Hong Yi-xiang.

"Politics is a specialized profession. It isn't something we ordinary people should meddle in," Chen Mei-shou advised.

"I don't think it's a profession. It's a scam," Hong Yi-xiang said.

"Maybe. Another thing I must remind you first. Westerners do things straightforwardly and seek truth from facts. Everything must be in the right order when you teach them martial arts, don't just talk, use comparisons, they won't eat a set menu," Chen Mei-shou said.

"Understood. Only the real deal convinces them," Hong Yi-xiang said.

"I guess they'll ask you to teach fisticuffs," Chen Mei-shou said.

"Need we speculate? Is it possible they'll want me to teach dancing!" Hong

Yi-xiang joked.

"The level shouldn't be rudimentary, otherwise it won't seem mysterious. Teach something not similar to their usual style," Chen Mei-shou said.

"Foreigners are also people, not necessarily all of them are so straight-forward," said Hong Yi-xiang.

"I know you are not short of cash, but I still hope you can take what they offer," Chen Mei-shou said.

"Why?" Hong Yi-xiang asked.

"Since you don't want to take your dad's baton as a businessman, you still must make your own career. This opportunity is definitely the best learning experience," Chen Mei-shou said.

"Well, handling these big American soldiers is the best way to forge myself," Hong Yi-xiang reflected.

"They are going to fight in Vietnam right away. If they want to go back to the United States alive, they have to train hard. If you are not good enough, they won't waste their time and life on you. What can prove your own worth better than this? Contact with Western culture will make us more pragmatic. You won't be off in an ivory tower, ignorant of how high is heaven or how deep the earth. Japanese judo and Western boxing were all tested under practical tempering like this," Chen Mei-shou said.

"I know that through constant sparring, putting my body on the line to experience the pain and cost of making mistakes, if the pain is enough, corrections will definitely be made quickly. And the tricks to fight for survival on the battlefield must be simple and easily grasped, easily applied. A move that is too complicated and too difficult carries mortal risk," Hong Yi-xiang said.

"Although the Americans and the Japanese are equally pragmatic, Americans are more assertive in their opinions when learning things, not as obedient as Japanese students. To teach Americans martial arts, you can't stand by and hold the pencil in their hand. They are used to finding their own answers. If the technique can reach the objective, there's no need to explain too much. Leave some space for them to fly by themselves. According to how strong you are now, finding good sparring partners will become harder and harder for you. If you want to improve further, this is a God given opportunity. Internal Boxing needs five to eight years to get through. I doubt that foreigners really want this kind of stuff?" Chen Mei-shou asked rhetorically.

"The problem of time commitment should be solved by classification and grading. First choose techniques that are simple, easy to learn and easy to use, and teach those," Hong Yi-xiang said.

"On the battlefield, preserving one's life is the most important thing. And saving one's life is inseparable from taking out the enemy. So the move's design can't be soft hearted," Chen Mei-shou said.

"This I understand. I'll take care of it. Can't be sloppy when dealing with the things passed down from the Grand Master. For some things once the chain is broken, they can't be recovered," said Hong Yi-xiang.

"You'll have to deal with that separately. The present era is progressing, time and efficiency are the key to survival. In the future, you have to distinguish between two paths to follow," Chen Mei-shou said.

"Okay. The advanced courses focus on the theory of boxing and the exploration of latent abilities, the difficulty level is higher. I'll select them and teach them individually. Xingyiquan was originally a combat technique in the army of antiquity. It is long spear techniques evolved into boxing technique. It has two different combat functions: armed and unarmed. When holding a spear, it is the art of splitting, chopping, snapping up, and piercing. Putting down the weapon, it is a method of unarmed close combat using splitting, drilling, crushing, pounding, and crossing," Hong Yi-xiang said.

"Great. I didn't expect that the conversion of traditional martial arts into modern combat skills would fit so well," Chen Mei-shou said.

"Just the opposite of Baguazhang, Xingyiquan's moves are concise, simplifying a great number of attack and defense concepts into 'from top to bottom,' 'from bottom to top,' 'from inside to outside,' 'from left to right,' 'rise and fall,' 'open and close,' 'contracting and springing out'… A few simple elements, originally for the convenience of rapidly transmitting military combat skills to a large number of soldiers. After being passed down to the civilian population, the twelve forms of five animals and seven beasts and were added," Hong Yi-xiang said.

"Don't forget the External Boxing you practiced, there are many practical things in it," Chen Mei-shou said.

"I will use External Boxing for the rudimentary foundational skills, after they have picked up the fundamentals, then I'll pass on the Internal School boxing techniques," Hong Yi-xiang said.

"Good idea," Chen Mei-shou said.

"The sixty-four palms of Post-Heaven Bagua have many freestyle fighting moves that catch people off-guard. Provided they conform to the principles of simplicity, ease of learning, and ease of use, they can also be incorporated. Thus, the deceptive and obvious give rise to each other, with the additional help of hard and soft, it should be enough to meet the needs of the battlefield," Hong Yi-xiang said.

"This is the essence extracted from traditional martial arts. You should choose a name that will live on," Chen Mei-shou said.

"It should be an extension of Master Zhang Jun-feng's school "Yizong" and must also be able to embrace the External and Internal martial arts taught by my other masters, worthy of all the teachers. It should let people see at a glance that this is an orthodox school of Chinese martial arts. Before the name 'China' was used, traditional martial arts had an ancient name called "Tang

Shou" Tang was the foreigners' name for ancient China from the Tang dynasty, and "Shou" means hand or fighting skills. The original characters for Japanese 'kara-te' were just these two characters Tang Shou[24]. The name 'kara-te do,' or way of the empty hand, was later used to replace the word "Tang" to erase the Chinese flavor. So, let me think…," Hong Yi-xiang said.

"Okay. Just call it 'Yizong Tangshou,' a Chinese martial art based on the *Book of Changes* and the transformations of yin and yang. It emphasizes that opposite sides must exist at the same time and when something reaches an extreme, it can only reverse," Hong Yi-xiang said.

"Hmm! It has historical depth serving as a link between past and future, and the breadth to encompass yin and yang complementarity, internal and external. It's really good," Chen Mei-shou said.

The symbol worn on the uniform for Yizong Tangshoudao students with the elements of Bagua Trigrams, Dadaocheng (rice stalks), Taiwan and the fist arts, circa 1963.

---

24 The original kanji for karate in Okinawa were 唐手, in pinyin Tang Shou, Tang (dynasty) hand denoting the Chinese origins of the art. When Gichin Funakoshi popularized Okinawan karate in mainland Japan, he changed the name to the homonym karate 空手.

Blurred Boundaries

Ceremony to establish the new school at Anxi St, 1983.

71– OUTWITTING THE EBONY STUPA

Many things are the same: if the orientation is wrong, it's just wrong. The incorrect thing, even if it is done effectively, is still incorrect.

Scene: US military advisor base, Linkou

A BLACK AMERICAN SOLDIER WHO WAS OVER 190 CENTIMETERS tall and weighed over 100 kilograms, with a muscular neck bigger around than his head, entered the field carrying a long staff. He first clasped his fist to bow to the officers and distinguished guests at the table, then grabbed the long stick in his hand and swung it alternately, spinning it to the left and right. The blur of the stick was a shadow guarding his body, the sound a mighty wind. He immediately won thunderous applause from the audience.

"I heard that Chinese martial arts have a kind of clever skill, using 'four ounces to parry a thousand pounds.' This Mr. Kent who just performed is a combat skills instructor in our army. He has studied long staff and stick skills in Japan. Today he will ask the masters present for advice with his long stick. All masters are welcome to come up to the stage and give him some pointers." The moment the translator said this, the black soldier used the technique *One Staff to Control the Universe*, dropped into a deep horse stance, his thighs parallel to the floor, his feet a little over shoulder width apart, his two hands holding the staff in a mixed grip and pressing down, the long staff with a diameter of more than six centimeters held tightly at thigh level, the tip quavering after being snapped down. To all appearances he was just like an ebony stupa.

Faced with the challenge of such a powerful opponent, all the invited martial arts masters on the scene immediately became restless and whispered to each other to exchange views. Some of the thinner, weaker martial arts masters introspected that they were not well-matched adversaries for this challenger, and each tactfully shuffled to less conspicuous corners. Several sturdy External School masters rubbed their palms and perked up, eager to discuss countermeasures to the challenge.

"Okay. Let me try first." A master martial artist from the Southern Shaolin Golden Lion Martial Arts Hall, his build wider than he was tall, was sent out by the crowd to test the temperature of the water. Several other senior brothers nearby shouted out his praise.

"And you are…?" the host asked.

"The Golden Lion Martial Arts Hall Liao Shui-sheng. So tell me, after all what is this black temple guardian's challenge?" Master Liao asked.

"It's very simple. If you can use another wooden staff to lift up his stick from the bottom, that's your win," the host said.

"No matter what method is used?" Master Liao asked.

"Yes. If you can lift it up, or make him loose his foothold as you lift, you win," the host said.

"Okay," Master Liao said.

After listening to the host's clear explanation of the rules of the test, everyone re-examined the test situation the black soldier had set. All they saw was this huge man with strong muscles, a broad, ripped body, at least two or three sizes bigger than the build of an average Asian man. Judging from the action of holding a stick and pressing down, he was obviously a martial arts master who combined God given talent and hard practice. Because he was so tall, it was not easy to notice that his horse stance was actually quite low. The shiny black hardwood staff in his hand seemed to be specially tailored to his height and build. In this wide horse stance pose he pressed the staff less than 2 feet above and parallel to the ground. In other words, the space he reserved for the challenger to exert force had been compressed to a limit. Anyone who has played with staffs knows that this is a well-designed and difficult challenge. In that limited space, power, and technique are both difficult to deploy.

Master Liao picked up an eyebrow height staff and twirled the stick to warm up. Because they were all coach-level teachers, his stick twirling was also a lively blur and rush of wind. When the martial artists on the sidelines saw this, they all cheered, rooting him on. Master Liao then performed several tries of snapping his staff up in the open air according to the test posed from the other party. Every time he snapped the staff upward, he issued a terrifying roar. Most traditional martial arts training in Taiwan was from the Southern Shaolin school. External School gongfu employs battle cries when exerting strength. From Master Liao's imposing manner on those several tries, stern in voice and countenance, it could be seen he was taking this very seriously.

"Tell him to pay attention now, I'm going to start," Master Liao said.

"Anytime," the black temple guardian gestured with a confident smile to welcome him "to start the lesson" at any time. Master Liao then stepped forward and extended the front tip of his wooden staff directly under the opponent's stave, and then after a few wriggles to relax his shoulders and neck, suddenly his back foot skipped forward a half step, and the front foot slid forward at the same time, the front heel dug in transmitting full strength into his waist twist, snapping up the tip of his stick forcefully releasing power. The expert's shot was surely clean and on target, it was indeed an extremely powerful one. However, when his "give it all you got" upward snap came into contact with the upper stick, apart from the crisp sound of the two wooden staffs violent clash, the upper stick remained motionless as before. At this time, the martial artists in the audience awakened to the realization that hidden deep in this ebony stupa, was unfathomable strength. So, a few more masters came up to try to challenge in various ways, but choked to death by the limited space, no one could successfully lift the long staff in the hands of the black temple guardian.

Just as the hall was sopping with an atmosphere of failure, a huge figure stood up from the corner of the martial artists seats. He was Master Huang of the Xinzhuang Martial Arts Center. From the beginning of the challenge, he had hidden in the least noticeable spot, calmly observing the process and details of the challenge, trying hard to search for any weakness in the black soldier. Master Huang was a giant in the Taiwan martial arts world. He was close to 200 centimeters tall and weighed more than 130 kilograms. He was the champ of unlimited weight class competitions in Chinese martial arts, judo, wrestling, and mixed martial arts. At this stage of the challenge, he was probably the last hope to determine whether the Taiwan martial arts world could turn things around.

"I don't want this toothpick. Give me a decent staff."

When he saw this opponent with a tonnage equal to his own, like two matched armies, this got the Black Temple Guardian's adrenaline moving, but his disciplined face only displayed a confident smile. To meet the counterattack of this giant, he especially rose from his stance and did a few warm-up movements to relax his muscles and bones, and then resumed his deep stance to meet this round from a new challenger. Master Huang took up the long staff that the US military man handed him. While grabbing the stick to warm up, he strolled all around the Black Temple Guardian and sized him up, as if looking for a convenient place to make an incision. He first tried snapping up two or three times lightly in the same way that the previous masters had tried and decided to give up this method that had already been proven invalid. He switched to a pole-vaulter's grip, with both hands tight on the rear third of the long staff, and then extending the front section of the long stick diagonally onto the ground under the Black Temple Guardian's stick. The other tail end of the stick was put on Huang's own shoulder for purchase, forming three supporting points in the front, middle, and back, so that the upper and lower staffs were closely intertwined, and ready to use the principle of leverage to crack this difficult challenge.

"Yeah. Finally, a guy who knows how to use his head has arrived," Dolenz said.

After the two giants exchanged glances at each other, they mobilized the entire force of their bodies and started a wonderful duel. The Black Temple Guardian did not change the original defensive deep horse stance. Master Huang used the bow and arrow stance to push up. The two roared almost at the same time declaring their determination to win. The volume of the sound shocked the audience and was immediately followed by the sound of the wooden staves pressing, twisting, and grinding, as well as the sound of the two men straining for breath to generate each last ounce of power. The two giant stupas locked in a stalemate, one face puffed out and red, eyes ferocious, the other black as lacquer, it was more difficult to make out his expression. Entwined in this struggle for nearly three minutes, there was a sudden loud crack, and the long staff held by Master Huang shattered at the intersection of the two sticks into hundreds of wood fibers and dusty fragments.

All the guests breathlessly watching the battle let out a gasp at the same time. The upper stick had maintained its original position to maintain his victory, and after the match the two shook hands with each other in mutual respect. The scene burst into thunderous applause for this rare and wonderful fight.

"Wow! It's really evenly matched."

"If they switched positions, I'd be willing to bet Master Huang would definitely win." While everyone was busy applauding the wonderful performance of the two giants, there was a faint sigh from the VIP seats: "Um. Just another bull that can only use brute force," Jim Dolenz leaned back in his chair with his arms folded across his chest not sharing in everyone's enthusiasm. It seemed that this kind of contest relying on raw force was not the real skill he hoped for. He wondered, could it be that after the spread of Chinese martial arts to Taiwan in the south, those astonishing realms were all lost and made extinct on the way to exile? Or were those things in the legends, from start to finish just the fanciful creations of literati's romantic crazy talk, and never truly existed in the real world. If so, then he might as well bring today's event, a preposterous plan to lure these skills into the open, to a quick close.

"Mr. Hong. Won't you come up and give it a try?" asked the director general of the National Martial Arts Association. Witnessing the entire martial arts world in Taiwan being capsized, his face a bit losing control, he could not resist calling on Hong Yi-xiang in the hopes he would go up on the stage and give it a go.

"No need. He has already dealt with so many people single handedly, it's not fair to him," Hong Yi-xiang said.

Through the translator, the Black Temple Guardian conveyed that he was okay and was happy to accept the challenge of others.

"Okay. Let him relax and rest first," the host said. On orders from the officer an army medic immediately gave the Black Temple Guardian a relieving massage to relax his muscles and bones. About ten or twenty minutes later, the Black Temple Guardian appeared again in the venue like a lively dragon and prepared to continue accepting challengers. Hong Yi-xiang had used the same idle interval to complete some simple warm-ups.

On the Black Temple Guardian's entry, he again adopted the deep horse stance with the staff held parallel to the ground. As soon as Hong Yi-xiang came up, just like other challengers, he gave two tries using the long staff to snap upward from bottom to top according to the rules of the contest. At first, everyone expected that he would really hit hard on the third try, but suddenly he circled the stick in the opposite direction and whipped the stick straight down from above. This tactic was tantamount to pushing heavily in the same direction of the Black Temple Guardian's original downward pressure, completely disrupting the Black Temple Guardian's center of gravity and composure.

Hong's powerful strike downward was directly followed by pressing into the body of the Guardian's staff using the "sticking stick technique," forcing the Black Temple Guardian to take a big step forward in an attempt to stabilize his balance. Unexpectedly, the instant his body pulled back to regain balance, Hong Yi-xiang's long staff, like a giant python coiled and looped under the Guardian's staff only this time Hong Yi-xiang snapped upward from below by complete surprise. The direction from bottom to top, added to the energy the Black Temple Guardian had put into pulling up, far exceeded the power he had calculated to need. By the time the Black Temple Guardian realized that this pushing force was way over the top, he knew it was too late to recover. It turned out that this returning rising staff was Hong Yi-xiang's main attack. Even more deadly, this snap-up used spiraling energy, and the Guardian's body could not avoid being controlled by his heavy staff as it was sucked into that huge whirlpool. The Black Temple Guardian lost complete control of his body, so his only choice was to move along with that invisible force rising from the ground and roll forward on the ground before he could break away and regain control.

The only point of contact between the two men was the two staffs, yet the Black Temple Guardian took a mighty spill, in front of everyone. Only when the soldier got up from the ground and bowed to Hong Yi-xiang recognizing defeat, did all the spectators seem to awaken from a dream and burst into applause. No one had imagined that such an intractable problem could be cracked with such a simple method.

The masters burst into comments:

"How can it be this way?"

"It was always so simple."

"Isn't this entry-level, basic stick method for beginners?"

"Right. Isn't it just a simple pressing staff and coiling staff?"

"I didn't say it earlier. I can do this too. Give me a try and for sure that Black Temple Guardian will take five, six, seven, eight tumbles."

"Ah. If it wasn't for being misled, who couldn't do this?"

"We all deceived ourselves, we only knew how to press up."

"I didn't think this black guy's stance was so weak."

"This was just a mental trick, it's not really gongfu at all."

"Fuck! Every time Hong lets us take point, and in the end it seems like were just carrying that guy in a sedan chair."

"No, things are not as simple as you thought."

This was originally just a banquet jointly hosted by the American military advisers and the National Martial Arts Association. The post banquet entertainment program was lively with diverse discussion until the curtain came down.

※ ※ ※

"Mr. Kent's skill in weaponry is very strong. I tried snapping up a few times and knew if I opposed the direction of his force with a stronger snap, I had no chance at all. Besides, even if I won, it would not be considered as 'using four ounces to parry a thousand pounds,'" said Hong Yi-xiang.

"What do you think was the key to his loss?" Dolenz asked.

"It should be the same as the key to his earlier wins," Hong Yi-xiang said.

"Can you please be a bit clearer?" Dolenz asked.

"Okay. Mr. Kent is very smart and very experienced. He compressed the space for us to exert force to a narrow range, making it difficult for the challengers to use all their strength," Hong Yi-xiang said.

"Yes. But he was using static force after all, how else could he withstand the challenger's dynamic force?" Dolenz asked.

"No. It looks like this on the surface, but in fact his power was dynamic," Hong Yi-xiang said.

"Really? Didn't he always stand there quietly?" Dolenz said.

"Yes. On the surface, he seems to have been standing there motionless all the time. But when the challengers snapped up hard, he slyly caused the weight of his body to press down, counteracting the challenger's opposing force. Seriously, he moved slightly at the moment when the two sides touched, he wasn't completely immobile," Hong Yi-xiang said.

"Okay. What was your strategy for cracking him?" Dolenz said.

"First, destroy his balance, then follow the direction of his force to help him along," Hong Yi-xiang said.

"Help him along? Oh. You mean 'push him to help him fall,'" Dolenz said.

"Put it this way, I just added a little more power to what he thought he needed, destroying his balance," Hong Yi-xiang said.

"A little more? How much more? Four ounces?" Dolenz asked.

"Close enough. Because he uses the instant the two sticks come in contact to shift his body weight and press down, so he must find a new fulcrum from the enemy to maintain his own balance. This is a type of 'borrowing balance' skill, the 'Eight Drunken Immortals' in Chinese martial arts also practice this similar technique, which uses the reverse resistance from the opponent to establish a dynamic balance point." Hong Yi-xiang said.

"So…"

"So, I didn't provide him with a point of borrowing force, and instead followed the direction of his force, again gently pushing him. It was enough,"

Hong Yi-xiang said.

"So, not only did you not let him lean on you, you also pushed him?" Dolenz said.

"That's why I hit the staff down first," Hong Yi-xiang said.

"And…?"

"Since the challenge was to move the stick from bottom up, I had to go against that direction and then repeat the original tactic," Hong Yi-xiang said.

"Why? Doesn't this return to the original problem of insufficient space to generate force?" Dolenz asked.

"On the surface, it may look the same, but in that instant the direction of his force was the opposite. Because he had to regain his balance quickly, his strength was pulled back during the short interval. I just had to grab that point in time, follow his direction, help him along and it was enough," Hong Yi-xiang said.

"Helped him!" Dolenz laughed.

"Anyway, it is necessary to use this 'following energy' to satisfy the principle of 'using four ounces to parry a thousand pounds,'" said Hong Yi-xiang

"The power of the second stick strike seemed to be different, otherwise, how could he have taken such a tumble," Dolenz observed.

"I adhered to his staff and used a bit of spiraling force. I just wanted to disarm him. I didn't expect that his grip was so tight, that he would fall so hard with his staff. I was just as shocked as him," Hong Yi-xiang said.

"You startled yourself. Ha-ha-ha…," Dolenz laughed.

"…"

"One last question, when you took that first strike down on his staff, why did you strike so close to Mr. Kent's hand? Was it accidental? Or did you deliberately startle him?" Dolenz asked.

"Oh. That was just an accidental 'foul ball,'" Hong Yi-xiang said.

"Really? The way I see it, it's not that simple," Dolenz said.

Dolenz originally thought that this huge black guy suddenly tumbling in this embarrassing outcome was too exaggerated. After the test, he conducted a private interview with Hong Yi-xiang through a translator to determine whether Hong Yi-xiang had only won by luck or really had ability. He had not imagined that this brief skirmish would reveal such meticulous observations, skill, and technical mastery.

"So that's it. You must first destroy the opponent's position, must never follow the direction the opponent is guiding. You must guide his direction, not directly oppose it. It turns out the key is to master the direction and timing—such techniques really exist. It turns out it's just a simple truth, a small curve or circle can create such a formidable power. It turns out that gongfu is not just a technique of fists and feet, knowing how to use your head is the real gongfu. Wow! He's really amazing. So, he's the one."

Hong Ze-han demonstrates Zhou Tong Staff, 2020.

Group photo of American GI students with Hong Yi-xiang, 1962.

Group photo of American GI students destined for the Vietnam battlefield with Hong Yi-xiang and assistant instructors, 1963.

72- THE SECRET TRAINING BASE IN THE CENTRAL MOUNTAIN RANGE

All beings fear consequences, the bodhisattva reveres the cause. During a lifetime, every single thing that happens is just an independent point, and it becomes obscure whether what is happening in the now is a cause or an effect. But at the end of the road all the points will form a line interlinking start to finish. So, making your prayers, your Hail Mary's and expressing regrets after the matter is of no use!

Scene: Linkou US military consultant's base

"I'M AFRAID THE KMT INTELLIGENCE NETWORK IN CHINA HAS been corrupted and must be completely dismantled and rebuilt," said Robert Smith.

"Is the rebuilding project too big to just identify the people with problems?" said Jim Dolenz.

"In espionage one inflamed hair can infect the whole body, we can't rely on luck," replied Robert Smith.

"Just because of your 'don't employ those you distrust, trust those you employ' motto?" asked Jim Dolenz.

"No. You're only half right. 'Trust those you employ' is not the motto of an intelligence agency. 'Don't trust those you employ' is correct," replied Smith.

"What about the people you have doubts about?" asked Jim Dolenz.

"Let them be decommissioned in advance, or they will be transferred to other unimportant logistical units. But their files, records and contacts must be archived first, and they will be checked one by one after the new system becomes operational. Anyway, our task is to rebuild a complete network here. A new intelligence network without doubts about loyalty," said Robert Smith.

"I have to communicate with the Taiwan authorities. Do you have any other requests?" Jim Dolenz probed.

"I must participate in the recruitment of every new member in the future, and I must have full power of appointment and removal."

"After such a severe setback losing the Chinese mainland, I think this government should care even more about the loyalty of the intelligence system now than we do," Dolenz observed.

"Besides that, I need an expert who understands martial arts to participate in the training," Robert Smith requested.

"This shouldn't be difficult. There are many "Budokan" specializing in Japanese kendo and judo, and there should be many martial arts masters in them," Dolenz offered.

"All well and good. But none of these people can be used," Smith said.

"Why?"

"It has to be traditional Chinese martial arts," Smith said.

"Why?"

"Because you want to infiltrate the mainland to work behind enemy lines, you must never use martial arts from outside of China. A small inadvertent slipup is enough to destroy everything you have worked so hard to build."

"Okay. Understood. I know that there are many folk religious organizations here. The locals call them 'Lion Dance Troupes.' They are the kind of people who specialize in religious activities such as dragon and lion dance and martial parades. These people practice. All of them are southern Chinese martial arts, I think you can find the person you want from among them."

"The south is not the nerve center for China's intelligence gathering, the focus should be on the north. Are there any locals familiar with northern boxing?" Smith drilled down.

"Among the crowds who retreated with the Nationalist government in 1949, there must have been many masters who were familiar with northern Chinese martial arts, but why the locals?"

"According to our intelligence, there are a large number of moles among the people who retreated here, and I don't want to take this risk," Smith said.

"Okay. So you're looking for a native Taiwanese with a simple background and good at northern Chinese boxing?" Dolenz sorted out the request.

"That's right. But it's not just about punching well. It's…"

"A martial artist who can instantly control the enemy and get out of trouble quickly. Right?" Dolenz interjected.

"That's right. Do you have someone like that in your pocket?"

"I'll have to spend a little more time investigating and figuring out if he's exactly what you're looking for."

"How many days?" Smith asked.

"Gimme five or six days."

"Three days."

"God had six days to create the first human, how could three days be enough?" Dolenz shot back.

"Three days."

"Why the rush?"

"I just want you to find that someone, I don't want you to be God. Three days, this isn't haggling in the vegetable market and you are not my mother-in-law who loves to bargain."

"Okay. I'll try my best," Dolenz said.

"Also, don't let the other party know the real purpose of this plan," Robert Smith added.

"What reason can I use?"

"Use Vietnam as an excuse."

"Okay. It just so happens that the Linkou base wants me to help them select a coach for the Marine Corps' unarmed combat skills, so just let your people mix in and participate in the training."

"This is a good cover story. Then I can make a decision based on the situation. The key is whether you find the right people."

※ ※ ※

Robert Smith was assigned to Taiwan to assist the local government in training intelligence personnel working behind enemy lines. Due to various security concerns, in addition to professional intelligence training, he also had some special requirements for training in unarmed combat skills. He needed someone who could adjust depending on the time, place, and opponent. With these special ideas and needs in mind, Hong Yi-xiang was selected and Smith approached him after observing a training session at Linkou.

"Hello. I'm Robert Smith. I'm with the American CIA's Asia division. I'm working on developing forces to use behind enemy lines in the Vietnam War," Smith said.

"..." Hong Yi-xiang.

"We are running a special program to train a group of special operators and special agents who will be dropped behind enemy lines in North Vietnam. It needs to be completed within half a year. "

"You mean airdrop?" Hong Yi-xiang asked, not sure where this was going.

"Yes, a parachute drop from a transport plane, at night, into North Vietnam."

"Understood."

"Because this is a very dangerous mission with a high expected casualty rate, we have some special requirements. Can you train a person to subdue an opponent within, say, five moves and escape dangerous situations safely?"

"I don't think I have that ability," Hong Yi-xiang demurred.

"I spoke with Anderson Lin, the judo guy—didn't you once negotiate with a bunch of local hooligans at the back station and take out your opponent with two or three moves?"

"That was just catching him off-guard. It's not a normal fight, it doesn't count."

"I want this kind of surprise."

"I think you misunderstood. I said, 'catching him off-guard.' The key to its success or failure was their lack of preparation, not my surprise."

"No. In our concept, the states of "surprise" and "unpreparedness" that you mentioned can actually be simulated and rehearsed. We are responsible to simulate the unfavorable conditions, you just need to tell us whatever works best to create the outcome we want," Smith pushed back.

"Why do you do this?"

"Because I have the responsibility to protect the personnel I have worked so hard to train. They must be able to escape quickly from dangerous situations, I don't care how cruel, how dark the techniques are, the purpose is not to leave the enemy alive. Otherwise not only are they not dead, but they may also implicate other personnel and even bring down the entire intelligence network," Smith explained.

"You just said leave no one alive? So you have to kill someone?"

"The accurate statement should be that the other person's life must be ended in the shortest possible time."

"I'm just a common guy, I don't understand 'killing,'" Hong Yi-xiang said, not comfortable with the direction the conversation was heading.

"No. You are not a common man in our eyes."

"..." Hong Yi-xiang.

"You're a deadly fighting expert."

"You must have mistaken me for some other guy," Hong Yi-xiang said.

"I think you'll remember that my job is gathering intelligence," Robert Smith continued.

"My martial arts is only suitable for winning or losing in the ring, it is not the same thing as fighting for life and death."

"That's why I say you're not like the other martial artists I've interviewed. Those guys can't tell the difference between the techniques of 'Win and Lose' and 'Fight to Die.'"

"Mr. Smith, my family and I have no intention of getting involved in your war. I think you must have enough ability and influence to help you find many more suitable candidates than me."

"There are indeed a lot of people who are eager for this opportunity. But, Mr. Hong, I believe you must know that war is deadly serious. It's got to be you, I'll make it hard for you to refuse," Smith said with chilly cordiality.

"..." Hong Yi-xiang.

"I'll show you something, and you'll believe we're serious. This is a photo we took a while ago." Robert Smith spread all the information he had collected in front of Hong Yi-xiang.

"What I want is not what you teach in the evening, what I want is what you and the three brothers Hong Yi-wen and Hong Yi-mian practice against each other in the morning."

"..." Hong Yi-xiang focused on every photo that was laid out in front of him.

"I'm really curious. How did these skills come about, did it really come from a rusted iron box?" Robert Smith asked pointedly.

"..." Hong Yi-xiang had no intention of answering this question.

"It doesn't matter. I just want to tell you from the bottom of my heart that only by taking this job will you live up to the person who wrote that book. And you won't waste your own martial arts and talents on mediocrity."

"The problem is that what you want is not my original intention to practice martial arts."

"Okay. I won't force you about this. But, can I simply learn martial arts from you?" Robert Smith seemed to be changing the subject.

"If it's a simple apprenticeship, of course you are welcome."

"Aren't you worried that in the process of studying, I will indirectly get from you what I want to get?"

"I'm sure you will find a way to get what you want, but that's your problem, not mine."

"Don't you think your position is as absurd as the person who eats meat but insists others not beat the cow?"

"Yes. It's the same as the current situation. Martial arts were originally used to protect one's own life, but then it's just as absurd to be asked to use it to kill people, isn't it?"

"Looks like I didn't underestimate you. I sincerely hope to learn from and collaborate with you," Smith said, bringing the meeting to a close.

After this unsuccessful interview, Robert Smith was more certain that Hong Yi-xiang was the person he and his organization were looking for. At that time, there was nothing in Taiwan that his organization could not arrange, including manipulating Hong Yi-xiang. A few weeks later, Hong Yi-xiang and Robert Smith met again under the vigorous insistence of the relevant authorities.

(The following is Mr. Smith's monologue)

"These special forces recruits are all one in a million.

"After an airdrop, they all have to fight on their own, and there is no backup.

"Of course, the more mature the warrior, the more assertive they are.

"Yes. Assertive means independent, strong-willed, disobedient.

"But we believe you have enough wisdom and skills to 'convince' them.

"Time and efficiency are the top priorities.

"Because you always seem to employ the smartest, easiest path to fix your opponents and problems. Your fists are very persuasive.

"It is necessary to strengthen their ability to source materials locally and adapt accordingly.

"What special operations and agents need most is to be able to escape undetected in the shortest possible time, yes. No matter what means are used.

"You have complete autonomy, decide for yourself what to teach.

"This is a top-secret plan.

"If you can, you must be away from home for half a year.

"No. Not in Vietnam. In Taiwan. In a special training base in the Central Mountains.

"Until the training is over, no contact with the outside world is possible.

"Yes. Including your family.

"The equipment and expenses you need will be entirely the responsibility of the US military and have nothing to do with your government.

"But about you, we have already informed the people of the government of your country.

"Today is mainly to confirm your wishes again.

"Of course, it also expresses our high respect and sincere regard for you.

"To provide assurances to you, we will ask the relevant units in your country to officially notify you.

"I hope to hear from you within a week."

73- AGENT SMITH OF THE CIA PART I— UNDILUTING DILUTED SECRETS

Just as one hundred percent alcohol is only suitable for fuel, and not suitable for humans to drink directly, even the strongest espresso coffee is a dilution of coffee beans, extracted with water.

Scene: Linkou US Military consultant's base

"Besides those unarmed fighting skills practiced by the Thirteenth Air Special Forces at Linkou, I don't know if you have other things in your bag of tricks?" Smith queried.

"In principle, the priority of hand-to-hand combat techniques used on the battlefield should be to simplify them and make the skills easy to acquire. If you require these GI brothers who have not been trained in regular martial arts to use those overly complicated and precise actions, I think it is playing with their lives," Hong Yi-xiang replied.

"What about warriors off the battlefield?"

"I don't understand what you mean."

"I mean special personnel like those working behind enemy lines, or secret agents. They generally have a better foundation in martial arts. What they require should be close quarter combat techniques that are not diluted, and even more authentic," Smith clarified.

"Does that mean there are such people mixed in with these GI brothers here?" Hong Yi-xiang asked.

"I didn't say that, I just want to know if you have the kind of fighting skills that are suitable for use in special conditions."

"I only know so much, beyond this level you may have to seek some lofty master," Hong Yi-xiang yielded.

"Is that so?"

"..." Hong Yi-xiang was not sure how to respond.

"Is this really the case?" Smith drilled down.

"..." Hong Yi-xiang still kept silent.

"According to the information provided by relevant units of your government, mixed within the many martial artists from the mainland who got shelter and aid from the Hong family, many were gang members in hiding, or Yiguandao cult members. I have sufficient reason to believe that because of the generous assistance provided by the Hong family, these martial masters in exile and demimonde ronin certainly exposed the Hong brothers, especially you, to these special combat skills."

"Alas, this is your own wishful speculation, but speculation is just that, speculation. Unfortunately, this time your inference is incorrect." Hong Yi-xiang yielded again.

"No. I believe my intuition."

"No, no. You should believe in facts, not intuition," Hong Yi-xiang rejoined.

"No…no, no! The intuition I am speaking of is a comprehensive judgment after careful comparison, not the kind of baseless conjecture to which you are referring."

"If you really want to insist on this, as much as I would love to help, there is really no way," Hong Yi-xiang said with finality.

※ ※ ※

A few days later, Smith and Hong Yi-xiang arranged to meet at the pensioner's teahouse on Liangzhou Street.

"I think I have some good news for you," offered Smith

"…" Hong Yi-xiang waited for the good news.

"I know you have always wanted to have your own studio, right?" Smith said.

"I'm listening,"

"But don't misunderstand. I can't really give you a studio."

"I think so too."

"But I can help you negotiate with relevant units in Taiwan. I can convince them to rent to you, at a very low price, space at the Yongle Elementary School, near your home. You need only pay a token rent; basically, the water, electricity, and cleaning costs," Smith said.

"Only that?" Hong Yi-xiang tugged.

"Of course, not only this."

"So, do you still insist on those non-existent things?"

"No. The reason I am doing this is for another above-board purpose—I was ordered to assist the US military in Taiwan in finding a proper large-scale outdoor training venue, and a coach outside the base. I know that all along you have been teaching boxing in abandoned warehouses or haunted empty houses provided by friends, otherwise you teach in open outdoor spaces or parks. I believe you also understand that these places are not suitable for the development of a martial arts system. They are not long-term bases of operation, and are especially unsuitable for openly teaching specialized skills," Smith said.

"Where did you hear this news?" asked Hong Yi-xiang.

"Have you forgotten that my profession is gathering intelligence?" Smith said with a smile.

"No. This is the second time you have pulled this shit out. I just thought that your professional skills should not be used on your friends, just like martial arts," replied Hong Yi-xiang.

"Yeah, so it would seem, correct. On top of persuading you to accept my proposition, I also had to make certain you were standing on the right side of the fence. I had sufficient reason and needed to do it."

"…" Hong Yi-xiang spoke silently with the concern in his eyes.

"Of course, you can choose to refuse, but even so, it will not affect the commitment I just made. I'm really just naturally curious, sincerely hoping to see with my own eyes those kinds of things you describe as 'Taking the Least Expected Action and Attacking the Unprepared,'" Smith said.

"Okay. Give me a week to think it over."

※ ※ ※

Just like that, a month later, a US military helicopter flew Robert Smith and his carefully selected hand-to-hand combat instructor Hong Yi-xiang to somewhere in Taiwan's Central Mountains, landing at a secret military base that technically never existed, and began executing a plan unrecorded in history. It was as if this never documented, confidential training program never existed.

"Actually, 'Attacking the Unprepared' is talking about 'when,' taking advantage of the moment the enemy is not paying attention to strike out. Taking the 'Least Expected Action' is talking about 'what,' employing techniques or angles of attack unanticipated by the enemy. The first speaks to 'When do you make a move?,' the second is selecting 'What moves do you use?,' is this clear enough?" Hong Yi-xiang explained to the group of hardened special forces operators, with Smith looking on.

"Do you mean, the question of when is that I must see the opportunity and seize it, right?"

"Yes."

"What about what? How to commence? How to strike? Where to strike?" Smith drilled down.

"*Shunqiao*—Use an Available Bridge, that is what you were just talking about 'see the opportunity and seize it,' take the moment," Hong Yi-xiang said.

"What if there is no bridge?"

"Then take the initiative to build a bridge, concoct a ruse."

"How do you build a bridge?"

Without waiting for Smith to finish his question, Hong Yi-xiang moved his left foot with a lateral button step behind Smith, and closed his right rear foot to his left, and precisely smacking Smith's right cheek with a right backhand slap. Although he had dialed down the power, Smith still saw stars.

"This is just a sneak attack. This isn't what I want!" Smith exclaimed.

"Nothing has started yet. This was just a probing hand to establish the bridge. You were the one not paying attention, so you got smacked."

Several of the soldiers looking on stifled their snickers.

"How should I know you'd suddenly take a shot?"

"You and I were standing within range of each other, how could you not know?" Hong Yi-xiang said.

"Okay. That one is on me. Bring it on! This time don't even think about Attacking the Unprepared," Smith challenged.

"Good. Since you insist on not getting the diluted stuff, it is a reminder that you must take care."

Hong Yi-xiang once again used his right backhand to slap at Smith's right cheek, Smith instinctively used his right hand to block. He didn't anticipate that as soon as he made contact with Hong's right hand, Hong's left hand would pierce under and securely grab Smith's right wrist opening Smith's center and triggering the release of power for a repeat attack from Hong's right backhand at the same angle. Smith immediately used his left hand to intercept Hong's second attack. He did not expect that Hong would seize Smith's left wrist from the bottom upward, with his left hand, but this time not only grab it, but also adding twisting energy to pressure Smith's left elbow joint. He became aware of the threat and that at any moment his left elbow joint might be torn by Hong Yi-xiang's powerful spiraling energy. Immediately he dropped the elbow joint, sinking down, hoping that the action would dissolve Hong Yi-xiang's purchase on him. He had not realized that Hong's right palm controlled the elbow joint, affording him no way to drop down.

"You lose," Hong Yi-xiang locked him in that position and did not continue to exert more pressure downward.

"Where is the loss?" Smith said, clueless and ignorant.

"I just need to advance a half step forward while pressing, then retreat a half step while rolling back, and your elbow joint will be trashed."

"Bold words, you can't necessarily do it." Smith was still intransigent in his refusal to admit defeat.

The words had not left Smith's mouth when Hong Yi-xiang, who controlled Smith's left elbow joint with both hands, suddenly "swallowed" in retraction and "spit," Smith immediately kneeled onto one knee.

"What is this?" Smith winced.

"This technique is called "Separate the Connective Tissue, Subdue the Bones." The semicircle push forward separates the tendons and sinews, forcing the tautness of your elbow joint and the surrounding muscle groups to dissipate. The step back with the rollback down is the Subdue the Bones part, but I did not press this to the terminal point."

"Why not?"

"If I pressed the locked elbow all the way, you'd probably have to go to the hospital to repair it. If you still insist that these are just bold words, then you may think it is worth the trip." Hong Yi-xiang lifted Smith up while using his right hand to clamp into the soft flesh of Smith's inside left upper arm, and then employed an inwardly twisting energy to adhere to a shallow layer of delicate epidermal tissue gathering it into the heart of his palm. The searing pain of the skin and flesh being separated instantly forced Smith to rise up on his tiptoes shouting in anguish.

"What sort of devilish trick is this?"

"Grabbing Skin," Hong Yi-xiang said.

"Whew! You see skin, you grab it!"

"If you still insist on seeing the true gongfu that is not diluted, then I may have to rip your skin off," Hong Yi-xiang chided.

"What the hell is this? Which evil martial arts cult do you belong to? How can it be so vicious?"

"This is not martial arts. Nor does it belong to a particular sect. These are just kinds of practical skills that have been layered within martial arts. It has a name not widely known 'Dark Arts and Dirty Tricks.' This is exactly what you spoke of, skills used by gangster martial arts masters and demimonde ronins to escape danger in an instant and survive. No one knows from whom such tactics originated. When they originated. Venomous, evil, unrestrained by rules or morals, these practices have been held in contempt and rejected by famed, decent schools, but they persist as a name not widely known, to survive and develop in the dark. Are you sure these are the things you want?" Hong Yi-xiang pressed.

"Whew! It's too incredible. There are actually such dark and venomous things in this world."

"So, do you still insist on summoning these fighting techniques that have been sealed in a dark world for so long?" Hong Yi-xiang warned.

"This ... I will have to think about carefully."

74- THE HERMIT DEEP IN THE MOUNTAINS

In the eyes of an assassin, no one is innocent. Every target is the same. If the orders are clear, there is no need that the target be bloated with vice, no need for evidence of a crime, no excuses "that we cannot live under the same sky." But when an assassin becomes the target of the hunt, the only option he preserves is often not a cold-blooded counter-attack, but a hasty run for his life.

Scene: Central Mountain Range

ON THE MID-AUTUMN FESTIVAL, THE FOLLOWING YEAR, HIDDEN deep in the mountains of the Central Mountain range, there was a simple, hidden cabin constructed of discarded building materials. Outside the quiet hut were scattered various old daily necessities and tools. At a glance, one would know that apart from sleeping, this loner would spend most of the time outside the house.

Under the shade of a century-old tree, a wooden log constructed about the same height and with the shape of a person, stood on the ground. From external appearances, it did not seem to be a wooden dummy for martial arts training. Such wooden dummy shapes are very simple, just a few short wooden sticks inserted horizontally on a large wooden figure. This wooden man had a head, a neck, and four limbs. On the wood, there were meticulously drawn channels where vital energy flows, striking points, nerve networks, and other strange lines and totems. Several parts looked well-worn from being pounded, with depressions and parts peeling off. If one looked closely, it was a bit like a giant "voodoo" doll, used by remote ethnic minorities to curse enemies in Southwest China, a wooden figure in the moonlight, adding a bit of weirdness and gloom.

The autumn night on the high mountain already carried with it a bone-chilling nippiness, and the dim candlelight shone on two people having a drink. Some people say that people forced into exile in a foreign land do not watch the moon during the autumn festival because they are afraid…afraid of stirring emotions of homesickness and despair…On the table were only a few dishes of home-made sour and fragrant vegetables of the Yunnan Bai minority group style, two pairs of hand carved chopsticks, two coarse pottery bowls that have long been rare in the city filled with amber spirits. If it were not for the bottle of Johnnie Walker Black Label whiskey that was placed on the table, it would really make observers wonder in which dynasty, in the long flow of Chinese history, this scene was set.

(The following is the monologue of the hermit in the mountains)

"I'm a criminal.

"I shoulder the blood debts of dozens of people I have killed.

"The ghosts of those who died unjustly remain at my side, even now.

"The accumulated rancor doesn't disappear, demons of the wronged never take a rest!

"They would rather not reincarnate until they have tortured me enough and their resentment dissipates.

"Retribution paid out in kind, fair to the extreme. Can't blame those I killed and can't blame ghosts searching for their souls. The missions I was carrying out were ordered by my superiors, but after all, the treachery was by my hands.

"It is a secret organization that has been around a long time.

"Various matters inconvenient for the Mandarins to take care of openly were all handled by this organization.

"All were entrusted to me by my superior. I don't even know how many hands the order passed through.

"Actually, it doesn't make a difference.

"Just execute, never ask questions.

"Afraid if I know too much, I won't be able to take action.

"Was it for personal grudges? Or eliminating an enemy of the State? Even personal grudges must have been packaged as State enemies early on, who knows!

"Later I realized that the original organization had long been dispersed, orphaned by the State. It was cut to pieces, no explanation, no secondment to a new job, and no funds to settle down. Just like that, it was dubiously disbanded. We all relied on the elders to find a way out for everyone and they turned this organization into a private agency. A secret organization that specialized in taking care of political enemies or private grievances for bureaucrats and gangsters. So overnight, from cadres loyal to the country, the brothers all became criminal hit men wanted for murder. That's how people kill one, then two, two then three, so…

"I never doubted the intentions of the elders…

"We are all men far from home and impoverished, there is no reason to kill each other.

"No one can say they knew nothing…

"The question is, in knowing, then what…

"Men in a foreign land, no other ability to earn a living, can only drift where their instincts tell them to follow, and live day by day.

"Naturally you persuade yourself, rationalizing that which you cannot but do.

"Finally, there are few who shouldn't be killed. Especially those who are mixed up in politics and organized crime…

"In the end, something really bad happened, the Big Boss told us we had to run for our lives, with only two escape routes…

"If you don't want to go into exile overseas, you have to escape deep into the mountains.

"I changed mountain hideouts several times, and later was still rooted out by my enemy's assassins, two brothers in crime were killed in an ambush and left me alone with serious injuries…

"Originally, I thought I didn't want to live anymore, simply go down the mountain to fight for my life, whack a couple, sell my life dearly…

"Unexpectedly, I ran into this woman, she nursed my wounds, and the thought of throwing my life away vanished. So, I tried to settle down like this. As soon as people have someone to care for, everything changes.

"She has suffered, driven crazy by her parents and first husband when she didn't deliver a son, sometimes good in the head, sometimes bad, it was all about money.

"Years living in the mountains alone and rough, I had to find a partner, it doesn't matter whether or not she is bad in the head, it's good to have company. Actually, after a long while, I really can't tell, is she crazy? Or, am I?

"When we first got together, every time the moon was full, I felt homesick. She said she was scared to death. In fact, I don't remember anything about it myself, but afterwards every time I saw cups, saucers and chopsticks dashed to pieces on the ground, I slowly came to believe that there was such a thing.

"People can't be without a home. Once you lose your roots, you feel like a lonely ghost. I'm old now. Weary. But I'm also alive. I didn't expect my heart to feel so at ease.

"Give me your hands and close your eyes.

"Use your intuition to answer my questions, don't think about it.

"Yes. This is 'Connecting to Another's Mind,' it's like hypnosis.

"What are you?

"Where from?

"Who else in the family?

"Again, your real name is?

"What is the purpose of coming deep into this mountain?

"What is the purpose of your martial arts training?

"Xingyi, Bagua, Taiji, External School and miscellaneous styles?

"Why do you practice so many, so complicated?

"Is it because of the 1949 retreat?

"How many martial artists instructors has the Hong family accepted in total?

"They taught it voluntarily, or instruction was bought with money?

"Do they mind if you cross over into so many styles?

"The February 28 Massacre had no effect on the relationship between masters and students?

"Why does the Hong family take special care of these foreigners in exile?

"Really no other purpose?

"Afterward, where did those masters go?

"In martial arts, who do you think influenced you the most?

"Why is it called 'Yizong Tangshou'?

"Why did you promise to teach these American soldiers?

"Do you understand their mission and purpose?

"Okay. It's okay if you don't answer.

"I live here, there is nothing I don't know about that happens in the mountains.

"It's okay, answer the questions you can answer.

"But don't think and resist.

"Have you heard of 'The Art of Controlling the Bull'?

"It is neither the Internal School nor the External School.

"This is not a martial art.

"This is a secret 'Art of Instantly Controlling the Enemy.'

"Are you willing to swear to not seek profit from this for life or be cursed?

"There is no appropriate heir, I would rather let it die in your hands.

"It is a mysterious technique that specifically targets the principal artery, the nerve plexus, and the lymphatic plexus.

"It's not really used to control cattle…

"It uses special techniques to strike several specific foramen and acupuncture points on the human body, instantly blocking blood flow and nerve signals, making people paralyzed or temporarily incapacitated…

"Even practice can cause permanent damage.

"You remember all the indents and scars on the wooden dummy outside the house?

"Those are the vital spots.

"Keep in mind. You can only practice against the wooden dummy.

"Just use your brain to remember it. If you forget it, you forget it.

"Accept it. It just means it was the Will of Heaven that it vanish. These things shouldn't exist in the first place.

"Never leave any written records.

At this time, the face of the old man reflected a beam of red fire light shining in from outside the wooden window. Looking out the window alongside the table, one could only see that wooden voodoo dummy was engulfed in raging flames, and near the flames squatted the old man's troubled partner…

"You have been here so many times. If you have never paid attention to the wooden dummy or the vital points, I am afraid it is too late. If you don't remember, don't feel it's a shame, it wasn't fated. Not fated, that's all right, and maybe not a bad thing.

"Tomorrow after you finish training, don't come looking for me again.

"The places I hide in the mountains are not just this one.

"You can't find them. And I'm afraid the traps I have set will hurt you.

"You and I are not a master and disciple.

"You and I only share the friendship of this box of whiskey.

"When the liquor is gone, I will forget about this.

"Including you and your name…

"I don't have a name, I mean I have, it's just…

"In the organization, there were only code names, no real names…

"Deep in the mountains, there is no need for names…

"You and I chanced upon this opportunity, that is enough.

"There is no need for any additional memories.

"Take to heart the memory of the vital points and the oath you swore, that's enough.

"It's just…

"No. No 'it's just.'

"This is all…

A period of clandestine teaching in the Central Mountain Range, unexpectedly produced the fateful transmission of a "secret art." Fateful origins and fateful endings, in the unseen mystical world it seems this was scripted long ago, but no one knows, was this a beginning or an end…

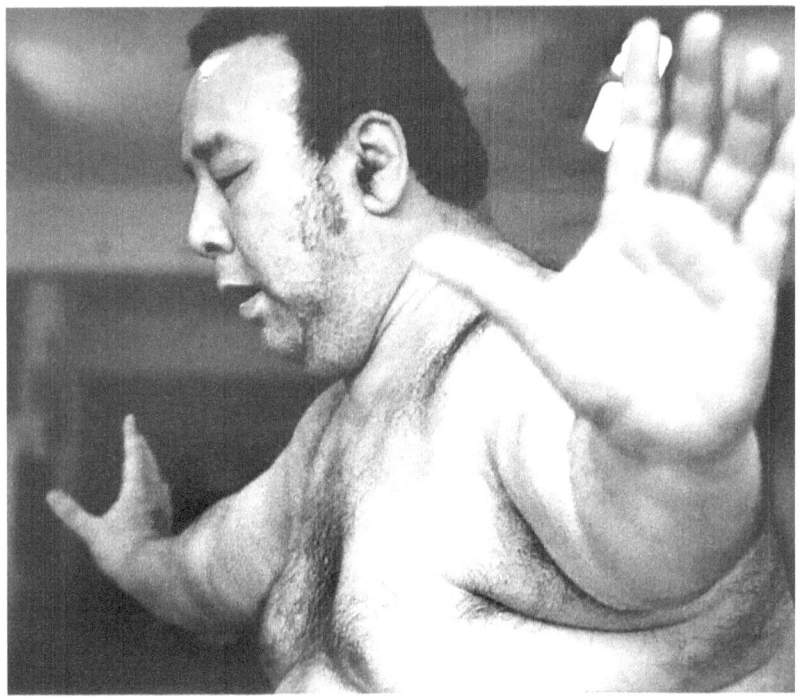

Besides studying point striking and seizing techniques with the hermit in the mountains, Hong Yi-xiang also learned longevity exercises, 1965-1968.
©Robin Moyer

Hong Yi-mian, Robert and Alice Smith, Hong Yi-xiang and Hong Ze-han, 1989.

75– AGENT SMITH OF THE CIA PART 2— ALL WARFARE IS BASED ON DECEPTION

Some seemingly formless, dimly discernable fantasies are often the guiding star that leads civilization. Some seemingly impossible, unbelievable things or phenomena, they once existed, as attested without doubt by the site of an ancient civilization at Machu Picchu.

Scene: Rough Brave Shantou-style hotpot al fresco restaurant

IN 1960, ONE COOL EVENING, SOMETIME AFTER RETURNING FROM the secret training in the mountains, Smith and Hong Yi-xiang had just completed one-on-one training and entered The Rough Brave Shantou-style *shacha* hotpot restaurant at the intersection of Guisui and Minle streets for a meal. During the meal, they encountered several rich second-generation princelings who operated tea houses, Chinese herb, and comestibles shops on Dihua Street. These people were playmates who had practiced gongfu together with the Hong family when they were young. Because they shared a similar age, a similar history during WWII, the prosperity and rise and fall of Dadaocheng, they shared a deeper level of trust and friendship than just common neighbors. In that spirit they merged their tables at the restaurant to better enjoy what was in those years common streetside haut cuisine.

During the dinner, a relaxed and happy atmosphere pervaded, featuring cup-on-cup toasting and mutual wine jousting, as if time had suddenly jumped back to that age of their carefree youth. Fueled by the catalyst of shot after shot of Johnnie Walker Black Label 80 proof Scotch whiskey, everyone began to share scenes and entertaining anecdotes recalled from the halcyon days when they practiced boxing under the martial arts masters recruited by the Hong family. These past scenes brought so vividly to mind seemed to particularly relax Hong Yi-xiang, and Smith, knowing Hong rarely unguarded his heart, took the opportunity to feign a drunken slip of the tongue to ask, "I bet in addition to grabbing skin and subduing the bones, you all must have practiced or been exposed to more ferocious gongfu, right?"

"Our group, we were all prodigals. In those days, the lot of us faked training martial art in name only, as we scrounged for meals at the Hong's, just hell-raisin' meat and wine lovin' friends. If it's about gongfu, you still have to ask Brother Yi-xiang," Kai Fuzi said.

"Yeah. That's right. We lot were all meat and wine lovin' buddies. I remember when Teacher Zhang Jun-feng took us along the embankment to practice his Splitting Fist, he shouted from the front in his heavy Shandong accent: one-two, one-two…a few of us troublemakers hid behind the ranks and followed his trailing sound to shout: Wine-Tuna…Wine-Tuna, not a one of us were serious. Unlike the Hong Brothers Three, so serious and stubborn. Ha-ha-ha!" Shui Chengzai added affably.

"Remember that whenever Teacher Zhang wanted to demonstrate a boxing application, everyone would deliberately choose to distance themselves from him and hide as far away as possible, in the most inconspicuous position, so as not to be grabbed for use as a human chopping board," Wan Dezi jumped in.

"Those days. Brother Yi-xiang was the most pitiful. Every time Teacher Zhang couldn't catch someone to be the target of his fist, he would shout: 'Fatso! You come here.' Half the muscular physique you see now was pounded out on that chopping board. Ha-ha-ha!" Yan Shi Zi pointed out.

"What about Hong Yi-wen and Hong Yi-mian? Why didn't they take a beating?" Smith asked.

"There is less meat on their bodies. When you hit 'em, the sound wasn't loud enough, and the shock effect was insufficient. No way to display the power of Teacher Zhang's Bagua palm and Xingyi boxing."

"Is this really the case?" Smith stirred the conversation.

"Actually, to get the worst of it is to benefit at the other's expense. Being the chopping board has advantages. You can trade in the suffering of a little surface pain for the opportunity to learn hands on, to experience the exquisite techniques of listening energy, changing energy, and issuing energy, and profit thereby. It's worth it," Hong Yi-xiang said, to keep the conversation real.

"You always had a strange way of calculating profit in business. Ha-ha-ha!" Wen Tongzai poked fun at his friend, "Isn't your Western Boxing very powerful? What's with wasting your time to learn these has-been relics?" he asked of Smith.

"I have always appreciated the ancient martial arts of the East. I think the offensive and defensive logic hidden inside is delicate, varied, elusive, intriguing. It is different from the direct, who is faster, force meets force flavor of Western Boxing. Especially Teacher Hong's seemingly silky soft and harmless sticky play, it can generate pain like an electric current to the soles of the feet, it's really incredible."

"What you are talking about, that isn't enough to be called 'incredible.' He has even stranger and more powerful things yet," Kai Fuzi said, sniffing around the trap Smith had laid.

"Is that so? What have you seen that is even more ferocious?" Smith asked innocently.

"Have you let him to grab your tendons?" Wentong Tsai asked.

"No. I don't know what that is," Smith said.

"This was originally a folk medicine treatment for heatstroke in our subtropical area, but I don't know why these therapeutic hand methods changed as soon as he got his mitts on them," Black Dog Tuanzi jumped in.

"Let him try it and then you'll understand," Kaifuzi urged him, and sure enough, a lot of people started to cheer them on.

Seeking to use the crowd's encouragement to his own advantage, Smith asked, "Can I give it a try?"

"Okay. Shush up. Don't you see these other guests dining next to you?" Hong Yi-xiang really couldn't resist this group of old friends, who loved to make a fuss.

"This is a public place and it's not convenient to do a bridging ruse. Just turn around and face me, yes. From where you are sitting just hit me in the face," Hong Yi-xiang instructed.

As Hong Yi-xiang had urged, Smith greeted Hong Yi-xiang's nose with a straight right punch. Hong Yi-xiang raised his right palm to intercept it from bottom to top, and on making contact, he wrapped his hand on Smith's wrist and tugged him to the right. Smith's body, sitting on the round plastic stool, involuntarily followed the huge, guiding force, which turned him at a large angle, almost with his back facing Hong Yi-xiang. He originally thought to simply follow the direction of the turn, raise his left elbow to strike Hong Yi-xiang's temple, but he did not anticipate that Hong Yi-xiang's hands were already placed behind him on the left and right sides of his neck. He felt Hong Yi-xiang's fingers burrowing into his shoulder methodically, and then these fingers hooked a string or tendon-like tissue under the clavicle. He plucked lightly on the string. At that moment Smith's vision was blocked by an impenetrable black curtain. When his vision cleared and he saw the scene in front of him again, the group of people who had been eating at the small table now gathered round him and stared.

"Wake up! Wake up. It's alright." Everyone babbled.

"Are you okay?" Hong Yi-xiang looked apologetic.

"I'm alright. It's okay. Really. I just took a nap. Whoa. People with chronic insomnia will love you for this technique," Smith said. "I've been choked out many times with judo's shime waza chokeholds, but nothing like this."

"Is it instantly disrupting the pulse? A nerve bundle? Or lymphatics? I'm not sure myself, I just know the position and how to apply the hands," Hong Yi-xiang said.

"Can you show me a little more?" Smith urged.

Perhaps it was out of guilt that he had gone too far, or perhaps because of the instigation and coaxing of a group of friends on the side, Hong Yi-xiang reached out and removed the pencil stuck in Smith's shirt pocket, and then marked secret points on Smith's arms and shoulders followed by repeated warnings that they must not be casually tried or disclosed to the public. Later, however, Hong seemed to regret his reckless behavior. At the end of the dinner, he suggested that everyone go to the public bath "Yongle Pool" on Minle Street to bathe and boil off the alcohol. Those acupressure striking and pinching points that he had incautiously drawn on Smith's body were naturally destroyed and hence expediently secreted by Hong's deceptive strategy in going to the big public bathhouse.

Postscript

In his later years, Hong Yi-xiang mentioned that when he first learned these techniques, the master who taught him had very solemnly warned him not to try them arbitrarily. When training the US special forces, he relied on military doctors to accompany him. After obtaining the commander's acquiescence, he couldn't help but use the techniques on those robust special forces recruits to verify the effectiveness. Later, they were used on several unbelieving disciples in the gymnasium on Anxi Street and almost killed them. Later, he rarely risked other people's lives to do human experiments with these special techniques.

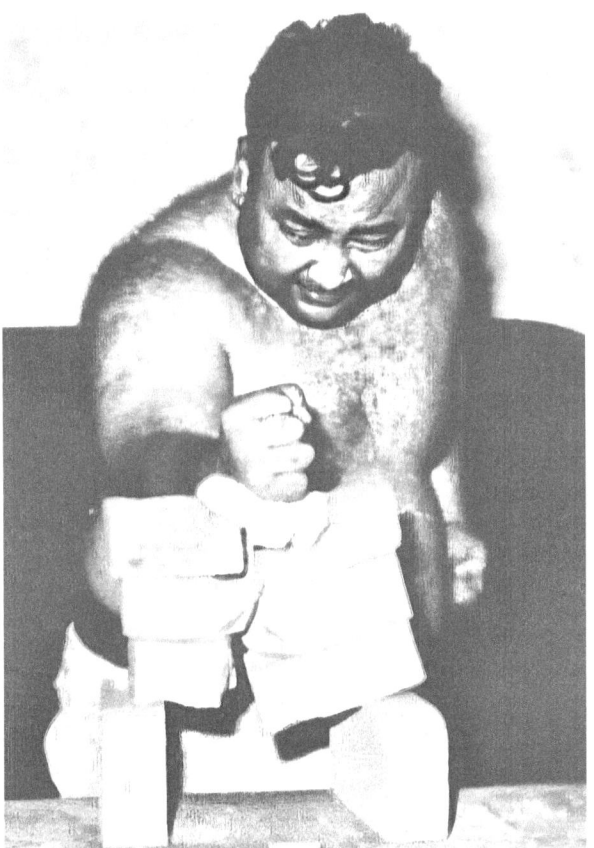

Hong Yi-xiang demolishes three bricks without spacers, circa 1964.

76– THE LONG MARCH TO JAPAN PART 1

Now that you are a warrior, you have no right to choose the battlefield!

Scene: Tokyo Budokan, Japan

The Tokyo Budokan was built in Japan to host the 1964 Tokyo Olympic Games. After the end of the Olympics, this venue was provided for the use of judo, kendo, karate, wrestling and other competitions, or concerts and other large-scale indoor events. The Japanese surrender at the end of World War II is commemorated here, each year on August 15, and the emperor of Japan and the prime minister always participate in the "National Mourning Ceremony for the Martyred."

On this day in the performance hall of the Budokan, huge red cloth banners were pasted with the white cut words "1969 All Japan Karate Championships." The audience seats were crowded with local and foreign martial art spectators. Taiji master Yang Ming-shi and Shaolin master Gao Sen-huang from Taiwan were both exponents who accepted an invitation from the competition to demonstrate Chinese martial arts. They went on stage, individually, to perform their expert routines, and the audience applauded loudly from time to time.

In the VIP seats on the sidelines, Ambassador Ma of the Embassy of the Republic of China (Representative Office) delicately conferred with the special guest, Hong Yi-xiang, who was preparing to go on stage, explaining a last-minute request made by the chairman of the competition.

(The following is the monologue of Ambassador Ma)

"Karate is the most popular Japanese national art in the world today.

"Getting invited to serve as a special guest in this World Cup competition, and to represent your country to demonstrate Chinese martial arts is a supreme, unparalleled honor.

"Mr. Hong, please take this rare opportunity to really show off your martial arts.

"Ryoichi Sasakawa, the honorary chairman of this world competition, is a celebrity in the Japanese business world. He has a strong influence in Japan's political and business circles and has always been enthusiastic and supportive of the diplomatic relations between the Republic of China and Japan…

"Although he is a businessman, he has been obsessed with martial arts and chess all his life. He also has a deep knowledge of the Chinese art of war and culture…

"He is also the biggest supporter and greatest hero behind the scenes promoting Japanese karate to the world stage…

"In the Japanese martial arts world, there are some legends spread about you in the Taiwanese martial arts world. Mr. Sasakawa is very interested in these legends, especially the fact that you used a staff to tumble that big American soldier. That created quite a stir here in the martial art world.

"It is said that this big American soldier once studied in a dojo in Japan. He used the same trick to challenge many well-known dojos here, but no one was able to figure out how to defeat him. Mr. Sasakawa never dreamed that you could use such a simple, clever way to unravel it so easily, so he also looks up to you very much.

"The Japanese business community has always respected the traditions shared in *Romance of the Three Kingdoms* and *The Art of War*. He believes that these simple and effective strategies could become a model and reference for the trade war.

"Just now the chairman specifically requested, if you can…

"In addition to your routine demonstrations arranged in advance by the competition, he sincerely hopes that you will deign to instruct several Japanese juniors on the spot and show them how it's done.

"He said that he is already tired of watching the pre-arranged duels and performances, he thinks that only sweat, blood, and tribulation accomplish anything. Like the guys who stood on the stage and represented their own dojo's in the sparring competitions, were any not trained like this?

"But watching pre-arranged duels and performances is no indicator of whether a competitor or martial artist can become a world class martial art master. He said that in the business world he has had to 'read' countless people, and he has great confidence in physiognomy. He hopes that he can witness with his own eyes today the birth of a world-class master.

"A martial artist of a high level is like a successful big business entrepreneur. In the face of crushing pressure and crisis, he will be able to use the wisdom accumulated in his life and instantly transform the energy into a strategy that can change his life and the world…

"He said that he is not twisting anyone's arm, he thinks you can understand his meaning…

"He believes that the venue and pressure of today's event will certainly surface unlimited hidden human potentials, and he dares use today's All Japan Cup competition to make a bet. He is counting on witnessing with his own eyes your miraculous ability to use wisdom to change and transform in the spur of the moment, Mr. Hong.

"What I am good at is diplomacy and negotiation. It should be my function and expertise to be prepared for all contingencies. But from my point of view, this request of Mr. Sasakawa presents only challenge and risk, with no upside. When facing such a person, in such a venue, and such a request, I really don't know what is best…

"Perhaps everything is as sincere and simple as he himself said, but in such a venue, winning or losing is no longer just a matter of *personal* honor or disgrace…

"Experience tells me not to be gullible and trusting in good faith, but…

"Accepting or rejecting the challenge, both carry unpredictable risks. The embassy has no special position or request, I am only conveying the wish of the chairman of the assembly…

"The request referred only to you, but not the other two.

"I reasonably suspect that they must have been preparing this for a long time. Although not necessarily malicious, in matters related to national honor and disgrace and the dignity of a martial artist, certainly they have no good intentions.

"I'm really terribly sorry. Letting you shoulder such a big challenge and risk by yourself.

"Alas. I should have turned down their request in the first place.

"What do you think?"

Suddenly, everyone's ears were filled with an announcement filling the arena: "Dear guests, the organizer has specially invited Master Hong Yi-xiang, a martial artist from Taiwan, to be present, and he will demonstrate orthodox Chinese internal martial arts for everyone. At the same time, the chairman is involved now in communicating with Master Hong through Ambassador Ma of the Republic of China. We hope that in addition to demonstrating the routines, he can have a brief technical exchange with a Japanese karate *kohai*. Let all martial artist *kohai* take this opportunity to expand the horizons of their knowledge and inspire even greater cultivation of their martial arts. We hope everyone will warmly and loudly give their applause, to invite Master Hong to generously share his teachings without holding back…"

"What a mess. Did the master of ceremonies make a mistake? How can he directly announce this request to all the competitors and the audience on the spot? Ai! Seems like it is already too late to get off the tiger."

The entire audience not only burst into thunderous applause when they heard the broadcast of the Master of Ceremonies, they even stood up to try to catch a glimpse of the action. A large number of media and photojournalists were on the scene, and with their professional instincts, rushed to the VIP seats where Ambassador Ma and Hong Yi-xiang were sitting, seeking to capture the first shots of the parties' initial reactions and expressions…

In the face of such unscripted hospitality, Hong Yi-xiang got up calmly, and took off his suit jacket with the blue sky, white sun and red earth flag of the

Republic of China Taiwan on his chest, exposing his bear-like build (it is said that the national flag was opportunistically cut by Ambassador Ma from the profile of the one on the Embassy of the Republic of China in Japan's competition program, and that he pasted it on for Hong Yi-xiang with his own hands). At this time, Hong Yi-xiang had completed the secret training mission of the US special forces in the Central Mountain Range of Taiwan. He had been hired by the Taiwanese-American military adviser to train US troops bound for the war in Vietnam at the Yongle Elementary School in Dadaocheng. Due to the day and night exercises, his figure that was originally portly, had metamorphosized into a build with the so-called "sturdiness of the ape's back and bear's shoulders," and his weight was maintained at about one hundred kilograms. Instantly, the camera flashbulbs in the hands of the media reporters flared in front of him like a string of pearls exploding and they chattered among themselves.

"It's the Taiwanese guy who broke the kiln bricks last time." Some sharp-eyed reporter recognized Hong Yi-xiang's identity at a glance.

"Yeah. The program doesn't mention this special demo."

"It must be a pleasant surprise, arranged in advance by the conference."

"How do you know?"

"No matter what the Japanese do, they only take action after planning thoroughly."

"Are you talking about Pearl Harbor?"

"Pipe down, aren't you afraid of getting a surprise attack in the ribs?"

"Will they really fight?"

"Fight who? Oh. You mean that Taiwanese. Who knows."

"I heard that he had disappeared for a couple months…"

"It must be he holed himself up to secretly train some special martial skill."

Amidst the roar of the crowd, Hong Yi-xiang strode with the majestic gait of a dragon or tiger and walked towards the martial arts performance stage where tens of thousands of people were fixing their gaze. After courteously bowing to the chairman, he turned his head and looked around at the large arena and the crowded auditorium and raised his hands in response to thunderous applause and cheers. At this time, Takushoku University, Keio University, and Okinawa University student karate club representatives one by one took to the stage to show their respects, thanking Hong Yi-xiang for the many years of enthusiastic tutelage he gave them during their winter vacation breaks. After these student representatives finished offering flowers, the tumult of emotions in the whole venue gradually subsided.

Before setting foot on this huge stage in a foreign land, Hong Yi-xiang had experienced many different obstacles and battles, but the affirmation he faced today was definitely within the biggest venue and the biggest challenge of his life. However, at this moment, his heart was as clear and tranquil as when he was practicing in the deep mountains. In his mind flickered the image of those simple wooden hand carved chopsticks and the rough thrown pottery bowl filled with amber wine, and that wooden dummy in the strange and gloomy atmosphere of the dark woods, and the position of every indent denoting vital points to strike. A man's life is so weirdly magical. He can be a down and out hermit in the deep mountains; he can also be standing on the stage of the World Cup like a hero in the clouds, accepting the respect and acclaim of the multitudes. Although he did not know what kind of benefit or harm he might receive after the demonstration, his heart was extremely calm at this time, and he swore quietly to himself: "Ancestors, from now on, I dedicate all of my honor in the martial arts to you."

Hong Yi-xiang stood alone in the center of the most conspicuous stage at the "Tokyo Budokan," facing the attention of tens of thousands of eyes, and he knew from the bottom of his heart that in this time and place, he was standing alone and helpless on the knife's edge of the ultimate peak, welcoming the call of glory and danger. At this moment, no one could help him or replace him at this juncture to receive this fateful baptism. He slowly shifted his stance, allowing his feet to deeply sink and lock into the tatami. His eyes were slightly closed, his gaze on the tip of his nose, his nose gazing inward at his mind, as he blended the secret techniques practiced on the mountain with the mind method of the Hunyuan posture, quietly completing three slow breath circuits of the Microcosmic Orbit to settle his state of mind. He resolved with absolute certainty he could face any upcoming challenge.

Since his childhood, Hong Yi-xiang was clearly aware that he possessed a special potential in the face of major crises. He became stronger when faced with tougher opponents. When dealing with particularly intractable problems ordinary people grab hold of the Buddha's feet at the last moment and intensify their practice. Instead, Hong would clear out all the distracting thoughts and obstructions in his mind. Besides striving to cultivate abundant vital energy, he would do nothing in that interval. To the depth of his soul, he was clear that provided his vital energy was sufficient, the feeling was right. If the correct feeling welled up, he believed, even should heaven collapse around him, he would remain standing. From the beginning he relied on this powerful conviction and aura, allowing him to always confront all manner of intractable challenges bravely and directly. And in this moment, he had calmed down sufficiently to clearly hear the movement of his blood sent from the heart and the exchange of breath in his lungs.

For the opening, he chose the Five Elements Consecutive Linking Form to best express the unadorned simplicity and Overt Energy of Xingyiquan, closely followed by the Sealing posture of Xingyiquan. He then took cues from the architecture of the arena and used the center as the axis. He chose inside swinging steps and outside button steps and walked in circles to demonstrate the comprehensive form of Bagua palm "Black Dragon Whips its Tail." Although the two routines demonstrated two distinct energies, overt and hidden, Hong Yi-xiang employed "Q"[25] Spiraling Energy's indirect tenacity to display hand techniques completely different from the bipolar hand techniques of ordinary Internal School boxing, which is either hard or soft. What emerged was a way of exerting force new to the audience, hard *and* soft, yin *and* yang, overt *and* hidden, mutually complementing each other. The movements were graceful and lively like a dragon and snake entwined in a struggle while flying through the heavens and leaping from the earth, a spectacle for the whole audience. When he finished the demonstration and returned to his original position, he performed the relaxing Sealing posture. Only then did the audience and the competitors in the arena stir from their breathless intoxication, and follow the lead of Ryoichi Sasakawa, who stood and started the applause, and one after another all stood up to deliver a warm ovation.

This special way of exerting force between hardness and softness had been swirling in Hong Yi-xiang's mind for many years, but he had never been able to find an appropriate method of interpreting it. It was not until he met the hermit hiding in the mountain forest of the central range, that he saw embodied in the hermit the way forward. But before this demonstration, his technique of controlling internal energy was yet in an extremely unstable state. However, just when his Xingyiquan demo was cutting over to Baguazhang, in a eureka moment as he turned around, a flash of understanding, like a teaching of the Buddha opening a window of enlightenment or a computer installing a higher-level operating software, suddenly he acquired extraordinary perception and skill. Some people say: "stimulation and stress are catalysts for the fusion of creativity and capability."

This aphorism thus provides the best explanation for this miraculous transformation.

After composing himself, he said to the emcee of the competition, in fluent Japanese: "Bring it on. I'm ready," After receiving a formal response from Hong Yi-xiang, the emcee immediately turned around and asked the chairman of the conference for instructions. After Ryoichi Sasakawa nodded, six heavyweight competitors sporting faded black belts tightly tied to their waists, jogged onto the stage. After completing the requisite courtesies and bows, they formed a line kneeling directly opposite Hong Yi-xiang, and then the karate-ka on the far right stood up first, shouting out his name, the school he represented, his teacher's name and his rank, and then took a step forward and bowed to Hong Yi-xiang, "Please, Elder, condescend to instruct me!"

---

25 For a discussion of Q elastic tenacity, see Chapter 51.

77– THE LONG MARCH TO JAPAN PART 2

Going all out is the highest praise to a swordsman!

Scene: Tokyo Budokan, Japan

"Shotokan karate, third-dan black-belt, Iwata Masaichi asks for advice from my Elder. Please grant instruction," The first Japanese exponent to "ask for instruction," stopped five steps away from Hong Yi-xiang, and in accord with the traditional courtesies of karate after he straightened his uniform, he respectfully bowed to his opponent with a 90-degree bow at the waist, and immediately assumed the preparatory fighting posture of Shotokan Karate, a deep horse stance. He did a few agile warm-ups and firepower tests, the thick canvas gi popped audibly between his punches and his kicks in the dank air of the venue, allowing the audience to clearly appreciate the speed and power of his every strike. At that time, this kind of low-extended stance was the most classic fighting stance chosen by karate practitioners. To overcome the inconvenience of moving and stepping out of the low horse stance, during a sparring match, most players would adopt a hopping method to compensate for its inherent limitations and deficiencies.

Hong Yi-xiang facing Iwata, watched his magnificent movements— one hundred percent of his focus went into Iwata's displays of firepower. Hong Yi-xiang did not deliberately warm up his body, but just like some celestial crane displaying its wings, his two hands lifted and opened, his body was slightly slanted as he stood on the spot. A door wide open, not a hint of defense, which is completely contrary to the "three-tips" (nose tip, hand tip, toe tip) required by the Internal school of boxing and the Santi three-body posture in which the fist does not leave the center. However, in the eyes of the opponent, this seemingly empty and undefended posture looked like a giant bear standing up and getting ready to pounce, making people shudder. In the eyes of the audience, the two experts in this confrontation — one active, lively, solid, magnificently full of energy to be released, the other soft and relaxed, the spirit calm and composed —epitomized the clear distinction in martial arts of the polarities of the Yin and Yang opposition of hardness and softness.

Iwata Masaichi saw that the opponent was ready, so he began to move, hopping forward and backward on his feet, slowly compressing the safe range between the two, and constantly probed the opponent's defensive perimeter with his front hand. Besides Hong Yi-xiang making minor adjustments of his angle to the attack, no meaningful response could be seen. He remained in "if the enemy doesn't move, I don't move" stillness. From these passive responses, Iwata reached the conclusion that the opponent insisted to adopt this tactic of biding his time, using the open door to lure the enemy in deep. For the sake of security, he used a feint again to confirm the level of sensitivity of the opponent's response. After repeated probes like this, Iwata was now convinced that even though he might underestimate the opponent's ability to respond, he could rely on his tried-and-true *seiken* straight punch which had been honed for years under cold waterfalls and in rushing water. He had an absolute advantage in terms of speed and strength, and he had sufficient certainty he could achieve the effect of a one punch kill, so he decided to take the initiative to strike first.

Once his mind was made up, Iwata immediately boosted the energy of his whole body. A loud *kiai*, like a peal of thunder, propelled him straight forward, and with his most assured right hand straight punch locked on target for his opponent's throat he launched the attack with all his might. Seeing that the opponent was coming on fiercely, Hong Yi-xiang first drew his body back half a step, then moved his left foot half a step to the left, dodged to Iwata's right flank, and at the same time his right hand intercepted the opponent's straight punch from the inside, hooking over it then pulling Iwata's punch to Hong's right. He stepped the right foot to change direction and push forward at a 45-degree angle to the right, while using the left hand to lift Iwata's right elbow from the bottom to the top, so that Iwata's right rib became a defensive gap. When Iwata realized this crisis, it was too late. At this moment, Hong Yi-xiang changed his direction again and took a step towards his left. At the same time, a right palm drove into Iwata's right ribs, and Iwata instinctively lowered his right elbow. The crisis was averted but he never dreamed that Hong Yi-xiang's palm was a feint. When Iwata's right elbow dropped to block Hong Yi-xiang's right palm strike, the feigned palm immediately turned over and slapped Iwata hard on the face with the back of his hand.

Fortunately, Iwata's reaction was fast enough, and he blocked the crocodile-like tail flicking attack with his left hand again, but his instinctual response was no match for Hong Yi-xiang's intentional or unintentional attacks. Taking the initiative to attack, Hong Yi-xiang's right hand borrowed the power of Iwata's block, turned down again, then circled inward and up and hooked Iwata's left shoulder as his right foot executed a swing step and his left foot followed with a button step. Now standing behind Iwata, right hand and left hand met on Iwata's left shoulder and pulled back. Iwata instantly lost his center of gravity and sense of direction. His opponent Hong was no longer in sight, Iwata only saw the ceiling of the immense hall as he plummeted backwards. The target of Hong Yi-xiang's "Z"-shaped stepping three-dimensional attack crashed to the floor in the center of the Tokyo Budokan ring.

Sitting next to Chairman Ryoichi Sasakawa was Suzuki Masafumi, the headmaster of the Shobukan school in Tokyo. He was ranked a ninth dan master of karate, which is the highest rank recognized by the All-Japan Budo Federation. Sasakawa had always been the biggest patron behind Shobukan so for this significant and extraordinary occasion he personally made on-site analysis and commentary for the Chairman. (The following is a narration by Master Suzuki for the chairman Sasakawa):

"Mr. Iwata originally wanted to leverage the home court advantage and the speed he is good at to launch a quick surprise attack as his opening move while the opponent's body and mind have not yet fully settled into the situation. By launching a rapid surprise attack, he was attempting to catch the opponent by surprise…

"He is no match for the opponent, and he was countered.

"This is how masters fight. On the surface, it looks like a simple two or three moves, but it is incomparably treacherous…

"Because both sides are experts, more importance is attached to the one initiating attack. As soon as you misjudge, you lose.

"The exponent makes a move, and loses with a move, it is a loss of judgment. It is not like he could not withstand a blow. This is not a matter over which face is lost.

"A straight punch is a linear attack, focusing on speed and angle. The opponent used a circle, which looked like a tornado. Advancing in a selected direction rotating at full speed, it is extremely powerful.

"All the power of Mr. Iwata was sucked into a vortex by the opponent.

"This was a duel between the circle and the line.

"A key was stickiness.

"As soon as Iwata's punch was entwined by the block, he was immediately reeled in. Lost control all of a sudden.

"Because he was controlled by the opponent's direction, he dropped into the vortex of Hong's attack.

"Multiple continuous attacks, like waves crashing on a beach.

"Iwata had to respond to each wave, but each wave was never the last.

"It's a decent outcome.

"Stickiness is one of the characteristics of Chinese Internal boxing.

"In addition to Taiji's 'Pushing Hands,' Hong Yi-xiang's system has a special technique called 'Strolling Hands.'

"It trains this kind of sticky gongfu. There are no fixed moves, it is learned in direct contact with the master, one move at a time.

"This is not Baguazhang technique, nor was it passed down to him by his master Zhang Jun-feng, basically no one knows where he learned these skills.

"I once sent people to his gym to observe for a long time, and I also asked friends in Taiwan to secretly take many photos and 8mm videos. I have studied it for a long time, but I still can't figure out its operation or the logic of its attack and defense.

"You just can't capture that kind of unconventional tactile feel in a photograph.

"It destroys lines with circles and overcomes hardness with softness.

"It's all a clever skill of borrowing energy to generate power…

"That Z-shaped stepping was intentional, intentionally deceptive. I have heard China has a famous style of boxing called Mizong—Deceptive Stepping — maybe that is what we have just observed.

"One more thing, only sharp-eyed masters can see this clearly…

"Hong Yi-xiang's right middle finger, it's the lock that controls Iwata-kun's wrist. And his left palm grabbing Iwata's lymph up near his armpit.

"Only when this key point is locked can the subsequent actions yield destructive power.

"To sum up, it is a delicate uniting of posture, footwork, hand technique, and fingering. Real gongfu using body shape to inflict injuries, admirable!

"This proves that what we know is quite limited.

"In the vast field of martial arts, there yet exist many elements that we don't understand, and it is far beyond our simple logic to fully understand them.

"Circles. Sticking. Entwining. The Internal School of Boxing really provides food for thought.

After all, Iwata was a veteran of the ring. He flowed with the throw and slapped the mat protecting himself on impact and got up in one go. The two who had contested won the warm applause of all the audience, regardless of whether they had won or lost.

"Thank you for your instruction." Although defeated in battle, Iwata Masaichi still maintained the demeanor of a warrior. He quickly straightened out his disheveled *gi*, and respectfully bowed to Hong Yi-xiang at 90 degrees, then returned to his original position, kneeling on the tatami. In his mind swirled thoughts of how to convert this unexpected failure into valuable practical experience for his future martial arts career.

On the fifth anniversary of the Tokyo Budokan, Hong Yi-xiang is invited to demonstrate Chinese internal martial arts, 1969.

78– THE LONG MARCH TO JAPAN PART 3

When the bear shows a generous smile and opens his arms in a friendly way to hug you, never forget: it's a bear!

Scene: Tokyo Budokan, Japan

"Goju-ryu Karate-do third-dan black belt, Tokyo Seibukan, Toyoda Higashio seeking instruction from my senior, please condescend to teach me."

"Goju-ryu Karate-do" and "Shotokan Karate-do" are similarly derived from the Shaolin boxing system of China. The difference is that Goju-ryu belongs to the branch of the "Southern Shaolin White Crane Style" transmitted to the east and was founded by Miyagi Chojun. The name of this style is derived from a mantra contained in the secret book "The Ideal of Martial Preparations" passed down within the White Crane school: "With the method of hardness and softness, swallowing and spitting, the body can adapt to change." Goju-ryu karate-do has obvious characteristics derived from Southern boxing, mainly the focus on the compact Sanchin stance, cat stance, a stress on merging hard and soft, and emphasizing the tempering of Qi, breathing, and the body.

Toyoda Higashio was a devoted disciple of Suzuki Masafumi from the Seibukan and with whom he underwent nearly ten years of rigorous training. He was also one of the coaches Suzuki relied on. He was a calm and practical exponent, gentle and courteous on the surface, yet in actuality he was heavy artillery, who could break 19 Japanese curved black roofing tiles with his bare hands. In fact, with full strength, he should be able to break even more tiles, but in order to express the highest respect for his teacher Suzuki Masafumi, he always insisted on not daring to go beyond that number. In the Japanese karate world, Suzuki Masafumi was most respected for his miraculous skill of "jumping vertically and breaking 20 tiles with bare hands." Suzuki's body was short, about 155 centimeters tall, and it was no easy matter to break a pile of 20-curved black roofing tiles nearly 60 centimeters high. To overcome the challenge of his inherent limitations, he undertook bitter research and severe training to finally create a unique method of breaking. He would stand in front of the tower of tiles and use his natural flexibility to jump vertically on the spot, and then utilize the increased height and momentum of his body from above to descend vertically onto the pile of tiles. His fist became a sharp wedge cleaving straight to the bottom. Instantly a high pile of tiles would be reduced to rubble, the V shape splitting to the left and right sides. This miraculous tile-breaking skill has never been surpassed in the Japanese martial arts world. Because of this, many of his students and successors performing breaking performances in public, even if they had the strength to surpass this limit, would deliberately constrain themselves. They would keep it below his number of tiles to show respect for Suzuki Masafumi!

Toyoda Higashio rapidly analyzed his observations and learnings from the previous demonstration and made a further detailed study of the instant replays being projected in the Budokan hall. The video recorded all the data of Hong Yi-xiang's fights with different schools in an open public forum. Even Hong Yi-xiang himself may not have seen such complete analysis before. This spirit of preparatory homework is precisely why in the short interval of a hundred years Japan could quickly absorb the culture and technology of the world and develop into a military, industrial, and economic power. This is also the key reason Japanese karate quickly developed into a complete system after separation from the tributary of Chinese External School martial arts and then morphed into a world-class sports suzerain.

After intensive and rapid research and judgment, Toyoda Higashio had a countermeasure in his mind. He decided to execute this rare "Right to Request a Boon" in a way that contributed the most to the Japanese martial arts world. He walked to the original position where former challenger Iwata Masaichi had stood, bowed respectfully and then kneeled and bowed again.

"May I use inquiring?" Toyoda asked.

"Yes," Hong Yi-xiang said.

"Excuse me, what is *Neijiaquan*?" Toyoda asked.

"This is a big question. I suggest putting it at the end. It would be more appropriate for me to answer with actions," Hong Yi-xiang said.

"Okay. In that case, what is so-called 'Internal Power *Nei Jin*?'" Toyoda asked.

"If you want to discuss internal power, it will inevitably link to 'Whole Body Power *Zheng Jin*' and 'Releasing Power *Fa Jin*,' so let's talk about them together. Do you know the principle of how a mechanical watch operates?" Hong Yi-xiang asked.

"I only know that it is the function of coil springs and gears working together," Toyoda said.

"Correct. The coiled springs provide power, pushing all the parts in the watch, including a variety of gears of different sizes. By means of a common frequency, the least common multiple, they create precise and regular operation, and work together to achieve the purpose of precise timing," Hong Yi-xiang said.

"Excuse me, what is the connection with inner strength?" Toyoda asked.

"The muscles, bones, joints, and connective tissue are just like the various parts in the watch. When we perform martial arts movements, these tissues will each produce circular rotations of various magnitudes, just like gears, each performing its own duties, each turning on its own. A good martial artist knows how to discover the most efficient common frequency and use it to unify all the energy generated by these discrete circular rotations, so that they can release the maximum energy at the same point in time, achieving the maximum destructive power," Hong Yi-xiang said.

"Excuse me, what is the difference between this and the power generated by External School martial arts?" Toyoda asked.

"Strictly speaking, the innate character and purpose of the power differ to some extent. External Boxing attaches great importance to the impact effect brought on by high-speed collision, which is more like the force released by a car engine operating in high gear. Internal Boxing pursues more attention to the bodies in physical contact, the affect produced under conditions of high resistance. Relatively speaking, it is more like an engine's high torque output in low gear," Hong Yi-xiang said.

"Which of these two forces in fighting produces the more lethal force?" Toyoda asked.

"What do you think? Shouldn't this be determined by the road conditions?" Hong Yi-xiang retorted.

"Yes. I understand. So, in what situations is Internal Strength most suitable?" Toyoda asked.

"I think it should be used when time and space are constricted at the same moment, this way it generates unimaginable results," said Hong Yi-xiang.

"Can you explain it further?" Toyoda asked.

"Inner strength utilizes the physical techniques of swallowing and spitting, opening, and closing, expansion and contraction, relaxation and tensing, and rise and fall to unify the body's intent, breath, and power, liberating a huge amount of energy in an instant. The force released may not be greater than a normal straight fist or uppercut. But because it directly acts on the enemy's body in an instant when the enemy is caught off guard, a deep crushing effect is produced causing serious damage to the internal organs in the body cavity. Therefore, the destructive power of internal strikes is mainly concentrated on deep cavities and permanent damage with what we call 'post-impact force,'" Hong Yi-xiang said.

"May I combine the speed of External boxing with the post-impact force of the Internal boxing strikes to form a power that is fast and deep?" Toyoda asked.

"I think if one works tirelessly towards this goal, when the required basic knowledge and technique accumulated is sufficient, this state will naturally be realized. Let's research hard together," said Hong Yi-xiang.

"Understood. What is 'sticking and adhesion'?" Toyoda asked.

"'Sticking' was originally a mutual interaction between the bodies and limbs. My elders in the martial arts gained some insights from it, and deliberately developed it into a kind of 'intentional contact,' detecting, cheating, and controlling his intent," Hong Yi-xiang said.

"What is the purpose of sticking?" Toyoda asked.

"To build a bridge. A channel that can send messages to each other," said Hong Yi-xiang.

"Then, please, I want to ask, what's the use of it?" Toyoda asked.

"To probe and control," Hong Yi-xiang said.

"Probe what?" Toyoda asked.

"Probe the dynamic information and hidden motives of the opponent's body," said Hong Yi-xiang.

"Control what?" Toyoda asked.

"Control the opponent's movements, distance, angle, balance, and mind, as well as all possible variables," Hong Yi-xiang said.

"Is it enough to just rely on sticking?" Toyoda asked.

"When the bridge is connected, the messages of body and mind are naturally connected. But the masters who approach the sublime can also connect to those messages even without physical contact," Hong Yi-xiang said.

"What about after receiving the message?" Toyoda asked.

"Make judgments and respond as necessary," Hong Yi-xiang said.

"When you get the information you want, do you want to withdraw your hand?" Toyoda asked.

"Why do you want to withdraw it?" Hong Yi-xiang asked back.

"Withdraw it to launch a quick and powerful attack," Toyoda said.

"Why not handle it at close quarters?" Hong Yi-xiang asked.

"Because it'll be difficult to exert strength without withdrawing it," Toyoda said.

"Not difficult. The difficulty lies in your concept and habituation, because the way you are accustomed to exerting force is straight back and forth, so…," Hong Yi-xiang said.

"Otherwise?" Toyoda asked.

"Use a circle," said Hong Yi-xiang.

"Circles have to go around, isn't it slower?" Toyoda asked.

"It's not slow. Sticking utilizes small circles," Hong Yi-xiang said.

"Stick and not leave?" Toyoda asked.

"Right. Then use the joints in the body 'swallowing and spitting' and the circulation of internal energy to recycle the power," Hong Yi-xiang said.

"Please explain," Toyoda asked.

"Please stand up and give me your right hand," Hong Yi-xiang gently contacted Toyoda's right arm with his right-hand palm up, his shoulders performing the action of "swallowing and spitting" to allow the opponent to feel how internal swallowing and spitting operated.

"To aid the spectators understanding, please use your fastest speed to attack me," Hong Yi-xiang ordered.

"Okay. Take care," Toyoda said.

Toyoda immediately assumed the Cat Stance and gathered his internal energy thinking to use the withdrawal of his right hand and following the power generated by the turn of his body to the right at the same time to attack Hong Yi-xiang's temple with a left punch. He did not anticipate Hong Yi-xiang would rapidly step his left foot forward, buttoning down Toyoda's foot while turning his palm, which was originally supporting Toyoda's right arm, in a semi-circle. The front quarter circle destroyed the opponent's center of gravity with "Supporting Pushing Energy." The back quarter circle coordinated with the right foot's withdrawal, so as to lead the opponent into falling forward with "Yanking Pulling Energy."

These two different directions of hidden energy made Toyoda's body first look up with the supporting pushing force, while the yanking pulling force that closely followed sent him snapping forward. Caught off guard, Toyoda's brain couldn't cope with the high velocity with which his body was pulled down and he collapsed heavily. Like a computer crashing, for an instant he lost consciousness and control of his body. This totally unexpected change not only made it so his original left punch to his opponent's temple could not be launched, but made his body unresponsive to him, causing him to collapse. Fortunately, Hong Yi-xiang at the last moment grabbed him, avoiding an even more devastating outcome.

The audience burst into enthusiastic applause, drowning out the detailed narration from the MC.

"Now you understand?" Hong Yi-xiang asked.

"Was it one circle? Producing two opposing forces at the same time?" Toyoda asked.

"Yeah. Push forward yank backward, with a slight delay," Hong Yi-xiang said.

"Can you try it again?" Toyoda asked.

"The second time you will have an informed resistance, but you can still try again," Hong Yi-xiang said.

Accordingly, the two did the same action again, Toyoda with new experience and wariness. As would be expected, when the two of them joined hands, Hong Yi-xiang could clearly sense the other side struggling to detect his own dynamic information from the contact between the two parties, so that at the most appropriate time, he might counterattack. Thus the two men's movements were frozen under the rapt attention of the audience. Time passed minute by second, and after about two or three minutes Toyoda finally dropped his hands and gave up.

"I see. It turns out that this is Neijiaquan. Thank you for your guidance," Toyoda Higashio took a step back respectfully, bowed deeply to Hong Yi-xiang, and returned to his position. With the posture and depth of the bow, the audience was deeply impressed by his heartfelt appreciation and respect for Hong Yi-xiang.

"Why did Toyoda give up attacking?" Sasakawa asked Suzuki in the VIP box.

"Because of that one punch, he couldn't launch it at all. He was under control and if he made a move he would lose," Suzuki said.

"Why? I don't believe his right hand was stuck and couldn't be pulled back?" Sasakawa asked.

"Yes. If he forcibly pulled it back, I am afraid he would have lost even worse. I originally thought that after knowing the opponent's moves and methods, he could easily crack it. It seems that things are not that simple. He must have encountered more serious problems," Suzuki said.

"Wow! What magical Internal boxing," Sasakawa exclaimed.

"I heard that the masters of Chinese Internal School of Boxing can prevent a bird on their hand from flying away from their palm. They can use the 'Listening Energy—*Tingjin*' in their hand to instantly negate the pressure of the bird's feet when it takes off. When a bird wants to take to the air, it must break away from the bounds of the earth. In addition to vigorously beating their wings, they also need to push both feet hard to increase the lift against gravity. With an Internal School master yielding, they basically can't take flight," Suzuki said.

"Toyoda is the bird that can't fly?" Sasakawa asked.

"That's right," Suzuki said.

"Just like chess masters facing off, they don't need to play to the last piece, they can determine victory and defeat, it's really wonderful," Sasakawa said.

Suzuki Masafumi, utilizing his life's cultivation and experience in martial arts, had wholeheartedly interpreted everything that he had seen and understood from the ring move by move for Sasakawa's benefit.

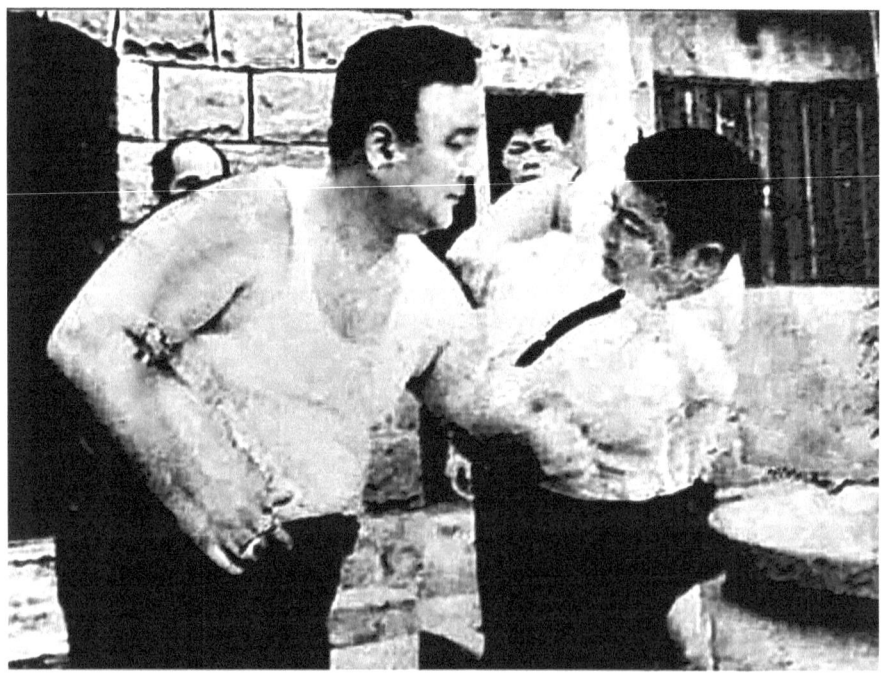

Hong Yi-xiang demonstrates joint locking technique on a visiting Okinawan karate teacher, circa 1965.

79– THE LONG MARCH TO JAPAN PART 4

The king's authority comes from conquest, not inheritance!

Scene: Tokyo Budokan and hotel coffee shop

"Kyokushinkai karate-do third-dan blackbelt, Yokoyama Tatsuhito requests of his elder, please enlighten me."

Kyokushinkai Karate-do emphasizes "full contact sparring." It was founded by Mas Oyama in 1964. It is a style narrowly focused on practical combat. Its moves are unpretentious, simple, capable of hitting, and being hit as signature features. Commonly used moves in Kyokushin Karate include straight punches, uppercuts, front kicks, spin kicks and other basic moves. The usage is quite simple, unadorned, and uniform, such as: hitting the chest with a straight punch, hitting the ribs with an uppercut, using a front kick to attack the heart, using a sweeping leg to attack the knees, and using a hook kick to hit the back of the head…fists meeting muscle, techniques exposing bone, it is extremely destructive. Because it emphasizes full contact sparring, it is different from other Karate styles with their "score a point and stop" habit. One can often see two exponents pushing through the pain to continue. They don't jump around, don't clinch, don't side-step, and don't even move much, standing opposite each other trading body blows with the opponent, until one of them falls or admits defeat.

The tall and sturdy Yokoyama was like a brown bear, step by step facing square and ready to pounce. Confronted with this strong enemy, Hong Yi-xiang as before did not shift forward or backward. He merely used a simple technique to pry open Yokoyama's right straight punch and seize Yokoyama's center of gravity to the left and support the ground with the sole of the left foot. The intention was such that at the instant when Yokoyama lifted his right foot to launch a head attack with a spin kick or a hook kick, Hong Yi-xiang used his right hand, already attached to the opponent, to apply "Clever Energy—*Qiao Jin*" and lightly pull down. Yokoyama's left support foot immediately slid forward, causing his attacking tempo to slow down slightly. Hong Yi-xiang seized the delay and snaked his left palm slapping the opponent's right neck. Because the method employed was a consecutive and hooking palm, Yokoyama was caught by the palm and was irresistibly moved forward by the palm strength. The instant his body was out of balance and he stumbled, Hong Yi-xiang's right knife hand gently chopped the artery between the left side of Yokoyama's throat and the collarbone. Afterwards he saw Yokoyama's eyes go blank, the body deflated, as he collapsed to his knees on the spot. Hong Yi-xiang immediately took a half step forward and braced Yokoyama under his armpits, not letting him collapse in front of the tens of thousands of spectators on hand. When the other five karate exponents watching the exchange at close range saw this, they immediately rushed up to catch Yokoyama's paralyzed body. Before the audience could figure out what had happened in the ring, Yokoyama had already been caught and first aid was on the scene…

"Enough! Put a stop to this." Taking into account the consequences of this spectacle and the emotions of the audience, Ryoichi Sasakawa immediately made a decision to stop all subsequent arrangements, and personally went on stage to take charge of the situation, expressing the thanks of the organizer directly to Hong Yi-xiang for his instruction.

"I sincerely appreciate Hong Sensei's generous and selfless demonstration, so that we can experience the vastness and unpredictability of martial arts in such a grand event. I hope all lovers of martial art attending today, regardless of nationality or style, can unite hand in hand to vigorously explore even more profound hidden vistas of the martial arts."

High up in a row far from the VIP seats, a thirty-one-year-old Matsuda Masashi, later to be known as Ryuchi, sat spellbound. Sasakawa's words spoke directly to his heart. He had started teaching himself to fight in elementary school but began to train karate in earnest in middle school, setting up his own karate club in high school. He had studied with "The Cat" himself, Gogen Yamaguchi, in Goju-ryu and with Mas Oyama. He had trained in Jigen-ryu and Daito-ryu Aikijutsu. His first exposure to Chinese boxing had been a demonstration by Wang Shu-jin at the Meiji Jinggu Shrine after which he had sought Wang's instruction in Xingyiquan in Tokyo. But today's demonstration blew him away. He had to get to Taiwan to taste this for himself.

※ ※ ※

Under instructions from Ryoichi Sasakawa, that evening Suzuki Masafumi invited Hong Yi-xiang and Chen Xi-zhao to visit Tokyo's Seibukan dojo for practice and arranged for all the senior cadres of the black belt group to host a banquet to treat Hong Yi-xiang and his accompanying friends. Everyone quickly completed the preparation of tables, chairs, dishes, and drinks. Except for the main folding table with chairs, the other black belt members all sat on the floor at unique low Japanese-style tables. In addition to a variety of sushi and yakitori skewers and other convenient take-out treats and dishes on the table, there were rows of large bottles of Japanese Hakutsuru Dai Ginjo and Gekkeikan sake and all kinds of beer.

"Toyoda, shouldn't you be the first to toast Master Hong, thanking him for his guidance at the Budokan today," Suzuki encouraged warmly.

"Yes. Sensei," Toyoda said, "Master Hong. Toyoda Higashio would like to thank you for your guidance today. Kampai!"

"Who taught you to ask questions? Are you afraid of being dressed down in public," Suzuki said.

"I really wanted to solve a puzzle baffling me, because all along I couldn't understand why Chinese culture and martial arts attach so much importance to the operation of the 'circle,'" Toyoda said.

"Do you understand now?" Suzuki asked.

"Actually, I should be thankful to Toyoda. Because of his question, I could share with so many people at the same time my own superficial experience of Internal boxing," said Hong Yi-xiang.

"Since you got Master Hong's personal guidance on the stage, do you want to demonstrate what have you learned from Master Hong today?" Suzuki invited.

"*Hai*!" Toyoda Higashio signaled his *kohai* in the neighboring seat to get up quickly, and went with him into the U formed by the tables. The two demonstrators bowed in front of the main table. Based on Hong Yi-xiang's method in the Budokan, he recreated a paint-by-numbers image, and carefully explained his own sensations at the time. He carefully explained how a small circular movement during sticking, when targeting the body's balance produces a disruptive effect. When his body was pushed by the front semicircle, to stabilize his center of gravity, his body instinctively leaned into the push so as not to be overpowered by an expected subsequent shove. What he didn't expect was that when the force of his pushback surged out, he would suddenly discover that the original opposing force had disappeared. The force he returned found nothing solid to receive the force, no fulcrum or obstruction to press against to maintain his balance. His entire body was being pulled down by a powerful vortex, and in that moment all he felt was the blood and qi of his entire core flowing in reverse and his brain going blank. When consciousness was restored, it seemed the whole thing was over too suddenly, and he had lost all memory of what had happened until he returned to the sidelines and knelt down. Then slowly his brain reconnected the blank spaces.

To demonstrate, Toyoda began to repeat the same actions over and over on the *kohai*, and the shots were merciless, using more and more force, until he was so proficient that he could use a Yanking Palm to drag the *kohai*, forcing him to sprawl on the ground. Under the arousal of applause and alcohol, Toyoda made many derivative changes and improvements, such as Yanking Palm followed by a reverse choke and a leg sweep to make the opponent fall face up on the floor.

"Look how happy they play," Suzuki said.

"Such a spirit of research is admirable," Hong Yi-xiang said.

"Japan's cultural foundation is shallow and resources are scarce. If we can't rely on this kind of spirit, turning one into ten, turning less into more, and turning roughness into refinement, Japan would never have a chance to compete with the great powers in the world," Suzuki declared.

"Toyoda is dishing it out quite heavy," Hong Yi-xiang said.

"This is the tradition of the dojo. He is training all the *kohai* to let them understand that it was not because he was too weak in the ring just now, but because you were too strong. He wants them to experience what he felt at the time when he was knocked out. This is sort of passing down the experience, especially after ladling on a little more pain, will be remembered more deeply," Suzuki said.

In such an atmosphere of refined martial study, everyone ate and drank this simple meal, talked and tested skills until nearly midnight.

※ ※ ※

The next day, at seven o'clock in the morning, Ryoichi Sasakawa and Suzuki Masufumi met to have a Western breakfast together at the coffee bar in the hotel lobby.

"In the final analysis, what system of martial arts does that technique belong to?" Sasakawa asked.

"It should be a deliberately hidden 'secret skill,'" Suzuki said.

"Is this the reason why he mysteriously disappeared a while ago?" Sasakawa asked.

"I don't know, but I believe that he sensed Yokoyama's strong intention and eagerness to win, which was far beyond the boundaries of a 'well intentioned request for instruction,' such that it pushed Hong to the point whereby he had no choice but to really 'teach him a lesson,'" Suzuki said. "I think by executing such a surprise attack on such an occasion, Yokoyama has really made the host lose face."

"Don't blame him. I asked him to do this," Sasakawa said.

"Why?" Suzuki asked.

"If not done, we will never see real gongfu. If not this way, karate will arrogantly stop learning and progressing. If not this way, the Japanese karate that we have cultivated so hard will wither like the brief moment of a flower, and will decline and wane in the martial arts world," Sasakawa said.

"Chairman…" Suzuki said.

"The technique is mysterious and unfathomable to be sure, but the key lies in his wisdom to respond in the moment," Sasakawa said.

"Yokoyama originally calculated that he would move to the left and right first as was his habit, so it was rather gutsy he thought to use a feint to force Hong to move, and then use the moment at which he was occupied to attack him with a high spinning kick to the head, hoping to flatten Hong, but he didn't expect to be the one carried out. Sooo! After all, the ability to adapt varies widely among people," Suzuki said.

"When confronting an enemy, habituation is a fundamentally fatal weakness, but I never expected it to be turned into a tactic to deceive the enemy," Sasakawa said.

"Also, Yokoyama relied too much on his own ability to take a hit with his nogare and ibuki training, he guessed wrong. At best, it is just that he figured he could take one or two strikes from Hong and would be able to recover. Unexpectedly, one wrong move on the chessboard, the entire game was lost," Suzuki said.

"When trading blows with a master, there is no tolerance for even a slight margin of error," Sasakawa said.

"He first used his right hand to suck in Yokoyama's body, and then used that left palm strike to clock the back Yokoyama's head. Yokoyama's neck was hit by such a heavy hand, his brain would instantly lose consciousness and control. This one palm strike was the equivalent of popping Yokoyama's 'balloon'…," Suzuki said.

"If the body is not filled with protective Qi, people will be vulnerable to even one strike," Sasakawa said.

"The most amazing kiss of death was after he slapped Yokoyama's neck, his palm was like an elephant's trunk wrapping around the neck, and he pulled Yokoyama into a collision with his right knife hand chop. This combination is so refined and hard to get out of. This is an opposing force that accelerates the collision at the same time. Even though it doesn't employ any special secret skills, people can't withstand such an attack, especially on the carotid artery. Yokoyama's loss today is just a loss of self-confidence in his ability to take a heavy blow. In the future, we must keep this in mind and take it as a warning lesson. By the looks of it, when this Mr. Hong is facing hostile intent and plotting, he is not such a soft-hearted and charitable character," Suzuki said.

"At the critical moment, one must be able to harden your heart. Only then have you the creds to become a world-class master," Sasakawa said.

"I dare to predict that Hong Yi-xiang will become a world-class martial arts master in the future," Suzuki said.

"No. After running the gauntlet yesterday and taking care of nearly all the exponents we put up against him with only one move, Hong Yi-xiang has proven his strength to the world: he is *now* a world-class martial arts master. Moreover, I think I can confirm what his secret technique is," Sasakawa said.

"Oh. Really?" Suzuki asked.

"It should be the 'Art of Controlling the Bull.' A soldier who served during the Second World War in the Yunnan-Burma border area in southwest China witnessed it and told me about it," said Sasakawa. "Art of Controlling the Bull? Isn't that the technique that Kyokushin-kai's Mas Oyama used to overpower and demolish a wild bull?" Suzuki asked.

"No. Not overpowering. Humans have always used intelligence to bring down animals larger than themselves. Not raw strength," Sasakawa said.

After this long conversation, Ryoichi Sasakawa's mind was clearly resolved. For his remaining years, he would dedicate himself to the ultimate goal of promoting the great Japanese nation's karate. He would mobilize the wisdom, wealth, and contacts he had accumulated over a lifetime in the commercial world to go all out, to not give up until the goal was reached...

"For the long-term development of our Japanese karate, we must find a way to obtain this secret technique. No matter how much time, money, and also by any means," Sasakawa said.

Hong Yi-xiang and Suzuki Masafumi hold a press conference in Tokyo, 1972.

Hong Yi-xiang imparts knowledge of Neijia boxing to the Tokyo Seibukan main dojo at the invitation of Suzuki Masafumi, 1972.

80– DARK ARTS AND DIRTY TRICKS

Black and white, dark and light, all exist in relation to each other. In a world that has no light at all, with nary a beam of sunshine or colors, no one knows whether one can still differentiate gradations of black? In the eyes of ordinary people living in a dark and disorderly country, is there another set of completely different rules of survival and moral code, and an operational logic that allows everyone to maintain ecological balance?

Scene: Anxi Street

"Mr. Hong, thank you for your ardent hospitality during this period, I will leave tomorrow."

"Where do you plan to go?" asked Hong Yi-xiang.

"Hualien."

"Okay," Hong Yi-xiang said.

The man was silent, as if waiting for Hong Yi-xiang to say something important.

"Tomorrow, I would like to treat all the masters to a farewell dinner in your honor at Another Heaven," Hong Yi-xiang said.

"Oh. Save it for my wake. No need."

"Okay. If that's what you want."

"I will make a move early in the morning. I won't be saying goodbye then."

"Alright. Just a toast with this glass of wine now, to thank you for everything," Hong Yi-xiang said.

"Bottoms Up!"

The man resumed his silence, shyly searching for words. "Mr. Hong, I want to sell a book to you to raise a little cash."

"I have no need of books. How much money do you need?" inquired Hong Yi-xiang.

"Ten taels." In that era of turmoil, solid gold was the only thing that made people feel most secure. It is just that coming from a teacher employed by the family, the number he proposed to the boss was not a reassuring number.

"Whew! Okay. I'll have to get it from my mother." Facing the request of such a significant sum, Hong Yi-xiang was a little surprised, but he didn't inquire further.

"This is not extortion."

"Don't speak that way. It's ten taels—done. I will deliver it to you later tonight," Hong Yi-xiang said conciliatorily.

"Thanks!"

The next day, before sunrise, Hong Yi-xiang got up, hoping that he could see off the teacher who hadn't even left a name. When he arrived at his residence, the door was open, the lights were on, but the man had gone. Only a piece of paper and a dilapidated handwritten manuscript were left on the desk. The paper read:

> *Physical Strength - Gongfu Skills - Strategies and Tricks - Dark Arts and Dirty Tricks*

Looking at the empty scene left by this man, Hong Yi-xiang understood in his heart he had lost the opportunity to say goodbye to the unknown master, last night was their final farewell. The realization cut into him, since this unnamed master was going to disappear from the world forever. Even the records of their meetings, traced in time, would be lost in drips and drabs. With some disappointment he picked up the dog-eared manuscript on the table, opened the cover to the place inscribed "Dark Arts and Dirty Tricks," and read the header of the homepage:

> *One leaf to obstruct, no view of Mount Taishan!*
>
> *After removing the leaf, you will discover all that you are facing. In fact, it has always been a world in which the successful are "kings" and the defeated are "bandits," without right and wrong, crooked and straight, ethical and moral!*

Postscript:

"Dark Arts" are kinds of techniques not practiced openly. They use secret arts employing some specialized inventions, tools, or techniques to achieve the goal of destroying targets.

"Dirty Tricks" is to hide in dark places waiting for the opportunity to attack. It is clearly understanding humanity's blind spots, the limits of human thinking, and the limits of experience. Using a tool, technique, or trap that ordinary people can't imagine, striking when it is difficult for them to be on guard, during an awkward situation in which there is no way to counterattack.

Hidden in the dark and employing methods, tools, or techniques not openly trained, such techniques are able to leap over the boundaries of innate human strength. They transcend acquired skills intensely trained in martial arts, bare-hand, and weapons. They even exceed the practiced strategies and schemes of military commanders. They render people incapable of making sense of them. Defenseless. "Dark Arts and Dirty Tricks" was like a turbocharger, making the original engine's output more powerful. They can take innate talent, techniques, and strategies and generate a more potent killing effect. But they have a fatal and insoluble flaw. That is, they cannot exist independently. They must first find a host. A host sufficiently intelligent, phlegmatic, and cool under pressure. Only in this way can such omnipresent and omnipotent value be embodied. And such people or hosts are not common.

Opportunity seeking people and people looking for opportunities. Equally unpredictable, elusive.

Physical Strength ~ Gongfu Skills ~ Strategies and Tricks ~ Dark Arts and Dirty Tricks.

81– THE AMERICAN MILITARY TRAINING BASE

In extraordinary times, one must take extraordinary steps. The jungle warfare in Vietnam was not a place fussy about fairness and principles. For the purposes of proving your strength and virtue, you needn't sacrifice your physical advantages. In fighting to the death, only survival is the truly virtuous path.

Scene: Dadaocheng—Yongle Primary School auditorium

IN THE AUDITORIUM OF THE YONGLE PRIMARY SCHOOL IN Dadaocheng, a whole row of tatami mats leaned against the wall at a 15-degree angle. In front of each tatami mat stood a bare-chested American soldier, entirely showered in sweat, training straight punches on the mats serving as punching bags. This group of American soldiers of various heights, skin colors, and hair colors all volunteered to participate in the training at their own expense. Since their first step into this dojo, they had regarded this place as a sanctuary for the body and mind outside the barracks. Punch after solid punch on the tatamis, more coarse and harder than punching sandbags. They faced this simple, make-do equipment with no complaints in their hearts. With this short-term reinforcement training they only sought to improve their chances of surviving the Vietnamese battlefield.

The most conspicuous thing about the three tatami mats tightly bound together were red splotches of fresh blood stains from the three soldiers bravely mortifying their flesh with this drilling. In order of height from tallest to shortest they were: Blunder, Rocco, and Johnson. All three of them had beautiful blue eyes. Blunder was the tallest, about 195 centimeters tall, with a small face and a high nose, a long and thick neck, a slender figure with a pure baby face, like a high school student. He was a big boy with a gentle personality. Rocco was about 185 centimeters tall, with a moderate build, a handsome face, bashful and introverted. If he was not heading to Vietnam to fight, but going to Hollywood to act in a movie, he would be another Alain Delon (the handsome French guy who co-starred with the Japanese actor Toshiro Mifune in *Red Sun*). Johnson was about 178 centimeters tall. He was an American of Swedish descent, with distinctly craggy facial features and a smart, sharp, decisive, and valiant leader's persona. The three of them were the first wave of the US servicemen who entered the dojo for training. It was also through their enthusiastic behind the scenes arrangements and support from the troop drillmaster that the representative of the US military was persuaded to come forward and ask Taiwan counterparts to assist in the loan of Yongle Elementary School. Local authorities agreed to rent the school playground and auditorium at night for a token sum, to provide them a training base for unarmed combat skills.

After completing the necessary boot camp training in the United States, these American GIs were first moved by warships or military aircraft to several bases in Asia to await orders for Vietnam deployment. They were members of the Air Task Force 13 (Provisional) numbering over 10,000 GI's in Taiwan. With a call up from the commander of the Vietnamese military region, they would enter yet another unfamiliar country, engaging in a fight for survival in a jungle where they did not belong. To facilitate this large number of American soldiers trying to obtain effective survival skills within a limited time, Hong Yi-xiang had already conducted training for a cadre of Taiwanese assistant teachers as early as half a year ago. He selected ten senior disciples from the original "Guandu Dragon Boat Team" for hellish training, and consonant with the goal of 'quick results in a short time,' he had prepared the new course.

"In extraordinary times we must use extraordinary means," Hong Yi-wen said.

"We must make good use of the innate physical advantages of Westerners. Don't reject the advantage of size and strength, as long as you can win," Chen Mei-shou said.

"The moves must be practical, simple, and easy to learn. Regardless of the Internal School or the External School, if it can take out the enemy and preserve life, use it. Don't use long training routines, just single, and sparring techniques, best practiced with both the right and left hands," Hong Yi-mian said.

"If you want 'quick results in a short time,' you have to go with the Internal School trained like the External School," Hong Yi-wen said.

"Where human life is concerned, we can't cling to traditional moves and teaching methods. If they have a chance, and come back alive in the future, then we can try to teach the original traditions," Hong Yi-xiang said.

Based on the "think-tank's" brainstorming discussions these Yizong Tangshou basic rudimentary learnings were created: "*BaBuDa*—Eight Step Fighting," "*BaLianShou*—Eight Consecutive Hands," "*BaShou*—Eight Hands," and "*BaTi*—Eight Kicks." In addition to these thirty-two simple, short techniques, the key was to drill them against a variety of different opponents every day in the hopes that they could quickly accumulate in the shortest period a variety of actual combat experiences and the courage not to shrink in the face of the enemy. There were six classes in the dojo every night practicing together at the same time, and each class counted about fifty people. In sparring, the fifty people were divided into two rows. They bowed to each other, then started one-on-one sparring. Every twenty minutes of sparring, they would rest for ten minutes. After the break, they would change partners and spar again. Individuals would have to engage at least four matches a night, facing four different opponents and styles of play. Between the six classes, there was yet another cross confrontation every week. This was to employ a realistic, concrete method of actual combat to make these soldiers experienced, hand-to-hand fighters before entering the jungle.

The emphasis on actual combat training methods generated many limb injuries in the initial stage. To avoid the impact these injuries had on training, Hong Yi-xiang borrowed from the design of special armor used when practicing Japanese kendo and commenced research and improvement into protective gear. In that era, the sports equipment industry was not as developed as it is today, and almost all needed items relied on one's own brain power and handicraft. Fortunately, there were many diverse talents in the gym, from all walks of life.

After the general design direction was established, Hong Yi-xiang personally drew the original sketches of the soft-shell armor and handed it over to the disciples from various professions to procure related materials and make a proof-of-design. Whereupon the world's first flexible protective gear especially designed for free-hand sparring was born. The innermost layer of the prototype soft shelled protective gear was stitched from a double layer of extra-thick cow hide leather. A layer of high-density foam rubber was strongly glued to the outer layer of the leather. The purpose was to buffer the force of the collision. Both hitters and those getting hit were properly protected. The outermost layer of the protective gear was made of a special durable canvas.

Wearing flexible armor while sparring generated a lot of sweat. The original cotton straps used to tie on the gear easily rotted and broke. Later, all the armor was retrofitted with parachute-grade nylon cords provided by the US military for strapping on the protective gear, solving the cotton rot problem. And because rawhide soaked in a lot of sweat for a long time would easily get moldy and smelly, after several discussions it was decided to adopt the suggestion of the US military supply officer to change the innermost leather protection layer to a special industrial rubber as an alternative material. At this point, the specifications and materials for the flexible protective gear were finalized.

Hong Yi-xiang felt that the ideal self-defense armor for practice must not only be able to effectively protect the user, it must also not impede movement and flexibility. Therefore, the seams of the protective gear should also be designed in accordance with the structure of the human body and the range of motion. The ideal was to achieve the purpose of protection, but not over-protection such that there would be no pain or sense of risk of injury. Otherwise, the person wearing the armor would have no sensation, and his lack of fear would become a dangerous illusion on a real battlefield.

The operation of a martial training hall is like this; from scratch, step by step, and placing attention everywhere, with effort it unfolds gradually. When the Vietnam War reached its peak, an average of about 350 locals and foreigners would squeeze in the auditorium and playground of Dadaocheng Yongle Elementary School every night, together participating in the formation of this martial arts system. For Taiwan, which was still in the period of mobilization and martial law, this colossal and specialized "military organization" was an "arsenal" to which national security and intelligence agencies paid special attention. Therefore, it was inevitable that mixed among the many students were undercover agents and informers sent by the security units. Their main mission was to prevent this powerful civilian force from causing national security or public security problems.

Many years later, a retired informant invited to a banquet to thank the teacher timidly revealed the truth of this untold secret under the influence of liquid courage. Fortunately, this Hong family never had a special political stripe, and the massive martial arts system never had any political inclination or activities, thus avoiding many possible troubles and entanglements.

This special disciple who had exposed these secrets hidden for so many years, later died. His family ran a restaurant serving fresh fish and free-range chicken and offering hot-spring baths. The spring had become clogged and the two workers in charge of maintenance were overwhelmed by the sulfur gas and passed out in the bottom of the well. The boss, in a rush to save them, didn't wait for the arrival of the firefighters, so he first used ropes to descend into the well to rescue the unconscious workers. Because of his courage and decisiveness, both workers were rescued. Fortunately, they dodged their brush with death, but regrettably it was he himself who succumbed to inhaling too much sulfur gas and died at the bottom of the well.

His surname was Zhang; he had a strong build and swarthy complexion, a gentle and kind personality, sober and calm, prudent in action, an exponent worthy of respect. I remember back then, every hot summer, he would provide gratis to the training hall bunches of Chinese herbs his family had dried themselves such as: Smallflower Beggarticks, Rough Leaved Holly, Mint, etc. used to decoct into a cooling herbal tea to share with all the students. To think back that such an enthusiastic and kind-hearted young life was extinguished in such an accident truly makes one weep. (Those of you students in the school, whoever drank this herbal tea, should know the Mr. Zhang mentioned here and raise a glass in remembrance).

Hong Ze-han

Hong Yi-xiang and a GI student sent to do battle in Vietnam, Martin Brond, 1967.

Hong Yi-xiang with American students, 1970.

Hong Yi-xiang with the disciples of the Dadaocheng Yongle Elementary School group, 1971.

82– THE MASTER PREPARES A BANQUET PART 1

If the bullock cart doesn't go, hit the cart? Or whip the ox? The tea is not good, hit the monkey? Or pillory the plantation owner? Monkey picked tea is not a product of happiness. The monkey is only avoiding starvation and a drubbing when it helps picking tea mired in a swamp. How can you hope a monkey working under these conditions will pick good tea leaves worth drinking?

Scene: Anxi Street

IN ADDITION TO FOCUSING ON THE STUDY, INTEGRATION, AND improvement of martial arts throughout his life, Hong Yi-xiang's biggest indulgence was to chat with martial arts fellow enthusiasts, visitors, and old friends, while brewing tea and discussing the world. He liked high mountain Oolong, Biluochun, green tea, Pekoe Oolong (white haired monkey), wild big leaf Pu'er, and Japanese green tea, and even the British Earl Grey tea with grapefruit fragrance. He would never refuse a good cuppa. However, he was slightly less interested in heavily fermented teas, such as aged Pu'er and Laoshan Tieguanyin, which were regarded as good drinks after a meal to resolve greasy food. When he was with friends outside brewing tea, what he cared most about was his interaction with others, whereupon he didn't care so much about what he drank. Whatever they ordered he would drink, seldom exposing his likes or dislikes in front of others, lest others deliberately suppress their own preference just for him.

Once he was invited to a cross-strait martial arts exchange conference in Fujian, China, and an enthusiastic admirer gave him a can of "Monkey Picked Tea," a specialty of Wuyi Mountain in the province. I don't know if it was a fake bought by mistake, or if the reputation of this class of tea exceeds its quality. After returning to Taiwan, he enthusiastically invited a bunch of his tea drinking buddies to share the enjoyment. The person who had gifted him the tea had given him earnest instructions, so he specially sent a business friend to Qixing Mountain to get fresh mountain spring water for making the tea and brewed it according to the water temperature indicated on the exquisite packaging. Who would have known that as soon as the tea entered their mouths, the group of tea friends couldn't wait to tease him: "This must be the guaranteed authentic or your money back monkey-picked tea alright," they chided.

"And it sure is monkey tea, not fit for human consumption."

"Really?" After he took a skeptical sip, he knew what these fussy old tea connoisseurs were going on about. Sure enough, the bitterness of the tea was hard to swallow.

"These deadbeat monkeys, picking what kind of crap tea?"

"Why is the monkey to blame? Monkeys don't drink tea, how are they gonna know if it is good or not?"

"That's right. If it weren't for you, why would a monkey pick tea out in miserable wet mud and suffer."

"It's the monkey who is smarter than us. If you made me pick tea and suffer, I would let you drink bitter and astringent monkey piss."

"If people don't consume it, monkeys won't suffer. People! We're greedy, and we get what we deserve."

"Tea bushes shouldn't be grown on swamps. How could this aberration of nature taste any good?"

"Yes. This is basic common sense, how come I forgot it."

"You forgot it. Serves you right."

"Yes. I deserve it. Deserve to drink monkey piss."

"Okay. Then let's enshrine the remaining tea leaves and wait for the giver of the tea to come some day and drink a pot by themselves."

"Right, right, right. Return to the original owner. When the time comes, I'll invite you all over."

"Ha-ha-ha."

Thus was his tea klatch and his tea talk. Although they talked a bunch of nonsense, their feelings were as warm as the tea. He often said that in general, when natural law is violated, most often there is some hidden problem. This monkey-picked tea was an example.

In addition, Hong Yi-xiang was also an authentic foodie. Besides his passion for tasting all kinds of delicacies, he liked to mess around in the kitchen, especially when he had eaten something special and unusual outside he would then try his hand at it at home. He always hoped that his family could share that happiness, passing straight through the tastebuds to the heart. Perhaps it is people who know how to eat and love to eat who have this kind of talent. A cuisine that moved him, no matter how complicated its process and ingredients, once he tasted it, he could replicate it with seventy to eighty percent fidelity. With this innate talent, the whole family often acted as his happy guinea pigs.

People who love to cook often like to wander the vegetable markets. He enjoyed passing through the market to observe the seasonal supply of melons, fruits, vegetables, chickens, and fish, and to appreciate the changes in the four seasons, coming to understand what is most abundant in the fields and seas. He said that the Shanghainese are fussy about 'not eating out of season' — that this is the most accurate predictor of fine food. If he had not accumulated sufficient life experience and wisdom, he could not have uttered such a natural rationale for the ages. In short, following the cycle of nature's solar terms,[26] it's best to eat whatever Heaven serves up at the time. For him, a master with rich experience, the ambiance of each distinct solar term, each course of varied delicacies, was always accompanied by distinct vicissitudes of life and memories of the past. Only by embracing the patience to ruminate fully, while extracting the full flavor of a situation, can one understand the breadth and depth of one's own life.

As he walked through the wet markets he was too well known a character and was not good at refusing. If a fishmonger familiar with him called out a greeting, he could not resist going over for a visit. Especially irresistible to him were those seasonal seafoods with a short production period rarely available in the market. Therefore, running into these situations where he felt it ungracious not to accept the vendor's kindness, he always overbought, settling the bill first and the vendor would help deliver it to his house after the market closed. Later, this transaction model became the normal state of affairs.

Whenever some butchers or vendors encountered a slowdown in the market, they would directly send the day's unsold leftovers to the Hong family, almost a forced sale. However, these unsalable products had been kept at room temperature for too long, and some of them had started to turn and could not be eaten at all. However, out of consideration for the vendor's feelings, Hong Yi-xiang would settle the bill according to the price set by the owner. Every time this situation was encountered, his attitude was, "Take it as helping to reduce their losses," to console himself. However, his eldest son, Hong Ze-zhou, was disapproving of his way of getting along with everyone. He thought that accommodating such people encourages their conniving. So, no matter what his dad said, he loyally played the role of the black-faced temple guardian. His scowl read, "Let those unscrupulous vendors never dare to come here and pretend to be pitiful, begging for unearned advantage."

The thirteenth day of the fifth lunar month is the birthday of Dadaocheng's "Lord of the Xiahai City God Temple." According to traditional customs, the night before, the constables and servants of the Lord of the City God roam the streets to make secret inquiries. According to folklore legends, this is to reconnoiter and arrange the route of the Lord's inspection tour. Just past noon the next day, the annual folklore procession begins. Among the ranks, including the birthday city god who will ride a royal palanquin for the inspection tour, and the worshippers in the district worshiping for his birthday, the indispensable frontline troops are:

The dragon dancers, lion dancers, and Masters Seven and Eight who mete

---

26 The Chinese annual calendar is divided into twenty-four periods of approximately fifteen days each, called Solar Terms in English.

out punishment and reward, He with the Eyes Seeing 1000 Miles and He who Hears Everything on the Wind, traditional music, opera performers, and stilt walkers, The Eight Generals, a parade of martial art performers, parade marshals, Dancers of the Cloth Boat, and other groups performing along the route. There are even music performances by Western music groups. Sharp-eyed people seeing this parade squad playing western instruments would notice that this is the same bunch that performed yesterday for a funeral, and even the music they played was all the same. The old "One hundred and one standards," only the tempo and beat was changed. People! To Gods, to demons, and to other people, they are all the same. They just want to muddle through. If they really cared about all the details and facts, they would not be able get through a day.

In that year, on the birthday of the King of the City God, apart from welcoming the gods, the most important part of the scene was tables every household had to set up to entertain distant relatives and friends, and customers who had business dealings in the market, upstream and downstream business partners. No one knows when this tradition of hosting a table and entertaining guests was established, but everyone became accustomed to regarding it as "family banquet annual public relations day." Under the dictates of the prevailing social atmosphere, some families that were not well off felt no choice but to take out loans or pawn valuables to shore up their sagging prestige on this special day. When one's own family had gone to similar banquets hosted by relatives and friends, then based on the principle of fairness and reciprocity, they had to return equal invitations.

Sanchong, which is separated by a river from Taipei City, also hosted grand devotions, religious parades, and table banquets on the twenty-fifth day of the lunar calendar on the "Emperor Shennong's Birthday." The birthdays of the patron saints of the two jurisdictions on both banks of the Tamsui River are less than a month apart. Before it was rebuilt and widened, Taipei Bridge, which connected Taipei City and Sanchongpu, looked like the Xiluo Bridge. It was also a steel-framed iron bridge. It had the rustic charm and appearance of that bygone era. Every year on the twenty-fifth day of the fourth month and the 'thirteenth day of the fifth month in the lunar calendar, just after noon on the Taipei Bridge, all motor vehicles were banned. The entire bridge was only open to pedestrians. It's just like today when streets are closed off for running marathons, except that all the people on the bridge and on the road were going to banquets. To allow the flow of people to circulate smoothly, the pedestrian traffic on the two-way lanes between the two places during the day and night must also be carefully planned for; otherwise, once the crowds got to pushing and trampling on the bridge, the consequences are not difficult to imagine. The newspaper once published an aerial photo, taken from a helicopter. From the picture, one could clearly see all the streets and alleys connected to the

Taipei Bridge in Taipei City, like unfolding branches, densely covered with pedestrians , heading to Sanchongpu. This tide of people flooded and finally converged and concentrated towards the bridge. On the Taipei Bridge, the crowds clustered until it was a dense mass, and the road and the bridge were not seen at all in the photo. It was not until after the Tamsui River that this black tide was gradually diverted and distributed along the streets and lanes of Sanchongpu. This was the special atmosphere in that era where all the city folk of the two locations, undaunted by hardship or danger, mobilized to get a free banquet meal.

Later, social problems such as family disputes, money borrowing disputes, drunk and disorderly conduct, and other pernicious problems caused by extravagant banquets, even drunken banqueteers falling from the bridge and drowning in the river, etc., emerged. Whereupon, with massive government promotion and persuasion, this general social tendency to extravagantly entertain slowly disappeared in the metropolitan area. This was an unavoidable process in the transformation of an agricultural society into a commercial society. In the process of metamorphosis, a half and half mix of good and bad things are overthrown, destroyed, or forgotten. Although, looking back from today's perspective, it is inevitable that one recalls fondly the cherished feelings between people in the past, but this kind of past can only be remembered and called to mind in words. To actually go back to the past, to face the plots, schemes, and stories that existed, in fact, may not really be as colorful, compelling, or wonderful as imagined…

That year, for Zhang Luo's great prayer banquet on the thirteenth day of the fifth month, Hong Yi-xiang had an inspiration; he wanted to invite those American boys who were about to go to fight in Vietnam to experience the flavor of Taiwan human feeling and cuisine before departing. He decided to put his talents on display and arrange a table to entertain guests. He indulged in this wild fantasy of holding a large-scale banquet with the enthusiastic support of all his friends and diehard supporters. To decide on the dishes and to sort the conflicting opinions of the peanut gallery, he chose to start with a small-scale tasting. After the menu was revised and nailed down, he then moved to the Yongle Elementary School's auditorium to expand the scope of this formal banquet to entertain those American boys who were thousands of miles from home, treating them to taste Taiwan's unique banquet culture. This can be regarded as a youthful fantasy of his clique of rich young men in Dihua Street and at the core of Hong Yi-xiang's being. But the final scale was really shocking.

Three special forces soldiers who survived their tour in Vietnam prepared a plaque of appreciation to Hong Yi-xiang, circa 1968.

83– THE MASTER PREPARES A BANQUET PART 2

You don't even know who it is you are helping? You just wishfully do what you think is right. In the eyes of the Viet Cong though, you are just an accomplice, a collaborator who cultivates killing machines!

Scene: Anxi Street, Yongle Elementary School

Taiwan's food culture has been influenced by foreign rule and colonization over ages. It is a mix of eating habits and cooking elements that these foreign rulers intentionally or unintentionally left behind. Nevertheless, the elements of food preparation gongfu do not deviate from steaming, cooking, stir-frying, deep-frying, stewing in sauce, and stewing in soy. The selection of ingredients also does not fundamentally deviate from the principle of "sourcing local." The essential ingredients for the average banquet menu include chicken, duck, fish, pork, abalone, lobster, shark fin, miniature Nine Holes abalone, sea cucumber, seasonal fruits and vegetables, sweet soup, desserts and so on. What distinguishes most courses used for banquets is the selection of precious and high-end ingredients, or the complicated preparation process of the dishes. The generous presentation of these mouthwatering items not normally available allows the invited guests to indulge their appetite for fine food to their fill. In that era of sadness and shortages, this should be seen as the people's wanton counterattack against the long-term repression of their lives and emotions. So, Hong Yi-xiang put out the call to the "YiZong TangShou Support Association," and those with money gave money, those with manpower gave manpower, those with chickens gave chickens, with meat gave meat, and with seafood gave seafood, as all were fully mobilized in this effort.

Chen Yan-sheng offered up big black sea cucumbers and sea cucumber intestines (this is a rare delicacy among the common people, the consistency is like dried scallops).

Harbor Uncle offered up wild, deep ocean pomfrets and giant prawns.

Hong De-xiong provided premium shark skin and fresh sharks fin (in those days it was still fashionable among Taiwanese to eat shark's fin).

Chen Xun provided Guandu's Muscovy Ducks and red yolk duck eggs.

Chen Qing-bo provided Guandu Iberico pig trotters, thigh bone marrow, liver, kidney, pork belly, pork intestines.

Chen yan-shi provided green bamboo shoots and seasonal vegetables, melons & fruits from Sanxia.

A-Linzai offered up free-range chickens and tripes.

Black Turtle supplied turtle doves and quail eggs.

Cai Wan-cheng provided Wheel brand Mexican canned abalone.

Chen Shi-teng offered wild, large spotted eel and eel.

Black Snake sponsored the Heisong soda pop, Santa Claus brand guava juice, and Shaoxing wine.

Lin No. 3 provided all the kitchen utensils, dishes, water cups, tables and chairs needed to run the banquet.

Everyone enthusiastically sponsored, each fearing to be outdone, lest the event suffer from a lack of support. And this groundbreaking "taste testing activity" should also be regarded as this martial arts system's first major mobilization of people and resources. Of course, this purpose of bringing a small bit of wonder and joy to ordinary lives with simple and honest enthusiasm untainted by haggling over gains and losses now seems to have been eradicated by current social norms. They only value efficiency and cost-to-earnings ratios. Traditional norms are replaced by: "Why should I help this event?", "What is the benefit to me in doing this?", "How much profit can I turn these advantages into?", "Why do I have to pay more than him?" Everyone has become smarter because of utility and pragmatism. Smarts and pragmatism don't approve of anything you unselfishly contribute to an organization to which you belong. (Of course, the generous temple donations—bribes—to gods are not included in this. Those should be regarded as investments to hedge risk).

A small taste testing dinner was held before the big banquet. The main chef, Hong himself, cooked it so this was to be a grand affair. Early in the morning, bit by bit all the ingredients were delivered to the scene from the sources and were handed over to Black Turtle and Black Snake for collection. At that time, small-scale banquets of this kind would usually have open-air catering next to the archway in front of the house, or on the side of the road, and they would rarely expend money to rent indoor venues. However, the ground floor space in the back street arcade was too narrow, the rental meal preparation sites were too large, so they set up a kitchen area in the rear courtyard of the Hong mansion on Anxi Street but struggled with the placement of the large woks and steamers. Suddenly, faced with such a variable on the battlefield, he didn't know where the inspiration came from, but Hong Yi-xiang adapted to the circumstances and assigned two of his boys to dismantle the doors of the house to serve as temporary work counters. Hong Yi-xiang's two baffled sons got their marching orders to tear down the doors, and then the two, one in front and one behind, crossed from Minle Street, cutting through Sanyi Wet Market with the door panels on their heads. All along the way they attracted the curious eyes of neighbors. Some naughty friends their age followed close behind, mimicking the sight and sound of a religious procession musical troupe, like the old city god on his inspection tour, marching to Anxi Street, until the door panel was put down, and they saw that the eldest son, Ze-zhou, was about to pop, like a volcano going to erupt. This group of naughty little urchins fell over each other in their rush to scatter. Ze-zhou's powerful reputation as someone not to be messed with was so trained all the way from childhood.

The spectacle of dismantling the door panels to act as preparation tables kicked off this parade. Hong Yi-xiang's cooking skills belong to the Niten Ichi-ryū, but the Japanese two sword style founded by Miyamoto Musashi uses one long and one short samurai sword, while the big steel cleavers wielded by Hong Yi-xiang employed "August 23rd Artillery War" blades. These were forged from unexploded artillery shells the Chinese People's Liberation Army had lobbed at Kinmen. Employing the "Two (Kitchen) Sword Style" he chopped prawns to make "Taiwan Coin Shrimp Toast." This dish is authentic Taiwanese cuisine, not an imitation of a similar Thai dish.

So-called Taiwanese Coin Shrimp Toast takes shelled shrimps smashed with the side of the cleaver, with pork lard mixed in, which is then chopped into a shrimp paste with a double knife action, then mixed with smaller shrimps so as to improve the texture. One stirs the shrimp paste and the small shrimps together uniformly, then spreads a tablespoon amount of shrimp paste on a small slice of toast with the edges removed (a large slice of toast is cut into four small pieces), and after dunking this toast in egg and crumbs, puts it in a large wok. Deep frying is done, until the surface of the shrimp cakes is golden brown, then they are dredged out and the oil drained off, and they're called a success. Because of the genuine, fresh ingredients, the shrimp cakes are really thick, substantial, juicy, flavor bombs with the zestfully chewy quality the Taiwanese call QQ, beating out the currently popular Thai Shrimp Cakes. The toast base tends to absorb fat when it is fried, so this traditional Taiwanese delicacy, convicted of harming public health, with no appeal for good behavior, was sentenced to life imprisonment with no possibility of parole or stay of execution, leaving its supporters wringing their hands in disappointment.

"Crispy Skinned Chicken" is made from a tender hen that has yet to lay eggs. After completing a complex marinating process, the most important thing is not to submerge the whole chicken directly into the hot oil when frying it, because the most essential juices originally sealed in the chicken would be evaporated and dried out. Rather one must suspend the chicken over the vat of hot oil and then use the iron ladle to continuously scoop hot oil from the pan to pour over the chicken. This pouring action has to be repeated until the skin of the chicken is amber colored and stopped when the bird is seventy to eighty percent done, so that the residual body cavity temperature finishes the cooking process. Even the driest gnarly breast meat, when so cooked, will have a juicy light pink color. It must be cooked until the skin is crispy and the meat is juicy, to be considered as having passed the test of a "Taiwanese Crispy Skin Chicken."

"Large Braised Knuckle" is actually pork trotters stewed in a fragrant soy sauce. Hong Yi-xiang once said that the key to the success of this dish is to use the native black pigs. They are raised naturally outside the pen and roam to eat, different from the captive white-haired pigs that are fed artificial feed and growth hormones. The skin of these Iberico pigs is thicker and tastier. At the same time, because of the large amount of exercise they get, the fat under the skin is firmer. After a long time of marinating, it does not become flaccid and disgusting. And the key to the deliciousness of this dish in those days was an extremely important element — soy sauce. To reach the limits of consummate tastiness, the sauce used by Hong Yi-xiang for marinating was hand brewed soy sauce and soy paste made of black soybeans by the wife of Hong Li's noodle maker. In those days, people who knew how to put up pickled vegetables and make fermented bean curd, usually also made their own brewed soy sauce. The fermentation and probiotic cultivation methods are almost the same, but brewed soy sauce has more processes employed for squeezing out the sauce and extracting the essence through long boiling. The homemade soy sauce is not only distributed to relatives and friends but is reserved for personal use. Stored in a cool place, it can usually be kept for three to five years without deterioration.

The braised trotters must be patiently plucked of all the hair on the skin to avoid damaging the "mouth-feel." The pig bristles must be plucked, you can't be lazy and use a knife to shave it or burn it off, lest the black hair remaining in the pores be consumed and the uneasy diners will feel the food is not clean. After the pig bristle is cleaned, it must be submerged in hot water to remove the blood, after which it is placed in ice water to cool down quickly, increasing the elasticity and taste of the pig skin and fat layer. Before braising, you have to deep fry the whole trotter in a frying pan until the skin is golden brown, and then remove the excess oil before putting it into the marinade. In the beginning, soy sauce is usually used to marinate and braise, so that the flavor penetrates, and the soy paste is added at the end when the whole trotter is crispy, so that the surface of the finished product is golden and oily. This is the traditional method of Taiwanese braising. If you follow this ancient method to prepare it, it is guaranteed the aroma of the marinade will be abundant, and only inhaling the aroma with your nose is guaranteed to increase your cholesterol and triglycerides level. This is the most wickedly delicious and irresistible dish in Taiwanese cuisine. So, just like this, guided by the principle of pursuing deliciousness regardless of cost, he completed twelve dishes of the most common Taiwanese banquet fare of that era.

01 Family Fortune Platter—Cold Bamboo Shoot Salad/Five Flavors Nine Hole Abalone/Lobster Salad/Canned Diced Abalone/Crispy Deep-fried Cashew Nuts/Bundled Thin Slices of Pork
02 Steamed Pidgeon Broth
03 Fried Prawns/Taiwan Coin Shrimp Toast
04 Duck Soup with Sour Vegetables
05 Sharks skin pottage (Taiwanese style "Buddha Jumps Over the Wall")
06 Fried Crispy Skinned Chicken
07 Sea Cucumber Braised Abalone
08 White Eel Stewed with Goji berry
09 Large Braised Pork Trotters
10 Smoked Pomfret
11 Eight Treasure Masked Taro
12 Golden Lion Peach + Almond Bean Curd Soup

After those relatives and friends who sponsored the ingredients had earnestly tucked into the "taste test," "seven mouths and eight tongues" all had different opinions. Several debates and amendments later, basically the original menu remained unchanged, only the flavoring, portions, and order of the dishes were adjusted and the gavel came down on the final verdict. The catering chef who had participated in the whole process ramped it up to expand, according to the plan. Whereupon a ground-breaking special feast, having gone through trial cooking and trial tasting, was fixed for the thirteenth day of the fifth month of the lunar calendar, the day of Haicheng God's birthday.

The banquet was set up in the auditorium of Yongle Elementary School. Fifty tables set for 600 guests were laid out with all the unique local cuisine and the inviting warmth of the Taiwanese people for the US soldiers trained at the gymnasium and that year invited to participate in the birthday banquet of the "Xiahai City God on Dihua Street." Although these American soldiers who believed in Christ's salvation had no clue what the City God was, but this did not dampen anyone's enthusiasm for participating in the feast. They organized a band and went up on the stage to sing, livening things up. Hearing the songs of home so far away, the young men's eyes misted over and became red. For them, the home on the other side of the Pacific was too far away. Here was love, and this was their home before getting mobilized to the battlefield in Vietnam. In addition to teaching them the combat skills to survive and protect themselves, Hong Yi-xiang also showed them the care and love they needed at this moment.

In this feast, Hong Yi-xiang specially invited two masters, Tu and Zhang Junfeng, to join in the fun. In addition, those martial arts teachers who had instructed the Hong family brothers when they were young who could be reached were invited, otherwise they appointed disciples to come to the banquet. Even Teacher Peng of the invisible Green Gang was invited. For the teacher of "The Art of Controlling the Bull" hidden in Central Mountain Range who had turned his back the mundane affairs of the world of dust, Hong Yi-xiang made a special trip to the mountain just to invite the husband and wife down to have fun together. He said that how many fortuitous and precious friendships a person can have in their life all depends on whether they actively and personably cultivate them. Whether a person's life is splendidly romantic or not is also a question of personal attitude.

Perhaps because he had a rich dad he could indulge in his passions throughout his life and create a romantic life story difficult for the average person to achieve. I am convinced, however, that without his free and easy personality, even had his father been wealthy beyond all reckoning, it would have turned out this way. Hong Wan-mei's candle business had become less and less expansive with the changes in society and was no longer as grand as before, but so long as people have been wealthy once, even if the financial might in their pockets is not what it used to be, that traditional pride could not be swallowed for a lifetime. The memories of those past years are still vivid, and I always felt that the American President owed Hong Yi-xiang a medal, a commendation for the heartfelt care he offered to his countrymen so far from home.

Chairman Eiichi Miyazato leading an Okinawan Goju Ryu black belt study group on a visit to Master Hong, 1987.

Receiving a visit from Hong Kong Choi Li Fut Wude Hall Chairman Huang Lun, with Hong Yi-xiang, Hong Jiao-zhen, and Hong Ze-zhou standing in the back, 1970.

84– TAIJI MASTER CHEN PAN-LING

When centrifugal and centripetal forces are in balance, they will be in a static state. This stillness is a 50:50 state of equilibrium, not nothing. The stillness pursued by Internal Boxing is exactly the state of balance between yin and yang and harmony between hardness and softness.

Scene: Master Chen Pan-ling's home, Taichung

(The following is a monologue of Master Chen Pan-ling)

"It can only be said that the Lord above takes special care of you. Some masters have been striking at it almost their entire lives, but in the end they have nothing to show for it…You really have Heaven's blessing, famous after one fight, and every time you get in the ring, it's with a huge crowd witnessing a crucial battle. However, it's not fair to you. Which critical battle hasn't also put you in a thorny dilemma? If it weren't for other people retreating their heads back into their shells like turtles, according to your personality, you wouldn't necessarily stick your head out. If those people had been allowed to use their fists to solve those difficulties, I am afraid they would have made a mess of things. The key to battles is not just gongfu and ruthlessness. It is courage and wisdom in the field. You were born for this role.

"Those who oppose you teaching foreigners, what they really care about is not those high-sounding words they spout on the surface. It's your prestige and increasing influence in the international martial arts world. In Japan, you used Internal School Boxing to demonstrate to the world its practical fighting prowess. In Taiwan, you smashed the kiln bricks with one fist, and with one stick you overturned the black giant that was invincible in Japan. You used your wits to overturn the Westerners' contemptuous view of Chinese martial arts, views they have had ever since the Boxer Rebellion…Maybe it's because you grew up in Taiwan and don't have too much Chinese historical burden on your shoulders. You let us clearly see that traditional martial arts have hope to become reborn in a new generation. Every time you fight, you leapfrog the traditional thinking and logic, like a rebellious, genius chess player, every chess move makes people look ahead in wonder.

"I can't see the limit in you, I can't see the limit of Chinese martial arts. Teaching Chinese martial arts to American soldiers going to fight in Vietnam, it seems is a predestined necessity of Internal Boxing to return to the battlefield. Xingyiquan was originally a combat technique trained in the army of old, and it has become refined and diverse due to its influx into the civilian population. When folk arts are passed down it is inevitable to avoid them becoming sensational claptrap and showy bullshit to please crowds. This makes the martial 'art' enter into a flashy, impractical dead-end. Only by returning to the battlefield, with its life and death baptism, can we restore the original intention and original appearance of martial arts.

"If Westerners are willing to learn Chinese traditional martial arts after they defeated China's broadswords, spears, thrusting swords, and halberds with foreign guns, there must be some empirical evidence behind their rationale. Putting to good use the Western emphasis on the logic of natural selection and 'survival of the fittest' and employing the most pragmatic and objective standards to screen the survival value of traditional Chinese martial arts. We can boldly eliminate the weak and retain the strong, allowing excellent martial arts to seek out superior genes with high survivability. This can be regarded as 'borrowing strength to augment strength,' a good strategy for win-win.

"No matter what decision is faced, the strong seek solutions, the weak seek excuses. Are you the kind who looks for a solution as a countermeasure or the kind looking for an excuse to shirk responsibilities. Those who have been gifted with good fortune must bear the responsibility of passing it on. A serendipity of turbulent times, and it is also the will of heaven. If there was no conflict between the Kuomintang and the Communist Party, there would be no large-scale migration of famous teachers to the south. And even more so, there would have been no large-scale transmission of Northern boxing styles to the South. Without the rich financial resources of the Hong family providing timely help, like delivering coal in winter, absent the talents residing here and chance encounters, then there would be none of today's achievements…through the exchange and sharing of Xingyi and Bagua, to be able to find reconciliation.

"You should already have received the full true transmission of this art of fighting from Master Zhang. Passing it on is the cost of receiving it. Why not pass it on to outsiders, and to whom does 'outsider' refer? What criteria are used to choose and define?

"In my opinion: 'outsiders' refers to people with whom one does not share a common temperament and values. It doesn't mean 'people outside of your school,' and they are definitely not the people referred to as foreigners. If you don't pass it on to 'outsiders,' and those insiders are unworthy, then what? Just look on idly and let the life be sucked out of it until there is nothing left to pass on? Remember. In this world the smart will always be in the minority, standing on the crest of a great age leading the mediocre majority. If you don't break with tradition, you won't stand.

"You can't narrowly use skin color and nationality as a barrier. You can't be hindered by what pedantic traditions say. Before it was recognized and accepted, which tradition and orthodoxy was not built up from the ruins of destruction. Without destruction and innovation at the beginning, where did today's tradition and civilization come from.

"What is tradition? Is it Beijing Man devouring raw meat and drinking blood? Or stone age man running around naked? If it is not built on innovation after the destruction of the existing situation, then where did today's martial arts, civilization, and tradition come from. In a nutshell, only by virtue of continuous innovation, constant renewal, is the universal principle of Taoism passed down for a hundred generations and thousands of years. Using traditional elements as the foundation to advance bold creativity. Then return the innovation gained back into the tradition, so that tradition can steadily keep up with the times. Master Zhang often said: "If you win, you are correct." Well said. He gets right to the point and draws blood.

"Let's chat about your Yizong Tangshou again. What you need now is not the external framework, but internal training. So-called 'Refining Cinnabar' means an alchemic practice guiding the concentration of inner essence. The only thing that does not overlap your past training, should be '99 Taiji.'

"Ninety-nine Taiji, also called GuoShuTaiji, is a method integrating the essence of various schools of Taiji into one grand achievement. Each school, each style has its own strengths and weaknesses…if they all draw their own boundaries, they isolate themselves. The research and creation of 99 Taiji is the brainchild of selfless contributions from famous Taiji masters of various schools sharing the essence of their hard won wisdom…it gathers together Chen, Yang, Sun, and Wu Schools of Taiji, and merges some characteristics of Shaolin, Xingyi, and Bagua…After removing repetitive and duplicate moves, we extracted those techniques having the highest practical effectiveness, the greatest physical benefits, the most natural and complete, and the best potential for developing latent cosmic abilities. These were refreshed and rearranged to create a form with the aim of best embodying 'the simple controlling the complex' and 'the soft overcoming the hard.' It is a holistic routine with depth and breadth.

"External martial arts are a must for entering the gate of Chinese traditional martial arts training. The emphasis is on the foundation, creating a platform on which to build, and pursue the transformation of tendon, bone, and marrow… Xingyiquan emphasizes Rising-Drilling-Dropping-Overturning, the scraping step to develop power, 'Direct Force' spiraling and drilling-in like the bore of a gun arcing inward. Bagua Palm requires walking, piercing, twisting, turning, button in and swing out stepping, overturning, and rolling, with 'Transverse Energy—Hengjin' to flank, yank and drop, and hence abandons the direct in favor of the angle to strike true.

"Taijiquan stresses 'silk reeling' twisting into eddies, moving in arcs that become circles, first relaxing the body to allow the inner Qi to sink and settle into the soles of the feet. Next keeping the upper body free and supple, it uses 'Vertical Strength' to guide the internal Qi from the ground up through the spine, unifying the three types of spiraling energy—Direct, Horizontal, and Vertical—into one, the entire body moving as one, so-called 'Holistic Energy' or 'Silk Reeling Energy'... advancing and retreating forward and backward, practicing 'Direct Energy,' left and right opening and closing practices 'Horizontal Energy,' up and down, rising and falling trains 'Vertical Energy,' its 'Holistic Energy' trains the whole body, inside and outside, to deliver one unified force.

"This unites advance and retreat, left and right, and up and down — the Six Harmonies —and establishes the concept of a three-dimensional combative space. Direct, Horizontal, and Vertical, these three types of force embody directional 'spiraling energy.' 'Silk reeling energy' is directing these horizontal, vertical, inside and outside interacting spiraling forces, such that it becomes a field that unfurls the outer circle from within. This is a most complete and all-encompassing energy field that can calmly respond to threats coming from all compass points...After a person has practiced Shaolin, Xingyi, Bagua, and Taiji, he can use this routine to encompass what he has learned. '99' implies extending boundlessly to unlimited size...Once you have mastered the form, use it as a medium in which to transplant the essence of what you have trained for a lifetime. First to exemplify, second to string together.

"Use this form to integrate what you have learned in your life. Then this will contain the essence of your learning as a 'Form of Forms.' This is the ultimate state of 99 Taiji, if you only follow the standard routine like a military drill, you can train a lifetime with no great achievement...The emphasis in the transmission of boxing arts is on explaining the concept and extending it... Regrettably, the more profound the method, the more that only the wise can really understand. That's why it is said of 99 Taiji, it is simple in style but deep in meaning, easy to learn but difficult to master.

"The key lies in the concept, not in the movements and applications. When you learn 99 Taiji, you must first let go of past established subjectivity...The emptier the cup, the more that can be added, and the greater the malleability. You must return to zero and learn from scratch. There can be no obstructions.

"I can't come to Taipei to teach you. If so, we should rather maintain the original friendship. Taipei is too humid. I could not get used to it. Besides, there are so many disciples here, I can't let them go.

"Just use the time you spend on business trips to Taichung collecting payments, twice a month... Don't you bring such a big gift each time you come... The Hong family already has no need, we're old friends, save a little bit. It takes at least three or four years for ordinary people to grasp it. Let's see after you return to Taipei, what your own training regimen is like... Master Zhang's there, I'll pay you a visit myself, there will be no problem.

"With your local and foreign contacts and networks to promote it, I believe that 99 Taiji can be promoted more effectively at home and abroad…The elevation and improvement of internal martial arts has always lacked a permanent organization capable of continuing its research and development. If you look at the tradition of the Japanese and Westerners in learning, they are constantly innovating and developing. It will take less than a few years for them to catch up and even surpass us… If we can't continue to explore higher realms, it will be like the three "unsung gifts to the world," gunpowder, printing, and paper.[27] One day, I'm afraid our offspring will have to go abroad to learn traditional Chinese martial arts."

Before Hong Yi-xiang practiced Xingyiquan and Baguazhang, he had already studied Yang Style Taiji for several years, but after all, at that time, he was young and shallow, and his understanding of Neijiaquan was still muddled. When he gradually mastered the essence of Xingyiquan and Baguazhang, his heart always carried a regret, and he hoped to find a renowned Taiji teacher to relearn and fill in this piece of the Neijiaquan jigsaw puzzle. As fate would have it, he came to know the Taijiquan master Chen Pan-ling who lived in Taichung. Hong visited many times on official business trips and called on him. After many intimate conversations, Master Chen Pan-ling agreed to Hong Yi-xiang's request and personally taught him the 99 Taiji Form compiled from the wisdom of many masters in China. Totally different from the past years, when he always invited the teachers to his home to live and teach, Hong Yi-xiang respected Master Chen's wishes and started the long-distance learning journey, scurrying between Taipei and Taichung.

Master Chen Pan-ling was talented in both the literary and martial worlds. He had a deep understanding and comprehension of the ancient text, *The Illustrated Book of Boxing Verses*. Hong asked his help with all kinds of thorny questions in boxing. With a word he could always break through the mystery to reveal the essence, giving people flashes of insight. This was unlike ordinary masters. With their limited level of discursive attainment, it was impossible for them to accurately employ contemporary language to describe the theory and abstract meaning of the boxing principles. They could only take out *The Illustrated Book of Boxing Verses*, nod their heads with an air of self-satisfaction, and repeat the ancient poems, leaving people more confused the more questions they asked.

Hong Yi-xiang said that only those who can clearly express profound theory in plain language and logic are the real masters. Those who seek to overly mystify or merely teach according to the book, most all are dilettante half-wits. Whereupon the relationship between Hong Yi-xiang and the Taiji master Chen Pan-ling, commenced a five-year long-term, long distance commuting study. According to Hong Yi-xiang, the study of 99 Taiji itself did not actually

---

27 He is counting gunpowder, the printing press, and paper as three "unsung gifts" of Chinese culture to the world.

take him too much time. During the period spent with the master, most of the time was to explore the higher realm of internal martial arts. Also, he dug into and researched the many old boxing manuals preserved after Old Father Hong's significant investment in the care and feeding of the exiled martial art masters. He said that this period should be considered as the most comprehensive and rapid cultivation of martial arts in his life —because of the caliber of his opponents, because opposites attract, and in so knowing each other, they cherished each other.

Famed Taiji Master Chen Pan-ling.

85– MOVIES, GONGFU, AND TEA PART I

Don't let past success limit your future development. Continuous revision is the only virtuous way of everlasting renewal!

Scene: Anxi Street

THE RISE OF "KUNG FU MOVIES" INJECTED MANY NEW AND interesting popular elements into traditional martial arts. Besides physical cultivation, self-defense, and protecting oneself from bullying, in the past, martial arts practice at best allowed that one could enter tournaments, accumulate experience in the ring and gain some reputation, then progress into a qualified martial arts teacher, and officially open a gym to teach disciples. Compared to the career prospects of other specialized technical skills, this profession was relatively narrow and limited in career development. Leaving aside those who practice martial arts purely for the love if it, if one can't become a famous martial art teacher, one can only retreat to the next best thing. This meant employment as personal protection for rich people or diving into various high-risk entertainment industries, such as dance halls, nightclubs, bars, illegal casinos…as hired muscle. Otherwise, you could hook- up with gangsters and the underworld and dine on the fat profits at the trough of this dark, hidden world. However, since kung fu movies became a worldwide trend, apart from inspiring the enthusiasm of the general audience falling over each other to train and the great business opportunity resulting for martial arts teachers, young people embracing dreams of a life in the movies especially sought out the martial arts techniques necessary to enter show business circles. Among them were the visually striking External systems such as Shaolin Hongquan, Praying Mantis, Choi Li Fut, Shenda, Wing Chun, Karate, Taekwondo, Aikido…these schools springing up like bamboo shoots after a Spring rain.

In those days of the kung fu movie craze sweeping the world, the beauty of speed, power and masculinity was sought after by filmmakers to excite the visual senses. Originally very plain and practical, unflowery Internal Boxing was not only not able to catch that wave of popularity, but was overwhelmed by the new wave, dragged under and mocked with ridiculous cameo characters. At best, it just filled the needs of the plot by providing one or two villains who practiced Bagua Palm or Xingyi Quan, inserted so as to contrast with the hero's and heroine's extraordinary bravery and invincibility. In the real world, those masters of internal martial arts who had spent their entire lives practicing real gongfu were rendered socially helpless in the face of the huge popular impact of kung fu movies.

During that period, I often heard the "time has passed me by" sighs of my elders, feeling that they were mocked by the movies and helplessly abandoned by the times. But if you really wanted to be able to portray the mood of these masters, then nothing could surpass the great film that came a few years later, *Pushing Hands*, directed by Ang Lee, as the most profound and realistic. In the screenplay, the Taiji master played by the aged movie star Lang Xiong, went to the United States to be cared for by relatives after his spouse died. Because of the language barrier and the culture gap, it was difficult to solve problems between the three family members: father, son, and foreign daughter-in-law. Therefore, the aging master wandered into a restaurant opened by Chinese compatriots and took refuge in a damp kitchen as a dishwasher. Forgetting why he had argued with the others, we only saw a Taijiquan hero standing in a narrow, greasy kitchen in a foreign place, far from home, all alone, facing a group of diehard young toughs who wanted to drag him out. This kind of helpless isolation, the forlorn desperation with no outlet to complain…made people truly feel the state of mind and emotions of those internal martial artists in that era. There are many things in the world which, only after sufficient life experience and setbacks, can one gain the sympathy of putting their heart in another's chest. The sympathy mentioned here is not compassion, but is empathy directed at the person involved with the same mood and mental state. Of course, this may only be because of the pathos stirred up in that unforgettable scene.

"Yi-xiang, is your gym affected?"

"Still okay," Hong Yi-xiang said.

"Wow! Young people are all running to learn Hong Quan and practice Taekwondo. This old stuff we're offering, no one wants."

"Adjust the teaching materials and teaching methods, it should be okay," Hong Yi-xiang said.

"Difficult. Even my own children ran to practice Taekwondo, who else can I look forward to training?"

"It's just the height of the kicks and how they use their feet is a little different. The techniques of kicking are minor variations on a theme," said Hong Yi-xiang.

"To speak of it makes me want to puke. The kid said he practices Taekwondo just because the uniform looks slicker. You tell me, are you pissed or not."

"Young people chase popularity and love fashion. This is a motivation and impetus for training. Weren't we the same back in the day? Brother, we need some empathy, if the principles are preserved, package it as necessary, and accommodate the needs of the market," Hong Yi-xiang said.

"Vacuous displays are not real, this kind of student I won't accept."

"It's not that serious. What we experience today will all be a part of history. This is an inevitable process. Just maintain your equanimity and it will all turn out fine," Hong Yi-xiang said.

"I understand all these arguments. It's just that our generation is so clueless. Putting up with crap for an entire lifetime. We are getting older and we still have to put up with it."

"Ai! Me too, it's not that I can't adapt, it's just I am not happy about it."

"Yes. Just not happy about it."

"Brothers, our generation has all experienced the trials of the great war and the mass exodus, we survived such suffering, and you still sweat this stuff?" Hong Yi-xiang asked rhetorically.

"That's right. So, it should be even clearer, people can't fight the tide of the times. Isn't it?"

"It's as you said. When I was young, I always thought that I could right myself among crashing waves and hold my stance on the top of a 100' bamboo pole. Who knew my whole life I was just drifting with the current."

"This is something I also worry about. When I was young, martial arts practice paid attention to respecting the teacher and the Way. By the time I became a master, the era had changed. If you become a teacher, now you must respect the students. How come it was never my generation's turn? Really, fucking A."

"Someone is spouting obscenities."

"Yi-xiang, sorry, I'm sorry."

"It's okay. In fact, it is not easy to be able to drift with the flow, it requires strong and flexible fortitude. Like a Western surfer, relying on just a board of wood so he can stand on the top of the wave and ride the wind and surf. Isn't this also 'going with the wave'? Providing you grab the correct angle and speed, people can stand on the waves," Hong Yi-xiang admired.

"Yi-xiang. You are young and have new ideas. We are old and I'm afraid we don't have the capacity to change."

"Don't think about it this way, you might be long in years, but don't let your mind be old. This is adaptation, not a change of principles, so don't be so serious. What young people want is really not that much, why not satisfy them first. Wait until some opportunity in the future to think of a method to guide them in the right direction. The route is just a little circuitous," Hong Yi-xiang said.

"Younger and older brothers all so advise. What else good do you old stick in the muds have to gripe about, if not the twists in the road? Drink up! Drink this year's newly picked Spring tea, it is a specialty of Alishan Shizhuo." Brother Wang, who oversaw making tea, exhorted everyone to drink the freshly steeped tea leaves.

"Alright. Drink tea and listen to the old tall tales. Life is one big enjoyment."

"No. I would rather like to hear Yi-xiang chat some more about new concepts.

We have little information in the countryside. Every time I come to Taipei, I spend a whole year digesting what I've learned."

"That's a symptom of your physiology deteriorating, leading to indigestion. Ha-ha-ha…"

"Go ahead, Yi-xiang."

"My kids often show me nature documentary videos about the world of wildlife. These documentaries are really filmed very well," said Hong Yi-xiang.

"What are you doing watching those boring things?"

"At first, I wanted to see how various wild animals fight for survival. I wanted to learn more about their techniques and ways of exerting power," said Hong Yi-xiang.

"This method is good. It is worthwhile to draw on their experience. After this, I will also put a video player in the gym and research together with the students."

"Continue."

"In nature, the normal state is the use of force to determine everything. Combative struggle happens anytime and anywhere, sometimes for food, sometimes for mating, sometimes for leadership. In short, in that world, only to the victor goes the spoils. I also inadvertently discovered that even ferocious beasts like tigers and lions, when they determine they can't beat an opponent, they will turn around and run without demur. They will certainly not fight to the death for the sake of face," Hong Yi-xiang said.

"This technique doesn't need to be taught by lions, I am also very good at it."

"Ha-ha-ha…"

"I know what you mean. What about if you can't escape?"

"It's the same as plants, although they cannot move, but when they encounter unavoidable natural disasters changing the landscape, they will find ways to change themselves and survive into the future," said Hong Yi-xiang.

"You want to turn me into a mental vegetable, that's easy, but I am afraid wanting me to learn how to change is harder than asking me to climb to Heaven."

"No. There are many ways, it's a matter of attitude, providing you can let go. Take plants as an example, when they encounter an unavoidable threat, some will choose to change themselves, let themselves become smelly, disfigured, or hard. They become more difficult for an intruder to penetrate," Hong Yi-xiang said.

"Like cactus and durian?"

"Yes. But some plants will adopt a completely different strategy. They make themselves more aromatic, fresher, sweeter, and more delicious, and in so doing attract more invaders to eat it," Hong Yi-xiang said.

"Isn't this suicidal, taking a dead-end path?"

"No. They envelop a larger number of seeds in the sweet and juicy flesh, thus turning every intruder into a host, to spread their offspring with the movement of the host, seeking a better environment for the next generation," Hong Yi-Xiang said.

"This method is too unsanitary."

"Why?"

"Because won't it be mixed in a pile of shit?"

"Ha-ha-ha! Survival. If it works, use it."

"That's right. Who would do this if there was a better way."

"Master Zhang used to remind us: 'If you can't beat 'em, just run!' Later, when I taught foreigners, I learned that they have a completely different concept. They say, 'If you can't beat 'em, join 'em.' These are all expedient adaptations, don't pay too much heed to how you feel about the process. Think about a little longer term and you shouldn't feel the diversion is intolerable," Hong Yi-xiang said.

"Yeah. Well said. Really interesting."

"Ai! Isn't it just the two choices of shit-smell or death?"

"Not necessarily. There are many methods, just think about it and they will come up," said Hong Yi-xiang.

"That's right. When you encounter this kind of mega-trend, you can only submit yourself to its flow, otherwise you will be crushed into meat paste."

"In fact, many things are not absolutely black and white. Recently, I have made some small discoveries when I studied the Taiji emblem," Hong Yi-xiang said.

"Oh? I'm interested in this, let's hear it."

"The two Taiji fish on the Taiji emblem, don't they interlock in two semicircles with one convex when the other is concave?" Hong Yi-xiang said.

"Yes. This represents an endless cycle, growing, and multiplying ceaselessly."

"When most people see the two colors of black and white, they will mistakenly think that the world is either black or white, either right or wrong," said Hong Yi-xiang.

"Isn't that the case?"

"Supposing it is. Then in the emblem, to demarcate black and white, why isn't a straight line used to cut the circle in half?" asked Hong Yi-xiang.

"Actually, I have seen ancient illustrations of the Taiji symbol where it was cut in half, but in later eras the change was made to the curved line."

"Eh. Yet another example of the evolutionary change in our understanding. This is symbolic of kinetic energy. If you use a straight line to cut the Taiji circle in half, then the endless dynamic will stop. It is not the idea that Taiji is meant to convey," Hong Yi-xiang said.

"Yes. So, you can't just look at the still image."

"Oh, really? So how do you look at it?"

"Take a look." Hong Yi-xiang casually drew a Taiji diagram about twenty centimeters in diameter on the paper, used the drawing pen to penetrate the center of the Taiji emblem, and then picked up the pen that pierced the Taiji emblem in front of everyone. He turned it slowly.

"Do you see the two Taiji fish, one black and one white, chasing each other's tails?" Hong Yi-xiang said.

"Interesting. I've practiced Taiji all my life, but this is the first time I have seen this trick indeed hiding such a mysterious secret, that it can be played like this."

"More than that. I'll spin it even faster. Okay. What do you see now?" Hong Yi-xiang prompted.

"Faster, the fish become blurry, and you can't see them clearly."

"So, what *do* you see?" Hong Yi-xiang asked.

"It blurs into one ball. There is nothing left."

"Okay. Don't pay attention to the fish. Are you seeing black? Or white?" Hong Yi-xiang asked.

"Neither. It's…"

"It's neither black nor white. How to say?"

"Neither black nor white, isn't it gray, idiot?"

"Yes, yes. It's gray."

"Okay. I'll stop it, now everybody look again, see how many colors are there on the Taiji emblem now?" Hong Yi-xiang asked.

"What's the trick? Isn't it the original black and white?"

"Then where did the gray you saw just now come from and where did it go?" Hong Yi-xiang asked.

"Isn't it caused by your turning?"

"Then why is it missing now?" Hong Yi-xiang.

"Because you brought it to a stop."

"So?" Hong Yi-xiang said waiting for them to catch on. "So, the world is not what we see with the naked eye. Between black and white, there is obviously a blurred world that is yet to be explored and defined. All the problems and all the possibilities encountered between black and white, perhaps the solutions to them are hidden in that fuzzy, blurred space."

"You mean there is a third thing between black and white?"

"Hmm. It can only be regarded as a broad theory," Hong Yi-xiang said. "Because at different speeds, gray will develop more different shades. Look…," Hong Yi-xiang said.

"Yeah. That's right."

"Therefore, when abnormal changes occur due to shifts in the environment or our own illness or aging, then it means we need to adapt," Hong Yi-xiang said.

"Use change to drive change, isn't that your Baguazhang tactic?"

"Change or Not Change, yes. Also seeming to change without changing, seeming not to change but changing, these are all possibilities within this idea. YiZong martial art pursues creating new possibilities in the midst of change, so it emphasizes that 'two opposite sides must exist at the same time' and 'when things reach an extreme, they can only move in the opposite direction' these two important principles. In other words, when a crisis arises, don't be affected by negative emotions and only see the harm, but not the opportunities and infinite possibilities hidden within," said Hong Yi-xiang.

"Within our systems there are similar boxing principles."

"Although our schools are different from each other, when viewed from the pinnacle of skill, they are in fact different routes to the same destination. The difference is only the starting point. It is said in the Five-Character Rhyming Mantras:

> If double weighting is not working, single weighting is successful;
> Single and double alternation should be quick, victory is in your grasp;
> Focus on intent more than strength, dodge the heavy and counter the light.
> Focused on intent, not power, deliberately, like a cat
> Determine arcs and angles, a thousand pounds four ounces overcomes;
> Approach the opponent from the outside, then surge in, small angles can have big effects.
> When stepping in directly, the front foot seizes the rear ankle;
> The hindfoot follows the front, the hand attack will be successful;
> Take advantage of the side to enter, success is ruthless;
> Changes should be fast and decisive, and the force should issue from the dantian;
> The outside angle is best, seize the outside then decisively surge in.
> Give birth to techniques according to opportunity, change is limitless;
> Too much or too little neither works, forget this and fail;
> No good comes of the martial, do not let your outside reveal your abilities or intent;
> The miraculous in martial art is when what is seen is not what occurs.
> The operation of the Yin Yang Way, its wonder and profundity is contained above.

"Among them, these simple words, 'Focus on intent more than strength, dodge the heavy and counter the light,' these simple words have a great impact on my life," Hong Yi-xiang said.

"Then I'll also share a story."

"Come and add some tea, moisten your throat first."

"On a bright moonlit autumn night, in an ancient Buddhist temple deep in the mountains, there was a group of stone-carved arhat statues chatting under the moon. An arhat pointed to the bright moon in the sky and asked everyone, 'Is the moon moving? Or are the clouds moving?' Someone answered 'Of course, the clouds are moving, because clouds are lighter and move as soon as the wind blows.' Another Arhat did not agree with him. They believed that movement and weight were not related. One cannot use this kind of false benchmark to judge right and wrong. You must use objective proofs to be convincing. Everyone was silent for a while when another Arhat pointed to the branch of a tree in front of him and said that the branch is fixed. Use it as the point of reference to prove that the cloud is moving, not the moon. This idea was immediately demonstrated and a consensus almost reached, but just as the Arhats nodded in agreement, one of the venerables with profound knowledge spoke to correct their perspective."

"Oh. Can there be yet a different perspective?"

"He said: 'It's not the cloud that is moving, or the moon that is moving, but your mind that is moving!'"

"It makes sense. Ai. Exploring the principles of the world is like peeling an onion, layer after layer, and you can exhaust a lifetime and not penetrate the learning."

"Hold up a bit. How is it I don't feel it's just the clouds moving, the moon moving, or the mind moving alone?"

"That must be the earth moving. Hey. Isn't the earth moving all the time?"

"Old brother, what you said doesn't sound like Zen. May I ask what kind of sect you are from?"

"Do you really want to know? Okay, I'll tell you. This is 'The More Things Change, the More They Stay the Same Sect.'"

"Ha-ha-ha…"

Hong Yi-xiang visiting Kyoto Japan with good friends Mr. Zheng and Chen Xi-zhao, 1972.

Hong Yi-xiang and old tea drinking partner Jiang Kai-fu on an excursion, 1980.

86– MOVIES, GONGFU, AND TEA PART 2

The object is easy to break if it is too hard, easy to be bound if it is too soft.

—*Xunzi*, Exhortation to Learning

Scene: Anxi Street

"We should complain less and look on the bright side. The benefits brought about by the change movies drive must be more than the drawbacks," Hong Yi-xiang said, "Buy a ticket and go to the cinema to take a gander. Only then will you know how it affects the world."

"In order, as Sunzi said, to 'know yourself and know the enemy'?"

"I'm still with 'the enemy hidden and I am exposed.' It's not that serious. Watching a movie is watching a movie. Can't you just go for your own pure entertainment?"

"Aren't they all stupid stories in which bad guys beat good guys, and then the good guys train in some unique martial skill and wreak vengeance?"

"That's right. But you're leaving out quite a bit. Don't forget, the course of the plot unfolding is the most important key."

"Have you seen the *Kung Fu* series on TV recently? It's really good. It has the artistic conception and depth of Neijiaquan. The only regret is that we have to rely on the foreigner's touch to depict Chinese martial arts and philosophy in film."

"This series boosts Chinese martial arts a bunch. It lets young people know that in addition to practicing martial arts, through the process of hard, painful cultivation and training, gongfu also imperceptibly enhances our perspective and level of understanding of the totality of life. A good boxing teacher should also play the role of a good spiritual mentor. This is where we should be working hard," Hong Yi-xiang said. "A movie is a very good vehicle, like a ship—today loaded with this, tomorrow loaded with that, the cargo will never be limited. If you know how to navigate, it can magnify your ideas and influence by tens of thousands fold."

"You guys, you're like mental vegetables."

"What are you braying about?"

"Isn't this a deluded attempt to use natural enemies as hosts?"

"You mean I use a movie as a vehicle. Ha-ha-ha…You're not senile! Your brain is firing on all cylinders."

"Don't keep burying your head in the sand like an ostrich, bird brain. After drinking tea, I invite everyone to watch a movie together. I will tell the kids to go buy the tickets first. A-Han, which one is good to see?" Hong Yi-xiang asked.

"*Way of the Dragon*. Bruce Lee stars in it," Ze-han said.

"Is it good?"

"Just started showing, it's super awesome, I'm afraid it is all sold out now."

"Then let's watch the next show. This evening, I'm inviting everyone to eat red yeast eel, dumpling soup, and Fuzhou dishes at Another Heaven."

"No. This round is on me, since Yi-xiang is inviting everyone to watch a movie, I'll pick up the tab for dinner."

"Good!"

"Pa, do you want to call Black Snake and 'squeeze' some tickets first?" Ze-han asked.

"Go and wait in line, how would I feel right troubling people with such a small thing," said Hong Yi-xiang.

"Come. It's still early, let's switch to this newly picked fresh spring tea."

"Which tea?"

"Pengfeng—Wind-Puffed-Up Tea."

"Eh?"

"It's also called Oriental Beauty Tea! My wife's mother's family has land in Emei, and she grows it herself."

"Eh! The brew is bright red, so beautiful."

"That's why the Queen of England praised it as Oriental Beauty Tea."

"Is that so? It's not your own BS puffing it up."

"It's true. 'Wind Puffed Up' is because this kind of tea does not undergo the process of rolling, so the tea is fluffier than Oolong tea, even a can stuffed full feels light and empty in your hand, just like it was deliberately pumped with air to cheat people, and so it was crowned with such a funny name."

"I thought it meant if I drink it, it will puff me up."

"Your belly is so big, even if you don't drink it, it's bloated."

"Ha-ha-ha…"

"Eh. A little fruitier flavor than ordinary tea leaves. A good cuppa."

"This kind of tea was originally an undesirable discard of tea farmers."

"Huh? You take tea that was discarded by others to offer guests."

"Let him finish."

"Because my own tea plantation sprays no pesticides, there are some small bugs in the tea bushes. Among them is a small bug called green leaf cicada and they like best to chew on the new leaf shoots. Once this kind of bug has taken a bite of the tender leaves, enzymes in the saliva of the little green leafhopper will wither away the pistils. Tea farmers, because they are afraid that it will affect the appearance and quality of their tea, deliberately pick out these bitten withered leaves. Mountain folk are thrifty by nature and cannot bear to throw them away, so they keep them to make their own big family pot of tea… Unexpectedly, a wholesaler merchant brought a few tea experts to visit the tea plantation. After inadvertently drinking its heavenly flavor, he mistakenly thought that we were hoarding the best stuff, deliberately keeping the best tea at home to drink. Later, after research, news of this kind of tea slowly spread, and it became the hottest first-class tea on the market, especially because of the value added by the small green leafhoppers, and indirectly it provided proof that no pesticides are used. The endorsement of the British Royal family is even more precious."

"You let us drink tea the same tea as the Queen of England. Wow! What an honor."

A tea leaf bitten by a small green bug, because of abnormal fermentation and missing bits, was originally regarded as rotten tea, unpresentable, and unsellable. After the packaging of the story and the artificial hype, it became highly prized by the British Royal family, and became a good tea loved by all. It can be seen that the determination of good or bad is not based on the quality of the tea itself, and the relationship between good tea and bad tea is also not so absolute and unchangeable. "Good tea" might be abandoned due to a lack of understanding, while ordinary, nothing-special tea leaves with beautiful packaging and hype can be touted as noble and expensive. And these miniscule, little green leafhoppers are for tea, just like what movies are for gongfu. If you don't know how to make good use of its value, you just treat it as a pest. You must know how to make good use of its benefits, then a rising tide lifts all boats and there is the advantage of mutual support.

"We brothers drink tea and crack watermelon seeds with our teeth, but what we *savor* is the mellow and rich affection among friends. No matter how highly valued is my tea, it is not as valuable as the friendship we share among brothers. If you all don't find it too difficult to swallow, I will have the delivery man take two catties of tea per person to your homes next week."

"Excellent. Let me thank you now."

"Brothers. What's this, a trifle? Every time I come to Yi-xiang's house I have so much to be grateful for, this is an appropriate way to thank everyone."

"Ai! Everyone only cares about the tea in the cup, but nobody has noticed that Brother Yi-Xiang's purple clay teapot must have a story behind it, wasn't it thrown by a famous potter?"

"It's an Yixing pot, but it's not from a famous potter. It was given to me by an American student the other students have taken to calling Sweet Potato," Hong Yi-xiang said.

"Is that the foreigner who busted up a bunch of dojos and hurt people?"

"He's a young Western man crazy about martial arts, but his method of handling interpersonal relationships leaves much to be desired. He wants to study with me," Hong Yi-xiang said.

That weekend, this group of internationally ranked senior martial artists whose black belt degree ranks together measured in the many dozens, who came up from Kaohsiung, and Tainan, Taichung, Hsinchu, Taoyuan, and other places by train, gathered at Hong Yi-xiang's gym at No. 36 Anxi Street in Taipei City to participate in the "Old Fist Club" that had four meetings at fixed times in the year. Different from the past gatherings of tea drinking, chatting, showing off moves, and fine dining, on this occasion, with the encouragement of Hong Yi-xiang, together they went to buy tickets and enter a movie theater, an unprecedented evening.

Among these seniors, there were people who had not seen a movie for more than twenty years. In the pitch darkness where they could not see their hands in front of their faces, these twelve, among the most influential masters and lineage holders of martial arts schools in Taiwan, were all fascinated by the new martial arts rising star, Bruce Lee, performing on the silver screen. They all felt pores that had been blocked for a long time open up with their goosebumps. The movie, the ups and downs of the plot and the battle cries of Bruce Lee when he punched and kicked, like raging waves battering a shore, time and again lifted the bold and unrestrained blood and passion they had felt as young men.

They couldn't help but look sideways to observe the young audience next to them. So profoundly inspired were they by Bruce Lee's acting and gongfu, they completely forgot their rejection and prejudice against Kung Fu movies before entering the cinema and observed in minute detail the powerful influence of movie art on the future world. A fictitious plot and characters, under the manipulation of this process and technology, undergoing various film tricks and processing, can deliver such a strong impact into the real world. Its influence completely crossed cultures, language, race, stigma, age, gender, beliefs, national boundaries, time, and space.

Finding himself amid this torrent of great change, Hong Yi-xiang understood that as the leader of a lineage, facing the wheel turning in an epoch of transformation, he could not be just awe-inspiring. He must also come up with detailed countermeasures and smart propositions. He must humbly explore the possible impact of this emerging force in the world. He deeply understood that what he was facing was no longer a single opponent in the ring, but the changes and impacts of an entire era. He could not solely rely on his personal willpower and strong body to make a stand against It. It was a mighty force—all the king's horses and all the king's men. It was the trend of the world and its people. It was another flood bigger than the one after 1949. In the face of this unopposable momentum, only by choosing the precise angle in which to insert himself could he harmonize and coexist with It, create mutual benefit with It. Only in this way could he find a new way. But how could he find a new method to serve the tastes of the people of the new era without departing from the core principles of Neijiaquan?

He must humbly return to the embrace of Nature and learn from Creation a new way of survival, making Neijiaquan transform into something as interesting, as useful, as universally appealing, and all-embracing, just like the movies. Otherwise, traditional internal gongfu would become like the dinosaurs at the end of the Cretaceous Period. Although they were mighty enough to be called the Masters of the Planet, ultimately, they could not escape the misfortune of extinction, eventually becoming just bones and fossils in a museum for future generations to ogle. It was necessary to learn modern languages and tools, and to make good use of two-way interactive communication, so as to give Internal martial arts a more approachable new-era appearance. But was this a compromise? Or an evolution? During his lifetime, he was afraid that there would be no clear answer.

He silently observed his son sitting beside him, intently watching the movie. The light beam spread by the film projector clearly outlined his lean silhouette. A doubt suddenly welled up in Hong Yi-xiang's heart. He didn't understand this obstinate, disobedient boy. Was he just trying to chase the trend of the times? Or did he really observe something in the movie? A new opportunity and turning point? Or the 'possibility' of a lifetime pursuit?

"Ai! If I pass the martial art baton to him, I'm afraid this kid…it's safer yet to have A-zhou and A-pei."

Facing the rapid changes in the macro-environment and with the family business declining day by day, Hong Yi-xiang clearly sensed his gradual loss of influence over and grasp of this changing world. He could not resist the rise of an indescribable anxiety about how his children would provide for themselves in a new and unfamiliar future world. This uneasiness hidden deep in his heart never stopped swirling in the subliminal currents of his mind, just like the two fish, one black one white, on the Taiji emblem chasing each other's tails to take a bite, continuously, always, endlessly cycling…

87- OLD BAI

Howard Brewer, Chinese surname Bai, was an elder brother disciple in the school, so he was called "Old Bai" by our brothers and sisters. Old Bai and my father were about the same age. After he retired as a senior intelligence officer in the US Navy, he chose to stay in Taiwan to develop his own business. For decades he followed Hong Yi-xiang to practice "Yi Zong Tang Shou," and he always contributed money and effort to the gymnasium, with no complaints and no regrets. Although my father did not want to encourage any money exchange between the brothers and sisters in the school, Howard was always the eldest brother or godfather of all the young foreign students who came to Taiwan to pursue their "kung fu dreams." He provided accommodation, monetary assistance, and did not expect anything in return. This kind of person in the Western world, not to mention in Taiwan, is indeed a rare outlier.

Scene: Yongle Elementary School

THAT YEAR, FOR THE TWENTIETH ANNIVERSARY OF THE GYM, MY father asked me to pair up with Howard Brewer to perform a two-man facing form on television. But at nearly 190 centimeters in height, he was too tall. At that time, there was no suitable partner to perform the Xingyiquan "Body Guarding Cannon" two man facing form with him at the gym. In the end, I was chosen mainly because I was good with my feet and could make up for the gap in height.

In Hong Yi-xiang's martial arts system, Old Bai was not the most senior (in terms of earliest arrival at the school) foreign disciple, but none of the brothers did not know Old Bai. So, in this huge martial arts family, he was the "eldest brother" of the three brothers of our Hong family, and also the eldest brother of all the senior brothers in the school.

Old Bai could speak fluent Japanese, so the communication between him and Hong Yi-xiang was unimpeded. But his communication with me always remained at the Lesson One level of a middle school English course.

Fortunately, this is not a problem in martial arts. Every time we encountered a communication problem, I would spout many English words and let the old man arrange and combine them by himself, adding some of my facial expressions and body movements. As a retired senior US Navy intelligence officer, he decoded this transmission. The partnership between the two of us was developed on the basis of this blurry communication. After we practiced together for a week or two, we discovered that the problems integrating the form were getting bigger and bigger, because he was really too tall. If one wanted to integrate the "Body Guarding Cannon" form according to the design of its techniques, huge gaps created by the difference in speed and distance were difficult to resolve.

Later, after we communicated several times like a chicken and duck clucking at each other, I unilaterally decided that he agreed with me to use the "Body Guarding Cannon" as the main structure, but redesign new moves to replace some repetitions that were not exciting or difficult, and to add high kicks and roundhouse kicks that were rarely used in Neijia Quan at that time. In addition, we also tried to adjust the speed of the sparring action, deliberately adding some slow-motion moves in the fast sparring, adding some delicate and hidden movements of Neijiaquan, and deliberately amplifying its stage effect. This special way of performing made up nicely for the difference in height between the two of us. From then on, he no longer had to strain his spine to bend all the way over to my height, and I didn't need to judge his speed.

So, Old Bai and I practiced against each other for nearly half a year, from 19:00 to 22:00 every night, six nights a week. The more we practiced the more skillful the moves, the more exciting the movements became. I sincerely thank him for his generosity and tolerance. My nitpicking, quirky personality was tolerated time and again, over and over, repeatedly... constantly revising the facing movements, but I never understood the consternation these revisions caused him. At that moment, I convinced myself: our performance must be the highlight of the entire anniversary show.

It's just that I never thought that people are not as good at calculating outcomes as heaven. On the day of the performance, Old Bai arrived late for some reason, leaving no opportunity for a pre-show rehearsal. He hurried to the studio to change into his uniform, he didn't have the slightest moment to adjust his frame of mind. Forced to perform in a hurry, the result of the performance can be imagined, he forgot the moves. After less than ten sequences of our fist and foot, he got stuck. I will never forget the suffocating feeling of time and space freezing at the same time.

After being booed off the stage, I ignored him for nearly half a year. I couldn't forgive him for being late and forgetting things, and I didn't want to know why he was late that day. I didn't think there was any reason or redemption that could make up for the grievance and humiliation we suffered at that time.

Until one day, he asked me to talk, a chicken and duck clucking at each other again. He made no explanation for what happened that day, he just told me:

"That's right! We screwed up a performance we'd been preparing for so long. So what? Why should we give up continuing to practice? Abandon the moves we spent so much time designing, modifying, and communicating? I don't think it's necessary for us to punish ourselves in such a self-defeating way because of one mistake. We should keep practicing and correcting. Until it's perfect. Only in this way will we have a chance to reverse this loser's mentality and lift this gloom. Only then will we have a chance to win back the applause with a better performance."

So, every night, our figures, one tall and one short, began to use different practice speeds in the auditorium and playground of Yongle Elementary School again, while I continued my incessant modifications.

Three months later, in the KPS Television studio on Dunhua South Road, we accepted the invitation of the TV station to give our first public performance after starting again. I remember that the KPS studio was crowded with employees from various departments of their company, scrambling to watch our wonderful performance. In the following six months, we successively appeared on several large-scale TV shows and interviews. It was not until after the Shaw Brothers Hong Kong film studio sought me out to make a film, a proposal rejected by my father, that we stopped all public performances.

I recalled this history with my elder brother Ze-zhou, after going to visit Old Bai before his death. On the hospital bed, the American was no longer as tall and sturdy as he used to be. The frailty and shrinkage of old age made me feel a pain in my heart. This thin old man with silver hair in front of me had overlapped my life for forty or fifty years. He tolerated my naivety and arrogance, taught me to face setbacks with a broader mind, and let me know that failure is not the end of the world, because only after failure will we have enough determination to challenge higher difficulties and opportunities.

Because of the extended experience of getting along and communicating with him, I had greater wisdom and courage to face various difficult challenges and tests in the workplace.

During my tenure at Jihsun Financial Holdings, I dealt with the procurement of the core banking software system. Facing the arrogance and threats of the German supplier, I had enough composure and courage to see at a glance through the hidden costs layered within the false hype and shaved off the difference of nearly NT$100 million in cost in one go. It also allowed me to accompany Mr. Cai Chen-yang and Ms. Lai Ying-li to Singapore to communicate with a design company during the renovation project of the Taipei Sheraton Hotel. When facing a tall and arrogant European catering consultant, I had enough courage to request the boss to take a break for a smoke, during which time I dressed down the consultant, allowing him to understand what he did not understand about Chinese banqueting and the deficiencies of his approach. Through the accurate translation of my colleague, he gave up his stubborn resistance and complied.

If I didn't have the benefit of the dribs and drabs of interaction and wisdom accumulated in the past from Old Bai, I would not have been able to face all kinds of challenges and bullying in the workplace.

When I went to see him in the hospital, I was not sure if Old Bai still clearly recognized me. Would he recognize me as that arrogant and ignorant little fart from way back when? I was not sure if he could still remember everything we'd been through together? At that moment, I could only hope that he would receive the best care and blessing from his Buddhist monk.

Old Bai passed on shortly thereafter. I sincerely hope that having completed his mission in the human world, he successfully found the old tea table that my father has set up in the other world and has reconnected with my father and the martial art sages in the gym there, to sip tea and talk of gongfu.

Howard Brewer, friend, brother, Old Bai—Rest in Peace.

Howard Brewer pays his respects at Hong Yi-xiang's grave, 1994.

88– THE WESTERN FANATIC OF MARTIAL ARTS PART 1[28]

For a species with no natural enemies, modesty is an abstract concept difficult to comprehend.

Scene: Yongle Elementary School

"Your friend has watched too many movies. We don't accept challenges here," said the assistant instructor.

"Why?" the female visitor asked.

"This is a place to practice Chinese boxing. If you want to make a challenge, the only correct way is to compete in the ring," said the assistant.

"Why do other martial gyms allow it then?" the female visitor asked.

"Well, then please go find one which allows it, but not here," said the assistant.

"Isn't this Hong Yi-xiang's gymnasium? Let him speak for himself," said the female guest.

"Why would he want to see you two? Miss, do you know Hong Yi-xiang?" the assistant instructor said.

"Since he is considered a master of martial arts, he should dare to accept the challenge of a young martial artist. Fearful from head to tail, is that the way of a great master?" said the female guest.

"Who said that the master is obligated to give you a martial demonstration. We practice martial arts here, we don't fight to show off. There is the door," the assistant instructor responded.

"He flew over especially from Japan. Why not let him give it a try?" the female visitor asked.

"Miss, exchanging blows, fists and feet flying, isn't like a wet-market where you can sample the vegetables, it's very dangerous," said the assistant.

"If one can't sample the sparring, then how do you prove you're qualified to teach people?" the female visitor asked.

"We prove our strength in the arena. You tell him that if he is really interested, he should do it the correct way. We have no need and no interest to prove

---

28 Chapters 88–91 regarding the foreigner Mr. K., aka Sweet Potato, were kindly translated by Marcus Brinkman OMD, who trained directly with Master Hong and also knew the subject of these chapters after he returned to the USA.

anything to him," said the assistant.

"He said 'if he doesn't fight he's a coward,' afraid of losing," the female visitor added, further provoking the assistant instructor.

"In this case, just go ahead, do and say whatever you like. That is your freedom. Finally, I repeat, if he is interested in martial arts, we welcome him to join in the practice, but if he just wants to provoke a fight, then no need to waste his time," said the assistant.

Yongle Elementary School Auditorium was an early training base of Hong Yi-xiang. Besides the specialized training of America's Vietnam GIs, it was as well the training base for representatives of Taipei's National Martial Arts Team. Almost all the players who participated in the national martial arts championships were trained here. Therefore, in addition to ordinary students, many of the people who practiced here were the main players of the sparring competitions and were ranked as assistant instructors. Most of them were current champions for their weight class.

The training here at night was always open to outsiders, free to observe, but often times, young martial artists admiring the master's reputation dropped by to issue challenges. Then, when they lost, they would go to file a complaint with public security, simply increasing a great deal of meaningless trouble. From that time forward, Hong Yi-xiang had strictly prohibited all the instructors from casually accepting challenges from outsiders to avoid disputes. On one particular day, a man and a women couple, who had previously come to visit the training hall several times, showed up just as two-person fighting drill practice commenced. The foreign man wanted the local girlfriend he brought along to step forward and issue a challenge for him. Because the tone was not very friendly, the originally well-intentioned assistant instructor who had kindly received them, lost patience with their impolite pestering, and turned around to continue training.

"Mr. K is a very powerful martial artist. He has practiced karate, Taekwondo, Chinese boxing, and various other martial arts. He is also an Indian yoga exponent. While standing upright on one foot he can kick dozens of times in succession…," said the female visitor.

"Enough. We're not interested in listening to this. If he wants to let people know how terrific he is, he should advertise in the newspaper," said the assistant.

"You're mistaken. Mr. K's reputation is well earned. There is no need to advertise. In Taiwan and Japan, he has defeated dozens of well-known martial artists. Your martial arts academy has such a tremendous reputation, however if you don't dare to fight then it's really quite awkward," replied the female visitor.

"Miss, be careful, talking such nonsense can stir up trouble, you're hurting his case, you know?" the assistant said.

"He said in Taiwan there remains no match for him. If even Hong Yi-xiang's training academy won't dare fight, then all of Taiwan must be the same. Such a disappointment," she said.

"I don't want to bicker with you anymore, the two of you please leave now," said the assistant.

"What's going on? Why do you talk to guests like this?" Hong Yi-xiang's eldest son, Hong Ze-zhou had just completed the physical training class for the competitors and was leading the team onto the mats for the next wave of sparring practice. This unpleasant dialogue was unfolding just as he was at the entryway of the door.

"Big Brother. This foreigner continues his senseless pestering, keeps demanding a challenge," the assistant said.

"Hey, who is he to you?" Ze-zhou asked the woman.

"I'mmm…" The female visitor gazed at the eldest brother Ze-zhou as he entered the arena leading a herd of burly, bear waisted, tiger-backed athletes. She was momentarily awed by the powerful aura exuded by these beasts of prey. Combined with the awkwardness of addressing his question about her identity, her original words of empty boastful provocation deflated, and for a while her deep-seated dread arrested her tongue.

"Miss, no matter what your relationship is, we all respect it. But do you know the risk of dropping in to kick down the door of a studio? Let me ask, just in case he has a mishap, are *you* willing to be responsible, can you take responsibility?" Ze-zhou asked.

"This is just what he wants me to say. His aim is to study real gongfu, and he just hopes to first get a taste, so he doesn't waste his time and money. Foreigners speak relatively more direct, please don't misunderstand," the female visitor replied.

"It's okay, we can understand this. However, there is a great deal of risk in exchanging blows between different types of martial arts. He's a foreigner in Taiwan, so he probably doesn't have any family here. What if he suffers an injury, will you take care of him?" Ze-zhou asked.

"I only…but you needn't worry. He is really a good fighter, he can take a hit. I've seen him fight many times and he has never been injured before. So, can you make an exception this time. Let him have a go. He made a special trip to come to this famous location from Japan," she replied.

"Okay, in that case I'll discuss it with my father. But it won't be today," Ze-zhou replied.

"Okay. Sorry to trouble you. This is my phone number, if you can, please contact me at your convenience," the female visitor said.

※ ※ ※

"I know of this guy. Mr. Suzuki told me about his behavior in Japan, and the trouble he caused the Japanese martial arts world. He not only created a ruckus and assaulted people everywhere; he also swaggers around provoking people with his slanderous intentions. I heard that he had ruffled the feathers of the Yamaguchi Gumi, a Yakuza organization, and they were getting ready to settle the score. Within the Japanese martial art circles, they are however worried that in the off chance something really bad happens, there may be no way of explaining it to the American government, so they have purposely created a plan to lure him to Taiwan. They prepared a bribe for Taiwan gangsters to take care of him, passing the problem over to Taiwan, to avoid offending the American government. So, if we let those underworld-linked martial arts gyms fight with him first, then this guy will probably return to America in a pine box… Okay. So, contact him and tell him to come to the gym tonight," Hong Yi-xiang said.

"Pa, do you want to notify some of the black belts to come over?" Ze-zhou asked.

"No need. Have a few younger contestants preparing for the provincial tournament come over and have a try, that's good enough. Just treat it as pre-training sessions before the competition. That's good. Along the way, have the police station dispatch someone to come for a look, just in case there is some kind of trouble afterwards," Hong Yi-xiang responded.

"Dad, can I take part?" Ze-zhou asked.

"What are you up to? Are you trying to save him? Or kill him?" Hong Yi-xiang said.

"I heard that this Sweet Potato once attacked Master Chang Dong-sheng, I just want to teach him with my own hands how to respect the old and honor the worthy," Ze-zhou said.

"This guy isn't necessarily a terrible person; he's just using an incorrect method. Although nothing short of fists and feet will subdue him, nothing said gets through to him, on the other hand don't go overboard, use just the appropriate degree and he should get it immediately," said Hong Yi-xiang.

"Right. That's also what I was thinking," said Ze-zhou.

"How could you think I don't know what's at the bottom of your heart? You are absolutely forbidden to enter the ring. You understand? Forbidden," said Hong Yi-xiang.

"Okay," Ze-zhou replied. However, if I'm never permitted to take on a challenge, then there's no need to teach me gongfu! However, this last heartfelt sentence he dare not speak out loud.

※ ※ ※

"The students in the gymnasium all pay tuition and come here to learn boxing. They are not obliged to accept a challenge. These ten players are preparing to participate in this year's Provincial Games. They are brown belt students and have an average of three years of martial training. They all agreed to accept your challenge. May I ask you, how much do you weigh?" Ze-zhou asked.

"He said that he weighs around eighty-five kilograms," said the female visitor.

"It doesn't look like it. At least over one hundred kilos," Ze-zhou said.

"He said he couldn't be more than one hundred kilos," she replied.

"Okay. In the interest of fairness, it is acceptable to move either up or down one weight class, choose any opponent you wish to challenge, please," Ze-zhou said.

The contestants ranged from fifty kilograms to more than ninety kilograms in the unlimited weight class and a total of ten people lined up awaiting the Mr. K challenge. After listening to Hong Ze-zhou's brief introduction and explanation, Mr. K first faced Hong Yi-xiang sitting at the table and politely bowed with some ceremony while stringing together a polite greeting in Japanese. Afterwards, like a diner at a buffet carrying a plate and surveying dishes, he eagerly looked back and forth at the ten willing to accept his challenge. This must have been his most formal and respectable challenge since he left Japan and began hunting in the martial arts halls and parks of Taiwan.

"Can I challenge this guy?" Mr. K asked.

"The opponent you have picked weighs no more than 55 kilograms. You are over one hundred kilograms. Are you okay with that?" Ze-zhou asked the Taiwanese student.

"Brother, no matter. I'll give it try," Chen Can-yao said.

"Okay. Then put on the protective gear and a few of you come and assist Sweet Potato for a moment," Ze-zhou said.

"Sorry. He says he has practiced qigong, so he does not need to wear protective gear. If your people are afraid of injury, you can wear it, he has no objection," said the female visitor.

"Okay. Then don't wear protective gear on either side. But for safety's sake, neither side can attack the opponent's head and groin area," Ze-zhou said.

"Any other requirements?" Ze-zhou asked.

"He said he wants full-contact strikes, not just touch and stop!" said the female visitor.

"Okay. Please tell him that our gymnasium does not have a touch and stop rule. Ask him to just let go, no problem," Ze-zhou said. "Chen Can-yao, the foreigner has practiced qigong, so just let your punches fly."

In the auditorium of Yongle Elementary School, no one knew how many challengers the Sweet Potato originally planned to take on, but if it was according to the habit he had when challenging Japanese and other Taiwanese gyms, he would have continued fighting until there were no opponents remaining before relenting. Only on that night, after his third opponent, he was unable to continue the fight because of the stomach cramps caused by a hit to the solarplexus and left ribs. His entire body leaned against the wall with an extremely pained expression on his face. At that moment, the girl who had accompanied him to the challenge had already shrunk aside and didn't know what to do.

"Find someone to take care of him," Hong Yi-xiang couldn't bear to see Mr.

K's misery and asked the assistant instructors to help him.

"Wait a bit. Don't move him. He made a special trip to see if we lived up to our reputation, isn't it so? Let him savor the moment a little longer. Let him really remember this feeling. Then he won't go everywhere stirring up trouble," Hong Ze-zhou said.

※ ※ ※

A few days later, the Sweet Potato carried a cardboard box with the words 'Chinese Mary Soap' written in simplified characters, containing a courtesy gift of several Yixing, purple sand teapots, wrapped in newspaper from the People's Daily of China, and a boxing book *Mizong Fist* written by Sun Xi-kun. This formal visit to Hong Yi-xiang was to ask for permission to enter the training hall to learn Eight Trigram Palm (Baguazhang).

"It seems that all your martial arts training doesn't seem to be of much help to you. As I watched you fight, all the moves you used were street fighting techniques, I really couldn't see any trace of the martial arts training in your past," Hong Yi-xiang said.

"Ordinary martial arts are too idealized, I want something that can really work, martial skill that's effective," Sweet Potato said.

"The routines provide the concepts and principles of offense and defense. Turning moves into effective combat skills requires a process of transformation and wisdom. That part must be done by yourself through hard work. Without this process of transformation, you can practice but it may not be useful," Hong Yi-xiang said.

"I understand this principle. The problem is that up to now, no one has been able to use proper martial arts to beat my street techniques. I can't persuade myself to practice a thing which has no practical value," Sweet Potato said.

"I can understand your feelings, and your logic isn't entirely wrong. But I think you should spend a little more time to master a martial art. Just like when you buy a new car, you have to learn to drive it before it will take you where you want to go, instead of doing nothing and just complaining about the car. When the ox cart does not go, if you want the cart to move, should you whip the ox? Or, should you whip the cart?" Hong Yi-xiang asked.

"I know what you mean. But I don't understand, why can't you just directly teach some practical things?" Sweet Potato asked.

"The Chinese say, 'The Master points to the door, Cultivation is up to you.' Because everyone has different talents and needs, teachers cannot tailor individual courses for each student. Therefore, instead of pushing others, it is better to push yourself, internalizing what you have learned to make it your own is the most important part of the martial arts training process. I think your problem lies here," said Hong Yi-xiang.

"But why do I think the things here are more suitable for my needs?" Sweet

Potato asked.

"It's just a coincidence. Maybe you won't think so in a while," Hong Yi-xiang said.

"Then I would like to ask Master Hong, why when martial artists encounter my style of street fighting, are they entirely unable to put theirs to use?" Sweet Potato asked.

"It's a matter of courage and insight. They may be intimidated by your reputation and build. That day, I saw that you picked someone smaller than you to fight. May I ask, if you face opponents who are bigger than you? Is that the way you fight?" Hong Yi-xiang said.

"Eh, what you said seems right. But I chose the small guy to fight because I think the value of martial arts should be the 'weak overcoming the strong and the few overcoming the many.' It's not that I purposely take advantage of them," Sweet Potato said disingenuously.

"That is indeed the purpose of martial arts, but the weight class should not be too different. A house cat cannot beat a leopard, no matter how strong it is, and a leopard cannot beat a lion, no matter how strong it is. If you have come to verify whether the gongfu is good or bad, don't you think it's a bit too demanding and unrealistic?" Hong Yi-xiang asked.

"I've overlooked this point, thank you for your reminder," Sweet Potato said.

"Victory or defeat in martial arts is inseparable from three key elements, one is courage, two is strength and three is skill. In fact, you are quite smart. You made good use of the first two advantages and won many challenges, and consequently you fell into a trap," said Hong Yi-xiang.

"I don't understand what you mean," he said.

"I mean, you use messy street fighting to test the practicality of martial arts, but in the end, you got caught up in the habits of street fighting. Think carefully, isn't it street fighting which you are best at right now? When you do meet a stronger and superior opponent, I would ask, where has the real gongfu, you originally learned, run off to?" said Hong Yi-xiang.

"Are you saying that to overcome street fighters, I have contrarily turned into a brawler?" Sweet Potato asked.

"This is the problem as I see it," Hong Yi-xiang said.

"Can it be changed?" he asked.

"As I just said, courage, strength, and skill, if you really want to change, you can only practice backwards. Start with your *skills* and work hard. This practice will gradually increase your ability to adapt. We often say that the boldness of execution stems from superb skills. With real ability, you naturally won't be afraid of messy brawlers. Just like riding a bicycle or driving a car, after learning, you naturally won't be afraid of the various situations that you encounter on the road, right?" Hong Yi-xiang said.

"But, with so many training halls, how can I tell which master is worth learning from?" Sweet Potato said.

"You can't always use your body in exchange. It's dangerous for you to do it this way. You're just fortunate so far that you haven't encountered an even more horrible outcome," Hong Yi-xiang said.

"I have no ill intent, but those people are too weak. I can't convince myself to learn from someone I don't respect," he said.

"You can't always use victory or defeat to decide everything. In that way, you can only find someone who can beat you, not someone who can really make you stronger," said Hong Yi-xiang.

"Then can you tell me a better way?" asked Sweet Potato.

"If you don't let go of your subjectivity, as I said, you may not be able to accept what you hear. What you need most now is to let go of the belligerent attitude and accept your transformation through martial arts. If you don't have this kind of determination, there is really no need to waste your time everywhere seeking skill," Hong Yi-xiang said. "Don't doubt whether the grapes that you have put in the barrel are good, just let them rest in oak barrels to ferment and age. After enough time, they will naturally become fine wine," Hong Yi-xiang said.

"I...," Sweet Potato muttered.

"In Japan, in Hong Kong, and in Taiwan, you gave people the impression that you are not a sincere seeker of skill, but a *ronin* who loves to brawl and stir up trouble. Unless you sincerely want to change, I don't think I can help you," Hong Yi-xiang said.

"In you I think I have found a skilled master with whom I can sincerely study, can you teach me Xingyiquan and Baguazhang?" Sweet Potato asked.

"It's not impossible, but you have to learn from the beginning," Hong Yi-xiang said.

"Master Hong, I already have a very good foundation and I don't want to repeat the basics. Can I pay a higher tuition to learn the highest-level courses with you alone?" Sweet Potato angled.

"A school isn't a restaurant. It's not 'you order what, we must teach you what.' Here we have our own logic and steps. If your cultivation doesn't reach the level of attainment, I will not teach you more helpful things," Hong Yi-xiang replied.

"Too drawn out. I really don't want to waste such a long time," he said.

"It seems that you still lack trust and confidence. Your mind is already full of such negative things, how can it contain anything else?" Hong Yi-xiang said.

"I just hope that I can learn the good stuff quickly. There is no other intention. In America there are many courses that are sold separately. I really have no bad intent," Sweet Potato said.

"With us, martial arts are taught, not sold," Hong Yi-xiang said.

"Okay. I will try to adapt to this idea," he said.

"What I really think you need right now is not to learn more Xingyiquan or Baguazhang. Perhaps these things may not help you. Maybe you already have enough martial arts to make you a top master, but you have never given them a chance to change *you*. Just like an anorexic patient, clearly, he has eaten a lot of stuff, but he still can't create any growth of flesh," said Hong Yi-xiang.

"I am willing to change myself, I am willing to sincerely follow your teachings," the Sweet Potato promised.

"I won't specifically reject or specifically welcome you to join my school, but if you want to become my disciple, you must stop your past behaviors, and you must not continue to make trouble outside," Hong Yi-xiang said.

The tediously long conversation continued through an interpreter from about two o'clock in the afternoon and ended just before dinner. Both sides exchanged their points of view without reservation. In the end, Hong Yi-xiang failed to discourage the Sweet Potato from the idea of studying martial arts with him, and he didn't seem to be too sure that he could shift this young man's various biased viewpoints. For the time being he should shelter him as a disciple, keep a close watch on him and guide him; maybe time truly could change all.

Hong Yi-xiang referees a full-contact provincial match, circa 1965.

89– THE WESTERN FANATIC OF MARTIAL ARTS PART 2

The key is not how much worldly knowledge you can cram down your throat, rather it is how much you can digest.

Scene: Yongle Elementary School

From that day on, the Sweet Potato entered Hong Yi-xiang's "*dao-guan*" (martial gym), to receive internal martial arts training. Under normal circumstances, new students would start with the four sets, Babuda, Balianshou, Bashou, and Bati, (Eight Step Hitting, Eight Linking Hands, Eight Hands, and Eight Kicks). These basic skills were courses tailored specifically for the US military who fought in the Vietnam War. The purpose was to enable them to learn the most basic and practical offensive and defensive techniques in the shortest period of time increasing their chances of survival on the battlefield.

Subsequently, with changes in the prevailing traditional environment, the generation of youth desired to do and study everything very quickly. After some fine-tuning, these movements were fashioned to be used in line with current martial trends and became a compulsory course for ordinary students. As these four sets of martial arts movements were easy to learn and not complicated, and their usage was simple and clear, they fit the needs of the younger generation. In addition, they are highly effective when used in *leitai* (full contact sparring) competitions.

Hong Yi-xiang was determined to embark on this path of martial arts reformation. A traditional martial artist, however, he couldn't help but consider the martial inheritance he received from the previous generation. The elder generation of masters who had passed the arts to him, later received orders from the government to decamp to the mountains to cultivate fruit orchards or to participate in the tunneling of the Central Cross Island Highway construction project. They discontinued the grand undertaking of handing down martial arts. Facing them one by one on their deathbeds, Hong made earnest commitments, there was no escaping the responsibility to shoulder the Confucian duty of passing down the history.

After thinking it over, he chose to use the newly developed routines as the adhesive agent gradually bonding the students to the orbit of traditional martial arts. As such, the external boxing and weapons taught by his elder generation became the compulsory courses for the second stage of training. Besides the above consideration of passing down the art, the main purpose was to enlist the External School of Boxing's focus on changing muscle, bone, and marrow exercises, enhancing the student's physical constitution and foundational power. After the students are comparatively mature in body and mind, and have a basic understanding of their body, strength, thoughts, and internal qi (energy), they may begin to receive the methods of internal martial arts.

Some of the high-level disciples already had a considerable degree of martial arts skill and some were chief instructors with over ten training halls or were military instructors. They were, however, willing to let go of their posturing and follow Hong Yi-xiang's teaching. It was simply a desire, through the guidance of a master, to penetrate and explore the deep mysteries of the Internal School of Boxing, completely different from young beginners' motivations to practice martial arts. Providing they could pass a qualification test, they could directly enter into the realm of internal boxing, starting from Xingyiquan, so as not to waste too much time repeating boxing basics. This was a necessary expedient and was mindful of some down-island students and foreign national students who could not stay in Taipei for a long time to learn boxing.

After years of exploration, Hong Yi-xiang had gradually developed a unique teaching model. He required beginner disciples to learn boxing with him more than three years to establish their own core concept based on their hidden potential, strengths, and weaknesses. Using this core concept as the central axis, it gradually developed into a complete, logical system.

In the third stage, various types of boxing forms were used to entice students to walk out with their own martial arts style, instead of stepping in the footprints of their predecessors and mechanically copying by rote. This also helped students avoid wasting time learning something that was not suitable for them, using twice the effort for half the result. Innate endowments differ. From outside appearance, average people can be divided into at least four major categories of tall, short, thin, and fat. In combination with the differences in people's inner personality, there are more types than can be quantified. If N is used to represent various personality types, then the differences between a single individual is at least at the Nth power of these four body types. As a single individual is a combination of various internal and external elements, if they are strictly required from beginning to end to practice the same martial art, then many potential and obvious talents will inevitably be suppressed, decline, and be completely lost. Therefore, after completing the required fundamental courses, students should be guided in a timely manner to develop boxing and techniques suitable for their potential talents.

The Twelve-Shaped Fist within Xingyiquan's boxing methods emulate nature's wild animals, of which there are five types of birds and seven types of beasts.

Their body type, natural instincts, and fighting characteristics are extracted as a model and used to fit the characteristics of human beings. Through the study of these models, it is hoped the deficiencies of human temperament and fighting skills can be reinforced. So, each person must use their heart to discover their own extraordinary potential and strive to establish a personal fighting method that fully expresses their unique quality. If not constructed on such logic, learning will be restricted by a unified expression of martial arts and severely suppress the development of self.

Take a big tree as an example. New students with different talents and gifts are like the roots of a tree buried in the ground; however, in accordance with unified teaching materials and training, everyone will converge within a single big tree trunk, learning the same art. At the same time, as one is simultaneously accepting these restraints, one directly progresses to the very top of the tree, then at its peak in space, at the very top, a stem will sprout and disseminate leaves. Thus can each branch and each leaf extract more air and sunlight resulting in the potential to blossom. From the convergence at the roots, to the unification and promotion in the trunk, to the opening and dispersing of branches, flowering, and fruiting, this is a complete learning process.

Over the years, this "Tree-like Development" concept was always Hong Yi-xiang's unique pedagogy principle—to pass on the Way. On the one hand, the operation of this mechanism helps students find the most suitable martial arts for their lifelong study. On the other hand, it also locates the most suitable descendants for the various kinds of martial arts, so that this Taoist tradition can continue to evolve.

Before he became a student of Hong Yi-xiang, the Sweet Potato had indeed acquired quite a wealth of martial arts accomplishments. After Hong Yi-xiang's examination, he agreed to start learning from Xingyiquan's third-level, internal martial art methods. To mend his past mistake of broad, mixed but shallow study, Hong Yi-xiang asked him to temporarily abandon his former subjectivity, start from the beginning and recognize his own hidden potential and needs anew, and establish his own offensive and defensive logic. Thus could he avoid the past problem of repeating the same error.

Would such a mechanism have the same strength of influence on this naturally pugnacious and extremely unstable foreigner? In fact, not many people were optimistic about his diligence and effort, and there were even many seniors within the martial arts circles who continued to lodge complaints and exert pressure upon the martial arts association and Hong Yi-xiang, not to accept this martial-arts *ronin* who caused trouble everywhere. Under pressure from many varied opinions, Hong Yi-xiang committed to keep the Sweet Potato 's behavior under strict control, with his understanding that any out-of-line behavior and the teacher apprentice relationship would be terminated immediately.

This simple verbal promise was of course unconditionally accepted by the Sweet Potato, who was eager to devote himself to Hong Yi-xiang's school. Ever since the day of his challenge when he suffered defeat in three consecutive matches, Sweet Potato had clearly realized that he was unbearably inadequate when facing orthodox internal martial arts. Especially when Hong Yi-xiang baldly pointed out the reality that he was unable to draw on any real gongfu to protect himself when faced with a strong counterattack. It was like an accurate deep and heavy left hook to the head. In his career of martial challenges, although Sweet Potato had won more than he lost, this caused him to realize that for many years, at the critical moment, he had never mounted a persuasive attack. No wonder people were always left with the negative impression that he relied only on his physique, like hard teeth biting soft tofu.

Faced with this series of facts and impacts, the Sweet Potato vowed to master all this profound knowledge that had brought him embarrassment, to use weakness to overcome strength as his classmates did and use skills to convince people. As a result, his absorption was like a dried sponge being placed back into the sea. As the scale of the gymnasium was large and there were a lot of people, there were many proficient fighters with whom to practice. This was tantamount to providing him with an ideal practice environment for combat.

Utilitarian and practical in nature, whenever he learned a new move, he would always find a rookie student to start testing the move's practicality and injuriousness. Moreover, the Sweet Potato showed no mercy to those newbies who were not yet aware of the situation, to the extent that during class breaks minor and major dustups with other students occurred. Although his ability to take advantage of others was limited, his popularity amongst the other students in the *daoguan* got worse by the day.

Eager to dig up more skills in the shortest period of time, the foreigner would often use holidays to visit senior students and disciples individually and exhaust every artifice and indirect approach in hoping to more quickly piece together the complete picture of Hong Yi-xiang's martial arts. If you think about the benefits, such a learning attitude should be considered commendable, but the problem was this embodied no systematic learning, and the result was that he once again dropped into his past erroneous pattern. Time passed day by day, but in the formal sparring practice, as usual, he always took a beating. In the end, he could no longer stand this stagnation in his studies, and took the initiative to seek Hong Yi-xiang's understanding of the reason.

"Master, I have been practicing here for nearly six months. I unfailingly practice every day, so why do I feel that I haven't made progress?" Sweet Potato asked.

"Why do you have that feeling?" Hong Yi-xiang asked.

"Because, six months ago, the guys I couldn't beat, I still can't beat," the foreigner grumbled.

"Where do you think the root of the problem is?" Hong Yi-xiang asked.

"I just don't understand it, that's why I am seeking Master's guidance," he said.

"Okay. Simply put, in these six months, your opponents have improved more than you, so they should win."

"Why? I believe I practiced with more conviction than all of them," K said.

"You have conviction. Even more conviction than them. This is really rare," said Hong Yi-xiang.

"Then, why am I still…?"

"Because you didn't really change your own shortcomings, you still keep repeating your past mistakes," Hong Yi-xiang said.

"But I have been really diligent in my training," he said.

"No. You are just studying hard, not using diligence to change. You still haven't gotten rid of your greed and impatience, and you still haven't really settled down to study one firm step at a time," Hong Yi-xiang said.

"I just hope I can learn more."

"This is the crux of the problem, too much without refinement is not helpful," Hong Yi-xiang said.

"But I picked their best and most powerful fighting moves," Sweet Potato said.

"It's one thing to remember movements and usage, but it's another thing to use these tricks cleverly. You didn't spend enough time teaching your body how to use those skills properly, so it is understandable why they are not useful," Hong Yi-xiang said.

"I accept this. I just want to commit to memory as many moves as possible during this time. After I return to the United States, I will gradually mull over and practice them," Sweet Potato said.

"I think this is not the correct way. In studying here, you should first establish your own core system, and then use this core to develop a complete encompassing logic, positioning you to continue your growth and development. Now you are only picking some random moves to learn, fundamentally mistaking the branch for the root. You should give it a good think, otherwise we are really wasting each other's time," Hong Yi-xiang once again clearly corrected the Sweet Potato's problem, and strictly required him to practice step by step in accordance with the method established by the gym, otherwise he would be asked to withdraw from the school. Under such clear instructions, he begged Hong Yi-xiang to give him another chance. He was willing to work hard to correct his shortcomings and study with all his heart.

※ ※ ※

That weekend morning, after Hong Yi-xiang finished the Taiji class, he chatted with his three sons in their living room.

"Pa, let him go. The other senior students are complaining, Sweet Potato still stubbornly resists change, and is getting everyone wound up wanting to steal their skills. They are all annoyed by him," Ze-zhou said.

"Such a committed person is rare to see," Hong Yi-xiang said.

"Pa, you can't just look at his merits. This person is bullying the newcomers. If it weren't for my scowling at him, I'm afraid those newcomers would be driven away," Ze-zhou said.

"I think he is most afraid of you now. He takes off like a shot as soon as you call, really obeys you," Ze-pei said.

"If it wasn't for Pa not allowing me to make a move on him, I'd really like to stomp him flat. This guy is messy, no manners. Every time after class, when everyone is changing clothes, he always runs everywhere bare-assed, for real," Ze-zhou declared.

"Foreigners are more open. Fortunately, there are no girls in our gym," Ze-pei laughed.

"Pa, I've carefully watched him sparring. In fact, his basic moves look good, so why is it when he is really fighting that he just can't use it?" Ze-han asked.

"Because his approach is always too shallow, he doesn't get close enough and is then unable to sink his teeth into his opponent," Hong Yi-xiang said.

"Why is this?" Ze-pei asked.

"The underlying reason is fear," Hong Yi-xiang observed.

"Afraid? This guy dares run around butt naked. What else would he be afraid of?" Ze-zhou asked.

"Afraid to fight?" Ze-pei asked.

"No way, Pa! We are talking about the Sweet Potato. Isn't he so belligerent?" Ze-zhou said.

"The fear I'm talking about is the deepest level of fear. The existence of this fear is sometimes unknown even to the person themselves," said Hong Yi-xiang.

"Is it because of fear he loses his cool and dares not let the enemy come in closer, even a little bit, so he can't latch on to the opponent?" Ze-han asked.

"That's right. Because he's unable to close in on the opponent's movement, so no matter how good the technique is, it won't be easy to execute, and in the end, it becomes the kind of sloppy brawling that you have all witnessed," Hong Yi-xiang said.

"Can't it be corrected?" Ze-pei asked.

"Innate true nature, like a birthmark, will stay with you for a lifetime. It can be changed, but not necessarily discarded. But if you know how to make good use of training and reverse the action of your shortcomings, you can have a lot of success. There are plenty of successful examples of remedial study, but the chink in the armor will never disappear," Hong Yi-xiang said.

"On the other hand, if you can grab the chink in an opponent's armor, will you win?" Ze-han asked.

"Is it a guaranteed win, I dare not say, but when I was in Japan, I heard an old ballet teacher who told a very interesting story, do you want to hear it?" Hong Yi-xiang asked.

"Yes," Ze-pei insisted.

"One year, in Japan, a professional baseball team hired a strong foreign player for a big salary to reinforce its batter lineup. Before the end of the first season the first year this foreign athlete entered Japanese baseball circles, he had blasted out home runs against the pitchers of almost every team. As time went on, all he had to do was step up to the batter's box and the pitcher's legs would start to tremble. Against this kind of all-rounder batter, they were completely helpless. It wasn't until the end of the season, that a coach from a certain team sought a breakthrough solution. He brought a super high-speed professional camera to take slow-motion video shots of this foreign player at the moment of the ball's impact by the bat. He showed the videos to high-level kendo master who was also a baseball fan," said Hong Yi-xiang.

"Why didn't he consult a pitching coach instead of consulting a kendo master?" Ze-pei asked.

"This is a good question. But after listening, you'll find the answer yourself, so I won't tell you. They repeatedly played slow motion video from every angle to let this kendo exponent observe, hoping he could find a weakness in the batter's movement or habits. After watching a few replays, the elderly kendo master closed his eyes for a moment, then smiled and said a key word: 'Inside corner ball,'" Hong Yi-xiang said.

"I thought he would say 'murder him,'" Ze-zhou said.

"Hey, that's not funny at all," Ze-han said.

"The baseball coach was completely unable to understand the meaning of this sentence and asked the kendo master to further elucidate. In return however, the Kendo master asked the coach to freeze the film frame on the facial expression of the foreign batter. It was a freeze-frame picture of a 'blinking eye,' and then he said that this was his hidden 'death point,'" Hong Yi-xiang said.

"Blinking? You mean…," Ze-han started to explain.

"If you already know the answer, please don't reveal it. I'll finish the story and then make a point," Hong Yi-xiang said.

"Okay," said Ze-han.

"This is a kind of body language that can't be concealed. This hitter was born with sharp eyesight like a hawk, he could clearly see the gesture and angle at the moment the ball left the pitcher's hand. Better than ordinary people, he knew the path and the angle of the approach of the ball from the pitcher's mound. Add to this his batting power, acquired through relentless practice, he hit the center of the ball with precision every time, causing the ball to explode out over the stadium wall. However, he couldn't conceal his inherent dread of an inside corner ball. As he himself is more aware than anyone of the threat to him of an inside corner ball, when the pitch trended slightly to the inside corner of his body, he wasn't able stop from blinking his eyes. It was an instinctive reflex. Even he himself was completely unaware of it," said Hong Yi-xiang.

"So, if you wanted to subdue this heavy hitter, the ball must pressure him as close to his body as possible. If necessary, let the pitcher feign loss of control and deliberately pitch the ball at his body to increase his fear, in which case he'll be unable to calm down and hit the ball," Ze-Zhou said.

"Correct," Hong Yi-Xiang said.

"What was the result?" Ze-Pei asked.

"Consequently, as soon as the season ended, the powerful foreign batter's contract was terminated ahead of schedule, and he packed to go home," Hong Yi-Xiang said.

"Wow! So ruthless. Such a tiny movement as the blink of an eye can topple a batting superstar," Ze-Zhou said.

"A showdown between masters is just that cruel. The outcome isn't determined by technique. Bet on the psychological mettle. And another thing not to overlook, the terrifying insight of the kendo master, even such a small movement could not escape his all-seeing eye. It's amazing," Hong Yi-xiang said.

"So, Sweet Potato's problem is just that he is restless," Ze-pei said.

"It's no wonder that when he learns things, he can only learn about five or six points, and can't completely settle down, put his mind at ease and just let go and allow what he is learning to change him. If he can't break free of this life-long limitation, it will be difficult for him to have great achievements in his life," Ze-Zhou said.

"Still you can't put the final nail in the coffin. Don't forget that people have the power to correct themselves. Maybe someday he'll figure it out, and he will naturally get out of his delusion," Ze-han said.

"I hope this is the case, too," Hong Yi-xiang said.

Martial arts are an empirical science. If their practicality is not verified through hands-on training, then forms become only romantic assumptions. The contest of hands-on practice, however, is not about winning or losing, but is about the post-winning or losing amendments. Winning or losing is only a temporary state and once past, it is past. But if through the interaction you can find your own shortcomings and insufficiencies, in time mending your flaws, thereby you unearth your own hidden advantages. Even if you lose in a contest, you actually win. You win the chance to make an adjustment and win the chance to make yourself better. When correction and growth are continuously maintained, the accumulated effect over a long period of time is quite impressive.

Hong Yi-xiang with eldest son Hong Ze-zhou and third son Hong Ze-pei at Yong Le Elementary School training hall, 1971.

Bob Yu left with Hong Yi-xiang and another student, circa 1971.

90– THE WESTERN FANATIC OF MARTIAL ARTS PART 3

The purpose of exchanging blows is to realize: What are you capable of now and what can you do in the future? But what one should recognize is: the person who can defeat you may not necessarily make you stronger; the person who can make you stronger may not necessarily be able to beat you. Fouls and tricks are an inevitable part of the competition. They are one way to win. You can't rely too much on strength and rules and sticking to convention; ignoring this reality is just the beginning of a disaster.

Scene: Yongle Elementary School

"SWEET POTATO, I DON'T WANT TO WASTE ANY MORE TIME bickering, I only have two suggestions. First, until you have fully learned spiraling force, we won't teach you Baguazhang and Sanshou. Second, do not bring up the thought of using money to buy gongfu again. Please keep this in mind. Here we only teach gongfu, we don't sell gongfu. I hope you make good use of this month, put away your demands and go traveling everywhere. In addition to gongfu, Taiwan is a very beautiful place. It's worth your time to look around."

"Big Brother, if you insist on this, maybe I won't come back to see you again in the future."

"That's a pity. We will always treat you as a friend. If this is your decision, then it is best we just sincerely wish you well."

And so, we thought we would not see the Sweet Potato again. However one day…

"How did you get in?" Hong Ze-han stared in surprise at the Sweet Potato.

"I came in by climbing over the wall."

"What the heck are you planning to do?"

"I don't really want to leave this training hall, I really respect Master Hong Yi-xiang."

"Well, there's no need to do it like this."

"I just want to learn the things I want a little faster. Leaving Hong Yi-xiang has depressed me. The problem is, I don't even know where I made a mistake?"

"This is really your biggest problem. You're rarely able to empathize with someone else's perspective."

"Which perspectives are you talking about?"

"My dad often reminds us brothers that if one wants to be a real master, one should know how to look at things from the other side's point of view."

"Isn't that controlled by the other party?"

"No, it's the opposite. Before you can control the opponent, you must first understand the opponent's thoughts and your own situation."

"So, from whose perspective should I think?"

"You should think about if you are ready, did Hong Yi-xiang deliberately make things difficult for you to learn? Baguazhang and Sanshou are included in the high-level courses, is there any reason for him not to teach you?"

"So, what about it?"

"What about it? The problem is that your current condition is not suitable for learning these things. Is this clear enough?"

"No. I've been ready since the first day I entered this gymnasium. I'm very aware of my condition, I'm quite good."

"You just have a great sense of your own ego. From the master's perspective, he hoped that by first tempering yourself with hard training, you would become more suitable."

"I'm really in good shape, I can prove it to you."

"Prove it to me, what's the use of that, you are going the wrong direction."

"No. You are Hong Yi-xiang's son, so if I can knock you down, that should be the best proof."

"That's why you made a special trip climbing the wall to come in and wait for me? And you chose the first day after you left this gymnasium. If you had this in mind then why didn't you do it before today?"

"I figured that if more people were around they would get in the way of a real challenge between you and me."

"You just want to confirm whether Hong Yi-xiang teaches his own son a special kind of thing, right?"

"You got that right. That's one of the reasons."

"In choosing now, aren't you afraid that people will suspect your motives?"

"You are not just an ordinary opponent; you are Master Hong Yi-xiang's beloved son. Although you are much younger than me, you and your brothers must have practiced gongfu since childhood. We have been practicing fisticuffs for about the same length of time. I feel choosing you as an opponent is quite reasonable, no?"

"Sure. From your subjective point of view, of course it's reasonable. You rarely make things difficult for yourself. And it's more reasonable to choose a time when there is no one here in the gym. Isn't that right?"

"I'm not as complicated as you think."

"No, you must have planned this for a long time, you are very smart, very calculating. You win. It proves that you are sooo tough. Even Hong Yi-xiang's son is no challenge for you. In case of defeat, no one in the world will know about this outcome. Right?"

"Even if everything you said is true, what difference does it make?"

"Sweet Potato, you use your cleverness in the wrong place. What else can you prove besides deceiving yourself?"

"I don't understand your blather. I just want to know will you accept a challenge or not?"

"If that's the case, then bring it on. But first, you have to help me with something."

"Help you with what?"

"Help me sweep the floor of the gym."

"You trying to stall for time?"

"No. I'm just afraid that when you go down, you'll get covered with dust."

Consequently, the two people who were about to face off, each armed with a broom, worked together to sweep clean the nearly 10,000-square-foot large auditorium of Yongle Elementary School, all in one go. However, this capricious request requiring Mr. K to help clean the floor in order to fulfill his wish made him anxious all along the way. He was constantly on guard for any potential variables and contingencies. Only after the two people cooperated, after the floor was cleaned up, he became aware that he was perhaps too suspicious. He couldn't help whispering to himself: "Have they really been looking out for me? Can it be I suspect their motives too much?"

The time was about 7:20 in the evening, and there were at least forty minutes before the formal practice time. Judging from past experience, it would take thrity minutes before the earliest students would enter the gymnasium to warm up, so the Sweet Potato and Hong Ze-han had at least twenty to thirty minutes to deal with their problem.

"Except for the head and groin, all contact is real," Ze-han said.

"Good," the foreigner replied.

"When one party calls to stop, you must stop," Ze-han said.

"Okay," he replied. The Sweet Potato clearly knew that these restrictions would place no formal constraints on him, especially since there were no other people to witness this situation. Moreover, since this foreign martial artist had cut off the master-disciple relationship with the training hall, any unexpected mishap could occur. But in that situation, it seemed Hong Ze-han had no other choice except to face it with all his strength.

In the gym, Hong Yi-xiang's second son, Hong Ze-han, was not like his battle-tested, full-contact sparring master, elder brother Hong Ze-zhou. He was frail and sick since he was young, due to severe asthma that made him almost inseparable from his medicine, twenty-four hours a day. Therefore, the Hong family never had high hopes that this child could take on such challenges. The reason why Hong Yi-xiang forced him to practice martial arts was simply so he could boost his immunity through exercise, reduce the frequency of asthma attacks, and reduce his daily use and frequency of the American magical elixir, steroids.

During that era when medicine was not very well developed, asthma was not just considered a disease, it was a killer. Only steroids could effectively relax the trachea to relieve its syndrome of breathing difficulties, since other drugs were basically ineffective placebos. According to Chinese medicine theory, the only chance for a person suffering from congenital asthma to take a turn for the better during their lifetime was in "turning the bones" and transforming one's constitution through lots of physical activity. Therefore, in the martial gymnasium Hong Ze-han, who was in the process of this bone transformation, was responsible for opening the door to Yongle Elementary School at 7 o'clock every night and preparing the gymnasium. Apart from cleaning, he was regarded as an ordinary student at best, not a warrior who could be sent to represent the gym. So, Sweet Potato chose Hong Ze-han as his challenger simply for the reason he was Hong Yi-xiang's son. Basically, his opponent was not a representative of the school.

However, under the impulse to fight, Sweet Potato still wanted to defeat someone to prove it was a mistake to believe he was not qualified to practice Bagua Palm and Sanshou. He was convinced that the most appropriate decision was to choose this occasion and this opponent. Of course, the other reason was that elder brother Hong Ze-zhou was just too strong. He figured, "If I fight him, it would only be proof of my own foolishness and deficiencies."

So, a "hunting tiger" and a "grass-eating sheep," would carry out a contest that only they would know about. The three simple rules of their agreement before the fight would really have no binding force upon the Sweet Potato. He knew the danger of attacking the head and groin, but for those who are determined to win, it can increase the threat felt in the opponent's heart of getting his "hit by an inside corner baseball pitch." So as soon as Sweet Potato started to engage, he couldn't wait to enthusiastically greet his opponent with these techniques. Both of them were expert in kicking attacks, only one was composed and the other was fast. In the process, both sides had hits on each other. As well, each successive kick was clearly felt to be heavier than the last. In this showdown, the rationality and restraint one should have, was buried by the idea of striving for victory. After the two sides had fought for several rounds, Sweet Potato determined the situation was not as optimistic as he had anticipated.

To get close to the opponent, he executed a risky feint, deliberately slowing down the speed of his retracting right kick and letting Hong Ze-han hook his foot with one hand. As soon as the Sweet Potato perceived his opponent's response he then immediately moved forward skipping on his left foot, accompanied by a stomping right foot, attacking the pit of his opponent's stomach. At the same time, he used a straight right fist toward his opponent's chin, hoping to end the battle. Objectively speaking, against an opponent with little actual combat experience, this combined attack contains a deceptive strategy that may be considered a good ploy, one difficult to deal with. He did not believe that the opponent had enough wisdom or ability to deal with this predicament.

The moment he was about to transform this feint into an actual attack, before his eyes that docile lamb suddenly evinced the strange glimmer of a wolf's spirit, and he heard a voice in his ear, "the ferocity of the second son is not in his body and hands but in a place that can't be seen." He had not been able to decipher this whisper in his ears for nearly a year, but before he could make the connection between the glimmer in the lamb's eye and this whisper, the fight ended. When he finally regained consciousness, he was already seated on the ground supported by his opponent. How could it be that he had no recollection of what strange things had happened during his period of unconsciousness, and why he was sitting on the ground? Why was he covered with dust? What hand technique did his opponent use and what had he done to me? Why was the left side of his throat slightly painful? What skill lay at the bottom of this? How could this guy in front of me, weighing less than 60 kilos, have so much power? Was this the spiral force? The dragon and the snake writhing? Or the legendary "Art of Controlling the Bull?" Why did the ancient people of China develop so many weird things? And during the Great Retreat of 1949 how many of these unusual skills had been absorbed by this stubborn, old, family clan? How many of these hidden secret techniques remained unexposed to the world? What kind of method should I use to get the Hongs to pass these special techniques on to me?

The showdown started and ended without even a third person knowing neither heads nor tails of this situation. Except for the two people involved, it can even be said that this incident never took place. It did not exist, so naturally there was no problem of losing and winning. The outcome was that the Sweet Potato's heart would carry an unreconcilable doubt from then on.

Of course, this foreign chap did not disappear from the martial arts world. After leaving Hong Yi-xiang's gym, he returned to America. Later, it was heard tell that he continued to use his usual methods to look for and challenge martial artists and fighters in his search for the secret techniques that his heart desired. One also heard that he had entered the mainland and used the same ploy, the same broth without adding new herbal medicine, to start challenges everywhere. Even later, he returned to Taiwan and sought out Hong Yi-xiang's beloved pupil, Mr. Howard Brewer, to accompany him for a visit to the Hong household. In addition to expressing his gratefulness and memories of Master Hong Yi-xiang, he vividly recounted his various deeds on the mainland, about seeking skill and his adventures with masters of Baguazhang, who passed down to him their unique hand methods. When he had spoken to his heart's content, he got up and moved about to demonstrate the substance behind his words. All the brothers who were sitting there drinking tea expressed admiration and respect. One would not have imagined that after he finished recounting a whole volume of assorted mythological stories, Hong Yi-xiang would indifferently ask:

"Aren't all the moves you demonstrated just now, methods that I taught you in the past?"

Sweet Potato couldn't conceal the awkwardness of his thick skin being laid bare, whereupon he performed the "Sichuan Changing Faces Opera" to everyone present. His complexion instantly became the color of a fully ripe beefsteak tomato and thus thoroughly red in the face, he immediately altered his words, saying, "Right. Right. I just used the moves passed on to me by Master Hong to defeat those teachers…"

It seems that his adventures attaining skill in China were truly quite peculiar. In those few years in China, did no one know what kind of high-level exponents he really chanced upon? Or were they dwarves? What magical skills and profound learnings from the martial forest did he master? We only know the linear trajectory of the Sweet Potato whirlwind. Besides his weight having shot straight up, the starchy Yam before our eyes was the same as the Sweet Potato from several years before, essentially unchanged. In regard to his renewed request to return to the gymnasium to study again, of course Hong Yi-xiang tactfully but clearly refused. The weight of the baggage attached to teaching him by his associates in the martial arts community was just too heavy. Later we heard that he had returned to China again and continued his career as a *ronin*, seeking skill and challenges, and was also seriously injured after suffering a rollover accident in his car. He was lying in the hospital for several months. Even later, after he returned once more to Taiwan to seek Master Hong Yi-xiang's transmission of Pre-Heaven Baguazhang and Sanshou and was turned down, news of him began to slowly fade away.

Why spend so many pages introducing this person? He made no contributions to Master Hong Yi-xiang or to YiZong TangShou. On the contrary, his unconventional and combative personality provoked a lot of trouble and disturbance. He also brought countless challenges and vivid lessons to the Taiwan martial art community, similar to stories in China's *Wuxia* genre novels. But even so, in private, Hong Yi-xiang still couldn't bear to criticize his actions. He felt that the Sweet Potato's enthusiasm for Chinese martial arts was on the verge of obsession. If not for the trouble that this foreigner stirred up everywhere, and the serious impacts it had on the harmonious environment of Taiwan's martial arts society, Hong Yi-xiang really hoped to teach him a bit more legitimate gongfu. The wisdom of our ancestral sages, however, guide us to "not pass on instruction to suspect people." So, one can only hope that this Sweet Potato will chance upon a superior man to transform him, eventually master amazing powers, and repent his past mistakes, to become a chivalrous knight upholding justice and benefiting the weak.

What is Sanshou?

Within the martial art taught by Hong Yi-xiang, "Sanshou" Strolling Hands is a comparatively unique, incomprehensible, and difficult to practice gongfu. This is an internal technique that uses the contact of both hands to know and control the opponent and subdue the opponent. It is a quintessential blend of form, intent, method, overt, covert, and evolutionary elements of the internal style. To master the indirect tenaciousness of "Q," the mystery of the virtual and the real, the tangible and intangible, one must first have a deep foundation in the Internal school. If practice is not on this right track, it's easy to use brute force with the hard always coming out on top for a superficial benefit. This will backfire and run counterproductive to mastering this technique. When two opponents engage in a match, it is like billowing waves rolling in, so "Strolling Hands" is also called "Colorful Wave Hands."

To compare Hong Yi-xiang's Strolling Hands and Taiji Boxing's "Push Hands," their respective surface appearances share some likeness, but the way the body works is freer and more unconstrained. Both employ the left and right hands to adhere in contact, and then based on constant mutual probing of internal energy, a full press, a hooking pluck, a pull in, a rollback and cast away, a yanking down, an evasion, and throw etc., is applied. There is no fixed method or mode of operation. It relies entirely on subliminal instincts. In the moment all information that is sensed creates an intuitive reflex, from the toes to the ankles to the knees, the hips, the waist, the chest, and the shoulders, to the elbows, wrists, fingers, and the vision. All potential energy and spaces of the average human body, joints, connective tissue, and muscle, not a single part is not put to full use. When Hong Yi-xiang practiced Strolling Hands, he would often close his eyes to "listen" and "understand" energy, to overcome the opponent. At that moment, his body shape was "focused on intent, not power, deliberately, like a cat," as described in the Five-Character Rhyming Mantra. Not only could he easily avoid and dissolve incoming force, but he could also launch continuous attacks at any time. At this pinnacle of skill, it is like returning to the aboriginal instinctive gongfu of humans. To faithfully fulfill his pledge to the original teacher of the art, Hong Yi-xiang did not easily impart this technique. On completing the required training courses and after a long period of observation, one on one with the students he would impart knowledge as the student wrote down character by character the learning. Therefore, unless a student brings out the scripts recorded one by one in his own hand, his is only a pirated version of a paint by numbers approach, and he is by no means a true inheritor of this art. Among the many disciples of this unique gongfu principle, except for Hong, and apart from the Hong Yi-xiang's three sons, Lei Hao-long was the only disciple to receive his confirmation of true transmission.

Hong Yi-xiang and his student and instructor at CCK airbase, Qin Ming-shan demonstrate Strolling Hands, circa 1968.

Hong Ze-han demonstrating flicking hands from a tip-toe stance, 1977.

Hong Ze-han

Hong Ze-han performs a roundhouse kick, 1980.

91– MATSUMOTO AND OKUYAMA

The fist does not leave the center, defend the body's central axis, don't lightly pursue easy wins before your eyes, let these advantages become an invisible restraint to your opponent. Just like an interlude in a musical piece and the field of white in a painting, it is not inaction but leaving more space for possibility and imagination.

Scene: Anxi Street Yongle Elementary School

(THE FOLLOWING IS A MONOLOGUE OF MATSUMOTO SHUHIRO.)
"Look at my fingers, and you will know the determination with which I have drawn a line separating me from my past.[29]

"I can't blame others for what I have suffered in the past…

"After graduating from Tokyo University, originally I tested into a very good, large trading company…

"For the benefit of the market, Japanese trading companies and gangsters are always linked together…

"Actually, not only the commercial world, but even the political world cannot cast aside its links to the Yakuza…

"These big bosses and politicians know very well that to get more money and power, they have to take advantage of this force that is not bound by conventions and laws. However, just a momentary reliance on their help, quickly becomes a dependence they will never be able to break free of, because it is too easy to use.

"I was the one sent by the trading company to connect with the Yakuza.

"Later, the Yakuza learned shrewdly, and they didn't want the scraps left after the trading company had finished its exploitation…

"So, their boss took the initiative to find me…

"What they needed was my corporate experience, and what I needed was the opportunity and promotion to a higher level they could give me, so the two sides hit it off.

"If I had worked two or three lifetimes at the trading company, it still would not have equaled the reward and influence the Yakuza gave me.

"When I returned to the trading company, representing the Yakuza, to negotiate with a senior manager, and saw the former high-ranking officer sitting

---

29 Matsumoto is referring to his severed pinky finger, a sacrifice or punishment among Japanese gangsters.

on the same level as me, I really believed that I was the alpha male lion, a lion that had found its own savanna. On this grassland, violence could achieve anything. If I could benevolently use wisdom to employ this evil force draped in a cloak of justice, then I would be as a God.

"There is no such thing as a dark path and a righteous road in this world, it's all BS, there is only the law of three meals a day to survive.

"My connections and expertise overlapping the black and white realms made me a most difficult opponent at the negotiating table.

"While *I* believed I could just reach out and touch the sky with my hand, I never really gave it much thought that I was only a pawn being passed between the hands of the two elders.

"I thought naively, to the extent I am being used, it is worth it.

"Don't people want to constantly create value to be exploited?

"It's just, thinking like this, so stupid…

"There were several incidents, and because I took the fall for others I have been in prison several times.

"Silly me, I thought that this is the demimonde. This is righteousness and justice.

"Every time I finished my time in the slammer, my status in the gang elevated and my vested interest expanded, so I mistakenly thought that doing time was a necessary evil in the struggle for existence.

"Not only did I have no regrets, but I also vowed secretly to strive to reach the top in the underworld…

"Until one day, I brought a large number of toughs onto my kid's school campus to teach a lesson to the teachers and students who bullied my kid. There I saw the shamed expression on my kid's face, right in front of the teachers and classmates, forbidding me from touching a hair on their heads. The expression, that kind of determination and unfamiliarity, made me feel extremely confused. That night, my heart was so painful that it was hard to go to sleep…

"I couldn't understand having made such a living, in the end what did I really have to show for it? And what did I lose?

"According to the rules of the gang, after cutting off the tip of my little finger, I had a high fever for several days, but when the fever subsided, I was still unable to fully wake up and pull myself together.

"So, I went to live in an ancient temple deep in the mountains. I hoped I could slowly settle down and after recovering my zest for life, could make plans. But every day, except for the moments when I transcribed the Heart Sutra, I constantly had a splitting headache, my life was worse than death…

"On a frosty winter's night, I went crazy and ran to the waterfall at the top of the mountain alone, and let the icy water cascade over the top of my head and body to cleanse me, stupidly believing that this could drive out the demon that had possessed my mind…

"I fell gravely ill again.

"When I got better, I understood clearly.

"Your own affairs can only be faced and resolved by yourself.

"The monks in the ancient monastery, the *Paramitas* in the Heart Sutra, the good spirits in the statues of the gods, the evil demons, and the icy waterfall in the deep mountains, none were of any help.

"To be alive, to be able to look one's conscience in the face, is good enough…

"The black, the white, they are all fake, and the places invisible to the naked eye, are they not always a riot of colors, completely mixed up and running together?

"The dark path is okay, the light path is okay, just getting by okay, each is okay.

"A person's life, isn't it all about standing on a black and white seesaw moving back and forth to find a balance?"

"Or just like a hamster, trapped on the wheel in its cage for a lifetime. People can only make a living by going with the grain.

"When the situation is dire, aren't good guys forced to do bad things? When the situation is good, can't bad guys do good things, with a wave of their hand?

"A good person can become a bad person, and a bad person can also become a benevolent person…

"There is no dividing line at all.

"I am no longer foolishly stuck on that dividing line.

"I just live my life consciously, with kind thoughts in my heart.

"When I had thought it through, my mental illness was also healed.

"On the mountain, I met the great calligrapher, Okuyama, who came to the temple to seek Zen. Every year at a fixed time he regularly went to various ancient temples in the mountains to meditate, seeking the inspiration and energy for his calligraphy creations.

"He is renowned for calligraphy, and also a top master of Japanese kendo.

"The Okuyama family is a famous orthodox samurai clan in Japan.

"He was the 'mad calligrapher' who opened my eyes to wielding the brush like a sword in a wild and unrestrained way and wielding the sword like a brush, hidden and understated.

"Meeting him was fate, and it was also the turning point of my life.

"After retiring from the mountain, I opened a shop specializing in tourist souvenirs and did some small business.

"Later, I got help from confidantes in the gang, and a connection with some second-tier politicians in Taiwan, and we cooperated to establish this travel agency specializing in the development of bilateral tourism between Taiwan and Japan.

"Okuyama Taiho loves Chinese culture and calligraphy, and every year leads a group from the Japanese Calligraphy Society to Taiwan to learn from calligraphers and have cultural exchanges.

"He is also qualified as a kendo teacher, and he will arrange for Japanese kendo masters to go to various universities in Taiwan for grading tests and to teach advanced courses.

"Behind both of his positions, he has a wealth of connections, so he has always been a well-spring of revenue for travel agencies.

"Okuyama Taiho once witnessed Master Hong Yi-xiang utilize his superb wisdom and sublime internal martial arts in the Tokyo Budokan, subtly subduing the top Japanese karate masters. Since then, he has held Master Hong in the highest esteem and admiration, so he directly requested me to beg Barrister Zhan Cong-yi to introduce us to call on you.

(The following is the monologue of Okuyama Taiho)

"Master Hong. After a glimpse of beauty at the Tokyo Budokan, I later read a critic in a famous Japanese martial arts magazine report the legend of your wily use of a long staff to outwit the big Westerner. This only increased my reverence for Master Hong's wisdom and level of mastery in overcoming opponents.

"Being in a samurai family lineage gives me a strong mission to inherit traditions and maintain the family calling. Since I was a teenager, I have received strict training from the family elders.

"Unexpectedly, as my skills gradually matured, Japanese kendo was itself in decline.

"After all, old things can't withstand the impact and neglect of new fashions…

"This skill symbolic of Japan's Bushido spirit has become a nostalgic ritual and soulless model in the fighting ring. It has completely lost kendo's true spirit of honing strong awareness.

"Not to mention how it explores the inner spiritual qualities and survival philosophy of a samurai.

"A desperately hopeless situation gradually drowned out my original thinking that I could swim against this riptide of ignorance.

"But to aspire to martyrdom like the great writer Yukio Mishima and commit suicide, I think I don't have that kind of determination and courage. I can't do it.

"But to just sit back and watch the Bushido spirit that supports Japan sink into the oblivion of the modern world without taking action, this I can't do either.

"What I can do is demand that the skills and spiritual tradition of kendo not be lost during my generation.

"What can I do for the future?

"The samurai and swordsmen in the past often said: Kendo does not die. But in this age, I am afraid that not perishing will be hard.

"For this, while I still have a breath, I am determined to express my accumulated pent-up frustrations on the decline of the old ways through calligraphy, and thereby expand the horizons and expand the vision of my kendo club friends…

"To me…calligraphy is kendo employing a brush, kendo is calligraphy employing a sword. In my final years I hope I can use calligraphy to pass on a record of these experiences and learnings, to at least let people in the future have a clue to explore the civilization that once existed in Japan and the lofty spirit of Bushido.

"Yes. Just like the Kinkaku-ji Temple in Kyoto, resolute in the torrent of history and time, heedless of wear and the change around it, it remains a body of resplendent golden light.

"You have to prop it up in order that it can be seen again."

※ ※ ※

That year, Matsumoto Shuhiro and Okuyama Taiho formally visited the Hong family through the introduction of lawyer Zhan. In accordance with ancient customs for a first meeting, they brought with them gifts of a porcelain Fortune Lion from the famed Kutaniyaki kilns and a copper helmet attributed to the age of Toyotomi Hideyoshi and requested a time for an official visit to the training hall. A few days later, Matsumoto Shuhiro and Okuyama Taiho formally came to ask for instruction. In seeking to be proper, Okuyama Taiho deliberately changed into a formal kendo uniform, and kneeled on entering the training area, then waddled his way in on his knees. This kind of sincere reverence a budoka demonstrates to a senior exponent leaves quite an impression. Such ancient samurai style of respect and dignity is probably rare even in Japan.

The samurai sword he wore was a famous *katana* passed down by his samurai ancestors. This sword was said to be forged by the most prestigious master swordsmith in Japan's capitol. It was tailor-made for the needs of his great samurai ancestors and was worth several ingots of gold. If measured by contemporary value, it would be a staggeringly astronomical number. If not for the expression of supreme respect to Master Hong Yi-xiang, this famous sword would never be taken out of the home lightly. Okuyama Taiho was an eighth dan teacher of kendo, so after a formal application he successfully received approval from the Taiwan and Japan Customs to bring the sword with him. Because of the requirement the famous sword not to leave his side, Okuyama Taiho was reluctant to hand over the famous sword to the freight forwarders for transportation, but was hindered by the flight safety restrictions, After special packing, the flight attendant on the plane locked it in a safe for special storage. It was not returned to the heir of this historic blade until customs clearance was completed after the plane landed.

Taking on the responsibility of referee for this cross-examination was Dr. Ye, who had studied kendo with Hong Yi-xiang when he was in school. Dr. Ye hailed from an influential family of doctors who lived in Dadaocheng. He had studied in Japan and obtained the qualification of Doctor of Medicine. In that era, it was a tradition for doctors to learn kendo. When he heard that Okuyama Taiho would bring his family heirloom sword to the visit, there was nothing further to say, he had to shoulder the responsibility of facilitating this friendly exchange, all the better to be able to gaze on the elegance of the renowned blade. Dr. Ye's build was small and thin, but his voice was booming and his movements agile, leaving a strong impression. He was a person who devoted two hundred percent to everything and liked to play the role of interlocutor. When he served as a referee, he concentrated on the details, and he was always more enthusiastic and busier than the players facing off on the field. No one in the world was more suitable to be the judge of this contest.

Okuyama Taiho waited for Hong Yi-xiang to complete his preparations for battle, first letting the tip of the sword hang down in a show of respect, and then raised the point of the sword to aim at the tip of his opponent's nose, assuming a stance well defended while preparing for battle, the two of them stood, the point of the sword a distance from the point of a wooden stave, their minds fully concentrated, their energy mobilized ready for an attack at any moment. Time moved slowly second by second, like a viscous river of tar. The students and VIPs were sitting cross-legged in the dojo. Save their eyes scanning back and forth between the two players in the battle, all appeared to be in a frozen state. After refusing to budge for about two minutes, Okuyama Taiho began probing to left and right, trying to find a gap to break through the defenses, but except for small adjustments of angle Hong Yi-xiang kept the tip of his staff locked on the sword's owner, pointed right at the tip of the sword, still maintaining a rear weighted Santi stance, solid as a mountain. His search to left and right for a defect in the defenses having failed, Okuyama Taiho returned to his original position.

Although the two men had yet to unleash powerful attacks, strained senses and rapid calculations in his mind had already dotted Okuyama Taiho's forehead with countless beads of sweat. Just as a pearl of sweat that rolled from the center of his eyebrows and along the bridge of the nose was about to drop off, Okuyama Taiho let out a loud roar from his dantian, the rear foot surged forward, and at the same time, his two hands lifted the sword over his head with the intention of deflecting the tip of the stick with the spine of the sword the instant he lifted it, so as to seize the brief interval when the staff was knocked off center, in order to cut forward and down. He never imagined the sword would land in emptiness, as the technique fell into a vacuum, and instinctively he arrested the subsequent attacks, quickly pulling back, withdrawing the sword to guard his central axis, thus preventing the other party from entering the void created. Unexpectedly, the counterattack he was worried about did not materialize. In his heart, he quickly reflected on what countermeasures the opponent made at the moment Okuyama launched his move. Why had he been incapable of deflecting the tip of the staff? But he drew a blank. So the two returned to the initial opposing stances, as if nothing had ever happened... Okuyama Taiho made two more similar attempts, until the fourth attempt, when he raised the sword above his head and he was shocked to realize that Hong Yi-Xiang's staff all along had been trained on his throat. He need only launch a drilling stab with spiraling energy released forward from his rear hand, the tip of the staff would pass through the throat like a spear. However, Hong Yi-xiang never made a move. In this instant, Okuyama had a flash of insight, understanding that the duel between the two men; victory and defeat, had already been determined from the moment he raised his sword, but all along he had no capacity to perceive it. The instant epiphany was like the purification rite of a new monk, he felt a chill from the soles of the feet through his spine and up to the top of the forehead, and his body shivered involuntarily. He respectfully retreated two steps, then knelt down, ceremoniously sheathing his sword, and reverently thanked Master Hong Yi-xiang for his gift of enlightenment. All the guests watching the match awaited a skirmish that never erupted; indeed it had only just begun when it was all over.

(The following is Hong Yi-xiang's commentary monologue)

"Wooden staffs and steel swords, one long and one short, one rigid and one flexible, each has its own strengths on the field of battle...

"Squaring off with a wooden staff to receive an enemy, although it is long, it may not be able to take advantage.

"Even when choosing an indirect flanking attack of Bagua, it still cannot avoid the direct frontal assault of weapons...

"Additionally, Bagua is based on a *ge*—a poleaxe. Its strength is a piercing thrust after a hooking and pulling back. A wooden staff has no hook. It is difficult to make the fine precise movements like a palm rising drilling overturning and dropping.

"Xingyi is based on a long spear, and trains spiraling energy. You can use the spear's tassel to entwine the opponent's weapon, and use binding energy to entangle and snap up the opponent's weapon, disarming him and letting the weapon fly...

"The wooden staff has neither the spear head to pierce nor the tassel to entwine...

"One can only control movement accurately, by drawing small circles with the tip of the staff to avoid your first wave of deflections, and then quickly circle the tip of the staff back to the original point and guard the center line. It is a micro movement, the motion of the staff's tip is not easy to perceive.

"The fist not leaving the center and the stick not leaving the center are both a dynamic way of defending the central axis, but you definitely don't want to rigidly attach to that defense, not moving at all…

"Change and no change, movement and quiescence, the profound and subtle mystery of winning or losing lies within this.

"An ancient boxing manual mentions a reminder, "the situation may be the same but the form can vary, and who can know clearly the form," which is saying that in a confrontation between the two parties, the first to reveal its form will not succeed.

"The reason why I didn't thrust out…

"Because the overall trend was set, there was no need to make superfluous actions.

"Furthermore, no real attack can be made without some risk or worry. I have a senior who hides in the mountains who said that when your arrow is aimed at the prey, you only see the prey, but you can't see your own danger—what is stalking *you*.

"This is the same as the passage in the *Book of Changes:* 'The Dragon Hiding in Deep Waters'—a person biding their time.

"Once you turn a threat into a specific attacking action, what was originally an accumulating power of unlimited potential in an instant becomes one single action, which is no longer an unpredictable and hard to fathom threat to the opponent.

"This is the advantage of uncertainty. It is more valuable in being stayed than in being executed, isn't it?"

Two years later, Hong Yi-xiang brought his eldest son, Hong Ze-zhou, and two disciples Su Dong-cheng (Fujita Higashinari), and Li Chun-sheng, to Tokyo Saitama Prefecture to cut the ribbon on the opening ceremony of "Yizong Tangshou Budokan Kobukan." In addition to the official public ceremony and martial arts performances to the media that day, Hong Yi-xiang clearly assigned Su Dongcheng to be responsible and promote this gym in the role of Chief Instructor. The establishment of this "Kobukan." the land and the buildings, was entirely sponsored by local entrepreneurs and foundations, but was under the authority and reputation of the main Taiwan school. It was another milestone of internationalization for the "Yizong Tangshou" system created by Hong Yi-xiang. It is a pity that the coaches selected to pass it on were weak, language barriers could not be overcome, and the succession lacked vitality. A true pity.

Japanese martial artist Matsuda Ryuichi sought the teachings of Hong Yi-xiang in Internal School boxing, 1973.

Hong Ze-han and Matsumoto Shuhiro, center, 1983.

92– LUODONG SHAOLIN HONG BOXING

Winning or losing in the ring is not enough to define a martial art lineage as good or bad. With the same grape varieties produced in Burgundy, different vineyards produce different flavors of red wine. So, the key is not in the body of techniques in the school, but in the ability to interpret them and make innovative inferences.

Scene: Yilan, Luodong

YILAN AND LUODONG ARE SITUATED IN THE EASTERN PART OF Taiwan. Obstructed by natural terrain and restricted by inconvenient transport links, before the Taipei-Yilan Expressway was punched through the mountains, most people who wanted to go to Jiaoxi, Yilan, Luodong, Hualien, and Taitung usually chose to take the train. If you chose to take the Taipei-Yilan road on the mountain route instead of taking the train, you had to go through the mountains and pass the test of "nine bends and eighteen hairpins," and run the gauntlet of wild lands fabled with many a frightful legend of various mountain folk before arriving at your destination.

Compared with the prosperous western part of Taiwan, the folk customs in these areas in the east are simpler and more old-fashioned, possessing a more intense traditional style and human touch. The retention of folk customs and traditional culture far exceeds that in the towns of western Taiwan, especially the pole climbing competition in Toucheng in the seventh lunar month of the lunar calendar. It is one of the best traditional folk activities in the country.

Li Chun-sheng was the chief of the "Luodong Shaolin Hongquan Martial Arts Center." Over the years, Yilan and Luodong have used the "Charitable Association" as means to promote Shaolin Hongquan and have actively participated in competitions organized by the National Martial Arts Association. In the county level martial arts competitions, whether it is routines, weapons, or sparring, they always walked away with most of the trophies, and he was the most influential leader in the region. In addition to his dedicated promotion of martial arts and folk activities, in those days, he also owned one of the best pipe chenille factories in the world.

The Southern Shaolin martial arts taught by Li Chun-sheng's gym were the most common hard gongfu taught in Taiwan's martial arts gyms and lion dance clubs. He completely followed the traditional methods and exercises taught by the old masters when they were young, especially "Hard Qigong," which is their special skill in Weizhen Eastern Taiwan. There were over half a dozen affiliated martial arts gyms and community organizations up and down the.

That year, using a large local folk worshipping ceremony as an excuse, Li Chun-sheng and several famous local martial arts clubs jointly invited Hong Yi-xiang acting as head coach of the national team, to Yilan and Luodong to a ceremonial banquet. Such hospitality is hard to turn down, and with the call of local seafood specialties, Hong Yi-xiang brought his three sons Ze-zhou, Ze-han, and Ze-pei to accompany him. The train tickets that were originally booked were changed to the Taipei-Yilan Road bus line, because they could not refuse the invitation of several small martial arts gyms in Shiding and Pinglin. And so the journey went stop by stop visiting, from early in the morning until the dead of night before reaching their destination. There are relatively few heavyweights in the martial arts world visiting the eastern region, so the local martial art gyms fell over each other to invite them. Therefore, from the moment they came out of the bus station the four Hongs, father and sons, were Shanghaied with good intentions by the local martial arts community for three days and three nights.

To avoid favoritism between one and the other, they arranged to visit every local martial arts gym, where they were invited to demonstrate and explain internal martial arts. In the process, they always asked Hong Yi-xiang to recall the various challenges he had experienced and offer anecdotes about martial arts training when he was young. These oral histories were a great inspiration and motivation for a younger generation of martial artists.

During their several days sojourn in Luodong, it was arranged that they stay in a guest house run by Mr. Hong De-yu's family (Hong De-yu was one of Li Chun-sheng's disciples). Every day upon finishing the daytime visits and banquets, Hong Yi-xiang visited Li Chun-sheng's martial arts gym to observe their routine training. The main gongfu taught in Li Chunsheng's martial arts gym was Shaolin Hongquan, which was quite popular at the time. The gongfu they were most proud of was "hard qigong." The initial practice of this kind of gongfu is to flog various parts of the body with bundles of thin steel rods. When slapping, one must move the Qi into the parts of the body being hit, and gradually increase the force from light to heavy, not giving up until the entire body is red through and through. The master must first nod before one can rest.

Intermediate training is to switch to a canvas bag filled with steel ball bearings to slap the body. When the heavy canvas bag hits the body, it will make a dull thudding sound like a drum. Students must move sufficient qi to the abdominal cavity to increase their resistance. The whole torso is like a basketball full of qi. Qi is used as a barrier to protect the various organs in the body cavity. Compared to sitting in an audience watching a performance, observing their training up close was more real, more stunning, and carried more immediacy, with no hint of chicanery.

The highest level of hard qigong is to use a big iron "bell" to peen the body. People who can practice to this level are already extraordinary. Once you have seen a performance of them using their flesh to resist the ferocious impact of heavy metal objects, then it is not difficult to understand why the Empress Dowager Cixi and the great politicians of the Qing court believed that the Yihetuan[30] were soldiers sent from heaven to defend the Qing Dynasty Empire.

"They must train until they can withstand hammer blows to be qualified to represent Yilan County in the national competition, but even so they have never made it into the championship finals or runner-up slots," Li Chun-sheng said.

"What do you think is the problem? The rules of the game? Or is the referee unfair?" Hong Yi-xiang asked.

"I did have this idea, always needing to console myself. But after fighting with your winning contestant again after the tournament, I won't further delude myself. Although they practice as usual every day, but deep down in my heart I still can't help but ask, 'Why can Iron Shirt training resist the iron bell, but can't ward off a human fist? If it can't be used in actual combat, then what is the point of the hardship of training this kind of gongfu?'" Li Chunsheng said.

"Did you find where the problem resides?" Hong Yi-xiang asked.

"The same student has lost twice in a row. If his skill is not inferior to other people, then what is it? Regrettably, it's nothing more than an Iron Sand Palm that can't knock people down, and an Iron Shirt that can't stop punches," Li Chun-sheng said.

"The problem is not in the gongfu, it is in the strategy," Hong Yi-xiang said.

"Why?" Li Chun-sheng asked.

"The tactics in the ring and out of the ring are different. Tournament sparring relies on scoring points. No matter how good a defense is, it does not score points," said Hong Yi-xiang.

"Can you not defend?" Li Chun-sheng asked.

"No, first tell me the difference between a good defense in the ring and a normal defense," Hong Yi-xiang said.

"Aren't they all about protecting themselves?" Li Chun-sheng asked.

"Yes, and then?" Hong Yi-xiang continued to ask.

"I get it. What you mean is that I should seize the opportunity to counterattack and increase my chances of scoring," Li Chun-sheng said.

"Yes, in the ring, defense is not defense, but a setup. Also, attack and defense must be flexibly interchangeable, so that people cannot see through your tactics at first glance," Hong Yi-xiang said.

"Understood," Li Chun-sheng said.

---

30 The Yihetuan 義和團 is the Chinese name of the Boxers of the Boxer Rebellion at the end of the 19th century.

"To protect himself, it is your fighter's habit as soon as he enters the ring to take in a deep breath generating internal energy to protect his body. This is the Achille's heel of hard qigong. To hold that breath, the body's flexible mobility is degraded, so that it naturally falls into the disadvantageous position of being reactive and taking a thrashing," Hong Yi-xiang said.

"Do you want to let go of that protective breath?" Li Chun-sheng asked.

"Can it be practiced to the level it becomes natural?" Hong Yi-xiang asked.

"Difficult, but it should be possible," Li Chun-sheng said.

"Only in that case is practicing it useful. Coupled with some complementary striking methods, then qigong will not have been practiced in vain," said Hong Yi-xiang.

"In short, we have to change, to be able to use it freely while moving, instead of holding it in all the time. Wow. Such a simple truth, why didn't I think of it?" Li Chun-sheng said.

"So, don't give up what you have learned before. Martial arts, the ability to overcome the enemy and arrive at victory is the key. If you can cross-train, you will have an advantage over others," said Hong Yi-xiang.

"It's clear now," Li Chun-sheng said.

"So, when you encounter an opponent whose resistance to a punch is weaker, you can use hard qigong to lure them into an over-committed showdown. This is the purpose of the hard qigong 'sacrificing body method,'" said Hong Yi-xiang.

"Yes. In the county games, we have used the same strategy to win many matches," said Li Chun-sheng.

"But the risk remains very high, the key is to strengthen the ability to initiate attacks," Hong Yi-xiang said.

"Master Hong, can you please explain the characteristics and differences between Xingyiquan and Baguazhang in the simplest way?" Li Chun-sheng asked.

"Xingyiquan and Baguazhang are both martial arts evolved from ancient polearms. Xingyiquan is the transformation of the long spear techniques of ancient mounted warriors into boxing techniques, so the "front hand parries, rear hand strikes" was developed into the Five-element striking methods. The Baguazhang hand method is like the ancient halberd polearm, Changji, with the pointed tip and the crescent blade. An overturning hook with a stab, so in the Bagua Palm's method of attack, the straight stab is an empty feint. When the enemy reaches out to block, then use the 'hook' of the Changji halberd to overturn, hook and pull back, first breaking the opponent's balance and then stabbing out. This is the *real* attack. This small action of inverting, hooking, and pulling back can not only break his balance, but is also a special technique used to deal with the Iron Shirt. A 'rise, drill, sink, and overturn' technique will shake the opponent to their feet, and the 'protective Qi' will be scattered. So, if you can flexibly interchange the tactics of the spear and the halberd and render the opponent unable to distinguish between the fake and the real, you can become the most difficult opponent in the ring to tangle with," Hong Yi-xiang said.

"This is what we want the most, Master Hong, are you willing to teach us? Can you let our system be under your mentorship?" asked Li Chun-sheng.

"Oh. This is a big deal. Don't do it rashly. If you need these techniques, I am willing to share them with everyone, but, truly, there is no need to pay such a price," said Hong Yi-xiang.

"Master Hong, the main purpose of this invitation to visit Luodong was to let you see if we latecomers can join Yizong Tangshou to pursue your study of internal martial arts, not just to seize the crown in the ring and do our hometown proud. It's that everyone is determined to pursue advancement," said Li Chun-sheng.

"Go on," said Hong Yi-xiang.

"In fact, for this purpose, some of our disciples had made a special trip to Taipei and spent the whole night at the window outside the Yongle Elementary School watching you practice, watching for five or six days in a row, every day. Every night they returned to the hotel to discuss it until midnight. In the end, everyone's consensus was that the gap is too great. One can no longer build a cart behind closed doors, blind to the conditions of the road," Li Chun-sheng said, "We have already practiced the External boxing taught by my master as far as it can go, and if we don't find a new way out, then I'll have to apologize to my disciples for following me so many years.

"Yilan County is a remote place. In days gone by, of the martial arts masters who came to Taiwan from China, exceedingly few set foot in the East to hand down their art. Therefore, everyone here is very unfamiliar with the internal martial arts. We are deeply indebted to your open explanations and break down, providing the only opportunity to get a glimpse of the mystery of internal boxing. I have a responsibility to lead everyone on the right path and ask Teacher Hong to help us achieve this aim. My master has passed away many years ago, and our brothers have always had a mind to continuously improve, so please don't refuse," Li Chun-sheng said.

"On the matter of making obeisance to the master, let's take our time on reaching that decision, but the question of passing down techniques, let's start there. The National Martial Art Association here has appointed me to train contestants for next year's international competition. You can select a few strong hands to participate in the training. One problem, all my protective gear and equipment are in Taipei, so is it convenient for you to come to Taipei?" asked Hong yi-xiang.

"A wish come true," Li Chun-sheng said.

"What about the contestant's work, livelihood and income?" Hong Yi-xiang asked.

"Rest assured; this is not a problem in Yilan," Li Chun-sheng said.

So, three months later, Li Chun-sheng personally led Li Shi-chu, Hong De-yu, Chen Hong-peng and other triumphant students to Taipei together with a few martial brothers of his generation. According to the traditional ancient rituals, they formally sent a letter to the Master to enter the Yizong Tangshou system. So began an organized transfer of key learnings and techniques, to facilitate the transplant of Yizong Tangshou system's essence to eastern Taiwan in the shortest period of time.

It was hoped that by means of this opportunity, Internal boxing technique would take root in Yilan, and it would continue to multiply and develop into a boxing technique with local characteristics. To fulfill their wish, in addition to the existing training in the evening, Hong Yi-xiang chose to open a special training session for Li Chun-sheng and his martial brothers during the day to reinforce their training, so that they could smoothly integrate the basics of their External boxing with the Internal school. The transplant plan at the time was roughly as follows:

Li Chun-sheng and his brothers: specializing in Xingyi/Bagua/Taiji Li Shi-chu: specializing in sparring practice Hong Deyu/Chen Hong-peng: specializing in Basic Forms and Applications

In an all-out effort implemented over several years, Hong led his three sons to divide up and implement the training plan. During the special training period, Hong Yi-xiang on several occasions led Hong Ze-zhou and Hong Ze-pei to the gyms in Jiaoxi, Yilan, and Luodong to establish a standard and assist Li Chun-sheng in the transformation of the entire system.

In the first year after Luodong Shaolin Hongquan was merged with Yizong Tangshou, Li Shi-chu completed intensive special training in Taipei, and underwent a radical transformation. Subsequently, he took the crown at regional and national Sanda sparring championships. These brilliant concrete achievements on the field of battle became the talk of the town in the Yilan Luodong region. Behind the scenes, Li Chun-sheng and his junior brother Fang Jia-jun, as well as Li Shi-chu, Hong De-yu, and Chen Hong-peng, actively promoted the transformation of local martial arts.

Seeking to apprentice an entire school to become the students of a new Master is different from transferring to a different department or school at university. Especially where the folk customs were more conservative, naysayers are easy to find . If this change was handled with only slight impropriety, it would inevitably lead to treachery from all walks of life. The positive image of Hong Yi-xiang's repeated exhibitions abroad that graced Taiwan's martial arts scene virtually resolved the static and interference that might have occurred in these places. Hong Yi-xiang's insistence that Li Chun-sheng should retain his original mentorship and school name eliminated much malicious gossip and made the whole thing seem fitting and proper. So, this major event of the system transformation, with the full support of Hong Yi-xiang and his sons, was a smooth integration, creating a successful model and a good example for the contemporary martial arts world.

There were many unanticipated hardships transitioning from External boxing into Internal boxing—the process of transforming techniques, especially in the ring. In that era, the so-called National Martial Arts sparring tournaments did not have any qualification restrictions. Chinese martial arts had always been advertised as broad, profound, and all-encompassing. Therefore, this fondness for the grandiose determined its destiny, such that it became difficult to regulate and develop. In national competitions, one often saw contestants from judo, boxing, karate, kick-boxing, and Thai boxing all mixed in, competing on behalf of their counties and cities. There were even hoodlums from the temples and street ruffians. Anyone who could fight and loved to fight could sign up to participate in the competition. Therefore, in the entire arena, it was go for broke, there was no technique at all. Some players would hurl raw language, cursing the opponent's ancestors, while pounding away, to boost their power. To emerge victorious in this kind of competition, besides having a tough mental constitution, rich pre-match experience was absolutely indispensable.

To enhance the actual combat ability of the contestants, Hong Yi-xiang mobilized many apprentices who had once seized the crown in ring competitions to take turns fighting against Li Shi-chu, so that he could adapt to various fighting styles.

During training, Li Shi-chu and Hong Ze-han, the coach in charge of kicking techniques, sparred. Li Shi-chu miscalculated the angle and speed of his opponent and was hit in his right ribs around his liver. His comrades training next to him knew that Li Shi-chu had practiced "hard qigong" and should be able to withstand this soft kick. They did not expect that Li Shi-chu's body would collapse like a sudden power failure and crash instantly. He was halfway through launching a heavy punch when he just fell flat. Startled teaching assistants rushed to give him first aid. After regaining consciousness, Li Shi-chu rested briefly and as before insisted on resuming the tough workout, not succumbing to stage fright, and fleeing.

Trophies won in the ring rely on this "tooth busting, blood-swallowing, set the jaw and persist with the bitter training" kind of willpower. Since that time, he radically converted from the "sacrifice style" of external boxing's "hard swallowing hard," and pivoted to the Three-Body style (Santi Shi) that Xingyiquan uses to meet the enemy. Moreover, in practicing "The General's Column" he mastered the body shape of sinking the chest, rounding the back, dropping the shoulders and extending the shoulder blades, successfully morphing into a difficult opponent who is good at internal techniques. Of course, after Hong Ze-han proved the power of "The Art of Controlling the Bull" on the Sweet Potato and Li Shi-chu, both of whom had practiced hard qigong, he never again dared to lightly try this secret technique capable of instantly knocking out and paralyzing people.[31]

Hong Ze-han performing Shaolin Hong Tiger-Crane Fist, circa 1980.

---

31 After winning many championships in the ring, Li Shi-chu was later hired by the Taiwan ambassador to the Philippines as the military attaché. He was responsible for the safety of the ambassador.

93– BBC WAY OF THE WARRIOR PART 1

If it is to be mortal combat, you need a reason to fight that is more important than life. If it is a debate, you need a motivation more reasonable than just winning or losing. However, we always try to utilize the truths in which we believe to persuade the other party, instead of utilizing ways that the other party can comprehend and find agreement with so as to help them understand our perspective, whereupon communication becomes endless wrangling, and minor differences become insurmountable gulfs.

Scene: Taipei Hilton Hotel

"I'm Assistant Director Li from the Press Bureau of the Executive Yuan. Howard Reid, a producer at the British BBC Broadcasting Corporation, asked me to call you. The BBC plans to produce a series of documentary films on traditional martial arts in Asia. They hope they can visit you and understand whether there is an opportunity for further cooperation?"

"Okay. In that case please contact my son first…"

So, two days later, Hong Ze-han, who served as a director at a local TV station, was invited to the Hilton Hotel to meet with BBC producer Howard Reid and the Assistant Director of the Press Bureau. In that era, the Hilton Hotel, the most luxurious international hotel in Taiwan, was *the* landmark in the square in front of Taipei's main railway station, and it was a favorite meeting spot for many young men and women. This hotel has now changed hands, changed name, undergone a major renovation, and the entire city has changed around it even more. It has never reclaimed its former glory and status.

The place where the two parties agreed to gather was not like a standard meeting in the lounge bar of the hotel, but directly in the producer's guestroom. When Hong Ze-han arrived for the appointment, the assistant director of the Press Bureau was also present. He was a mild mannered and polite young man responsible to translate and record the minutes for both sides. Although Hong Ze-han could understand and speak some simple English, Hong Yi-xiang specifically instructed him to conduct the meeting in Chinese. In managing this on his behalf, Ze-han was expected to make clear the thinking of both parties, and not, in an effort to show off his ability, make wild guesses jeopardizing this major event.

Howard Reid was a young, tall, blonde, blue-eyed, and handsome British guy topped off with the halo of a Ph.D. in Anthropology from the UK's University of Cambridge . He looked more like a film star than a producer at work behind the camera.

"Hello. Nice to meet you. Are you the son of Master Hong Yi-xiang?" Reid asked.

"Yes, I am. Nice to meet you," Hong Ze-han said.

"Do you know the British Broadcasting Corporation? We are a world-renowned broadcasting company. We have the best production teams in the world, and the documentaries we produce are critically acclaimed, internationally," Reid said.

"His purpose in stating this is to emphasize that they are not a fly-by-night independent production company," Assistant Director Li said.

"I understand. May I present my business card," Hong Ze-han said.

"Oh. Are you a TV director? Aren't you a martial arts coach?" Reid asked.

"Both. Being a director is my day job, and being a martial arts coach is a family affair," Hong Ze-han said.

"So, you know the BBC?" Reid asked.

"Not in depth, but it should be that I know more than the average person," Hong Ze-han said.

"Very good. Choosing you as the first candidate for interviewing should be a good start," Reid said.

"Mr. Hong, the Director of the Press Bureau attaches great importance to this filming plan, which will greatly enhance Taiwan's international visibility," Assistant Director Li said.

"I know. Don't worry," Hong Ze-han said.

"When I made the pre-planning in the UK, I did not expect that there would be so many traditional martial arts masters in Taiwan. Please understand. This is the reason why we could not meet in the lobby bar. You can see we collected so much research that even a king-size double bed can't fit it. I really don't know where to start," Reid apologized.

"Although Taiwan is small, there is still plenty of talent," Assistant Director Li said.

"During the exodus to the south of the Nationalist Government in 1949, there were many Chinese martial arts masters who accompanied the government and the army," Hong Ze-han said.

"Oh? Really. We originally planned to select only one topic and one personage for an in-depth profile in each country, so I have to pick one candidate out of so many…," Reid said. "So, I thought up a good way. Can you please give me a reason, a reason that can *convince* me, why choosing Hong Yi-xiang is a must for me?"

"I understand. Only one can be selected. This is indeed not an easy task. So, in order not to put you in a tough situation, we are willing to give up this opportunity. I hope this can reduce your troubles a little bit," Hong Ze-han said.

"Ah. Why?" Reid queried.

"Mr. Hong, this can't be what he intended," Assistant Director Li said.

"Don't worry, I'm not pouting. We just don't want to participate in this kind of competition," Hong Ze-han said.

"Mr. Hong, this is not a good outcome. Master Hong Yi-xiang has always been our primary candidate. I don't want to just give up like this," Reid said.

"Okay. Since you said Hong Yi-xiang is your first candidate, can you please give me a reason, a reason for me to go back and persuade my dad to let you shoot the documentary," Hong Ze-han said.

"Oh, I think I underestimated your ability to negotiate," Reid said.

"No. You misconstrue," Hong Ze-han said.

"No, no. I would rather hope I didn't make a mistake, since I like to work with smart people. Of course, I expected you would be an outstanding Kung Fu master," Reid said.

"I, too, wish it was like this, but it's a pity I am not. Also, I just glanced at the pile of dossiers on the bed: Wang Shu-jin, Qiao Chang-hong, Han Qing-tang, Chang Dong-sheng, Shen Mao-hui, Gao Dao-sheng, Liu Yun-qiao, Gao Sen-huang, Gao Fang-xian, Fu Shu-yun, Zhang Xing-y… These are the top masters of the contemporary era, even if you close your eyes and choose one, they are all qualified to be the headliner. Trust me," said Hong Ze-han.

"I think Mr. Hong is right," Commissioner Li said.

"My professionalism does not allow me to do this. I have to choose the best one from so many masters. Mr. Hong, can you give me a suggestion," Reid said.

"Then, what is the standard to apprise 'best?'" Hong Ze-han asked.

"Well, the one best able to represent the entire essence of Chinese traditional martial arts," Reid said.

"Still too abstract," Hong Ze-han said.

"Well. Why did I not have these problems when I chose the principal karate figure in Japan?" Reid asked.

"The first reason may be that you originally had a good understanding of karate, and the second is that you already had a strong subjective predisposition," Hong Ze-han said.

"Yeah. That's right. I practice karate," Reid said.

"So, your current troubles weren't caused by me. I didn't make your work too complicated, right?" Hong Ze-han said.

"No. Your point is well taken. It means things are far more complicated than we originally thought. Good. I have an idea. You are a film director, right? Then I will ask you in turn, if you were given the chance to use the influence of the BBC to introduce Taiwan's traditional Chinese martial arts to the world, how would you do it?" Reid said.

"Are you giving me a job interview now? Why do I get the impression that the question you are asking me now is your job?" Hong Ze-han said.

"No. My job is to make the best show, no matter what method is used, and I am doing this now. I just happened to have run into someone who can help, and now I'm convincing this person, at least that's what I think," Reid said.

"Mr. Hong, our Minister...," Assistant Director Li said.

"Don't worry. I'm just creating an opportunity to guide the content," Reid said.

"If you segment by sect, Chinese traditional martial arts include at least Northern and Southern Shaolin, Xingyi, Bagua, Taiji, and wrestling etc. If you only segment by Shaolin schools there is still much to consider, like White Crane, Taizu, Choy Lee Fut, Wing Chun… If the BBC only uses one episode for the whole package, it is not hard to imagine the result, and I am afraid that the audience will already know more than you can present. This should not be the outcome you are seeking," Hong Ze-han said.

"So then?" Reid asked.

"Unless you confirm that one episode is not enough, there is no need to continue discussing it," Hong Ze-han asserted.

"Even though it would increase the budget a lot, I am willing to try. It's just, if you want to request each sect to shoot an episode, then I think…" Reid hesitated.

"Rest easy. Although Chinese martial arts have many schools, there is another simple way to categorize them," offered Hong Ze-han.

"I got it. You mean Internal School and External School,—great. How could I forget this method. Starting out with this classification, divide the production into two episodes…," Reid hypothesized.

"Did the BBC consider shooting in mainland China?" Hong Ze-han wondered aloud.

"For the time being we don't have this plan. We have considered Hong Kong," Reid admitted.

"China is the source after all. Setting aside political factors for the moment, there must be some reasonable formula. I suggest perhaps using 'Northern Boxing Spread to the South' as the theme," Hong Ze-han said.

"Elucidate please," Reid insisted.

"The origins of traditional Chinese martial arts each developed against backgrounds distinctive in time and place and with special characteristics. Like the Boat Stance and the Horse Stance, they evolved corresponding to the special conditions of boats being used in the south and horses being used in the north. Without the intervention of external forces, the mutual influence between each other would be very slow and gradual," Hong Ze-han explained.

"What do you mean by external forces?" Reid asked.

"Famines, diseases, and wars are all irresistible external forces. And 1949 was an era of huge change in China, which resulted in the greatest human migration south in modern Chinese history. It influenced population, culture, wealth, political power, *and* martial arts," Hong Ze-han detailed.

"At that time, Taiwan and Hong Kong were the largest bases for absorbing these resources. Due to these human factors, many martial arts masters were forced to gather in these tiny hot-houses, and there resulted inevitable collision, integration, and transformation. Northern Internal boxing techniques rarely seen in the past converged overnight on this small southern island of Taiwan. Clashes with the unfamiliar and resistance led to mutual fusion and absorption. This flood of propagation to the south obviously produced qualitative and quantitative changes to the martial arts ecology of the south and the structure of Southern boxing. Isn't this kind of clash of eras, places, and cultures the best angle of entry for this documentary?" Hong Ze-han inquired.

"Excellent," Reid replied, his anthropologist's muse had been tickled.

"So, at least two episodes. Fewer and you might as well not bother," Hong Ze-han expressed.

"I'll figure out how to get it done," Reid agreed.

"Sweet!" Assistant Director Li couldn't hide his inner joy and gave a thumbs up of approval.

"Also, please accept my most sincere advice. In selecting these masters please don't continue to employ this kind of competitive 'Hollywood audition to win a chance at performing.' It is really unsuitable," Hong Ze-han suggested.

"I know, but please tell me, what is a better way?" Reid solicited.

"Go to visit them one by one, with your sincerity. Then make a choice based on the result of your visits, instead of summoning them one by one to be inspected, unless what you want is not a real master."

"Sorry. I severely misunderstood the culture here," Reid confessed.

"I think Mr. Hong's suggestion is correct," Assistant Director Li said.

"Okay. After I have paid a visit to all the masters, can we meet again? At the coffee shop on the first floor, not in here anymore. My instincts tell me you are willing to help. I hope I am right," Reid persisted.

"Mr. Hong, from the standpoint of the Press Bureau, I would like to ask you to provide this assistance. The BBC is worthy of this," Assistant Director Li enjoined.

The three parties completed their first meeting in a harmonious atmosphere and established good communications. In this series of documentaries, these changes increased the length and proportion of exposure for Taiwan, compared to the original plan. Production costs also increased. Fortunately, a large-scale broadcasting network such as the BBC has sufficient resources to bear these additional expenditures. Of course, even more important was to have a producer like Howard Reid who had high context Emotional Quotient skills and could act decisively. Otherwise, such a negotiation may not have resulted in satisfaction for all three parties.

Hong Ze-han had sent several proposals to the TV station and competent authorities to film a documentary to faithfully explore the legacy of Chinese martial arts, and even actively sought financial sponsorship from the corporate world. In that age when the economy was just starting to take-off, everything was tied to commercial preconditions alone, and the legacies of culture and martial arts were not considered essential to society.

The appearance of Howard Reid in that milieu was as an angel descended from the sky. When there is something that you desperately want to do, but never could achieve with your own hands, if in the process of helping others you can draw on their resources and reputation to help them realize their objective, it should count as self-realization in disguised form. In that case you suppose it doesn't matter if you don't appear in the whole completed event.

With this state of mind, Hong Ze-han decided to use the strategy of "retreat to advance" to guide this negotiation. Only through the BBC's professional skills and ubiquitous broadcasting network could Hong Yi-xiang and his Yizong Tangshoudao be pushed out onto an elevated world stage. He was convinced that only in this way would it have a chance to be seen by the world.

When Ze-han stepped out of the Hilton Hotel and faced the wide Taipei main station plaza, he vaguely experienced the nameless jitters felt by his grandmaster Zhang Jun-feng as he stepped out of the same station rear plaza for the first time, facing Taiwan, a small southern island, unfamiliar yet full of infinite possibilities. A timer in Hong Ze-han's heart began a countdown to the next scheduled phone call with Howard Reid. So, dreaming about it all the way home, he calculated and strategized: How can the essence and mystery of the Internal School of boxing be conveyed in a brief forty-five minutes? What kind of film language should be employed to convey the beauty and philosophical thinking hidden deep within the fisticuffs of authentic gongfu? What kind of camera angles and perspectives should be used to allow the audience to absorb the legend and unique knowledge of Hong Yi-xiang…

Hong Ze-han and his cousin Hong Ze-hao practice flying sidekicks along the Danshui River in front of the Temple of Heavenly Waters, 1974.

Hong Ze-han and his friend Jungle Lu practice kicking along the Danshui River flood control wall, 1974.

94– BBC WAY OF THE WARRIOR PART 2

Logical reasoning can only progress from one to two, and from less to more. Imagination on the other hand can create something out of nothing and produce infinite possibilities.

Scene: Homes in Anxi Street and Minle Street

"Won't this affect your work?" Hong Yi-xiang asked.

"Of course, it will. But this is an opportunity to speak directly to the world, you can't miss it," Ze-han said.

"You have anything important to say, you gotta tell the world? Can't you tell your brother first," Ze-zhou insisted.

"Do you know why mating rights in the wild are only reserved for the strongest winner?" Ze-han demanded.

"I never imagined this matter would suddenly be related to animals fucking around!" Ze-zhou joked.

"Stop interrupting. Let him talk," Hong Yi-xiang instructed.

"Because of fierce competition for survival in the wild, opportunities for reproduction must be reserved for the strongest genes to ensure that the species can continue to reproduce," Ze-han explained.

Hong Yi-xiang sat quietly still trying to grasp what his some was communicating.

"Times are constantly advancing, and new and interesting things are constantly emerging. In the future, the environment faced by Chinese martial arts will become more and more nasty. The Kung Fu boom of the recent past may not return. After such a big surge, once the tide subsides, it will inevitably be quiet for a long time."

"No doubt. If nothing new of value continues to be developed, even the best things will die out," Ze-zhou admitted.

"Like some old crafts and tastes that we miss, if there is no inheritor or successor, and no one leaves any record, once it disappears, it disappears forever. Dad, the Yizong Tangshoudao you created with a lifetime of hard work must be passed on in a planned way. By fighting for the BBC episode I hope the power of TV broadcasting will attract more outstanding people, we can select the best of these talents, let them plant the seeds of Yizong Tangshoudao, and so pass it on. The BBC has a superior communication network, we mustn't miss this opportunity. They need us to make this episode, and we need them, too," Ze-han said, promoting.

"And afterwards?" Ze Zhou asked.

"That's it, what other 'afterwards' is there," Ze-han rejoined.

"Do you know why the disciples of the older generation were taught by oral transmission? Even if the technique had been written in boxing manuals, beginner disciples would still have to hand transcribe them. Do you know why?" Ze-zhou queried.

"I know, but you still want to tell me again, right. Just say it," Ze-han replied.

"It means that the disciples should read while transcribing. Don't let them get away with the illusion that this knowledge is easy to grab, otherwise it will not be held as precious. It can only be learned one on one, one technique at a time. Absolutely no photos, let alone making a movie, just to avoid all the secrets of this sect leaking out. Once secret techniques and skills are public, no matter how good the tactics are, they all become ordinary common knowledge, so your opponent can easily counteract them. This violates the maxim 'The Exposed Technique Will Not Land,' don't you know? You play around with TV and movies, don't you know that a two-hour video tape can capture the essence of a master's entire life's learning, leaving nothing, true or not?" Ze-zhou retorted.

"Sure," Ze-han confirmed.

"Then why do you still want to persuade dad to accept this interview?" Ze-zhou asked.

"These are two completely different things. Of course, this is not to say that if we don't shoot, things will turn out this way. There are still other ways to meet our needs…," Ze-han claimed.

"Yes. That's what I meant," Ze-zhou said.

"But on the other hand, all the things you are worried about may not happen after the filming. There are countermeasures for avoiding such results. Handled well, it can be a win-win, even a win-win-win situation, isn't this better? I think we should lead things in this direction," Ze-han affirmed.

"Yes. I believe this. Isn't complicating simple things your specialty? You always had this natural gift, this skill to wear out our family more than those British people, believe me. But I beg you, give it up, let others do it," Ze-zhou responded.

"Thank you for such praise. But this is a big deal, how about we just put a bit more effort into it?" Ze-han urged.

"No. You still haven't grasped my thinking. Do you know why the 'face change' of Chinese Sichuan opera has been able to attract the eyes of audiences of different generations for hundreds of years?" Ze-zhou asked.

"You ask, you answer, okay. Anyway, you have already set the riposte. I don't play your fool," Ze-han replied.

"It's interesting. If the progenitor who invented this performing art did not tightly hold the secret of this key technique, do you think an audience would be willing to shell out the cash and politely sit down to watch their performance?" Ze-zhou questioned.

"These are the most meaningful words I have ever heard come from your mouth. Admirable. Respects," Ze-han exclaimed.

"Admirable your ass! On the surface, keeping secrets seems to be a negative and selfish practice, but history tells us that this is the best choice. Why can a restaurant that sells Peking duck be handed down for generations and hundreds of years without falling into disrepute? Not guarding the core techniques and secrets is a short cut to ruin, there is no way it can last a long time, you know, oh, Great Director!" Ze-zhou spat.

"You think too much. We're just filming a documentary episode, you make it seem like we're leaking state secrets, is it that serious?" Ze-han asked.

"A-zhou's words are not without reason. Martial arts are injurious techniques, it's unacceptable if we don't take this risk into account," averred Hong Yi-xiang.

"Dad. I agree with this," Ze-han pleaded. "But those concerns can basically be controlled from the source. Coupled with the assistance of some film technology, there will not be a problem," Ze-han responded.

"Okay. Maybe it really can be done like that. But is it necessary? Think about it carefully. After the BBC film is made, they can sell the rights around the world, they can make a lot of money, who's to say they won't win a big prize and get a lot of fame and fortune from it. I ask you, what do we get in the end?" Ze-zhou remained uneasy.

"What we get are the possibilities—possibilities that will not happen if we don't do it,'" Ze-han retorted.

"What kind of BS is that? Your imagination is too rich," Ze-zhou disagreed.

"Yes. To accomplish this, one *must* have more positive imagination and less negative worries. If this episode is made and broadcast, there will be some response. These reactions will give rise to many opportunities we cannot even imagine right now. Maybe in the process we can learn from some experiences we didn't have in the past, we can get to know some special people, we can win more recognition, and maybe many unexpected good things will happen…," Ze-han speculated.

"Don't waste your energy. In all the world, there is no such thing as a free lunch," Ze-zhou said.

"Sure. So, in the same way, isn't it that the BBC can't eat our free lunch for nothing? If you have food, provide food, if you have energy, provide labor, each according to their means. I don't know what is wrong with it," Ze-han replied.

"Pointless arguing with you. If dad doesn't object, you can do whatever you like. I don't want to be dipped in these muddy waters. I'll say it again," Ze-zhou insisted.

"What?" Ze-han asked.

"Stupid… idiot," Ze-zhou could not bear his younger brother's careless romanticism, so he turned around and walked away full of resentment, ending this inconclusive debate.

"Those calling other people Idiot are the real idiots. Dad, you won't oppose this?"

"I really can't tell which one of you is the real idiot. If you have thought it through clearly, then do it. Can I stop you? Just don't let it affect your work, and don't get twisted inside out, okay."

"Dad, don't worry. I already quit my job, so there is no work to be affected."

"You! Did you tell your mother beforehand? Ai! Really? Don't wind up empty handed."

"No."

"Will the BBC support you with a stipend for the research work of filming?"

"No, even if there was, I don't want it."

"Then what do you want?"

"The possibilities that won't happen if we don't do it."

"Okay. Maybe you should think about it first, in case nothing happens, and you gave up your job, how might things go for you."

"This is a possibility."

Provoked by a bunch of as yet unrealized "possibilities," in his younger brother's speech full of impractical, romantic thoughts, Hong Ze-zhou swore to have nothing further to do with the mess. And Hong Yi-xiang, like an old cat crouching in the eaves, quietly watched the battle of words between the two brothers. As was his habit, he maintained an "okay to take it or leave it" mentality about the cooperation plan with the BBC. He just wanted to figure out why this child was so enthusiastic about such an uncertain thing, what was he thinking? What clues did *he* see? If the child, like his grandfather before him, really had the ability to see key issues at a glance, how should he, as a good father, help him at a critical moment? However, as he listened, the signals were yet very weak. Hong Ze-zhou only had a little bit of fuzzy intuition and premonition, still far away from the degree where awareness rapidly converges into detailed judgement. No one knew whether this predictive ability would continue to develop, maybe it was just a temporary phenomenon. If this was the case, would it be a good thing to have this unstable and unpredictable ability?

"Ai! This kid jumps off and does this stuff even he is not clear about. Why can't he be as pragmatic as his older brother? Only, is it good to be as pragmatic as his older brother? Will something be missed? Even I am mixed up by this guy. Is it possible I too care about the miraculous "possibilities" he talked about? This kid, who dreams all day. Even quitting such a good job. I really don't know how he'll tell his mother without making her pop. Didn't he love that job very much. Did he forget how much he looked like a happy monkey when he was promoted to be a director? Three out of five times this kid runs into big trouble, and this time I don't know what result may arise…"

As Hong Yi-xiang grew longer in years, the authority that a strict father should have exercised was massaged by these children into helpless nagging from a loving father. He originally expected the children to grow up one by one without a hitch, marry wives and have children. If the environment permitted and the children were willing, of course, he hoped he could pass on the wisdom and connections he had accumulated in the martial arts over a lifetime. Fortunately, the aptitudes and talents of these three children were not too bad, and they were all serious in practicing boxing, save for the worries about second son A-han's asthma. It would be no major problem for eldest son A-zhou to pick up the baton. If you added two younger brothers to help, this combination should be enough to support this system. But should he allow them to continue down this path?

A seemingly ordinary media interview made the Hong family's second son quit his admired job as a director, without hesitation, just to swing for the fences and strive for an inexplicable possibility. Was this possibility somewhere between all and nothing just an illusion? Or could he really grasp this blurry intuition and spin it into a concrete accomplishment? Who knew…?

Zhu Ming, famed for his sculptures of Taijiquan, meeting Hong Yi-xiang during the filming of the BBC documentary, 1982.

95– BBC WAY OF THE WARRIOR PART 3

What cannot be achieved now may not be possible in the future. But if we give up now, it will never be done.

Scene: Hilton Taipei Hotel

"A TOTAL OF TWENTY CANDIDATES WERE IDENTIFIED, AND THEY have all been visited according to your suggestion. In the end, only five are left. After I return to the UK to discuss with the planning team, I will lead my production team back here for the final screening. We decided to cut Chinese martial arts into two themes based on the Hard and the Soft. The External School of Boxing representing hardness is expected to be researched and filmed in Hong Kong, and the Internal School of Boxing representing softness will be filmed in Taiwan. For Chinese martial arts I'm sure to shoot two episodes, so there should be plenty of space for in-depth exploration and reporting. What do you think of our arrangement?" Reid inquired.

"This is a smart decision," Hong Ze-han replied.

"Thank you for your suggestion. It helped us find the best production direction. During these interview visits, we heard of some special kung fu, I thought it was very interesting. Assistant Director Li suggested that I come to ask you about this. Is that okay?" Reid asked.

"You should go to the old masters for their advice," Hong Ze-han suggested.

"I did ask. But the more it is spoken of, the more mysterious it is. The more one listens, the more blurred it becomes," Reid replied.

"Oh? No wonder my father always says that an old master can only prove his age, not necessarily how good he is at kung fu," Hong Ze-han offered.

"Ha-ha-ha…This statement really draws blood with the first poke. Really interesting. I have to remember this idea, otherwise, if I don't pay attention, it's easy to fall into these myths. But I must admit, the long white beards and deep wrinkles are really convincing in front of a camera," Reid responded.

"Yep. So, what's the question?" Hong Ze-han asked.

"Palm Wind," Reid said.

"How could you ask such an awesome question," Hong Ze-han queried.

"Is it really awesome?" Reid wondered. "Have you studied it?"

"No," Hong Ze-han said.

"Have you seen it?" Reid queried.

"Nope," Hong Ze-han replied.

"Have you heard of anyone practicing it?" Reid proceeded.

"Sure. All inside of novels," Hong Ze-han said.

"So, this thing doesn't exist at all?" Reid speculated.

"This way you have answered your own question, not good," Hong Ze-han pointed out. "What you haven't seen or heard doesn't directly infer that it doesn't exist," Hong Ze-han claimed.

"Unless you can prove it exists," Reid retorted.

"No. Unless you can prove that it doesn't exist. Otherwise, this kind of logic would smother many possibilities," Hong Ze-han persisted.

"Hey, gentlemen, are you discussing this? Or are you arguing?" Assistant Director Li intervened.

"Calm down. We are just 'discussing vigorously,'" Hong Ze-han replied.

"Aren't martial arts supposed to be pragmatic, fist on face," Reid proposed.

"You're only speaking to one component, if it were only this, then it is not Chinese martial arts," Hong Ze-han related.

"Is that right? The other part, what is it?" Reid asked.

"Eh. Are you trying to trick me into answering your question?" Hong Ze-han asked.

"This is a necessity of my profession. Aren't you also a director?" Reid asked.

"Alright. There is yet a domain, which is to explore inwardly some things that seem to be non-existent or impossible…," Hong Ze-han responded.

"Explore inwardly?" Reid asked.

"Yes," Hong Ze-han said.

"Explore the various possibilities of the human body, using Qi and Daoyin," Hong Ze-han put forth.

"What is that?" Reid asked.

"Western civilization has created many great inventions, including movies and television, but the tools to propel these civilizations require a very powerful internal force," Hong Ze-han said.

"What does this have to do with what you said?" Reid queried.

"I mean the exploration of the inner universe, a non-invasive inner exploration," Hong Ze-han replied.

"Like Indian yoga and Tibetan meditation?" Reid asked.

"Yes. If martial arts lack the inner spiritual level of cultivation, only muscles, fists and violence remain. Especially for internal boxing," Hong Ze-han clarified.

"Tell me about 'Qi and Daoyin.'" Reid drew him out.

"Internal training has two parts: psychology and physiology. The psychological part is mainly for the exploration of life and existential philosophy. The United States once filmed a Kung Fu television series. This was the best interpretation of the psychological training…," Hong Ze-han said.

"I understand this part, no need to elaborate," Reid confirmed.

"The physical part is the exploration of the essence of life, let's talk about 'Daoyin' first. 'Daoyin' is a mind control technique which the Internal School calls 'Yi' or Intent, different from ordinary sensory feelings," Hong Ze-han explained.

"Mr. Hong, you are now using one abstract thing to explain another abstract thing, so how can I understand it?" Reid exclaimed.

"Okay. Let's put it this way. 'Yi' means that we have the ability to sense our internal organs and inner workings," Hong Ze-han said.

"We use our mind[32] to sense the activities of internal organs and glands in the body, and then learn to control the originally involuntary autonomic muscle tissues and organ functions of the body, including: the frequency of operation, circulation, metabolism, and endocrine release," Hong Ze-han related.

"I find that the ancient civilizations of the East seemed particularly interested in such invisible and abstract subjects," Reid offered.

"Yes. But since it can't be seen, it's easy to con people with tricks. Others can be cheated, but we mustn't deceive ourselves. Our tradition instructs us, we should respect yin and yang and the harmony of internal and external. This may be an unfamiliar field to which you should pay attention," Hong Ze-han said.

"Agreed. What again is 'qi'?" Reid inquired.

"This qi does not refer to the air you breathe. There are many things that cannot be explained clearly in simple language or words. If 'intention' is an inwardly directed response and control technique, then 'qi' should be considered as an energy that assists intention with its execution," Hong Ze-han clarified.

"So, Yi and Qi are two very important elements in Eastern civilization and the Internal School of Boxing? Therefore, there are many things in Chinese martial arts for which their existence cannot be proven, neither can their non-existence be proven?" Reid pondered.

"Between you and me, yes, you can say that, but I think it is best not to lead everyone to think in that direction, especially before you have a correct understanding of Chinese martial arts," Hong Ze-han suggested.

"I'm just curious about such a thing as 'Palm Wind.' In essence, atop what theoretical assumptions is it constructed?" Reid asked.

"If you use a researcher's mentality to probe, 'Palm Wind' should be an expression of qi or a kind of inner energy released and projected," Hong Ze-han said.

"Assistant Director Li, you were right. I think Mr. Hong understands," Reid said.

"No. I really don't understand. It is only with very limited knowledge that I am trying to understand," Hong Ze-han said.

---

32 It should be noted that in TCM and CMA, the mind corresponds to the *Xin*, heart, not the *Nao*, brain.

"No problem. At least so far, I am satisfied. Please continue," Reid assured.

"Up to now, it is known that deadly weapons or martial arts all must pass through a physical medium and contact with the body before they produce their effect, isn't it?" Hong Ze-han said.

"The physical media you are talking about is solid, like knives, arrows, bullets, and people's fists and feet, right?"

"If the physical medium is removed, can the energy that originally impelled the weapon still be deadly?" Hong Ze-han asked.

"No way. Well, no. I remember, things like sound waves and lasers can directly injure without the need for solid media…," Reid considered.

"I've heard of singers in Italian operas, who can break a glass with their high-pitched vibration frequency?" Hong Ze-han asked.

"Yeah. That's right," Reid agreed.

"If I control the opponent with my hand first, and then by chance suddenly yell in his ears, at least it can startle him unexpectedly, right? If I can take advantage of this gap, won't my chances of winning become greater?" Hong Ze-han posited.

"It's possible. This is at least a smart diversionary tactic," Reid affirmed.

"If we use the palm of our hand to compress the air directly into the opponent's ear, can it also hurt his hearing?" Hong Ze-han postulated.

"It's possible," Reid responded.

"If I use a Taiji 'Pressing Palm' against your chest, seize the moment you exchange your breath and press it down like this…?" Hong Ze-han placed his right hand on Howard Reid's chest then, taking advantage of the instant he was not paying attention as he breathed, Hong pressed down with penetrating energy. Reid showed the discomfort of someone having trouble breathing. "Uncomfortable, right?"

"Wow! What an unpleasant feeling. Is this the palm wind?" Reid asked.

"Of course not. This is just a hand method to compress the breath, attack the 'qi,'" Hong Ze-han explained.

"Then, what about Palm Wind?" Reid wondered.

"How do I know how the Palm Wind operates. Aren't we just now researching its theoretical basis?" Hong Ze-han returned. And put a ball point pen on the table. "Watch what happens when I flick it with my finger. When the pen flicks off my finger, it will continue to surge forward until the resistance cancels out all the momentum. It will stop, right? This means that the energy that we project through our fingers can continue to exist for a period of time after it leaves the hand. If this condition is employed in golf, the energy knocking ball out will exist longer and farther, right? So, energy can continue to exist alone after leaving the hand, but if there is no ball or pen, it is just harder for us to observe," Hong Ze-han substantiated.

"Okay. You explained that power can continue to exist alone after leaving the hand, and then?" Reid questioned.

"Therefore, we can reasonably infer that if one undertakes enhanced training to intensify and concentrate energy, can't it be like the resonant vocals of a high-pitched singer or a laser beam, using a very concentrated and coherent energy, to project it directly out of the body, and achieve the purpose of injuring people? I dare speculate that this is the theoretical basis for the existence of 'Palm Wind,'" Hong Ze-han illuminated.

"Yeah. It seems to make a little sense," Reid agreed.

"'Things that make sense but can't be done' are abundant," Hong Ze-han conceded.

"Okay. Do you have any other thoughts on the 'Palm Wind?'" Reid inquired.

"There is one. This is not to be spoken of in your film. We are just speculating with known science and imagination to decipher an unknown domain, so this is not ready for the light of day. Unless you go back to the UK to practice behind closed doors until you have magical skills to demonstrate to people. Then you can make a special episode to interview yourself," Hong Ze-han joked.

"Mr. Hong, don't underestimate your own conclusion today. A wise man in the West said: Logic can help you change one into two, from less to more. But imagination can help you change nothing into something. The ability to change nothing into something is creativity. Usually, we must imagine something first, before people concentrate their knowledge and effort to find a solution for making it real. This is also the main purpose of my further exploration of the topic of 'Palm Wind.' The last thing I want to ask is, does Master Hong Yi-xiang agree with you?" Reid wondered.

"I use the genes he gave me to explore these things that only exist in legends. Basically, my mother is not interested in these abstract things," Hong Ze-han related.

"Oh. So, you mean that I should be able to observe more, and more special, things from your esteemed father?" Reid speculated.

"He is the master. I'm just the master's son. Speaking from the principle of proportions, you should be able to learn more and more convincing things from him," Hong Ze-han corroborated.

"Interesting. Through the communication with you, I am full of expectations for the meeting with Master Hong Yi-xiang!" Reid exclaimed.

"I believe you two will have a very delightful conversation," Hong Ze-han confirmed.

This second meeting was still at the Hilton Hotel, but this time it was in the Italian restaurant. Together with Assistant Director Li from the Information Ministry, the three people ordered a large brick oven baked pizza and red wine, and conversed in a harmonious atmosphere, like friends of many years dining and chatting. They did not discuss whether Master Hong Yi-xiang had entered the BBC's list of five finalist candidates. Their focus was on abstract topics from folklore legends. No one knew what kind of link these discussions would have with the future documentary, and what kind of conclusions might be drawn. But some topics have such a powerful magnetic attraction, people fall over one another to explore them, until they find a way to make them believable.

In the development of human civilization, besides the accumulation of experience and its inferences slowly forming effective survival skills and upgraded logic, imagination played another role in making something out of nothing. Always seeking methods and possibilities that exist between the "possible" and the "impossible," blurring hard and stubborn boundaries, moving the line of self-imposed limits, mankind is guided to bravely explore new opportunities and new possibilities in the unknown. Perhaps in the future, "Palm Wind," supported by a scientific understanding of the human body, will become a real ability, just as human beings can step on a wooden board to ride the wind and waves. What people will observe at that time will be an outward manifestation of civilization, rather than a kind of gongfu that is internal energy released to the outside. Maybe. Under the leadership of technological civilization, the exploration and development of the inner universe may eternally remain just crazy talk, always just idle dinner chatter; the only difference is, whether melon seeds, peanuts and tea are served on the table? Or pizza and wine.

Hong Yi-xiang demonstrates a Taiji throwing technique during the filming of the BBC documentary, 1982.

96– BBC WAY OF THE WARRIOR PART 4

A Russian prima ballerina said: Even if you are relegated to the edge of the stage, where there is no spotlight, and no one cares about you, from start to finish you must maintain your poise, only in this way can you have a chance to be seen.

Scene: Anxi Street

IN THE WILDERNESS, THE CUCKOO BIRD DELIBERATELY LAYS ITS own eggs in the nest of other species of birds, allowing the other female bird to help incubate the eggs and nurture its offspring. No one knows why it behaves this way. No one knows, after the hatched little bird grows up and knows the world, who will he recognize as his mother. Maybe in their world, the relationship between birds is relatively simple, only a question of DNA passed on, with no recognition of ancestry or squabbling over the distribution of inheritance. Perhaps it is because ever since Pangu created the heavens, they have been incubated and raised in other bird's nests. Therefore, in its awareness, the other mother bird is its real mother. So, when it becomes an adult, laying eggs in other bird's nests is the will of Heaven!

There are many matters which at the beginning are perhaps just a mistake made in a rush, but later it is found within the mistake resides a truth, so it is accepted and adapted. Once the mistake is perpetuated long enough, perpetuated with sufficient conviction, the wrong concept becomes right. Isn't it the case? Until one day, another stronger, even more self-interested new idea is promoted, until it is sufficient to topple the original tradition and understanding…

To succeed in depositing one's ideas into another person and use their opportunity to propagate the ideas is not unlike the cuckoo bird, since placing one's own eggs in other people's mental or operational nests is not so simple. Especially when facing a production team with the world's leading technology and experience. This is not merely a bird's nest that would casually accommodate foreign things, unless they are like succulent berries, providing delicious taste and nutrition as an inducement to spread and propagate the new seed, otherwise all the scheming and calculations would be just a trunk full of daydreams.

"Leave the opportunity to others. We don't want to compete with our good friends for this documentary opportunity," Hong Yi-xiang said, demurring.

"Pa, small matters can be yielded to others, big deals can't. In Taiwan we won't have a second chance to let such a professional team and such a strong communication network generate interest in us. Only if you stand up, only then is there an opportunity for the world to see how Chinese Internal Boxing has taken root in Taiwan over these years," Hong Ze-han insisted.

"If this is the case, should you not first think about what is the benefit to the BBC in choosing us? Why did they give this opportunity to us instead of others?" Hong Yi-xiang speculated.

"Pa, before I set foot in the Hilton Hotel, I already thought this through," Hong Ze-han assured.

"But there are some things that can't be forced," Hong Yi-xiang insisted.

"Pa, this is a big deal. I must have the determination to do something I know may be impossible. I can't passively rely on water carving the canal I want. If I don't force it, I'll never get it, so I have fight for it with all my might. Even if I don't get anything in the end, providing I try my hardest, I will be the better for it, right?" Hong Ze-han declared.

"Very well. But determination is not enough. Do you have any reliable way to know what is impossible?" Hong Yi-xiang responded.

"We must first win the chance to be in the documentary," Hong Ze-han contended.

"Yes, but how to win?" Hong Yi-xiang wondered.

"The key is in you," Hong Ze-han pushed.

"No. The key should be at the BBC," Hong Yi-xiang objected.

"No, it's you!" Hong Ze-han argued.

"Isn't the master control in the hands of others?" Hong Yi-Xiang asked.

"Yes. But I understand the thinking of the production team. They want more than gongfu, they want a story with tension, a story that makes the whole documentary look more interesting and inspiring."

"Then what can you do?" Hong Yi-xiang inquired.

"Help them understand your martial arts and your story in a simpler way," Hong Ze-han suggested.

"Do you think they will listen to you?" Hong Yi-xiang doubted.

"At least they have to listen again one more time before they make the final decision," Hong Ze-han asserted.

"Listening and listening *to* you are two different things," Hong Yi-xiang related.

"Yes, so before they tell the audience about your story, I have to seize this opportunity to use them as *my* audience first, and tell them your story in my way," explained Hong Ze-han.

"Yeah. Not a bad idea," Hong Yi-xiang agreed.

"Don't you always remind me not to help by making decisions for others, but to form an environment wherein they can make their own decisions under their own free will, such that the results that you want to occur naturally," Hong Ze-han recalled.

"What makes you so certain it will work this time?" Hong Yi-xiang questioned.

"Other martial artists are obstructed by the 'dignity of the master,' such that they will only passively wait to be understood. But you have me, I can actively provide them with some interesting and useful ideas and information, allowing them in the shortest time to grasp the essence and characteristics of the Internal School of boxing. When they layer on their expertise, we should be able to help them to complete the best documentary. Therefore, unless they decide not to make this episode, it's hard for them not to seek my help," Hong Ze-han promoted.

"I never saw that you could have such a confident and imperious manner," Hong Yi-xiang exclaimed.

"Pa, in fact, my inner strength is formidable, I just suppress it like grandpa did," Hong Ze-han confided.

"Oh. Why didn't I know you were so repressed," Hong Yi-xiang joked.

"It's not like that. Just to let you know that the battlefield I am familiar with is the negotiating table, not the ring. When using my brain power to fight tit-for-tat, I am not a weakling, even if I must sometimes show weakness due to the circumstances, but this kind of weakness is only a temporary expedient, not true weakness. I did this just so that they can truly appreciate our assistance without worrying that I will try to take over. Only by creating this win-win situation, can we get all we want, can this episode become the real highlight of this entire documentary series," proclaimed Hong Ze-han.

"If you do it this way, don't you feel it's very unfair? Letting others use your ideas like this for free," argued Hong Yi-xiang.

"Yes."

"Then why bother?" Hong Yi-xiang continued.

"Pa, in Taiwan, the reality of creative endeavors is that 'if you can settle for second best it is already considered a victory.' Having my capabilities validated by this cooperation is enough for me. If not, I will never know what I am capable of," Hong Ze-han said.

"Hmm. I thought that politics and the economy had changed for the better, and in a more liberal environment everyone could expand their freedoms. I didn't expect that repression still exists," Hong Yi-xiang sighed.

"Pa. We are a small island-bound country, what else do we have to compete with others? If it weren't for this impetus, the situation might be even more dire. I am used to finding new pathways under this pressure. I believe that 'settling for second best' will one day become 'pushing for No. 1,'" Hong Ze-han urged.

"It's fine to think so. But I can't help but remember what the old friend I met on the mountain once said. He said that there is a traditional puppet show in the southwest border of China called 'Water Puppets.' The puppet master must wear black clothes, black pants, and a black hood, hiding behind a black curtain, forever isolated from all the applause, the lights and glory behind the black curtain concealing his existence…," Hong Yi-xiang related.

"Pa, rest assured. If the performance is good enough, I believe that one day we can take off the black masks, step out from behind the black curtain and stand on the stage to face the audience, take our bows, and accept their applause," Hong Ze-han reasoned.

"Yeah? Very well. I really hope that in my lifetime, I can see my child standing on the stage, receiving the glory and applause he deserves," Hong Yi-xiang supported.

Before the era of cable television, in an age when there were only three broadcast channels, TTV, CTV, and CTS, the local television production ecosystem was very tough. Due to the limitations of market size and production funding, the pre-production time for a special documentary was often no more than a week, and the director often wore several hats, doing drafting and editing. On one hand, the production team had to interview at the shooting location, while on the other hand, looking for creative inspiration on the spot, making sure to backfill any missing materials on location.

For programs produced in such a nasty ecosystem, the difficulties exploring the core of an issue in depth were many, maintaining high production values sufficient to make business owners cough-up ad spend, pleasing to the big boss of the TV station, was even more difficult. The innate persistence and lofty spirit of a productive, creative person like Hong Ze-han became incomparably humble and unbearable.

Seeing the explosive power and infinitely extending possibilities behind this transnational cooperation, Hong Ze-han secretly iterated countless wargame outcomes. He surmised that the BBC would put the visit to Hong Yi-xiang last. After summarizing the experiences of the first four interviewees, their questions would be more direct and in-depth. To accurately convey the concept of internal martial arts, he accepted the advice of Deputy Director Li of the Information Bureau, and specifically asked Daniel Reid to serve as the interpreter for this visit, so that Deputy Director Li would no longer be burdened translating the mind-numbingly difficult martial arts terms.

Daniel Reid was an American freelance writer, a high achiever who graduated from the Chinese Department of an Ivy League school. He spoke, read, and wrote Chinese fluently. In addition to writing books, he also helped many airlines write special travel reports for their airline monthly magazines. After completing a translation of Taoist health techniques, he had taken a keen interest in Chinese martial arts, and after reading Robert W. Smith's chapter on Hong Yi-xiang, he took the opportunity of a request by China Airlines to visit Taiwan. He was introduced to Hong Yi-xiang by Howard Brewer, and he entered Hong Yi-xiang's school and was formally apprenticed to learn the art. Reid assuming the role of translator for this crucial interview was the most ideal choice for both parties. After completing these pre-arrangements, Ze-han could only quietly wait for things to happen.

About half a year later, Howard Reid brought his production team to Taiwan to inspect the shooting environment, and at the same time conduct the final interview and final selection of the person of interest. Counting from the first meeting, over a period of twelve months, the British production spokes team had made three visits to Taiwan to do pre-work before the official interview. Such a pragmatic and prudent production approach, besides requiring strong financial backing, also revealed the persistence and effort behind the BBC as a leading brand in the communication industry. This time, the production team was still led by producer Howard Reid and the interview location was fixed at No. 36 Anxi Street, in Taipei. Accompanying him were the directors of the episode, photography and lighting, whose job it was is to simultaneously reconnoiter the conditions of on-site shooting, to confirm that when the official shooting took place, they would have all the required equipment and hook-ups.

Sure enough, before interviewing Master Hong Yi-xiang, they had already completed the interviews with the other four candidates, and they had also filmed and recorded the entire interviews. This production team was experienced and professional. After each staff member entered the interview environment, they worked separately without any communication and assistance. Such a deliberate professional work standard might be just a normal state in the European and American film and television circles, but in Taiwan, where production funding was limited, they were simply a dream team. It allowed Hong Ze-han, who was accustomed to making do and settling for the lowest common denominator, to see a different work attitude and insistence.

"Excuse me, where do the Internal and External Schools of boxing differ?" Howard Reid asked.

"Mainly in the use of the mind and control techniques," conveyed Hong Yi-xiang.

"Controlling what?" inquired Reid.

"Controlling Yi—intention, Qi—intrinsic energy and Li—strength; the three elements of martial arts," Hong Yi-xiang explained.

"Can you use kata forms and movements to show me the difference?" Reid wondered.

"Usually, that is the way it's done. Correct. But that is not the proper way," Hong Yi-xiang replied.

"Why?" Reid asked.

"If I perform the routine movements of External Boxing with the operation mode of Internal Boxing, like this…" Hong Yi-xiang got up and taking a Shaolin Arhat Boxing routine as an example, performed a short section applying principles of Taiji. "Do you think this is Internal or External School boxing?" Hong Yi-xiang queried.

"If you don't specifically remind me, of course I will think it is Taiji," Reid offered.

"So, the routine and the movement itself is not the key. The technique of control is," Hong Yi-xiang upheld.

"Thank you for your demonstration, we fully understand your meaning. Okay. Since this is the case, is there a special reason to differentiate the External School from the Internal School of boxing?" Reid pursued.

"In the early stages of the development of boxing, there probably wasn't any such deliberate segmentation, but later the types and schools of martial arts developed more and more, so later generations arranged things with similar attributes and complementary effects together, so that it should be like this. Got it?" Hong Yi-xiang expounded.

"Between the Internal and External Schools do there exist mutually exclusive, incompatible issues?" Reid asked.

"If there are, they are human problems, not a fisticuffs problem. To me, the difference between the Internal and External Schools is just a matter of sequencing. It just follows the process of human physiological and psychological maturation and development from the external to the internal, the process of harmonizing from hard to soft, nothing more than that. In fact, no clear boundary exists between them," Hong Yi-xiang pointed out.

"Can you speak a bit about the difference of hard and soft?" Reid requested.

"Internal and external, hard and soft, are two sides of the same body, they are mutually dependent on each other and exist at the same time, and they can switch back and forth freely at any time," averred Hong Yi-xiang.

"So how do you distinguish the difference between the two?" Reid wondered.

"You can use your original perspective, how you look at them, so how they exist. I just want to remind you that these concepts of internal and external, hard and soft, they are not clearly and mutually delineated and in conflict with each other," confirmed Hong Yi-xiang.

"Okay. We will find a way to use the Western scientific point of view to clarify this point. Thank you, Master, for your reminder. Then is there a simpler way of talking about Xingyi, Bagua, and Taiji?" Reid queried.

"Xingyiquan is an unarmed boxing technique derived from the spear techniques of the ancient army. Soldiers were mounted on a war horse and could not move as nimbly as if they touched the ground with their feet. The techniques are designed to be very simple and effective, a martial art that emphasizes using the simple to control the complex. It is the best entry point for awakening one's innate vitality and inner strength," commented Hong Yi-xiang.

"Excuse me, what is inner strength?" Reid asked.

"Inner strength is a holistic unified force that manifests from the inside to the outside. Before making physical contact, it is not easy to sense its existence and power, easy for people to ignore and underestimate its injurious potential. As soon as it is brought in contact, in an instant all the stored power is released into the enemy's body," Hong Yi-xiang explained.

"Can you demonstrate some real moves?" Reid solicited.

"Sure. Please give me your hand," Hong Yi-xiang said. Reid stretched out his right hand at the request of Hong Yi-xiang and held it palm upwards at the height of his waist.

"Brace your hand a little bit. Protect yourself. I'll use an External Boxing striking method—let you try that," Hong Yi-xiang directed.

"Okay. No problem," Reid acknowledged.

For safety's sake, Hong Yi-xiang carefully reconfirmed that Reid's palm was ready before acting. He used his right hand to draw a circle from inside to outside, and with an External Boxing smashing hammer technique, he quickly slammed the back of his fist against Reid's right palm. The instant the two hands made contact, an explosive sound erupted, which almost made the BBC work team drop what they were doing and looked worriedly at Reid's reaction.

"Hurt?" Hong Yi-xiang asked.

"Really hurts. But I'm okay. Don't worry," Reid assured.

"Okay. Is this method of striking the same as the karate you learned in the past?" Hong Yi-xiang inquired.

"Same. But it's a little more painful," Reid offered.

"Right. Now I want to demonstrate the movement of inner strength again. Can your hand take it?" Hong Yi-xiang asked.

"Relax. I'm fine," Reid confirmed.

Hong Yi-xiang resumed to his position again, changed his fist to an open palm, and struck down from the same posture, but it seemed that the speed and power was not nearly as fierce and powerful as the previous strike. Unexpectedly, this palm, flowing as effortlessly as a soft fluff of silk, made Reid suddenly withdraw his right hand like he had grabbed a live electric cable. His face twisted from what was obviously extreme discomfort and pain.

"Yow! Really hurts…," Reid said. It took at least twenty or thirty seconds before he slowly recovered his ability to converse.

"Hey! It's really so painful. How could it be like this? My whole body was like a strong electric current running through it directly from the palm to the sole of the foot. What's going on and why is it like this?" Reid asked.

"I just used a most natural way to release my power onto your body," Hong Yi-xiang relayed.

"Doesn't the first strike look faster and harder? Why does this relaxed method hurt more?" Reid puzzled.

"Improper technique cancels out our innate power. I just remove those obstacles and let the original power flow into your body naturally. That's it," Hong Yi-xiang described.

"Are you saying that some techniques increase our effort, but diminish our power?" Reid asked.

"Yep. It sounds contradictory, but it's true. To make a technique look or sound forceful, near the end of the technique we will make a quick braking action. This brake or pull back action will make our clothes or pants make a snapping sound like a whip cracking. Some coaches use this sound to judge whether the students are punching hard enough, but they didn't expect the action of making this sound is the biggest culprit in destroying the generation of power," said Hong Yi-xiang.

"Why?" Reid asked.

"All the outward force that hits is locked up at that braking point. If the force fails to penetrate the enemy's body from the front of the chest to the back, the damage will remain in a shallow layer, and it will not be able to damage the internal organs in the opponent's torso. And if I had put full power into the palm I just released, the capillaries in your finger may have burst due to the sticky pressure of this strike. This is the power of Xingyiquan's 'one punch kill'! Is it still painful now?" Hong Yi-xiang asked.

"It's getting better already. I was thinking that if the palm was thrown on my chest just now, how many ribs would be broken?" Reid speculated.

"Not necessarily. Both sides are moving during a match, the lethality is often weakened by the opponent's self-defense instinct in the moment of contact. When you can accurately capture the moment of the opponent's breath relaxing or use a feint to destroy the opponent's balance first and guide the opponent's body to fall and collide into your strike, under these conditions the collision of the opponent into the blow makes it even more frightening."

"Are there such techniques?" Reid questioned.

"This is an aspect of Bagua Palm training," confirmed Hong Yi-xiang.

"Can you talk about Bagua Palm?" Reid requested.

"Yes. But I must briefly summarize the part about Xingyiquan. Xingyiquan trains Ming Jin, Obvious or Overt Energy. It requires producing motion from stillness, emphasizing that if the enemy does not move, I don't move, if the enemy moves slightly, I move first. The key lies in the mastery of the angle and the moment. Of course, you still need to have enough internal energy to injure the opponent. Bagua Palm's stepping is to confuse and lure the enemy. There are many changes in tactics, but the key tactic is 'Destroy first, then Strike,' so the sixty-four hands of the Post-Heaven Bagua sets are all 'building the bridge and crossing the bridge…,'" Hong Yi-xiang explained.

"What is 'Destroy first, then Strike'?" Reid asked.

"The original purpose of martial arts is to mow down the opponent so that the opponent can't harm you. But if you want to take down the opponent, one doesn't just blindly strengthen one's own power. Instead, one uses a smarter and simpler methods to allow the same force to generate greater lethality. Among various ways, the best method is to first destroy the opponent's balance and guide the opponent's body to make him fall into a collision with my attack, producing a multiplier effect."

Hong Yi-xiang used the Yanking Palm of Post-Heaven Bagua as a demonstration, circling to the left, he used a right piercing palm to lure Reid's defense, when the two sides joined hands, he immediately overturned his hand, seized Reid's right wrist, and dragged him down. One only saw Reid's body immediately topple in direction of the yank, but his head could not keep up with the speed of the upper body dropping in that instant and snapped back abruptly, the cervical vertebrae making a cracking sound of bones squeezing each other. This explosive release of force startled Reid who quickly released his hands and rubbed the back of his neck, his expression one of frightened astonishment, provoking uncontrolled laughter from all the onlookers.

"Are you okay?" Deputy Director Li inquired.

"I'm fine. I was just startled by the sudden change. Wow! What an uncomfortable feeling. It felt all at once like my whole rhythm of breathing and blood circulation was disrupted. Even now it is not very comfortable; Mr. Hong, I'll be okay, right? How can I have such a peculiar reaction?" Reid wondered.

"This is a typical response to this attack. Bagua Palm will give the person struck this kind of topsy-turvy, chaotic blood flow experience," declared Hong Yi-xiang.

"This is my first experience of power being employed to such an extent, it's incredible," Reid exclaimed.

At the instant when Hong Yi-xiang took his shot, Hong Ze-han, who had been calmly watching the skirmish on the sidelines, confirmed the results of the day's visit in his mind. He knew this demonstration had offered a unique insight into the internal martial arts. He knew his intuition and predictions were, and had been, spot-on…

Hong Yi-xiang personally directs the training of Xingyi Five Element Consecutive Linking form, 1982.

Hong Yi-xiang personally directs disciples in the training of Great Roc Spreads Its Wings form, 1982.

97– BBC WAY OF THE WARRIOR PART 5

People narrating past events and history are always loyal to the narrative. As for how much is heard? How much is understood? It's not that important. Isn't it?

Scene: Anxi Street, Danshui River, Hilton Hotel

After a long period of time, the BBC finally sent a letter formally inviting Master Hong Yi-xiang, to serve as the subject of the "Chinese Internal Martial Arts" documentary in the series *The Way of the Warrior*, and asked Hong Yi-xiang before the official filming work started to set aside two weeks for detailed consultation and confirmation with the production team on the content and locations of the actual shooting.

It was also agreed that the BBC directors could involve themselves in the day-to-day life of the subject at work and in repose to capture the most realistic portrait. The cultivation and professionalism of BBC's team allowed them to capture these moments without disrupting the family.

To help the BBC understand the origins of this martial arts system, and to leave some historical record of an extraordinary generation, Hong Yi-xiang led the BBC production team to visit the home on Dihua Street of his father, Mr. Hong Wu-fan. This afforded them an opportunity to have a face-to-face dialogue with the key figure and driving force behind the martial arts master.

It was a winter morning. Mr. Hong Wu-fan had just finished breakfast and was sitting alone by the stove in the store, warming by the fire. Hong Wan Mei Trading had undergone a half century of severe decline, and was no longer a prosperous, bustling shophouse. However, in order not to disturb the elder's feeling of consistency, every day the shop opened and closed according to the schedule of decades past.

After he was widowed, the elder Hong Wu-fan continued his habit of forty years to rise at dawn and hike in the mountains. Finishing a thousand-step walking exercise in the house every morning, he sat on the rattan-armchair next to the counter and read copies of rubbings he had made of sutras carved into the cliffs when he scaled Taiwan's hundred peaks in his early years. The place in which he now sat, was originally the place of *his* boss, his wife, Mrs. Hong Li-mian, who used to occupy the post every day when she was alive. Just as when Madam Hong was around, atop a grate on the stove simmered "Danggui, Ginseng, Milk Vetch and Wolfberry Tea" based on a formula her son Hong Yi-xiang obtained from a hundred-year-old Chinese medicine doctor for Health Promotion Tea. The steam slowly emitted from the mouth of the pot always added a warm and humid atmosphere to this corner of the house. She used to put her two wrinkled and spotted hands on a wooden grate at the stove, the golden and jade bracelets adorning her wrists heated gently by the fire. After her departure from this life, all that was left was Mr. Hong Wu-fan alone, insisting on living in this old shop, this old home, and this old bed, leading an old life he knew so well.

After Zhang Jun-feng recommended he convert to the Yiguandao religion, Mr. Hong Wu-fan became a vegetarian at sixty years of age. On the passing of his wife, his five daughters-in-law took turns to cook his three meals every day in a seven-day cycle. All his remaining daily life necessities were taken care of by Hong Yi-xiang's eldest daughter, Hong Shu-zhen. The formerly bustling enterprise of this traditional family faced another major transformation. The great helmsman, Mr. Hong, who had reached for the sky, gradually aged, while the second generation that should have taken over according to tradition was only passionate about martial arts. With no way to leverage the resources accumulated by the family, nor utilize a lifetime of established marketing channels to transform the family enterprise in a timely and effective way, the business inevitably entered into a fateful decline.

After brief introductions, the BBC engaged in some simple question and answer dialog through an interpreter. Although Mr. Hong was already a venerable ninety years old, regarding all the past events they raised, he could clearly explain and respond. Perhaps the questions raised by the BBC unintentionally liberated memories long locked up and buried deep in his heart. A panorama of that big era unfolded scene by scene, next to the warm stove in the cold winter, according to their sequence in time. If the topic of the filming not been fixed on a martial arts lineage, the oral history shared by Mr. Hong Wu-fan would surely make another deeply moving, poetic saga.

The old man still had a clear memory of past events, succinctly and accurately recounting the first time that Master Zhang Jun-feng came to the Hong's. The situation at home, where Zhang stood, what he said, in what he was attired, Hong painted a vivid oral description, as if it had just happened the day before. In the end, he personally led the BBC staff to climb a wooden ladder up into the attic storage of the shop, and sorted through large bundles of long spears, wooden staffs, and single-handed swords that were provided to neighborhood youths to practice martial arts together…plus all manner of long and short weapons with peculiar shapes. In the clouds of dust undisturbed for decades, past events were vividly reanimated before their eyes. For Westerners who did not have the same culture nor were raised in the same background, the implications, meaning, and value of some images and sentiments were difficult to fully comprehend. But those who recall history and past events are always eager to recollect. As for how much is heard? How much is understood? It is not that important, is it?

The BBC team filming Hong Ze-han on the banks of the Danshui River in Dadaocheng, 1982.

98– BBC WAY OF THE WARRIOR PART 6

"A foot may be too short, an inch may be too long"—right and wrong, correct and erroneous is a relative, corresponding, comparative relationship, not an absolute relationship. It cannot be measured with a rigid scale and criterion. All aspects of the environment and needs of the current moment must be considered to come to a solution to a problem. Using the same principle, advance preparation versus adapting to changing circumstances are two completely different mindsets and countermeasures. To survive and seek living in this world, a person cannot always rely on one set of immutable principles by which to live.

Scene: Anxi Street

AFTER ALMOST ANOTHER THREE MONTHS, THE BBC's LOCATION team finally came to Taiwan to shoot the official documentary film, and everything unfolded step by step, according to the original plan. Hong Ze-han saw with his own eyes the blueprints he had drawn in his mind, realized one after another into real images in the hands of the professional BBC team. He felt an indescribable sense of comfort. Although the harvest of these things would eventually be in the hands of others and would contribute to their international fame, just to have seen his own ideas transformed by the might, professionalism, and broadcasting reach of the BBC, projecting the great achievements of Master Hong Yi-xiang in the field of martial arts onto the world stage, this was enough to fill his heart with satisfaction.

Hoping to present the best face in front of the camera, the son, Hong Ze-han, a person always prepared in advance for everything, and the father, Hong Yi-xiang, a person who always insists on adapting to changes, were a pair with completely different natures. It was difficult not to produce some friction and confrontations during the filming of the documentary.

"Actual combat has to adapt to a situation. If he doesn't hit at me, how will I have that sense." The master was like a willful child, making trouble with his son even before the shooting of the BBC cameras had started.

"Pa! It's making a film. It's not a fight! It's not about taking out the opponent. It's about letting the audience know why you fight like this. Think of it this way," his son Ze-han directed.

The father's silence showed that he had no intention of giving in.

"You have to let the photographer know how you want to attack. How you'll position yourself. How you'll conclude. Otherwise, every time you go out of the frame, it's always 'NG—Do Over!' How can he work this way?" Ze-han pressed him unrelentingly.

"You understand what he wants. So, you do it." It looked like he was on fire. He started to shamelessly bail on the project.

"This is your special record. How can I do it for you," the son was also riled by the father's willfulness.

"What's the matter?" Howard Reid asked.

"It's alright. I just wish he'd first let the cameraman know the way he is going to attack and the position he's going to demonstrate. But he insists on improvising."

"A-han, it's okay. I totally understand his ideas and principles. Please, you don't need him to change," Reid assured.

"But it's been 'NG' all the time."

"No matter. We brought a lot of film. You don't have to worry. Just let it go and let him express himself his own way," Reid tried to settle Ze-han's concerns.

The scene of a dustup between a father who always adapted to circumstances based on his feeling, and a son who always required preparation in advance, was captured on film by Zhuang Zhi-cheng, a master photographer making behind-the-scenes records of the shoot. Looking at the characters, situation, and atmosphere in this photo, many complex emotions are frozen in time and space.[33] Although the still photos cannot speak, what is remembered is that in the end everyone succumbed to Hong Yi-xiang's persistent willfulness.

---

33 I had completely forgotten that in the photo, my back to the camera, I had said something unpleasant, which made my old man on the left look helpless and innocent! Looking at this old photo, a thought I had not had before suddenly emerged in my heart: is this family's martial arts legend to come to this end? I think the conflict between father and son came from misaligned mutual expectations!

There is no doubt about Hong Yi-xiang's martial arts level of mastery and his interpretation of martial art body language. However, his spoken language skills left others feeling that his words could not express the meaning intended. On this point even he himself had the same regret. A master like him, who had experienced the tempests of multiple epochs and great changes in his life, had he more eloquence or expressive ability, could fully spread what he felt in his heart and comprehended in his mind, and share it with all. He could have contributed more and had higher achievements. But he always said: "A-han. You understand. You're able. You take it further."

Maybe it was because Ze-han, the film industry professional, knew very well that once the BBC's documentary was delivered, would it even matter if the performance was naturally revealed? Or deliberately staged? Or was just a momentary blunder, or utterly out of control? Eventually it would all be part of history. Strangers or your future descendants, can only look at the perspectives stated and all that was recorded in the documentary, to define the apex and meaning of your life. So, in front of the camera, you'd better not leave any 'NG' pictures. In the end, you'll never know whether that part will be edited in. But the old man always said: "A-han. It's okay. Just go with the flow. Don't pay too much attention to the opinions of people you don't even know."

In the three months prior to the actual shooting work, hoping to faithfully present the intentions of the training forms and the physical beauty of their movements, Hong Yi-xiang asked Hong Ze-han to practice from nine o'clock to 12 o'clock noon every morning. After a brief lunch and rest break, practice resumed from two o'clock to five o'clock in the afternoon. From 7 to 10 o'clock in the evening, it was the regular class time. Hong Yi-xiang personally supervised the self-training every afternoon, applying the most rigorous standards to review and correct him. The training continued night and day, driving him to reach Master Hong's standard. This unseen training process allowed him to enjoy one minute on the stage, but behind the stage was ten years of joy, sorrow, and hardship.

One repetition of the Xingyiquan Swallow Form did not take more than ninety seconds in the film broadcast by the BBC. However, the person demonstrating had to endure at least a thousand strictly practiced repetitions before it appeared in the film and was reviewed by the world. Sometimes, for a short-range objective, people will set up some self-training regimen to achieve the requirements of that goal. If the existing gongfu is deep, after hard training one will often unconsciously enter another new level of martial arts. This unexpected attainment made Hong Ze-han deeply aware of the infinite possibilities of human potential… But just like other types of documentary films, there are many wonderful shots that were taken with great pains on the set. In the end, they often cannot be squeezed into a film of less than an hour.

It is always hard to understand the world's paradoxes. During the shooting, the things most eye-popping and greatly affirmed were deleted from the entire documentary in the editing room, as they took too long. And as for the things that were selected in the editing room, after the final broadcast, would the audience really be receptive to them? Even experienced directors can't be completely spared from this kind of unbearable regret!

The BBC production team in Taiwan to film Hong Yi-xiang's martial art and introduce the Chinese Internal School of boxing, 1982.

The BBC production team and disciples of the Guandu branch of the Yizong Tangshou school, 1982.

99- ACROSS THE EQUATOR TO TRANSMIT THE ART IN AUSTRALIA PART 1

It only takes a little courage and fervor to destroy an enemy, but it takes more wisdom and commitment to leave them be.

Scene: Anxi Street

ALTHOUGH THE BBC *THE WAY OF THE WARRIOR* MARTIAL ARTS documentary was not broadcast in Taiwan, as expected, it really aroused the interest and enthusiastic response of many martial arts fans in other countries who flocked to Taiwan to pursue the original and unfamiliar Internal School of martial arts. This included fans from South Africa, Germany, France, Britain, the United States, Australia, New Zealand, Israel, Japan, Malaysia, Hong Kong and so on.

Regrettably, the training hall on Anxi Street was too small to accommodate all the students. To preserve the quality of the lessons, it was for the best that we reluctantly turned away most of the young people committed to only a short period of time to train in Taiwan, rather to concentrate the opportunities on enthusiasts with considerable martial arts roots and time to commit, not blindly chasing a temporary fad.

Why had the training retreated to the small studio on Anxi Street, the reader might well ask? Long before the BBC went to Taiwan to film, there had been an unpleasant event on which the dust had long settled. This is also the reason why Hong Yi-xiang gave up large-scale teaching of boxing. In order set the record straight, we must employ a most sober, calm mind to provide an abbreviated account. This is to inform those who did not know the whole inside story, who never understood the source of Mr. C's "Tang Shou Dao" and the "Yizong Tangshou" originated by Hong Yi-xiang and at the bottom of it, what was their relationship.

In the heyday of the Kung Fu boom, the dojo hosted by Hong Yi-xiang had an average of two to three hundred students every night, and they received rigorous training in Yizong Tangshou on the grounds of the Yongle Elementary School.

To accommodate the large quantity of students unable to participate in training due to the limitations of the venue, Hong Yi-xiang began to systematically support disciples who already had coaching qualifications to open branches in various places promoting Yizong Tangshou, for example: Chen Xun at the Guandu Tangshou dojo, Li Chun-sheng of Luodong Tangshou dojo, Huang Qing-xiang of Nangang Tangshou dojo, Su Dong-cheng of Tokyo Xingwu Tangshou dojo, and Tang Feng-qi of Miaoli Tangshou dojo, were all cultivated under this plan. But the lure of this apparent business opportunity was too much for one Mr. C. Originally working as an English translator at the dojo, Mr. C without the certification and authorization of Hong Yi-xiang set up a gym outside under the name of "Tang Shou Dao," and some middle-level cadres who had not yet qualified as instructors served as coaches of the gym. In fact, given the friendship between Hong and C's father, if Mr. C really wanted to open a branch gym to make a living and openly applied to Hong Yi-xiang, he would not have been rejected. Even though he did not have a formal martial arts background, he would have gotten the full support of qualified teachers of the school. However, Mr. C chose a path that ordinary people do not take.

His gymnasium not only imitated everything in the main hall in terms of name, teaching materials, clothing, and equipment, but he also claimed to be a closed-door disciple of Grandmaster Zhang Jun-feng. Whereupon, Mr. C who had not received formal martial arts training, relying on some martial arts concepts and vocabulary accumulated during his work as a translator in the gym, plus some clever packaging and a talent for self-promotion, transforms overnight from an amateur into a martial arts Master. Certainly, this kind of queer event can only happen in Taiwan, a society full of tolerance. And this retrograde betrayal of the master immediately angered all the members of the "Black Belt Group" who strongly recommended teaching him an appropriate "lesson":

"Master, let's go and fight for justice."

"What is justice? How can it be achieved?" Master Hong responded.

"At least he should remove the three words 'Tang Shou Dao.' Otherwise, this hard-earned reputation will be ruined by this wise guy."

"Are we the underworld? We couldn't stop him opening a gym, do you still care what name he uses? Don't make things difficult for them."

"Master, are you not angry at all?"

"Of course, I'm pissed. But I don't want to have this kind of splintering."

"However, this guy keeps claiming outside that he is Zhang Jun-feng's closed-door disciple, the next thing he will upgrade to become your younger brother in the school, so won't we all have to call him senior uncle?"

"Would you really call him Senior Uncle?"

"Of course not. What is he?"

"Then you haven't suffered any loss. Why care about what he said?"

"But, if we don't deal with him, wouldn't it mean we don't distinguish between right and wrong?"

"You fix him, are right and wrong then clearly distinguished?" The black belts were not convinced. "Right, wrong, and fairness don't prevail in some people's minds. Otherwise, he would not dare to do it. If there is no right and wrong in a person's mind, anything said to him is a waste of air."

"You can't mean to let them do whatever they desire?"

"Cool down and think about it. Your big group comes angrily busting down his door on some punitive expedition for me, and you aren't aware of how the neighbors would view this, what the neighborhood would think? In case of an argument with them, do *they* become your opponents? In this case, what the general public sees, isn't it the big bullying the weak?"

"These ungrateful tools."

"Don't bring up kindness and reasoning anymore, it seems such things are long gone. We will let it go this time and see how God deals with it. Anyway, you are not allowed to do it yourself. Understood?"

"Master, you're too indulgent of these swine."

"Why perpetuate this karma?"

Under Hong Yi-xiang's strong restraining hand, a potentially violent and bloody response to this act of betraying the master's school was avoided. But the character of despicably selfish people severely damaged his trust in human kindness. Those who understood the real situation knew that it was not Mr. C who hurt him the most, but that Hong Yi-xiang had diligently cultivated some of the cadres who betrayed him. Although they were still not good enough to stand on their own, but with their aptitude and acquired effort, given time they would eventually make people take notice. Unexpectedly, they chose a shortcut at the crossroads of life, a shortcut that chilled the hearts and vexed those who loved them. Two were young men possessed of martial art talent from an impoverished family unable to pay any tuition. To nurture their talent, Hong Yi-xiang not only allowed them to study for free in the gym for many years, but never received a cent or a gift from them. During the festive season, the Hong family often received too many gifts and cakes to be consumed. While they were fresh, Hong Yi-xiang's wife, Hong Wang Ai-qing, would let these children take some home to share with their family.

Perhaps it is just like Confucius said: "The superior man may indeed have to endure want, but the mean man, when he is in want, gives way to unbridled license." Thus does poverty really make some people disloyal, dispirited, and demented. Unbearable after so many years of considerate loving kindness. Man, such a truly complicated and incomprehensible species.

Since that incident, Hong Yi-xiang had a different understanding of fragile and untested human nature. He began to seriously think about what Master Zhang Jun-feng once said: "Every master will inevitably tutor some traitors and scumbags." He began to have serious doubts about the large-scale promotion of martial arts. His original, wishful thinking was that it was easier to select good talent from among a large number of people to cultivate, but this did not take into account the impact of losing sight of moral character. He began to believe that he had unwittingly tutored some scoundrels that harmed society. And was it good to share the martial arts that he taught, without exception, techniques that could instantly break people's bones, and perhaps even cause permanent damage, to people without holding back at all? Who really knows whether these students, deep in places that eyes cannot peer, had done anything to benefit mankind? Or done damaging things?

Although he was a great master, he was also a human being, not immune from being wounded by treachery and low people. He resolutely canceled the lease of the Yongle Elementary School venue and dispersed most of the students. Those who insisted on not leaving, he referred to the regional gyms to continue their training. The central training hall stopped lessons for a long, long time. In 2022 online, one of Hong Yi-xiang's "great grandson students" (a third-generation student) mockingly related a story he said Su Dong-cheng had shared in jest and under the influence of alcohol regarding the incident with Mr. C. To avoid misunderstanding caused by rumors passed on by those who were not present, or perhaps not even born, at the time of the real event, I use this opportunity to set the record straight.

It was not until the old family home on the back section of Anxi Street was demolished and rebuilt into a new building that he bought the second floor from his brother Hong Yi-wen as his residence, and then converted his fourth-floor unit into a training hall, restoring the small class format of training courses. These classes were mainly provided to some disciples already serving as coaches at home and abroad, so that they could return for advanced training. Of course, there were occasionally favors called in that could not be rejected to teach new students. Besides this, the training hall had no official activities to encourage enrollment. During this time, if there was any doubt about a student's character, they would be tactfully persuaded to leave, and no matter how many strings were pulled or favors called in, he would not accept them, period.

In terms of teaching materials, some of the more lethal methods were always downplayed, and he no longer required students to practice repeatedly until he was satisfied as he had in the past, so this period was the greatest ebb in his decades of teaching. Many years later, the students who had betrayed the teacher were condemned by their conscience and beseeched the senior disciples to bring them back to apologize to Hong Yi-xiang and bow down in front of the statue of Bodhidharma for forgiveness. But Hong Yi-xiang strictly rejected Mr. C's multiple requests to return to the fold. Ze-zhou, Ze-pei, and all the disciples who had entered the gate strongly opposed Mr. C's entreaty, and Hong's enthusiasm for helping others without complaint or regrets had not been restored. If it weren't for the BBC interview rekindling his enthusiasm for martial arts, this school would have indeed experienced a crisis of continual decline.

※ ※ ※

That day, a middle-aged Australian with blonde hair and blue eyes and an interpreter went to the training hall at No. 36 Anxi Street and sought to call on Hong Yi-xiang. At that time, a light and breezy Hong Yi-xiang was drinking tea and chatting in the coffin shop run by Jiang Kai-fu in Dihua Street. This was the largest casket shop in northern Taiwan, and the shop had been stocked with a large quantity of the finest raw wood materials for many years; Chinese cedar approaching a thousand years old, Slippery elm, camphor wood… To sample and savor tea here, amidst the unique aroma of logs and phenol made people feel like they were in a secret mountain hideaway, but to most people being in the coffin store while drinking tea and chatting, sounds really creepy. When this foreign guest came to knock on the door and pay a visit, only the eldest son, Hong Ze-zhou, was present.

"This is Mr. Dean Rainer; he came all the way from Australia to visit Master Hong Yi-xiang."

"My pa is not around. What's up?"

"Dr. Dean used to study Tang Shou Dao for many years under the followers of a Mr. C. He hopes to learn more advanced internal martial arts from Master Hong."

"We don't teach the students of that person."

"Why?"

"Since he is a student of that person, it is only right he should continue to learn from him."

"Mr. C has passed away for some years. We have no other way to…"

"If he learned from other people, we would still consider it, but having learned from that person means no dice."

"Can you tell me why?"

"We don't want to have any association with that person."

"You are Master Hong's…?

"I am his eldest son, I represent my father."

"Please finish listening to my explanation before you decide. Okay? Back in the day, after watching the BBC documentary in Australia, I really admired Master Hong Yi-xiang's internal boxing method. I made a special trip from Australia to Taiwan. I hoped he would accept me as his student, but when I found the old Yongle address, you were no longer there. Later I heard that Master Hong Yi-xiang no longer accepted disciples, so I wandered into Mr. C's to learn Tang Shou Dao. I had absolutely no idea about what happened in Taiwan, why Master Hong Yi-xiang suddenly ceased teaching boxing? But for a long time, I thought that what we were learning was his martial arts. I love Taiwanese culture and martial arts, especially Tang Shou Dao and the Internal School of boxing created by your esteemed father. We have been developing in Australia for many years, and now we have tens of thousands of members.

We sincerely hope that we can get the approval and guidance of Master Hong Yi-xiang."

"My father no longer teaches boxing. And we don't have a fully equipped, large-scale dojo. I would love to help with your problem, but my hands are tied. Please find your own solution."

"Can I speak with Master Hong Yi-xiang himself? I believe he will realize how sincere we are."

"I said, I represent him. I can answer any of your questions clearly, I have already told you clearly, please don't waste your time."

"Alright. Then I have only one cordial request. In this envelope, there is all the historical information on the development of Tang Shou Dao in Australia. There are photos of us practicing together these many years and a special card made by everyone. Please be sure to pass it on to Master Hong Yi-xiang to look over. My apologies for taking up so much of your time."

100– ACROSS THE EQUATOR TO TRANSMIT THE ART IN AUSTRALIA PART 2

Communication is not "You listen to me!" but "Okay, I'm listening."

Scene: Anxi Street, Sydney, Australia

IN FRONT OF THE SOFA ON A SHORT MAHOGANY AND MARBLE TABLE were scattered yellow manila folders sent by Dr. Dean, as well as dozens of photos taken at different times and in different scenes. Some were taken in the dojo and some were photos taken during field practice. There was a large card with several hundred signatures. Hong Ze-han with red pen in hand was immersed industriously counting names one by one and putting a red dot next to each to avoid double counting.

"Don't be stupid, how about it," Hong Ze-Zhou barked.

"If we don't count 'em, how do you know altogether how many people signed it," Ze-han said.

"You take this thing seriously," Ze-zhou said.

"Is there any reason to come from so far as the southern hemisphere and prepare a fake card to deceive people?" Ze-han asked.

"Who knows whether or not he's here to con some Gongfu," Ze-zhou said.

"If it's a con, so what? The bee takes the nectar of the flower, doesn't it also spread the pollen for the flower?" Ze Han opined.

"You bug-brain! Are people as simple as honeybees?" Ze-zhou sarcastically rejoined.

"Are people as bad as you think?" Ze-han asked.

"A single bad one is worth tens of thousands of stupid ones like you," Ze Zhou rudely remarked.

"Nonsense. Such good people don't exist anymore," Ze-han satirically reflected.

"I've eaten more salt in my life than you've eaten rice, what do you know," Ze-zhou irritably responded.

"Yeah. That's why your blood pressure's so high," Ze-han snidely stated.

"You…"

"Enough! What we should think about is, if I don't accept them. What will happen to these people…," interjected Hong Yi-xiang.

"Pa, that's their problem. Before they found the path to our door, didn't they live well? Don't bother to worry about them," Ze-zhou urged.

"The Australian said that he came to Taiwan after watching the BBC documentary?" Hong Yi-xiang inquired.

"Yes, he said that he came to Yongle Elementary School to look for us, but later somehow found an introduction to the C side," Ze-zhou offered.

"Right, it's not their fault. We don't have to be like this…," Ze-han responded.

"Let me give it a think—alone…," Hong Yi-xiang concluded.

So, after nearly three months letting the dust settle and reflecting on the situation, Hong Yi-xiang and the brave and battle tested Hong Ze-zhou, were invited to take a Cathay Pacific flight to Sydney, Australia. This was Dr. Dean's suggestion. He invited Hong Yi-xiang to personally inspect the level of development of the Tang Shou Dao school he had built with his own hands in Australia, and then decide whether to accept the school's return to the fold. From a traditional point of view, traveling far away is always a big deal, especially if you must fly across the equator to an unfamiliar country in the southern hemisphere.

For this expedition, Hong Ze-zhou trained alone for nearly a month before the trip. As the eldest son of a master of martial arts, Hong Ze-zhou was dutybound to serve as the first brave general to accompany his father pioneering new frontiers. In Yilan, in Okinawa, in Kitakyushu, in Tokyo, and in Miaoli in the future, when facing this kind of unknown challenge, he was an indispensable figure at his father's side. His expertise was not in the performance of forms or explaining technique, but in close combat. In particular, he possessed a 110 kilo, unlimited super-power physique. Speed and heavy punching had always been his two deadly weapons in the gym, rattling the courage of his opponents. His personality and sense of responsibility behooved that he take his preparation training seriously. He burst a heavy punching bag, spilling the sawdust filler all over the place.

This expedition would be regarded as Hong Yi-xiang's journey of recovery out of the shadow of betrayal.

This inspection tour to Sydney, Australia, was a peculiar trip for the Hong family, father, and son, both filled with mixed emotions. It was like trekking a vast distance to visit a biological son adopted by a strange family. Before they set foot in this southern hemisphere country, they had no idea how Rainer would appear in their eyes. But when the two of them, father and son, sat in VIP seats and watched hundreds of Australians in the spacious dojo earnestly practicing the Tang Shou Dao that Hong himself had created, the strange yet familiar subtle feelings completely dissolved their previous doubts and reignited his passion for martial arts.

"Before I saw your earnest performance with my own eyes, I dare not believe my heart could be this moved. I want to sincerely thank Dr. Dean for his dedication to the promotion of Tang Shou Dao in Australia over the years, producing such a bountiful result. Also, if he hadn't kept chipping away, running around to get things done, persistently persuading us to come here, I would have missed meeting everyone because of my subjectivity and prejudice. Thank you for your devotion to Tang Shou Dao. I also thank Dr. Dean for his enthusiasm in his painstaking arrangements. As the founder of Tang Shou Dao, I sincerely welcome everyone's involvement. I will discuss with Dr. Dean and plan for advanced courses and techniques of Tang Shou Dao, structured guidance to share with everyone, thank you one and all," Hong Yi-xiang said.

This two-week visit to Australia was carefully arranged by Dr. Dean. In addition to attending interviews with various local TV stations, they also visited the Sydney Opera House, the Sydney Bridge, and the neighboring scenic spots, sampling the finest local cuisine and seafood. They paid a call on the Chinese Martial Arts Association founded by local Chinese and several large-scale Chinese martial arts clubs. These training halls were founded by early immigrants from Guangdong, Hong Kong, and other places. They mainly trained Choy Lee Fut, Hongquan, Wing Chun and other External School styles.

These were self-preservation organizations that their ancestors established to make a living in a strange place. Perhaps it is an immigrant society's nature to not forget, so they retained an extremely traditional martial arts ethic and ancient customs. It was as if the traditions and etiquette brought by the immigrants from their ancestral homes had allowed the visiting Hong's, father and son, to enter a time tunnel strengthening the bonds of friendship spanning time and space with a group of ancient people in the overseas Chinese community. However, the tenacious character of these immigrants, tempered by living abroad in a foreign land, will inevitably carry some standoffishness.

Fortunately, Hong Yi-xiang and Huang Lun, the director of Hong Kong's Choy Lee Fut Wude Hall, were close friends. At the same time, he had also accepted the Hong Kong IKO's Goju-ryu karate head coaches, Chen Ji-zhi and Huang De-ming, as disciples. They had considerable influence in the Hong Kong martial arts world. Boosted by the global popularity of the BBC documentary, his visit was welcomed by them with great enthusiasm.

The members of this martial arts club were mainly Chinese. Toward Dr. Dean, a white Australian promoting Chinese martial art, they had not been too receptive or friendly. But leaning on Hong Yi-xiang's soft demeanor and personal visit, it effectively dissolved the original barrier. Of course, Hong Yi-xiang mentioned to Dr. Dean in advance some unspoken rules for interaction between Wushu training halls, so he gave sufficient face to the president of the Wushu Federation. In the demimonde, there are always many loyalties and passions hidden in dark corners to be taken care of; how to identify these unspoken boundaries and proprieties is not a cultural characteristic familiar to Western society. Fortunately, Dr. Dean was a smart person with high IQ *and* EQ, and he quickly grasped these unnecessary and elaborate formalities.

With such ability, it is no wonder that in just a few years he could develop the Tang Shou Dao founded by Hong Yi-xiang to such an extent and pile up such achievements. A martial artist's life-long achievement is, of course, corelated to his martial arts cultivation level. Equally it stands on this foundation, how high his achievement is, will be more highly corelated to his situational IQ. Both Hong Yi-xiang and Dr. Dean had this natural trait and charm. They could overcome the shadow of Mr. C's betrayal of the teacher, and achieve a sincere friendship based on mutual respect, as teacher and friend.

Ocean excursion during the second trip to Australia to train Dean Rainer and his students, 1984.

On the third trip to Australia to teach the arts, Hong Yi-xiang is invited to demonstrate joint locking at a living history museum, 1985.

101– ACROSS THE EQUATOR TO TRANSMIT THE ART IN AUSTRALIA PART 3

People from vanquished lands, can't see a better tomorrow and easily become desperados.

Scene: Sydney, Australia

After the inspection tour to Sydney, the Hong family thoroughly swept away any previous doubts and accepted Dr. Dean's requests. He and his assistant instructors were given several two-week training courses in Taipei to correct some errors they had learned in the past and appropriately strengthen their unarmed fighting skills. During this period, the Hongs, father and son, were invited to Australia for a second time to inspect the revised results and set out to develop an advanced training course. To expand the promotion of Tang Shou Dao in Australia and strengthen Internal boxing skills, Dr. Dean proposed to hold a two-week senior student advanced training camp in Sydney. Enrollment was expected to be more than thirty students.

The distance between Taiwan and Australia was far and the cost of moving people around relatively high. To achieve the highest cost-benefit ratio for the transfer of knowledge, it was decided after discussion that this time, Hong Ze-han would be added, a total of three people, to go to Australia to teach the new courses. Hong Ze-pei was left alone at the Taiwan headquarters in charge of the educational affairs. After finalizing the task assignments and preparations, the Hong family, father and two sons, flew Cathay Pacific transiting in Hong Kong and on to Sydney, Australia.

Dr. Dean booked them into first-class seats to repay the Hong family's uncompensated gifts of learning every time they went to Australia. It was hoped that Hong Yi-xiang and Hong Ze-zhou, with their large sturdy builds, would have no need to endure the narrow seats of economy class on such a long flight. Sure enough, you get what you pay for. The first-class cabin was wide, with comfortable seats and exquisite fare, adding many enjoyable pleasantries to the long journey. However, God seems to have deliberately played a little joke on them. Less than an hour after the plane departed Hong Kong for Australia, the flight attendants having just delivered the dinner on the plane, the pilot announced that for an undisclosed reason they must return to Hong Kong's Kai Tak Airport immediately. As soon as the broadcast ended, they saw the flight attendants with stern smiles quickly collect all the meals that had just been delivered according to the guests' orders. Ze-han's eyes longingly followed the shelled whole Australian lobster he had not yet savored as it was hurriedly taken away by the flight attendant. Hong Ze-han felt distressed as if he had encountered an armed robbery on the plane.

"Fortunately, Pa and I eat fast," Ze-zhou quipped.

"Will they bring it back later?" Ze-han asked.

"You're dreaming," Ze-zhou replied.

"Why is this?" Ze-han wondered.

"Definitely a problem with the airplane," Ze-zhou commented.

"I mean, God, why take my lobster away?" Ze-han emphasized.

"Ask him. Anyway, you are closer to him on the plane," Ze-zhou responded.

"You mean we are closer to heaven?" Ze-han asked.

"Don't fear that all the passengers are going to cheat you out of your lobster," Ze Zhou exclaimed.

"Then I'll ask the stewardess. I made a mark on my tray," Ze-han objected.

"Don't make a spectacle of yourself. It's just a small lobster, as long we survive flying to Sydney, I promise to order you a lobster five times the size, so you can scarf down lobster until you cry 'uncle,'" Ze-zhou promised.

"Okay. On your word," Ze-han reacted.

"First, pray for the plane to land safely," Ze-zhou insisted.

After alighting, all the passengers on flight sat idly in the empty transit hall of Kai Tak Airport until past midnight, suffering for over three hours, during which time the airline's ground staff only appeared once to distribute cold drinks, non-alcoholic beverages, and an unappetizing sandwich, then disappeared, never to be seen again. Besides the boarding pass in their pockets proving that they were first-class passengers, basically, they were no different from refugees fleeing the chaos of war. With great difficulty they waited for the eventual transfer to a replacement airliner, but because it was outfitted in the middle of the night, everything was kept simple. Except for being able to fly, there was nothing loaded on board, not even a lowly cup of instant noodles. And so, the Hong family, father and sons, with empty tummies and full of remorse, completed their first super-duper, prestigious, luxurious first-class trip.

By the time the plane arrived at Sydney Airport, all the people who had been sent to warmly welcome them were at their wits end. Fortunately, on the fly, the smart and considerate Dr. Dean made some emergency rescheduling of the itinerary. He assigned a student, Mark, who had been to Taiwan for training, to take the Hong family to a villa at Bondi Beach, New South Wales, to freshen up and take a rest, while he split off to turn this emergent variable into a welcoming banquet.

"Pa and I came here twice, both times everything was A-okay. This time thanks to you, your highness, adding on, it became topsy turvy," Ze-zhou complained to his younger brother.

"Damn right. So don't forget that lobster—five times the size," Ze-han reminded.

"Still thinking about that lobster. Grow up," Ze-zhou said. "Ai! There is a McDonald's down the road, Mark, can you stop the car first and let my younger brother fill his gourd. He is still fretting over a lobster he didn't get to eat on the plane," Ze-zhou explained.

"Sure. But I can't order a lobster burger here," Mark chuckled.

"Anything to fill his stomach is okay," Ze-zhou said.

The car parked in front of a fast-food restaurant by the road. The four of them got their order and just as they sat down and were ready to enjoy it, they saw the guests in the dining area hurriedly pack their belongings and head for the door.

"What's up?" Ze-zhou asked.

"Don't tell me we have to return to Hong Kong," Ze-han groused.

"I'll go suss it out," Mark returned shortly and said with a wry smile, "It's okay. Two gangs of high school students made an appointment here to negotiate some trivial matter, but one of them is from the 'Vietnamese Green Gang.' Although they said it is a negotiation, I think they're young and frisky, it's possible a fight might still erupt."

"Oh. What do we need to do to help?" Ze-zhou asked.

"No need. I have already greeted the leaders from both sides, the table there is a boundary they better not cross, otherwise, there are three martial arts masters from Taiwan here," Mark responded.

"Okay. Let's just watch like a reality show," Ze Zhou returned.

Whereupon the four adults watched as a group of young Asians and Australians fought in the fast-food restaurant. Fortunately, they were fighting with bare hands, and there was no deep hatred to be avenged. In the end, the gang with fewer people was soundly defeated and fled, and the gang with more members took advantage of the victory, shouting and chasing them out. The gang leader keeping up the rear faced the Hong's, gave a short bow, and then left triumphantly.

"What the fuck?" Ze-zhou spouted.

"He is thanking us for not interfering," Mark replied.

"Oh. Is that gratitude? Or ridicule?" Ze-han wondered.

"It depends on what *you* think," Ze-zhou considered.

"Are all the fights here like this?" Ze-han asked.

"It's hard to say. After this kind of trouble, it may come to knives, eh. The gang that just fled was a member of the Viet Green Gang, backed up by a bigger gang," he sighed. "Vietnamese refugees were originally taken in out of humanitarian regard and compassion, but no one anticipated the many social and public security problems this policy has brought to Australia. In the past, these undesirable elements were limited to activities in the Chinese community. Now there are more people, so they expand their turf. People really worry about the future of law and order in Sydney," Mark explained.

"I have also interviewed Vietnamese refugees in Penghu, Taiwan," Ze-han remarked. "They are housed on a small island called Chimei. The Taiwan government dare not allow them to enter the main island, for fear that this kind of problem would arise. Fortunately, they are only transiting in Taiwan. The purpose of the resettlement is to allow the US CIA to have ample time to filter their backgrounds, to prevent North Vietnamese spies being mixed in with refugees and disrupting public order. In the end, these people will be arranged to work and settle in the United States, Canada and Australia. To help them, the Taiwan government also organized many vocational training courses. Those willing to receive training get salary and bonuses. There are still a small number of young people who are unwilling to accept their fate and work a job. They prefer to go through life in a daze, loafing, causing trouble…"

"A person who no longer has a country should love and improve himself all the more," Hong Yi-xiang interjected.

"Seeking to make a life in a foreign land, if you refuse to bow your head, accept your fate, and you're unwilling to work harder than others, you'll never escape your limitations, fated to sink to the lowest levels of society. Mingling with gangs may be the last resort for these people. But this road, in the end, puts your life on the line," Ze-han reflected.

"With this going on, many Australian parents hope that their children, in addition to playing rugby, learn some self-defense martial arts, at least to know something to protect themselves," Mark replied.

"Martial arts is like a sharp knife, it can protect you or hurt another, but the key is not the knife, it's the person wielding it," Hong Yi-xiang declared.

"Understood. Dr. Dean has always cared about students' morality. There are no gang members in our system, please rest assured," Mark confirmed.

At the welcome dinner that evening, highlights of the BBC documentary were played on a big screen at the hotel, and then Dean Rainer introduced the Hong family, father and sons, one by one, as well as the event schedule, and describing the mood of his first visit to the Hong family. He used self-deprecating humor to describe how he was rejected by Hong Ze-zhou at that time, as if he was a delinquent who had committed a bunch of faux pas with the Hong family.

"I only remember that this strong, but unfriendly young man, was like a keg of gunpowder which could be detonated by my words at any time. However, I believed that I could convince him. I had missed the chance once already and knew full well that if I missed it this time again, God would not give me a third chance. When a person knows that there are no more opportunities, he becomes more pragmatic and positive. I only knew for sure that I should never use the direct power of Xingyiquan, let alone the turning tricks of Baguazhang, I could only use the softness of Taijiquan. It turns out that I used the right Kung Fu, so today we have this honor. At the same time, we have invited two generations, three martial arts masters, from the Hong family to Sydney, to share their martial arts and wisdom with everyone. I hope everyone will cherish this opportunity to learn from these three…"

That night, the three only ate, drank, and chatted without training. Everyone was thirty percent tipsy and employed simple single words of English to form a myriad of happy and unrestrained conversations. No one cared whether the other party really understood what was expressed. Anyway, when drinking, it is always a conversation between the alcohol of one and the alcohol of the other. Provided people are responsibly happy, that's good. Isn't it?

It's worth mentioning that the main course of the banquet that night was lobster. When the waiter brought out a large silver platter with three Australian extra-large lobsters piled on it, all the guests cheered the exaggerated spectacle, and the humorous Dr. Dean specially brought that tray of large lobsters over to Hong Ze-zhou. "This is not for you. You're too fierce. This whole platter of giant lobsters was prepared for a certain person. That person is in Australia for the first time, but his lobster was confiscated by the stewardess on the plane for some unknown reason. To mend his great sorrow and to avoid this loss affecting his mood of teaching boxing, we specially prepared these three extra-large lobsters to give him, hoping that he can eat joyfully, and hoping he can use three times the enthusiasm in Australia in the next few days to help us learn more Tangshoudao, okay," Dr. Dean used seafood specialties of the southern hemisphere and humor to commence a martial arts training camp with a prologue full of laughter. A team leader can be forceful and imperious, can be clever and insightful, or can be funny and humorous. Dean Rainer obviously had the characteristics of the latter two. No wonder that in his hands, the Yizong Tangshou created by Hong Yi-xiang could expand so rapidly in this country.

Hong Ze-han and two of the Australian students at the Anxi St Gym, 1988.

102– ACROSS THE EQUATOR TO TRANSMIT THE ART IN AUSTRALIA PART 4

Why not take the unfairness you are experiencing as a temporary loan to God. When the time comes, the balance of capital and interest will be transferred back to your passbook account.

Scene: Sydney, Australia

BACK IN THOSE DAYS, WHEN FACED WITH MR. C'S BETRAYAL, HONG Yi-xiang chose to deal with it in a tolerant but unforgiving manner. In the eyes of most of his disciples, this decision seemed to have forfeited the satisfying, bold revenge a martial arts master deserved. No one would have thought that after some years these tributaries that had branched out would eventually return to the mainstream. When he heard the news of the death of Mr. C, he still felt regret for his persistent unforgiveness. Whereupon, under the ingenious arrangement of providence, the Hong family father and sons, regarded as serendipitous this branch and leaves. They worked hard to help this offshoot isolated below the equator to replenish the blood and nutrients of genuine orthodox Yizong Tangshou.

The three of them rose at 5 o'clock in the morning each day to perform morning exercises on the empty Bondi Beach, returning to the villa at 6:30 to tidy up, and at 7 o'clock Mark would pick them up and drive them over to have breakfast with Dr. Dean. Leveraging his friendship with the owner, the Bondi Beach Villa was specially borrowed by Dr. Dean. Every Saturday and Sunday, the entire beach filled with young men and women of all colors. It was a holiday mecca full of joyful energy. But come Sunday night, the beach was filled with the roar of evacuating cars, leaving behind an empty, rippled sand spit facing a dark ocean of stars. From Monday to Friday evening, the entire beach was almost deserted, and handed over entirely to the Hong family. The father and sons were teaching boxing in downtown Sydney all day, so it was only this brief period of little more than an hour every dawn during which they could relax and enjoy the beauty here by the sea.

There was a bridge separating Bondi from the center of Sydney. Every time the bridge was crossed, it was necessary to throw a few coins into a toll booth basket to pass the gantry. It was much more convenient than the manual toll method of Taiwan's highways in the past, and it didn't force the toll collectors to stand at the toll gate and breathe the exhaust emitted by cars all day. However, once the automated collection was enabled in Taiwan, those people were unemployed. The impacts brought about by the progress of technological civilization are always mixed. At the same time as new technologies are developed, people must inject more wisdom, so as to consider and solve possible negative effects, but until better solutions are available, people who did not want to be replaced or eliminated by technology and machines must first find a way to squeeze themselves into the top one-third of the leading group, so they can gain the lion's share of resources. Thus, one will have enough surplus to take care of the disadvantaged and backward groups.

The venue for the training was located at the Olympic Center in Sydney. There is a dining center in this building, but to avoid eating the same thing every day, Dr. Dean arranged for the three of them to eat a bountiful breakfast with different flavors, at different restaurants and discuss the focus of the day's training or coordinating the equipment needed. The daily training course started at 9 o'clock in the morning, with a break every 90 minutes for 20 minutes They were usually busy until 1:30 in the afternoon, when they would take lunch. In order not to waste everyone's time, the daily lunch was Greek food from the Olympic Center restaurant. There were no Greek restaurants in Taiwan back then, and no photos were printed on the menus for reference. To prevent the scene from *Way of the Dragon*, in which the country bumpkin, Bruce Lee, orders three bowls of soup due of language barriers, lunch for the father and sons was almost entirely handled by Dr. Dean.

Observing table etiquette, Dr. Dean always looked for expressions of the Hong family father and sons after their first bite of the meal. After confirming that the dishes were in line with their taste, he would, rest assured, eat. Therefore, making a satisfied and grateful expression each time they dined became a necessary homework for the Hong family. Later, these expressions became a source of mirth among all the guests at the table. Dr. Dean knew that Hong Yi-xiang liked to eat seafood, so he had the restaurant prepare a dozen fresh oysters for Hong Yi-xiang at lunch and dinner, almost every day,. But no matter how rare a delicacy is, once it becomes a must-eat for every meal, it also becomes a nauseating stomach turner, even more so with raw oysters. The first few days he ate them with reckless abandon, but after eating oysters daily for a whole week, despite his cultivation as a ninth dan international martial art instructor, he could not endure these extravagant delicacies. In the end, he had to reluctantly beg Dr. Dean "No more oysters!" At that time, consuming raw oysters until the person raised the white flag and surrendered was really inconceivable. However, south of the equator, this played out live before our eyes and should also be regarded as one of the master's happiest encounters.

The students participating in the training were all instructor "seedlings" specially selected by Dr. Dean, so the speed and effectiveness of learning obviously surpassed the average. Hong Yi-xiang often said, "Only by asking the right questions, can one get the correct answers." From students' questions during a break, a diligent teacher can certainly determine the results of the instruction. Therefore, in just two weeks, all the forms and applications of Xingyiquan had gone through one round of teaching, including: Xingyi Five Elements Mother Boxing, Five Birds—Seven Beasts 12 Forms, Five Tiger Boxing, Twelve Flooding Hammers, The Sheltering Cannon, and Zhoudong Staff, and others. To facilitate the review and passing down the art, Hong Yi-xiang made a generous exception and agreed for Dr. Dean to arrange a professional photographer to make a complete video of the entire training course. During that period, everyone was completely focused and free of distractions, just seeking to complete the entire training course within two weeks according to the established plan. It proved that if one can overcome the mind's weakness and the body's failings when stamina hits a wall, human potential is truly infinite. The person who has challenged their limits is no longer the same person.

They got up in the dark every morning and were busy until nearly eleven o'clock in the evening and would return, in the dark, to the sea view villa. Upon returning they would wash their clothes, and at about midnight would pass out on their beds, oblivious to others, sleeping through the night until the next morning without even having the strength to turn over and change sides, until awakened by the loyal and steadfast alarm clock. In the villa's refrigerator, Mark had gifted them two tubs of vanilla and chocolate ice cream, that the weary warriors never had time open the entire stay, leaving them for Mark to enjoy with his family.

Despite hardship on top of exhaustion, everyone was quite happy being very busy. On weekend afternoons and Sundays, local teachers, and students took the trouble to organize outdoor social activities. The first event was a barbeque at a very beautiful lakeside. Of course, Dr. Dean personally took over the responsibility of main chef. He was worried that people not good at cooking would ruin the premium Australian beef and the sacrifice of the cow would not be properly eulogized by the guests' tastebuds. So, except for Hong Yi-xiang, who liked to cook accompanying him at the grill, the others all played with frisbees and boomerangs on the grass by the lake.

Boomerangs are a hunting tool used by the indigenous peoples of Australia. Young Australians today, not to mention indigenous youth, at most can only let the boomerang return into their own hands. To employ it like their ancestors, to hunt moving prey as a source of sustenance, would certainly put everyone on a weight-loss diet.

In Australia premium beef is usually served with, at most, a little bit of sea salt so that one can savor the most fundamental flavor of the meat juices. When grilling, one must patiently wait, cooking it only on one side, until juice appears on the topside of the meat before turning it over. Taiwan tastebuds have long been accustomed to black pepper and mushroom sauces on steak, so they always felt that eating steak in Australia seemed to be missing something. Also of note, leafy vegetables are rare unlike in Taiwan when dining on Western fare, where the first course is definitely a large salad followed by a bowl of thick pumpkin soup or borscht.

The people here usually eat very simply, but dessert after every meal is a must. Among them, the most impressive to the visiting Taiwanese was "Rice Pudding." As the name suggests, rice is added to fresh milk and eggs, and then baked into solid pudding in the oven. They never imagined a staple of the Taiwanese people could be added to a Western-style dessert and become the star, so fragrant, thick, and delicious.

One evening, they ate at the Maxwell House Seafood Restaurant by the sea. The whole restaurant is made of logs inside and out. The restaurant's business was so good, even if you called to make a reservation in advance, you might not get a seat. The owner of this seafood restaurant was named Maxwell. The restauranteur did his own cooking. He was one of the earliest students of Dr. Dean, so his rank in the organization was not low. He got married and due to the booming business at the restaurant, he could no longer go to the gym to practice every day, but he continued to have a strong relationship with the gym. He knew that the Hong's had come to Sydney to teach boxing, and he insisted Dr. Dean invite them to his restaurant. People with real character are always very enthusiastic about the people they like. When this Mr. Maxwell greets people he likes, it's never a handshake, but a tight bear hug. After hugging Hong Yi-xiang and Hong Ze-zhou, he espied the diminutive Hong Ze-han, and couldn't help but jokingly say, "Are you sure this is the Kungfu Man punching away in the BBC documentary?"

For this meeting, Maxwell also prepared a copy of *The Way of the Warrior* book written by Howard Reid for the Hong family to autograph. After looking at the Chinese calligraphic autographs, he felt that the Chinese characters were so beautiful, he went into the kitchen and took out a special heavy felt-tip pen to ask Master Hong and sons to autograph the biggest log column in the restaurant. He said with the martial art master's autograph, in the future his restaurant would charge an extra dollar for each diner enjoying seafood, as they would be freely availing themselves of the blessings of good fortune the master had shared.

That meal was the most enjoyable time for the three Hongs, , during their two-week trip in Australia. Taiwanese people love seafood, but also were warmed by the wit and friendliness of the boss and the enthusiasm of all the students. The hospitality made that bowl of seafood soup full of fresh scallops and small cuttlefish even more sweet and delicious. Having drunk and eaten to their heart's content, Mark was still responsible for driving the Hong family back to the beach villa. Before Mark left, Hong Yi-xiang finally couldn't help but ask:

"Mark, do you need to rest for a few days?"

"I'm fine. It's just my back got a little injured. I can make it, don't worry," Mark replied.

"I did a thorough ultrasound scan for him a few days ago. From the report I couldn't see what the matter was, but his back just can't straighten up. I could only prescribe some anti-inflammatory pain relievers and muscle relaxants for him, but they don't seem to help," Dr. Dean offered.

"It's a problem with his main and collateral qi channels. I observed it on the first day, but my kids don't want me to do any medical treatments, just teach martial art," Hong Yi-xiang responded.

"Can you help him?" Dr. Dean inquired.

"It should be no problem. But the problem is that you have to convince my kids first. They are their mother's spies!" joked Hong Yi-xiang.

"It shouldn't be a problem, right, young Mr. Hong's?" Dr. Dean queried.

"My mother is worried that my dad is always overly enthusiastic, so before leaving, she made it clear that we should not let him do any medical treatments, just martial arts. Moreover, traditional Chinese therapies may not be suitable for you," Ze-zhou commented.

"How can that be? I'm a doctor, I understand the structure of the human body. We just look different on the outside is all," Dr. Dean reflected.

"No, we are talking about treatment methods. My father's methods, we know, will be very painful," Ze-zhou asserted.

"Pain I can bear. I'm willing give it a try." So Mark followed Hong Yi-xiang's instructions to lie on his back on the dining table, then raised his feet until they draped on both sides of his head, just like the yoga Shrimp pose.

"You all help him hold his feet, don't let him retract," Hong Yi-xiang directed.

"Okay," Ze-zhou and Ze-han complied.

"If Dr. Dean is open-minded about traditional oriental therapies, there is no harm in seeing how I can deal with this," assured Hong Yi-xiang.

"Good. Thank you." Dr. Dean replied.

Hong Yi-xiang used the traditional Chinese method of relaxing the muscles and connective tissues to help Mark, to deal with the lumbar injury that had plagued him for many days. Dr. Dean carefully observed the steps and the several key acupressure massage points. The whole course of treatment lasted for about ten minutes. Mark constantly gritted his teeth against the unrelenting pain, more than most people could bear, without crying out. When his feet were laid flat again, they could see his face fully flushed and, sopping with sweat beads as big as soybeans…

"You still okay?" Hong Yi-xiang asked.

"No problem. Just let me take a rest," Mark confirmed.

"Does he need to take medicine?" Dr. Dean asked.

"I won't dispense medicines. If it hurts in the middle of the night, you can take some anti-inflammatory and painkilling medicine," Hong Yi-xiang suggested.

"Alright. I already gave this to him," Dr. Dean allowed.

"Drink as much water as possible the next few days, don't drink alcohol, especially beer. Also avoid fried and barbequed foods," Hong Yi-xiang instructed.

"Alright. Understood. It's feeling much better now," Mark replied.

"If it's normal, you should be able to recover eighty percent by tomorrow," Hong Yi-xiang predicted.

When Hong Yi-xiang was studying medical arts at a young age, he already had attained the professional qualifications and skills in the treating of trauma, However, to avoid a multiplicity of liabilities when abroad, the two brothers of the Hong family repeatedly urged their father not to go over the top. Dr. Dean himself was a locally respected doctor, so they should respect the local medical profession.

The sharp-eyed Hong Yi-xiang observed on day two of the training that Mark had obvious symptoms of a back injury, but due to the ground rules between father and son he had no choice but to restrain himself. However, seeing this young man of South African descent enduring his severe injuries every day just to come pick them up, he really couldn't bear it. He knew very well Western medicine treatment modalities at that time for connective tissue and sports injuries were cold compresses, hot treatments, and a lot of painkillers, basically clueless remedies. In addition, during the barbecue that afternoon, he inadvertently caught a glimpse of Mark alone behind a big tree massaging his back and resting, and he decided to go for it, to extend a helping hand and save the day. When he had seen Mark sweating profusely just then, in the bottom of his heart he knew the patient's symptoms should abate, but when he turned around and saw the expressions of his two sons, he realized *his* troubles were getting worse.

Hong Yi-xiang and Dean Rainer in Sydney, Australia, to complete the third session of cadre training, 1985.

103– ACROSS THE EQUATOR TO TRANSMIT THE ART IN AUSTRALIA PART 5

A person need not bow and scrape for five scoops of rice, rather focus on the work he likes every day. In such a way, work is a supreme enjoyment.

Scene: Sydney, Australia

AT 7 A.M. THE NEXT MORNING, WHEN MARK ONCE AGAIN APPEARED in front of the Hong family, he was no longer the stiff, pained, and stooped person who had been injured a few days earlier. He was completely restored to the appearance of a young man in glowing spirits. As soon as he saw Hong Yi-xiang, he came forward to give him a big hug. For the curative effects to have transformed him into a new man in just one night forced the two Hong brothers to relinquish any shred of doubt left hanging. It seems that they had not fully understood their father's true ability, just myopically used a common yardstick to measure his talent. Fortunately, he who had crossed great rivers and seas and been cultivated by the challenge of tempests and storms, did not seem to mind the limitations of this kind of affection. After all, in the eyes of his family, he was just a dad, an ordinary but family-loving dad.

On the successful completion of the scheduled training, the last weekend remaining in Australia became a relaxing moment for the Hong family father and sons. On Friday evening, Dr. Dean gave special advance notice to the Hong family of a big surprise. Sure enough, on Saturday morning, he drove them to a large equestrian center in the Sydney suburbs to watch an equestrian show. During the performance, the compere also introduced the three martial arts masters from Asia, who received warm applause and welcome from all the performance staff, which goes to show the huge reach of the BBC documentary.

At noon, everyone ate at the restaurant attached to the equestrian show arena. They ate grilled steaks larger than the plates on which they were served. Hong Ze-han didn't dare to eat beef too rare, so the waiter wrinkled his eyebrows and asked him repeatedly to confirm his order, then respecting his decision gave him the first well-done steak grilled there since the restaurant opened. After only one bite of that steak, it was displayed on the table like some inedible preserved religious relic, to be revered but not consumed. A traveler going abroad must have the wisdom to "do in Rome as the Romans do" and possess the ability to adapt. The locals consumed their steaks rare. It is correct to acquiesce accordingly and eat like they do. Don't insist on your own point of view and thinking you are always right.

Departing the equestrian center, they visited a private textile studio. It was nestled beside a quiet country lane. The house was built about five steps above the ground, and the view of the countryside was extraordinary. Inside was only one middle-aged Australian with great red sideburns and beard. He didn't pay much mind to the guests and seemed a bit roughhewn.

His specialty was to use traditional wooden looms and pure wool yarns, naturally dyed various colors, and weave them into fabrics exclusively for fashion. There were no fixed design patterns. How to weave, how to match colors, all depended on the mood of this Mr. Red Beard sitting at the loom. Ordinarily he would not deign to perform for visitors but Dr. Dean charmed him and he made an exception for them. He took his time, stopping to think, considering his color choices, then knitting a row slowly. From his work attitude and tempo, it could be seen that this guy was not short of money. Otherwise, at his rate of output, people would really wonder how this fellow could make a living. After he finished a simple demonstration, Dr. Dean led everyone in a round of applause and thanked him for his enthusiastic performance. Seeing his happy yet shy appearance, one would know that he was a haughty old man who grew up seeking applause. Only after further conversation did they learn this arrogant Mr. Weaver was a fabric designer who specialized in helping the world's well-known fashion brands and top designers make new fabrics. He was not an ordinary textile worker. Therefore, strictly speaking he should be regarded as an artist.

After Dr. Dean introduced the Hong family father and sons to this Mr. Weaver, it was obvious that his demeanor changed 180 degrees. For people roaming the demimonde, one's reputation in the demimonde more easily wins the respect of the other party than genuine talent. Due to this respect, Mr. Weaver agreed to make an exception for Master Hong Yi-xiang and to tailor for him a hunting jacket. When a person can achieve this level in business, can choose customers based on his own likes and dislikes, then that's really enjoying work. Since this fellow was not willing to bow and scrape for five bowls of rice, the Hong brothers were even less pleased when extorted the exorbitant price of five sacks of rice times two, just for the privilege of watching his masterful bowing and scraping.

Dr. Dean insisted on paying this considerable sum for Hong Yi-xiang. In Australia if the label says "Handmade," you should keep your distance for safety. These hand-made items are all frighteningly expensive, they'll give you a heart attack, especially the things that have been blessed by the name of the artist, their lethality is even more alarming. Dr. Dean said that he hoped Master Hong Yi-xiang would wear it in the future and recall the good times everyone had spent together in Australia. This was a thoughtful gift particularly because, for Hong Yi-xiang, it was difficult to buy such large-size, ready-made clothes in Taiwan. What was more unexpected was that after the measuring and payment were sorted, the haughty Mr. Weaver took out a register of famous customers and asked Hong Yi-xiang to sign it as *his* souvenir. It turns out that this cool guy, underneath his cold appearance had a bit of warm heart.

After Hong Yi-xiang finished autographing the register, the man took out another piece of fabric from storage. He said it was a precious work that he had kept for many years. He had retained it in his warehouse as he didn't want it to be copied commercially in large quantities. He said that he felt very close to Hong Yi-xiang's aura, so he wanted to give this cloth to Hong Yi-xiang for free. The only request was that Dr. Dean agree to use *this* cloth for Hong Yi-xiang's tailored hunting jacket. As for the piece of fabric that had already been selected and purchased, Mr. Hong was asked to take it back to Taiwan for the best tailors to work on there. The style of artists is truly different from that of ordinary people, and they frequently manifest conduct that ordinary people can't understand, but the conduct is never divorced from the pursuit of perfection.

The next day, early in the morning, a motorcade led by Dean hit the highway. The convoy continued to hurtle down the expressway for more than two hours, as the houses and signs of habitation along the way became less and less, and the eye only saw undulating wilderness and grassland.

"I think your goose is cooked," Ze-han ribbed his brother.

"Why?" Ze-zhou asked.

"This should be the way to a horse ranch," Ze-han replied.

"What about it?" Ze-zhou wondered.

"I guess they are taking us to go horseback riding," Ze-han guessed.

"Horseback riding is great! I like riding horses."

"Yep. You're the one who loves to brag about your equestrian skills in front of everyone, so they made just such an arrangement," Ze-han postulated.

"I really like riding horses," Ze-zhou repeated.

"In Taiwan, it's just trotting on a field. Don't forget that this is Australia. Riding here is in the open wild. I think your goose is really cooked this time," Ze-han shook his head.

Ze-zhou looked perplexed.

"Don't scare him," Hong Yi-xiang intervened.

"Pa. Can you ride?" Ze-han asked.

"Nope," Hong Yi-xiang said.

"Neither can I. Brother, congratulations. This time you enjoy it all by yourself," Ze-han suggested.

Hong Ze-han was not wrong in his guess, this trip *was* really to let the father and sons experience the most primitive and authentic Australian outback. Dr. Dean and the students decided that Master Hong and his sons should enjoy the delight of galloping a horse in the wilderness, so they secretly arranged this surprise. However, there is a certain degree of danger with horses galloping in the wilderness. After further consideration, they dare not rashly cajole Hong Yi-xiang and Hong Ze-han, neither who had ever ridden a horse, to take risks. Originally Mark offered to stay with them, but after discussion, Mark agreed to accompany the group with Hong Ze-zhou into the Australian outback.

The greater surprise was the weather in the Australian prairie that changes on a dime. Before the posse pulled out, the sun was beautiful and the breeze lovely. Within a half hour the wind and the clouds had changed their color. First, wind raised dust up from the ground and blotted out the sky and the sun. Thunder and lightning erupted simultaneously, and suddenly there was a torrential downpour. This kind of wild wind and rain continued to fall savagely for around forty-five minutes and then a moment later the beautiful sun and lovely breeze returned as if nothing had happened. After another ten minutes, they saw the drenched posse return like the defeated soldiers of a routed army struggling home!

"This was my surprise excursion in Australia?" Ze-zhou inquired.

"Yes! Not including the huge thunderstorm just now, that was specially added to the performance by the Australian god of the wilderness, no extra charge," Dr. Dean's timely humor transformed the sudden thunderstorm into a special favor from God. The third round of transferring the art to Australia for Hong Yi-xiang and his sons wound down with this special excursion, a sopping wet exclamation point!

To thank the Hong family father and sons for their uncompensated, selfless sharing of their experience and achievements in martial arts, at the airport, Dr. Dean produced another surprise. He secretly modified their itinerary for returning to Taiwan, inviting them to a five-day Hong Kong stop-over in the hopes that Master Hong and his sons could enjoy a vacation and the pleasures of shopping in Hong Kong before returning to Taiwan. In short, this trip to Australia was full of warmth and pleasant surprises, never to be forgotten.

Hong Yi-xiang with black belt students of the Hong Kong International Karate Organization Gojuryu dojo who had received training from him. He stopped in to see them on the way back from Australia, 1985.

104- MIAOLI VAGRANT BOXING

The kind of martial art that can be tested for its practical life and death value in the Vietnam War and can also accept challenges from the international martial arts world should be passed down for generations and millennia.

Scene: Miaoli

"Fighting on the battlefield is life or death. We need simple and effective moves that increase the probability of survival, so some overly technical things must be removed. Moreover, folk martial arts are riddled with complicated and showy techniques becoming flowery boxing in fancy uniforms that collapse at the first blow. A martial art that can be employed on the Vietnam battlefield, and at the same time, whose techniques can be put to the test in international martial arts circles, this is a proven martial art. Not just practical fighting capability, but also a high degree of technical sophistication. Only one person can do this," Mr. Tang said.

"Hong Yi-xiang," Mr. Chen said.

"Yep. Just him," Mr. Tang replied.

"Why?" Mr. Chen asked.

"Because of my work and hobbies, I've been privately observing this person for many years," Mr. Tang explained.

"Do you know who wrote the poison pen letter? How could there be such a person?" Mr. Chen wondered.

"Not a peer from the martial arts world. Just someone who can't bear seeing someone good," Mr. Tang replied.

"Do you know who it is?" Mr. Chen asked.

"Why ask so pointedly?" Mr. Tang rejoined.

"Mr. Hong is a good friend of my father, need I remind you," Mr. Chen conveyed.

"Their names are best left unsaid. I can only tell you that one of them is also a relatively well-known internal boxing master. I heard he accepted a challenge from the Sweet Potato, a foreign student of Hong Yi-xiang, and was defeated, thus tarnishing his reputation. He is full of resentment," Mr. Tang clarified.

"Masters also muck around with this kind of petty affair," Mr. Chen remarked.

"Despicable behavior and talent are two separate things. Talented immoral people abound. Bureaucrats and politicians in government, principals and professors in schools, priests, and lay-clergy in religion. Even more are those who are sweetness and light on the stage and filthy contemptible characters in the shadows," Mr. Tang opined.

"Are they still writing the letters?" Mr. Chen asked.

"That was a long time ago. It should be over with," Mr. Tang replied.

"That's good," Mr. Chen said.

"Brother Chen. Is it convenient for your father to introduce me to Master Hong?" Mr. Tang asked.

"Aren't you already a master of Vagrant Boxing[34] and Taekwondo? Put another way, if you are so busy, where will you find the time to study?" Mr. Chen queried.

"No matter how busy I am, I can still find a way to squeeze out a little spare time to do something I really want to do. Please, brother," Mr. Tang supplicated.

Under the recommendation of his friend's father, Chen Jun, Mr. Tang, who held an important post as head of the police, and Teacher Liao, the chairman of the Miaoli Taekwondo Association, formally apprenticed to Hong Yi-xiang as their teacher. At the same time, they also invited several friends from the same hometown in Miaoli to learn Yizong Tangshou at the gym on Anxi Street. Early every Saturday morning, they would rush to catch a train from Miaoli to the class in Taipei. The classes were from 9 a.m. to noon. They were taught by Hong Yi-xiang, Hong Ze-zhou, and Hong Ze-pei. Only one student, a Ph.D. in animal husbandry teaching pig rearing, did not have a foundation in martial arts. Mr. Tang was originally a master of Vagrant Boxing, and due to his years of service in both the military and police, he also maintained his personal training regimen. Teacher Liao was ranked at fifth or sixth dan in Taekwondo, so after six months study, he already developed quite good skills. With such results, Mr. Tang boldly proposed a larger plan to Hong Yi-xiang.

He said that he had obtained the support of the local education authority and planned to replace the Taekwondo classes in the elementary, junior high, and high school curriculum with Yizong Tangshou. However, to accommodate a large-scale promotion, it would be necessary to train all the local PE teachers as seed coaches. Mr. Tang entreated Hong Yi-xiang to appoint Hong Ze-zhou as the Chief Instructor of this special program. From that time onwards, Hong

---

34 Vagrant Boxing 流民拳 is a martial art self-protection system passed down within the Hakka community. Hakkas or 客家人, The People Who are Guests of the House, as the name suggests, do not have a provincial homeland within China and, like the Romani, spread their communities around China and their diaspora. They were formerly treated with aloofness and sometimes downright prejudice by local communities, but in the Chinese melting-pot of Taiwan in the present era, they are a vibrant, proud, and accepted community.

Ze-zhou conversely took the train to Miaoli every Saturday, and then was transported to Miaoli municipal gymnasium for training the recruits. With monthly regularity, Hong Yi-xiang would go to the site to inspect the progress and results of the training. They continued to progress through six months of training, then began certification of qualifications, after which qualified physical education teachers began to comprehensively promote Tangshoudao in schools at all levels in Miaoli.

To comply with local conditions and the consideration of the education system, Hong Yi-xiang agreed with Mr. Tang's suggestion to integrate the traditional Chinese martial arts he had spent his entire life on, under the name of "Chinese Tangshoudao," and include this in the curriculum of the elementary, junior, and high schools' PE program formal classes with the vigorous assistance of the local government. Taiwan's educational institutions had never faced up to the promotion of traditional martial arts. At best, they allowed students to establish after-school training clubs. This time, the formal curriculum could be widely promoted in schools at all levels. This was mainly due to Mr. Tang's enthusiasm and coordination, as well as his abundant connections and resources in the local area, plus his special military and police background. His ability to organize and mobilize was indeed beyond the reach of ordinary people.

The promotion process coincided with Taiwan's initiation of the largest anti-crime-syndicate operation in the history of local public security, the "Yiqing Project." Mr. Tang was ordered to Green Island to take up an important position in the "Vocational Training Corps" and was responsible for managing those gang leaders who were imprisoned. On this isolated island formerly famous for incarcerating political prisoners, he had to mix with these gang leaders and big bosses daily and maintain harmony. Besides the essential possession of absolute authority, in addition, Mr. Tang said he had the vital energy and drive derived from his martial arts training. Without "qi," no matter how much authority and force are given to you, it may be insufficient to suppress mobsters who have long been struggling amidst the gleam of swords and the reports of guns. Between the manager and the managed exist many subtle interactions, and unless you have been there it is difficult to understand that "This old boy can chuck away his life, so what can you do to me?" sense of powerlessness.

During the Mid-Autumn Festival of that year, Mr. Tang had gotten orders to stay on Green Island to hold down the fort and could not return to Taiwan to celebrate the festivities. He asked a favor of a colleague returning to the main island of Taiwan for the holiday to carry a pair of deer antlers freshly sawed off that day, and several monstrous looking Green Island Coconut Crabs, to present to Master Hong Yi-xiang as festive gifts.

It is said that on that isolated island, in addition to the detainees and the detainers, there were many sambar and Sika deer native to Taiwan, the horns of which are an expensive Chinese medicine ingredient. The deer antler, usually seen in traditional Chinese medicine shops, is cut into thin wafers and dried. However, the pair delivered to Hong's house were whole antlers, with blood still oozing out of them. At first glance of that sight, it was hard not to imagine the carnage during the sawing of the antlers. The Hong family, who rarely used traditional tonics, really didn't know what to do with those two animal horns. Later, Yi-xiang asked Hong Yi-wen, who was well-versed in Chinese medicine, to help draw-up a precious Chinese medicinal prescription.

A traditional Chinese medicine shop on Dihua Street cut the antlers into slices and steeped them with Chinese medicinal materials and half a dozen bottles of aged Kinmen Gaoliang sorghum white spirits, to create a long-life, longevity enhancing, essence nourishing and Qi replenishing tonic wine. That large earthen ware jar of nourishing, life enhancing, tonic wine was always viewed by the family like it was an animal specimen in a laboratory. No one ever thought of opening it to try its legendary miraculous curative effect. A few years later, when Mother Hong was mopping the floor one day, she accidentally tapped that earthen ware jar with a mop, and the medicinal liquor that had been sealed up for many years exploded. Since then, the only trace of the secret life-extending prescription of the palace was the smell of wine permeating the room, but the mystery of the omnipotent cure of legend has been completely lost to mankind.

As for the several hideously armored coconut crabs, Mother Hong originally thought to release them under the coconut trees in the nearby park, and let dust return to dust, but when she went to the park, she shockingly discovered that what she thought were coconut palms were, in fact its close relative, the betel nut tree. She saw only bare yellow earth under the tree. To release them there would be no better than killing them. After an emergency family meeting was convened, it was decided that her son Hong Ze-pei would take them to the trees and shrubs on the banks of the Danshui River, letting them make their way in the world. No one knows whether these coconut crabs which had immigrated from Green Island to the banks of the Danshui River, bare of coconuts, survived swimmingly or not. If so, today they are blessed with generations of children and grandchildren.

After nearly three years of development of Chinese Tangshoudao in Miaoli, among one in ten thousand students, Mr. Tang unearthed a ring fighting contestant, Xu Run-cai. After training, he bravely seized the championship of the Chinese Wushu World Cup for many years running. In taking the ring to measure one's strength against players from different martial arts, the most important thing is courage combined with insight. The martial arts world has a saying "First is courage, second strength, and third skill." One phrase right to the point: only courage is the primary key determining winning or losing in the ring. If you lack courage, no matter how much strength you are born with, and how high the skill you have developed, if you panic, and your inner resolve is shattered, you have nothing. Sometimes this variety of inborn gift or deficiency, may not be able to change even with a lifetime of effort.

Among Hong Yi-xiang's disciples was a student who practiced boxing at the gym for many years surnamed Zou. He was always the first to sign up for the annual competitions, but he always got cold feet and dare not compete in the ring. One time he even burned up the uniform for the competition the day before the bout. His whole life he never overcame this demon obstacle in his heart. In fact, whether one participates or not in a competition, whether one gets the crown or not, neither represents nor proves that a person's abilities are good enough, because everyone has different natural endowments. The danger, though, is when the time comes one displays and does not hide weakness.

Xu Runcai and this disciple Zou are exactly two extreme opposites. In ordinary practice, one may not necessarily be able differentiate any particularly distinctive skills. Once in the ring, Xu looked just like Rambo returning to the jungle of the Vietnam War, back to the battlefield he was familiar with, as if he was completely transformed into another person. This is all due to his natural endowments. Whether you can apply yourself and work hard to reverse innate weaknesses to become strong depends on your own luck. Even if you meet the best teacher, you can't necessarily turn shit into gold and trying to force it is endless torture for both sides.

Thanks to the great assistance of Mr. Tang in the Miaoli area, Hong Yi-xiang and his martial arts blossomed everywhere. Behind this spectacular achievement an undeniable truth was revealed: in the incessant evolutionary process of human civilization, although traditional martial arts have endured wave upon wave of tests of the times and continue to survive, they can no longer exist in isolation within future generations. Without the support of the public and administrative policies, it is inevitable: after a night of tempest, the ground will be covered in fallen blossoms…

Hong Yi-xiang demonstrates the monkey and crane postures from Taizu Transforming Crane form, circa 1983.
©Robin Moyer

105– A POT OF TEA SHARED IN THE DEMIMONDE

What is Jianghu? The demimonde. It could be anything, or nothing. You can only say it is a situation resulting when your awesomeness meets up with the awesomeness of another, perhaps combining perhaps colliding with each other. A situation in which neither party has a choice and neither can extricate themselves, like the great ocean's rip tide or waterspouts. Some people are sucked down with the action of the whirlpool never to recover, and some people are lifted by the waterspout, as if they are going to ascend to heaven. But whether it is sinking down or rising up, everyone is the same, they are all sucked into it.

Scene: Chinese Tea House on an Alley off of Bade Road

"Brother Yi-xiang, we are all just trying to make a living here, is it necessary to adopt those protective body armor gear for sparring..."

Sitting in front of me was one of the top masters in Taiwanese martial arts circles. The tea house he selected was located in a secluded alley, and we were the only occupied table in the spacious shop. In those days, tableside service was not fashionable, and the topic discussed by the two parties was sensitive, related to the face of many masters. After the tea leaves, tea set and boiling water were brought up, the master gave the shop owner a signal that he was dismissed. As I was the most junior, I was naturally responsible for making tea. In fact, every time my father had friends from the martial arts world come to the gym to make tea and chat, it was my duty to play the tea lackey. I still remember that Jinxuan Oolong from Plum Mountain terroir was brewed that day. This brewed tea was different from the typical creamy fragrance of Jinxuan tea but had a faint scent of peach and fruit.

"You know, this is everyone's thought. It's not just my opinion," the master continued.

"I understand. Keep talking," Hong Yi-xiang replied.

"Also, can you stop teaching those foreigners," the master pushed.

"Why?"

"The war is over. They are not staying here to learn gongfu to preserve their own hides in battle."

Hong Yi-xiang sat silently in quiet disagreement.

"These people are here to steal our things. The Vietnam War was over long ago and all those soldiers have withdrawn. You teach without reservation, and sooner or later they will excavate all your secrets. Also, mixed within these foreigners are people whose backgrounds are not straightforward. Especially the tall guy who retired from US Naval Intelligence. As far as I know, this person was not low-ranking. He must be staying here for another purpose. You have to be careful."

The object of his insinuation was my training partner, Howard Brewer, and with the unrestrained agitation of my youthful self, I blurted out, "He's long since retired. Now he's just an ordinary antique dealer. Also, aren't you teaching boxing in Los Angeles?"

"A-han! You brew the tea. I'll ask you if I don't understand. Zip it!" My father requested me to accompany him mainly to let me act as an interpreter of some of the dialect accents he did not readily understand.

I was dumbfounded.

"I heard that your son is working as a director on a TV station. Why don't you consider passing the martial arts hall to the young people to manage?"

"Young people have their own ideas. You can't understand 'em and you can't change 'em. Why bother?" I could see my father's frustration.

"Brother Yi-xiang, I reached out to discuss these two matters with you today. This is everyone's suggestion. What do you think?" He brought up these thorny issues again.

"I totally understand your good intentions," Hong Yi-xiang replied.

"I'm not stopping you from teaching real gongfu. But how to teach it? Who to teach? How many students? You have to exercise more discretion. You can't treat everyone equally, no class discrimination. You should always hold back the good bits for yourself, isn't it?"

"Times have changed. No matter how good the bits, I won't hold them back," Hong Yi-xiang remonstrated.

"Why? At least save some for your children."

"No. My three boys all have their own ideas. What can I use to make demands of them? When I was their age, didn't I just engross myself in martial arts and neglected to take over my old man's candle business," Hong Yi-xiang said, expressing his regret.

"Young people may just want to see more of the world. Sooner or later, they'll return to the fold."

"No. I often tell them, if you have the ability, go out and develop yourselves, I'll save this swallow of rice for the disciples who train with me," Hong Yi-xiang said.

"Your sentiments are admirable. But I'm a few years older than you. During the Great Retreat, I saw too much of the ugliest side of human nature. One must always leave a back door escape route, otherwise…"

"Understood. Thank you very much for the reminder," Hong Yi-xiang said, his patience frayed.

"When I first arrived in Taiwan, I also received assistance from your father. I have a special affection for the Hong family. You mustn't misunderstand that I am uniting everyone to gang up on you to restrain your development."

"You don't have to worry about this. I understand completely. But let me take this opportunity to share some different ideas with everyone," Hong Yi-xiang said.

"Okay. Your turn."

"I think at our age, we are all faced with the problem of continuing traditions and passing the baton. Times, traditions, constantly change. The value of these things continuing to exist encounters increasingly severe tests," Hong Yi-xiang predicted.

"That's right."

"I think if the road of empirical proof is not taken, they will decline all the way. Decline until they are unrecognizably degraded," Hong Yi-xiang warned.

The master was silent."The production, maintenance and improvement of these protective armors for sparring, they consume the extremely limited income of my gym. But to not do this is unacceptable. If we want to hold international competitions, we must show our firepower to hold on to the trophies. Some martial arts gyms only sign up for forms competitions, not sparring, why? You know better than me," Hong Yi-xiang dug in.

When the master listened to these words, his eyes never dared to face Hong Yi-xiang.

"Every time I participate in a discussion on the rules of the Guo Shu Federation ring fighting, isn't it the martial arts gyms that *never* send people to participate in the ring competition who are pushing their agendas the most?" Hong Yi-xiang expressed his frustration.

"Actually, everyone knows that you have always been shouldering this burden, you needn't bother haggling with them."

"Western boxing, Japanese judo and karate, Muay Thai and Taekwondo, no matter what angle you use to evaluate them, there is one fact that we can never deny. They are constantly improving their practical value through competition in the ring, and this practical utility is the reason why they will continue to survive in the future, isn't it?" Hong Yi-xiang observed.

The master looked on with no response.

"Today, I brought two sets of brand-new protective gear just for you, each a top and a bottom four pieces. I hope you will have the opportunity to let your students wear them and beat up on each other. I believe that after they have clashed hard with each other, they will have a completely different understanding of their old training when they return to it," Hong Yi-xiang offered.

"These things are so precious; I'd be embarrassed to take them." At that time, no such products were available in Taiwan's sporting goods stores.

"Also, I can provide you with the production methods and material specs of these protective gears unconditionally, so that everybody can make and use them," Hong Yi-xiang extended the offer further.

"These things are too precious. Everyone is just eking out a living teaching, how can they afford to take on the expense."

"If really in need, some of the used protective gear in my gym can also be lent to everyone for free," Hong Yi-xiang said. The men sat in silent resistance to his offer. "The reason I do this is in the hope of raising the overall level of training. Only this kind of martial arts is alive. It's not just living in a boxing manual and past myths," Hong Yi-xiang finished.

"Alright. In that case, it would be rude of me to refuse."

"And you just mentioned that you don't want me teaching foreigners boxing anymore; why?" Hong Yi-xiang asked.

"Actually, your son just made a good point. I am teaching foreigners myself; everyone is teaching them. Why not teach them if there is money to be made? But the problem is, your foreign students are challenging the locals and trying out their gongfu everywhere. Our rice bowls are at risk of being broken by them."

"Pa, he means…," I blurted out.

"I know who he is talking about," Hong Yi-xiang interjected.

"Yi-xiang. These foreigners are tall and sturdy. When they make a challenge, they don't pay attention to seniority, respect for teachers, and their messing around makes everyone miserable."

"They're not ill intended. It's just cultural and differences in awareness that cause this misunderstanding. They value practicality and don't want to waste time on uncertain things. Coupled with their intense curiosity, as soon as they see those esoteric, illogical, incomprehensible amazing powers and tricks, they can't help but try them out to see if those things are really so awesome," I couldn't help but interject, however my old man still held my hand and wouldn't let me go on. "Okay. Don't worry about this. I will strictly restrain them. As for the troubles caused to the many old masters, I am really sorry. I would like to ask you to help convey my regards."

Then, the conversation drifted to something less important, until my dad and I watched the master get into the cab, shouldering the four heavy pieces of equipment. After I settled the bill for the tea, I walked along the alley with my old man and chatted:

"Pa. This is just dragging you down, isn't it?" I spoke.

"Nah. It's just the way life is."

"Do you think they will use that protective gear?" I asked.

"That's my intention. Why speculate about the results?" Hong Yi-xiang said. "A-Han. Chinese martial arts were passed down in Taiwan in that age of great change when circumstances were favorable and took root in our family. But sooner or later, both sides of the Taiwan straits will be re-opened. What face do you think the traditional martial arts inherited in Taiwan will present when confronted with the traditional martial arts from the source?" Hong Yi-xiang queried.

"I don't know. What do you think?"

"I don't know either. But what if we just respect the ancient method and brew it exactly the same way?" Hong Yi-xiang asked, by way of drawing out my thinking.

"Then it would certainly be like the Jinxuan Oolong tea I just brewed, the more times it is steeped, the weaker it gets," I said.

"So then?" Hong Yi-xiang drew me out further.

"So, one has to keep adding new elements, incessantly researching, developing, improving?"

"Yes. But you still can't give up the core concepts that already exist, otherwise you'll be giving up something near when grasping for something afar," Hong Yi-xiang pointed out.

"That's why you've been spending time categorizing and improving those source materials?"

"Actually, I really hope you can continue to research these things to completion," Hong Yi-xiang said.

"Pa, I'm not up to it. I'm too weak. I can't shoulder this burden."

"No. Not weak. You can shoulder it," Hong Yi-xiang did not relent.

I understood what he meant, but I didn't want it to turn out like this.

"If you were already strong enough, you needn't rely on these techniques anymore. Isn't it so? Take my word for it, A-Han, you'll be able to. One day you will."

Hong Yi-xiang and students on the way to perform at a television station.

106– NATURAL BOXING'S MASTER WAN LAI-SHENG

An advantage momentarily held back, is a type of restraint; effective restraint can create infinite possibilities.

Scene: Fuzhou City, China

ONE YEAR, HONG YI-XIANG WAS INVITED TO FUZHOU, CHINA TO serve as the chief referee of the "Cross-Strait Chinese Wushu Observation Tournament." He led three generations from the Taiwanese martial arts world to Fuzhou to participate in this event. This was also the first time since he learned Chinese traditional martial arts from Master Zhang Jun-feng when he was young, that Hong Yi-xiang himself had set foot on Mainland China. He joined hands with fellow enthusiasts of martial arts on the mainland for the exchange and development of Chinese martial arts on both sides of the straits. At that time, the Taiwan martial art world's level of development of competition rules was relatively advanced and complete. To shorten the gap between the two sides of the Taiwan Straits, he arrived in Fuzhou one week in advance to assist in training the local referees and have a complete exchange on the relevant support needed during competitions.

Master Wan Lai-sheng was from Gexian Town, Echeng County, Hubei Province. Born in 1903, he formally apprenticed himself to train in martial arts in Beijing since the age of thirteen, along the way training in Shaolin Six Harmony Boxing, Arhat Boxing, Monkey Boxing, Pigua, Xingyi, Bagua, Taiji and other Internal Schools of boxing. He had deeply researched all manner of traditional weapons, swords, and staves and was the author of many martial arts books such as *Wushu Compendium*, *Original Taijiquan Illustrated*, and *Manual of International Martial Arts*. In the past he had taught boxing and practiced medicine in Shanghai, Henan, Wuhan, Guangxi and other places. The "Natural Boxing" he founded seeks to reach a level of martial art in which "motion and stillness have no beginning, change is endless, deception and reality cannot be differentiated, thus natural." He was also a political commissar of Fujian Province and the vice chairman of the Provincial Wushu Association.

"Master Wan has very high seniority in the Chinese martial arts world, and he is our respected elder."

"The heroic deeds of Wan Lai-sheng when he was young, I have long heard in Taiwan," said Hong Yi-xiang.

"Master Wan has always provided guidance and supported new martial artists, but his whole life he paid particular attention to those with real learning and genuine talent. About those counterfeit martial artists always practicing lip-service gongfu, he has nothing nice to say."

"I agree. *That* kind of person should be a tournament announcer or salesman. Immersing themselves in the martial arts world, they are not only abusing themselves, but also doing crappy martial art. Master Wan is the real deal," Hong Yi-xiang said.

"Master Hong, you are a celebrity in the international martial arts world, and we all know that you are an expert of actual combat using the Internal School Boxing. Although we have reported your qualifications to Master Wan a few days ago, this old man's competitive spirit has not waned with the years, so I take the liberty to remind you that when Wan Lai-sheng meets other people for the first time, he can't help but have a sly go at them, testing whether the other party has got what it takes. Please be aware Master Hong, and please be tolerant."

"Understood. Thanks for your reminder and taking the trouble to tell me," Hong Yi-xiang said.

At the welcoming dinner that day, Master Wan Lai-sheng was invited to a get-together with the martial arts representatives from Taiwan. Master Wan was very old but his step was still light and graceful, and he radiated health and vigor. After a brief introduction, Hong Yi-xiang, hoping to honor the old worthy, stepped forward to politely shake hands. He didn't expect that as soon as the two sides joined hands, his right hand would immediately feel it was being compacted inward by a hidden force. Hong Yi-xiang's palms were thicker than ordinary people, unless the opponent was also born big boned, it was difficult to exert force on his giant palm. Master Wan Lai-sheng was of a lean body type, and his hand bones no different from those of ordinary people. That he could exert such power against such a disparate size ratio clearly showed that his skill was extraordinary. On this first meeting, Hong Yi-xiang did not expect such a heavy handshake. Reacting instinctively, Hong Yi-xiang immediately resisted with hidden energy to avoid the joints being squeezed by the other party to the point he would no longer be able to counter. The moment the two powers cancelled each other out, he could instantly feel the opponent's grip increase greatly. Hong Yi-xiang understood that *this* wave was the real main attack.

Facing such a powerful challenge, Hong Yi-xiang not only did not feel unhappy, conversely it returned him to his youth and the secret pleasure of comparing martial stills with others here and there. Naturally following his body's step forward of welcome greeting, he took another small step forward. At the same time, he used the palm of his left hand to cover the hands of the two of them, and locked Wan Lai-sheng's thumb with the middle finger of his right hand. Applying only thirty percent of his strength gave a hint to the opponent to stop before going too far. If the opponent did not stop exerting force, his broken thumb joint would be the regrettable outcome. Sure enough, after sensing this subliminal threat, Master Wan Lai-sheng immediately let up on his grip, and also used *his* left palm to cover Hong Yi-xiang's left hand to express a warm greeting. Thus, in this "four hands overlapping, enthusiastic greeting" was a hidden test of strength between the two masters of two generations completed. At that moment, Hong Yi-xiang considered himself lucky that someone had given him a heads-up, otherwise, if he had only relied on natural reactions in the spur of the moment, one fears that the scene that day would not have been so peaceful and harmonious.

"Master Hong, good gongfu."

"My Elder Master Wan, please teach me more."

It was not until the two legends released their handshake that the gentleman in charge of introducing the two sides could fully off-load the secret anxiety in his heart. Among the hundreds of guests on the scene, apart from the two masters involved, he alone knew what had happened in the test just then.

According to Hong Yi-xiang's later memories, Master Wan Lai-sheng's internal strength was indeed greater than he had expected. He speculated that while he might not necessarily lose the fight, in that kind of situation, if the two masters really wanted to have at it in front of everyone, then it would truly damage the harmony between comrades across the straits. Coupled with the fact that the opponent was already advanced in years, he must not take any offensive actions. Therefore, utilizing the half step forward, he deliberately pressed the opponent's right wrist down into a lock from which no force could be issued. On the one hand, this checked the opponent's ability to continue exerting coercive force while obviating the need to respond with a heavy-handed counterattack. On the other hand, he locked the opponent's thumb with his middle finger and thumb and pressed his left palm covering the opponent's thumb. If the opponent insisted on trying to parse victory, he need only grip tight, twist the opponent's right hand down and back, while his middle finger and thumb twisted in the opposite direction. To keep the thumb from dislocating, the opponent would have to kneel to escape this miniature joint lock. If the opponent made a big move to resist, he need only further press his left hand forward, and the opponent would have no speck of a chance to escape. This is the inescapable "Three Locks" seizing technique. Fortunately, both sides signaled the end. If they really wanted to continue the skirmish, he was not sure whether he would have gone easy against the elder at that juncture.

In the evening, after a busy referee's seminar, several old apprentices accompanying Hong-Chen Xun, Huang Qing-xiang, Li Chun-sheng, and some fellow enthusiasts from Taiwan martial arts circles, gathered to sip tea and chat in Hong Yi-xiang's suite. About ten o'clock in the evening, when he had only just bid everyone return to their rooms to rest, he heard the doorbell ring, opened the door, and took a look. Two strapping men about forty years old had brought a basket of delicately packaged fruits to pay a visit.

"Master Hong, we are Master Wan Lai-sheng's disciples. Master asked us to send you a sample of Shandong Pears for you to taste. This is to express our welcome and admiration of you."

"How can I accept this, Master Wan is the elder, and I am all prepared to visit him tomorrow. Unexpectedly, I am one step behind him, you are here first. Come, come, come, please come inside."

"Master Hong, you're too polite. Here we are the host, it is we who should call on you."

"Ai! The two sides of the straits have been separated for decades. To get to this stage was truly difficult. You don't know how happy my masters would be to see this day."

"In fact, seeing Master Hong's achievements in the world of martial arts, their souls should be equally happy in Heaven."

"Just to not shame the masters is already a blessing. With such an illustrious teacher as Master Wan leading the way, the future achievements of you two will eclipse the brilliance of we old men."

"Master Hong, to tell you the truth, our teacher was deeply impressed with the technique you used during the day. The whole afternoon, I don't know how many times he brought it up to we two. Just praising you not only for your fine technique, but also for your generous and compassionate heart, your technique was right to the point, but then not released, it's really not easy."

"Ai! Spur of the moment. I should offer up a humble apology."

"No. Master Hong, over here, who doesn't know our master's lofty view, he can't stomach fake experts who rely on their mouths to train the martial art of saying 'gongfu.' He is truly happy from the bottom of his heart to see while he is still alive that after several decades since Chinese martial arts left these shores, an exponent such as Master Hong can be produced. Truly not easy."

"Shucks, here I was just now encouraging the guys from Taiwan to seek the benefit of further instruction from Master Wan and the elders. By no means should they miss this rare one in a million opportunity. From our perspective, Master Wan is a living encyclopedia and witness to China's modern martial art history."

"Master Hong, you are too kind. Master instructed us both that tomorrow we definitely have to seek the opportunity to ask Master Hong to teach us a few hand joint control techniques, so that we will not miss the opportunity to learn from the master."

"Good, good. No problem. From now on, together we should cross the boundaries restricting us and we should exchange and learn from each other, swap pointers and encourage each other to grow."

This fated meeting with Master Wan Lai-sheng in Fuzhou, by means of a mutual tacit understanding and hidden test of strength, added to the shared admiration and friendship, and also preserved a resplendent bright spot and happy memory for the cross-straits meeting of martial arts luminaries.

Hong Yi-xiang with Guandu branch instructor Chen Xun and Nangang branch instructor Huang Qing-xiang, invited to attend the Fuzhou China Wushu Training Exchange, 1989.

Grand Master Wan Lai-sheng and Master Hong Yi-xiang on their meeting in Fuzhou, China, 1989.

107– CONVERSATIONS WITH MY OLD MAN ON THE BALCONY PART 1—THE STRATAGEM OF WITH THE GRAIN VERSUS AGAINST THE GRAIN

Sunzi's Art of War states:

> *When laying siege to a city, leave an egress for the enemy do not restrain returning combatants.*

Scene: On the Balcony at Anxi Street

"When I picked up that dense piece of wood, in the bottom of my heart I knew where things stood," my father said.

"What kind of wood was it?" I asked.

"Judging from the grain and the weight that should've been beech wood. A-Han do you know beech wood?"

"In Taiwan, isn't its hardness second only to oak?"

"Yep."

"It's a kind of wood harder than Magnolia Compressa! And its tough fibers and ductility are really strong! It shouldn't be used by people in breaking demonstrations."

"I reckon the thickness was three to three and a half inches!"

"Wow! This thickness coupled with the tough ductility; I imagine it would be tougher to break than fired bricks."

"And there's something else that is hard for most people to perceive."

"Yeah?"

"When you pull materials for building a house, it's customary that the long side of the lumber is with the grain and the short side of the lumber is against the grain, right?"

"Yeah, unless you especially specify, otherwise then it'll be this way."

"But this three-and-a-half-inch thick piece of beech wood was conversely the opposite."

"So you had to break against the grain?"

"Not necessarily. It depends on how you hold the wood up, doesn't it?"

"Right! Why didn't I think it could be struck this way? Heh-heh. So, this is the way you cracked it?"

"Sort of. But I couldn't be sure if this selection of wood was just a mistake by the organizer or if he intentionally was setting a trap for me."

"You mean to say… if you held the board up so as to make it easier to break with the grain then this guy would jump out and ridicule you for taking the easy way out?"

"Wouldn't you if you were him?"

"Wow, what a snake in the grass… So what did you do?"

"If I didn't want to take a risk I still could've thought of a way to back out, but in that moment my fighting spirit got the best of me."

"You bit the bullet?"

"Yeah, I didn't want to let myself back out and regret it."

"Dad, maybe this guy had already figured that out!"

"A-Han. Once I was standing at that juncture it didn't matter whether he had planned for this, the most important thing was that the four people gripping the wood could hold fast when I released my power into the strike. If they didn't put up an opposite and equal opposing force, then it would be over."

"Even if there was just a slight slip of a couple of centimeters then all of your incoming force would be dissipated, right?"

"Fortunately, Ye Zhen-fang, Lee Qing-xiang, and Lin the chicken seller had all been with me for many years. I trusted they could catch my tempo and certainly could stand firm."

"Dad, if I was that guy then I would've just bribed those men. Because at that critical moment the cost was lowest, it was most environmentally friendly, and the opportunity for success was highest! Wasn't it? Ha-ha-ha!"

"Yep, so it's better you are my son! Ha-ha-ha." Rare humor from my dad.

"So afterwards? I can't see the results from this photo."

"I broke it. But it was really difficult to break. To tell you the truth I really crushed it, from the bottom of my heart I really admired that tricky guy."

"Afterwards did you find out who that guy was?"

"Yeah, I know. Actually, you've seen him and helped serve tea to him."

"Who would mess around with these kinds of cheap tricks and still dare to come to the school and drink tea?"

"You go figure it out. You should be good for more than just knowing how to bribe people. Use a little of your genius and think about it and when you've figured it out, then I'll tell you."

If everybody only knew… just how many people had come to our school to drink tea… then you wouldn't be laughing.

Why is it that until today I still can't figure out who this guy was hiding in the shadows making his plans and still daring to come and drink tea at our school.

Besides demonstrating raw power, Hong Yi-xiang shows an understanding of physics and materials as he demolishes a single thick board, circa 1974.

108– CONVERSATIONS WITH MY OLD MAN ON THE BALCONY PART 2— FOCUS ON STRENGTH AND GET POWERFUL, FOCUS ON MIND, AND GET THE TOTAL SOLUTION

Fast frying and slow cooking each achieve different flavors of dishes. Pressure cookers try to overcome the problem of slow cooking time, but the compressed time is often offset by the diminution of the delicate flavors!

Scene: Yongle Elementary School

"Pa, one-thousand reps done." Me.
 "Oh? So fast." My old man.
 "I doubled my practice. Twenty times a day." Me.
 "A rep normally takes twenty minutes. Did you practice seven or eight hours a day?" Dad.
 I could see where this was going and stayed silent.
 "Did you speed it up?" My old man.
 "Yeah. But I did practice the number of reps you specified. Sometimes I exceeded it."
 "Oh. That's good. But it's also a pity."
 "Pa. The speed is too slow. I can't practice power at all."
 "If you are only seeking speed, don't practice this."
 "But it's so slow and soft. It's really incompatible with concepts of actual combat."
 "Oh? Is that so?"
 "I've carefully examined every move and application, but not many are practical in a fight."
 "A-Han. The quality and effectiveness of training are reciprocal. You seek speed and sacrifice all the qualities hidden in the details."
 "This method needs to be upgraded. It's so inefficient."
 "No. Your attitude's got to change. It's too rough."
 "Pa. Don't you seek to be single weighted at all points? But these moves are all double weighted. Power must be there somewhere. But the movement is

slow. How do you hit people?"

"When you shift position, is it double? Or single?"

"Single weight of course. Otherwise, how can you move."

"Eh. So, isn't that right?"

"Right, what?"

"You're all about speed. You're all about power. That's why you ignore all the 'Movement within the Transition' and 'Transition within the Movement,' right or not?"

"You didn't say to pay attention to this and practice it."

"I thought you were smart. That you'd figure it out yourself."

"Pa. You want me to practice this, just say so. Wasting so much of my time in vain."

"Focus on strength and get powerful, focus on mind and get the total solution. Practice makes perfect. It's just a pity that you are not as smart as I thought."

"Pa! It hurts when you say that."

"No pain, no gain."

I had no words.

"Double weighting is the only way to build the foundation of internal boxing. The wave motion during the transition between single and double is the key. It's a way to find the source power, unify the power, and release the power." My father tried to temper the wound by way of attempting deeper explanation.

I still had no words.

"Whether competence improves or not depends on the quality and direction of one's training. Focus on strength and get powerful, focus on mind and get the total solution, only mental and physical effort used together can find the key to unlock the inner universe."

"Pa. You're talking like some demimonde wizard. It's too mysterious. Can't you arrange a standard curriculum that is more unified, simpler, and easier for people to understand?" I took an indescribable delight in this successful ambush.

"Although the mechanism of energy gathering and transformation in people's bodies is largely similar, it is different due to each person's innate understanding and acquired ability. It's difficult to use a unified and systematic formulation or teaching method to cover everything, and each student must be reviewed case by case. Like the old expression 'Direct Oral Transmission inspires True Understanding.' However, this special situation has been used by some fake and shoddy teachers with a mind to deliberately manipulate. They use this veil of mystery to exaggerate unrealistic power and go about everywhere conning people." Dad.

"So, we just let those people continue to manipulate and hype these things?"

"You have a better way?"

"What can I do? I practiced it wrong myself. What else can I do?"

He let out a laugh, "You who seize every chance to gain advantage through trickery, dare to blame others."

"Is it really important to *Fajin*-Issue Force? No, that's not the right question. It should be, is it really that powerful?" I asked.

"*Fajin* is just one compulsory class in martial arts training. As for how powerful it is? I don't know. It depends on the limits to which human beings can develop the inner universe within the body. But I personally think it is not truly necessary and am not overly superstitious about it."

"That's right. If *Fajin* was so powerful, were I the leader of the country, then I would try to convince those masters to dedicate these skills to the nation and teach them to our military or special forces, so that they can use these techniques defend the homeland."

"Ha-ha-ha! You are so naive. What are you going to use to persuade the Masters."

"Use a lot of money."

"Some things can't be bought with money."

"Then beautiful women."

As I would have predicted, my old man declined to respond, but I still had a good time making fun. "If that doesn't work, pull a gun."

"Then you are a tyrant."

"So how?"

"Isn't that the reason why it remains a Gordian knot?"

"Pa. What about your own opinion?"

"I don't have a special opinion. In fact, I want to see such miraculous powers with my own eyes. Those who claim to be able to make opponents magically fly away, put 'em in the ring, exchange punches with any kind of boxing champion and see what happens. See if he can stand his ground and continue to BS."

"Wow! You could definitely sell the broadcast rights to that for a profit."

"Alright. So what about it? Do you still want to continue training?" My old man got back to business.

"I'll have to start all over again. It's just, Dad, are there any *more* important points you're not mentioning? Please clarify once and for all," I entreated.

"Ha-ha-ha! Wherever the boat goes, that's the scenery you see. Now, do you get it?"

Imagine here a cartoon caption balloon filled with stars and lightning ... (Being the master's son, in fact, most of the time is unhappy!)

"A-han, tell me from the bottom of your heart. After knowing the truth, why choose to continue practicing?"

"I want to go on stage, make people fly away and pocket the broadcast rights."

This time, my old man was speechless, floored by this skillful left hook.

"Ha-ha-ha..." There is an invigorating feeling in defeating the master.

Because, until one trains to the very end, no one knows if there remain further possibilities.

Because, when the sport of basketball was just emerging, no one knew that it was possible to jump high enough to slam dunk.

Because, in the past, no one would believe that today we could all learn astronomy or geography on a mobile phone.

Because something is not known openly, does not mean it doesn't exist, does it?

However, I sincerely recommend that you:

Don't spend a fortune looking for peerless martial arts. Sincerely seek a teacher whose virtue equals his skill, and make your practice grounded. Don't cut corners. Maybe, you will discover earlier than me the method that can effectively develop your inner potential. Rest assured. I'm over sixty. I can't beat you for sure. Pedal to the Metal!

Hong Yi-xiang smashing two bricks placed flat on the floor when requested to perform an impromptu breaking demo, circa 1975.

109– CONVERSATIONS WITH MY OLD MAN ON THE BALCONY PART 3— INVOLUNTARY MUSCLES

Perhaps the scope of what we can control through thought is not limited to those things which we know as naturally passed down. However, awakening the internal control techniques are too difficult, too unpredictable. Hence, we habitually employ external technologies to gain access to skills we lack, including telescopes, microscopes, computers, mobile devices and all manner of firearms and ammunition.

Scene: On the balcony of the Anxi Street villa

"A-han, what is internal practice?" Dad.
"Some say it's massaging the internal organs, some say it's cleansing, nourishing, and guiding the Qi, isn't that the case?" Me.
"What's your own opinion?" Dad.
"How do I know. I really don't have any concept of such things that can't be seen or touched." Me.
"Aren't you curious?" Dad.
"Curious minded, yeah. But the concept is too abstract and opaque. It's too easy to be manipulated by people's claims, too easy for erroneous ideas to be spread. I really detest such deliberately mystified and purposely obscured things, stuff that can't be tested as true or false." Me.
"How do you verify it then? Go to the ring and fight? Or enter a laboratory and test it?"
"Whatever, don't you feel that people who over-hype mysterious gifts falling from heaven eventually end up exposed to the light of day?"
"Maybe. However maybe you haven't found the right way to verify it for yourself yet."
"Pa, isn't this the way they talk? Never commit to a description or explain clearly, deliberately reserving a blurry space for people to fathom and fill with their own imaginings. Don't you think this is the acme of manipulation and deception."
"Yes. However, when you write a screenplay for a movie, don't you like to keep a vague or fuzzy space for the audience to use their imagination? Why are you the only one allowed to do this?"

"That's different. That's literature, fiction. It's not martial arts. Martial arts are an empirical science, relying on evidence. You can't mess around ambiguously like this."

"Okay. You set your own rules, and therefore you can say anything you like. Remember when you went to visit the one-hundred-year-old monk on Thumb Mountain with John? Didn't you take the opportunity to ask him such questions?"

"Yeah. How could I forget this?"

"What did he say?"

"He said: Internal work is the technique of focusing on the interior of the body. It uses the mind to train the usually 'involuntary muscles' connected to the autonomic nervous system in the body to become 'voluntary muscles.' These muscles can then be used as one likes. Yeah. How could I forget this part?"

"A-han, you shouldn't rush too quickly to conclusions about some things. Since you have this reminder, why don't you try first to verify the information with your own body? Didn't you say that in writing you only need deduce a single 'pivot point' around which a complete story turns? Isn't control of involuntary muscles such a focus point, what do you say?"

"Argh! But how to start?"

"Haven't you always had your own way?" Dad knew my deep-rooted habits all too clearly.

"Should I use my breath to guide my mind? Or should I use my mind to guide my breath? Then, focus on some point or organ, and then…"

"No need to tell me what you want to do. You just need to know what you are doing."

So, in my mind, I felt like a humpback whale blowing bubbles to herd a school of herring, various ideas of different significance emerged, such as: how to use the breath to control the lung capacity, to use thought to regulate the heart rate and adjust gastrointestinal peristalsis, to use micro-motions to entrain the peripheral nervous system, the contraction and release of the posterior ophthalmic muscles, and controlling the secretions of various glands in the body…

No one knows whether the inner universe of the human body really hides secret codes and interrelated possibilities that can be changed and regulated by mind? If you want to figure this out, how can you truly understand the processes if you don't start with your own body and mind.

Human organs can be roughly divided into three categories: voluntary, partially voluntary, and involuntary. If you are right-handed, then your right hand is a voluntary muscle, your left hand is a partially voluntary muscle, and your internal organs are involuntary muscles. Through deliberate training we can make the left hand, which is not as completely dexterous or responsive to thought, become as fluid and responsive as the right hand. We can even decrease or increase the speed and frequency of lung and heart operation through mind control, meditation, and guided breathing, so we are indirectly controlling other uncontrollable internal organs, glands, and nervous systems through heartbeat and breathing control.

The purpose of generating control. Of course, these techniques belong to the category of exploring and developing the inner universe of the human body, and they are also the highest level pursued by many yoga and inner strength enthusiasts. As for whether humans can achieve the ability to directly control involuntary muscles through acquired inner training, it is still unknown. But what cannot be achieved now may not be impossible in the future, right? However, we can't imagine what the relationship between people and the external world will look like when all the originally involuntary organs, systems, and glands in the human body become controllable.

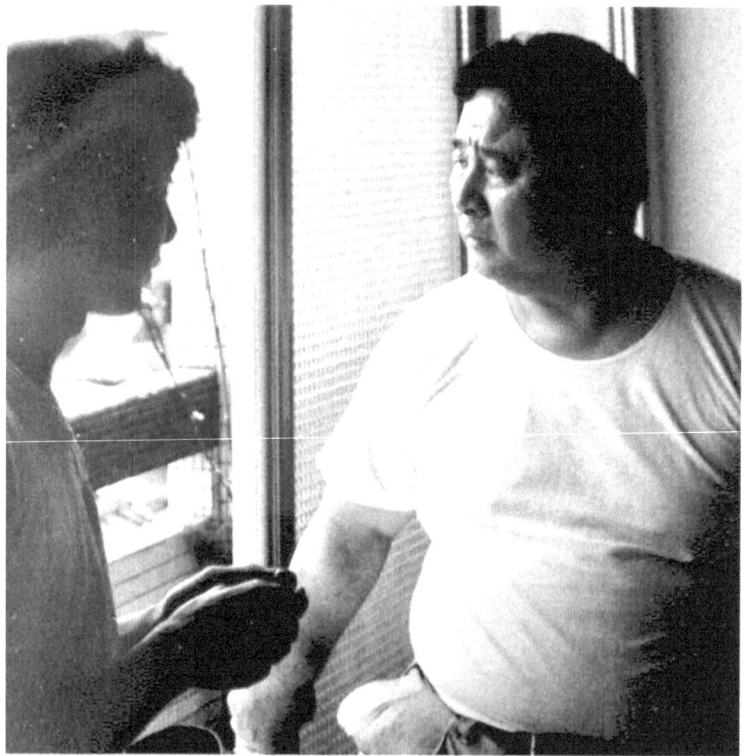

A conversation on the balcony between Hong Ze-han and Hong Yi-xiang, 1990.

110– CONVERSATIONS WITH MY OLD MAN ON THE BALCONY PART 4—TILT YOUR HEAD, DON'T TILT THE TACO

"Don't worry. My speed is very fast. You can't catch me," I said.

"No matter how fast you go, there is a limit! Once locked, you can't escape," Dad replied.

"Look! Like this!" I used a very short inhalation to demonstrate a double kick, roundhouse, and hook. "Can you catch it?"

"It's fast. But speed is not the key." He disapproved of my wanton arrogance, but he still held back his anger.

"Of course, it's not just speed! What's more important is that this kind of kick is two-way, and the speed of retracting is equally fast. Like a double-edged sword, both the roundhouse kick and the back hook can hurt people."

"It doesn't matter how many edges on the sword! What I care about is what if I get caught?" he said.

"I will immediately skip forward and make up for it with a shortrange elbow attack, definitely the opponent will not be able to take advantage of me," I said.

"Okay. Since you are so confident, then you kick me."

"No, it's too dangerous."

"You have no idea how I'm going to deal with you, the one who should be careful is yourself," he said.

"Okay. Then I will kick slower."

"Kick as fast as you can. Otherwise, you'll never know where your problem is," he said

So, I inhaled, stepped in, raised my foot…

Then, a palm slap inexplicably landed on my cheek. It didn't hurt, but it stung. It hurt not my body, but my ego.

"How?" I searched.

"Angles."

I still did not get it.

"And a half step!"

"Oh?" I was still thinking about how to get my face back.

"I seized the moment when you took in a breath and skipped forward, and used a step forward to block your space," he said.

"I'll try again." I figured that since he had revealed his move, I should have a chance to win it back.

This time I struck with a backhand to lure him to make a bridge, planning to clasp his wrist and then step up and kick. Unexpectedly, the result was still the same.

"How could this be?" I asked.

"The key is your breath," he said.

I was dumbfounded.

"The strong breath you are most proud of and rely on the most.

It provides you with speed and strength, but it also exposes your secret at the same time."

"Then I just need to improve the way I breathe! Isn't it?" I said.

"Yeah? I don't know. Maybe it's worth you giving it a try. But this way of inhaling and holding your breath is, after all, an unnatural way of practicing, and it's not good for your body. Why burden your body so?"

"You don't know. I've tried many different methods, but this one is the fastest and strongest. I just have to hide the change of breath." I stuck to my guns.

"The method you are practicing now, whether you are pursuing skills, strength, or speed, is inseparable from physical principles and limitations. You must start with body structure, mechanics, and inertia, but these techniques cannot escape the constraints of gravity after all."

"Aren't you limited by the same?"

"Yes! So I choose to follow the natural way."

"Dad, that's what you old people think! I'm still young. For young people, speed and strength come naturally. I think my problem is that I'm not fast enough, you see. If I can practice speed like whipping a towel, you won' be able to catch it." I whipped the towel in my hand into the air, and then pulled it back instantly, the end of the towel made a crisp sound of flicking in the air and ejected a fine mist.

Half a year later, in the middle of the night, I passed out inexplicably in the bathroom. I didn't realize it until my elder brother Ze-zhou got up to brush his teeth in the morning. The entire family mobilized to move me into the best clinic in the area, Dr. Yang's Surgery. I stayed in the hospital for three full weeks before going home. Only my father and I understood the real cause of this severe stomach bleeding, but to the end he never gave any blame, just said lightly:

"Your congenital condition is weak, after recovering, don't practice in that way again."

Another year later, the same story played out again.

"Ah Han, don't be stubborn! Practice internal boxing instead! Preserving your health is more important than looking flashy. Don't 'play' martial arts anymore." His words pierced to my core.

Two or three years ago, a German from Austria came to our Zhishanyan training area. He said that he was introduced by Ms. Violet Rao in Vienna. I didn't want him to come, but he still came. He was nearly two meters tall, taller than our student Aaron Arnold. His height like an NBA star made me wonder how to refuse him to avoid unimaginable consequences. He was an expert in a sports science named Philip. In order to help Olympic athletes challenge the limits of human physical fitness in the arena he uses computer programs to analyze the smashing movements of volleyball attackers, and researches whether they should shoot at the highest point of the jump? Or should they take advantage of the time difference and shoot at a certain point when the body starts to descend? He said that the purpose of jumping in volleyball is to score points, not to jump higher than anyone else. He used the latest scientific tools and methods to seek new answers following natural laws and methods.

"In addition to this method, do you think there are other possibilities?" he asked.

"Only if the physical training is connected to or transformed into a chemical change." I repeated what the old monk who lived on Thumb Mountain and who had been exiled in the deep mountains of Nanyang for many years had said in my ear.

"You mean adrenaline? Steroids? Or other banned drugs that can't be tested in the Olympics?" Philip asked.

"No. I'm talking about inner alchemy. It's like endorphins or some glands and secretions in the human body that humans haven't been able to understand yet."

"Wow! Do you understand?"

"Of course not."

"Oh." I couldn't tell if he was a little disappointed or not.

"The human body is a powerful chemical factory. This vast inner universe still contains a lot of energy and knowledge that has yet to be exploited. It is worth exploring and digging with various tools or methods, isn't it?" I said.

"How?" asked Philips.

"Tilt your head, don't tilt the Taco, let the Taco alone."

The last portrait of Master Hong Yi-xiang practicing Xingyiquan, 1993.

III- DOWNFALL OF THE STRONG

So large one cannot see beyond it, so loud one cannot hear, so mournful one cannot find tears. The achievements of the king can neither be continued, nor duplicated.

Scene: Anxi Street

That year, Hong Yi-xiang was sixty-six years old. His wife, Ms. Hong Wang Ai-qing, was admitted to Taipei MacKay Hospital for gallstones. Due to the negligence of the attending physician, the biliary tract was not cleansed during the operation, causing embrittlement and obstruction of the tract, inducing jaundice. When a second operation was carried out, the attending physician changed to orthoscopic surgery, but then accidentally injured the internal organs and caused massive bleeding. After an overnight rescue failed, she left this world in the early morning of the next day.

I stayed in the hospital to take care of my mother, that day I was outside the operating room. I listened to the news of deteriorating conditions in the operating room through the night. Until the doctor came out and announced that the operation had failed, I could not believe how a simple procedure could change into a sudden rending of heaven and man. And that grievous day, fell on my thirty-sixth birthday.

Hong Yi-xiang lost his reason to go on living and day by day became increasingly lonely and depressed. Even though his children tried their best to maintain the daily routines and traditions of their mother to avoid stirring his sadness, a widower's grief and loneliness still erodes his will to survive.

"I want to hand over the martial arts training hall federation to A-zhou to lead and leave those secret techniques to A-pei to inherit and let them share the work and cooperate and manage it together. What do you think?" Hong Yi-xiang asked.

"Pa, do what you think needs to be done. I have no opinion," Ze-han replied.

"A-han, I do this for my own reasons. Managing a martial arts system is very different from simply teaching martial arts. There are very complicated people and matters to interact with inside and outside the organization. You are serving in the financial industry, so it's best to avoid being involved with these characters. Some people seeking personal gain will feign morality and righteousness to enhance their reputation, and they will try to get entangled with you. Once they benefit from your morality and justice, nothing will wash you free of them.

"A-zhou and A-pei don't have this to worry about, and their personalities are more resolute. Just like a knife blade, they can chop and they can break, and they won't give quarter to any slackers. You are gentle by nature, and you are not good at refusing others, just like the back of a knife, it's thick, but it isn't suitable for the role of being the headman of a martial arts school. So, I want you to be the invisible blade behind the planning in the strategy tent, be their wise brother and backup, or simply stay in the business world like grandpa, who can say you might even breakthrough in some resounding way not apparent now," Hong Yi-xiang speculated.

"Pa. You overestimate my ability to develop in the business world. I just work as a part-time worker, a mouthful of rice handed out by in-laws, and my title is also bestowed by them. How can I accomplish anything," Ze-han demurred.

"That's okay. So long as you don't go hungry. I'm afraid you will persist to burn the candle at both ends," Hong Yi-xiang worried.

"Pa, work and martial arts balance out my life. How so ever you want to arrange matters at the school, I will do what you want, no objections," Ze-han promised.

"For a long time, this system has been mine alone to manage. If I depart, I know exactly what it will become. Although you have put a lot of effort into improving its status in the international martial arts world, you also know that some things cannot be just handed down. Unless you make yourself as formidable as me. But is it worth it?" Yi-xiang queried.

"Pa. You are right. Not only can I not change myself, nor can I change my opponent or my battlefield," Ze-han admitted.

"I don't want you to surrender to your fate and give up, but to put yourself on the correct stage. Only in such a way will your efforts get the affirmation and applause you deserve," Yi-xiang observed.

"Pa, don't worry. I'll always strive to play the competent supporting role. Help them from the side," Ze-han avowed.

"A-han, although I have let you learn boxing from your second and third uncles since you were young, strictly speaking, you are not a typical martial artist. What you like is the theory behind the martial arts, not martial art itself. You always practice very hard, but that is your nature, you just don't want to lose *my* face, isn't it? A-han, that's a sense of duty, not destiny," Hong Yi-xiang elucidated.

"Pa, that's not the only reason. I really enjoy the feeling of hard training and self-improvement. Besides, I have been practicing for decades, and I can't give up. As for my skill adapting to the marketplace, they are just unconscious reflexes at the spur of the moment, purely for work needs, not a special ability," Ze-han replied.

"Unconscious reflex at the spur of the moment, is talent. Don't neglect your potential at the negotiating table. A-han, your battlefield is not here. Staying in the business world, I believe your whole life will be more excellent, more remarkable," Hong Yi-xiang offered.

"Pa, haven't you ever thought that using the resources in the business world to support the development of martial arts has always been the tradition of our Hong family? Why don't we continue to do this? Maybe one day, I can integrate these commercial resources with martial arts," Ze-han speculated.

"In fact, this was originally my hope. However the business world and the martial arts world have had no intersection over the years, how could it be easy to talk across-the borders," he sighed. "In this day and age, to find an entrepreneur like Hong Wu-fan was back then, willing to support the continuation and development of martial arts without asking for a reward, it's impossible. So, I would rather remind you to listen carefully to the heartfelt advice of Master Nan Huai-jin and make good use of your innate business wisdom. Concentrate on making yourself a businessman gifted with civil and martial skills. In that sphere, my network of contacts has all withered away, and is really of no help. I can't be like Grandpa, who could have provided you with a decent stage on which to grow," Hong Yi-xiang expressed his regret.

"Pa, what's with the self-deflating talk. If I truly want to have this skill, I should raise my family up from scratch like a grandpa did," Ze-han protested.

"Alas. If your brothers were born one generation earlier, maybe Hong Wanmei Trading Company would not be like today, thriving for only one generation, and then falling into silence on Dihua Street," lamented Hong Yi-xiang.

"Pa, without the legendary stories created by your generation, even if Hong Wanmei's business was greater still, it would be no more than an ordinary merchant on Dihua Street. Every footprint left by your father and his sons, whether it is concerning the Taiwan martial arts world, or the culture and history of Dihua Street in Dadaocheng, far exceed the significance and value to the world of business," Ze-han asserted.

"Is that so?" Hong Yi-xiang wondered.

"Pa, please think about something that can make you happy, okay. Don't trouble yourself any further with those inexplicable things," Ze-han urged.

"Sure, alright. Let me finish explaining the whole plan. I know you, though mild mannered and conflict averse, you basically don't like food that others put on your plate. You like to hunt your own food, eat what you kill, right? You always want to look beyond traditional applications to create new possibilities. In your spare time, I want you to study the material collected by our Hong family during its long period of decline. This untouched research has been sealed up to now, but in the day, they were all obtained in exchange for gold, one volume and one scroll at a time. The words used in these boxing manuals to record the secret techniques of strange schools is so obscure and concise. They are abstruse and difficult to understand, and they are impossible to inquire about with anyone, or to verify. So, it was all kept locked in grandpa's iron chest. I fear if left this way, these techniques will disappear from the earth," bemoaned Hong Yi-xiang.

"Didn't you and your brothers ever attempt their practice?" Ze-han inquired.

"Yes. Like 'Dragon and Snake Writhing'[35] and 'Strolling Hands,' under the guidance of Teacher Peng and Teacher Chen Pan-ling, we invested a long time to digging them out. After the two masters passed away, no one remained who could pry open anything further. I grew up reading Japanese books, and those Chinese cursive hand-written boxing manuals, to me, are simply unintelligible," complained Hong Yi-xiang.

"Pa, if the reading of these old boxing manuals is not guided by the experts of your generation, cracking them today would be adding trouble to difficulty," Ze-han pointed out.

"If this is the case, it's Heaven's will. Anyway, the training hall and the transmission have been arranged, and there should be no worries about it not being passed on for the time being. Now my only wish is that through *you*, these ancient boxing tomes can be deciphered. As for how much you can accomplish, do what you can, it is left to fate. Naturally, your willingness to find answers and your ability to find answers, depends on your aspirations," Hong Yi-xiang reflected.

"Pa, even you couldn't crack the problems, how am I going to solve them on my own," Ze-han doubted.

"Take it as my reward to you, or my punishment. Back then, you asked me to receive the BBC reporters and put me on the big worldwide stage. Now I leave this task to you, count it as courtesy demanding reciprocity," Hong Yi-xiang gently chided.

"Pa, you've overcome one difficulty after another, and every trial you have gone through had its meaning and value. In fact, we have also benefited a lot in the process. It was really worth it," Ze-han expressed.

"It's fine for you all to think this way. Now I plan to split the resources at hand into two avenues to be advanced, 'Promotion of the Legacy' and 'Stealthy Cultivation and Research.' You are responsible for the stealthy cultivation and research part, but I am afraid that you will have to be self-reliant. No one knows whether these old boxing tomes can stand up under scrutiny. If you rush to seek a commercial sponsor, and the breakthroughs are not as expected, people will mistake you for deliberately selling them a bill of goods. So, it's best to break with the idea of getting outside help. In short, for you to do this not only requires a long-term investment, but also you must endure the possibility and disappointment of no future pay back. This is a long and lonely road,"

---

35 龍蛇滾 LongSheGun—a description of the internal body mechanics used in YiZongTangShouDao Bagua in which the spiraling energy of legs, waist, spine, shoulders, and arms in motion gives the sense that a dragon and snake are fighting entwined within the practitioner's body.

Hong Yi-xiang advised.

"Pa, me working behind the scenes, always nose to the grindstone, I like it. You can rest assured," Ze-han confirmed.

"Then that's settled. In fact, the promotion of the legacy part that A-zhou and A-pei are responsible for is also demanding. They are like goalkeepers; they have to guard the door for the rest of their lives to ensure that there is no leakage. Even if there is a chance for them to score, they still can't leave their post. Moreover, they must faithfully pass on the original legacy and cannot change the style at will. Once it is changed, there is no longer a benchmark, you know? This is the price of an orthodox inheritance. But I believe they can strictly abide by this rule. Providing they can join hands, cooperate and complement each other, they can ensure that these techniques will never deteriorate or be lost," dreamed Hong Yi-xiang.

"Pa, you're right. I'm not only not a good goalkeeper, I'm afraid that even with the ball you gave me I may not be able to score," Ze-han considered.

"A-han, between water solidifying into ice, and ice melting into water, there is a stage where it will become half ice and half water. I believe that at the edge of what ordinary people consider to be impossible, there must exist a similar frontier. If you persevere and explore with your heart, knowledge, experience, and energy accumulate. The essence will naturally release, and the released knowledge and human energy will not only force the frontier to recede, but also is a necessary precondition for the ice to melt. When you blindly accept the taboos and restrictions in others' eyes, without attempting and pushing back, the boundary will be pushed forward and continue to contract our living space. The field you want to explore in the future is the comings and goings along this verge, the fuzzy space created by this frontier, you know? No one knows how big this frontier is, just do your best is all," Hong Yi-xiang encouraged.

"Pa, have you ever thought if we were to reverse this plan?" Ze-han wondered.

"I knew you would ask this way. There is nothing wrong with it, provided you and your brothers all coordinate well," Hong Yi-xiang responded.

"Pa, I'm just curious, I don't mean anything else, please continue," Ze-han pleaded.

"I hope that in the future if you have any realizations or discoveries on that frontier, you will have to spend a little more time sifting and judging whether those things are suitable for public knowledge. Just like the master who taught me the Art of Controlling the Bull said, there are some things that just shouldn't exist in this world. You have to keep in mind that with excessively brutal and venomous skills, you should rather keep a lid on them or let it disappear forever, rather than indiscriminately abuse or spread it for personal fame and gain, you know?" Hong Yi-xiang advised.

"Pa, I'll remember. Don't worry," Ze-han reassured.

"Very well. No matter whether you wind up with nothing gained, or you find something strangely special, remember it must be handled with the coldest, rational attitude. Master Peng said that some dark, cold, and shadowy domains, like a bottomless black hole, have a magnetic magical attraction for people. Once you enter them, it is very easy to lose yourself, and you will fall in deeper and deeper. Like mind control, internal alchemy, and exploration of the inner universe, these seemingly grey areas are difficult to decipher or verify with modern human technology. One wrong step can easily place you on a demonic path. You must be cautious," Hong Yi-xiang advised.

"I know. I will keep this in my heart," Ze-han confirmed.

"The past few decades, my modest personal reputation was built on martial arts. To maintain this modicum of fame has made you boys burn candles at both ends, working by day and teaching boxing at night. I dragged you all into it," Hong Yi-xiang reflected.

"Pa, we all grew up eating the same rice, and no one ever complained. Don't think about bad things," Ze-han implored.

"If it weren't for me being obsessed with martial arts and missing the opportunity to transform the business, how could this family have gone into such decline. Thinking of it, I am unworthy of grandpa, I let down your mother and your brothers and sisters," lamented Hong Yi-xiang.

"Pa, like Grandpa, we have always been proud of your martial arts achievements. You were destined to be a great martial arts master, if you had done anything else, you would be out of place," Ze-han affirmed.

"Yeah, that, too. In the business field, I am a complete loser. Not a single business I invested in returned even a drop of blood," he sighed. "Apart from martial arts, there is really nothing I'm good at," Hong Yi-xiang deplored.

"Well, you are too humble. Grandpa said that in addition to martial arts, bankrupting business should also be regarded as another of your hidden talents," Ze-han joked.

"Ha-ha-ha! This is true. Hearing you talk nonsense; I feel a lot better. If your mother was still here, it would all be fine," Hong Yi-xiang wished.

"Pa, I had a weird dream last night. I dreamt that Ma was waiting in a huge luxurious airport departure lounge. She looked very young and was made up very beautifully. She was wearing her favorite burgundy velvet cheongsam. I think she was very contented there, as if she were going for a long vacation. Sooner or later our whole family will meet again," Ze-han predicted.

"She is waiting for me," Hong Yi-xiang said wistfully.

"Pa, Ma has a very good life there. Please let her enjoy her life of ease a few years, so let's not rush over and bother her," Ze-han advised.

It was just a few months after this conversation, that one morning Hong Yi-xiang prepared to go to the Chinese National Martial Art Association for a regular meeting. Life as usual. He not only shaved, trimmed his sideburns, and patted on after-shave cologne, but also cleaned the electric razor of stubble. Then, taking advantage of a delay in the pick-up car's arrival, he took Hong Ze-pei's eldest son, Hong Zhong-wei, and played with him for a spell in the living room on the second floor of Anxi Street. Everything was his normal routine before leaving home for a meeting. As soon as the scheduled time arrived, dressed neatly he went down to the ground floor and rode in the car of a disciple surnamed Kang to the National Martial Art Association. It was during this meeting to revise the rules of competition, that he chose to depart this world.

He chose to depart the world from the martial arts hall in which he had invested most of his life. He was sixty-eight years old. The cause of death was not that listed on the death certificate, but the loneliness of a middle-aged strongman unable to escape the grief of being widowed. Facing such heartfelt desolation and pent-up torment was the most fatal and untreatable terminal illness for a mighty man most respected for martial arts by the younger generation. Even if he availed himself of more love from his children and his disciples, it was of no use.

How strong and resilient is the life of a martial arts master, and how fragile. He can stand atop of the world's martial arts arena, face the challenges of various powerful enemies without showing fear, and lightly pass repeated trials, but on his own cannot emerge from a widower's haze of painful grief. This was not a soft-hearted iron man, it was just honoring a marriage contract and commitment between a husband and wife to remain together in life and in death… there was no regret or reluctance. Living to him was, by then, an endless torture. We should rather let him depart. Go be with our mother. Go to spend their happy time together. We are willing to bear the extreme sorrow of losing both parents in just two years… Pa, Ma, take care, see you soon.

Recognizing his lifelong devotion to the Taiwan martial arts world, the National Arts Federation honored Master Hong Yi-xiang's coffin to be draped with the national flag, 1993.

A procession of 120 students, local and foreign, pull Master Hong Yi-xiang's casket on one last trip around his beloved Dadaocheng area of Taipei, 1993.

112– THAT DAMNED "SWALLOW SKIMS THE WATER"

Are you the type of person who, before they have had a chance to verify something, believes: if you don't see something with your own eyes, it doesn't exist? Then you will definitely miss many beautiful things and pay the price for it.

Scene: More Coffee Shop, Wenlin

"A-han, we are all of an age now. It's not easy to do these movements," Chris opined.

Before Chris was to return to Seattle for the summer, we chatted in a small coffee shop owned by one of his distant relatives, on the one hand discussing the translation of this book and on the other hand having wide ranging discussions. I remember him saying this when we talked about performing two low moves—Taijiquan's Snake Creeping Down and Xingyiquan's Swallow Skims the Water.

"When Master Hong was your age, I rarely saw him personally perform these moves."

"Little Bai,[36] my father had operations on his knees, how could he do these moves again," I said.

"But why do you insist to never give up practicing these movements? After all, we aren't young,"

Like a blunt needle Chris' question unintentionally pierced a remorseful and uneasy point in my heart. "Me! Serves me right."

"What's the matter?" Chris could see his question had upset me more than he expected.

"I quit my job at the TV station to prepare for the BBC shooting the documentary in Taiwan. Every morning from 9:00 to 12:00, from 2:00 to 5:00 in the afternoon I trained alone, and then in the evening until 10:30 or 11:00 I practiced together with the fellows in the gym. I hoped that through this practice, our martial arts system would appear better than others in *The Way of the Warrior* series."

"I remember you mentioning this when we were translating the book

---

36 Chris Bates Chinese surname is Bai, same as Howard Brewer. Within the school, then, Howard was *Lao Bai*, Old Bai, and Chris is *Xiao Bai*, Little Bai.

together, you said you couldn't resist going all in with your chips on this hand when you had an opportunity like this."

"Little Bai, I was originally engaged in film and television work. What did I know about the BBC? I knew it was influential. Although I was lucky enough to win the negotiation in the selection process of 'who is the master of internal boxing,' I knew in my heart that the key to really reversing our fortune would be the quality of what was filmed and edited into the final documentary. I think it was very difficult for martial arts masters from other sects to understand the significance and value hidden behind this opportunity.

"We had the advantage and value of information asymmetry. That the system created by my father could be used in fighting should not have been news at that time. But his influence was limited to Taiwan, Hong Kong, Japan, Okinawa, around Asia and the US special forces he trained. If we wanted to expand into the world and increase his influence, there was no choice but to firmly grab onto the opportunity provided by the BBC."

"The facts show it, that was the right decision," Chris supported.

"One day, my father went up to the fourth floor to watch me practice boxing as usual, and he sat on the rattan chair behind the red line of the training area and stared at me practicing Xingyi's Swallow and Five Elements Consecutively Linked Forms."

"Didn't your mother object to you quitting your job to concentrate on doing this? What about the Master Hong's attitude? He didn't raise any objections?"

"He knew I was doing the right thing, nothing was uttered from his mouth, he just stared at me practicing."

"Did you ask him to watch you?"

"No. I only discussed with him what I wanted to present, and I told him that we had to control or guide the final result of the film from upstream, instead of passively cooperating with the requests of the director and cameraman at the moment."

"Did the BBC agree that you do it this way?"

"Their attitude towards documentaries is worth learning from. The director and producer had in-depth communication with me before shooting. Their camera only plays the role of an objective observer, and never interferes with the plot and development of the film as it unfolds. This of course also includes the good and the bad taking place in front of the camera."

Then, I explained to Little Bai the reasons why I was damned to do these low postures until today…

"Not only do you have to lower your body, but you also have to stretch your arms forward so that you can clasp the opponent's ankle," my father said.

I remained silent but strained to achieve the stretch."Still not enough. Your wrist must go beyond the ankle of your front foot. Do it again. Push a little more. What the fuck—are you giving up?"

"Pa, the tendons are only so long. I really can't stretch forward any further," I objected.

"No. You can."

"No. I can't! I know my own body."

My father was flustered.

"Don't you see? I am already putting my all into it. No is no. You can't stubbornly insist on me doing something you can't even do yourself," I said to drive the point home.

"No. You can." My father insisted on what he said.

"Pa. I've tried and tried. Tried and tried again. It's been almost a month. No way, no way, don't you see that?"

"No. The resistance is in your mind." My pa kept his head down and didn't look at me when he said this.

"I try every day, what am I resisting?"

"You resist going beyond yourself. Going beyond me."

"What reason do I have to resist going further?"

"Because that way you can always hide in my shadow. Isn't it so?"

"Why should I want this?"

"Once you excel past me, you no longer have any barrier or protection. Isn't it true?"

"Things aren't that complicated. It's just one movement. You're over-thinking this."

"A-han, what I see is different from what you see. It's not just a movement. You know better than anyone else that it's not just 'a movement.'"

"Then you can do it yourself. If you can do it, I can do it." I couldn't help making such an offensive remark.

Whereupon, I watched Hong Yi-xiang become so angry he couldn't utter a word.

Whereupon, I watched him step across the red line into the training area.

Whereupon, I watched an internationally recognized 9th dan martial arts master personally step before me to perform a model, deep, long but not entirely smooth, Swallow Skims the Water, with his nearly 120-kilogram body, on artificial knee joints…

And then, that damned impertinent young bastard looked on regretfully at his father's broad back as he crossed the red line without a word and took the iron gate out of the gym, going downstairs to take his leave.

Hong Ze-han teaches Swallow Skims the Water to Chris Bates, 2022.

113– THE PARADOX OF INCREASE IS DECREASE

Compilation is to integrate many similar moves and usages into one with the principle of removing the rubbish and preserving the essence. Therefore, the seemingly newly added combinations of punches actually exist to reduce many unnecessary repetitions. There are also many novel miscellaneous tricks and usages, which were often employed to increase the combat power taught by Hong Yi-xiang before his death. If they are not systematically compiled, it is likely that in the process of passing on the art, unique qualities defying definition will be omitted, forgotten, and quietly lost.

Scene: Molly's Hamburger Joint, Yusheng Street

THAT WEEKEND, A TIMELY RAIN FELL IN TAIPEI, WHICH EASED THE drought in Taiwan a little, but also disrupted our once-a-week practice opportunity. We couldn't go up the mountain to train our boxing for two weeks in a row, and the extra calories from eating and drinking during the Chinese New Year had nowhere to go, so we temporarily stored them on our waistline and belly in the form of low-interest fixed deposits. Chris asked me if I would be free to discuss the translation of *Blurred Boundaries* on a rainy day, so we met at the nearby Molly Burger, to discuss the manuscript, and to pass the boring afternoon.

"An American friend asked me how you can hold so many moves and applications in your head," Chris said as we took a break from translating this book.

"I don't understand what he meant by that."

"He's saying, with so many moves, when a situation arises how do you know which move to use?" Chris asked.

"Have you forgotten the lesson of the duel on the beach between Kojiro Sasaki and Miyamoto Musashi?"

"I think my friend must know the advantages and disadvantages of tricks and adaptability to circumstance, but he is probably more curious about your thoughts or tactics."

"I'm a person who is an easy-going laid-back kind of guy, where is my forethought and tactics; whatever I can grab in the moment, that's what I use. Where is there a set principle or logic?"

"Is this your fuzzy logic?" Chris asked.

"You mean if mixing things up when I am able? Or using what I grab in the moment?" I asked.

"I mean, it seems as though you never have a set, standard answer."

"Yes. It turns out I am such a mercurial unprincipled person. Ha-ha-ha! Logic and principles. Sometimes they are the answer, sometimes a trap. Once ensnared, you can't get out."

"You put it that way, you're right. But also, not right. To stick to no fixed principle is a principle. Isn't it?"

"I guess. But don't you think this is at least more elusive and unpredictable than clinging to a fixed logic?"

"Maybe. But you said you can latch on to whatever to use in the moment, so what about the off chance there is nothing to grab? Then you're dead."

"Then … then grab a stick or a kitchen knife. You can't just do nothing and wait to die," I said.

"Isn't that the logic of Miyamoto Musashi?"

"If necessary I can also be Kojiro Sasaki. In the face of the voluminous martial arts heritage handed down by my family, I think the only thing I can do is to learn first and then sift."

"The problem is, the 'you' we see seems to be constantly adding new things, but we never see what you have filtered out. Why?"

"Adding new moves is to simplify the old ones."

"That's too paradoxical. I don't get your meaning."

"I try my best to integrate moves that have high homogeneity, and then find a way to filter out the most reasonable, easy to execute and effective applications or sequences, reassemble them into a new combination, and then take the large number of traditional moves and record them on videos, to be archived and stored. So, in fact, behind every new move, there are a lot of similar moves that are simplified, archived, and put in the attic. What everyone sees is only the net increase side, the tip of the iceberg piling up on top, not the submerged iceberg from which things have been taken. So, they have this greater misunderstanding of 'only adding, never decreasing.' Only through this method will we have more time to concentrate on practicing those new, integrated combinations."

"So, what we've been through, for approaching twenty years, is this process of screening and integrating new creations."

"You could put it that way. At first, it was just a rough concept or a blind attempt, and it was only later that I found out that this was a way out."

"But don't you think it's still too much material?"

"If I completely return to the martial arts that Hong Yi-xiang collected back then, I'm afraid it will go far beyond this."

"But for my friend who's been practicing martial arts for decades, it's still too much. Don't you worry that once there's too much, you won't be able to specialize?"

"Of course, I'm worried. But what about after specialization? Have you ever thought about it becoming too narrow and limited. A lot of things have been lost because of this?"

"Things are also lost due to sifting and refinement," Chris pointed out.

"How so?"

"No need to talk about food, the example is clear. When it is refined, nutrition is usually the victim."

I thought about it and nodded in agreement. "Good thing we are training Bagua (八卦) and not Bahgua(肉乾 pork jerky). But give me an example in the martial arts."

"There is a good example in the martial arts. Morihei Ueshiba and Aikido. Before he founded Aikido, he had trained in Daito ryu jujutsu and had worked in northeast China where he was exposed to other martial arts. By all accounts, he was a tough cookie capable of defending himself with his art. But Aikido was a refinement of all he had learned and been exposed to. What he taught was only the refinement. Very few have been able to achieve his level of skill and effectively employ Aikido against all comers." "The students today can diligently train Aikido, but they have not walked the entire path Ueshiba walked, so they do not have the keys to unlock its mysteries."

"Yeah. So how to manage it? Do you have two brains?" Chris asked.

"Of course, there is only one brain. But you can still find a way to solve the conundrum."

"How to solve it?"

"Just like the hard disk of a computer, the capacity of a hard disk can be divided into several different partitions, and the original files and updated files can be stored and processed separately."

"And then what?"

"One partition represents one level, and one level only focuses on one topic, just like at the beginning, it took me nearly ten years to refine the 99 Form of Taijiquan into the current short version of Intensive Taiji, and in 2015–2016, we spent two years concentrating on integrating the Sixty-Four Post-Heaven Palms of Baguazhang. In 2017, we sorted out the sword techniques and stick techniques (Eight Battles Sword and Zhou Dong Staff), sorted out the elbow strikes (Zhougong) in 2018, and sorted out Xingyiquan in 2019. Twelve-Animals Boxing (Hong family Xingyi Twelve Animals), we refined in 2020, then organized Hong Yi-xiang's frequently employed techniques (Hong Family Xingyi Thirty-six Methods), Section 1-12 of the first section, and we continued to complete the second section 13-24 in 2021. In 2022, the third section, 25-36 methods, will be completed, and at the same time, the compilation of the whipstick (the dog-fighting style) will be carried out. In 2023…"

"Enough. Just listening leaves one breathless. Don't you think it's exhausting?"

"Of course, it's not easy. But since there is no way to escape, its best to turn around and face it. Along this road I can see the looming backs of my ancestors. Now I'm old myself, so I decided to turn around. Turn around, go back, and boldly reorganize our branch of this lineage. Only then can we mutually recognize and be recognized by each other, right? But once I choose this direction, I have to be like the Burlap Monk who bowed his head and planted rice. All the way, 'Backwards, ho!'"

> *My hand inserts the green rice shoots into the paddy,*
> *My lowered head sees the reflection of the sky in the water,*
> *My mind is tranquil square in the Way,*
> *To retreat in the end is to advance.*

"But, how do you distinguish and differentiate between so many diverse martial arts schools?"

"When I deal with Xingyi, I only have Xingyi in my mind. When I sort out Bagua, I also have only Bagua."

"I don't believe that you can so cleanly dissect these different concepts and techniques without mixing them up."

"You suspect correctly. But if you mix it up, you mix it up. Have you ever wondered why they can be mixed up?"

"I really can't imagine, maybe you have accidentally mixed-up different things yourself. What else is there to learn about?"

"Because in some deep recess that you can't see, they must have some common genes. So, if you mix them up, you mix them up. Isn't it the case?"

"You mean 'mixing together'? Or 'mixing-up'?"

"Whether it's this mix or that, is there any difference in the end?"

"You're mixing me up by saying that."

"Think about it carefully. People. They look at mountains that maybe aren't mountains or look at water that's maybe not water. Then you still care whether this one mixes with the other, and whether that one mixes with the other?"

"These principles you are talking about now should not apply to the issues we were discussing before."

"Then how do you know if the issue we were originally discussing wasn't mixed in with another issue we had been previously discussing?"

"Mama Mia! How you viciously mix things up. Ha-ha-ha..."

114– MY PLAN B: JERRY-RIGGED SAW ON A POLE

Martial arts must emphasize martial virtue and righteousness, technique is not the emphasis. To respect the art, one must first respect the teacher, what is given lightly is not received lightly.

Scene: Guanyin Mountain

RECENTLY, CHRIS BATES, AND MARCUS BRINKMAN PLANNED TO go to Guanyin Mountain to climb Tough Guy Ridge, but because a friend who was traveling with them had twisted his ankle, they decided on the spur of the moment to go to Dad's tomb for a visit. The following Wednesday, when Chris and I met at the American Club in Taipei to discuss the translation of *Blurred Boundaries*, he told me that there was a tree in the burial area next to my father that had fallen on the stone steps up the hill.

At the time I thought he was talking about a huge magnolia tree that fell many years ago, so I didn't pay much attention. Unexpectedly, after a few days, I had a dream one night. My father told me that his body was not very comfortable, and I was shocked to realize that perhaps the tree that Chris mentioned referred to another tree. Because I was quite worried, the next morning, after a hurried breakfast, I drove up to Guanyin Mountain with Mrs. Hong, and discovered that what Chris had described was a not-so-small banyan tree at the adjacent tomb. It had fallen head-to-toe on the stone steps. At the moment, Mrs. Hong and I were unarmed, so we could only take pictures with our mobile phones and then go home and think about how to take care of this big tree blocking the path.

The following Saturday afternoon when we were practicing at Zhishanyan, I mentioned this to Chris, and he took the initiative to tell me that he would go up the mountain with me and help me deal with the tree. Several days later, at 8:30 in the morning, Chris texted me: 'The weather is not bad today, do you want to go up the mountain to deal with that tree?' Because A-pei was busy with the breakfast shop business, I asked my eldest brother A-zhou to meet us in Luzhou, and the three of us went up the mountain together.

To deal with the big tree blocking the road, Chris brought his kukri knife, A-zhou brought a large shovel and a saw borrowed from the neighbors, and I brought all the accoutrements for tomb sweeping including: two machetes, long-handled pruning shears, a scraper for shoveling soil, three pairs of cotton gloves, and a white waxwood pole more than 170 centimeters long specially used to practice "Zhou Dong Staff," and packing tape, to extend the length of the saw if necessary, to deal with those branches hanging high in the air.

After the three of us arrived at the scene and made a rough inventory of the current damage and equipment, we decided to prune only the branches that were blocking the road, because the whole tree was too huge. I was also afraid that if we cut the trunk, it would smash the weak stone steps below. So, we decided to let Chris try his kukri knife first, to see if he could handle those Ficus branches that were about the thickness of a wrist, the Plan B being to use the saw mounted on the pole.

The Gurkha kukri knife was indeed very sharp and lived up to its reputation. We watched as he repeatedly raised the knife and struck. The thick branches were cut off neatly one by one. So, we asked Chris to cut down the branches one at a time without causing the whole tree to fall down, while A-zhou and I were responsible for cleaning up the weeds in Mom and Dad's cemetery and the fallen rocks and leaves. The three of us worked hard in our respective roles and were busy until about 12:30 before completing the task. At the end of the break, Chris poured two cups of hot tea and placed them on the stone table in front of my mother's and father's graves, and then elder brother, A-zhou on temporary duty as the Taoist priest, reported to the two elderly people that our work today was successfully completed.

Mom passed away at sixty-four years old and Dad passed away at sixty-eight years old. The two departed this world only a year and a half apart. From the current point of view, they were both young. It has been many years since the two old folks left us, but to have these old disciples who are willing to stand up and help in such a situation should bring a smile to their faces in the afterlife!

"Tiger" Hong-Ze-zhou and Chris Bates enjoying
tea after the tomb sweeping work, 2021.

The three Hong sons seated in the center with student friends
from the Danjiang University Tangshoudao Club, 2015.

Master Hong's three sons seated at a banquet held by students. Hong Ze-han (5th from right), Hong Ze-zhou (third from right) and Hong Ze-pei (first on right), 2013.

易宗唐手道創始人　洪懿祥先生

About the Author

HONG ZE-HAN IS THE SECOND SON OF HONG YI-XIANG. HE WAS born in 1955 and was admitted to the Department of Film Directing at the National University of Arts. However, during his summer internship, his boss, who was also the most famous film and television tycoon in Taiwan at the time, told him, "Stay here. In film school, you won't learn more real and useful things than here." So he dropped out of school to work as a director and screenwriter for the then three major TV networks, TTV-Taiwan Television Enterprise, CTV-China Television Corporation, and CTS-China Television System. Many of his works have won awards.

After getting married, he turned to advertising, working in sales and creative direction until he caught the eye of client Tera Electronics, which brought him into consumer electronics marketing and business management.

After successfully serving as Deputy General Manager at the Sheraton Taipei Hotel, where his main task was to carry out a challenging full renovation of the largest five-star hotel in Taipei, he joined Jihsun Financial Holding Group as Chief Executive Officer and Deputy Chief Executive Officer leadership until his retirement in 2014.

Zehan has a wife and two sons. In his spare time, he enjoys Chinese calligraphy, reading, writing, hiking, fine food, and Yizong Tangshou martial arts training.

He can be contacted at Facebook *Hong Ze Han*.

Blurred Boundaries is his first full-length narrative work.

About the Translator

CHRISTOPHER BATES HAS A BA ASIAN STUDIES AND A MASTER OF International Management and took his senior year of university in Taiwan in 1976 and is fluent in Mandarin Chinese. His interest in Asia was fueled by a passion for training in Asian martial arts. He holds the rank of 8th level black belt in American Bando and commenced training under Master Hong Yi-xiang in 1982 studying all the elements of Yizong Tangshoudao under Master Hong and his son Hong Ze-han.

His business career in Asia spanned 40 years in industrial product sales, business intelligence consulting, and executive search. He retired in 2016 to pursue interests in writing, motorcycle touring, and training martial arts. He has published two novels: *The Wave Man* is a crime thriller set in Thailand and Japan, and *Rise of the Water Margin*, a near-future cyber thriller set in China and the USA. His translations of Chinese have been published in *Journal of Asian Martial Arts*. He is also the co-author of *Culture Shock! Taiwan* now in its 4th edition. *Blurred Boundaries* is his first published long-form translation.

He and his Taiwanese wife of 45 years spend their retirement in Taipei and Seattle.

BOOKS FROM YMAA

- 101 REFLECTIONS ON TAI CHI CHUAN
- 108 INSIGHTS INTO TAI CHI CHUAN
- A WOMAN'S QIGONG GUIDE
- ADVANCING IN TAE KWON DO
- ANALYSIS OF GENUINE KARATE
- ANALYSIS OF GENUINE KARATE 2
- ANALYSIS OF SHAOLIN CHIN NA 2ND ED
- ANCIENT CHINESE WEAPONS
- ART AND SCIENCE OF STAFF FIGHTING
- THE ART AND SCIENCE OF SELF-DEFENSE
- ART AND SCIENCE OF STICK FIGHTING
- ART OF HOJO UNDO
- ARTHRITIS RELIEF, 3D ED.
- BACK PAIN RELIEF, 2ND ED.
- BAGUAZHANG, 2ND ED.
- BRAIN FITNESS
- CHIN NA IN GROUND FIGHTING
- CHINESE FAST WRESTLING
- CHINESE FITNESS
- CHINESE TUI NA MASSAGE
- COMPLETE MARTIAL ARTIST
- COMPREHENSIVE APPLICATIONS OF SHAOLIN CHIN NA
- CONFLICT COMMUNICATION
- DAO DE JING: A QIGONG INTERPRETATION
- DAO IN ACTION
- DEFENSIVE TACTICS
- DIRTY GROUND
- DR. WU'S HEAD MASSAGE
- ESSENCE OF SHAOLIN WHITE CRANE
- EXPLORING TAI CHI
- FACING VIOLENCE
- FIGHT LIKE A PHYSICIST
- THE FIGHTER'S BODY
- FIGHTER'S FACT BOOK 1&2
- FIGHTING ARTS
- FIGHTING THE PAIN RESISTANT ATTACKER
- FIRST DEFENSE
- FORCE DECISIONS: A CITIZENS GUIDE
- INSIDE TAI CHI
- JUDO ADVANTAGE
- JUJI GATAME ENCYCLOPEDIA
- KARATE SCIENCE
- KATA AND THE TRANSMISSION OF KNOWLEDGE
- KRAV MAGA COMBATIVES
- KRAV MAGA FUNDAMENTAL STRATEGIES
- KRAV MAGA PROFESSIONAL TACTICS
- KRAV MAGA WEAPON DEFENSES
- LITTLE BLACK BOOK OF VIOLENCE
- LIUHEBAFA FIVE CHARACTER SECRETS
- MARTIAL ARTS OF VIETNAM
- MARTIAL ARTS INSTRUCTION
- MARTIAL WAY AND ITS VIRTUES
- MEDITATIONS ON VIOLENCE
- MERIDIAN QIGONG EXERCISES
- MINDFUL EXERCISE
- MIND INSIDE TAI CHI
- MIND INSIDE YANG STYLE TAI CHI CHUAN
- NATURAL HEALING WITH QIGONG
- NORTHERN SHAOLIN SWORD, 2ND ED.
- OKINAWA'S COMPLETE KARATE SYSTEM: ISSHIN RYU
- PRINCIPLES OF TRADITIONAL CHINESE MEDICINE
- PROTECTOR ETHIC
- QIGONG FOR HEALTH & MARTIAL ARTS 2ND ED.
- QIGONG FOR TREATING COMMON AILMENTS
- QIGONG MASSAGE
- QIGONG MEDITATION: EMBRYONIC BREATHING
- QIGONG GRAND CIRCULATION
- QIGONG MEDITATION: SMALL CIRCULATION
- QIGONG, THE SECRET OF YOUTH: DA MO'S CLASSICS
- REDEMPTION
- ROOT OF CHINESE QIGONG, 2ND ED.
- SAMBO ENCYCLOPEDIA
- SCALING FORCE
- SELF-DEFENSE FOR WOMEN
- SHIN GI TAI: KARATE TRAINING
- SIMPLE CHINESE MEDICINE
- SIMPLE QIGONG EXERCISES FOR HEALTH, 3RD ED.
- SIMPLIFIED TAI CHI CHUAN, 2ND ED.
- SOLO TRAINING 1&2
- SPOTTING DANGER BEFORE IT SPOTS YOU
- SPOTTING DANGER BEFORE IT SPOTS YOUR KIDS
- SPOTTING DANGER BEFORE IT SPOTS YOUR TEENS
- SPOTTING DANGER FOR TRAVELERS
- SUMO FOR MIXED MARTIAL ARTS
- SUNRISE TAI CHI
- SURVIVING ARMED ASSAULTS
- TAE KWON DO: THE KOREAN MARTIAL ART
- TAEKWONDO BLACK BELT POOMSAE
- TAEKWONDO: A PATH TO EXCELLENCE
- TAEKWONDO: ANCIENT WISDOM
- TAEKWONDO: DEFENSE AGAINST WEAPONS
- TAEKWONDO: SPIRIT AND PRACTICE
- TAI CHI BALL QIGONG: FOR HEALTH AND MARTIAL ARTS
- THE TAI CHI BOOK
- TAI CHI CHIN NA, 2ND ED.
- TAI CHI CHUAN CLASSICAL YANG STYLE, 2ND ED.
- TAI CHI CHUAN MARTIAL POWER, 3RD ED.
- TAI CHI CONCEPTS AND EXPERIMENTS
- TAI CHI CONNECTIONS
- TAI CHI DYNAMICS
- TAI CHI FOR DEPRESSION
- TAI CHI IN 10 WEEKS
- TAI CHI PUSH HANDS
- TAI CHI QIGONG, 3RD ED.
- TAI CHI SECRETS OF THE ANCIENT MASTERS
- TAI CHI SECRETS OF THE WU & LI STYLES
- TAI CHI SECRETS OF THE WU STYLE
- TAI CHI SECRETS OF THE YANG STYLE
- TAI CHI SWORD: CLASSICAL YANG STYLE, 2ND ED.
- TAI CHI SWORD FOR BEGINNERS
- TAI CHI WALKING
- TAI CHI CHUAN THEORY OF DR. YANG, JWING-MING
- TRADITIONAL CHINESE HEALTH SECRETS
- TRADITIONAL TAEKWONDO
- TRAINING FOR SUDDEN VIOLENCE
- TRIANGLE HOLD ENCYCLOPEDIA
- TRUE WELLNESS SERIES (MIND, HEART, GUT)
- WARRIOR'S MANIFESTO
- WAY OF KATA
- WAY OF SANCHIN KATA
- WAY TO BLACK BELT
- WESTERN HERBS FOR MARTIAL ARTISTS
- WILD GOOSE QIGONG
- WING CHUN IN-DEPTH
- WINNING FIGHTS
- XINGYIQUAN

AND MANY MORE . . .

VIDEOS FROM YMAA

- ANALYSIS OF SHAOLIN CHIN NA
- ART & SCIENCE OF STAFF FIGHTING
- ART & SCIENCE OF STICK FIGHTING
- BAGUA FOR BEGINNERS 1 & 2
- BAGUAZHANG: EMEI BAGUAZHANG
- BEGINNER QIGONG FOR WOMEN 1 & 2
- BEGINNER TAI CHI FOR HEALTH
- BIOENERGY TRAINING 1 & 2
- CHEN TAI CHI CANNON FIST
- CHEN TAI CHI FIRST FORM
- CHEN TAI CHI FOR BEGINNERS
- CHIN NA IN-DEPTH SERIES
- FACING VIOLENCE: 7 THINGS A MARTIAL ARTIST MUST KNOW
- FIVE ANIMAL SPORTS
- FIVE ELEMENTS ENERGY BALANCE
- HEALER WITHIN
- INFIGHTING
- INTRODUCTION TO QI GONG FOR BEGINNERS
- JOINT LOCKS
- KNIFE DEFENSE
- KUNG FU BODY CONDITIONING 1 & 2
- KUNG FU FOR KIDS AND TEENS SERIES
- LOGIC OF VIOLENCE
- MERIDIAN QIGONG
- NEIGONG FOR MARTIAL ARTS
- NORTHERN SHAOLIN SWORD
- QI GONG 30-DAY CHALLENGE
- QI GONG FOR ANXIETY
- QI GONG FOR ARMS, WRISTS, AND HANDS
- QIGONG FOR BEGINNERS: FRAGRANCE
- QI GONG FOR BETTER BALANCE
- QI GONG FOR BETTER BREATHING
- QI GONG FOR CANCER
- QI GONG FOR DEPRESSION
- QI GONG FOR ENERGY AND VITALITY
- QI GONG FOR HEADACHES
- QI GONG FOR THE HEALTHY HEART
- QI GONG FOR HEALTHY JOINTS
- QI GONG FOR HIGH BLOOD PRESSURE
- QIGONG FOR LONGEVITY
- QI GONG FOR STRONG BONES
- QI GONG FOR THE UPPER BACK AND NECK
- QIGONG FOR WOMEN WITH DAISY LEE
- QIGONG FLOW FOR STRESS & ANXIETY RELIEF
- QIGONG MASSAGE
- QIGONG MINDFULNESS IN MOTION
- QI GONG—THE SEATED WORKOUT
- QIGONG: 15 MINUTES TO HEALTH
- SABER FUNDAMENTAL TRAINING
- SAI TRAINING AND SEQUENCES
- SANCHIN KATA: TRADITIONAL TRAINING FOR KARATE POWER
- SCALING FORCE
- SEARCHING FOR SUPERHUMANS
- SHAOLIN KUNG FU FUNDAMENTAL TRAINING 1 & 2
- SHAOLIN LONG FIST KUNG FU BEGINNER—INTERMEDIATE—ADVANCED SERIES
- SHAOLIN SABER: BASIC SEQUENCES
- SHAOLIN STAFF: BASIC SEQUENCES
- SHAOLIN WHITE CRANE GONG FU BASIC TRAINING SERIES
- SHUAI JIAO: KUNG FU WRESTLING
- SIMPLE QIGONG EXERCISES FOR HEALTH
- SIMPLE QIGONG EXERCISES FOR ARTHRITIS RELIEF
- SIMPLE QIGONG EXERCISES FOR BACK PAIN RELIEF
- SIMPLIFIED TAI CHI CHUAN: 24 & 48 POSTURES
- SIMPLIFIED TAI CHI FOR BEGINNERS 48
- SIX HEALING SOUNDS
- SUN TAI CHI
- SWORD: FUNDAMENTAL TRAINING
- TAEKWONDO KORYO POOMSAE
- TAI CHI BALL QIGONG SERIES
- TAI CHI BALL WORKOUT FOR BEGINNERS
- TAI CHI CHUAN CLASSICAL YANG STYLE
- TAI CHI CHUAN THEORY OF DR. YANG, JWING-MING
- TAI CHI FIGHTING SET
- TAI CHI FIT: 24 FORM
- TAI CHI FIT: ALZHEIMER'S PREVENTION
- TAI CHI FIT: CANCER PREVENTION
- TAI CHI FIT FOR VETERANS
- TAI CHI FIT: FOR WOMEN
- TAI CHI FIT: FLOW
- TAI CHI FIT: FUSION BAMBOO
- TAI CHI FIT: FUSION FIRE
- TAI CHI FIT: FUSION IRON
- TAI CHI FIT: HEALTHY BACK SEATED WORKOUT
- TAI CHI FIT: HEALTHY HEART WORKOUT
- TAI CHI FIT IN PARADISE
- TAI CHI FIT: OVER 50
- TAI CHI FIT OVER 50: BALANCE EXERCISES
- TAI CHI FIT OVER 50: SEATED WORKOUT
- TAI CHI FIT OVER 60: GENTLE EXERCISES
- TAI CHI FIT OVER 60: HEALTHY JOINTS
- TAI CHI FIT OVER 60: LIVE LONGER
- TAI CHI FIT: STRENGTH
- TAI CHI FIT: TO GO
- TAI CHI FOR WOMEN
- TAI CHI FUSION: FIRE
- TAI CHI QIGONG
- TAI CHI PUSHING HANDS SERIES
- TAI CHI SWORD: CLASSICAL YANG STYLE
- TAI CHI SWORD FOR BEGINNERS
- TAI CHI SYMBOL: YIN YANG STICKING HANDS
- TAIJI & SHAOLIN STAFF: FUNDAMENTAL TRAINING
- TAIJI CHIN NA IN-DEPTH
- TAIJI 37 POSTURES MARTIAL APPLICATIONS
- TAIJI SABER CLASSICAL YANG STYLE
- TAIJI WRESTLING
- TRAINING FOR SUDDEN VIOLENCE
- UNDERSTANDING QIGONG SERIES
- WATER STYLE FOR BEGINNERS
- WHITE CRANE HARD & SOFT QIGONG
- YANG TAI CHI FOR BEGINNERS
- YOQI: MICROCOSMIC ORBIT QIGONG
- YOQI QIGONG FOR A HAPPY HEART
- YOQI:QIGONG FLOW FOR HAPPY MIND
- YOQI:QIGONG FLOW FOR INTERNAL ALCHEMY
- YOQI QIGONG FOR HAPPY SPLEEN & STOMACH
- YOQI QIGONG FOR HAPPY KIDNEYS
- YOQI QIGONG FLOW FOR HAPPY LUNGS
- YOQI QIGONG FLOW FOR STRESS RELIEF
- YOQI: QIGONG FLOW TO BOOST IMMUNE SYSTEM
- YOQI SIX HEALING SOUNDS
- YOQI: YIN YOGA 1
- WU TAI CHI FOR BEGINNERS
- WUDANG KUNG FU: FUNDAMENTAL TRAINING
- WUDANG SWORD
- WUDANG TAIJIQUAN
- XINGYIQUAN
- YANG TAI CHI FOR BEGINNERS

AND MANY MORE...

more products available from...
YMAA Publication Center, Inc. 楊氏東方文化出版中心
1-800-669-8892 • info@ymaa.com • www.ymaa.com

www.ingramcontent.com/pod-product-compliance
Lightning Source LLC
Chambersburg PA
CBHW030507080526
44586CB00011B/106